The Complete Games of
World Champion Anatoly Karpov

The Complete Games of World Champion Anatoly Karpov

K. J. O'Connell, D. N. L. Levy, J. B. Adams

B. T. Batsford Limited *London*

First published 1976
© K. J. O'Connell, D. N. L. Levy, J. B. Adams 1976
ISBN 0 7134 3141 5 paperback
ISBN 0 7134 3140 7 cased

Printed in Great Britain by
The Anchor Press, Tiptree, Essex
for the publishers
B. T. Batsford Limited
4 Fitzhardinge Street, London W1H 0AH

BATSFORD CHESS BOOKS
Advisor: R. G. Wade
Editor: K. J. O'Connell

Contents

	Preface	vii
	Tournament and Match Record	viii
	Biographical Details	x
1	Early Years (1961–65)	1
2	1966 – The USSR's Youngest Master	20
3	Trinec	37
4	1967 Miscellany	42
5	Groningen	51
6	Two Matches	59
7	Moscow University Championship	62
8	USSR Team Championship	69
9	Leningrad Match-Tournament	75
10	1969 Miscellany	82
11	World Junior Championship	87
12	Hungary–RSFSR	104
13	USSR Armed Forces Team Championship zonal	108
14	Kuibyshev	113
15	Caracas	121
16	USSR Armed Forces Team Championship	132
17	38th USSR Championship	135
18	Korchnoi Training Match	146
19	Daugavpils	150
20	Student Olympiad	157
21	USSR Team Championship	160
22	USSR Armed Forces Team Championship	164
23	Leningrad University Team Championship	169
24	39th USSR Championship	172
25	Alekhine Memorial	182
26	Hastings	194
27	Training Game v. Spassky	207

28 USSR Olympiad   208
29 Student Olympiad   214
30 Skopje Olympiad   222
31 San Antonio   235
32 Budapest   251
33 USSR National Teams Match-Tournament   259
34 Leningrad Interzonal   263
35 European Team Championship   282
36 41st USSR Championship   287
37 Madrid   300
38 Candidates' Quarter-Final   308
39 Candidates' Semi-Final   314
40 Nice Olympiad   322
41 Candidates' Final   330
42 Ljubljana–Portoroz   348
    Appendix   355
    43 6th USSR Spartakiad   355
    44 Milan   356
    Index of Openings   361
    Index of Endings   367
    Index of Opponents   369
    Illustrations between pages 182–183

Preface

When the publishers expressed their desire for a book on Karpov in algebraic notation, the decision was made to write a new one, rather than reissue *The Games of Anatoly Karpov* with just the notation changed.

Although this book does not contain every game that Karpov has ever played, it does contain every one of his games that has been previously published (some of them in highly obscure places), every one that Karpov has in his possession, and some that he does not. It is unlikely that any of the missing games will now materialize, hence the claim to completeness.

The total number of games included is 569 – the opportunity being taken to include, at proof stage, Karpov's games from the 1975 USSR Spartakiad and Milan.

The work on this book was undertaken by Kevin O'Connell. David Levy and Jimmy Adams made readily available their previously published Karpov material.

We would like to thank the following for their help, translations and permission to reproduce annotations: Anatoly Karpov, M. Blaine, G. Chesterfield, A. J. Gillam, Peter Markland, Alan Perkins, Brian Reilly, Freddy Reilly, Dr Keith Sales, Charles de Villiers, R. G. Wade, Mike Wills, B. H. Wood and *The British Chess Magazine, Chess, Chess Life and Review, The Chess Player,* Robert Hale & Co. and R. H. M. Chess Publishing.

KJO'C, DNLL, JBA
London, November 1975

Tournament and Match Record

			+	=	−
1961	Zlatoust Town Ch		5	3	·
	RSFSR Junior Ch (5/10)		2	·	·
	various		5	1	1
1962	RSFSR Junior Ch (5/10)		·	·	·
	various		8	4	·
1963	various		3	·	·
1964	RSFSR Junior Ch		4	·	·
	Botvinnik simul.		0	1	0
1965	USSR Junior Ch (4½/8)		·	·	·
	Spassky simul.		0	1	0
	USSR Armed Forces, zonal		4	·	·
	9th USSR Schools' Spartakiad (7/9)		·	·	·
1966	USSR Junior Ch		4	4	1
	Masters v. Candidate Masters		5	10	0
	USSR Junior Team Ch (?/8)	bd. 7	2	·	·
	Scandinavia Juniors–USSR Juniors	bd. 6	1	1	0
	Training games		2	·	·
1966/7	Trinec	1	9	4	0
1967	RSFSR Spartakiad		3	1	1
	USSR Junior Ch, ½-final	5	3	1	3
	USSR Schools' Spartakiad (?/9 or 10)	bd. 2	3	4	·
1967/8	Groningen	1	6	8	0
1968	Ciric simul.		0	1	0
	USSR–Yugoslavia	bd. 12	3	1	0
	USSR Juniors–Scandinavia Juniors	bd. 2	0	1	1
	Moscow University Ch	1	7	6	0
	6th USSR Team Ch	bd. 6	9	2	0
1969	Leningrad Match-Tournament	1	5	5	2
	USSR Juniors–Yugoslavia Juniors	bd. 3	2	2	0

			+	=	−
	'Red Armies', Warsaw	res	1	0	0
	USSR Armed Forces Team Ch	bd. 2	5	1	1
	World Junior Ch, Stockholm	1	12	5	0
	Hungary–RSFSR, Budapest		0	2	2
1970	USSR Armed Forces Team Ch, zonal		3	3	·
	RSFSR Ch, Kuibyshev	1	8	9	0
	Caracas	4-6=	8	7	2
	USSR Armed Forces Team Ch		2	3	1
	38th USSR Ch, Riga	5-7=	5	14	2
1971	Training Match v. Korchnoi	Drawn	2	2	2
	39th USSR Ch, Daugavpils ½-final	1	9	8	0
	Student Olympiad, Mayaguez	bd. 3	7	1	0
	USSR Team Ch, Rostov-on-Don	bd. 6	6	1	0
	USSR Armed Forces Team Ch	bd. 1	2	4	1
	Leningrad University Team Ch		4	·	·
	39th USSR Ch, Leningrad	4	7	12	2
	Alekhine Memorial, Moscow	1-2=	5	12	0
1971/2	Hastings	1-2=	8	6	1
1972	Training game v. Spassky		0	0	1
	USSR Olympiad, Moscow	bd. 2	4	3	2
	Student Olympiad, Graz	bd. 1	5	4	0
	Skopje Olympiad	1st res	12	2	1
	San Antonio	1-3=	7	7	1
1973	Budapest	2	4	11	0
	USSR National Teams Match-Tournament	bd. 1	2	2	0
	Leningrad Interzonal	1-2=	10	7	0
	European Team Ch, Bath	bd. 4	4	2	0
	41st USSR Ch, Moscow	2-6=	5	11	1
	Madrid	1	7	8	0
1974	Candidates' ¼-final v. Polugayevsky	Won	3	5	0
	Candidates' ½-final v. Spassky	Won	4	6	1
	Nice Olympiad	bd. 1	10	4	0
	Candidates' Final v. Korchnoi	Won	3	19	2
1975	Ljubljana–Portoroz	1	7	8	0
	6th USSR Spartakiad, Riga	bd. 1	4	3	0
	Milan	1	4	16	1
			284	**269**	**33**

Biographical Details

Anatoly Evgenyevich Karpov

date of birth	23.5.1951
place of birth	Zlatoust, Southern Urals
mother	Nina Grigorievna
occupation	Housewife?
father	Evgeny Stepanovich
occupation	Chief engineer of a Tula factory

chess career

learnt chess	1955 age	4
3rd category	1958	7
2nd category	1960	9
1st category	1960	9
candidate master	1962	11
master	1966	15
international master	1969	18
grandmaster	1970	19
World Champion	1975	23

education

school   Zlatoust, School No. 3
Tula, ?

university   Moscow State University
1968–1969
Leningrad State University 1969–

personal

height (12.71)	5 ft 7½ in.
weight (12.71)	7 stone 12 lbs
colour of hair	Brown
colour of eyes	Green
family moved to Tula	1965

Elo rating

1971	2540	
1972	2630	World No. 7=
1973	2660	World No. 2=
1974	2700	World No. 2
1975	2705	World No. 1

(Fischer inactive for 3 years)

1 Early Years (1961–5)

This chapter begins with Karpov's earliest recorded games, played when he was 9 years 8 months old and already a second category player (we believe that Karpov received his first category rating after his result in the 1961 RSFSR Schoolboys Championship). The games against Korchnoi, Botvinnik and Spassky, all from simultaneous displays, are of special interest.

Cheliabinsk 1961

0101 Shusharin–AK

6.1.1961: Spanish

(Notes by Wade)

1 e4 e5 2 ♘f3 ♘c6 3 ♗b5 a6 4 ♗a4 ♘f6 5 ♘c3 b5 6 ♗b3 ♗b4 7 0-0 0-0 8 d3 d6 9 ♘d5 (All this is not far from the fount of opening theory. 9 ♘e2 ♘a5 was considered in discussions on the Schlechter–Tarrasch match, Cologne 1911.) 9 ... ♘×d5 10 ♗×d5 ♕e8 (Besides reserving development options for his c8 bishop, Karpov frees d8 for the knight as a means of releasing the pin d5–a8.) 11 c3 ♗a5 12 a4 ♗b7 13 b4 (13 d4 keeps Black's position under pressure, e.g. 13 ... ♘d8? 14 de de 15 ab ab 16 b4.) 13 ... ♗b6

14 a5 ♗a7 (This bishop is not without influence.) 15 ♖e1?! (1)

1
15W
B

(Now, which move should Black play in order to place his pieces both effectively and harmoniously?) 15 ... ♖b8! (Karpov, only 9 years 8 months old when this game was played, is as devoted to the harmonious disposition of his forces in his early games as he is today. How many players, sensing the congestion in the area a8–a6–c6–c8, would have played immediately 15 . . . ♘d8.? After 16 ♗×b7 ♘×b7 the knight is badly situated. Now the knight may go to e7 and g6, while on ♗×b7, . . . ♖×b7 followed by . . . c6 and the rook will be available for doubling on a number of files.) 16 ♗g5 ♘e7 17 ♗×e7 ♕×e7 18 ♕b3?? (This loses a piece.) 18 . . . c6 19 d4 cd 20 ed f6 21 de fe 22 ♖e2 ♔h8 23 ♘d4 ♗×d4 24 cd ♕f7 25 de ♗×d5 26 ♕g3 de 27 ♖×e5 ♖be8 28 ♖ael ♖e6! 29 f3 ♖g6 30 ♕f2 ♗×f3 31 g3 ♖f6 32 ♖e7 ♕g6 33 ♕d4 ♕c2! 34 ♕f2 ♕×f2+ 35 ♔×f2 ♗g4+ 36 ♔g1? **0–1** (36 . . . ♗h3) How many nine-year-olds have played as well as this?

0102   Lazarev–AK

6.1.1961: Q G D

1 d4 d5 2 c4 e6 3 ♘c3 ♘f6 4 ♗g5 ♗e7 5 ♘f3 h6 6 ♗h4 00 7 e3 ♘bd7 8 c5 b6 9 b4 c6 10 ♗d3 ♗b7 11 00 a5 12 a3 ♗a6 13 ♕e2 ♗×d3 14 ♕×d3 b5 15 ♘d2 ♘h7 16 ♗×e7

♕×e7 17 ♘b3 a4 18 ♘a5 ♖ac8 19 ♘b7 e5 20 f3 ♖c7 21 ♘d6 ♘g5 22 ♖ael ♘e6 23 ♘e2 ♘g5 24 ♘g3 ♘e6 25 ♘gf5 ♕f6 26 ♔h1 ♔h7 27 ♘g3+ g6 28 ♖d1 ♕e7 29 ♕c3 f6 30 ♕d3 ♖a7 *(2)*

31 h4? f5 32 h5? ♕h4+ 33 ♔g1 ♕×g3 34 hg+ ♕×g6 35 ♔f2 ed 36 ed ♘f4 37 ♕d2 ♕×g2+ 38 ♔el ♕×d2+ 39 ♖×d2 ♖f6 40 ♖hl ♘f8 41 ♖dh2 ♘8e6 42 ♖d2 ♘g5 43 ♔f2 ♖e4 44 ♘×f5 ♖f7 45 ♘h4 ♘g6 46 ♘×g6 ♖×f3+ 47 ♔gl ♔×g6 48 ♔g2 ♖×a3 49 ♖bl ♘e4 **0–1**

0103   Shneider–AK

8.1.1961: King's Gambit

1 e4 e5 2 f4 ef 3 ♘f3 ♘f6 4 e5 ♘h5 5 d4 d5 6 c4 ♗g4 7 ♗e2 ♗e7 8 00 00 9 cd ♕×d5 10 ♘c3 ♕d8 11 ♘e4 ♘d7 12 ♘f2 ♗f5 13 ♘el g6 14 ♗×h5 gh 15 ♕×h5 ♗g6 16 ♕e2 ♘b6 17 ♘f3 ♘d5 18 ♘e4 ♕d7 19 a3 ♕c6 20 ♘f2 ♗f5 21 ♘d3 ♗×d3 22 ♕×d3 ♔h8 23 ♕f5 ♕g6 24 ♕×g6 hg 25 h4 ♔g7 26 ♔f2 ♖h8 27 ♖hl *(3)*

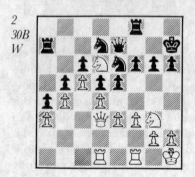

2
30B
W

3
27W
B

27 ... c5 28 dc ♗×c5+ 29 ♔e2 ♖ae8 30 b4 ♗e3 31 ♗b2 ♘b6 32 ♖ad1 ♖e7 33 ♘g5 ♘c4 34 ♗a1 ♘×a3 35 ♘×f7 ♔×f7 36 e6+ ♖×e6 37 ♗×h8 ♗d4+ 38 ♔f3 ♗×h8 39 ♔×f4 ♖b6 40 ♖he1 ♖×b4+ 41 ♔g3 ♖d4 42 ♖f1+ ♔e6 43 ♖de1+ ♗e5+ 44 ♔h3 ♖d3+ 45 ♖f3 ♖×f3+ 46 gf ♔f5 47 ♖d1 a5 48 ♖d5 b5 49 ♔g2 ♔e6 50 ♖d1 b4 51 ♖e1 ♔f5 **0–1**

Zlatoust 1961

0104   Tarinin–AK

16.1.1961: Spanish

1 e4 e5 2 ♘f3 ♘c6 3 ♗b5 a6 4 ♗a4 ♘f6 5 00 ♗e7 6 ♖e1 b5 7 ♗b3 d6 8 c3 00 9 h3 ♘a5 10 ♗c2 c5 11 d4 ♕c7 12 ♘bd2 ♗d7 13 ♘f1 ♘c6 14 ♘e3 ♖fe8 15 b3 ♗f8 16 dc dc 17 ♘d5 ♘×d5 18 ed ♘a5 19 ♘g5 h6 20 d6 ♗×d6 21 ♗h7+ ♔f8 (*4*)

4
21B
W

22 ♘×f7 ♔×f7 23 ♕h5+ ♔e7 24 ♕h4+ ♔e6 25 ♕g4+ ♔f6 26 ♕h4+ ♔f7 27 ♕h5+ ♔f8 28 ♗×h6 ♖e7 29 ♕f3+ ♖f7 30 ♕×a8+ ♗c8 31 ♗g5 ♘c6 32 ♗e4

♘e7 33 ♖ad1 ♘f5 34 ♗×f5 ♖×f5 35 ♖×d6 **1–0**

Zlatoust Town Championship 1961

0105   AK–Budakov

R1: 10.2.1961: Spanish

1 e4 e5 2 ♘f3 ♘c6 3 ♗b5 a6 4 ♗a4 ♘f6 5 00 ♗e7 6 ♖e1 b5 7 ♗b3 00 8 c3 d6 9 h3 ♘a5 10 ♗c2 c5 11 d4 cd 12 cd ♕c7 13 ♘bd2 ♗d7 14 ♘f1 ♘c4 15 ♘g3 g6 16 b3 ♘cb6 17 ♗e3 ♗f6 18 ♖c1 ♕d8 19 ♗d3 ♗b7 20 ♖e2 d5 21 de ♘×e5 22 ♘×e5 ♗×e5 23 ed ♕×d5 24 ♗e4 ♕×d1+ 25 ♖×d1 ♗×e4 26 ♘×e4 **½–½**

0106   Zadneprovsky–AK

R?: 22.2.1961: Nimzo–Indian

Karpov wins a pawn, then another, and another, and then a rook, all by move 32, but then takes another 33 moves to press home his advantage.

1 d4 ♘f6 2 c4 e6 3 ♘c3 ♗b4 4 a3 ♗×c3+ 5 bc 00 6 ♗g5 h6 7 ♗h4 d5 8 e3 b6 9 ♘f3 ♘bd7 10 ♕c2 ♗a6 11 ♘e5 g5 12 ♗g3 ♘×e5 13 ♗×e5 ♗×c4 14 f3 ♗×f1 15 ♖×f1 ♘d7 16 ♗g3 ♕g7 17 f4 f6 18 h4 g4 19 f5 e5 20 h5 ♕e8 21 ♖h1 ed 22 ♗f4 de 23 ♕e2 ♖g8 24 000 ♕e4 25 ♖d4 ♕×f5 26 ♕×e3 ♖h8 27 ♕e7+ ♔g8 28 ♗d2 ♖h7 29 ♕e2 ♔f7 30 ♖×g4 ♖e8 31 ♕d1 ♘e5 32 ♗e1 ♘×g4 33 ♔b2 ♘f2 34 ♗×f2

♕×f2+ 35 ♔b3 ♕×g2 36 ♖h4
♖g7 37 ♖d4♔e6 38 ♖d2 ♕g4 39
♕h1 ♖g5 40 ♖d4 ♕f5 41 a4
♖×h5 42 ♕g1 c5 43 ♖d2 ♖g5 44
♕h2 h5 45 ♕c7 ♕e5 46 ♕×a7
♕d6 47 ♕h7 ♖e7 48 ♕h8♔d7 49
♖f2 f5 50 ♖d2 f4 51 ♕a8 ♖f5 52
♕b7+ ♔e6 53 ♕c8+ ♕d7 54
♕g8+ ♔d6 55 ♕b8+ ♕c7 56
♕g8 ♖ef7 57 ♖e2 f3 58 ♖e3 f2 59
♕e8 ♕d7 60 ♕b8+ ♔c6 61
♕a8+ ♕b7 62 ♕e8+ ♔c7 63
♖e7+ ♖×e7 64 ♕×e7+ ♔b8 65
♕d6+ ♔a7 **0-1** (1·53 − 0·37)

0107 Kalashnikov–AK

R4: 1.3.1961: Queen's Indian

The nine-year-old Karpov
chooses not a tactical battle, but an
ending which he proceeds to play at
nearly five times the speed of his
opponent.
1 d4 ♘f6 2 ♘f3 e6 3 c4 b6 4 g3 ♗b7
5 ♗g2 c5 6 00 ♗e7 7 ♘c3 cd 8
♘×d4 ♗×g2 9 ♔×g2 d5 10 ♕a4+
♕d7 11 ♕×d7+ ♘b×d7 12 cd
♘×d5 13 ♘×d5 ed 14 ♘f5 g6 15
♘×e7 ♔×e7 16 ♖d1 ♔e6 17 ♗d2
♖ac8 18 ♗c3 ♖hd8 (5)

5
18B
W

19 ♖d4 ♘c5 20 f3 ♖d6 21 ♖ad1
♖cd8 22 g4 f6 23 h4 h6 24 ♖f4
♘d7 25 e4 ♘e5 26 ed+ ♖×d5 27
♖e1 a5 28 g5 hg 29 hg f5 30 ♖h4
♔d6 31 ♗×e5+ ♖×e5 32 ♖d4+
♔c7 33 ♖c4+ ♖c5 34 ♖×c5+ bc
35 ♔g3 ♖d2 36 ♖e6 ♔d6 37
♖e7+ ♖d7 38 ♖e5 ♔d6 39 ♖e8
♔c6 40 ♔f4 ♖d2 41 ♖e6+ ♔d7
42 ♖×g6 ♖×b2 43 ♔×f5 c4 44
♔e4 ♖d2 45 ♖a6 ♖×a2 46 ♔d4
c3 47 ♔×c3 ♖a3+ 48 ♔d4 ♖×f3
49 ♖×a5 ♔e7 50 ♔e5 ♔f7 51 ♖a6
♔g7 52 ♖h6 ♖f2 53 ♖d6 ♖f1 54
♔e4 ♖f2 55 ♖h6 ♖f1 56 ♔e5 ♖f2
57 ♔e6 ♖f3 58 ♖f6 ♖e3+ 59 ♔f5
♖f3+ 60 ♔e6 ♖e3+ 61 ♔f5
♖f3+ 62 ♔e5 ½–½ (1·55 − 0·35)

0108 AK–Gaimaletdinov

R?: 10.3.1961: Spanish

1 e4 e5 2 ♘f3 ♘c6 3 ♗b5 d6 4 d4
♗g4 5 d5 a6 6 ♗×c6+ bc 7 dc h6 8
00 ♘f6 9 ♕d3 ♗e7 10 ♘c3 00 11
♘d2 ♕e8 12 ♕c4 ♖b8 13 ♘b3
♖b6 14 ♘a5 ♔h7 15 b3 ♗e6 16
♕d3 ♘h5 17 ♖d1 f5 18 f3 f4 19
♘d5 ♗×d5 20 ed+ ♔h8 (6)

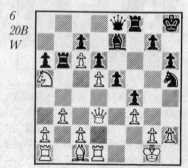

6
20B
W

21 ♘b7! (The black rook on b6 is surrounded and White systematically sets about winning the exchange.) 21 ... ♗f6 22 ♖b1 ♕f7 23 a4 ♗g5 24 a5 ♖b4 25 c3 ♖b5 26 c4 ♖×b7 27 cb ♖b8 28 b4 ♖×b7 29 b5 ab 30 cb ♕e8 31 ♕c4 ♕a8 32 ♕c6 ♕a7+ 33 b6 cb 34 ab ♕a6 35 ♗d2 ♘f6 36 ♕×d6 e4 37 ♗×f4 ♗×f4 38 ♕×f4 ef 39 ♕×f3 ♖×b6 40 ♖×b6 ♕×b6+ 41 ♔h1 ♕d6 42 h3 ♔h7 43 ♕e2 ♘g8 44 ♕e6 ♕×e6 45 de ♘f6 46 e7 ♔g8 47 ♖e1 ♔f7 48 ♔h2 ♔e8 49 ♖e5 ♘g8 50 ♔g3 ♘×e7 51 ♔g4 ♔f7 52 h4 ♘g8 53 ♔f4 ♘f6 54 g4 ♘e7 55 h5 g5+ 56 ♔e4 ♔f7 57 ♖a5 ♘g8 58 ♔e5 ♘g7 59 ♖a7+ ♔h8 60 ♔e6 **1–0** (7)

7
60W
B

0109   AK–Mukhudulin

R?: 19.4.1961: Sicilian

1 e4 c5 2 ♘f3 ♘c6 3 d4 cd 4 ♘×d4 ♘f6 5 ♘c3 d6 6 ♗e3 e5 7 ♘b3 ♗e7 8 f3 00 9 ♗c4 a6 10 ♕d2 ♕c7 11 ♗d5 ♘b4 12 ♖c1 ♘f×d5 13 ♘×d5 ♘×d5 14 ♕×d5 ♗e6 15 ♕d2 f5 16 ef ♖×f5 17 00 ♖af8 18 c4 ♕d8 19 ♘a5 ♗g5 20 ♗×g5 ♖×g5

21 ♔h1 ♖h5 22 g3 ♕c7 23 ♖fd1 ♗h3 24 ♕d5+ ♖f7 25 b4 ♕b6 26 c5 ♕b5 27 ♕c4 ♕×c4 28 ♖×c4 dc 29 ♖d8+ ♖f8 30 ♖×f8+ ♔×f8 31 bc ♗e6 32 ♖b4 ♗×a2 33 ♖×b7 ♗d5 34 c6 ♗×f3+ 35 ♔g1 ♗g4 36 c7 e4 37 ♘b3 ♖b5 38 ♖b8+ ♔e7 39 ♘d4 ♖c5 40 ♖b6 ♗c8 41 ♔f2 ♖×c7 42 ♔e3 ♗b7 43 ♘f5+ ♔f8 44 ♘d6 ♖c3+ 45 ♔e2 ♗c6 46 ♖×a6 ♔e7 47 ♘f5+ ♔f7 48 ♘d6+ ♔e7 49 ♘f5+ ♔e6 50 ♘d4+ ♔d5 51 ♘×c6 ♖×c6 52 ♖a7 ♔d4 53 ♖d7+ ♔e5 54 ♖×g7 ♖c2+ 55 ♔e3 ♖×h2 56 ♖e7+ ♔f5 57 ♖×e4 h3 58 ♖f4+ ♔g5 59 ♔f3 ♖h6 60 ♖g4+ ♔f5 61 ♖g7 ♔f6 ½-½ (0·45 - 1·45)

0110   AK–Zyulyarkin

R?: 3.5.1961: Sicilian

1 e4 c5 2 ♘c3 ♘c6 3 g3 g6 4 ♗g2 ♗g7 5 ♘ge2 e6 6 d3 ♘ge7 7 ♗e3 ♘d4 8 00 00 9 f4 ♖b8 10 ♔h1 b5 11 a3 d6 12 ♕d2 d5 13 ♖b1 a5 14 b4 ♘×e2 15 ♘×e2 d4 16 ♗f2 cb 17 ab a4 18 e5 ♘f5 19 g4 ♘h4? 20 ♗e4 f5 21 ef ♗×f6 22 g5 ♗×g5 23 fg ♘f5 24 ♗g3 ♖b7 25 ♗e5 ♖bf7 26 c3 dc 27 ♗×c3 h6 28 ♗f6 ♕b6 29 ♘f4 hg 30 ♗×g5 ♖h7 31 ♕g2 ♔f7 32 ♕g1 ♕d6 33 ♖bc1 ♖fh8 34 ♖f2 ♗d7 35 ♘×g6 **1–0** (1·10 - 1·40)

Cheliabinsk 1961

0111   Kalinkin–AK

7.5.1961: Spanish

1 e4 e5 2 ♘f3 ♘c6 3 ♗b5 a6 4 ♗a4

♘f6 5 00 ♗e7 6 ♖e1 b5 7 ♗b3 00 8 c3 d6 9 h3 ♘a5 10 ♗c2 c5 11 d4 ♕c7 12 ♘bd2 ♖d8 13 ♘f1 cd 14 cd d5 15 ed ed 16 ♗g5 ♘×d5 17 ♖c1 ♕d6 18 ♗e4 ♗×g5 19 ♘×g5 g6 20 ♕f3 ♗e6 21 ♗×g6 hg 22 ♖×e6 ♕d7 23 ♖d6 ♕f5 24 ♕×f5 gf 25 ♖×d8+ ♖×d8 26 ♘g3 ♘f4 27 ♔f1 d3 28 ♖d1 ♖d5 29 b3 *(8)*

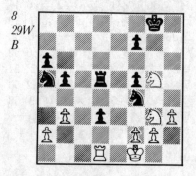

8
29W
B

29 . . . ♘c4 30 ♘f3 (30 bc bc∓ ∓)
30 . . . ♘b2 31 ♖d2 ♘c4 32 ♖d1 ♘b2 ½–½

RSFSR Junior Championship
Borovichi 1961

Karpov was the youngest of the 66 players who took part in this ten round Swiss tournament. Karpov scored 5/10 (the norm for the first category). The leading scores were: 1 P. Ilyaguev 8½; 2–3 M. Kogan, V. Tarasov 8; 4 V. Zilberstein 7½.

0112   AK–Nedelin

R?: 3.7.1961: Spanish

1 e4 e5 2 ♘f3 ♘c6 3 ♗b5 a6 4 ♗a4

♘f6 5 00 ♗e7 6 ♖e1 b5 7 ♗b3 d6 8 h3 00 9 c3 ♘a5 10 ♗c2 c5 11 d4 ♕c7 12 ♘bd2 ♖d8 13 d5 ♘b7 14 ♘f1 c4 15 g4 ♘c5 16 ♘g3 g6 17 ♔g2 ♘e8 18 g5 a5 19 ♗e3 b4 20 ♕e2 ♗a6 21 ♗×c5 ♕×c5 22 ♕d2 ♖db8 23 ♖eb1 ♗c8 24 ♘e2 ♘g7 25 b3 ♗a6 26 cb ab 27 bc ♗×c4 28 ♗d3 ♗×d3 29 ♕×d3 ♖a3? 30 ♕×a3 ba 31 ♖×b8+ ♗f8 32 ♖c1 ♕a7 33 ♖cc8 ♕e7 34 ♖×f8+ ♕×f8 35 ♖×f8+ ♔×f8 36 ♘d2 **1–0** (0·33 – 1·10)

0113   Timoshenko–AK

R?: 8.7.1961: French

This is the first available game played by Karpov against one of his three great 'rivals' – in succession Timoshenko, Vaganian and Korchnoi. Timoshenko and Karpov had met twice prior to this game, each player winning once.
1 e4 e6 2 d4 d5 3 ♘d2 de 4 ♘×e4 ♘d7 5 ♘f3 ♘gf6 6 ♘×f6+ ♘×f6 7 ♗e3 ♗e7 8 ♗d3 a6 9 00 00 10 ♘e5 ♘d5 11 c4 ♘×e3 12 fe ♗f6 13 ♖f3 ♗×e5 14 de ♕g5 15 ♕c2 h6 16 ♕c3 ♗d7 17 ♖g3 ♕e7 18 ♖f1 ♗e8 19 ♖b1 g6 20 ♖f6 ♔h7 *(9)* (White must be winning, though Karpov proceeds to defend himself extremely well. White should generally take his time and in particular to guard the entry squares at d1 and d2.) 21 h4 (21 ♖gf3!? Instead he allows his rook to be drawn away to g5. This is useful if his attack is going to succeed,

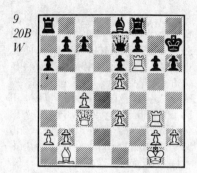

9
20B
W

which it would if his queen could
get to g5.) 21 . . . h5 22 ☐ g5♔g7 23
♕c2 ☐ h8 24 ♕e2 ♕c5 25 b3 ☐ d8
26 ♕f3 ♕e7 27 g4 ♕d7 28 ♕×b7
hg 29 ☐ fl ☐×h4 30 ♕e4 ♕d2 31
♕f4 ♔g8 32 ♕g3 ☐ h3 33 ♕f4
♕×e3+ 34 ♕×e3 ☐×e3 35 ☐×g4
☐×e5 36 ☐ g2♔g7 37 ☐ b2 ☐ d4
38 a3 ☐ g4+ 39♔f2 ☐ f4+ 40♔gl
☐ g4+ 41 ♔f2 ♗c6 42 ☐ gl ☐×gl
43 ♔×gl ☐ e3 44 a4 a5 45 ♔f2
☐ h3 46 ♔el ☐ hl+ 47 ♔d2
☐ h2+ 48♔c3 ☐×b2 49♔×b2 g5
50♔c3 g4 51 ♗d3 g3 52 ♗fl g2 53
♗×g2 ♗×g2 **0–1** (1·59– 1·26)

Zlatoust Town Ch 1961

0114 AK–Shefler

R?: 24.11.1961: French

l e4 e6 2 d4 d5 3 ed ed 4 ♘f3 ♘f6 5
♗e2 ♗d6 6 00 h6 7 ☐ el ♗e6 8
♘bd2 ♘bd7 9 ♘fl c6 10 ♗d3 ♕c7
11 ♕e2 000 12 ♗e3 ☐ de8 13 ♘g3
g6 14 c4 ♗g4 15 c5 ♗f4 16 ♕d2
♗×e3 17 ☐×e3 ♗e6 18 b4 ♘g4 19
☐ eel f5 20 a4 ♘gf6 21 ♘fl ♘e4 22
♕b2 g5 23 ☐ ebl g4 24 ♘3d2 ♕f4

25 ♗×e4 fe 26 b5 ♕c7 27 b6 ab 28
cb ♕d6 29 a5 ♘b8 30 ♘b3♔d8 31
♘c5 ♗c8 32 a6 ba 33 b7 ♗d7 34
♕b6+ ♕c7 35 ♕a7 ♔e7 36 ♘e3
☐ hf8 37 ♘×a6 ♘×a6 38 ☐×a6
♕f4 39 ♕c5+ ♕d6 40 ♕c2 ☐ b8
41 ☐ bb6 h5 42 ☐ a5 ♕c7 43
♘×d5+ **1–0** (0·46 – 2·02)

Magnitogorsk 1961

0115 AK–Maksimov

5.12.1961: King's Indian

l e4 g6 2 d4 d6 3 c4 ♗g7 4 ♘c3 ♘f6
5 f3 00 6 ♗e3 ♘bd7 7 ♗d3 e5 8 d5
♘c5 9 ♘ge2 a5 10 ♕d2 ♘×d3+ 11
♕×d3 ♘d7 12 000 f5 13 ☐ dfl f4 14
♗f2 ♘c5 15 ♗×c5 dc 16♔bl a4 17
☐ dl ♗d7 18♔al a3 19 b3 ☐ f6 20
♘cl (*10*)

10
20W
B

20 . . . b5 21 ♘×b5 ♗×b5 22 cb
☐ b6 23 ♘e2 ♕b8 24 ♘c3 ♕a7 25
♕c4 ☐ d6 26 ☐ cl ☐ b8 27 ♘a4
♕a5 28 ☐ hdl ☐×b5 29 ♘×c5
☐ b4 30 ♕c3 ♕b6 31 ♘a4 ♕b5 32
♕×c7 ♗f8 33 ♕c5 ♕b7 34 ♕c3
☐×a4 35 ba ☐ d8 36 ♕b3 ♕a6 37
d6+ ♔h8 38 d7 ♕e2 39 ☐ c8 ♗e7

40 ♔b1 ♔g7 41 ♖×d8 ♗×d8 42
a5♔h6 43 g4♔g7 44 h4 h6 45♔c1
g5 46 hg hg 47 ♕×a3 ♕c4+ 48
♔b1 ♕b5+ 49 ♕b3 ♕×a5 50 a4
♔f8 51 ♔a2 ♕a7 52 ♕b4+ ♔g7
53 ♖d5 ♕f2+ 54 ♕b2 ♕×f3 55
♖×e5 ♔g6 56 ♖e8 ♕×g4 57
♖×d8 ♕e6+ 58 ♕b3 ♕×e4 59
♖g8+ ♔f5 60 d8♕ **1–0** (1·00 –
2·25)

Zlatoust Town Ch 1961

0116 AK–Ponomarev

R?: 20.12.1961: French

1 e4 e6 2 d4 d5 3 ed ed 4 ♘f3 ♘f6 5
♗d3 ♗g4 6 00 ♗e7 7 ♖e1 00 8
♗g5 ♘bd7 9 ♘bd2 ♖e8 10 c3 c5
11 ♕b1 c4 12 ♗f5 ♗h5 13 ♗f4 ♘f8
14 ♘e5 ♘g6 15 ♘×g6 ♗×g6 16
♗×g6 fg 17 ♕c2 ♗d6 18 ♗×d6
♕×d6 19 ♘f3 ♘e4 20 ♘e5 (*11*)

11
20W
B

20 ... ♖e6? 21 ♘×c4 ♕f4 22 ♘e3
♘f6 23 ♘f1 ♖ae8 24 ♖×e6 ♖×e6
25 ♖d1 g5 26 ♕d2 ♕h4 27 ♘e3
♘e4 28 ♕e2 ♖h6 29 h3 ♖f6 30
♖f1 g4 31 ♘×g4 ♖f5 32 f3 ♘d6 33
♕f2 (33 ♕e6+ !? – Wade) 33 ...

♕g5 34 ♖e1 h5 35 ♘e5 b5 36 ♘c6
♖f7 37 ♕e3 ♕g3 38 ♘e7+ ♔h8
39 ♘×d5 ♘f5 40 ♕f2 ♕g5 41 f4
♕d8 42 ♘e3 ♘h4 43 g3 ♘g6 44 f5
♘f8 45 ♕e2 ♕g5 46 ♔g2 ♘d7 47
h4 ♕h6 48 ♕f3 ♖e7 49 ♕f4 ♕a6
50 a3 ♘f6 51 ♘c2 ♕c6+ 52 ♕f3
♕e8 53 ♖×e7 ♕×e7 54 ♘e3 ♕d6
55 ♔h3 a5 56 d5 b4 57 ab ab 58
♕f4 ♕d7 59 c4 ♕a7 60 d6 ♕a1 61
♕f3 ♕×b2 62 d7 ♕d4 (62 ...
♘×d7 63 ♕×h5+ ♔g8 64 ♕e8+
± ±) 63 ♘d5 ♕g4+ 64 ♕×g4 hg+
65 ♔g2 ♘×d7 66 ♘×b4 ♔g8 67
♘d5 ♔f7 68 ♔f1 g6 69 fg+ ♔×g6
70 ♔e2 ♔f7 71 ♔e3 ♔e6 72 ♔d4
♔d6 73 h5 ♘c5 74 h6 ♘e6+ 75
♔e4 ♘g5+ 76♔f5 ♘f7 77 h7♔c5
78 ♔f6 ♘h8 79 ♔g7 **1–0** (1·15 –
1·05)

Zlatoust 1961

0117 AK–Kalashnikov

25.12.1961: Spanish

1 e4 e5 2 ♘f3 ♘c6 3 ♗b5 a6 4
♗×c6 bc 5 d4 ed 6 ♘×d4 c5 7 ♘e2
♗b7 8 ♘bc3 ♘f6 9 f3 c6 10 e5 ♘d5
11 ♘e4 f5 12 ef ♘×f6 13 ♘d6+
♗×d6 14 ♕×d6 ♕e7 15 ♕×e7+
♔×e7 16 ♗g5 ♖ae8 17 000 d5 18
♘g3 ♗c8 19 ♖he1+ ♔f7 20 ♔d2
h6 21 ♗×f6 ♔×f6 22 ♖×e8 ♖×e8
23 ♖e1 ♖×e1 24 ♔×e1 ♔e5 (*12*)
('Study endgames!' – Karpov. He
takes 40 minutes for the whole
game – a precise average of 40
seconds per move.) 25 ♔d2. d4 26
♘e4 c4 27 c3 ♗f5 28 cd+ ♔×d4 29

12
24B
W

♘c3 ♗d3 30 g3 g5 31 a3 h5 32 ♘d1
♗f1 33 ♘e3 ♗d3 34 ♘d1 ♗g6 35
♘e3 ♗d3 36 ♘d1 ♗h7 37 ♘c3
♗g8 38 ♘e2+ ♔e5 39 ♔e3 ♔d5
40 ♘c3+ ♔e5 41 ♘e4 ♔f5 42 ♘c5
♔e5 43 ♘×a6 ♔d5 44 ♘b4+ ♔c5
45 ♘a2 c3 46 ♘×c3 ♔c4 47 a4
♔b3 48 a5 ♗c4 49 f4 gf+ 50 gf
♔b4 51 f5 ♔×a5 52 ♔d4 ♔b4 53
♘e4 ♗a2 54 f6 ♗f7 55 ♘c5 ♗d5
56 h4 ♗f7 57 ♘d3+ ♔b3 58 ♘e5
♗e6 59 ♘×c6 ♔×b2 60 ♘d8 **1–0**
(0·40 – 2·13)

Zlatoust 1962

0118 AK–Alexeyev

7.1.1962: Sicilian

1 e4 c5 2 ♘f3 e6 3 d4 cd 4 ♘×d4
♘f6 5 f3 d5 6 ed ♘×d5 7 ♗b5+
♗d7 8 ♗×d7+ ♘×d7 9 0-0 ♗c5 10
♔h1 0-0 11 ♘b3 ♗e3 12 ♕e2 ♗×c1
13 ♖×c1 ♕g5 14 ♘1d2 ♘f4 15
♕f2 ♘f6 16 g3 ♘g6 17 ♘c5 ♕d5
18 ♘ce4 ♘h5 19 ♖d1 ♕c6 20 ♘b3
b6 21 ♖d6 ♕c7 22 ♖ad1 ♖ad8 23
♖×d8 ♖×d8 24 ♖×d8+ ♕×d8
25 ♕d2 ♕e7 26 ♘c3 ♕d7 27 ♕d4
♕e7 28 ♕d6 h6 29 ♕×e7 ♘×e7 30

♘d6 ♘c6 31 c3 ♔f8 32 ♔g2 ♔e7
33 ♘b5 e5 34 ♘d2 ♔d7 35 ♘c4 f5
36 ♘bd6 ♔e6 37 b3 ♘f6 38 ♘b5
♘d5 39 a4 a6 40 ♘ba3 ♘a7 41
♘b1 b5 42 ♘b2 e4 43 ♔f2 ♔e5 44
c4 ♘b4 45 ♔e3 ♘c2+ 46 ♔d2
♘d4 47 f4+ ♔e6 48 ♔c3 ♘ac6 49
ab ab 50 b4 g5 51 cb ♘×b5+ 52
♔c4 ♘cd4 53 ♘c3 ♘×c3 54
♔×d4 ♘e2+ 55 ♔e3 ♘c3 56 ♔d4
♘e2+ 57 ♔e3 ♘c3 58 ♔d4 ½–½

0119 Kirillov–AK

8.1.1962: English

Karpov engineers a mating net
in a double rook ending.

1 c4 e5 2 g3 g6 3 ♗g2 ♗g7 4 ♘c3
♘e7 5 b3 0-0 6 ♗b2 ♘bc6 7 e3 f5 8
♘ge2 ♔h8 9 0-0 d6 10 d4 ♗d7 11 d5
♘b4 12 a3 ♘a6 13 ♖b1 ♕e8 14
♕c2 g5 15 f4 gf 16 ef e4 17 ♘d1
♕g6 18 ♗×g7+ ♕×g7 19 ♕b2
♘c5 20 ♕×g7+ ♔×g7 21 ♘e3
♔f6 22 b4 ♘a4 23 ♖b3 a5 24 ♖c1
ab 25 ab ♘b6 26 ♘c3 ♖a7 27 c5
♘bc8 28 ♗f1 c6 29 ♖d1 ♖a8 30 dc
♗×c6 31 ♘ed5+ ♗×d5 32
♘×d5+ ♘×d5 33 ♖×d5 ♖a1 34
♔f2 ♖a2+ 35 ♗e2 ♔e6 36 ♖d4
d5 37 b5 ♖c2 38 c6 bc 39 bc ♖×c6
40 ♖b7 ♘e7 41 g4 fg 42 ♗×g4+
♔f6 43 ♗a4 ♘g6 44 ♖aa7 ♘×f4
45 ♔g3 ♘d3 46 ♖×h7 ♔e5 47
♖he7+ ♔d4 48 h4 ♘e5 49 ♗e2
♖g6+ 50 ♔h3 ♖fg8 51 ♖a4+
♘c4 52 ♗×c4 dc 53 ♖d7+ ♔c3
54 ♖c7 ♖g3+ 55 ♔h2 ♖g2+ 56
♔h1 ♖2g7 (it seems more likely
that 56 ... ♖2g4 was played – see

White's 61st move.) 57 ♖a×c4+
♔d3 58 ♖c3+ ♔d4 59 ♖7c4+
♔e5 60 ♖c5+ ♔f4 61 ♖h5 ♖g1+
62 ♔h2 ♖8g2+ 63 ♔h3 ♖d2 **0–1**
(1·30 – 0·30)

0120 Kolishkin–AK

11.1.1962: Spanish

1 e4 e5 2 ♘f3 ♘c6 3 ♗b5 a6 4 ♗a4
♘f6 5 00 ♗e7 6 ♖e1 b5 7 ♗b3 d6 8
c3 00 9 h3 ♘a5 10 ♗c2 c5 11 d4
♕c7 12 ♘bd2 ♘c6 13 dc dc 14 ♘f1
♖d8 15 ♕e2 ♗e6 16 ♗g5 ♖d7 17
♘e3 h6 18 ♗×f6 ♗×f6 19 ♖ed1
♖ad8 20 ♖×d7 ♖×d7 21 a4 c4 22
ab ab 23 ♘d2 ♘a5 24 ♖b1 ♕d8 25
♘df1 ♗e7 26 ♖d1 ♗c5 27 ♖×d7
♕×d7 28 ♘g3 g6 (*13*)

13
28B
W

(Karpov has found good squares
for all his pieces. He gradually
increases the pressure until White's
whole position becomes overloaded
and falls apart at the seams.) 29 h4
h5 30 ♘gf1 b4 31 ♘d2 b3 32 ♗b1
♕b5 33 ♘d5 ♕a4 34 ♕d1 ♔g7 35
♘f3 ♗g4 36 ♕d2 ♕a1 37 ♕c1 f6

38 ♘d2 ♗e2 39 ♘c7 ♕f7 40 ♘a6
♗b7 41 ♘c7 ♘d6 42 ♘d5 ♗d3 43
♕d1 ♘×e4! 44 ♘×e4 ♗×e4 45
♘e3 ♕×b1 46 ♕×b1 ♗×b1 47
♘f1 ♔e6 48 ♘d2 ♗c2 49 ♔f1 ♔f5
50 ♔e2 g5 51 hg fg 52 ♘f3 g4 53
♘e1 h4 54 f3 g3 **0–1**

0121 Kalashnikov–AK

16.2.1962: Spanish

1 e4 e5 2 ♘f3 ♘c6 3 ♗b5 a6 4 ♗a4
♘f6 5 00 ♗e7 6 ♖e1 b5 7 ♗b3 d6 8
c3 00 9 h3 ♘a5 10 ♗c2 c5 11 d4
♕c7 12 ♘bd2 ♗d7 13 ♘f1 ♖fc8 14
d5 ♗f8 15 g4 ♘c4 16 b3 ♘b6 17
♗e3 a5 18 a3 a4 19 b4 cb 20 cb
♕×c2 21 ♕×c2 ♖×c2 22 ♗×b6
♖b8 23 ♗a5 ♖bc8 24 ♘g3 ♖8c3
25 ♔g2 h6 26 ♗b6 ♗e7 27 ♖e3
♖×e3 28 ♗×e3 ♘e8 29 ♖c1
♖×c1 30 ♗×c1 ♗d8 31 ♗e3 ♔h7
32 g5 hg 33 ♘×g5+ ♗×g5 34
♗×g5 ♔g6 35 ♗d8 f5 36 f3 f4 ½–½

RSFSR Junior Championship
Vladimir 1962

Anatoly, at eleven, was again the
youngest (jointly with Bora Men) of
the 86 players who competed in this
ten round Swiss. Once again
Karpov made a 50% score (5/10).
The leading scores were: 1 N.
Rashkovsky 10(!); 2 O. Averkin 8; 3
V. Krasnov 7½; 4–7 V. Tsesh-
kovsky, B. Kogan, V. Strebkov, N.
Mukhamedzyanov 7.

Simultaneous Display, Cheliabinsk 1962

0122   Korchnoi–AK

26.3.1962: Scotch Four Knights

1 e4 e5 2 ♘f3 ♘c6 3 d4 ed 4 ♘×d4
♘f6 5 ♘c3 d6 6 ♗b5 ♗d7 7 00
♗e7 8 ♖e1 00 9 ♗f1 ♖e8 10 h3
♘×d4 11 ♕×d4 ♗c6 12 ♗e3 ♕d7
13 ♖ad1 ♗f8 14 ♗g5 ♗e7 15 ♗c1
a6 16 g4 h6 17 f4 ♖ad8 18 ♗g2
♕c8 19 ♕d3 b5 20 a3 ♕b7 21 ♕f3
♗f8 22 h4 a5 23 g5 hg 24 hg ♘h7
25 ♗h3 d5 26 ed ♖×e1+ 27 ♖×e1
♗×d5 28 ♘×d5 ♕×d5 29 ♕×d5
♖×d5 30 g6 ♗c5+   ½-½

Cheliabinsk 1962

0123   AK–Tarinin

R1(?):15.6.1962:Spanish

1 e4 e5 2 ♘f3 ♘c6 3 ♗b5 a6 4 ♗a4
d6 5 ♗×c6+ bc 6 d4 f6 7 00 ♗g4 8
de fe 9 ♕d3 ♗e7 10 c4 ♘f6 11 h3
♗×f3 12 ♕×f3 00 13 ♘c3 ♘d7 14
♕g4 ♗f6 15 ♗e3 ♕e8 16 ♖ad1
♖b8 17 b3 ♖f7 18 ♖d3 ♘f8 19
♘e2 ♕d7 20 ♕×d7 ♖×d7 21
♖fd1 ♖bd8 22 ♘c3 ♔f7 23 g3
♔e6 24 ♔g2 ♔f7 *(14)*

25 f4 ef 26 gf ♗×c3 27 ♖×c3 c5 28
♔f3 g6 29 ♗f2 ♔e6 30 ♖cd3 c6 31
♗h4 ♘d4+ 32 ♖×d4 cd 33 ♗×d8
♖×d8 34 ♖×d4 ♔e7 35 c5 d5 36
ed cd 37 ♖a4 ♖a8 38 ♔e3 ♔d7 39
♔d4 ♔c6 40 ♖b4 a5 41 ♖b6+
♔c7 42 ♔×d5 ♖d8+ 43 ♖d6 ♖f8
44 ♖a6 ♖f5+ 45 ♔c4 ♖×f4+ 46

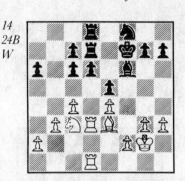

14
24B
W

♔b5 a4 47 ♖a7+ ♔b8 48 ♖×h7
ab 49 ab ♖f6 50 c6 ♖f3 51 b4 ♖f4
52 ♔a5 ♖c4 53 b5 **1-0** (0·48 -
2·20)

0124   Kolishkin–AK

R2(?):16.6.1962:Spanish

1 e4 e5 2 ♘f3 ♘c6 3 ♗b5 a6 4 ♗a4
♘f6 5 00 ♗e7 6 ♕e2 b5 7 ♗b3 d6 8
a4 ♗g4 9 c3 ♗×f3 10 ♕×f3 00 11
♖d1 ♘a5 12 ♗c2 c5 13 d4 ♕c7 14
d5 c4 15 ♘d2 ♖fb8 16 ab ab 17 ♘f1
♘d7 18 ♘e3 ♘c5 19 ♘f5 ♗f8 20
♕g3 ♔h8 21 f4 f6 22 fe fe 23 ♖f1
♘ab3 24 ♖×a8 ♖×a8 25 ♗×b3
♘×b3 26 ♗e3 ♖a1 27 ♖×a1
♘×a1 28 ♕f2 ♕f7 29 g4 ♘b3 30
h4 g6 31 ♘g3 ♕×f2+ 32 ♔×f2
♗e7 33 h5 ♔g7 34 hg hg 35 ♘f1
♗h4+ 36 ♔e2 ♔f6 37 ♘h2 ♗g5
38 ♘f3 ♘c1+ 39 ♔d2 ½-½ (1·15 -
0·45)

0125   AK–Karin

R3: 5.10.1962: Modern

1 e4 g6 2 d4 ♗g7 3 c4 c5 4 d5 d6 5
♘c3 ♘a6 6 ♗e3 ♘c7 7 ♕d2 a6 8

♗d3 ♗d7 9 ♘ge2 b5 10 00 ♖b8 11 ♖ab1 ♘f6 12 ♗h6 00 13 ♗×g7 ♔×g7 14 f4 ♘fe8 15 ♘g3 e6 16 b3 ed 17 ♘×d5 ♘×d5 18 cd ♖c8 19 ♗c2 ♔g8 20 e5 ♘g7 21 ♖be1 ♖e8 22 ♘e4 de 23 fe ♘f5 *(15)*

15
23B
W

24 ♘f6+ ♔g7 25 ♗×f5 ♗×f5 26 ♖×f5! ♖h8 (26 . . . gf 27 ♕g5+ ♔f8 28 ♘×h7 mate; 27 . . . ♔h8 28 ♕h6 and 29 ♕×h7 mate) 27 ♖f3 c4 28 bc bc 29 ♕d4 ♕a5 30 ♖ef1 ♕c5 31 ♕×c5 ♖×c5 32 ♘g4 (threatening mate) 32 . . . ♖f8 33 ♘f6 ♖fc8 34 ♖c3 ♖a5 35 a3 ♖ac5 36 ♔f2 a5 37 ♖b1 ♖5c7 38 ♔e3 ♖e7 39 ♔d4 **1–0** *(0·33 – 2·00)*

0126 Aroshiov(?)–AK

R4: 6.10.1962: French

1 e4 e6 2 d4 d5 3 ♘c3 de 4 ♘×e4 ♘f6 5 ♗d3 ♘bd7 6 ♘e2 ♗e7 7 00 ♘×e4 8 ♗×e4 ♘f6 9 ♗f3 00 10 c4 c6 11 ♗f4 ♗d6 12 ♗g5 h6 13 ♗×f6 ♕×f6 14 ♘c3 ♗c7 15 ♘e4 ♕e7 16 ♕b3 ♖b8 17 ♖ac1 ♖d8 18 ♖fd1 e5 19 d5 cd 20 cd ♗f5 21 ♘g3 ♗g6 22 ♕c3 ♗d6 23 ♗e4 ♗×e4 24 ♘×e4 ♖d7 25 ♕a5 ♖a8 26 ♖c4

f5 27 ♘c3 ♖ad8 28 h3 (28 ♕×a7?? b5 ∓ ∓) 28 . . . e4 29 ♘b5 ♗c5 30 ♘c3 b6 31 ♕a4 *(16)*

16
31W
B

31 . . . e3 32 fe ♕×e3+ 33 ♔h1 ♖e7 34 ♕c2 ♕g3 35 ♘e2 ♕f2 36 ♘g1 ♖ed7 37 ♕b3 ♖×d5 38 ♖c2 ♕e3 39 ♕×e3 ♗×e3 40 ♖×d5 ♖×d5 41 ♖e2 f4 42 ♘f3 g5 43 g3 ♔f7 44 ♔g2 ♔f6 45 ♖c2 ♖c5 46 ♖×c5 bc 47 gf ♗×f4 48 b3 ♔f5 49 ♔f2 ♔e4 50 ♔e2 h5 51 ♘e1 ♔d4 (51 . . . ♔d5 seems stronger) 52 ♘d3 ♗d6 53 ♘f2 ♗g3 54 ♘d3 g4 55 hg hg 56 ♘b2 ♗f4 57 ♘d3 ♗d6 58 ♔d2 g3 59 a4 g2 60 ♘e1 g1♘ (a rare case of under-promotion to a knight) 61 ♘c2+ ♔d5 62 ♔d3 ♘f3 63 ♘e3+ ♔c6 64 ♔c4 a5 65 ♘f5 ♘e5+ 66 ♔c3 ♔d5 67 ♘e3+ ♔e4 68 ♘c4 ♘×c4 69 ♔×c4 ♗f4 70 ♔×c5 ♗d2 71 b4 ♗×b4+ **0–1** *(2·50 – 2·20)*

Zlatoust 1962

0127 Zyulyarkin–AK

20.10.1962: Hungarian

1 e4 e5 2 ♘f3 ♘c6 3 ♗c4 ♗e7 4 d4

d6 5 c3 ♘f6 6 de ♘×e5 7 ♘×e5 de
8 ♕c2 OO 9 ♗g5 c6 10 ♗×f6 ♗×f6
11 ♘d2 ♕e7 12 OOO b5 13 ♗e2 ♗e6
14 ♔b1 ♖ab8 15 g4 c5 16 h4 ♕c7
17 g5 ♗e7 18 c4 a6 19 ♔a1 ♖b6 20
♘f1 bc 21 ♘e3 ♖e8 22 ♗×c4
♗×c4 23 ♘×c4 ♖b4 24 ♖d5 f6 25
gf ♗×f6 26 a3 ♖bb8 27 ♘d6 ♖ed8
28 ♕c4 ♔f8 29 ♖hd1 ♕b6 30
♖5d2? ♖×d6 31 b4 ♖×d2 32
♖×d2 cb 33 ♖d7 ♗e7 34 a4 b3 35
♔b1 ♕×f2 **0–1** (1·23 – 0·57)

Koyensk 1962

0128   Manakov–AK

5.11.1962: Spanish

1 e4 e5 2 ♘f3 ♘c6 3 ♗b5 a6 4 ♗a4
♘f6 5 OO ♗e7 6 ♖e1 b5 7 ♗b3 d6 8
♘c3 OO 9 ♘d5 ♗g4 10 h3 ♗h5 11
c3 ♘a5 12 ♘×f6+ ♗×f6 13 ♗c2
c5 14 b4 ♘c6 15 g4 ♗g6 16 ♗b2 cb
17 cb ♘×b4 18 ♗b3 ♘d3 19 ♗d5
♘×e1 20 ♗×a8 ♘×f3+ 21 ♕×f3
♕×a8 22 d3 ♖c8 23 ♗a3 ♕b8 24
♗b4 ♗g5 25 ♕d1 ♕b6 26 d4
♕×d4 27 ♕e1 **0–1**

Zlatoust 1962

0129   AK–Piskunov

12.12.1962: Alekhine

1 e4 ♘f6 2 e5 ♘d5 3 c4 ♘b6 4 d4
d6 5 ed ed 6 ♘c3 ♘c6 7 a3 ♗f5 8
♗e3 g6 9 ♗d3 ♕d7 10 ♘ge2 ♗g7
11 OO OO 12 b3 ♖ad8 13 ♕c2 ♗×d3
14 ♕×d3 ♘e7 15 ♘g3 c6 16 ♖fe1
d5 17 c5 ♘bc8 18 ♖e2 f5 19 ♗f4

♔f7 20 ♖ae1 ♖fe8 21 ♗e5 ♘g8 22
♗f1 ♘f6 23 ♘d2 ♘e4 24 ♗×g7
♔×g7 25 ♘f3 ♖e7 26 b4 ♖de8 27
♘e5 ♕d8 28 f3 ♘×c3 29 ♕×c3
♖e6 30 g3 ♕c7 31 ♕d2 ♘e7 *(17)*

17
31B
W

32 ♘d3 ♖×e2 33 ♕×e2 h5 34 ♕e6
h4 35 ♕d6 **1–0** (1·10 – 1·55)

Zlatoust 1963

0130   Korotayev–AK

15.2.1963: QGD

1 d4 ♘f6 2 c4 e6 3 ♘c3 d5 4 e3 b6 5
♘f3 ♗b7 6 cd ed 7 ♗d3 ♗d6 8 OO
OO 9 ♗b5 ♖e8 10 ♘×d6 ♕×d6 11
♘e5 ♘bd7 12 f4 ♘e4 13 ♖f3 f6 14
♘g4 c5 15 ♖h3 ♘f8 16 ♘f2 f5 17
b3 cd 18 ed ♖ac8 19 a4 ♕f6 20
♗b5 ♖e7 21 ♗b2 ♖ec7 22 ♗d3
♘e6 23 ♕h5 g6 24 ♕h6 ♘×d4 25
♘d1 ♘c5 26 ♗c2 ♘ce6 27 ♗d3
♕f8 28 ♕h4 ♘×b3 29 ♖b1 ♘d2
30 ♖c1 ♕f7 31 ♖a1 ♘e4 32 ♖b1
♘6c5 33 ♗f1 ♗a6 34 ♗e5 ♖d7 35
♗×a6 ♘×a6 36 ♘f2 ♘ac5 37
♘d1 ♘×a4 38 ♖a3 ♘ac5 39 ♕e1
d4 40 ♖ba1 ♘b3 41 ♖1a2 ♖c1 42
♖b2 ♘c3 **0–1** (2·07 – 1·23)

0131   Zyulyarkin–AK

22.2.1963: QGD

1 d4 ♘f6 2 c4 e6 3 ♘c3 d5 4 ♗g5
♘bd7 5 e3 ♗e7 6 ♘f3 OO 7 ♕c2 b6
8 cd ed 9 ♗b5 ♗b7 10 ♕f5 c6 11
♗d3 h6 12 ♗f4 ♗c8 13 ♗b1 ♗b4
14 ♕c2 ♘e4 15 OO ♗×c3 16 bc
♗a6 17 ♖e1 f5 18 ♘e5 ♘×e5 19
♗×e5 ♕h4 20 ♖c1 ♖f7 21 a4 ♗c4
22 f3 ♘g5 23 ♕f2 ♕×f2+ 24 ♔×f2
♘e6 25 ♗a2 ♗×a2 26 ♖×a2 (*18*)

0132   Kalashnikov–AK

14.6.1963: Ponziani

1 e4 e5 2 ♘f3 ♘c6 3 c3 ♗e7 4 d4 d6
5 ♗b5 ed 6 cd ♗d7 7 ♘c3 ♘f6 8 OO
a6 9 ♗a4 OO 10 ♖e1 ♗g4 11 ♗e3
d5 12 e5 ♘e4 13 a3 ♗f5 14 ♖c1
♘a5 15 ♘×e4 ♗×e4 16 ♘d2 b5 17
♘×e4 ba 18 ♕×a4 ♘c4 19 ♖×c4
dc 20 ♕×c4 ♕b8 21 b4 ♕b7 22 d5
♖fd8 23 ♖d1 (*19*)

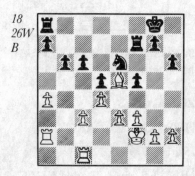

18
26W
B

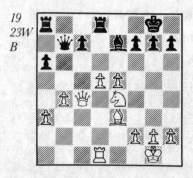

19
23W
B

26 … c5 27 c4 cd 28 cd ♘c5 29
♖d1 de+ 30 ♔×e3 ♖e7 31 f4 ♖d8
32 ♔f3 ♖ed7 33 d6 ♘b7 34 g4 fg+
35 ♔×g4 ♔f7 36 f5 ♖c8 37 ♖d4
♖c5 38 ♔f4 ♘a5 39 ♖g2 ♖×e5
(The initial move of a neat
simplifying combination, also
netting a pawn.) 40 ♔×e5 ♘c6+
41 ♔d5 ♘×d4 42 ♔×d4 ♖×d6+
43 ♔e5 ♖c6 44 ♖d2 ♖c5+ 45
♖d5 ♖×d5+ 46 ♔×d5 a6 47 ♔c6
b5 48 ab ab 49 ♔×b5 ♔f6 50 ♔c4
♔×f5 51 ♔d3 ♔g4 **0–1** (2·10 –
1·10)

(White has given up a rook for a
piece, two pawns, and what he
clearly thought to be a tremendous
position. However, Karpov neatly
infiltrates White's position and the
end product is that White has given
up a rook for nothing.) 23 … a5 24
♘c5 ♕c8 25 b5 ♕f5 26 ♗d4
♗×c5 27 ♕×c5 ♕e4 28 ♗c3
♖ab8 29 f3 ♕e2 30 ♕d4 ♖×b5 31
e6 f6 32 ♖e1 ♕a2 33 e7 ♖e8 34
♕g4 ♕×d5 35 ♗×f6 ♕f7 36
♗×g7 h5 37 ♕d7 ♖d5 38 ♕h3
♕×g7 39 ♕e6+ ♕f7 40 ♕c6 g5
41 h4 ♖g7 42 ♖e6 ♖×e7 **0–1**

RSFSR Junior Championship Vladimir 1964

0133 AK–Fedin

R?: 1.7.1964: Sicilian

1 e4 c5 2 ♘c3 ♘c6 3 g3 g6 4 ♗g2
♗g7 5 ♘ge2 d6 6 00 e5 7 d3 ♘ge7
8 f4 00 9 h3 f5 10 ♗e3 ♘d4 11 ♕d2
♕c7 12 ♘d1 ♗d7 13 c3 ♘e6 14
♘f2 ♖ab8 15 ♖ac1 ♗c6 16 b4 b6
17 c4 ♘d4 18 ♗×d4 ed 19 b5 ♗b7
20 g4 ♖f7 21 a4 ♖bf8 22 ♖c2 ♔h8
23 ♖a2 ♘g8 24 g5 ♖e8 25 a5 ♖fe7
26 ♘g3 d5 27 ab ab 28 ef ♖e3 29
♘fh1 dc 30 dc gf 31 ♖a7 ♖b8 32
♘×f5 ♖e6 33 ♗d5 ♖g6 34 ♘hg3
♕c8 35 ♗f7 ♖a8 36 ♖×a8 ♗×a8
37 ♔h2 ♕b7 38 ♗×g6 hg 39 ♘h4
♔h7 40 f5 gf 41 ♕e2 ♘e7 42
♕h5+ ♔g8 43 ♕e8+ ♔h7 44
g6+ ♔h6 45 ♕×e7 f4 46 ♘gf5+
1–0

0134 AK–Petrov

R?: 2.7.1964: French

1 e4 e6 2 d4 d5 3 ed ed 4 c3 ♗d6 5
♗d3 c6 6 ♘f3 ♘e7 7 00 ♗g4 8
♘bd2 ♕c8 9 ♖e1 00 10 ♘f1 ♘g6
11 ♘g3 ♗d7 12 h3 ♗×f3 13 ♕×f3
♕c7 14 ♘f5 ♖fe8 15 ♗g5 f6 16
♘×d6 ♕×d6 17 ♗d2 ♘df8 18
♕g4 ♕d7 19 ♗f5 ♕d6 20 h4 ♘e7
21 ♗d3 f5 22 ♗×f5 ♘×f5 23 ♕×f5
♕g6 24 ♕×g6 ♘×g6 25 g3 ♔f7 26
♔g2 h5 27 ♗g5 a5 28 ♔f3 a4 29 g4
hg+ 30 ♔×g4 ♘f8 31 f4 ♘h7 32
♔f5 g6+ 33 ♔g4 ♖e4 34 ♔f3
♖ae8 35 ♖×e4 ♖×e4 36 ♖h1

♘×g5+ 37 hg ♔g7 38 b3 a3 39 b4
b5 40 ♖b1 ♖e8 41 ♖b3 ♖a8 42
♔g4 ♘f7 43 f5 gf+ 44 ♔×f5 ♔g7
45 ♔e5 ♔g6 46 ♔d6 **1–0**

0135 AK–Simanov

R?: 6.7.1964: Sicilian

1 e4 c5 2 ♘c3 ♘c6 3 g3 g6 4 ♗g2
♗g7 5 ♘ge2 e6 6 d3 d6 7 ♗e3 ♘d4
8 00 ♘e7 9 f4 00 10 ♖b1 ♘ec6 11
h3 ♖b8 12 ♔h2 b5 13 ♕d2 ♕a5 14
a3 b4 15 ab ♕×b4 16 b3 ♗d7 17
♕c1 ♘×e2 18 ♘×e2 ♘d4 19
♘×d4 cd 20 ♗d2 ♕c5 21 ♖a1
♗b5 22 ♖a2 ♖fc8 23 ♕e1 a6 24
♕e2 f5 25 ♕e1 ♖e8 26 ♖f2 e5 27 fe
♗×e5 28 ♗f4 fe 29 ♕×e4 ♕c7 30
♕d5+ ♔g7 31 ♖a1 ♖f8 32 ♖af1
♕e7 33 ♖e1 ♖be8 34 ♗×e5+ de
35 ♖fe2 ♖f5 36 g4 ♖g5 37 ♖e4 h5
38 ♖×d4 hg 39 hg ♕f6 40 ♖de4
♗c6 41 ♕c5 ♗×e4 42 ♖×e4 ♕e6
43 ♔g3 ♔h6 44 ♕e3 ♖f8 *(20)*

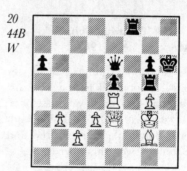

20
44B
W

45 b4 ♕f6 46 c4 ♕e6 47 c5 ♕d7 48
♗f3 a5 49 ba ♕e7 50 c6 ♖a8 51
♕e1 ♕f6 52 c7 ♖f8 53 ♕e3 ♖c8
54 ♖c4 ♕d6 55 ♖c6 ♕d7 56 ♔h4

♕e7 57 ♗e4♔g7 58 ♔g3 ♖h8 59 c8♕ **1–0**

0136 Sazontiev–AK

R?: 8.7.1964: QGD

1 d4 ♘f6 2 ♘f3 e6 3 ♗g5 d5 4 c4 ♗e7 5 ♘c3 00 6 e3 ♘bd7 7 ♗d3 ♖e8 8 00 ♘f8 9 ♘e5 c6 10 f4 ♘6d7 11 ♗×e7 ♕×e7 12 ♖f3 f6 13 ♘g4 ♘b6 14 c5 ♘bd7 15 ♖g3 ♔h8 16 ♘f2 e5 17 ♕h5 e4 18 ♗e2 g6 19 ♕h6 b6 20 b4 a5 21 b5 ♗b7 22 cb ♘×b6 23 bc ♗×c6 24 h4 ♖ec8 25 h5 ♕g7 26 ♕×g7+ ♔×g7 27 hg hg 28 ♖b1 ♖ab8 29 ♗a6 ♖c7 30 ♘fd1 ♘fd7 31 ♖h3 ♗a4 32 ♖h2 ♗×d1 33 ♘×d1 ♘a4 34 ♖a1 ♘c3 35 g3 ♘×d1 36 ♖×d1 ♖c3 37 ♖e1 a4 38 ♖d2 ♖b6 39 ♗f1 ♔f7 40 ♖ee2 a3 41 ♔f2 ♖b4 42 g4 ♘b6 43 ♖c2 ♖×c2 44 ♖×c2 ♖b2 45 ♖e2 ♘a4 46 ♔e1 ♘c3 47 ♖d2 ♘×a2 **0–1**

'Trud' Training School Moscow 1964 (1963?) .

As part of the training scheme (see p. 103), Botvinnik gave a six board simultaneous display with clocks. A. Dubinsky and Y. Balashov both beat Botvinnik, Karpov drew and Botvinnik won the other three.

0137 AK–Botvinnik

Caro Kann

1 e4 c6 2 d4 d5 3 ♘c3 g6 4 ♘f3 ♗g7 5 ♗f4 ♗g4 6 ed cd 7 ♘b5 ♔f8 8 h3

♗×f3 9 ♕×f3 ♘c6 10 c3 ♘f6 11 ♗d3 a6 12 ♘a3 ♕b6 13 ♕e2 ♘h5 14 ♗e3 ♕c7 15 00 ♘f4 16 ♕d2 ♘×d3 17 ♕×d3 h5 18 ♘c2 ♗f6 19 f4 e6 20 ♘e1 h4 21 ♘f3 ♘e7 22 ♘e5 ♘f5 23 ♗c1 ♔g7 24 ♖f2 ♗e7 25 ♕f3 b5 26 ♗d2 b4 27 ♖e2 a5 28 ♖ae1 ♖a6 29 ♕d3 ♕b7 30 ♖c1 ♖c8 31 ♗e1 a4 32 c4 ♘×d4 33 ♖d2 ♘f5 34 ♖dc2 ♘e3 35 ♖e2 dc 36 ♘×c4 ♘×c4 37 ♖×c4 ♖d6 38 ♕e4 (*21*)

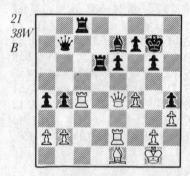

21
38W
B

38 ... ♖×c4?? 39 ♕×b7 ♗f6 40 ♗×b4? ♗d4+ 41 ♔h2 ♖b6 42 ♕e7 ♖c×b4 ½–½ 'He doesn't understand anything about chess' – Botvinnik speaking about Karpov circa 1963/4.

USSR Junior Championship Moscow, 4–?.1.1965

This tournament was an eight round Swiss. Karpov, at thirteen the youngest player, scored 4½. No games are available. Leading scorers in the tournament were 1 M. Mukhin 6½; 2 A. Petrushin 6; 3–5 A.

Goikhman, V. Zhelnin, V. Kupreichik 5½.

Vladimir 1965
Clock simultaneous

0138 AK–Spassky

24.1.1965: Caro Kann

1 e4 c6 2 d4 d5 3 ♘c3 de 4 ♘×e4 ♘d7 5 ♘f3 ♘gf6 6 ♘×f6+ ♘×f6 7 ♗d3 ♗g4 8 c3 e6 9 h3 ♗h5 10 ♕e2 ♗d6 11 ♗g5 ♕c7 12 000 ♗f4+ 13 ♗×f4 ♕×f4+ 14 ♕e3 ♘d5 15 ♕×f4 ♘×f4 16 g4 ♗g6 17 ♘e5 ♗×d3 18 ♘×d3 ♘×d3+ 19 ♖×d3 ♖d8 20 ♔d2 ♔e7 21 f4 (*22*)

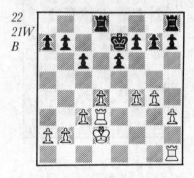

22
21W
B

21 ... h5 22 g5 ♖d5 23 ♔e3 ♖hd8 24 h4 c5 25 ♖hd1 c4 26 ♖3d2 ♖b5 27 ♖b1 ♖d6 28 b3 ♖db6 29 ♖db2 a5 30 ♔d2 a4 31 b4 f6 32 ♔e3 ½–½

Tula 1965
Armed Forces zonal

0139 Drizgalovich–AK

21.12.1965: Grünfeld

1 d4 ♘f6 2 c4 g6 3 ♘c3 ♗g7 4 ♘f3

00 5 e3 d5 6 cd ♘×d5 7 ♘×d5 ♕×d5 8 ♕c2 ♘c6 9 ♗c4 ♕d6 10 00 ♗g4 11 ♗e2 ♘b4 12 ♕d2 c5 13 a3 ♘c6 14 dc ♕×c5 15 b4 ♕b6 16 ♗b2 ♖fd8 17 ♕c2 ♗f5 18 ♕b3 ♘a5 19 ♕a2 ♗e6 20 ♕b1 ♗×b2 21 ♕×b2 ♘c4 22 ♗×c4 ♗×c4 23 ♖fd1 ♗d5 24 ♘d4 ♕f6 25 ♕e2 e5 26 ♘f3 a6 27 ♖ac1 b5 28 ♖d2 ♗c4 29 ♖×d8+ ♖×d8 30 ♕b2 ♕d6 31 h3 (*23*)

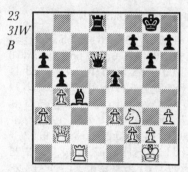

23
31W
B

31 ... f6 32 a4 ♔g7 33 ab ab 34 ♖a1 ♖d7 35 ♖c1 ♕d3 36 ♔h2 ♖a7 37 ♖a1 ♖d7 38 ♖a3 ♕d6 39 ♔g1 h5 40 ♖a1 ♕d3 41 ♔h2 g5 42 ♖c1 ♔h6 43 ♖c3 ♕d6 44 ♔g1 g4 45 hg hg 46 ♘e1 ♔g5 47 ♖c1 f5 48 g3 ♕d5 49 ♘g2 ♕e4 50 ♕c2 ♕×c2 51 ♖×c2 ♖d1+ 52 ♔h2 ♖b1 53 ♖d2 ♖×b4 54 ♘e1 ♖b1 55 ♘g2 b4 56 ♘h4 b3 57 ♘g2 b2 **0–1**

0140 AK–Polyakov

28.12.1965: Spanish

1 e4 e5 2 ♘f3 ♘c6 3 ♗b5 a6 4 ♗a4 b5 5 ♗b3 ♗b7 6 00 ♗c5 7 c3 ♘a5 8 ♘×e5 ♘×b3 9 ab ♕e7 10 ♘f3

♘f6 11 d4 ♗b6 12 ♗g5 ♗×e4 13 ♖e1 00 14 ♘fd2 d5 15 f3 ♗×f3 16 ♘×f3 ♗d6 17 ♗×f6 ♕×f6 18 b4 ♕f4 19 ♕e2 h6 20 ♕e5 ♕×e5 21 ♘×e5 ♖fe8 22 ♘d2 a5 23 ba ♖×a5 24 ♖×a5 ♗×a5 25 b4 ♗b6 26 ♘df3 ♖a8 27 ♘c6 ♖a3 28 ♘e7+ ♔f8 29 ♘×d5 ♗a7 30 ♘×c7 ♖×c3 31 ♖e8 **mate**

0141 Hampyuk–AK

28.12.1965 Spanish

1 e4 e5 2 ♘f3 ♘c6 3 ♗b5 a6 4 ♗a4 ♘f6 5 00 ♗e7 6 ♖e1 b5 7 ♗b3 d6 8 c3 00 9 h3 ♘a5 10 a4 ♘×b3 11 ♕×b3 ♗e6 12 ♕d1 c5 13 ab ab 14 ♖×a8 ♕×a8 15 d3 c4 16 ♗g5 ♖d8 17 ♗×f6 ♗×f6 18 d4 d5 19 ♕c2 de 20 ♕×e4 ♗d5 21 ♕e3 ♗×f3 22 de ♖d3 23 ♕f4 ♗e7 24 gf ♖×f3 25 ♕g4 ♗c5 26 ♖f1 h5 27 ♕g2 h4 28 ♔h1 ♖×h3+ **0–1**

0142 AK–Orekhov

French

The first game Karpov had published in *Shakhmatny Bulletin* (1965 No. 8).

1 e4 (*Shakhmatny Bulletin* gave the order 1 d4 e6 2 e4.) 1 . . . e6 2 d4 d5 3 ♘d2 ♘f6 4 e5 ♘fd7 5 ♗d3 c5 6 c3 ♘c6 7 ♘e2 f6 8 ef ♘×f6 9 ♘f3 ♗d6 10 00 00 11 ♘g3 ♕c7 (An immediate 11 . . . e5 leads to a double-edged position, e.g. 12 de ♘×e5 13 ♘×e5 ♗×e5 14 f4 ♗c7 15 f5 ♗×g3 16 hg ♘e4 17 ♗×e4 de

18 ♕b3+ ♔h8.) 12 ♗g5 ♗d7 13 ♕b1 (13 ♕c2 c4) 13 . . . h6 14 ♗×f6 ♖×f6 15 ♘h5 ♖f7 16 ♗g6 ♖e7 17 ♘h4 (threatening 18 ♗h7+ ♔f7 19 ♕g6+ ♔f8 20 ♘×g7 ♖×g7 21 ♕f6+ ♖f7 22 ♕h8+ ♔e7 23 ♘g6 mate) 17 . . . ♗e8 18 f4 cd 19 ♔h1 dc 20 bc ♕d7 21 ♕d3 ♗f7 22 ♖f3 e5 23 ♖g3 ♗×g6 (If Black eats the poisoned pawn by 23 . . . ef he dies as follows: 24 ♗×f7+ ♖×f7 25 ♖×g7+ ♔f8 26 ♘g6+ ♔e8 27 ♖e1+ ± ±) 24 ♕×g6 ♖f8 25 f5 e4 26 f6 ♖ef7 27 ♘f5 (*24*)

24
27W
B

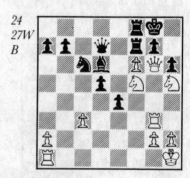

27 . . . ♖×f6 (27 . . . ♗×g3? 28 ♘×h6+ ♔h8 29 ♘×f7+ ♕×f7 30 fg+ ; 29 . . . ♖×f7 30 fg+ ♖×g7 31 ♕h6+ ♔g8 32 ♘f6+ ± ±) 28 ♘×f6+ ♖×f6 29 ♕×g7+ ♕×g7 30 ♖×g7+ ♔h8 31 ♖d7 ♖×f5 32 ♖×d6 e3 33 ♖e6! ♘e5 34 ♔g1 ♔g7 35 ♖e1 ♔f7 (35 . . . ♘c4 36 ♖e7+ ♔f6 37 ♖×b7 ♘d2 38 h3!± ±) 36 ♖×h6 ♘c4 37 ♖h3 ♖e5 38 ♖f3+ ♔e6 39 ♖f1 ♖e4 40 h3 ♔e5 41 g4± ± d4 42 ♖f5+ ♔e6 43 cd ♖×d4 44 ♖f8 b5 45 g5 ♖d7

46 ♔g2 a5 47 h4 b4 48 g6 a4 49 h5 ♖d5 50 h6 ♖g5+ 51 ♔f1 ♖×g6 52 h7 ♖h6 53 h8♕ ♖×h8 54 ♖×h8 b3 55 ab ab 56 ♔e2 b2 57 ♖e8+ ♔d5 58 ♖×e3 ♘×e3 59 ♔×e3 ♔c4 60 ♔d2 ♔b3 61 ♖b1 ♔a2 62 ♔c2 **1–0**

9th USSR Schools' Spartakiad
Harkov, 1965

Karpov's 7/9 was the best score on board three (for juniors under 16 years of age) jointly with D. Kudishevich. None of the games is available.

2 1966—The USSR's Youngest Master

This chapter contains the games played by Karpov in the USSR Junior Championship, the Leningrad match tournament in which Karpov became the youngest holder of the Soviet master title, the USSR Junior Team Championship, a match between junior teams of the USSR and Scandinavia and some training games against two well-known women players.

USSR Junior Championship
Moscow, 3-12.1.1966

This event took place in the club-house of the Hotel Altai. The results of the tournament, a nine-round Swiss were as follows: 1-2 M. Shteinberg, V. Lilein 7 (Shteinberg winning the title – he had won more games than Lilein); 3-4 Didishko, Kudishevich 6½; 5-6 Karpov, Timoshenko 6; 7 Manin 5½; 8-14 Karasev, Kirpichnikov, Samadov, Shakarov, Shereshevsky, Ubilava, Umansky 5; 15-18 Kolbanov, Nepomnyashchy, Shvarts, Tsikhelashvili 4½; 19-26 Chechelian, Kakageldiev, Kosikov, Krupenko, Pertsikavichus, Sazontiev, Shusterman, Vaganian 4; 27-28 Agzamov, Zernitsky 3½; 29-30 Aliev, Sangla 3; 31 Saifutdinov 1½; 32 Mukhamedzhanov 0.

0201 AK–Nepomnyashchy

R1: ?.1.1966: Spanish

1 e4 e5 2 ♘f3 ♘c6 3 ♗b5 a6 4 ♗a4 ♘f6 5 00 d6 6 d3 b5 7 ♗b3 ♘a5 8 ♘c3 ♘×b3 9 ab ♗b7 10 ♘e2 ♘d7 11 ♘g3 g6 12 ♗g5 f6 13 ♗d2 ♗g7 14 ♕c1 00 15 ♗h6 d5 16 ♗×g7 ♔×g7 17 b4 c5 18 bc ♘×c5 19 ♕e3 d4 20 ♕d2 ♖c8 21 ♘e2 ♕b6 22 ♖ad1 b4 23 ♔h1 b3 24 c3 dc 25 ♘×c3 ♖f7 26 ♕e3 ♘d7 27 d4 ed 28 ♘×d4 ♔g8 29 ♘d5 ♗×d5 30 ed ♘e5 31 d6 ♖d7 32 f4 ♘f7 33 f5 ♖×d6 34 fg hg 35 ♕×b3 ♕×b3 ½-½

0202 Shakarov–AK

R2: ?.1.1966: QGD

1 d4 ♘f6 2 c4 e6 3 ♘c3 d5 4 cd ed 5
♗g5 c6 6 e3 ♗f5 7 ♕f3 ♗g6 8
♗×f6 ♕×f6 9 ♕×f6 gf 10 ♘ge2
♗d6 11 g3 ♘d7 12 ♘f4 ♗f5 13
♗e2 000 14 ♗h5 ♗e6 15 000 ♘b6
16 ♘ce2 ♔b8 17 ♔b1 ♘c8 18 ♖c1
♘e7 19 a3 b6 20 ♖hd1 ♔b7 21
♗f3 ♘c8 22 ♔a1 ½–½

0203 AK–Tsikhelashvili

R3: ?.1.1966: Sicilian

1 e4 c5 2 ♘c3 ♘c6 3 g3 g6 4 ♗g2
♗g7 5 ♘ge2 d6 6 00 e5 7 f4 ♘ge7 8
d3 ♗e6 9 ♗e3 00 10 ♕d2 ♘d4 11
♘d1 ♕d7 12 c3 ♘×e2+ 13 ♕×e2
♖ac8 14 ♘f2 d5 15 ♗d2 d4 16 c4
b5 17 b3 bc 18 bc ♖b8 19 ♖fb1
♘c6 20 ♕d1 a5 21 a3 ♕a7 22 f5
♗d7 23 g4 ♘e7 24 h4 a4 25 ♕f3 f6
26 ♗h3 ♖b3 27 ♖f1 ♕b7 (*25*)

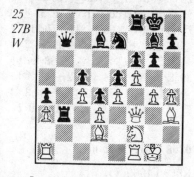

25
27B
W

28 ♔h1 h6 29 fg f5 30 gf ♗×f5 31
♗×f5 ♖×f5 32 ♕g2 ♖h5 33 ♕g4
♘f5 34 ♔g1 ♖b2 35 ef ♖×d2 36
♕×h5 e4 37 de ♕c7 38 ♕f3 d3 39
♖ad1 **1–0**

0204 Samadov–AK

R4: ?.1.1966: Caro Kann

1 e4 c6 2 d4 d5 3 ♘c3 de 4 ♘×e4
♘f6 5 ♘×f6+ ef 6 g3 ♗d6 7 ♗g2
00 8 ♘f3 ♕a5+ 9 c3 ♖e8+ 10
♗e3 ♕h5 11 ♘d2 ♗g4 12 ♕b3 b6
13 00 ♗h3 14 ♗f3 ♕f5 15 ♖fc1
♕c8 16 ♘e4 ♗c7 17 c4 ♘d7 18
♕a4 ♘b8 19 ♘c3 ♗d6 20 b4 ♕f5
21 ♗e2 ♖c8 22 c5 ♗c7 23 b5 bc 24
dc cb 25 ♘×b5 ♕d5 26 ♗f1 ♗×f1
27 ♔×f1 ♗e5 28 ♘d6 ♖f8 29 ♖d1
♕e6 30 ♖ac1 ♘d7 31 ♘b7 ♘b8
32 c6 g5 33 ♗c5 ♖c8 34 ♗d6 (*26*)

26
34W
B

34 ... a5 35 ♗×e5 fe 36 c7 ♘a6 37
♖d8+ ♔g7 38 ♕a3 ♘b4 39 ♕c3
h6 40 ♕c5 ♘a6 41 ♕f8+ ♔g6 42
♕g8+ ♔h5 43 ♕f8 ♘×c7 44
♖×c7 ♖×c7 45 ♖×a8 ♖c1+ **0–1**

0205 AK–Lilein

R5: ?.1.1966: Sicilian

(Notes by Karpov)

1 e4 c5 2 ♘c3 ♘c6 3 g3 g6 4 ♗g2
♗g7 5 ♘ge2 d6 6 00 e6 7 f4
(*Shakhmatny Bulletin* No. 3 1966

gives the move order: 7 d3 ♖b8 8
♗e3 ♘d4 9 ♕d2 b5 10 ♘dl b4 11
f4 ♘e7 12 g4 f5 13 h3 ♘a5 14 ♘g3
♕a4 15 c3 bc 16 bc ♘c2 17 ♖cl
♘×e3 18 ♘×e3 00. KJO'C) 7 ...
♘ge7 8 d3 ♖b8 9 ♗e3 ♘d4= 10
♕d2 b5 11 g4 b4?! (11 ... 00!?) 12
♘dl ♕a5 13 ♘g3 ♕a4?! (13 ...
00) 14 c3 (14 ♖f2? b3 15 c3 ♘c2; 15
cb ♘×b3 16 ♘c2 ♗d7∓; 14 ...
00?! 15 ♕cl± and 16 c3) 14 ... bc
15 bc ♘c2 16 ♖cl ♗×e3 17 ♘×e3
f5?! 18 h3?∓ (18 gf gf 19 ef ef 20
♘h5±) 18 ... 00 19 gf gf?! (19 ef!? ef
20 ♘d5∓) 19 ... ef 20 ef ♘×f5∓
21 ♘g×f5 ♗×f5 22 ♘×f5?!∓ (22
♘d5!?) 22 ... ♖×f5 23 ♗e4 ♖h5
24♔h2 ♖f8 25 ♖f2 ♕d7 (and here
Shakhmatny Bulletin, loc. cit., gives
the order: 25 ... ♗h6 26 c4 ♕d7
27 ♗g2. KJO'C) 26 ♗g2 ♗h6 27
c4 ♖hf5 28 ♖cfl ♕e7 29 ♗d5+
♔h8 30 ♕b2+ ♗g7 31 ♕e2 ♕h4
32 ♕g4 ♕×g4? (32 ... ♕e7 33
♕e2 ♕d8∓) 33 hg ♖×f4 34 ♖×f4
♗e5 35 ♔g2 ♗×f4 36 ♖bl= ½–½

0206 AK–Didishko

R6: ?.1.1966: Scandinavian

1 e4 d5 2 ed ♘f6 3 d4 ♘×d5 4 c4
♘b6 5 ♘c3 e5 6 ♘f3 ed 7 ♕×d4
♘c6 8 ♕×d8+ ♘×d8 9 ♘d4 ♘c6
10 ♘c2 g6 11 b3 ♗g7 12 ♗b2 ♗d7
13 000 000 14 ♘d5 ♗×b2+ 15
♔×b2 ♗×d5 16 cd ♘e5 17 ♗c4
♘g4 18 f3?? ♘f2 19 d6 ♘×dl+
20 ♖×dl ♗e6 **0–1**

0207 Timoshenko–AK

R7: ?.1.1966: Spanish

1 e4 e5 2 ♘f3 ♘c6 3 ♗b5 a6 4 ♗a4
♘f6 5 00 ♗e7 6 ♖el b5 7 ♗b3 d6 8
c3 00 9 d4 ♗g4 10 ♗e3 ♘a5 11
♗c2 ♘c4 12 ♗cl ed 13 cd c5 14
♘bd2 ♘×d2 15 ♕×d2 ♗×f3 16 gf
♕b6 17 dc dc 18 ♔hl ♖fd8 19
♕e2 c4 20 ♖gl ♘d7 21 ♖g2 ♘e5
22 ♗e3 ♗c5 23 ♖agl g6 24 f4 ♘d3
25 e5 ♖ac8 (*27*)

27
25B
W

26 h4 ♕b7 27 ♗×c5 ♖×c5 28 ♕e3
♕d5 29 b4 ♖c6 30 h5 ♕d4 31 ♕f3
♖·b6 32 f5 ♘×e5 33 ♕h3 ♖dd6 34
♖h2 ♕d5+ 35 ♖gg2 ♘f3 36 ♖g4
♘×h2+ 37 ♔×h2 ♕d2 38 hg hg
39 fg fg 40 ♖e4 ♕×f2+ 41 ♔hl
♕f7 42 ♖h4 ♕f6 43 ♖g4 ♕h8 44
♖h4 ♕al+ 45 ♔g2 ♖d2+ **0–1**

0208 AK–Sazontiev

R8: ?.1.1966: QP

1 d4 ♘f6 2 g3 d5 3 ♗g2 c6 4 ♘f3
♗g4 5 00 ♘bd7 6 ♘bd2 e6 7 c3
♗d6 8 ♕c2 00 9 e4 de 10 ♘×e4
♘×e4 11 ♕×e4 ♘f6 12 ♕c2 ♕a5

13 ♖el ♗f5 14 ♕e2 ♕c7 15 ♘e5 ♘d5 16 a3 ♖ad8 17 c4 ♘e7 18 ♘f3 ♕a5 19 ♗e3 ♖b8 20 ♖acl ♗g4 21 h3 ♗×f3 22 ♗×f3 ♘f5 23 ♖edl ♘×e3 24 ♕×e3 ♖d6 25 b4 ♕f5 *(28)*

28
25B
W

26 ♔g2 ♖fd8 27 ♖c3 a6 28 a4 ♗a7 29 c5 ♖6d7 30 b5 ab 31 ab cb 32 ♖a3 ♗b8 33 ♖b3 ♕f6 34 ♖×b5 ♖×d4 35 ♖dbl ♖d3 36 ♕e2 ♖d2 37 ♕e4 ♖8d4 38 ♕el ♖4d3 39 ♗e2 ♕g5 40 c6 ♖×g3+ 41 fg ♖×e2+ 42 ♕×e2 ♕×g3+ 43 ♔fl **1-0**

0209 Kudishevich–AK

R9: ?.1.1966: QGD

1 d4 ♘f6 2 c4 e6 3 ♘c3 d5 4 cd ed 5 ♗g5 c6 6 e3 ♗e7 7 ♖cl ♗f5 8 ♗d3 ♘e4 9 ♗×e7 ♕×e7 10 ♘ge2 00 11 00 ♘d7 12 ♖el ♖fe8 13 ♗bl ♘df6 14 f3 ♘×c3 15 ♘×c3 ♗×bl 16 ♖×bl c5 17 dc ♕×c5 18 ♕d4 ♕×d4 19 ed ♔f8 20 ♔f2 ♖ed8 21 ♖e5 ♖d7 22 g4 h6 23 h4 ♘e8 24 ♖bel ♘c7 25 ♔g3 ♖e8 26 ♖×e8+ ♘×e8 27 f4 ♘c7 28 f5 ♖e7 29 ♖×e7 ♔×e7 30 ♔f4 f6 *(29)*

29
30B
W

31 ♔e3 ♔d6 32 ♔d3 ♔c6 33 ♘e2 ♔d6 34 ♔e3 ♔c6 35 ♘f4 ♔d6 36 ♔d3 ♔c6 37 ♘h5 ♘e8 38 ♔e3 ♔d6 39 ♔f4 ♔e7 40 g5 hg+ 41 hg ♔f7 42 ♔g4 ♔e7 43 ♘f4 ♘c7 44 ♔h5 ♔f7 45 a4 a5 46 ♔g4 ♔e7 47 gf+ ♔×f6 48 ♘h5+ ♔f7 49 ♔f4 g6 ½-½

Masters v. Candidate Masters   Leningrad, 1-24.7.1966

By 1966 this had become an annual event in which young candidate masters were given the opportunity to win the master title. The tournament was played according to the Scheveningen system – each master playing only against the candidate masters. The results were as follows:

Candidate Masters	Masters	AK v. Masters			
Karpov 10/15	I. Zaitsev 12	1½	½	½	½
M. Mukhin 6	Chistiakov 10½	2½	1	1	½
Zotkin 5½	Alexeyev 9½	1½	½	½	½
Menkov 5	Noakh 7½	2½	1	1	½
Shakhtakhtinsky 2	Ravinsky 7	2	1	½	½

Each player played three games against each player of the other category. Karpov exceeded the master norm by two points.

0210   AK–Chistiakov

R1: ?.7.1966: Sicilian

1 e4 c5 2 ♘c3 ♘c6 3 g3 g6 4 ♗g2 ♗g7 5 d3 h5 6 h3 d6 7 ♗e3 ♗d7 8 ♕d2 a6 9 ♘ge2 ♘d4 10 ♘d1 ♕c7 11 ♘f4 e6 12 c3 ♘e7 13 cd cd 14 ♘×e6 fe 15 ♗g5 ♖c8 16 00 ♘c6 17 f4 ♘d8 18 f5 ef 19 ef ♗×f5 20 ♖c1 ♕×c1 21 ♕e2+ ♗e5 22 ♗×c1 ♖×c1 23 ♘f2 ♖×f1+ 24 ♔×f1 00 (30)

30
24B
W

25 ♗d5+ ♔g7 26 ♔g2 ♘e6 27 h4 ♖f7 28 b4 b5 29 ♗e4 ♔h6 30 ♗×f5 gf 31 ♕d2+ ♔g6 32 ♔f3 ♖g7 33 ♕c2 ♔f6 34 ♘h1 ♖c7 35 ♕d2 ♔g6 36 ♘f2 ♖g7 37 ♘h3 ♔h7 38 ♘g5+ ♘×g5 39 hg ♔g6 40 ♕c1 ♖f7 41 ♕c8 ♔×g5 42 ♕g8+ ♖g7 43 ♕d8+ ♔g6 44 ♕e8+ ♔f6 45 ♕f8+ ½-½

0211   Alexeyev–AK

R2: ?.7.1966: QP-Torre

1 d4 ♘f6 2 ♘f3 e6 3 ♗g5 d5 4 ♘bd2 ♗e7 5 e3 b6 6 ♘e5 ♗b7 7 ♗d3 ♘fd7 8 ♗×e7 ♕×e7 9 ♕g4 g6 10 f4 f5 11 ♕h3 ♘×e5 12 fe ♘d7 13 c3 000 14 ♕f3 g5 15 a4 c5 16 a5 c4 17 ♗c2 ♔c7 18 b3 b5 19 a6 ♗c6 20 bc bc 21 ♗a4 ♗×a4 22 ♖×a4 ♖b8 23 00 ♖b6 ½-½

0212 AK–Noakh

R3: ?.7.1966: Petroff

1 e4 e5 2 ᘔf3 ᘔf6 3 d4 ᘔ×e4 4 de
d5 5 ed ♗×d6 6 ♗e2 00 7 ᘔbd2
♗f5 8 00 ᘔc6 9 ᘔ×e4 ♗×e4 10
ᘔg5 ♗g6 11 ♗d3 ♕f6 12 ♗×g6
♕×g6 13 c3 ♖ad8 14 ♕b3 b6 15
ᘔf3 ♖fe8 16 ♗g5 ᘔa5 17 ♕b5 f6
18 ♗h4 ♕f7 19 ♖fd1 ♕c4 20
♕×c4 ᘔ×c4 21 b3 ᘔe5 22 ᘔd4 a6
23 ♗g3 g6 24 ♖f1 ♔f7 25 ♖d2 c5
26 ᘔe2 ♗c7 27 ♖ad1 ♖×d2 28
♖×d2 g5 29 f4 ᘔg6 30 ♖d7+ ♖e7
31 ♖×e7+ ♔×e7? (31 . . . ᘔ×e7
32 fg ♗×g3 33 gf ♗×h2 34 fe
♗e5!) 32 fg ♗×g3 33 gf+ ♔×f6 34
hg! ♔e5 (*31*)

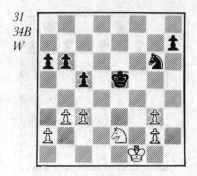

31
34B
W

35 ᘔg1 ♔e4 36 ♔e2 ᘔe7 37 ᘔh3
ᘔd5 38 ᘔf2+ ♔f5 39 ♔d3 h5 40
a4 b5 41 ab ab 42 c4 bc+ 43 ♔×c4
ᘔe3+ 44 ♔×c5 ♔e6 45 b4 ♔d7
46 ᘔe4 **1–0**

0213 Ravinsky–AK

R4: ?.7.1966: Spanish

1 e4 e5 2 ᘔf3 ᘔc6 3 ♗b5 a6 4 ♗a4
ᘔf6 5 00 ♗e7 6 ♕e2 b5 7 ♗b3 d6 8

c3 00 9 ♖d1 ᘔa5 10 ♗c2 c5 11 d4
♕c7 12 h3 ♖e8 13 de de 14 ᘔbd2
♖d8 15 ᘔf1 ♖×d1 16 ♕×d1 c4 17
♗g5 ♗e6 18 ♕e2 ᘔb7 19 ᘔg3?!
(19 ᘔe3 would have left open more
options for the knight.) 19 . . . g6 20
♖d1 ♖d8 21 ♖×d8+ ♗×d8 22
♕e3 ᘔd7 (22 . . . ᘔc5? 23 ᘔ×e5!
♕×e5 24 ♗f4±) 23 ♗×d8 (if 23
♗h6 f6 is good.) 23 . . . ᘔ×d8 (Also
23 . . . ♕×d8 24 ♕a7 ᘔdc5 25
ᘔ×e5 ♕d2 was possible, but
Karpov has his future well under
control by a solid, steady
improvement of his piece place-
ment.) 24 ♕h6 (Ravinsky, on the
other hand, still shows his
enthusiasm for tactical niceties: he
now intends 25 ᘔg5 ᘔf6 26 ᘔf5! gf
27 ♕×f6± ± ; 25 . . . ᘔf8 26 ᘔf5 f6
27 ᘔ×e6 f×e6 28 ᘔe3 with 29
ᘔd5 to follow.) 24 . . . f6 25 ♕e3 a5
(Black has a real future on the Q-
side, but White will come up
against a brick wall on the K-wing.)
26 h4 (if 26 a3 then 26 . . . ♕c5! 27
♕×c5 ᘔ×c5 with 28 . . . ᘔc6 and
29 . . . b4 to follow.) 26 . . . b4 27 h5
♔g7 28 ♗d1 ᘔf7 29 hg hg 30 ᘔd2
(*32*)

32
30W
B

30 . . . ♘c5 (With the clever threat
of 31 . . . ♘d3 32 b3 cb! 33 ♕×d3
ba and the pawn queens.) 31 b3 cb
32 ab (or 32 ♘×b3 ♘×b3 33
♗×b3 ♗×b3 34 ab bc∓ ∓) 32 . . .
♕b6 33 ♘gf1 ♘d6 (with the
mighty threat of 34 . . . bc 35 ♕×c3
♘b5! 36 ♕e3 ♘d4 with the
b-pawn getting the full Karpov
pile-up technique) 34 c4 ♕c6 35
♗c2 a4 36 ba ♗×c4 37 ♘g3 ♗f7
(not 37 . . . ♘×a4?? 38 ♕a7+ ± ±)
38 a5 ♕b5 39 f4 (Desperation –
now Karpov finishes in style.) 39
. . . ♕×a5 40 fe ♕a1+ 41 ♔f2 (if 41
♔h2 ♕×e5 42 ♘f3 ♘f5! is a nice
move.) 41 . . . ♕×e5 42 ♘f3 ♕b2
43 ♕×c5 b3 44 ♘d4 bc **0–1** (45
♕×c2 ♕×d4+ or 45 ♘×c2 ♘c4!
winning a piece either way.)

0214   AK–I. Zaitsev

R5: ?.7.1966: Sicilian

1 e4 c5 2 ♘c3 ♘c6 3 g3 g6 4 ♗g2
♗g7 5 d3 e6 6 ♗e3 d6 7 ♕d2 ♕a5
8 f3!? ♘ge7 9 ♖b1 ♘d4 10 a3 00 11
♘ge2 ♘ec6 12 00 ♘×e2+ 13
♘×e2 ♕×d2 14 ♗×d2 b5 15 c3 c4
16 d4 ♗b7 17 f4 ♖fe8 18 g4 ♘e7 19
♘g3 f5 20 gf ef 21 b3 cb 22 ♖×b3 fe
23 ♘×e4 ½–½

0215   Chistiakov–AK

R6: ?.7.1966: QGD

(Notes by Ravinsky)

1 d4 ♘f6 2 c4 e6 3 ♘c3 d5 4 ♗g5
♗e7 5 ♗×f6 ♗×f6 6 cd ed 7 e3 00 8

♗d3 c5 9 dc d4 (This leads to very
sharp play. 9 . . . ♕a5 and 9 . . .
♗e6 are the other possibilities.) 10
♘e4 de 11 fe ♗×b2 12 ♖b1 ♗f6 13
♘f3 ♗h4+ (A doubtful manoeuvre which loses time. 13 . . .
♕a5+ deserved consideration.) 14
g3 ♗e7 15 00 ♗h3 16 ♖f2 ♘d7
17 ♘d4! (A strong move, with the
unpleasant threat of ♕h5, forcing
Black's reply.) 17 . . . g6 18 ♖c2
(White overrates his position,
placing his hopes on his next move.
Simply 18 c6 would allow White,
after 18 . . . bc 19 ♘×c6 ♕e8, to
preserve his initiative with either 20
♗b5 or 20 ♖b7.) 18 . . . ♖c8 19
♘f2 (*33*)

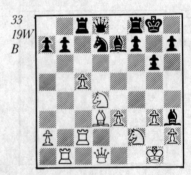

33
19W
B

19 . . . ♗g5! (Obviously White had
thought that Black only had the one
move, 19 . . . ♗e6, and then after
20 ♘×e6 fe 21 ♕g4± since if 21 . . .
♘×c5 22 ♗×g6 yields a very
strong attack. Karpov's unexpected
tactical stroke changes the picture
of the battle and the initiative
passes to Black.) 20 ♖e2 ♘×c5! 21
♗×g6 (Again the bishop on h3

cannot be captured on account of 21 ... ♗×e3+ 22 ♖×e3 ♕×d4 23 ♕e2 ♖fe8 and White loses a piece.) 21 ... hg 22 ♘×h3 ♘e4∓ (Though he has material equality White's position is clearly worse.) 23 ♘b5 ♕e7 24 ♘×g5 ♘×g5 (threatening 25 ... ♕e4) 25 ♕d5 ♖fd8 26 ♕g2 ♖d3 27 ♘×a7 ♖c7 28 e4? (This loses a piece. However, even after the better 28 ♘b5 ♖×e3! it is clear that White would still have to resign.) 28 ... ♕c5+ 29 ♔h1 ♕×a7 30 h4 ♘e6 31 ♖f1 ♕a3 32 ♔h2 ♖cc3 33 ♕f2 ♖f3 34 ♕e1 ♖×g3 35 ♖ef2 ♖h3+ 36 ♔g1 ♕c5 **0-1**

0216 AK-Alexeyev

R7: ?.7.1966: Sicilian

1 e4 c5 2 ♘c3 ♘c6 3 g3 g6 4 ♗g2 ♗g7 5 d3 d6 6 ♘ge2 e5 7 ♘d5 ♗e6 8 ♘ec3 ♘ge7 9 ♗g5 h6 10 ♗f6 00 11 00 ♗×f6 12 ♘×f6+ ♔g7 13 ♘fd5 ♗×d5 14 ♘×d5 ♘×d5 15 ed ♘e7 16 c3 ♕b6 17 ♕d2 ♖ac8 18 ♖fe1 ♖c7 19 ♔h1 ♘g8 20 h3 ♗e7 21 ♖e2 ♖fe8 22 ♖ae1 ♕a5 23 a3 b5 24 ♔h2 ♕b6 25 b4 a5 26 ♖b1 ♖c8 27 ba ♕×a5 28 ♕b2 ♖cc7 29 ♕×b5 ♕×b5 ½-½

0217 Noakh-AK

R8: ?.7.1966: Spanish

1 e4 e5 2 ♘f3 ♘c6 3 ♗b5 a6 4 ♗×c6 dc 5 ♘c3 ♗g4 6 h3 ♗×f3 7 ♕×f3 ♗c5 8 d3 ♕f6 9 ♕×f6 ♘×f6 10 ♗g5 ♘d7 11 ♗e3 000 12 ♖d1

♖he8 13 ♔e2 f6 14 ♔f3 b5 15 ♘e2 ♗×e3 16 fe c5 17 b3 ♘b6 18 g4 ♖d7 19 h4 ♖ed8 20 ♖df1 ♖f7 21 ♔g2 ♘d7 22 ♖f2 ♗e7 23 ♘g3 ♘f8 24 g5 fg 25 hg g6 26 ♔h3 ♘e6 27 ♔g4 ♖d6 28 ♖fh2 ♘f8 29 ♘f1 c4 30 dc bc 31 ♘d2 cb 32 ab ♖f7 33 ♘c4 ♖e6 34 ♖h3 ♖ee7 35 ♖a1 ♖e6 36 ♖a5 ♘d7 37 ♖f3 ♖×f3 38 ♔×f3 ♔d8 39 ♔e2 ♔c8 40 ♖d5 ♔d8 41 ♘b2 ♔c8 42 ♘d3 ♖e7 43 ♘b4 ♔b7 44 ♖a5 ♖e6 45 ♖a1 ♘c5 46 ♘d3 ♖×e4 47 ♔f3 ♘d2+ 48 ♔e2 ♘e4 49 ♔f3 ♘d2+ 50 ♔g4 (avoiding the draw) 50 ... ♖c6 51 ♖a2 e4 52 ♘e5 ♖c5 53 ♘d7 ♖f5 54 ♘f6 ♘f1 55 ♘×e4 ♘×e3+ 56 ♔g3 ♘f1+ 57 ♔g4 ♘h2+ 58 ♔g3 ♘f3 59 ♔g4 ♘e5+ 60 ♔g3 ♘f7 61 ♔g4 ♘b6 62 ♖a1 ♘e5+ 63 ♔g3 ♖f3+ 64 ♔g2 ♖e3 65 ♘f6 ♖e2+ 66 ♔g3 ♖×c2 67 ♔f4 ♘d3+ 68 ♔e3 ♘c5 69 b4 ♘e6 70 ♘×h7 ♖h2 71 ♘f6 ♖h3+ 72 ♔f2 ♖d3 73 ♘h7 ♖d5 74 ♖g1 ♔b5 75 ♖g4 ♖d4 76 ♖×d4 ♘×d4 77 ♘f8 c6 78 ♘×g6 ♘e6 79 ♔e3 ♘×g5 (*34*)

34
79B
W

80 ♘e5 ♘e6 81 ♔d3 ♘f4+ 82

♔c3 ♘d5+ 83 ♔b3 ♘×b4 84
♘c4 ♔c5 85 ♘d2 ♘d5 86 ♔a4
♘b6+ 87 ♔b3 a5 88 ♔c3 ♘d5+
89 ♔b3 ♔b5 90 ♘e4 a4+ 91 ♔a3
♘b6 92 ♘d6+ ♔c5 93 ♘b7+
♔c4 94 ♘d6+ ♔d5 95 ♘e8 c5 96
♘c7+ ♔d4 97 ♘e6+ ♔c4 98 ♘c7
♔c3 99 ♘a6 c4 100 ♘c5 ♔d4 **0–1**

0218   AK–Ravinsky

R9: ?.7.1966: Spanish

1 e4 e5 2 ♘f3 ♘c6 3 ♗b5 a6 4 ♗a4
♘f6 5 d3 d6 6 c3 ♗d7 7 00 g6 8 b4
♗g7 9 ♘b3 00 10 ♖e1 h6 11 ♘bd2
♔h7 12 ♗b2 ♘h5 13 a3 f5 14 ♕c2
fe 15 ♘×e4 ♘f4 16 ♔h1 ♗g4 17
♘g1 d5 18 ♘g3 h5 19 f3 ♗e6 20
♘3e2 ♕d7 21 ♖ad1 h4 (*35*)

35
21B
W

(It seems that Black has good
chances of a K-side attack, but
Karpov easily neutralizes the
threats.) 22 ♘×f4 ♖×f4 23 ♗c1
♖f7 24 ♗g5 ♗f6 25 ♗×f6 ♖×f6
26 ♕f2 g5 27 d4 ed 28 cd ♗f5 29
♗a4 ♖e8 30 ♗×c6 ♖×c6 31 ♕d2
♔g6 32 ♖×e8 ♕×e8 33 ♖e1 ♖e6
34 ♖×e6 ♕×e6 35 g4 hg 36 hg g4

37 ♔g2 gf+ 38 ♘×f3 ♗e4 39
♕g5+ ♔f7 40 ♕f4+ ½–½

0219   I. Zaitsev–AK

R10: ?.7.1966: Petroff

(Notes by I. Zaitsev)

**1 e4 e5 2 ♘f3 ♘f6 3 d4 ♘×e4 4
♗d3 d5 5 ♘×e5 ♘d7 6 ♘×f7!?**
(*36*)

36
6W
B

6 ... ♕e7 (In addition to this
reliable move there is 6 ... ♔×f7
e.g. 7 ♕h5+ ♔e7 (7 ... ♔e6 is no
stronger as then 8 ♕e2 ♕h4 9 g3
followed by 10 f3 is good for White.)
8 ♕e2 (8 ♕×d5 is weaker in view of
8 ... ♘df6 9 ♕e5+ ♔f7 10 ♗×e4
♗b4+ and 11 ... ♖e8.) 8 ... ♔d6
(or 8 ... ♔f7 9 ♕h5+ ♔e7 10 ♕e2
etc.) 9 ♗f4+ ♔c6 10 ♗×e4 de 11
♕c4+ ♔b6 12 ♕b3+ ♔a6 13
♕a4+ drawing.) **7 ♘×h8** (Forced.
After 7 ♘e5 ♘×e5 8 de ♕×e5
Black has a very strong attack.) **7
... ♘c3+ 8 ♔d2 ♘×d1 9 ♖e1
♘×f2 10 ♗×h7** (Not 10 ♖×e7+
♗×e7 11 ♗×h7 ♗g5+ ∓∓.) **10 ...
♘e4+** (The attempt to save the

queen by 10 . . . ♘e5 11 ♖×e5 ♗e6
is very risky for Black.) **11 ♖×e4 de
12 ♗g6+ ♔d8 13 ♘f7+ ♔e8 14
♘d6++ ♔d8 15 ♘f7+** ½-½

0220 AK–Chistiakov

R11: ?.7.1966: Sicilian

1 e4 c5 2 ♘c3 ♘c6 3 g3 d6 4 ♗g2
♘f6 5 ♘ge2 g6 6 d3 ♗g7 7 00 h5 8
h3 ♗d7 9 ♔h2 ♘e5 10 f3!? ♕c7 11
♗g5 ♗c6 12 ♕d2 ♘h7 13 ♗f4 h4
14 ♖ab1 hg+ 15 ♗×g3 ♘f6 16 f4
♘ed7 17 b4 cb 18 ♖×b4 ♘h5 19
♗f2 ♖c8 20 d4 b6 21 ♖c4 ♕b8 22
d5 ♗b7 23 ♖×c8+ ♕×c8 24 ♗d4
♗a6 25 ♖f3 f6 26 ♘g3 ♗×g3 27
♖×g3 ♔f7 28 ♗f3 ♘f8 29 e5
(Sacrificing a pawn to open lines
against the black king.) 29 . . . de 30
fe fe 31 ♗e3 ♖h4 32 ♗g4! ♕c4 33
♗g5 (*37*)

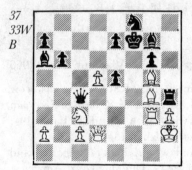

37
33W
B

33 . . . ♖×g4 (if 33 . . . ♖h8 then 34
♗×e7! ♔×e7 35 d6+ ♔f7 36 d7
♘×d7 37 ♕×d7+ ♔f8 38 ♖f3+
♔g8 39 ♗e6+ ± ±) 34 ♖×g4 ♕c7
35 ♘e4 ♔g8 36 d6 ed 37 ♕d5+
♕f7 38 ♕×f7+ ♔×f7 39 ♘×d6+
♔g8 40 ♖a4 ♗e2 41 ♖×a7 ♘e6

42 ♗e3 ♗f3 43 ♘e8 ♗h8 44 ♘d6
e4 45 ♖a8+ ♔h7 46 ♘f7 ♗f6 47
♖e8 ♘c7 48 ♖c8 ♘d5 49 ♘g5+
♔g7 50 ♘×f3 ef 51 ♗d2 ♗e5+ 52
♔g1 ♗d4+ 53 ♔f1 ♔f7 54 ♖a8
♔f6 55 c4 ♘e3+ 56 ♗×e3 ♗×e3
57 ♖a3 ♗c5 58 ♖×f3+ ♔e5 59
♖d3 ♔e4 60 ♔e2 g5 61 ♖d5 ♗e7
62 ♔d2 ♗b4+ 63 ♔c2 ♗e7 64
♔b3 ♔f4 65 ♔a4 ♔g3 66 ♖d3+
♔g2 67 ♔b5 ♗c5 68 a4 ♗f2 69 c5!
bc 70 a5 c4 71 ♖×c4 (Karpov gives
1–0 at this point. According to
Shakhmatny Bulletin No. 11 1966 the
game continued . . . .) 71 . . . ♗g1
72 a6 ♗b6 73 ♔b5 ♗g1 74 ♔c6
♗a7 75 ♔b7 **1–0**

0221 Alexeyev–AK

R12: ?.7.1966: QP–Torre

1 d4 ♘f6 2 ♘f3 e6 3 ♗g5 d5 4 e3
♗e7 5 ♘bd2 b6 6 ♗d3 ♗b7 7 00
00 8 c4 ♘bd7 9 cd ed 10 ♖c1 c5 11
dc ♘×c5 12 ♗e2 ♘fe4 13 ♗×e7
♕×e7 14 b4 ♘e6 15 b5 ♖ac8 16
♗d3 ♖fd8 17 ♘b3 ♕a3 18 ♕e2
♘c3 19 ♕d2 ♘×a2 20 ♖a1 ♕×b3
21 ♖×a2 ♘c5 22 ♖×a7 ½-½

0222 AK–Noakh

R13: ?.7.1966: Philidor

1 e4 e5 2 ♘f3 d6 3 d4 ♘d7 4 ♘c3 c6
5 ♗c4 ♕c7 6 00 h6 7 a4 ♗e7 8 a5
♘gf6 9 ♖e1 00 10 h3 ♖e8 11 ♗e3
♗f8 12 d5 cd 13 ♗×d5 ♘×d5 14
♘×d5 ♕d8 15 c4 ♘f6 16 ♕d3
♘×d5 17 ♕×d5 ♗e6 18 ♕d3 ♕c8
19 ♖ec1 f5 20 ♘h4 fe 21 ♕×e4

♗e7 22 ♘f3 ♗f6 23 ♖a3 ♕c6 24 ♕g6 ♗f7 25 ♔g4 ♗e6 26 ♔g3 ♔h7 27 c5 ♖ad8 28 ♖ac3 d5 29 ♘×e5 ♗×e5 30 ♕×e5 ♗×h3 31 ♕g3 d4 32 ♗×d4 ♕×g2+ 33 ♕×g2 ♗×g2 34 ♔×g2 ♖×d4 *(38)*

38
34B
W

35 a6 ba 36 c6 ♖c8 37 ♖a1 ♖c7 38 ♖×a6 ♖d6 39 b4 ♔g6 40 b5 ♔h7 41 ♖a5 ♖f6 42 ♖ca3 ♖ff7 43 f4 ♖ce7 44 ♔g3 g6 45 ♖c3 ♖c7 46 ♖×a7 ♖×a7 47 b6 ♖ac7 48 bc

♖×c7 49 ♔f3 ♔g7 50 ♔e4 ♔f6 51 ♔d5 ♔f5 52 ♖g3 g5 ½-½

0223   Ravinsky–AK

R14: ?.7.1966: Four Knights

1 e4 e5 2 ♘f3 ♘c6 3 ♘c3 ♘f6 4 d4 d6 5 ♗b5 ♗d7 6 ♗×c6 ♗×c6 7 ♕d3 ♕e7 8 ♗g5 h6 9 ♗h4 g5 10 ♗g3 ed 11 ♕×d4 ♗g7 12 000 ♘h5 13 ♕d3 000 14 ♘d4 ♗×d4 15 ♕×d4 ♔b8 16 f3 ♘×g3 17 hg h5 18 b4 g4 19 b5 ♗×b5 ½-½

0224   AK–I. Zaitsev

R15: ?.7.1966: Modern

1 e4 c6 2 d4 g6 3 ♗e3 ♗g7 4 c3 ♘f6 5 ♗d2 d6 6 f3 ♘bd7 7 ♗d3 00 8 ♘e2 e5 9 00 d5 10 ♔h1 ♖e8 11 ♖c1 b6 12 ♘g3 ♗b7 13 ♘b3 ♕c7 14 ♕d2 a6 15 ♖ce1 c5 16 dc bc 17 c4 d4 18 ♗g5 ♕b6 19 ♕a5 ½-½

USSR Junior Team Championship   Vladimir, 5-14.8.1966

The results of the A-final were: 1 Ukraine 34/50; 2 RSFSR 31½; 3 Moscow 26½; 4 Byelorussia 25½; 5 Georgia 24; 6 Latvia 8½. The RSFSR team headed their group of the preliminaries with 33½/40 ahead of 2 Latvia 19½; 3 Kazakhstan 18; 4 Estonia 15½; 5 Azerbaidzhan 13½.

Teams were constituted of 6 juniors and two girls under the age of 18 and two juniors under 15. The RSFSR team was G. Timoshenko, Y. Anikayev, A. Arkhipov, E. Sveshnikov, Z. Shteiner, V. Shepenkov, A. Karpov, M. Umansky, V. Ushakova, T. Konstantinova. Karpov played on the top board for his age group.

The prize for the best score on board seven (Karpov's) was won by E. Kim of Uzbekhistan with 8½/9. Asked about this event (at Bath 1973), Karpov thought he had won a board prize, so he must have made a good score and perhaps had the best result on his board in the A-final.

0225 Kudishevich–AK

R?: ?.8.1966: Spanish

(Notes by Karpov)

A stubborn, tense, it cannot be said faultless, struggle developed. At one moment it seemed that Black was near to victory. He seized the centre and gradually crushed the enemy with his pawns. But there followed White's own counter-stroke and the struggle flared up with renewed strength. Time trouble gradually approached (and this is a very fearsome thing for a chess player – avoid time trouble!) and Black again succeeded in seizing the initiative. The white pieces then found themselves in a tangle from which they were unable to emerge. 1 e4 e5 2 ♘f3 ♘c6 3 ♗b5 a6 4 ♗a4 ♘f6 5 00 ♗e7 6 ♖e1 b5 7 ♗b3 d6 8 c3 00 9 h3 ♘a5 10 ♗c2 ♗b7

    11 d4   ♘c4

In my remarks concerning . . . (Karpov–Zhelyandinov, game 1303) . . . I said that White often bases his play on the knight at a5. Thus the idea of this variation consists in the redeployment of the knight away from its unfortunate position on a5. At the same time, Black hinders, for a while, the emergence of the knight on b1. It is now disadvantageous for White to play 12 ♘bd2 as Black replies 12 . . . ♘×d2 and gets rid of one of the most dangerous 'Spanish' pieces.

    12 b3   ♘b6
    13 ♘bd2

It is obvious that in the variation 13 de de 14 ♕×d8 ♖a×d8 15 ♘×e5 or 14 ♘×e5, Black wins back the pawn by the move . . . ♘×e4 and gets a good game.

    13 . . .   ♘fd7
    14 ♘f1   c5
    15 d5

This leads to very sharp play. A quieter continuation for White was 15 ♘e3. Black accepts the challenge.

    15 . . .   f5
    16 ef   ♗×d5

An inaccuracy. Better was 16 . . . ♘×d5 17 c4 ♘b4 with fully satisfactory play. But during the game I was afraid that White would be able, successfully, to organize a central blockade and therefore I did not want to allow c4.

    17 a4   ♗c6
    18 ♘e3

A very original and interesting position has arisen. On the one hand, Black has a pawn preponderance in the centre, on the other hand, his K-side is somewhat weakened and White threatens, by the moves c4 or a5 and ♘d5, to blockade the pawns and transform Black's strength into a weakness. There is one defence to these plans.

    18 . . .   e4
    19 ♘d2   d5

At first sight it seems that Black has obtained an excellent position, but, by some energetic moves,

White shows that this is not quite so.

20 a5   ♘c8
21 c4!

A blow struck at the centre. It turned out that Black was just one tempo short for fortifying his better pawn centre (. . . ♘f6). Now Black is thrown headlong into a whirlpool of complications.

21 . . .   d4
22 ♘d5   ♗×d5
23 cd   d3
24 ♗b1 (*39*)

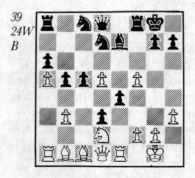

39
24W
B

The black pawns are far extended and they greatly restrict the opposing pieces, but at the same time they are vulnerable to immense danger. The question arises – how are they to be defended? After 24 . . . ♗f6 25 ♖a2 ♘e5 26 ♘×e4 ♕×d5 27 f4 the d–pawn is lost. More complicated is the variation 24 . . . ♘f6 25 ♘×e4 ♘×e4 26 ♖×e4 ♘d6 27 ♖g4 c4 28 bc bc 29 ♗a2 ♖×f5 30 ♗a3, and now against 30 . . . ♖×d5 there follows 31 ♖×c4! ♘×c4 32 ♗×c4±. Having calculated these

variations I decided to play the move . . .

24 . . .   ♘e5
25 ♘×e4   ♕×d5
26 ♗b2

An inaccuracy. It was better to play immediately 26 ♘c3 ♕d4 27 ♗b2 ♗f6 28 ♖a2! with great advantage to White. Possibly my opponent did not see 28 ♖a2 and therefore chose a different order of moves. Now I succeeded in evading this extremely unpleasant variation.

26 . . .   c4
27 ♘c3

Here White had at his disposal the very interesting and seemingly very strong move 27 bc! At the board I didn't much like Black's position, specifically because of this move. The following variations arise:

a) 27 . . . bc 28 ♗a2 and now if 28 . . . ♗b4 then 29 ♘c3 ♕d6 30 ♕a4±;

b) 27 . . . ♘×c4 28 ♗c3 b4 29 f6!±±.

Only at home, in calm surroundings, did I find the satisfactory continuation 27 . . . bc 28 ♗a2 ♘d6! (It is difficult to play such a move at the board because all the pieces in the centre are 'hanging'). White cannot win a pawn by 29 ♘×d6 ♗×d6 30 ♗×e5 ♗×e5 31 ♕g4 ♖ac8 32 ♗×c4 ♕×c4, and against 29 ♘c3 there is the reply 29 . . . ♕b7 with the threats . . . ♕×b2 and . . . ♖×f5.

27 ...   ♕c5

28 ♘a4

It was better to transpose into the variations given above, because against 28 ♘e4 Black cannot play 28 ... ♕c7 because of 29 f4. After the text move Black seizes the initiative.

28 ...   ba

Who could have foreseen that this pawn would decide the outcome of the game.

29 ♖×e5 ♕c7 30 bc♗f6 31 ♕×d3 ♖b8 32 ♕d5+ ♔h8 33 ♗d4 ♘e7 34 ♕e4 ♘c6 35 ♖c5 ♕a7

Having seized the initiative, Black accurately conducts this phase of the game. The white pieces mutually protect each other and any move brings with it material loss.

36 ♗e3 ♗×a1 37 f6 g6 38 ♖×c6 ♕d7 39 ♗c2 a3

A second queen is on the way, and not a single white piece can do anything about it.

40 ♗h6 ♖×f6 41 ♖×f6 ♗×f6 42 ♕f4 ♕d8 **0–1**

0226 AK–Arbakov

R?: ?.8.1966: Spanish

(Notes by Yudovich)

1 e4 e5 2 ♘f3 ♘c6 3 ♗b5 a6 4 ♗a4 ♘f6 5 OO ♗e7 6 ♖e1 b5 7 ♗b3 OO 8 a4 ♖b8 9 c3 d6 10 h3 ♘d7 11 d4 ♗f6 12 d5 ♘e7 13 ♘a3 g6 14 ♗c2 ba 15 ♗×a4 ♗g7 16 ♗c2 h6 17 ♘d2 f5 18 ♘ac4 ♘f6 19 ♘e3 ♕e8

20 ♗d3 ♘h5 (The opening has favoured White, but subsequently he conducts the regrouping of his position too slowly. Developing a K-side initiative, Arbakov does not refrain from material sacrifices.) 21 ♗×a6 ♗d7 22 ♗f1 ♘f4 23 g3 ♘h5 24 ♗g2 f4 25 ♘ef1 fg 26 fg ♕f7 27 ♖e3 g5 28 ♖f3 ♕g6 29 ♖a7 g4 30 ♖×f8+ ♖×f8 31 h4 ♕f7 32 ♕e1 ♘g6 33 ♖×c7 ♘hf4! 34 gf ef 35 ♘h2 ♘e5 (40)

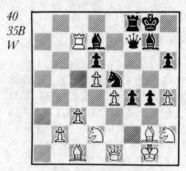

40
35B
W

36 ♘df3 gf 37 ♘×f3 ♕g6! 38 ♔f1 (If 38 ♔h1 then 38 ... ♗g4 is unpleasant.) 38 ... ♗g4? (38 ... ♗b5+ ∓ ∓, but Black was in serious time trouble.) 39 ♕f2 ♘d3?! (39 ... ♕×e4 is better.) 40 ♕d2 ♘×c1 41 ♕×c1 ♕×e4 42 ♕e1 ♗×f3? (In time trouble, Arbakov thought he was winning a piece. 42 ... ♕×d5 was necessary, still with good chances.) 43 ♕×e4 ♗×e4 44 ♗×e4 ... **1–0** (x moves)

0227–0232 Karpov's other six games from this event are not available, nor is it known against whom they were played.

Scandinavia–USSR Junior Match   Stockholm, 27-28.8.1966

This match was played on 15 boards. The result: USSR 23 Scandinavia 7.
There follow the results of the first six boards:

1 Gulko	½0	Sigurjonsson (IS)	½1
2 Kupreichik	1½	Bengtsson (S)	0½
3 Vorotnikov	11	Sirkiä (SF)	00
4 Dvoretsky	½½	Wibe (N)	½½
5 Bokuchava	11	Haldanarsson (IS)	00
6 Karpov	1½	Hatlebakk (N)	0½

0233   Hatlebakk–AK

R1: 27.8.1966: Spanish

(Notes by Vasilchuk)

1 e4 e5 2 ♘f3 ♘c6 3 ♗b5 a6 4 ♗a4
♘f6 5 00 ♗e7 6 ♖e1 b5 7 ♗b3 d6 8
c3 00 9 h3 ♘a5 10 ♗c2 ♗b7 11 d4
♘c4 12 b3 ♘b6 13 ♘bd2 ♘fd7 14
♘f1 c5 15 ♘e3 g6 16 ♗b2 ♗f6 17
♕e2 ♕c7 18 de ♘×e5 19 ♘×e5
♗×e5 20 ♗d3 (*41*)

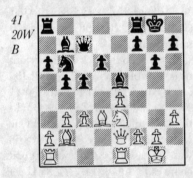

41
20W
B

20 . . . c4! 21 bc ♘a4 22 ♖ac1
(better 22 cb) 22 . . . b4! 23 ♘d1 a5
24 ♗a1 ♖fd8 25 ♕c2 (if 25 ♕d2
then 25 . . . ♘c5 follows.) 25 . . .
♗c6 26 ♖b1 ♘c5 27 ♘e3 ♗a4 28
♕d2 (Karpov gives the order 28

♘d5 ♕a7 29 ♕d2 b3 30 ♗f1 ba 31
♕×a2 ♖db8 32 ♕e2 ♗b3 33
♔h1. The move order in the text is
that given by Vasilchuk, the trainer
of the USSR team, in *Shakhmatnaya
Moskva*.) 28 . . . b3!∓∓ (Now the
bishop on a1 is shut out of play and
White's c–pawns are devalued.) 29
♘d5 ♕a7 30 ♗f1 ♖db8 31 ♔h1 ba
32 ♕×a2 ♗b3 33 ♕e2 a4 34 f4
♗g7 35 f5 ♖e8 36 ♕g4 (White
seeks counterplay on the K-side,
but in vain.) 36 . . . ♗c2 37 ♖b2
♖×e4 38 ♖×e4 ♗×e4 39 fg hg 40
♖d2 ♘b3 41 ♖d1 ♗c2 42 ♖e1
♕f2 43 ♕e2 ♕×e2 44 ♗×e2 ♖e8
45 ♗b2 ♗d3 46 ♘f4 ♗×c4 47
♔g1 g5 48 ♔f2 ♘d2 49 ♗d3 ♖b8
0–1

0234   AK–Hatlebakk

R2: 28.8.1966: Spanish

1 e4 e5 2 ♘f3 ♘c6 3 ♗b5 a6 4 ♗a4
♘f6 5 00 ♘×e4 6 d4 b5 7 ♗b3 d5 8
♘×e5 ♘×e5 9 de c6 10 c3 ♗c5 11
♘d2 ♗f5 12 ♘×e4 ♗×e4 13 ♗c2
♗×c2 14 ♕×c2 00 15 ♗f4 ♕d7 16
♖ae1 ♖ae8 17 ♗e3 ♗×e3 18

♜×e3 f6 19 ef ♜×e3 20 fg ♕×g7 21
fe ♜×f1+ 22 ♚×f1 ♕e5 (*42*)

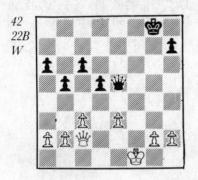

42
22B
W

23 ♕e2 ♕f5+ 24 ♚g1 ♕b1+ 25
♚f2 ♕×a2 26 b4 ♕b1 27 ♕g4+
♚f7 28 ♕d7+ ♚f8 29 ♕d6+ ♚f7
30 ♕c7+ ♚g8 31 ♕e5 ♕c2+ 32
♚f3 ♕d1+ 33 ♚g3 ♕e2 34 ♚h3
h6 35 ♕e6+ ♚h7 36 ♕f7+ ♚h8
37 ♕f4 ♚h7 38 g4 ♕e1 39 ♕f5+
♚g7 40 ♕d3 ♕f2 41 ♕d4+ ♚h7
42 ♕f4 ♕e1 43 ♕f7+ ♚h8 44 ♕e6
♚h7 45 ♕d7+ ♚g8 46 ♕c8+
♚g7 47 ♕b7+ ♚g8 48 ♕a8+
♚h7 49 ♕a7+ ♚g8 50 ♕d4 ♚f7
51 ♕e5 ♚g6 ½-½

Training Games   Yalta 1966

It seems probable that the two games which follow were played at some
kind of summer training event organized by the 'Trud' club. Both Kushnir
and Volpert at this time represented 'Trud' in the USSR Team
Championship and, of course, Karpov had been a member of Botvinnik's
Moscow 'training school', also organized by 'Trud', for some three years.

0235   AK–Kushnir

Spanish

1 e4 e5 2 ♘f3 ♘c6 3 ♗b5 a6 4 ♗a4
♘f6 5 00 ♗e7 6 ♜e1 b5 7 ♗b3 00 8
a4 ♗b7 9 c3 d5 10 ed ♘×d5 11 ab
ab 12 ♜×a8 ♗×a8 13 ♘a3 ♘f4 14
d4 b4 15 ♘c4 bc 16 bc ♘d5 17

43
29W
B

♘c×e5 ♘×c3 18 ♕d3 ♘d5 19
♘×c6 ♗×c6 20 ♗c2 g6 21 ♘e5
♘b4 22 ♕c3 ♗d5 23 ♗h6 ♘×c2
24 ♕×c2 ♜e8 25 ♘c6 ♕d6
26 ♘×e7+ ♜×e7 27 ♜b1 ♗b7 28
♕b3 ♕e6 29 ♕b4 (*43*)
29 . . . ♗×g2?? 30 ♕×e7! **1–0**

0236   AK–Volpert

Sicilian

1 e4 c5 2 ♘c3 ♘c6 3 g3 g6 4 ♗g2
♗g7 5 d3 d6 6 ♘ge2 e5 7 00 ♘ge7
8 ♗e3 00 9 ♕d2 ♗e6 10 h3 ♕d7 11
♚h2 f5 12 f4 b6 13 ♜ae1 ♜ae8 14 fe
de 15 ♗h6 ♘d4 16 ♗×g7 ♚×g7 17
ef gf 18 ♘×d4 cd 19 ♘e2 h6 20 c3
dc 21 ♕×c3 ♚h7 22 ♕×e5 ♗×a2

23 ♘f4 ♘g6 24 ♘×g6 ♔×g6 25 ♖c2+ 33 ♔g1 ♖c1+ 34 ♔f2
♕f4 ♗d5 26 ♗×d5 ♕×d5 27 d4 ♖c2+ 35 ♔e3 ♕b3+ 36 ♔e4 ♖c7
♖×e1 28 ♖×e1 ♖c8 29 ♖e2 ♖c6 37 ♖f5+ ♔e8 38 ♕g6+ ♔d7 39
30 g4 fg 31 ♕×g4+ ♔f7 32 ♖e5 ♖f7+ ♔c8 40 ♕g8+ **1-0**

	1	2	3	4	5	6	7	8	9	0	1	2	3	4	
1 **Karpov**	×	½	1	1	½	1	1	1	1	½	½	1	1	1	**11**
2 Kupka	½	×	·	·	·	·	·	·	·	·	·	·	·	·	**9½**
3 Kupreichik	0	·	×	·	·	·	·	·	·	·	·	·	·	·	**9½**
4 Smejkal	0	·	·	×	·	·	·	·	·	·	·	·	·	·	**8½**
5 E. Nowak	½	·	·	·	×	·	·	·	·	·	·	·	·	·	**8**
6 Sikora	0	·	·	·	·	×	·	·	·	·	·	·	·	·	**8**
7 Augustin	0	·	·	·	·	·	×	·	·	·	·	·	·	·	**7½**
8 Schoupal	0	·	·	·	·	·	·	×	·	·	·	·	·	·	**5½**
9 Blatny	½	·	·	·	·	·	·	·	×	·	·	·	·	·	**5**
10 Maroszczyk	½	·	·	·	·	·	·	·	·	×	·	·	·	·	**5**
11 Kornasiewicz	0	·	·	·	·	·	·	·	·	·	×	·	·	·	**5**
12 Walica	0	·	·	·	·	·	·	·	·	·	·	×	·	·	**4**
13 V. Nowak	0	·	·	·	·	·	·	·	·	·	·	·	×	·	**3**
14 Rutka	0	·	·	·	·	·	·	·	·	·	·	·	·	×	**1½**

Karpov's debut in an international tournament was made under very strange circumstances. The Soviet Chess Federation received an invitation to send two players to an international junior tournament. The choice fell on Anatoly and Victor Kupreichik. When Karpov and his companion arrived in Czechoslovakia, it turned out that an error had been made – the tournament turned out to be not at all for juniors, but for adults. There was nothing to be done, willy nilly the two youngsters had to be included in the tournament. The result was stunning; Karpov took first place without losing a single game. With hindsight this outcome does not seem so strange, but Kupreichik headed his article on the tournament in *Shakhmatny v SSSR* (No. 3 1967) with the words 'Tolya Karpov's Surprise'.

The games are presented in round order although, as can be seen from the dates (taken from Karpov's scoresheets), the first round game was played after round three.

0301 Kupreichik–AK

R1: 28.12.1966: Spanish

1 e4 e5 2 ♘f3 ♘c6 3 ♗b5 a6 4 ♗a4 ♘f6 5 ♕e2 b5 6 ♗b3 ♗c5 7 c3 00 8 d3 h6 9 00 d6 10 h3 ♖b8 11 ♖d1 ♖e8 12 ♘bd2 ♘h5 13 ♘f1 ♘f4 14 ♗×f4 ef 15 d4 ♗a7 16 a4 b4 17 ♗×f7+? ♔×f7 18 ♕c4+ d5!∓∓ 19 ed (or 19 ♕×c6 ♗b7 20 ♘e5+ ♖×e5 – perhaps Kupreichik overlooked this) 19 ... ♘a5 20 ♕d3 ♕×d5 21 ♖e1 ♗b7 22 ♕h7 ♘c4 23 b3 ♘d6 24 ♖e5 ♕×b3 25 ♘1d2 ♕×c3 26 ♖ae1 ♗×d4 27 ♘g5+ hg 28 ♕h5+ g6 29 ♕h7+ ♔f6 30 ♖e7 ♗×f2+ 31 ♔f1 ♕d3+ 32 ♖1e2 ♗×g2+ 33 ♔×g2 ♕g3+ **0–1**

0302 AK–Smejkal

R2: 27.12.1966: Sicilian

(Notes by Wade)

A meeting between two future grandmasters must arouse interest. 1 e4 c5 2 ♘c3 ♘c6 3 g3 g6 4 ♗g2 ♖b8!? 5 d3 b5 6 ♗e3?! b4 7 ♘ce2 ♗g7 8 ♕c1 d6 9 f4 ♗d7 10 ♘f3 f5! 11 00 ♕b6 (11 ... e6 12 e5) 12 h3 e6 13 ♖d1 (A curious move, suggesting that White plans 14 c3 bc 15 bc ♕b2?! 16 ♖d2. It is most unusual to see Karpov with such a congested position, e.g. ♖d1, ♖a1, ♕c1.) 13 ... ♘ge7 14 g4 00 15 ♘g3

♘d4 (Smejkal must sense that his position is comfortable and therefore feels the need to do something to exploit his advantage.) 16 ♔h1 e5? (This needed very exact calculation as it extends the c1–e3 diagonal and gives White counterplay. 16 ... ♘×f3 17 ♗×f3 ♗c6 or 17 ... a5, planning a5–a4–a3, retains a satisfactory position for Black.) 17 gf gf 18 ♘h5 (Now White is going to have as many pieces on the K-side as Black.) 18 ... ♗h6? (This overlooks the effect of White's 21st. 18 ... ♘g6! should hold the position.) 19 fe f4 (*44*)

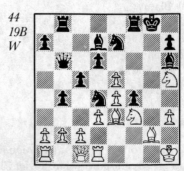

44
19B
W

20 ♗×d4 cd 21 ♘f6+ ♖×f6 22 ef ♘g6 23 ♕d2 ♕d8 24 a3 b3 25 cb ♕×f6 26 ♖ac1 ♖×b3 27 ♕f2 ♘e5 28 ♕×d4 **1–0** (time) A disappointing game.

0303 Blatny–AK

R3: 27.12.1966: Spanish

1 e4 e5 2 ♘f3 ♘c6 3 ♗b5 a6 4 ♗a4

♘f6 5 00 ♗e7 6 ♕e2 b5 7 ♗b3 00 8 c3 d6 9 a4 ♗b7 10 d4 ed 11 cd ba 12 ♖×a4 d5 13 e5 ♘e4 14 ♘c3 ♘b4 15 ♖d1 a5 16 ♘d2 ♘×d2 17 ♗×d2 c5 ½–½

0304 AK–Augustin

R4: 28.12.1966: Sicilian

1 e4 c5 2 ♘c3 ♘c6·3 g3 g6 4 ♗g2 ♗g7 5 ♘ge2 ♖b8 6 00 e6 7 f4 d6 8 g4 h5 9 g5 ♘ge7 10 d3 b5 11 ♕e1 ♘b4 12 ♕d2 ♘bc6 13 ♔h1 d5 14 f5 ef 15 ♘×d5 ♘×d5 16 ed ♘e5 17 ♕c3 ♕d6 18 ♗f4 b4 19 ♕b3 00 20 d4 cd 21 ♘×d4 ♗b7 (*45*)

45
21B
W

22 ♘c6 ♗×c6 23 dc ♕c5 24 ♖ad1 ♖bd8 25 ♗e3 ♕b5 26 a4 ♕c4 27 ♗×a7 ♕×b3 28 cb ♖×d1 29 ♖×d1 ♖c8 30 ♖c1 ♘d3 31 ♖c4 ♗e5 32 ♗b6 ♘×b2 33 ♖×b4 ♗c3 34 ♖b5 ♘d3 35 c7 ♖e8 36 ♗a5 ♖e1+ 37 ♗f1 ♖×f1+ 38 ♔g2 ♖f2+ 39 ♔g1 ♗d4 40 c8♕+ ♔h7 41 ♖d5 ♘c2+ 42 ♖×d4 **1–0**

0305 Maroszczyk–AK

R5: 29.12.1966: QGD

1 d4 ♘f6 2 c4 e6 3 ♘c3 d5 4 ♗g5 ♗e7 5 e3 00 6 ♘f3 ♘bd7 7 ♖c1 b6 8 cd ed 9 ♗d3 ♗b7 10 00 c5 11 ♗f4 a6 12 ♘e5 ♖c8 13 ♗f5 g6 14 ♗h3 ♖a8 15 ♗h6 ½–½

0306 AK–Walica

R6: 29.12.1966: Sicilian

1 e4 c5 2 g3 ♘c6 3 ♗g2 g6 4 ♘e2 ♗g7 5 00 d6 6 c3 e5 7 ♘a3 ♘ge7 8 ♘c2 00 9 d4 ed 10 cd f5 11 ♗e3 fe 12 dc dc 13 ♗×c5 ♗g4 14 ♕×d8 ♖f×d8 15 ♘c3 ♗d5 16 ♘×e4 ♗e2 17 ♖fe1 ♗d3 18 ♘d6 ♘f6 19 ♘×b7 ♗×c2 20 ♘×d8 ♖×d8 21 ♖ac1 ♖c8 22 ♗×c6 ♖×c6 23 ♖×c2 **1–0**

0307 V. Nowak–AK

R7: 30.12.1966: Nimzo-Indian

1 d4 ♘f6 2 c4 e6 3 ♘c3 ♗b4 4 ♕b3 c5 5 ♗d2 ♘c6 6 dc 00 7 e3 ♗×c5 8 ♗e2 d5 9 cd ed 10 ♘f3 ♗e6 11 ♘g5 ♗f5 12 ♘a4 ♗d6 13 ♕×b7 (*46*)

46
13W
B

13 ... ♘b4 14 ♗×b4 ♖b8 15 ♕c6 ♗×b4+ 16 ♔f1 ♗d7 17 ♕c2 ♕a5 18 ♘c3 ♖fc8 19 ♖c1 d4 **0–1**

0308   AK–Sikora

R8: 31.12.1966: Sicilian

1 e4 c5 2 ♘c3 ♘c6 3 g3 e6 4 ♗g2
♘ge7 5 ♘ge2 d5 6 ed ♘×d5 7
♘×d5 ed 8 d4 ♗g4 9 h3 ♗e6 10
♗e3 c4 11 b3 b5 12 a4 cb 13 ab bc 14
♕×c2 ♘b4 15 ♕b3 ♗e7 16 ♖a4
a5 17 ba ♕b6 18 ♗d2 0-0 19 0-0
♖fb8 20 ♖b1 ♖×a6 21 ♖×b4
♗×b4 22 ♕×b4 ♕×b4 23 ♖×b4
♖×b4 24 ♗×b4 ♖a1+ 25 ♔h2
♖a2 26 ♗f3 (*47*)

47
26W
B

26 . . . g5 27 ♔g2 h5 28 ♘c3 ♖b2
29 ♗c5 ♖b3 30 ♘×d5 ♗×h3+ 31
♔×h3 ♖×f3 32 ♔g2 ♖d3 33
♘f6+ ♔g7 34 ♘×h5+ ♔g6 35 g4
f5 36 ♘g3 fg 37 ♗f1 ♔f5 38 ♘e3+
♔f4 39 d5 ♖d2 40 ♗d6+ ♔e4 41
♔g3 ♔d4 42 ♗e7 **1–0**

0309   AK–E. Nowak

R9: 1.1.1967: Spanish

1 e4 e5 2 ♘f3 ♘c6 3 ♗b5 a6 4 ♗a4
♘f6 5 0-0 ♗e7 6 ♖e1 b5 7 ♗b3 d6 8
c3 0-0 9 h3 ♘a5 10 ♗c2 c5 11 d4
♕c7 12 ♘bd2 ♘c6 13 d5 ♘d8 14
♘f1 ♘e8 15 g4 f6 16 a4 ♖b8 17

♘g3 g6 18 ♔h1 ♘f7 19 ♘h2 ♘g7
20 h4 ♗d7 21 ♖g1 ♕c8 22 ♕e2
♗d8 ½–½

0310   Kornasiewicz–AK

R10: 2.1.1967: Spanish

(Notes by Kupreichik)

1 e4 e5 2 ♘f3 ♘c6 3 ♗b5 f5 4 d4 fe
5 ♘×e5 ♘×e5 6 de c6 7 ♗c4
♕a5+ 8 ♗d2 ♕×e5 9 ♗×g8
♖×g8 10 ♘c3 d5 11 ♕e2 ♗d6 12
0-0-0 ♗d7 13 f3 0-0-0 14 fe ♖de8 15
♖de1 d4 16 ♘d1 ♗e6 17 ♔b1 c5 18
b3 c4 19 bc ♗a3 20 ♕d3 ♕c5 21
♘b2 ♗×b2 22 ♔×b2 ♔b8 23
♕b3 ♗×c4 24 ♕b4 ♕c6 (*48*)

48
24B
W

(The open b–file makes the white
king uncomfortable. White's best
defensive resource is probably 25
♗f4+ ♔a8 26 ♗d6. However, he
played . . .) 25 e5? ♖e6 26 a4 ♖c8
(threatening 27 . . . ♕×g2) 27
♖hg1 ♕d5 28 a5 ♖c5 29 ♕a3 b6
30 ♖a1 d3! (With unanswerable
threats. If 31 cd then 31 . . . ♖b5+
32 ♔c2 ♗×d3+ ! is decisive.) 31 ab
♕d4+ 32 ♕c3 ♖×b6+ **0–1**

0311   AK–Kupka

R11: 2.1.1967: Spanish

1 e4 e5 2 ♘f3 ♘c6 3 ♗b5 a6 4
♗×c6 dc 5 00 ♗g4 6 h3 h5 7 c3
♕f6 8 d4 ♗×f3 9 ♕×f3 ♕×f3 10 gf
ed 11 cd 000 12 ♗e3 f5 13 ♘c3 ♘f6
14 ♖ad1 ♖e8 15 e5 ♘d5 16 ♘×d5
cd 17 ♔h2 ♖e6 18 ♖g1 ♔d7 19 ♖
c1 g6 20 ♖c2 ♗e7 21 ♗g5 ♗×g5
22 ♖×g5 h4 23 ♖c5 b6 24 ♖c3 a5
25 ♖g1 ♖c8 26 ♖gc1 c6 27 f4 ½–½

0312   AK–Schoupal

R12: 3.1.1967: Petroff

1 e4 e5 2 ♘f3 ♘f6 3 ♘×e5 d6 4 ♘f3
♘×e4 5 d4 ♗e7 6 ♗d3 d5 7 c4
♗g4 8 ♕b3 ♘c6 9 cd ♘×f2 10
♔×f2 ♗×f3 11 gf ♗h4+ 12 ♔g2
♘e7 13 ♘c3 00 14 ♗f4 ♘g6 15
♗×g6 fg 16 ♗g3 ♗f6 17 d6+ ♔h8
18 dc ♕×d4 19 ♖ad1 ♕c5 20 ♖d5
♕c6 21 ♖d6 1–0

0313   Rutka–AK

R13: 4.1.1967: Spanish

1 e4 e5 2 ♘f3 ♘c6 3 ♗b5 a6 4 ♗a4
♘f6 5 d3 b5 6 ♗b3 ♗e7 7 c3 00 8
♘bd2 d6 9 ♘f1 ♘a5 10 ♗c2 c5 11
h3 ♕c7 12 g4 ♖d8 13 ♕e2 ♗b7 14
♘g3 d5 15 g5 de 16 de ♘d7 17 ♘f5
♗f8 18 h4 c4 19 h5 ♘c5 (Who will
come first – White on the K-side or
Black through the centre?) 20 g6
♘d3+ 21 ♗×d3 cd 22 gh+ ♔h8
23 ♕e3 ♘c4 24 ♕g5 ♗×e4 25 h6
f6 26 hg+ ♕×g7 (The text is
aesthetically pleasing and probably
stronger than 26 . . . ♗×g7 which
was also possible.) 27 ♕h5 (if 27
♘×g7 fg 28 ♘e6 ♗×f3 29 ♘×d8
♖×d8 30 ♖h3 d2+ 31 ♗×d2
♘×d2∓ ∓ or 27 ♕×g7+ ♗×g7 28
♘×g7 ♔×g7 29 ♖g1+ ♔×h7 30
♘d2∓ Black is doing well in all
cases) 27 . . . ♕d7 28 ♕g4 ♗c5 (49)

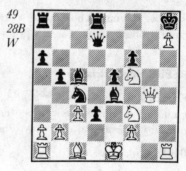

49
28B
W

29 ♕×e4 d2+ 30 ♗×d2 ♘×d2 31
♘h4! (hoping for 31 . . . ♘×e4?? 32
♘g6 mate) 31 . . . ♗×f2+! 0–1

4 1967 Miscellany

This chapter contains games from the 1967 RSFSR Spartakiad, (0401–0405), the USSR Junior Championship (0406–0412) – Karpov's only failure in his entire career to date!, and the USSR Schools' Spartakiad (0413–0421).

10th RSFSR Schools' Spartakiad, Zonal — Bryansk

Karpov, playing on board one, scored 7½/8. No games are available. The event probably took place in January or February.

RSFSR Spartakiad — Vladimir, February 1967

Karpov, playing on the second 'adult' board for Tula, met his first grandmaster (in serious competition) in this event (game 0402). It has proved impossible to trace any other details of this tournament.

0401 Sadovsky–AK

R1: ?.2.1967: English

1 c4 ♘f6 2 ♘c3 e5 3 g3 g6 4 ♗g2
♗g7 5 e4 d6 6 ♘ge2 ♗e6 7 d4 0-0 8
d5 ♗d7 9 0-0 ♘h5 10 ♗e3 f5 11
♕d2 ♘a6 12 f3 ♖f7 13 a3 ♘c5 14
♕c2 ♕e8 15 b4 ♘a4 16 c5 f4 17
♗f2 fg 18 hg ♘×c3 19 ♘×c3 ♕e7
20 ♕d2 ♖af8 21 ♕e3 a6 22 a4 (*50*)
22 . . . ♗f6 23 ♕d3 ♗g5 24 ♖a3
♘g7 25 ♘e2 ♕e8 26 ♕c2 h5 27
♗e1 ♖f6 28 ♗f2 ♔h7 29 ♗e1
♗h6 30 ♗f2 ♗c8 31 ♖fa1 ♗g4! 32

50
22W
B

f4 ♗×e2 33 ♕×e2 ef 34 ♗d4 ♖6f7
35 b5 ♘f5! 36 ♗f2 fg 37 ♗×g3
♘×g3 38 ♖×g3 ♕e5 39 ♖aa3 ab

40 cd b4 41 ♖ad3 cd 42 ♕e1 ♖c7
43 ♖gf3 ♖×f3 44 ♗×f3 ♖c2 45
♗g2 ♖c1 46 ♖d1 ♗e3+ 47 ♔h1
♖×d1 48 ♕×d1 b3 49 ♕×b3 ♕g3
50 ♕×b7+ ♔h6 **0–1**

0402 Antoshin–AK

R2: ?.2.1967: Queen's Indian

Karpov's first serious game
against a grandmaster.

1 d4 ♘f6 2 c4 e6 3 ♘f3 b6 4 ♘c3
♗b7 5 a3 ♗e7 6 d5 00 7 e4 d6 8
♗d3 ♘bd7 9 00 ♘e5 10 ♘×e5 de
11 f4 ♘d7 12 ♕g4 ♗c5+ 13 ♔h1
♕e7 14 ♕g3 ♗d4 15 ♘b5 ed 16
ed± c6 17 d6 ♕d8 18 ♘×d4 ed 19
f5 f6 20 ♗h6 ♖f7 21 ♖ae1 ♘c5 22
♗b1 ♕d7 23 b4 ♘a4 24 c5 ♘c3 25
♗d3 a5 26 ♗d2 ♘d5 27 ♖e4 ab 28
ab ♖a7 29 ♕e1 ♗a6?! 30 ♗×a6
♖×a6 31 ♖e8+ ♖f8 32 ♕e6+!
♕×e6 33 ♖×f8+ ♔×f8 34 fe± ±
b5 35 g4 ♖a2 36 g5! ♖×d2 37 ♖a1
g6 38 gf **1–0** An aesthetically
pleasing conclusion.

0403 AK–Detkov

R3: ?.2.1967: Spanish

1 e4 e5 2 ♘f3 ♘c6 3 ♗b5 a6 4 ♗a4
♘f6 5 00 ♗e7 6 ♖e1 b5 7 ♗b3 d6 8
c3 00 9 d4 ♗g4 10 ♗e3 ♕d7 11
♘bd2 ed 12 cd d5 13 e5 ♘e4 14 a3
♘a5 15 ♗c2 f5 16 ef ♘×f6 17 ♕b1
♖ae8 18 ♘e5 ♕c8 19 ♗g5 ♔h8
(*51*)

20 ♗×h7 ♘×h7 21 ♘g6+ ♔g8 22
♘×e7+ ♖×e7 23 ♗×e7 ♖f4 24
♕d3 ♘c6 25 ♖ac1 ♕d7 26 ♕e3

♖f7 27 ♗h4 ♖f8 28 ♕c3 ♘d8 29
f3 ♗f5 30 ♖e7 **1–0**

51
19B
W

0404 Zakhvatov–AK

R4: ?.2.1967: Catalan

1 d4 ♘f6 2 c4 e6 3 g3 d5 4 ♗g2 ♗e7
5 ♘f3 00 6 00 c5 7 cd ♘×d5 8 ♘c3
♘c6 9 e4 ♘×c3 10 bc b6 11 ♗f4 cd
12 cd ♗a6 13 ♖e1 ♗b4 14 ♖e3
♗c4 15 d5 ed 16 ed ♗×d5 17 ♖d3
♗×f3 18 ♗×f3 ♕f6 19 ♖c1 ♗c5
20 ♖×c5 bc 21 ♖d6 ♖ad8 22
♗×c6 ♖×d6 23 ♕×d6 ♕×d6 24
♗×d6 ♖d8 25 ♗f4 ♖d1+ 26 ♔g2
c4 27 ♔f3 ♖a1 28 ♗d5 c3 29 ♗b3
h6 30 ♔e2 c2 31 ♗×c2 ♖×a2 32
♔d2 a5 33 h4 g5 34 hg hg 35 ♗e3
♔g7 36 ♔c3 f6 37 ♔b3 ♖a1 38
♗d4 ♖c1 ½–½

0405 AK–Nizovsky

R5: ?.2.1967: Spanish

1 e4 e5 2 ♘f3 ♘c6 3 ♗b5 a6 4 ♗a4
♘f6 5 ♕e2 ♗e7 6 c3 00 7 00 d6 8 d4
♗g4 9 ♖d1 ♘d7 10 h3 ♗h5 11 g4
♗g6 12 ♗×c6 bc 13 de ♕e8 14 ed
♗×d6 15 ♖e1 ♘c5 16 ♘bd2 ♖d8
17 ♕c4 ♘d3 18 ♖e3 ♘e5 19 ♘×e5

♗×e5 20 ♖e1 h5 21 ♘f3 hg 22 hg ♕e7 23 ♔g2 ♖fe8 24 ♗g5 ♗f6 25 ♗×f6 ♕×f6 26 e5 ♕e6 27 ♕×e6 fe 28 ♔g3 c5 29 c4 ♔f7 30 ♖e3 ♗d3 31 ♖c1 ♖d7 32 ♖c3 ♖ed8 33 ♘g5+ ♔e7 34 ♖f3 ♗g6 35 ♖a3 ♖a8 36 ♖a5 c6 37 ♖fa3 ♖d3+ 38 ♖×d3 ♗×d3 39 ♖×c5 ♔d7 40 b4 a5 41 ♖×a5 ♖×a5 42 ba ♗×c4 43 ♔f4 ... **1-0** (x moves)

USSR Junior Championship

Moscow, March 1967

½-final	1	2	3	4	5	6	7	8	
1 L. Grigorian	×	1	1	½	1	½	½	1	5½
2 A. Bokuchava	0	×	½	½	1	1	1	1	5
3 A. Lukin	0	½	×	1	0	1	1	1	4½
4 G. Timoshenko	½	½	0	×	1	½	1	1	4½
5 A. Karpov	0	0	1	0	×	1	½	1	3½
6 M. Dvoretsky	½	0	0	½	0	×	0	1	2
7 R. Vaganian	½	0	0	0	½	1	×	0	2
8 S. Palatnik	0	0	0	0	0	0	1	×	1

Results of the other ½-final: 1-3 Y. Balashov, K. Grigorian, M. Shteinberg 4½; 4-6 Y. Anikayev, T. Georgadze, M. Mukin 3½; 7 V. Kupreichik 3; 8 M. Lebovich 1.

The double-round final, which began 27.3.1967, resulted as follows: 1 Lukin 6½; 2-3 Balashov, Shteinberg 5; 4-6 Bokuchava, K. Grigorian, L. Grigorian 4½.

The winner of this event was to represent the USSR in the 1967 World Junior Championship in Jerusalem (Lukin did not play there – a political repercussion of the Six Day War).

Karpov's failure to qualify for the final is the only real failure in his entire career to date.

0406 Timoshenko–AK

R1: ?.3.1967: Bishop's Opening

1 e4 e5 2 ♗c4 ♘f6 3 d4 ed 4 ♘f3 ♘×e4 5 ♕×d4 ♘f6 6 ♗g5 c6 7 ♘c3 d5 8 000 ♗e7 9 ♖he1 ♗e6 10 ♕h4 ♘bd7 11 ♗d3 c5 12 ♘e5 ♘×e5 13 ♖×e5 d4 14 f4 ♘d7 (Not 14 ... dc? 15 ♗b5+ when 15 ... ♗d7 16 ♗×d7+±± and 15 ...

52
18W
B

♘d7 16 ♗×d7+ ±± are equally hopeless for Black.) **15 ♗ b5 ♗×g5 16 fg ♕c7 17 ♗×d7+ ♔×d7 18 ♕e4** (*52*)

Black's difficulties are shown in the variation 18 . . . b6 (seemingly consolidating his pawn chain) 19 ♘b5 ♕c6 20 ♘×d4! cd (20 . . . ♕×e4 21 ♘×e6+ ♔e7 22 ♖×e4 fe 23 ♖de1±) 21 ♖×d4+ ♔c7 22 ♖×e6! ♕×e6 (22 . . . fe 23 ♖c4±±) 23 ♖c4+ ♔b8 24 ♕f4+ ♔b7 25 ♖c7+ ♔a6 26 ♕a4 mate.

However, Black could have tried 18 . . . ♖ad8 19 ♘d5 ♕d6 20 c3 ♔c8. In the game, Karpov continued with the outright blunder . . .

18 . . . ♕c6? 19 ♖×c5! ♕×e4 (Or 19 . . . ♕×c5 20 ♕×b7+ ♔d6 (20 . . . ♔d8 21 ♕×a8+ ±±) 21 ♘e4+ ±±) **20 ♘×e4 ♖hc8 21 ♖×d4+ ♔e7 22 a4 b6 23 ♖×c8** ♖×c8 24 ♔d2 ♗f5 25 c4 ♖c6 26 ♘g3 ♗e6 27 ♔c3 ♖c5 28 h4 h6 29 b4 ♖c8 30 ♘e4 f5 31 ♘f2 hg 32 hg ♖h8 33 ♘h3 ♗d7 34 b5 ♖h5 35 ♔b4 ♖h8 36 a5 ♗e6 37 a6 ♗f7 38 ♔c3 g6 39 ♔b4 ♖c8 40 ♘f4 ♖c5 41 ♘d3 ♖c8 42 c5 bc+ 43 ♘×c5 ♗e8 44 ♖d1 ♖c7 45 g3 ♖c8 46 ♖e1+ ♔d8 47 ♘b7+ ♔d7 48 ♖e3 ♗f7 49 ♖d3+ ♔e7 50 ♖c3 ♖×c3 51 ♔×c3 ♗d5 52 ♔d4 ♗g2 53 ♔c5 ♗f1 54 ♘a5 **1-0**

0407   AK–Palatnik

R2: ?.3.1967: Sicilian

1 e4 c5 2 ♘c3 ♘c6 3 g3 g6 4 ♗g2 ♗g7 5 ♘ge2 e6 6 d3 ♘ge7 7 00 00 8 ♗e3 ♘d4 9 ♕d2 ♕a5 10 ♘f4 d6 11 ♖ab1 ♖ec6 12 a3 a6 13 ♕d1 b5 14 ♘ce2 ♗b7 15 c3 ♘×e2+ 16 ♕×e2 ♖ac8 17 h4 b4 18 ab cb 19 d4 e5 20 ♖a1 ♕d8 21 de ♘×e5 22 ♗d4 ♖e8 23 ♖fd1 f5 24 ♕c2 fe (*53*)

53
24B
W

25 ♕b3+ ♘c4 26 ♖h3 ♗h6 27 ♕×b4 ♗a8 28 ♖×a6 ♗×f4 29 ♗×c8 ♗d5 30 ♖b7 ♗f7 31 ♖a8 ♕d7 32 ♖×e8+ ♕×e8 33 ♖a1 e3 34 ♖a8 **1-0**

0408   Lukin–AK

R3: ?.3.1967: Nimzo-Indian

(Notes by Karpov)

1 d4 ♘f6 2 c4 e6 3 ♘c3 ♗b4 4 ♗g5 h6 5 ♗h4 c5 6 d5 d6 (*Shakhmatny Bulletin* No. 9 1967 gave the order 6 . . . ♗×c3+ 7 bc d6 8 f3 00 9 e4 ♖e8 10 ♗d3. KJO'C) **7 f3 00 8 e4 ♖e8 9 ♗d3?** (9 ♗e2, 9 ♘ge2) **9 . . . ♗×c3+?** (9 . . . ed! 10 cd ♘×e4∓ 11 ♗×d8 ♘×c3+ 12 ♔any ♘×d1) **10 bc ♘bd7?** (10 . . . ed!? 11 cd ♘×e4! 12 ♗×d8 ♘×c3+ 13 ♘e2 ♘×d1 14 ♗c7 ♘b2 15 ♔d2 ♘×d3 16 ♔×d3

♗f5+ 17 ♔d2 ♘d7∓ ; 13 ♔f1
♘×d1 14 ♗c7 ♘b2 15 ♗e2 ♗f5∓)
**11 de fe 12 f4!? ♕c7 13 ♘f3 b5! 14
♗×f6** (14 cb c4 15 ♗c2 ♗b7 is
unclear.) **14 ... ♘×f6 15 e5 de 16
fe ♘d7 17 00** (17 ♕e2 ♗b7
threatening 18 ... ♗×f3 and 19 ...
♘×e5) **17 ... ♗b7** (17 ... ♘×e5?
18 ♘×e5 ♕×e5 19 ♕f3± ±) **18
♗c2** (threatening 19 ♕d3) **18 ...
bc 19 ♕e2 ♗d5 20 ♖ae1** (20 ♗b1
♖f8 21 ♕c2 ♖f5 22 ♘h4 ♖×f1+
23 ♔×f1 ♘f8∓) **20 ... ♕a5 21
♘g5! ♕×c3** (21 ... hg 22
♕h5± ±) **22 ♗h7+ ♔h8 23 ♗b1**
(23 ♖f7 ♘×e5; 23 ♕h5? ♕d2∓ ∓)
23 ... ♖e7 (23 ... ♖f8 24 ♘f7+
♔g8 25 ♘×h6+ gh 26 ♕g4+ ♔h8
27 ♕g6 ♕d4+ 28 ♔h1 ♖×f1+ 29
♖×f1 ♗×g2+ 30 ♕×g2 ♖g8 31
♕h3± ♕d2 32 ♗e4) **24 ♕h5
♕d4+ 25 ♔h1** (25 ♖f2 ♖f8 26
♘f3 ♗×f3 27 ♕g6 ♗e4!∓ ∓) **25
... ♗×g2+ ! 26 ♕×g2 ♕d2+ 27
♔h1 ♕×g5 28 ♕f3 ♖b8! 29 ♕e4
g6 30 ♖g1 ♕f5 31 ♕e3** (54)

**54
31W
B**

**31 ... ♖×b1∓ 32 ♖×b1 ♔g7 33
♖be1 ♖f7 34 ♕e2 ♕d3 35 ♖g3
♕d5+ 36 ♕g2** (36 ♔g1 ♖f4∓) **36
... ♕×g2+ 37 ♔×g2 ♖f5** (37 ...
♘b6!?) **38 ♖a3 ♘×e5 39 ♖×a7+
♔f6 40 ♖f1 ♘d3 41 ♖a4!
♘b2!?∓ 42 ♖a5 ♘d3 43 ♖a4
♔e5! 44 ♖×c4 ♔d5 45 ♖c2
♖g5+ ! 46 ♔f3 ♔d4∓ 47 h4 ♖e5
48 ♖d1 c4 49 a4 ♖f5+ ! 50 ♔g3
♖a5 51 ♖a2 c3 52 ♖f1 ♘c5 53
♖f4+ ♔d3 54 ♖a3** (54 ♖f3+
♔c4 55 ♖a3 ♔b4∓ ∓) **54 ...
♖×a4!∓ ∓ 55 ♖f3+** (55 ♖×a4
♘×a4 56 ♖×a4 c2 57 ♖a3+ ♔d2
58 ♖a2 ♔d1∓ ∓) **55 ... ♔d2 56
♖f2+** (56 ♖×c3 ♘e4+) **56 ...
♔d1 57 ♖f1+ ♔c2 58 ♖c1+** (58
♖f2+ ♔b1 59 ♖f1+ ♔b2∓ ∓) **58
... ♔b2! 0–1**

0409 AK–Dvoretsky

R4: ?.3.1967: King's Indian

(Notes by Karpov)

**1 d4 ♘f6 2 c4 g6 3 ♘c3 ♗g7 4 e4
d6 5 f3 00 6 ♘ge2 e5 7 ♗e3 ed 8
♘×d4 c6 9 ♗e2 d5 10 ed cd 11 00
♘c6 12 c5** (12 cd ♘×d5 13 ♘×c6
bc 14 ♘×d5 cd 15 ♗d4± ; 14 ...
♕×d5!=) **12 ... ♕c7 13 ♗f2±
♕e5?! 14 ♘cb5 ♗d7 15 ♖e1
♕g5 16 ♗f1± ♖fe8 17 g3** (17
♕c2!?, so that if 17 ... ♖×e1 then
18 ♖×e1, and 17 ... a6 18 ♘×c6
♗×c6 19 ♘d4±) **17 ... ♖×e1 18
♕×e1 ♖e8 19 ♕c3 ♘×d4** (19 ...
♕h5 20 ♘d6) **20 ♘×d4 ♕h5 21
♖e1 ♖×e1 22 ♕×e1 g5!? 23 ♕a5
♕g6 24 g4** (24 ♕×a7!? ♕b1 25
g4± ♕×b2 26 ♕b8+ ♗f8? 27
c6± ± ; 26 ... ♘e8 27 ♘f5±) **24**

. . . h5 25 ♕×a7 hg 26 ♕×b7 gf

(55)

55
26B
W

27 c6± ± ♕e4 h3 (28 cd ♕g4+ 29 ♔h1 ♘e4 30 ♕b8+ ♔h7 31 ♔g3, but not 30 d8♕+ ?? ♔h7!!∓ ∓ 31 ♗g3 ♗×g3+ 32 hg ♕h5+ 33 ♔g1 ♗×d4 mate, or 31 ♗g1 f2 32 ♘e2 fg♕+ 33 ♘×g1 ♘f2 mate) **28 . . . ♗×h3** (28 . . . ♘g4 29 cd ♘×f2 30 d8♕+ ♔h7 31 ♕×f7± ± ♘×h3+ 32 ♔h2!) **29 ♗×h3 ♘e8 30 ♘f5** (30 ♗f5?! ♕f4 31 ♕c8 ♗×d4 32 ♕×e8+ ♔g7) **30 . . . ♕b1+ 31 ♔h2 ♗e5+ 32 ♘g3 g4** (32 . . . ♕c2 33 ♔g1 ♕c1+ 34 ♘f1± ±) **33 ♕c8** (33 ♗×g4? ♕c2 34 ♔g1 ♗×g3 35 ♗×g3 ♕g2 mate; 35 ♕b6 ♕d1 mate) **33 . . . ♕×b2 34 ♕×g4+ ?** (34 ♕×e8+ ! ♔g7 35 ♕×e5+ ! ♕×e5 36 ♗d4! ♕×d4 37 ♘f5+ ± ±) **34 . . . ♔f8 35 ♕×f3 ♗d4 36 ♔g1** (36 ♘h1!? threatening 37 ♗e6± ±) **36 . . .**

♕c1+ 37 ♗f1 ♗×f2+ 38 ♕×f2 ♕×c6 39 ♕d4 ♘g7 40 ♗g2 ♕g6 41 ♘f1 ♘f5 42 ♕×d5 ♕b6+ 43 ♔h2 ♕h6+ 44 ♗h3 ♕f4+ 45 ♔g1 ♘d4 46 ♕a8+ 1-0

0410 Vaganian-AK

R5: ?.3.1967: Queen's Indian

1 d4 ♘f6 2 ♘f3 e6 3 c4 b6 4 g3 ♗b7 5 ♗g2 ♗e7 6 ♘c3 0-0 7 0-0 d5 8 ♘e5 c5 9 dc bc 10 ♕b3 ♕b6 11 ♕×b6 ab 12 ♖d1 ♖d8 13 ♗g5 ♘a6 14 cd ed 15 ♘g4 ♘c7 16 ♘e3 ♔f8 17 ♖ab1 b5 18 ♗×f6 ♗×f6 19 ♘e×d5 ♗×d5 20 ♘×d5 ♘×d5 21 ♗×d5 ♖a6 22 e4 b4 23 ♔f1 ♗d4 24 ♔e2 ♖f6 25 f3 ♗e7 26 a4 ba 27 ba ♖d7 28 ♗b7 g5 29 ♖d2 ♖h6 30 ♔f1 c4 31 ♖b4 ♗c5 32 ♖×d7+ ♔×d7 33 ♖×c4 ♗×a3 34 ♖c2 ♖b6 35 ♗c8+ ♔e7 36 ♗f5 h6 37 ♖c8 ♖b2 38 ♔g1 ♗d6 39 ♖c6 h5 40 h4 gh ½-½

0411 L. Grigorian-AK

R6(?): The score of this game is not available.

0412 AK-Bokuchava

R7(?): The score of this game is not available.

USSR Schools' Spartakiad
Leningrad, July 1967

The teams in this event were composed of six boys and two girls. Karpov played board two for RSFSR behind Gennady Timoshenko. Seiran Chechelian (board two for Georgia) had the absolute best result with 8½ /9, his only draw being against Karpov.

The scores in the A-final were: 1 RSFSR 25½; 2-3 Moscow, Ukraine 22½; 4 Georgia 21; 5 Byelorussia 15; 6 Moldavia 13½.

0413 AK–Tsamryuk

R1: 11.7.1967: Sicilian

1 e4 c5 2 ♘c3 ♘c6 3 g3 g6 4 ♗g2 ♗g7 5 ♘ge2 d6 6 00 ♘f6 7 d3 00 8 h3 ♗d7 9 ♗e3 ♖b8 10 ♕d2 b5 11 ♘d1 ♕a5 12 c3 ♖fc8 13 ♗h6 ♗h8 14 g4 ♘e8 15 f4 b4 16 f5 bc 17 bc ♘e5 18 ♘f4 ♕d8 19 ♘e3 ♘c7 20 ♕f2 ♕e8 21 ♖ad1 ♖b6 22 h4 ♖cb8 23 ♖d2 ♖b1 24 d4 cd 25 cd ♖×f1+ 26 ♗×f1 ♘c6 27 ♘ed5 ♘×d5 28 ♘×d5 (*56*)

56
28W
B

28 ... ♘b4 29 ♘f4 ♘c6 30 h5 ♖b4 31 ♘e2 a5 32 ♖d3 ♖c4 33 hg fg 34 fg hg 35 ♖f3 ♗g7 36 ♗×g7 ♔×g7 37 g5 ♗g4 38 ♖f4 ♗×e2 39 ♗×e2 ♖×d4 40 ♗b5 ♖d1+ 41 ♔g2 ♖c1 42 ♕b2+ e5 43 ♕×c1 ef 44 ♕×c6 ♕e5 45 ♕d7+ ♔h8 46 ♕e8+ **1-0**

0414, 0415 – These games are not available.

0416 Abetisian–AK

R4: 14.7.1967: QP

1 ♘f3 ♘f6 2 d4 e6 3 ♗f4 d5 4 e3 a6 5 ♘bd2 ♘bd7 6 c3 c5 7 ♗d3 b5 8 00 ♗b7 9 h3 ♗e7 10 ♘e5 00 11 ♘×d7 ♕×d7 12 ♘f3 ♖fc8 13 ♘e5 ♕e8 14 ♖c1 a5 15 ♗g5 b4 16 ♕e2 c4 17 ♗b1 ♘d7 18 ♘×d7 ♕×d7 19 ♗×e7 ♕×e7 20 e4 a4 21 e5 a3 22 f4 g6 23 ♖f3 b3 24 ♕f2 ♗c6 25 g4 ♖cb8 (*57*)

57
25B
W

26 ba ♕×a3 27 ♖f1 ba 28 ♗×a2 ♕×a2 29 ♕g3 ♖b1 30 f5 ♖×f1+ 31 ♖×f1 ♗d7 32 fg hg 33 ♕f3 ♗e8 34 ♖f2 ♕b1+ 35 ♔h2 ♖a1 36 ♖g2 ♕d3 37 ♕f6 ♖f1 **0-1**

0417 AK–Chechelian

R5: 15.7.1967: Sicilian

A fighting struggle in which Karpov wrests from Chechelian the only half point which the latter dropped on his way to winning the board prize with 8½ /9.

1 e4 e6 2 d4 c5 3 ♘f3 cd 4 ♘×d4 ♘f6 5 ♗d3 ♘c6 6 ♘×c6 dc 7 00 e5 8 ♘d2 ♕c7 9 a4 ♗e6 10 b3 ♗e7 11 ♗b2 00 12 ♕e2 ♘d7 13 ♘c4 ♗f6 14 ♗a3 ♖fd8 15 ♗d6 ♕c8 16 f4 ♗×c4 17 ♗×c4 ef 18 ♖ad1 ♘e5 19 ♗×e5 ♗×e5 20 ♗×f7+ ♔h8 21 ♕h5 ♕c7 22 ♗g6 h6 23 ♗f5 ♕b6+ 24 ♔h1 c5 25 ♖d5 ♖×d5 26 ed ♕f6 27 ♗d3 ♗d4 28 g3 ♗e3 29 gf ♗×f4 30 ♖e1 ♖f8 31 ♖e6 ♕d4 32 ♖e8 ♔g8 33 ♖×f8+ ♔×f8 34 ♕f5+ ♕f6 35 ♕c8+ ♔f7 36 ♕d7+ ♔f8 37 ♕×b7 ♕e7 ½–½

0418 Popov–AK

R6: 17.7.1967: Spanish

1 e4 e5 2 ♘f3 ♘c6 3 ♗b5 a6 4 ♗×c6 dc 5 00 f6 6 d4 ed 7 ♘×d4 c5 8 ♘b3 ♕×d1 9 ♖×d1 ♗d6 10 ♘a5 b6 11 ♘c4 ♗e7 12 ♗f4 ♗e6 13 ♘e3 ♗d8 14 ♘c3 h5 15 ♘cd5 ♖c8 16 h4 c6 17 ♘c3 c4 18 a4 ♘e7 19 ♗d6 00 20 a5 b5 21 ♗c5 ♖e8 22 ♘e2 ♘g6 23 g3 ♗g4 24 ♘×g4 hg 25 ♖d7 ♖×e4 26 ♘c3 ♖e5 27 ♗b6 b4 28 ♘a4 ♗e7 29 ♖ad1 ♖e2 30 c3 ♗f8 31 cb ♘e5 32 ♔f1 ♖c2 33 ♖d8 ♖×d8 34 ♖×d8 ♔f7 35 ♖d1 ♘d3 36 ♗d4 ♗×b4 37 ♘b6 c5 38 ♗c3 ♗×c3 39 bc ♖×f2+ 40 ♔g1 ♖f3 41 ♔g2 ♘e5 42 ♘a4 ♖d3 43 ♖c1 ♖d2+ 44 ♔f1 ♖a2 45 ♘×c5 ♖×a5 46 ♘e4 ♔e6 47 ♔e2 ♘d3 48 ♖b1 ♖e5

0–1

0419 AK–Lilein

R7: ?.7.1967: Sicilian

1 e4 c5 2 ♘f3 d6 3 d4 cd 4 ♘×d4 ♘f6 5 ♘c3 a6 6 g3 e5 7 ♘b3 ♗e7 8 ♗g2 ♕c7 9 00 00 10 a4 b6 11 ♗e3 ♗b7 12 f4 ♘bd7 13 f5 ♗c6 14 g4 h6 15 h4 ♘h7 16 ♗f2 ♖fc8 17 ♕d3 ♘df6 18 ♗f3 b5 19 ab ab 20 ♘d2 b4 21 ♘e2 ♕b7 22 ♖×a8 ♖×a8 (*58*)

58
22B
W

23 c4 bc 24 ♘×c3 ♕×b2 25 ♘c4 ♕b8 26 ♖d1 ♘e8 27 ♘b6 ♖a3 28 ♘c4 ♗b5 29 ♗e2 d5 30 ♕×d5 ♖×c3 31 ♕×e5 ♘d6 32 ♖b1 ♘f6 33 ♕a2 ♕e8 34 ♗×b5 ♘×b5 35 ♕a5 ♘×e4? (The knight on e5 has no flight square after 35 ... ♗c5‡ ∓ e.g. 36 ♖×b5 ♕×e5 37 ♕a8+ ♔h7 38 ♖b8 ♗×f2+ 39 ♔×f2 ♕f4+ or 36 ♘×c5 ♕×e5 remaining a safe piece up.) 36 ♕×b5 ♕×b5 37 ♖×b5 ♘×f2 38 ♔×f2 ♗×h4+ 39 ♔g2 ♗g3 40 ♘d7 ♔h7 41 ♖a5 ♗d6 42 ♖a6 ♖g3+ 43 ♔f2 ♖d3 44 ♔e2 ♖d4 45 ♔e3 ♖d1 46 ♖a8 ♖f1 47 ♔e4 h5 48 gh f6 49 ♘f8+ ♗×f8 50 ♖×f8 ♖h1 51 ♔f4 ♖×h5 52 ♔g4

♖h1 53 ♔f4 ♖b1 54 ♔g4 ♖b4+
55 ♔f3 ♔h6 56 ♖g8 ½-½

0420   AK–Dobkin

R8: ?.7.1967: Sicilian

1 e4 c5 2 ♘c3 ♘c6 3 g3 g6 4 ♗g2
♗g7 5 ♘ge2 d6 6 00 e6 7 d3 ♘ge7
8 ♗e3 ♘d4 9 ♕d2 00 10 ♘d1 ♖b8
11 ♘c1 b6 12 c3 ♘dc6 13 ♗h6 d5
14 ♗×g7 ♔×g7 15 ed ♘×d5 16
♘e3 ♘×e3 17 fe ♗b7 18 d4 e5 19
♖d1 ed 20 cd cd 21 ed ♘e7 22 d5
♕d6 23 ♘e2 ♖fd8 24 ♘c3 ♕c5+
25 ♔h1 ♘f5 26 g4 ♘d6 27 ♕f4
♕c8 28 ♖d3 ♕d7 29 ♖h3 f6 30
♖f1 ♖f8 31 ♖hf3 ♔g8 32 ♕g3
♕d8 33 ♖e1 ♖e8 34 ♖fe3 ♖×e3
35 ♖×e3 ♕f8 36 ♖e6 ♖d8 37 ♕f4
f5 38 g5 ♗c8 39 ♖e5 ♘f7 40 ♖e2
♕d6 41 ♕d2 ♗d7 42 ♗f3 ♖e8 43
♖g2 ♕e7 44 h4 ♕e3 45 ♖f2
♕×d2 46 ♖×d2 ♖e3 47 ♔g2 ♘e5
48 ♖e2 ♖×e2+ 49 ♗×e2 ♔f8 50
♔f2 ♔e7 51 ♔e3 ♔d6 52 ♔d4 a6
½-½

0421   Palatnik–AK

R9: ?.7.1967: Spanish

1 e4 e5 2 ♘f3 ♘c6 3 ♗b5 a6 4
♗×c6 dc 5 00 ♗g4 6 h3 ½-½

5 Groningen   27.12.1967–8.1.1968

		1	2	3	4	5	6	7	8	
1	Karpov	×	½	1	1	½	1	½	1	**5½**
2	Adorjan*	½	×	½	1	1	1	½	½	**5**
3	Lewi	0	½	×	1	0	1	1	1	**4½**
4	Timman	0	0	0	×	½	1	1	1	**3½**
5	Zara	½	0	1	½	×	0	½	1	**3½**
6	Hostalet	0	0	0	0	1	×	1	0	**2**
7	Ligterink	½	½	0	0	½	0	×	½	**2**
8	Moles	0	½	0	0	0	1	½	×	**2**

* *Adorjan played under the name of 'Jocha'*

The preliminaries were played in the form of a single seven-round Swiss:
1 Adorjan (H) 5; 2-6 Hostalet (E), Karpov, Lewi (PL), Ligterink (NL),
Timman (NL) 4½; 7-8 Zara (R), Moles (IRL) 4; 9 Jacobsen (DK) 3½; 10
Boersma (NL) 3; 11-14 Dudek (A), Maeder (BRD), Schaufelberger (CH),
Tate (ENG) 2½; 15-16 Fučak (Y), Meulders (B) 2.

The Success of Tolya Karpov   A. Bikhovsky

There was particular interest in this year's tournament, because, as
everyone knows, the World Junior Championship was held in August 1967
in Israel without the participation of the socialist countries. The
Groningen tournament is the largest since the World Junior and can
provide an answer to the legitimate question: 'Can we conquer the World
Junior Championship?'.

Why was Karpov chosen to represent the Soviet Union? The special
selection tournament held before the world championship in Moscow was
won by Andrei Lukin, Anatoly Karpov being unsuccessful. However, the
presidium of the chess federation supported Karpov's candidature after

considering future events; the choice was given to one of our junior masters who could participate in the world championship in 1969.

In a very short training session Tolya and I mainly concentrated on preparation for Timman and Adorjan . . . Our suppositions were justified, in that these players were the main opponents for Tolya Karpov in the fight for first place. Karpov's fine victory over Timman was the main factor in deciding the final outcome of the tournament.

0501 AK–Schaufelberger

PR1: 27.12.1967: Sicilian

1 e4 c5 2 ♘c3 ♘c6 3 g3 g6 4 ♗g2 ♗g7 5 d3 d6 6 ♘ge2 ♕d7 7 ♗e3 b6 8 f4 ♗b7 9 OO ♘d4 10 ♕d2 h5 11 h3 f5 12 ♗f2 OOO (Better was 12 . . . ♘×e2+ 13 ♕×e2 and only then 13 . . . OOO, though, with 14 a4, White still keeps the initiative.) **13 ♘×d4! ♗×d4** (Black realizes that he must swap the dark-squared bishops as after 13 . . . cd 14 ♘e2 e5 15 c3 dc 16 ♘×c3 ♘e7 17 a4! White serves up a tremendous Q-side attack in which his QB plays a leading role.) **14 ♗×d4 cd 15 ♘e2 e5** (*59*)

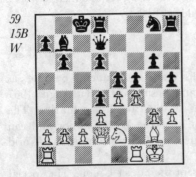

59
15B
W

16 c3! h4 (This is insufficient, but if 16 . . . dc 17 ♕×c3+ ♕c7 18 ♖ac1 ♕×c3 19 ♖×c3+ ♔b8 20 ef gf 21

fe de 22 ♖×f5± ± , or 16 . . . ♕g7 17 cd ed 18 ♕b4 and the d–pawn is lost.) **17 cd hg** (If 17 . . . ed 18 ♘×d4 hg 19 ♕c3+ ♕c7 20 ♕×c7+ ♔×c7 21 ♘e6+ or 19 . . . ♔b8 20 ♘c6+ wins the exchange.) **18 de ♘e7** (The best defence, threatening 19 . . . de 20 ♕c3+ ♘c6!, for if 18 . . . de 19 ♕c3+ ♕c7 20 ♖ac1 ♕×c3 21 ♖×c3+ ♔b8 22 ef ef 23 fg± ±) **19 ♕c3+ ♔b8** (Also 19 . . . ♕c7 20 ♖ac1 ♕×c3 21 ♖×c3+ ♔b8 22 ed ♖×d6 23 ♘×g3 and 19 . . . ♘c6 20 d4! both leave White set for victory.) **20 ♘×g3** (not 20 ef? ♘×f5 21 d4 ♗×g2 22 ♔×g2 ♘e3+ 23 ♕×e3 ♕×h3+ 24 ♔g1 ♕h2 mate) **20 . . . fe 21 de d5 22 ♖ad1** (If 22 ed then 22 . . . ♗×d5! 23 ♖ad1 ♕e6 gives Black dangerous counter-chances against White's weakened K-side.) **22 . . . d4 23 ♕d2 ♖×h3? 24 ♗×h3 ♕×h3 25 ♕g2 ♕h4 26 ♖f3! ♖h8 27 ♖×d4 ♘f5 28 ef gf** (or 28 . . . ♗×f3 29 ♕×f3 ♕h2+ 30 ♔f1 and no more checks) **29 ♖dd3 ♖g8 30 ♕h2 1–0**

0502 AK–Maeder

PR2: 28.12.1967: Sicilian

1 e4 c5 2 ♘c3 ♘c6 3 g3 g6 4 ♗g2

♗g7 5 d3 d6 6 ♘ge2 e5 7 ♘d5
♘ge7 8 ♘e3 ♗e6 9 00 00 10 ♘c3
♖b8 11 ♘cd5 ♗×d5 12 ed ♘d4 13
a4 (with the threat of 14 g4 and 15
c3, winning the knight) 13 . . .
♘df5 14 ♘c4 h5 15 ♗d2 ♘h6 16
b4 ♘g4 17 ♖b1 ♘f6 18 ♗g5 cb 19
♖×b4 ♕d7 20 ♗×f6 ♗×f6 21 a5
(*60*)

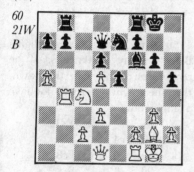

60
21W
B

21 . . . h4 22 c3 ♔g7 23 ♕b3 ♖h8
24 ♖b1 hg 25 hg ♕f5 26 ♘×d6
♕×d3 27 ♘×b7 ♖bc8 28 c4 ♕e2
29 ♘d6 ♖cd8 30 ♘e4 ♕h5 31 ♕f3
1–0

0503   Adorjan–AK

PR3: 28.12.1967: Spanish

1 e4 e5 2 ♘f3 ♘c6 3 ♗b5 a6 4
♗×c6 dc 5 00 ♗g4 6 h3 h5 7 c3
♕d3 8 hg hg 9 ♘×e5 ♗d6 10
♘×d3 ♗h2+ ½–½

0504   AK–Ligterink

PR4: 29.12.1967: Sicilian

1 e4 c5 2 g3 d5 3 d3 de 4 de ♕×d1+
5 ♔×d1 ♘c6 6 ♗e3 b6 7 ♘d2 g6 8
c3 ♗g7 9 f3 ♘f6 10 ♘h3 00 11 ♔c2
♗b7 12 ♖d1 ♖fd8 ½–½

0505   Zara–AK

PR5: 30.12.1967: Petroff

1 e4 e5 2 ♘f3 ♘f6 3 ♘×e5 d6 4 ♘f3
♘×e4 5 ♕e2 ♕e7 6 d3 ♘f6 7 ♗g5
♘bd7 8 ♘c3 h6 9 ♗h4 ♕×e2+ 10
♗×e2 ♗e7 11 000 a6 12 ♖he1 00
13 ♗f1 ♖e8 14 ♘e4 ♔f8 15 ♘×f6
♗×f6 16 ♖×e8+ ♔×e8 17 ♖e1+
♔f8 18 ♗×f6 ♘×f6 19 h3 ♗d7 20
♔d2 ½–½

0506   Timman–AK

PR6: 30.12.1967: Torre

1 d4 ♘f6 2 ♘f3 e6 3 ♗g5 d5 4
♘bd2 ♘bd7 5 e3 ♗e7 6 ♗d3 00 7
♕e2 c5 8 c3 b6 9 ♘e5 ♘×e5 10 de
♘d7 11 ♗×e7 ♕×e7 12 f4 f5 13 ef
♖×f6 14 e4 ♗b7 15 00 ♖af8 16 ed
♗×d5 17 ♖ae1 ♖×f4 18 ♗×h7+
½–½

0507   AK–Hostalet

PR7: 1.1.1968: Torre

1 d4 ♘f6 2 ♘f3 d5 3 ♗g5 e6 4
♘bd2 ♘bd7 5 e3 ♗e7 6 ♗d3 c5 7
c3 cd 8 ed ♕c7 9 00 00 10 ♖e1 a6 11
♘f1 b5 ½–½

0508   Zara–AK

FR1: 2.1.1968: Queen's Indian

1 d4 ♘f6 2 ♘f3 e6 3 g3 b6 4 ♗g2
♗b7 5 00 ♗e7 6 c4 00 7 ♘c3 d5 8
♘e5 ♕c8 9 cd ♘×d5 10 ♘×d5 ed
11 ♗f4 ♕e6 12 ♖c1 (12 ♕c2 c6 13
e4!± – Bronstein) 12 . . . ♗d6 13
♘d3 ♘d7 14 ♕b3 ♖fe8 15 e3 c6 16

♗×d6 ♕×d6 17 ♖c2 ♘f8 18 ♖fc1
♘e6 19 ♕b4 ♕×b4 20 ♘×b4 ♘d8
21 ♗f1 a5 22 ♘d3 f6 23 ♖c3 ♗a6
24 ♘f4 ♗×f1 25 ♔×f1 ♔f7 26
♖×c6 ♘×c6 27 ♖×c6 ♖ec8 28
♖×b6 ♖ab8 29 ♘×d5 ♖×b6 30
♘×b6 ♖c2 31 ♘a4 f5 32 h4 h6 33
a3 g5 34 hg hg 35 ♔g2 g4 ½–½

0509 AK–Moles
FR2: 3.1.1968: Spanish

(Notes by Karpov)

1 e4	e5
2 ♘f3	♘c6
3 ♗b5	a6
4 ♗a4	♘f6
5 ♕e2	♗e7
6 c3	b5
7 ♗b3	d6
8 a4	♗b7

Accurate response. If 8 . . . ♖b8
there would follow 9 ab ab 10 d4.

9 00	00
10 d3	h6

With this move Black begins to
follow a plan based on K-side play,
but, in my opinion, this is wrong
because White, at the right time,
can counter in the centre.

11 ♖e1	♘h7
12 d4	♘g5
13 ♗×g5	hg

A mistake. He should have
played 13 . . . ♗×g5. No doubt
Black thought that, with the bishop
pair, he would have a good game.

14 d5	♘a7

14 . . . ♘a5 would have been
better.

15 ♖d1	g4

Here I had to decide: how should
I place my knights? To prevent a
K-side attack White should station
one knight on f1, but there are so
many nice squares on the Q-side. I
decided to locate my knights in
such a way that one of them would
never be very far from f1.

16 ♘e1	♗c8
17 ab	

Straight away this spotlights
Black's many weaknesses. If he
recaptures on b5 with the pawn,
then the knight on a7 will not have
a single move.

17 . . .	♘×b5
18 ♗c4	♗d7
19 ♘c2	♕c8
20 ♘d2	g6
21 ♘b4	♗g5
22 ♖a5	♕b7

The best move. Black wants to
play . . . ♘d4 and, by getting some
play in the centre, to distract
White's pieces from the a–pawn.

23 ♘b3	♔g7
24 ♖da1	f5
25 ♘×a6	

White has won à pawn and
completely dominates the Q-side
while Black, apparently, has not
managed to achieve a thing. The
game unexpectedly takes on a
sharp character.

25 . . .	♕b6!

Black's only chance. He sacrifices
a piece, in return for which he gets a
fearsome attack thanks to White's
pieces being tied down.

26 ♗×b5   fe(*61*)

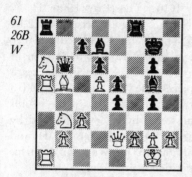

61
26B
W

27 c4

The best continuation. There was another variation, but, in the final analysis, it would only have been a draw: 27 ♗×d7 ♖×f2 28 ♕×f2 ♗e3 29 ♕×e3 ♕×e3+ 30 ♔h1. White has a rook and three pieces for the queen, but they are all on the one flank – far away from the king: 30 . . . ♖h8 31 ♗×g4 ♕g3 32 ♗h3 ♖×h3 33 gh ♕f3+ 34 ♔g1 ♕e3+ 35 ♔f1 ♕f3+ and not 36 ♔e1 on account of 36 . . . e3!

27 . . .   ♖×f2
28 c5   ♖×e2
29 cb   ♗e3+

Here, again, a decision is necessary. If 30 ♔f1 ♖f2+ 31 ♔e1 cb Black has an excellent position. But if I go to h1 don't I get mated?

30 ♔h1   ♗×b5

Another possibility was 30 . . . ♖h8 31 ♗×d7! (31 ♗×e2? g3 32 h3 ♗×h3 33 gh ♖×h3+ 34 ♔g2 ♖h2+ 35 ♔×g3 ♗f4+ 36 ♔g4 ♖g2+ draws) 31 . . . ♗f4 32 h3 ♖×h3+ 33 gh ♖h2+ 34 ♔g1 g3

and White has just the one defence: 35 ♖e1 .

31	b7		♖h8
32	b8♕		♖×b8
33	♘×b8		♗c4
34	♖5a3		♖×b2
35	♘a5		♖×b8
36	♘×c4		♗d4
37	♖d1		♖b4
38	♘e3		♖b5
39	g3		♖c5
40	♔g2		♖b5
41	♖c1		**1–0**

0510 Lewi–AK

FR3: 3.1.1968: English

1 c4 e5 2 ♘c3 d6 3 g3 g6 4 d4 ♘c6 5 de de 6 ♕×d8+ ♘×d8 7 ♘f3 ♗d6 8 ♘b5 ♗d7 9 ♘×d6+ cd 10 b3 f6 11 ♗a3 ♘f7 12 ♖d1 ♔e7 13 ♗g2 ♗c6 14 00 f5 15 ♘e1 ♘f6 16 ♘c2 ♖hd8 17 ♘b4 ♖ac8 18 ♖d2 e4 19 f3 ♔e6 20 ♖fd1 ♘e5 21 ♖d4 ef 22 ♘×c6 ♖×c6 23 ef ♖a6 24 ♗b4 ♖×a2 (*62*)

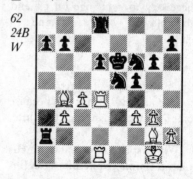

62
24B
W

25 ♖e1 (25 ♖×d6+ ♖×d6 26 ♖×d6+ ♔f7 27 ♗c3= White wants more.) 25 . . . g5 26 f4 gf 27 gf

♖g8 28 ♖d2 ♖×d2 29 ♗×d2 ♘e4
30 ♖×e4 fe 31 fe♔×e5 32 ♗c3+
♔f4 33 ♔f2 e3+ 34♔f1 b5 35 ♗d5
♖g5 36 ♗b4 ♔e5 37 ♗c3+ ♔f4
38 ♗b4 ♖g6 39 cb ♔e5 40 ♗c6
♔d4 41 ♗f3 ♔d3 42 ♗e2+ ♔e4
43 ♗d1 ♖f6+ 44 ♔e1 ♔d4 45
♗a3 ♔c3 46 ♗c1 ♔d3 47 ♗e2+
♔e4 48 ♗f1 ♖f2 49 ♗c4 ♖×h2 50
♔d1 ♔d4 51 ♗e2 d5 52 ♗a3 ♔c3
53 ♗f3 d4 54 ♗c5 ♖f2 **0–1**

0511 AK–Timman

FR4: 4.1.1968: English

(Notes by Karpov)

1 c4	e6
2 ♘c3	♘f6
3 ♘f3	♗b4
4 ♕b3	c5
5 a3	♗a5

The bishop on a5 is rather
lacking in prospects and White's
future plans are all built around this
circumstance. I think that it was
necessary to exchange on c3 and
then play . . . ♘c6, . . . d6 and . . .
e5.

6 e3	00
7 ♗e2	d5
8 00	♘c6

Of course 8 . . . d4 is bad because
of 9 ♘a4 with advantage to White.

9 ♘a4

White springs into action. His
plan is simple: while Black's KB is
on a5 the move . . . b6 is not
possible and so it is difficult to
defend the c–pawn.

9 . . .   ♕e7

10 ♕c2   ♘d7

If 10 . . . d4 11 ♘×c5 de (11 . . .
♕×c5 is no good because of 12 b4
♘×b4 13 ab ♗×b4 14 ed; and if 12
. . . ♗×b4 13 ab ♘×b4 then 14
♕b3 de 15 ♗a3 with an extra
piece) 12 fe ♕×c5 13 b4 ♘×b4 (13
. . . ♗×b4 14 ab ♘×b4 is still
answered by 15 ♕b3 followed by
♗a3) 14 ab ♗×b4 15 d4 and
although White is a pawn down his
position is promising.

11 d4

At last White plays d4. Black is
not well developed whereas White's
pieces are actively placed.

11 . . .   dc?

Black's position is worse but this
is an outright blunder. He could
have played 11 . . . cd 12 ed dc but
after 13 ♗×c4 White still has the
advantage.

12 dc	e5
13 e4	♘d4
14 ♘×d4	ed
15 ♗×c4	♘e5
16 b4	

Not precise. Just when the game
is almost won White makes a
mistake. 16 ♗d5 was correct.

16 . . .	♗c7
17 ♗d5	d3?

Black missed an excellent chance
to complicate matters by 17 . . .
♘f3+ 18 gf ♕h4 19 e5 ♗×e5 20 f4
d3.

18 ♕d1   ♗g4

On 18 . . . ♘g4, 19 f4 ♕h4 (19
. . . ♕f6 20 ♖a2) 20 h3 would have
followed.

19 f3   ♗h5
20 ♖a2

63
20W
B

Now Black's attacking prospects have completely disappeared. As the opportunity presents itself White will attack the K-side.

20 ...   ♔h8
21 g4   ♗g6
22 f4

22 ♖g2 would have been safer and then ♗b2 and ♘c3.

22 ...   ♘×g4
23 ♕×g4   f5
24 ef   ♗×f5
25 ♕f3   ♖ad8
26 ♘c3

The bishop must be over-protected so that Black is not left with any tactical possibilities.

26 ...   ♕f6
27 ♖g2   ♕d4+
28 ♔h1   ♖f6
29 ♗d2

29 ♗b2 would have been better but, in time-trouble, I decided that it was safer to blockade the d-pawn.

29 ...   ♖h6
30 ♕f2

We were both in time-trouble and I overlooked that my opponent could capture on d5. Fortunately this did not throw away the win.

30 ...   ♖×d5
31 ♖e1 ♖e6 32 ♘×d5 ♕×d5 33 ♖×e6 ♗×e6 34 ♔g1 ♕b3 (The threat was 35 ♗c3.) 35 ♕e1 ♔g8? (35 ... g6 was relatively best.) 36 f5 ♗f7 37 ♗h6 g6 38 ♕a1 ♗e5 39 ♕×e5 ♕d1+ 40 ♔f2 ♕c2+ 41 ♔g3 **1–0**

0512   Hostalet–AK

FR5: 5.1.1968: Nimzo-Indian

1 d4 ♘f6 2 c4 e6 3 ♘c3 ♗b4 4 e3 00 5 ♕c2 c5 6 a3 ♗×c3+ 7 ♕×c3 ♘c6 8 ♗d3? (8 dc is the right course.) 8 ... cd 9 ed d5 10 ♘e2 dc 11 ♗×c4 (*64*)

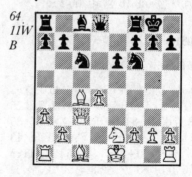

64
11W
B

(It is hard to believe that White's resignation is forced after only seven more moves, yet such is the impact of Karpov's style of play that this is exactly what happens.) 11 ... e5! 12 ♗e3 (Protecting the d-pawn. If 12 de ♘e4! 13 ♕e3 ♕a5+ 14 ♘c3 ♘×c3 15 bc ♘×e5) 12 ...

♘e4 13 ♕b3 ♕a5+ 14 ♔f1 (As 14 ♘c3 allows 14 ... ed, White's king is now very definitely held in the centre for good.) 14 ... ♘×d4 15 ♘×d4 ed 16 f3 (not 16 ♗×d4 ♘d2+ winning the queen) 16 ... de 17 fe ♕d2! **0–1** (it is a forced win for Black after 18 ♗e2 ♗g4! 19 ♖e1 ♖ac8 20 ♕d1 ♖c1 21 ♕×c1 ♗×e2+ 22 ♔g1 ♗f3!)

0513 AK–Adorjan

FR6: 6.1.1968: Sicilian

1 e4 c5 2 ♘c3 ♘c6 3 g3 g6 4 ♗g2 ♗g7 5 d3 d6 6 ♘ge2 e5 7 ♘d5 ♘ge7 8 ♗g5 h6 9 ♗f6 00 10 ♘×e7+ ♘×e7 11 ♗×g7 ♔×g7 12 ♕d2 ♗e6 13 f4 ♕d7 14 00 f6 15 ♖f2 ♖ad8 16 ♖af1 b6 ½-½

0514 Ligterink–AK

FR7: 8.1.1968: QGD

1 d4 ♘f6 2 c4 e6 3 ♘c3 d5 4 ♗g5 ♗e7 5 e3 00 6 ♘f3 ♘bd7 7 ♖c1 c6 8 ♗d3 ♖e8 9 00 dc 10 ♗×c4 ♘d5 11 ♘e4 ♗×g5 12 ♘e×g5 h6 13 ♘e4 ♕e7 14 ♘g3 ♘5b6 15 ♗d3 e5 16 ♗b1 ed 17 ♕d3 ♘f8 18 ♘×d4 ♗d7 19 e4 ♖ad8 20 ♕c3 ♗c8 21 f4 ♘a4 22 ♕e3 ♕b4 23 ♘df5 ♕×b2 24 ♗c2 ♘c3 25 e5 ♗×f5 26 ♘×f5 ♕b6 27 ♕×b6 ½-½

0515 Ciric–AK

simultaneous: 6.1.1968: Spanish

This game was one of a ten-board simultaneous display given by the Yugoslav grandmaster in the afternoon after the sixth round of the finals, played that morning. Maeder, Schaufelberger and Timman also drew, Ligterink won, and Ciric won the other five.

1 e4 e5 2 ♘f3 ♘c6 3 ♗b5 a6 4 ♗a4 ♘f6 5 00 ♗e7 6 ♖e1 b5 7 ♗b3 d6 8 c3 00 9 h3 ♘a5 10 ♗c2 ♗b7 11 d3 c5 12 ♘bd2 ♖e8 13 ♘f1 ♕c7 14 ♘g3 g6 15 ♗h6 ♘d7 16 ♘g5 ♘f8 17 b4 cb 18 cb ♗×g5 19 ♗×g5 ♘c6 20 ♕d2 ♘d4 21 ♗d1 ♘de6 22 ♗h6 ♖ac8 23 ♘e2 d5 24 ♕e3 ♕d6 25 a3 de 26 de ♖c4 27 f3 ♘d4 28 ♘×d4 ♖×d4 29 ♗e2 ♘e6 30 ♕f2 ♕d7 31 h4 ♖d6 32 ♗e3 ♘d4 33 ♗f1 ½-½

A lightning tournament, held on December 31st, was won by Karpov with 13½/16, followed by Adorjan 12½; Lewi 12, Timman 10½ etc.

6 Two Matches

USSR Yugoslavia   Sochi, 21.6–2.7.1968

1 Geller	½ ½ ½ ½ Gligorić	7 Gurgenidze ½ ½ ½ 1 Nikolić
2 Bronstein	½ 1 ½ ½ Ivkov	8 Ranniku 1 1 0 0 Liliak
3 Holmov	½ ½ ½ ½ Matulović	9 Alexandria 1 1 0 0 Jivković
4 Sakharov	1 1 1 ½ Ostojić	10 Konopleva 1 ½ 1 1 Belamarić
5 Platonov	½ ½ 0 ½ Minić	11 Shteinberg 1 0 1 ½ Fučak
6 I. Zaitsev	1 1 ½ ½ Bukić	12 **Karpov** 1 1 1 ½ Vujaković

The composition of the teams was boards 1–7 men, 8–10 women, 11–12 juniors. The Soviet Union won 30½–17½.

0601 AK–Vujaković

R1: Pirc

1 e4 d6 2 d4 ♘f6 3 ♘c3 g6 4 f3 c6 5 ♗e3 b5 6 ♕d2 ♘bd7 7 ♘ge2 ♗g7 8 g3 0-0 9 ♗g2 ♘b6 10 b3 a5 11 0-0 ♕c7 12 h3 ♗b7 13 ♘f4 ♖fd8 14 ♕f2 ♖ac8 15 ♘d3 ♘fd7 16 ♖ad1 b4 17 ♘e2 c5 18 f4 ♗a6 19 f5 ♖f8

65
28W
B

20 ♖d2 cd 21 ♗×d4 ♗×d3 22 cd ♗×d4 23 ♘×d4 ♕b8 24 h4 ♘f6 25 ♗h3 ♖c5 26 ♕e3 ♘bd7 27 ♘e2 ♕c7 28 g4 (*65*)

28 ... ♖c2? (This leads to the knight on d7 being undefended.) 29 ♖×c2 ♕×c2 30 g5 ♘h5 31 fg ♘e5 32 gh+ ♔×h7 33 d4 ♘c6 34 ♖c1
1–0

0602 Vujaković–AK

R2: Spanish

1 e4 e5 2 ♘f3 ♘c6 3 ♗b5 a6 4 ♗a4 ♘f6 5 d4 ed 6 0-0 ♗e7 7 e5 ♘e4 8 ♘×d4 ♘×d4 9 ♕×d4 ♘c5 10 ♘c3 0-0 11 ♗e3 ♘×a4 12 ♕×a4 d5 13 ed ♗×d6 14 ♗f4 ♗×f4 15 ♕×f4 ♗e6 16 ♖fe1 ♕d7 17 ♖ad1 ♕c6

18 ♖d3 ♖ae8 19 ♖de3 f6 20 h4 ♗d7 21 ♕d4 ♖×e3 22 ♖×e3 ♗e6 23 h5?! h6 24 ♖g3 ♖f7 25 ♕d8+ ♔h7 26 ♕d3+ f5 27 ♖g6? (unnecessarily entombing the rook) 27 ... ♕d7 28 ♕×d7 ♗×d7 29 ♘d5? f4 30 g3 fg 31 ♖×g3 ♖f5 32 ♘×c7 ♖c5! 33 ♖c3 ♖×c3 34 bc ♗g4 35 ♔g2 ♗×h5 36 ♘e6 ♗f7 37 ♘c5 ♗×a2 **0-1**

0603   AK-Vujaković

R3: Pirc

1 e4 d6 2 d4 g6 3 ♘c3 ♘f6 4 h3 ♗g7 5 ♗e3 00 6 ♕d2 c6 7 g4 e5 8 000 ♕e7 9 d5 c5 10 ♘ge2 ♘a6 11 ♘g3 ♘c7 12 ♔b1 ♘fe8 13 ♗e2 (Karpov gives the order 13 f3 ♖b8 14 ♗e2 b5 15 ♖dg1 b4 16 ♘d1

66
21B
W

♘b5 17 h4 c4 18 ♕×b4 ♘ec7 19 ♕d2 ♗d7 20 h5 ♖b7 21 c3 a5 22 ♔a1 a4 23 ♘f5 ♗×f5 24 gf a3 25 hg ab+ 26 ♘×b2 fg 27 fg **1-0**. The text is from *Shakhmatny Bulletin* No. 9 1968.) 13 ... ♖b8 14 ♖dg1 b5 15 h4 b4 16 ♘d1 ♘b5 17 h5 c4 18 ♕×b4 ♘ec7 19 ♕d2 ♗d7 20 c3 a5 21 ♔a1 a4 (*66*)

22 ♘f5! ♗×f5 23 gf a3 24 hg ab+ 25 ♘×b2 fg 26 fg ♖a8 27 ♗×c4 ♖a3 28 ♗h6 hg 29 ♖×g6 ♖f4 30 ♖hg1 **1-0**

0604   Vujaković-AK

R4: Spanish

1 e4 e5 2 ♘f3 ♘c6 3 ♗b5 a6 4 ♗a4 ♘f6 5 d4 ed 6 00 ♗e7 7 e5 ♘e4 8 ♘×d4 00 9 ♘f5 d5 10 ♗×c6 bc 11 ♘×e7+ ♕×e7 12 ♖e1 ♗f5 13 f3 ♘c5 14 b3 ♘e6 15 ♗a3 c5 16 ♘c3 c6 17 ♕d2 ♖fd8 18 ♘a4 ♕a7 19 ♕f2 c4 20 ♘c5 ♗×c2 21 ♖ac1 cb 22 ab ♗g6 23 f4 (Karpov gives the order 23 h3 ♖db8 24 ♖c3 ½-½. Again, the text is from *Shakhmatny Bulletin* No. 9 1968.) 23 ... ♘×c5 24 ♗×c5 ♕d7 25 h3 ♖db8 26 ♖c3 ½-½

USSR Juniors–Scandinavia Juniors

Tallinn, 17–19.8.1968

| 1 Miklyaev | ½ 1 | Andersson (S) | ½ 0 |
| 2 Karpov | 0 ½ | Jacobsen (DK) | 1 ½ |

The Soviet Union won this 15-board match 20½–9½.

0605 AK–Jacobsen

R1: Dutch

1 c4 f5 2 g3 ♘f6 3 ♗g2 g6 4 ♘c3
♗g7 5 ♘f3 00 6 00 ♘c6 7 d4 d6 8
d5 ♘e5 9 ♘×e5 de 10 e4 f4 11 b3 g5
12 f3 ♕d6 13 g4 h5 14 h3 hg 15 fg
♗d7 16 a4 ♕b6+ 17 ♔h2 ♔f7 18
♗f3 ♖h8 19 ♔g2 ♖h4 20 a5 ♕c5
21 ♗a3 ♕e3 *(67)*

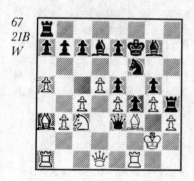

67
21B
W

22 ♕e1 ♗×g4 23 hg (if 23 ♗×g4
♘×g4 and if 24 hg ♖×g4+ ∓ ∓) 23
... ♘×g4 24 ♖h1 ♖×h1 25 ♕×e3
(not 25 ♕×h1 ♕f2+ 26 ♔h3 ♕g3
mate, nor 25 ♔×h1 ♖h8+ 26 ♔g2
♖h2+ ∓ ∓) 25 ... ♘×e3+ 26
♔×h1 g4 27 ♗e2 f3 28 ♗c5 ♗h6
29 ♖e1 (if 29 ♗×e3 ♗×e3 threat
mate) 29 ... b6 30 ♗×f3 (or 30
♗×e3 ♗×e3 31 ♗×f3 ♖h8+ 32
♔g2 gf+ 33 ♔×f3 ♗d2∓ ∓) 30 ...

bc 31 ♗d1 ♔g6 32 ♘b5 ♗f4 33
♖×e3 (if 33 ♔g1 g3 with ... ♖h8–
h2 to follow) 33 ... ♗×e3 34 ♘×c7
♖h8+ 35 ♔g2 ♖h4 36 a6 ♗f4 37
♔g1 g3 38 ♗f3 ♖h2 39 ♗g2 ♔f7
40 ♔f1 ♖h6 41 ♔e2 ♖b6 **0–1**

0606 Jacobsen–AK

R2: Bird

1 f4 d5 2 ♘f3 g6 3 g3 ♗g7 4 ♗g2
♘f6 5 00 00 6 d3 b6 7 e4 ♗b7 8 e5
♘e8 9 g4 f6 10 ♕e1 e6 11 ♘c3 f5 12
gf gf 13 ♔h1 d4 14 ♘e2 c5 15 ♖g1
♘c6 16 ♗d2 a5 17 a3 a4 18 ♘g3
♘e7 19 ♘h5 ♗×f3 20 ♗×f3 ♖a7
21 ♖×g7+ ♘×g7 22 ♘f6+ ♔f7 (if
22 ... ♔h8 23 ♕h4± ±) 23 ♕g3
♖h8 24 ♖g1 ♕f8 25 ♕g5 ♘g6 26
h4 ♘e8 27 h5 ♕e7 (not 27 ... ♘e7
28 h6 ♘g6 29 ♘×h7 ♖×h7 30
♕×g6+ ♔e7 31 ♕×h7+ ♕f7 32
♕×f7+ ♔×f7 33 h7± ±) 28 ♘×e8
(or 28 hg+ hg+ 29 ♔g2 ♘×f6 30 ef
♕×f6 and Black is alive and
kicking) 28 ... ♔×e8 29 hg hg+ 30
♔g2 ♕×g5+ 31 fg ♖c7 32 ♖h1
♖g8 33 ♖h4 ♔f7 34 ♖h7+ ♖g7
35 ♖h8 ♖g8 36 ♖h7+ ♖g7 37
♖h4 ♖g8 38 ♗d1 ♔g7 39 ♔f2
♖d8 40 ♗e2 ♖cd7 ½–½

7 Moscow University Championship 1968–1969

	1	2	3	4	5	6	7	8	9	0	1	2	3	4	
1 **Karpov**	×	½	1	½	1	½	½	½	½	1	1	1	1	1	**10**
2 Ageichenko	½	×	0	½	1	1	1	0	½	1	1	1	½	1	**9**
3 Gik	0	1	×	1	½	1	0	½	½	1	1	1	½	1	**9**
4 Vatnikov	½	½	0	×	1	0	1	½	1	0	½	1	1	1	**8**
5 Vibornov	0	0	½	0	×	1	½	1	0	1	1	1	1	1	**8**
6 Skvortsov	½	0	0	1	0	×	0	1	½	1	1	1	1	1	**8**
7 Krasnov	½	0	1	0	½	1	×	0	1	½	0	1	1	1	**7½**
8 Lepeshkin	½	1	½	½	0	0	1	×	½	½	½	½	½	1	**7**
9 Estrin	½	½	½	0	1	½	0	½	×	½	½	0	1	1	**6½**
10 Bitman	0	0	0	1	0	0	½	½	½	×	0	1	1	1	**5½**
11 Sukhanov	0	0	0	½	0	0	1	½	½	1	×	1	0	0	**4½**
12 Hramtsov	0	0	0	0	0	0	0	½	1	0	0	×	1	1	**3½**
13 Zilbert	0	½	½	0	0	0	0	½	0	0	1	0	×	½	**3**
14 Pronin	0	0	0	0	0	0	0	0	0	0	1	0	½	×	**1½**

Winning this tournament is the only recorded achievement of Karpov's year at Moscow University. During the summer vacation(?) he transferred to the Faculty of Economics, University of Leningrad.

There are many doubts about the order in which the following games were played. Gik, in his report on the tournament (*Shakhmatnaya Moskva* No. 3 1969) says that Karpov won his first six games. Karpov provided both date and round number for all the games which follow, except those against Bitman and Vatnikov. However, these do not fit in with Gik's report, nor do the round numbers fit in with the normal pairing for a fourteen-player tournament. There is room for research here. Because of these problems, the games are presented in order of date played.

0701 Hramtsov–AK

R11(?): 28.10.1968: English

(Notes by Karpov)

1 c4 e6 2 g3 d5 3 ♗g2 ♘f6 4 ♘f3
♘c6 5 0 0 ♗e7 6 b3?! (6 d4) 6 . . . 0 0
7 ♗b2 d4!∓ 8 d3 (8 e3!? e5 9 ed ed
10 d3 ♗g4) 8 . . . e5 9 a3 (9 ♘a3!?
planning 10 ♘c2, a3, ♕d2 and b4)
9 . . . a5 10 ♘bd2 h6 (intending 11
. . . ♗f5 or 11 . . . ♗e6) 11 ♘e1
♗e6 12 ♘c2 ♕d7 13 ♖e1 ♗h3 14
♗h1 ♗g4 15 ♖b1 ♔h8 (15 . . . f5!?)
16 ♗c1 f5 17 b4 a4 (17 . . . ab 18
♘×b4!) 18 c5 ♕e6 19 e3 (19 ♘c4
e4) 19 . . . de 20 ♘×e3 ♘×e3 21 fe
(*68*)

68
21W
B

21 . . . e4?! (21 . . . ♖ad8!? 22 ♕c2
e4!∓) 22 de ♘e5? (22 . . . fe, to
prevent 23 ♘f3, intending 23 . . .
♘e5) 23 ♘f3! fe (23 . . . ♖ad8 24
♘d4) 24 ♘×e5 ♕×e5 25 ♗b2 ♕f5
26 ♕c2 (26 ♕d4?? ♕f2 mate) 26
. . . ♗g5 27 ♗×e4 ♗×e3+ 28 ♔h1
(28 ♖×e3?? ♕f1+ 29 ♖×f1 ♖×f1
mate) 28 . . . ♕g5 29 ♗×g7+ !
♕×g7 (29 . . . ♔×g7 30 ♕c3+
♔g8 31 ♖×e3 ♖ae8 32 g4, but not
31 ♕×e3?? ♖f1+ ! 32 ♖×f1

♕×e3∓∓) 30 ♖×e3 ♖ae8 31 ♖f3
(31 g4!?) 31 . . . ♖×f3 32 ♗×f3
♖e3= 33 ♗×b7 ♖×a3 34 ♕e4 (34
♗g2!?) 34 . . . ♕f6 35 ♕e8+ ♔g7
36 ♗d5 h5! 37 ♕e2 (37 ♕×h5 ♖a1
38 ♕d1 ♖×b1 39 ♕×b1 a3 40 ♗g2
♗×g2+ 41 ♔×g2 ♕b2+∓∓; 37
♕e1 was the only move.) 37 . . .
♖a1!∓∓ 38 ♕c2 (38 ♕d1 ♖×b1
39 ♕×b1 a3∓∓) 38 . . . ♕f1+ !!
0–1

0702 AK–Pronin

R1(?): 2.11.1968: Franco-Sicilian

(Notes by Karpov)

1 e4	e6
2 d4	c5
3 d5	ed
4 ed	d6
5 ♘f3	♗g4
6 ♗e2	

6 ♗b5+ ♘d7 7 0 0 a6
| 6 . . . | a6 |
| 7 a4 | |

7 0 0!? b5 8 a4±
| 7 . . . | ♗×f3 |

7 . . . ♘f6 8 0 0 ♗e7 9 ♘c3 0 0 10
♘d2±

8 ♗×f3	♗e7
9 0 0	♘d7
10 ♘d2	b6

10 . . . ♘gf6!?
| 11 ♖e1 | |

11 ♘c4! (planning 12 ♗f4 and 13
♖e1±) 11 . . . b5 12 ab ab 13 ♖×a8
♕×a8 14 ♘a3 ♕b7 15 c4±
| 11 . . . | ♘e5 (*69*) |

11 . . . ♘gf6 12 ♘c4 0 0 13
♗f4±±

69
11B
W

12 ♖×e5!   de
13 d6   ♗×d6
14 ♗c6+   ♔f8?

14 . . . ♔e7 15 ♗×a8 ♕×a8 16 ♘c4 ♕b8 17 ♗g5+ with good compensation.

15 ♗×a8   ♕×a8
16 ♘c4   ♗c7
17 ♗e3!   ♘e7

17 . . . a5 18 ♕d7 ♕d8 19 ♖d1± ±

18 a5   ba

18 . . . b5 19 ♘b6 ♕c6 20 ♗×c5 f6 21 ♕d5 ♕×d5 22 ♘×d5 ♗d8 23 ♘b4± ±

19 ♗×c5   ♕c6

19 . . . ♕d8 20 ♘×e5! (intending 21 ♘c6) 20 . . . ♕×d1+ 21 ♖×d1 ♗×e5 22 ♖d8 mate!

20 ♘×e5!   ♕e8

20 . . . ♗×e5 21 ♕d8+ ♕e8 22 ♗×e7+ ♔g8 23 ♕×e8 mate.

21 ♕d4   h5
22 ♖e1   **1–0**

0703 Vibornov–AK

R 13(?): 4.11.1968: Sicilian

(Notes by Karpov)

1 e4 c5 2 ♘f3 a6?! 3 ♘c3 (3 c4!?; 3 c3!?) 3 . . . b5 4 a4?! b4 5 ♘d5 ♗b7! (5 . . . e6 6 ♘e3 ♗b7∓) 6 d3 ♗×d5!? 7 ed ♘f6 8 d4 ♘×d5 9 ♗c4 (9 dc e6∓) 9 . . . ♘f6 (9 . . . e6? 10 ♗×d5 ed 11 dc±; 9 . . . ♘b6?? 10 ♗×f7+ ! ♔×f7 11 ♘e5+ ♔g8 12 ♕f3 ♕e8 13 a5± ±) 10 dc (10 d5!? g6 11 00 d6 12 ♖e1 ♗g7 13 ♕e2 ♖a7 14 a5 with compensation) 10 . . . e6 11 ♗e3 ♕c7 12 ♕d4 ♘c6 13 ♕d3 ♘g4! 14 ♗×a6 (the only move; 14 00 ♘×e3 15 ♕×e3 ♘a5 with 16 . . . ♗×c5 to follow) 14 . . . ♘×e3 15 fe ♗×c5 16 ♗b5 00 17 00 d5 18 ♔h1 (18 ♗×c6!?) 18 . . . ♘e5! (*70*)

70
18B
W

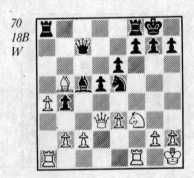

19 ♕e2 (19 ♘×e5 ♕×e5 threatening both 20 . . . ♗×e3 and 20 . . . ♕×b2) 19 . . . f5!? (19 . . . ♘g4 20 e4 de 21 ♕×e4 ♘f2+ 22 ♖×f2 ♗×f2 23 ♗d3 g6 24 ♕×b4∓) 20 ♖ael ♘g4 21 ♕d2 ♖f6 22 g3 ♖h6 23 ♔g2 ♕b6 24 ♘h4 ♘×e3+ ∓ ∓ 25 ♖×e3 ♗×e3 26 ♕×b4 f4 27 ♕e7 ♖f6 28 ♘f3 ♗c5 29 ♕d7 ♗d6 30 c3 ♖d8 31 ♕c6 ♕e3 **0–1**

0704   AK–Gik

R2(?): 15.11.1968: Sicilian

(Notes by Karpov)

1 e4 c5 2 ♘f3 d6 3 d4 cd 4 ♘×d4
♘f6 5 ♘c3 g6 6 ♗e3 ♗g7 7 f3 0-0 8
♗c4 ♘c6 9 ♕d2 ♕a5 10 0-0-0 ♗d7
11 h4 ♘e5 12 ♗b3 ♖fc8 13 h5
♘×h5 14 ♗h6

14 ♔b1 was played in Spassky–
Stein, RSFSR–Ukraine 1967,
when Black obtained counterplay
with the exchange sacrifice 14 . . .
♖×c3 15 ♕×c3 ♕×c3 16 bc ♖c8
17 ♔b2 a5.

In the last Student Olympiad in
Austria (Ybbs), the West German
players succeeded in strengthening
White's play, so White does not
have to waste a tempo with his king.

14 . . .   ♗×h6

14 . . . ♘d3+ brings about an
extremely sharp situation: 15 ♔b1
♘×b2 (not 15 . . . ♗×d4 because of
16 ♘d5!) 16 ♔×b2 ♗×h6 17
♕×h6 ♕×c3+ (Karpov wrote
these notes seven years ago, during
which time 17 . . . ♖×c3 has
become the theoretical recommendation – KJO'C.) 18 ♔b1.

15 ♕×h6   ♖×c3
16 bc   ♕×c3
17 ♘e2 *(71)*

Black overlooked this move. Now
17 . . . ♘d3+ does not work: 18
♖×d3 ♕a1+ 19 ♔d2 ♕×h1 20 g4
♘g3 21 ♕×h1 ♘×h1 22 ♔e3 and
the knight is trapped. So Black must
retreat his queen.

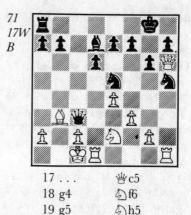

71
17W
B

17 . . .	♕c5
18 g4	♘f6
19 g5	♘h5

Here I was about to play 20 ♘g3
when I noticed that after 20 . . .
♗g4! White's queen is shut out of
play. If 21 ♘f5 there follows 21 . . .
♗×f5 22 ef ♕e3+ 23 ♔b1 ♕f4 and
it is not at all clear how to continue
the attack.

20 ♖×h5!

The only way forward!

20 . . .	gh
21 ♖h1	♕e3+
22 ♔b1	♕×f3

Clearly not 22 . . . ♕×e2 because
of 23 ♕×h5 and mate is inevitable.

23 ♖×h5   e6

23 . . . ♕×e4 does not work on
account of 24 g6! when the brave
pawn is attacked four ways but
remains inviolate! Possibly better
chances of salvation are to be found
in 23 . . . ♘g6 24 ♕×h7+ ♔f8 25
♖h6 e6 26 ♖×g6 fg 27 ♕×d7
♕×e2.

(Subsequent analysis, by V.
Priimachenko in *64* No. 32 1971,
suggests that Black can draw the
ending. From the end of Karpov's

analysis: 28 ♕×d6+ ♔g7 29 ♕e7+ ♔h8 30 ♕f6+ ♔h7 31 ♕f7+ ♔h8 32 ♕×g6, which Gufeld and Lazarev claimed to be winning for White, 32 . . . ♕d1+ 33 ♔b2 ♕d4+ 34 c3 ♕d2+ 35 ♗c2 ♕d7 and Black has sufficient counterplay, e.g. 36 ♕f6+ ♔g8 37 g6 ♖e8 38 ♕d4 ♕×d4 39 cd e5. Also, immediately after 23 . . . ♘g6, there is nothing in 24 ♕×h7+ ♔f8 25 ♕h6+ ♔e8 26 ♕h8+ ♘f8. – KJO'C)

24 g6!   ♘×g6

Forced, since after 24 . . . fg 25 ♕×h7+ ♔f8 26 ♕h8+ ♔e7 27 ♖h7+ ♘f7 28 ♕×a8 ♕×e2 29 ♕×b7 White wins.

25 ♕×h7+   ♔f8 (72)

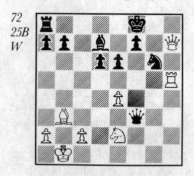

72
25B
W

26 ♖f5!

This blow was not expected by my opponent.

26 . . .   ♕×b3+

26 . . . ef is not possible in the face of mate, so Black gives up the queen for rook and bishop.

27 ab   ef
28 ♘f4   ♖d8

If 28 . . . ♘×f4 then, naturally, 29 ♕h8+ and 30 ♕×a8.

29 ♕h6+   ♔e8
30 ♘×g6   fg
31 ♕×g6+   ♔e7
32 ♕g5+   ♔e8
33 ef   ♖c8
34 ♕g8+   ♔e7
35 ♕g7+   ♔d8
36 f6   **1–0**

0705   Krasnov–AK

R5(?): 16.11.1968: QGD

1 d4 ♘f6 2 c4 e6 3 ♘f3 d5 4 ♘c3 ♗b4 5 ♗g5 h6 6 ♗×f6 ♕×f6 7 e3 00 8 ♗e2 dc 9 ♗×c4 b6 10 00 ♗b7 11 ♖c1 c5 12 ♘b5 a6 13 ♘d6 ♗×f3 14 gf cd 15 ♘e4 ♕e5 16 ed ♕f4 17 d5 b5 18 ♗b3 ♘d7 19 de ♘e5 20 ef+ ♔h8 21 ♔g2 ♘g6 22 ♘g3 ♖ad8 (? Karpov) 23 ♕e2 ♕×c1 24 ♖×c1 ♘f4+ 25 ♔f1 ♘×e2 26 ♘×e2 ♖c8 27 ♖a1 ♗d6 28 f4 g6 29 ♔g2 ♗e7 (Karpov gives the order 29 . . . ♖fd8 30 ♔f3 ♗e7. The source of the text is *Shakhmatny Bulletin* No. 4 1969.) 30 ♔f3 ♖fd8 31 f5 g5 32 ♘g3 ♖d3+ 33 ♔g2 ♔g7 34 ♘h5+ ♔f8 35 ♖e1 a5 36 f6 ♗b4 37 ♖e4 ♖×b3 38 ab ♔×f7 39 ♖e5 ♖c5 40 ♖e7+ ♔g6 41 ♘g3 ♔×f6 42 ♖e2 ♖e5 43 ♖c2 ♖e6 44 ♔f3 ♔e5 45 ♖c8 ♖f6+ (Karpov gives the order 45 . . . ♗d6 46 ♔e2 ♖f6.) 46 ♔e2 ♗d6 47 f3 ♖f4 48 ♘e4 ♗b4 49 ♔e3 ♖h4 50 ♖e8+ ♔f5 51 ♘g3+ ♔f6 52 ♖b8 ♖×h2 53 ♖b6+ ♔f7 54 ♖×b5 ♖×b2 55 ♔e4 (Karpov

gives the order 55 ♘f5 ♖×b3+ 56 ♔e4.) 55 ... ♖×b3 56 ♘f5 a4 57 ♘d4 ♖b2 58 ♖b7+ ♔e8 59 ♘c6 ♗c3 (? Karpov) 60 ♖a7 ♖a2 61 ♔f5 a3 62 ♖e7+ ♔f8 63 ♔g6 (Karpov gives the game as being drawn at this point.) 63 ... ♖d2 ½–½

0706 AK–Sukhanov

R9(?): 20.11.1968: Sicilian

1 e4 c5 2 ♘c3 ♘c6 3 g3 g6 4 ♗g2 ♗g7 5 d3 ♘f6 6 ♗e3 d6 7 h3 ♘d4 8 ♘ce2 ♕b6 9 c3 ♘×e2 10 ♕×e2 ♗d7 11 ♘f3 ♕a6 12 ♘h4 (? Karpov) 12 ... ♗c6 13 ♕c2 d5 14 e5 ♘d7 15 f4 ♗b5 16 ♗×d5 ♗×d3 17 ♕g2 000 18 ♖d1 c4 19 b3 e6 20 ♗×c4 ♗×c4 21 bc ♕×c4 22 ♕e2 ♕×e2+ (? Karpov) 23 ♔×e2 f6 24 ef ♗×f6 25 ♘f3 e5 26 fe ♘×e5 27 ♗×a7 ♖de8 28 ♘×e5 ♗×e5 29 ♔d3 ♗×g3 30 ♖hf1 ♖e6 31 ♗d4 ♖d8 32 ♖f7 h5 33 ♖b1 b6 (? Karpov) 34 a4 ♗c7 35 ♔c4 ♖c6+ 36 ♔b5 ♔b7 37 ♖e1 ♖d5+ 38 ♔b4 ♖f5 39 ♖×f5 gf 40 ♔b5 ♖d6 (! Karpov) 41 ♔c4 ♖g6 42 ♖e7 ♔c6 43 ♖h7 f4 44 ♖×h5 f3 45 ♔d3 ♖g2 46 ♖f5 ♖a2 47 ♖×f3 (Karpov gives 1–0 at this point. The source for the continuation is *Shakhmatny Bulletin* No. 4 1969.) 47 ... ♖×a4 48 h4 ♖a5 49 ♖f6+ ♔b7 50 ♖h6 ♖f5 51 ♔e4 ♖f1 52 ♔d5 ♖f5+ 53 ♔e6 ♖f3 54 h5 ♔c6 55 ♖f6 ♖h3 56 h6 ♗d8 57 ♖g6 b5 58 ♔f7+ ♔d5 59 ♔g7 b4 60 cb ♔×d4 61 ♖d6+ ♔e5 62 ♖×d8 ♖g3+ 63 ♔h8 ♔f6 64 h7

♔f7 65 ♖d1 ♖b3 66 ♖f1+ ♔e7 67 ♖f4 **1–0**

0707 AK–Estrin

R4(?): 29.11.1968: Spanish

1 e4 e5 2 ♘f3 ♘c6 3 ♗b5 a6 4 ♗a4 ♘f6 5 00 ♗e7 6 ♕e2 b5 7 ♗b3 d6 8 h3 ♘a5 9 ♘c3 00 10 d3 c6 11 ♘h2 ♘×b3 12 ab ♗e6 13 f4 ef 14 ♗×f4 d5 15 e5 ♘e8 16 d4 ♕d7 17 ♘f3 ♘c7 18 ♗g5 ♗×g5 19 ♘×g5 ♗f5 20 b4 ♗g6 21 ♕d2 ♖ae8 22 ♘e2 ♕e7 23 ♘f3 ♗e4 24 ♖ae1 (? Karpov) 24 ... ♗×f3 25 ♖×f3 f6 26 ♘c1 fe 27 ♖×e5 ♕d6 28 ♖fe3 ♖×e5 29 de ♕h6 30 ♘b3 ♘e6 31 c3 ½–½

0708 AK–Zilbert

R8(?): 30.11.1968: Spanish

1 e4 e5 2 ♘f3 ♘c6 3 ♗b5 a6 4 ♗a4 d6 5 d4 b5 6 ♗b3 ♘×d4 7 ♘×d4 ed 8 a4 ♗b7 9 ♕e2 ♕d7 10 c3 d3 11 ♕×d3 ♘f6 12 ab ab 13 ♖×a8+ ♗×a8 14 00 ♗e7 15 ♖e1 00 16 ♘a3 ♖e8 (? Karpov) 17 ♕×b5 ♗c6 18 ♕f5 ♗×e4 19 ♕×d7 ♘×d7 20 ♖×e4 ♘c5 21 ♗a4 **1–0**

0709 AK–Bitman

R?: 15.1.1969: Sicilian

(Notes by Karpov)

1 e4 c5 2 ♘f3 e6 3 c3 d5 4 ed ed 5 ♗b5+ ♘c6 6 00 ♗d6 7 d4 cd? 8 ♘×d4 ♗c7 9 ♕h5 ♘ge7 10 ♗d3! a6 11 ♖e1 ♘e5 12 ♗b5+ ♔f8 13 ♗e2? h6 14 h3 ♘g8 15 ♗f1 ♘f6 16

♕d1 g5?! 17 ♘f3! ♘c6 18 b3 g4 19 hg ♗×g4 20 ♗a3 ♗×a3 21 ♘×a3 ♖g8 22 ♕d2 ♕d6? 23 ♘c4 ♕d8 24 ♕×h6+ ♖g7 25 ♘ce5 ♗×f3 26 ♘×f3 ♘g4 27 ♕f4 ♕b6 28 ♖e2 ♕c5 29 ♖c2 ♔g8 30 ♖e1 ♖f8 31 ♗d3 ♘d8 32 ♗f5 ♘f6 33 ♖e3 b5 34 ♕h6 ♘g4 35 ♗×g4 ♖×g4 36 ♘g5 **1–0**

0711   Vatnikov–AK

R?: ?.?.196?: Four Knights

1 e4 e5 2 ♘f3 ♘c6 3 ♘c3 ♘f6 4 ♗b5 ♘d4 5 ♘×d4 ed 6 e5 dc 7 ef ♕×f6 8 dc ♕e5+ 9 ♕e2 ½–½

0711   Ageichenko–AK*

(* Colours?) This game is not available.

0712   Skvortsov–AK*

(* Colours?) This game is not available.

0713   Lepeshkin–AK*

(* Colours?) This game is not available.

8 USSR Team Championship,
Riga, 10–24.12.1968

Karpov played on board six for the Armed Forces team which came second, with 72½/110, behind 'Burevestnik' (Students) with 78. Karpov's result of 10/11 was the absolute best result of the event.

			1	2	3	4	5	6	7	8	9	0	1	2	3	
1	**Karpov**	M	×	1	½	·	1	1	1	1	½	1	1	1	1	**10**
2	Miklyaev	M	0	×	1	·	1	1	½	1	1	1	1	½	1	**9**
3	Vaganian*	M	½	0	×	×	½	·	·	·	·	1	·	·	½	**2½**
4	Shteinberg*	M	·	·	×	×	·	½	½	1	1	·	1	½	·	**4½**
5	Popov	C	0	0	½	·	×	½	½	1	1	1	1	1	½	**7**
6	Tsikhelashvili	C	0	0	·	½	½	×	1	½	½	1	1	1	1	**7**
7	Nisman	C	0	½	·	½	½	0	×	½	0	1	1	1	1	**6**
8	Kirpichnikov	C	0	0	·	0	0	½	½	×	½	1	1	1	1	**5½**
9	Lisenko	C	½	0	·	0	0	½	1	½	×	½	1	½	1	**5½**
10	Reiman	1	0	0	0	0	·	0	0	0	0	½	×	1	1	½	**3**
11	Peshina	C	0	0	·	0	0	0	0	0	0	0	×	1	1	**2**
12	Romanishin	M	0	½	·	½	0	0	0	0	½	0	0	×	½	**2**
13	Sangla	C	0	0	½	·	½	0	0	0	0	½	0	½	×	**2**

7

* *Vaganian played the first five rounds, Shteinberg the last six.*

0801 Popov–AK

R1 v. Moldava: Spanish

1 e4 e5 2 ♘f3 ♘c6 3 ♗b5 a6 4 ♗a4 ♘f6 5 00 ♗e7 6 ♖e1 b5 7 ♗b3 d6 8 c3 00 9 d4 ♗g4 10 d5 ♘a5 11 ♗c2 c6 12 dc (if 12 h3 then 12 ... ♗×f3 is much better than 12 ... ♗d7? 13 ♘×e5!) 12 ... ♕c7 13 h3 ♗h5 14 ♘bd2 ♖ad8 15 ♕e2 ♘×c6 16 ♘f1 ♖fe8 17 ♗g5 ♘d7 18 ♗e3 ♗g6 19 a4 ♕b7 20 ab ab 21 ♖ed1 ♘f6 22 ♗g5 ♘h5 23 g3 ♗×g5 24 ♘×g5 ♘f6 25 ♗d3 b4 26 ♘f3 ♘b8! 27 ♘1d2 (73)

27 ... d5 28 ♘h4 (if 28 ed e4 wins a piece.) 28 ... de 29 ♗b5 ♖f8 30 ♘×g6 hg 31 ♖a4 bc 32 bc e3 33 fe

73
27W
B

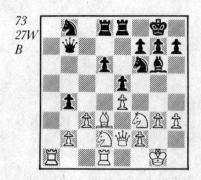

♘d5 (with the idea of 34 ... ♘×c3 with a family fork) 34 ♘e4 ♘×e3 35 ♖b1 ♘d5 36 c4 ♘e7 37 c5 ♘f5 38 ♗d3 ♕d5 39 ♗c4 ♕d7 40 ♗b5 ♘c6 41 ♗×c6 ♕×c6 42 ♖a6 ♕c8 43 ♔h2 ♖d4 44 ♖ab6 ♖fd8 45 ♖1b2 ♖4d7 46 h4 ♘d4 47 ♕e3 ♕a8 48 ♘d6 ♕d5 49 ♖b8 ♖×b8 50 ♖×b8+ ♔h7 51 ♘e4 f6 52 ♖b2 ♖a7 53 ♖f2 ♕a8! (54 ... ♖a3 55 ♕e1 ♘f3+ , or 55 ♘c3 ♕a5, is the threat.) 54 ♔h3 ♖a3 55 ♕e1 ♘f5 56 h5? (56 ♖e2 would have been better.) 56 ... ♖e3 57 ♘×f6+ gf 58 ♕d1 ♖×g3+ 59 ♔h2 ♕e4 **0–1**

0802   Sangla–AK

R2 v. Kalev: Torre

1 d4 ♘f6 2 ♘f3 e6 3 ♗g5 c5 4 c3 cd 5 cd ♕b6 6 ♕b3 ♘e4 7 ♗f4 ♘c6 8 e3 ♗b4+ 9 ♘bd2? (9 ♘fd2) 9 ... g5 10 ♗×g5 (or 10 ♗g3 g4∓ ∓) 10 ... ♗×d2+ 11 ♘×d2 ♕a5 **0–1**

0803   AK–Vaganian

R3 v. Spartak: Alekhine

1 e4 ♘f6 2 e5 ♘d5 3 d4 d6 4 ♘f3 g6

5 ♗e2 ♗g7 6 c4 ♘b6 7 ed cd 8 b3 00 9 ♗b2 ♘c6 10 00 ♗g4 11 h3 ♗×f3 12 ♗×f3 d5 13 c5 ♘c8 14 ♕d2 e6 15 b4 a6 16 a4 ♘8e7 17 ♘a3 ♘f5 18 ♘c2 h5 19 b5 ♘a5 20 ♕b4 ♘c4 21 ♗e2 a5 22 ♕c3 ♘×b2 23 ♕×b2 ♕g5 24 ♖fd1 e5 25 de ♘h4 26 ♘e1 ♗×e5 27 ♕c1! (cleverly saving the exchange) 27 ... ♕f6 28 ♖a2 ♗d4 29 ♘d3 ♖fe8 30 ♖c2 ♖ac8 31 ♗f1 ♘f5 (with the idea of playing 32 ... ♘e3 33 fe ♗×e3+ 34 ♖f2! when 34 ... ♕h4 and 34 ... ♕d4 are both awkward for White.) 32 ♔h1 ♕h4 33 ♕d2 ♗g7 34 ♕×a5 ♖a8 35 ♕b4 ♖×a4 36 ♕×h4 ♖×h4 37 g3 ♖c4 38 ♖dc1 ♖×c2 39 ♖×c2 ♘d4 40 ♖c1 ♖c8 41 ♗g2 ♘×b5 42 ♖b1 ♘c3 43 ♖×b7 ♗d4 ½–½

0804   Nisman–AK

R4 v. Trud: Nimzo-Indian

1 c4 ♘f6 2 ♘c3 e6 3 d4 ♗b4 4 a3 ♗×c3+ 5 bc c5 6 e3 ♘c6 7 ♘e2 b6 8 ♘g3 ♗a6 9 ♗d3? (This is a mistake that should lose a pawn. The critical variation is 9 e4 00 10 ♗g5 h6 11 h4! cd 12 cd hg 13 hg g6 14 e5! ♘h7 15 ♕g4! ♘×g5 16 ♘e4 ♔g7 17 ♘×g5 ♖h8 18 ♖×h8 ♕×h8 19 ♖d1 with a dangerous attack.) 9 ... ♘a5 10 ♕e2 d6? (10 ... cd 11 cd ♖c8 wins the c–pawn straight off.) 11 ♗b2 ♕d7 (Intending to occupy a4 to increase the pressure on c4.) 12 e4 000! (if 12 ... ♕a4 13 e5 de 14 de ♘d7 15 ♘e4!) 13 a4 h5! 14 00? (14 h4 was

the only move, but then Black could proceed with 14 ... e5 15 f3 g6! with ... ♘g8, ... f6, ... ♕g7, ... ♘e7, ... ♖dg8 and ... g5 to follow.) 14 ... h4 15 ♘h1 e5 *(74)*

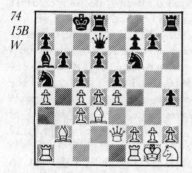

74
15B
W

16 f4 (Blocking the centre with 16 d5 would be met by 16 ... ♘h5 with a tremendous attack, e.g. 17 g3 ♕h3 18 ♗c1 f6! 19 ♗d2 g5 20 ♗e1 ♖dg8 21 ♖a2 ♔b8! 22 ♖b2 ♗c8! 23 ♖a2 ♘f4!∓ ∓) 16 ... ♘h5 17 fe de 18 d5 ♘f4 19 ♖×f4 (Forced, otherwise 19 ... ♘×d3 and White's position falls apart at the seams.) 19 ... ef 20 e5 h3 21 g4 (The alternative, 21 g3 fg 22 ♘×g3 ♔b8 23 ♖f1 ♕×a4 24 ♖×f7 ♗×c4, is hopeless for White.) 21 ... ♔b8 22 ♗c1 (Allowing a neat combination, but the obvious 22 ♘f2 is dealt with by 22 ... f3! 23 ♕×f3 ♘×c4! 24 ♗×c4 ♗×c4 25 d6 ♕e6 winning easily.) 22 ... ♗×c4! 23 ♗×c4 (23 ♗×f4 ♗×d3 24 ♕×d3 ♕×d5 25 e6+ ♔a8∓ ∓) 23 ... ♘×c4 24 ♕×c4 ♕×g4+ 25 ♘g3 ♖h4! (not, of course, 25 ... fg??) 26 ♕×f4 ♕×f4 27 ♗×f4 ♖×f4 28 ♖d1

(Protecting d5, but since the a-pawn is now lost, White could quietly resign.) 28 ... g6 (to play 29 ... ♖×a4 without allowing 30 ♘f5) 29 ♖d2 ♖×a4 30 ♔f2 ♖c4 31 ♖d3 a5 32 ♔e3 ♖e8 33 e6 fe 34 d6 ♖d8 35 ♘e4 ♗c8 36 ♘f6 ♖d7! 37 ♘×d7 ♔×d7 38 ♔d2 ♖h4 39 ♔c2 b5 40 ♖g3 ♔×d6 41 ♖×g6 ♖f4 42 ♔b3 a4+ 43 ♔a3 ♖f3 44 ♔b2 b4 45 cb cb 46 ♖g4 ♔d5 **0-1**

0805 AK–Peshina

R5 v. Zhalgiris: English

1 c4 g6 2 g3 ♗g7 3 ♗g2 c5 4 ♘f3 ♘c6 5 00 d6 6 ♘c3 h5 7 d3 ♘h6 8 e4 00 9 h3 ♖b8 10 ♗g5 a6 11 ♘d5 ♔h7 12 ♖c1 ♗d7 (if 12 ... ♗×b2 13 ♗×h6!) 13 a3 b5 14 b4 f6? 15 ♗d2 cb 16 ab bc 17 dc e6 (Black's pawn formation is reminiscent of Keres–Petrosian, Candidates' 1959, but less flexible.) 18 ♘f4 *(75)*

75
18W
B

18 ... ♘×b4 19 ♗×b4 ♖×b4 20 ♕×d6 ♖b6 21 ♕a3 e5 22 ♘d5 ♖c6 23 c5 a5 24 ♘d2 ♖e8 25 ♘c4 ♗f8 26 ♘cb6 ♘g8 27 ♖fd1 ♗e6

(Black is hopelessly lost: his pieces are unable to co-operate and he has absolutely no counterplay.) 28 ♕×a5 ♕b8 29 ♘b4 ♖c7 30 ♘a6 ♕a7 31 ♕b5 ♖ec8 (31 ... ♖ce7 32 c6 and 33 c7) 32 ♘×c8 ♖×c8 33 c6 **1-0**

0806   Kirpichnikov-AK

R6 v. Daugava: Spanish

1 e4 e5 2 ♘f3 ♘c6 3 ♗b5 a6 4 ♗a4 ♘f6 5 00 ♗e7 6 ♗×c6 dc 7 ♘c3 ♘d7 8 d4 f6 9 ♗e3 (9 ♗e2!, to use the knight on the K-side and to make possible c3 to bolster the centre, is best.) 9 ... 00 10 ♕e2 ♕e8 11 ♘h4 g6 12 ♘f3 ♗d6 13 ♖ad1 ♖f7 14 ♘d2 b5 15 f4 ed 16 ♗×d4 c5 17 ♗e3 ♗b7 18 a4 b4 *(76)*

76
18B
W

19 ♘cb1 (if 19 ♘d5 then 19 ... f5 and White's position still falls apart) 19 ... ♗×e4 20 ♘×e4 ♕×e4 21 ♕d3 ♖e7 22 ♕×e4 ♖×e4 23 ♗d2 ♘b6 24 b3 c4 25 a5 ♘d5 26 ♗c1 ♘×f4 27 ♔f2 ♖ae8 28 ♔f3 ♘e2 **0-1**

0807   AK-Lisenko

R7 v. Lokomotiv: Sicilian

1 e4 c5 2 ♘f3 ♘c6 3 ♗b5 g6 4 c3 ♗g7 5 00 ♘f6 6 ♖e1 00 7 h3 ♕b6 8 ♘a3 d5 9 d3 ♗d8 10 ♕e2 d4 11 ♗×c6 bc 12 cd cd 13 ♘c4 ♕c7 14 ♗d2 a5 15 ♖ec1 ♗e6 16 ♕e1 (a characteristic Karpov pile-up on a weak pawn) 16 ... ♗×c4 17 ♖×c4 ♕b6 18 b3 c5 19 ♖a4 ♕b5 (The counter-attack on the d-pawn saves Black.) 20 ♘e5 ♘d7 21 ♘c4 ♘e5 22 ♘×e5 ♗×e5 23 ♕e2 ♗c7 24 f4 ♕c6 25 ♖c1 ♕d6 26 ♕f3 ♗b6 27 f5 ♗c7 28 ♔f1 gf (A surprising move, but Black still uses White's d-pawn as a means of counter-attack.) 29 ♕×f5 ♕g3 30 ♕f3 ♕×f3+ 31 gf ♗b6 32 ♔f2 f6 33 ♖g1+ ♔f7 34 f4 e6 35 ♔f3 f5 36 ♖e1 ♔f6 37 ef ef 38 h4 ♖g8 39 a3 ♖a7 40 ♖c1 ♖ga8 41 h5 ♖c8 42 ♖ac4 ♖e8 43 ♖e1 ♖×e1 44 ♗×e1 ♖b7 45 b4 cb 46 ab a4 47 b5 a3 48 ♖c2 ♖a7 49 ♖a2 ♗c5 50 b6 ♗×b6 51 ♗b4 ♖a4 **½-½**

0808   Tsikhelashvili-AK

R8 v. Dinamo: Vienna

1 e4 e5 2 ♘c3 ♗c5 3 ♕g4? ♘f6 4 ♕×g7 ♖g8 5 ♕h6 ♗×f2+ 6 ♔d1 ♖g6 7 ♕h3 d5 8 ♕d3 ♗b6 9 ♘×d5 ♘×d5 10 ♕×d5 ♕f6 11 ♘f3 ♘c6 12 c3 ♗g4 13 ♕d3 ♕e7 14 h3 ♗d7 15 g4 000 16 ♕e2 h5 17 g5 f5 18 h4 ♖d6 19 ♗h3 fe 20 ♕×e4 ♗×h3 21 ♖×h3 ♖f8 22 d3 ♕d7 23 ♖g3 ♗f2! 24 ♖g2

🜚×d3+ 25 ♘d2 🜚e3 26 🜚×f2
🜚×e4 27 🜚×f8+ ♔d8 28 ♔c2
🜚e1 29 b4 e4 30 g6 ♔g7 31
🜚×d8+ ♔×d8 32 ♘×e4 🜚×e4
33 ♗g5+ ♔c8 34 🜚d1 b6 **0-1**

0809 AK–Romanishin

R9 v. Avangard: Richter-Veresov

1 d4 d5 2 ♘c3 ♘f6 3 ♗g5 c6 4 ♘f3
♘bd7 5 e3 g6 6 ♗d3 ♗g7 7 0-0 0-0 8
🜚e1 🜚e8 9 h3 ♕b6 10 🜚b1 e5 11
♗e2 ♘e4 12 ♗h4 ed (12 . . . ♘×c3
13 bc ♕a5!? is an interesting
possibility.) 13 ♘×e4 de4 (13 . . .
🜚×e4!?) 14 ♘×d4 ♘e5 15 c4 c5!?
(To free e6 for his bishop without
allowing it to be exchanged e.g. 15
. . . ♗e6 16 ♘×e6 🜚×e6 17 b4±
But the text weakens the Q-side
and, especially, d5.) 16 ♘b5! (*77*)

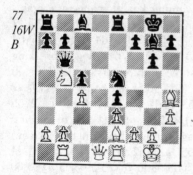

77
16W
B

16 . . . ♗e6 (Probably better than
16 . . . a6 when both 17 ♘d6!? and
17 ♘c3, with ♘d5 to follow, are
good for White.) 17 ♕a4 ♕c6
(threatening 18 . . . a6 19 ♘c3
♘×c4∓) 18 🜚ec1 h6 (Now 18 . . .
a6 19 ♘c3 ♘×c4 meets with 20
♗×c4 ♕×a4 21 ♘×a4 ♗×c4 22

🜚×c4 b5 23 🜚×c5 ba 24 🜚a5
🜚fb8 25 🜚×a4 🜚×b2 26 🜚×b2
♗×b2 27 🜚×e4± .) 19 🜚c2 g5 20
♗g3 🜚ed8 21 b4 cb 22 ♕×b4 ♘d3
23 ♕a3 a6 24 ♘c7 🜚ac8 25 ♕a5
b5 26 ♘×e6 fe 27 ♗g4± ♘e5 28
♗×e5 ♗×e5 29 🜚bc1 🜚d6 30 g3
♕b6 31 ♕e1 bc 32 🜚×c4 🜚×c4 33
🜚×c4 ♕b7 34 ♕c1 🜚b6 35 🜚c8+
♔g7 36 ♕c5 ♗d6 37 ♕c3+ e5 38
♔g2 🜚b1 39 a4 (preventing 39 . . .
♕b5 with 40 . . . ♕f1+ and 41 . . .
♕h1 mate) 39 . . . ♕f7 40 🜚d8 **1-0**
(After 40 . . . ♗e7 41 🜚d7 ♕f6 42
♕c7 ♔f8 43 ♕c8+ ♔g7 44 ♕e8
Black has no way to continue his
resistance.)

0810 Reiman–AK

R10 v. IUD: Nimzo-Indian

1 d4 ♘f6 2 c4 e6 3 ♘c3 ♗b4 4 e3 c5
5 ♗d3 0-0 6 ♘f3 d5 7 0-0 ♘bd7 8 cd
ed 9 a3 ♗a5 10 🜚b1? (Gligorić has
demonstrated in three famous
games against Damjanović and
Yanofsky in 1968, and against
Andersson in 1971 that White has
excellent chances after 10 b4!) 10
. . . ♗c7 11 b4 cd 12 ed h6 13 🜚e1
🜚e8 14 h3 🜚×e1+ 15 ♕×e1 ♘f8
16 ♗e3 ♗d7 17 ♕d2 🜚c8 18 ♘e5
♘e6 19 ♘f5 ♗×e5 20 de d4 21 ef de
22 ♕×e3 ♕×f6 23 ♘d5 ♕d8 24
🜚d1 b6 25 ♘f4 ♕e7 26 ♘d5 ♕e8
27 🜚d3 ♗b5 28 ♕g3 ♕d8 29 🜚c3
🜚×c3 30 ♘×c3 ♗c4 31 ♘e4 ♗d5
32 ♘c3 ♘d4 33 ♕e5? (33 ♗d3
would have been better.) 33 . . .
♗×g2 34 ♔×g2 ♕g5+ 35 ♔f1

♘×f5 36 ♕e4 ♕g6 37 ♕f3 **0-1** (time)

0811   AK–Miklyaev

R11 v. Burevestnik: Spanish

A fitting last round struggle to decide the destination of the board prize, and a win providing the absolute best result of the event. (Notes by Suetin)

1 e4 e5 2 ♘f3 ♘c6 3 ♗b5 a6 4 ♗a4 d6 5 c3 ♗d7 6 00 g6 7 d4 ♗g7 8 h3 ♘f6 9 ♘bd2 00 10 ♖e1 ♖e8 11 ♗c2 h6 12 a3 ♔h7 13 ♘f1 b5 14 ♘g3 ♘a5 15 b3 c5 16 d5 c4 17 b4 ♘b7 18 ♗e3 ♕c7 19 ♘h2 a5 20 ♕d2 ♖a6 21 ♖f1 ♖ea8 22 ♖ac1 ab 23 ab ♘g8 24 f4 f6 25 h4 ♗e8 26 ♘g4 h5 27 ♘h2 ef 28 ♗×f4 ♘d8 29 ♕d1 ♔h8 30 ♘e2 ♘f7 31 g4 ♘e5 32 gh gh 33 ♘g3 ♕f7 34 ♘f3 ♘g4 35 ♘d4 ♗h6 36 ♕d2 ♗×f4 37 ♕×f4 ♘8h6 38 ♘gf5 ♘×f5 39 ♘×f5 ♕f8 40 ♗d1 ♘e5 41 ♖c2 ♖a2 42 ♖×a2 ♖×a2 (*78*)

78
42B
W

43 ♘g3! (The black pawns come under heavy fire from the threats of 44 ♕×f6+ and 44 ♗×h5.) 43 ... ♔g7

(Black had an interesting possibility of creating counterplay with 43 ... ♖a3! immediately attacking the vulnerable base of the white pawn chain. The main variation occurs after 44 ♕×f6+ ♕×f6 45 ♖×f6 ♗d7! (45 ... ♖×c3 46 ♔f2!) 46 ♖h6+ ♔g8 47 ♖×d6 ♖×c3 48 ♘×h5 ♖c1! 49 ♘f6+ ♔f7! 50 ♘×d7 ♖×d1+ 51 ♔f2 ♔e7! – analysis by Geller and Furman – 52 ♖e6+ ♔×d7 53 ♔e2!! – already White has urgently to think about his own salvation; 53 ♖×e5 is bad because of 53 ... c3! and the pawn queens – 53 ... ♖d4 54 ♖×e5 c3 55 d6 etc. draws.)

44 ♕×f6 ♕×f6 45 ♖×f6 ♖a1 46 ♖f1 ♖c1 47 ♘e2! (The start of the winning knight manoeuvre, gaining a tempo on its journey to f5.) 47 ... ♖a1 48 ♘d4 ♔g8 49 ♘f5! ♖a6 50 ♔f2 (now the king successfully enters the action) 50 ... ♗g6 51 ♔e3 ♗×f5 52 ef ♖a2 53 ♔d4 ♖a1 54 ♗e2! ♖a2 55 ♗×h5± ± (Black is defenceless against the advance of the f–pawn.) 55 ... ♖h2 56 ♖f4 ♖d2+ 57 ♔e4 ♖d3 58 f6 ♖×c3 59 ♔f5! ♖e3 60 ♖f1 ♘d7 61 ♖g1+ ♔f8 62 ♖a1 ♖e5+ 63 ♔g6 ♖e8 64 ♖a7 ♖d8 65 ♖c7! (Karpov deprives his opponent of any hope of counterplay based on advancing his c–pawn.) 65 ... ♔g8 66 ♔g5 ♔h8 67 ♗g6 ♔g8 68 h5 ♔h8 69 h6 c3 70 ♖×c3 ♖f8 71 f7 **1-0**

1 Karpov	xxxxxx	$1\frac{1}{2}10\frac{1}{2}\frac{1}{2}$	$1\frac{1}{2}110\frac{1}{2}$	$7\frac{1}{2}$
2 Vaganian	$0\frac{1}{2}01\frac{1}{2}\frac{1}{2}$	xxxxxx	$\frac{1}{2}1\frac{1}{2}01\frac{1}{2}$	6
3 Shteinberg	$0\frac{1}{2}001\frac{1}{2}$	$\frac{1}{2}0\frac{1}{2}10\frac{1}{2}$	xxxxxx	$4\frac{1}{2}$

This event, which took place in the Leningrad Palace of Pioneers 'imeni Zhdanova', was held specifically for the purpose of determining who would represent the Soviet Union in the forthcoming World Junior Championship. Karpov quite clearly established his superiority over his rivals.

0901 Vaganian–AK

G1: 21.3.1969: Queen's Indian

(Notes by Karpov)

1 d4 ♘f6 2 c4 e6 3 ♘f3 b6 4 e3 ♗b7 5 ♗d3 ♗e7 6 00 c5 7 ♘bd2?! (7 ♘c3!?) **7 . . . ♘c6 8 a3 cd 9 ed d5 10 cd ♕×d5 11 ♗c4 ♕d6 12 ♘b3 00 13 ♕e2** (13 ♗g5!?) **13 . . . h6 14 ♖d1 ♖fd8 15 ♗e3 ♖ac8 16 ♖ac1 ♘d5∓ 17 ♗d2?! a5! 18 ♖c2 ♕b8 19 ♘c1 ♘f4 20 ♗×f4 ♕×f4 21 ♖cd2** (21 d5!? ed 22 ♗×d5 ♗f6∓) **21 . . . ♗f6 22 ♘d3? ♕c7! 23 ♘de5 ♘×d4 24 ♖×d4 ♖×d4 25 ♘×d4** (25 ♖×d4 ♗×f3∓∓ 26 ♕×f3 ♕×e5 27 ♖e4 ♖×c4!) **25 . . . ♕×e5 26 ♘b5 ♕×b2** (26 . . .

♕×e2!? 27 ♗×e2 ♗d5∓∓) **27 ♘d6 ♕×e2 28 ♗×e2 ♖c7 29 ♘×b7 ♖×b7 30 a4 ♖c7 31 ♗b5 ♖c2 32 h3 g6 33 ♖d6 ♖c1+ 34 ♗f1 ♖a1∓∓ 35 ♖×b6 ♖×a4 36 g3 ♗d4** (36 . . . ♖a2! 37 ♗c4 ♖c2 and . . . ♗d4∓∓) **37 ♖b8+ ♔g7 38 ♗e2 ♖a2 39 ♔f1 a4 40 ♖b4 e5 41 ♖b7 a3?? 42 ♗×f7+ ♔h8 43 ♖f8+ ♔g7 44 ♖f7+ ♔×f7 45 ♗c4+ ♔f6 46 ♗×a2 g5! 47 f3** (47 g4 e4 48 ♔e2 ♔e5 49 f3 ♔f4 followed by . . . ♔g3, . . . ♔×h3 and . . . h5) **47 . . . h5 48 ♔e2 e4!** (79)

49 fe (49 g4 h4 50 fe ♔e5 51 ♔f3 ♗c5 then, fantastic ending!, Black wins: 52 ♗f7 ♔d4 53 ♗g8 ♗d6 54 ♗f7 ♔d3 55 ♗g8 ♗e5 56 ♗f7 ♔d2 (draw after 56 . . . ♔c3 57

79
48B
W

♔e2 ♚b2 58 ♚d3 a2 59 ♗×a2
♚×a2 60 ♚c4 ♚b2 61 ♚d5 ♗f6
62 e5 ♗d8 63 e6 ♚c3 64 ♚d6 ♚d4
65 e7 ♗×e7+ 66 ♚×e7 ♚e5) 57
♗e6 ♚e1 58 ♗c4 ♗f4 59 ♚g2
♚d2 60 ♚f3 ♚c3 (tempo!!) 61 ♗f7
♚b2 62 ♚e2 a2 63 ♗×a2 ♚×a2 64
♚d3 ♚b3 65 ♚d4 ♚b4! (65 . . .
♚c2 – draw) 66 e5 ♚b5 67 ♚d5
♚b6∓ ∓) **49 . . . g4!∓ ∓ 50 hg hg
51 ♗b3 ♗e5 52 ♚f2 ♚e7 53 ♚e3
♗×g3 54 ♚d4 ♗e5+ ! 0-1**

0902 AK–Shteinberg

G2: 23.3.1969: Sicilian

(Notes by Karpov)

1 e4 c5 2 ♘c3 ♘c6 3 g3 g6 4 ♗g2
♗g7 5 d3 d6 6 f4 e5 7 ♘f3 ♘ge7 8
00 00 9 ♗e3 ♘d4 10 ♕d2 ♘ec6 11
♖ab1 (11 ♘d5? ef 12 ♗×f4
♘×f3+ 13 ♗×f3 ♗×b2) 11 . . .
♗g4 12 ♘d5 ♘e7 13 ♘×e7+
♕×e7 14 c3± ef 15 ♗×f4 ♘×f3+
16 ♗×f3 ♗e6 (16 . . . ♗×f3 17
♖×f3 f5) 17 b3 ♖ae8 18 ♖be1 (to
prevent 18 . . .f5) 18 . . .b6 19 d4 cd
20 cd ♕d7 21 ♕b4! ♖d8 22 ♗g2

♖fe8 23 d5 (23 ♖c1 ♗h3!) 23 . . .
♗g4 24 ♖c1 ♕e7 25 ♖c6 ♗e5 26
♖fc1 ♗×f4 (26 . . . ♖c8!? 27 h3
♗d7 28 ♖c7 ♗×f4 29 gf ♕h4∓ ; 27
♕d2±) 27 gf ♕h4 (27 . . . ♖c8?! 28
♖×c8 ♖×c8 29 ♖×c8+ ♗×c8 30
e5) 28 ♕e1! ♕f6 (28 . . . ♕×e1+ 29
♖×e1±) 29 ♕d2 ♕e7 30 ♖1c3
♖c8 31 h3 ♖×c6 (31 . . . ♗d7 32
♖c7 ♕f6 33 e5!± ± ; 32 . . . a6 33
♕d4±) 32 dc± ± ♗e6 33 ♖d3
♖d8 34 ♚h2 (34 e5 d5 35 ♗×d5?
♕c5+ 36 ♕f2 ♖×d5∓ ∓) 34 . . .
♖c8 (34 . . . f6!?) 35 ♖×d6 ♕c7 36
♕d4 ♕e7 37 ♚g3 (to prevent 37
. . . ♕h4) 37 . . . h5 38 ♗f3 (to
permit 39 h4 without allowing 39
. . . ♗g4) 38 . . . h4+ 39 ♚h2 ♕e8
40 ♕f6 ♕f8 41 e5 ♕e8 42 ♕×h4
♚g7 43 ♕f6+ **1-0**

0903 AK–Vaganian

G3: 24.3.1969: Alekhine

1 e4 ♘f6 2 e5 ♘d5 3 d4 d6 4 ♘f3 g6
5 ♗e2 ♗g7 6 00 00 7 b3 ♘c6 8 c4
♘b6 9 ed cd 10 ♗b2 ♗g4 11 ♕d2
(The last time they had this
position, Karpov played 11 h3 –
game 0803.) 11 . . . e6 12 ♘a3 d5 13
♖fd1 dc 14 ♘×c4 ♘×c4 15 bc
♕b6 16 ♖ab1 ♗f5 17 ♗d3 ♗×d3
18 ♕×d3 ♖fd8 19 d5 ♗×b2 20
♕e2 ed 21 cd ♘b4 22 ♖×b2 ♕c5
23 h3 b6 24 d6 ♖×d6 25 ♖×d6
♕×d6 26 ♕e4 ♘d5 27 ♖d2 ♖d8
28 ♘e5 (with the idea of 29 ♘g4
and 30 ♖×d5) 28 . . . ♕c5 29 ♕f3
f5 30 h4 ♖d6 31 ♖d1 ♚g7 32 h5
♚f6 33 hg hg 34 ♕g3 ♚g7 35 ♕g5

罝 e6 36 ②f3 ②f6 37 罝 c1 ♛e7 38
♛f4 罝 d6 39 罝 e1 ②e4 40 g4 ♛f6
41 g5 ♛e7 42 ♔g2 ♔g8 43 罝 h1
♛g7 44 罝 c1 ♛b7 45 罝 h1 ½–½ (A
most interesting position – Black is
close to winning, but if he tries for
the whole point he is liable to lose.
Two intriguing variations are: 45
. . . ②d2 46 ♛×d6 ♛×f3+ 47♔g1
♛d1+ 48 ♔g2 with perpetual
check, and 45 . . . 罝 d3 46 ♛e5!
♛g7 47 ♛e8+ ♛f8 48 罝 h8+ ± ± .)

0904 Shteinberg–AK

G4: 26.3.1969: Queen's Indian

1 d4 ②f6 2 c4 e6 3 ②f3 b6 4 g3 ♗b7
5 ♗g2 ♗e7 6 00 00 7 ②c3 ②e4 8
♛c2 ②×c3 9 ♛×c3 c5 10 罝 d1 d6
11 ♗e3 ♛c7 12 罝 ac1 ②d7 13 b3
②f6 14 ②e1 ♗×g2 15 ②×g2 ♛b7
16 ♛d3 cd 17 ♗×d4 罝 fd8 18 ②e3
罝 ac8 19 ♛b1 h6 20 罝 d3 罝 d7 21
罝 cd1 b5 22 ♗×f6 ♗×f6 23 cb
♛×b5 24 ②c4 d5 25 e4 ♗ cd8 26 ed
罝×d5 27 罝×d5 罝×d5 28 ♛c2
♗d4 29 罝 d2 ♛d7 30 ♛e4 f5 31
♛f3 ♔h7 32 ♔g2 ♛f7 33 ②e3
罝 d8 34 ♛c6 ♛f6 35 ②c4 罝 d5 36
罝 e2 f4 37 f3 fg 38 hg ♗e5 39 ②e3
♛g5 40 ♛c2+ ♔g8 41 ♛c8+
♔h7 42 ♛c2+ g6 43 ②g4 ♗g7 44
②f2 ♛e7 45 ②d3 ♛f7 46 ②f2 罝 f5
47 ♛c6 罝 e5 48 ②e4 g5 49 ♛c2
♔g8 50 g4 h5 51 ②d6 ♛f4 52 ②c4
hg 53 ②×e5 ♗×e5 54 fg ♛h2+ 55
♔f1 ♛h1+ 56 ♔f2 ♛h4+ ½–½

0905 Vaganian–AK

G5: ?.3.1969: Nimzo-Indian

(Notes by B. Vladimirov)

1 d4 ②f6 2 c4 e6 3 ②c3 ♗b4 4 e3
00 5 ②f3 c5 6 ♗e2 d5 7 00 ②bd7
8 cd ed 9 ♛b3 ♗×c3 (Black parts
with the bishop, but, in exchange,
secures control of the e4 square with
gain of tempo. In the event of 10 bc
c4 the position takes on a closed
character and White's two bishops
cannot generate activity.) 10
♛×c3 ②e4 11 ♛c2 b6 12 dc
(After 12 b3 ♗b7 13 ♗b2 罝 c8 this
move would have been forced.) 12
. . . bc 13 b3 ♗b7 14 ♗b2 罝 c8 15
罝 fd1 ?! (A superficial move. 15
②d2, to exchange the active black
knight and giving more room for
the bishops, is stronger.) 15 . . .
♛e7 16 罝 ac1 f5 17 ②e1 ? (The
logical continuation was 17 b4.
After 17 . . . cb 18 ♛a4, Black
would have been obliged to go over
entirely to defence. The extra pawn
does not play a significant role, and
what is more it is impossible to keep
it, for example 18 . . . ②dc5 19
♛×a7 罝 a8 20 ♛b6 罝×a2 21
♛×b4 ②×f2 22 ♗d4. Seemingly
Black would have been compelled
to reply 17 . . . c4 against which 18
♗d4 gives White quite good
chances.) 17 . . . ♛h4 18 g3 ♛h6
19 ②g2 ♔h8! (Creating the threat
20 . . . d4) 20 ♛d3 罝 ce8 (Because
White no longer has the move ♗b5,
Karpov develops the rook on to the

e-file, again threatening . . . d4. If 21 ♗f3 Black continues just the same with 21 . . . d4 22 ed ♗a6 23 ♕c2 ♘g5∓. In order to liquidate the attack White should play 21 f4, abandoning the e4 square to the opposing knight, but Vaganian decides against this and prefers the following weakening of position which leads to bankruptcy.) **21 f3 ♘g5** (*80*)

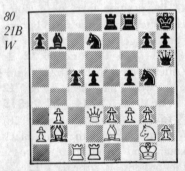

80
21B
W

22 ♘f4 (Black's task would have been more difficult after 22 h4. As the following variations show, Black must still win: 22 . . . ♘h3+ 23♔f1 d4 24 ed f4. How does White continue now? Let us say 25 g4, but now 25 . . . ♖e3 26 g5 ♕h5 27 ♘×f4 ♖×f4 28 ♕×e3 ♗×f3 29 ♔e1 ♗×e2∓∓. If 25 dc there follows 25 . . . fg and on 26 ♕×d7 then 26 . . . ♗×f3 is decisive. If, instead of 26 ♕×d7, 26 c6 ♗×c6 27 ♖×c6 ♕×c6 28 ♕×d7 then 28 . . . ♖×f3+ 29 ♔e1 ♖×e2+ 30 ♔×e2 ♕e4+ and mates. In the event of 25 d5 fg and White again cannot hold the position.) **22 . . . d4 23 h4** (If 23ed Black sacrifices the

exchange with 23 . . . ♖×e2, obtaining a winning position. Thus 24 ♕×e2 ♘×f3+ 25♔f1 ♘×h2+ 26 ♔f2 ♘f6 27 d5 ♖e8 28 ♘e6 ♘hg4+ 29 ♔e1 ♗×d5 30 ♖×d5 ♕h1+, or 29 ♔g1 ♖×e6!, forces White's resignation.) **23 . . . ♗×f3 24 ed ♘h3+ 25 ♘×h3 ♗×e2 26 ♕d2 ♖e3 27 ♔h2 ♘f6 28 ♘f4 ♘g4+ 29 ♔g2 ♗f3+ 30 ♔g1 ♗×d1 0–1**

0906 AK–Shteinberg

G6: 29.3.1969: Spanish

1 e4 e5 2 ♘f3 ♘c6 3 ♗b5 a6 4 ♗a4 ♘f6 5 ♕e2 b5 6 ♗b3 ♗e7 7 c3 00 8 d4 d6 9 00 ed?! 10 cd ♗g4 11 ♗e3 ♘a5 (11 . . . ♘×e4 12 ♗d5!± ±) 12 ♗c2 ♘c4 13 ♗c1 c5 14 b3 ♘b6 15 ♗b2 ♘fd7 16 a4 ba?! 17 ba a5 18 ♖d1 ♖c8 19 ♘a3 c4 20 ♗c3 d5 21 e5 ♗b4 22 ♘b5 ♘b8 23 h3 ♗h5 24 ♕e3 ♘c6 25 ♖d2 ♗×f3 26 ♕×f3 ♘a8 27 ♖ac1 ♘c7 28 ♗f5 ♘e6 (28 . . . ♖b8 29 ♘×c7 ♕×c7 30 ♕×d5± ±) 29 ♔g4 ♕e7 30 f4 ♖b8 31 ♔h2 ♘c7 32 ♘×c7 ♕×c7 33 ♕f3 ♘e7 34 ♗c2 f5 35 ♖f1 ♕d7 36

81
50B
W

g3 ♕e6 37 ♖g2 g6 38 g4 ♔h8 39
♖g3 ♖f7 40 ♕e3 ♖bf8 41 ♗b2
♕b6 42 ♖g2 ♕c6 43 ♖f3 ♕e6 44
♗c1 ♕b6 45 ♔h1 fg? 46 hg ♘c6 47
e6 ♖e7 48 f5 ♕×d4 49 ♕×d4
♘×d4 50 ♗b2 c3 (*81*)

51 ♖×c3! ♔g8 52 ♖e3 ♗c5 53
♖e5 ♖b8 54 ♗c3 ♘×c2 55 ♖×c2
d4 56 ♗×a5 ♗d6 57 ♖d5 **1–0**

0907 AK–Vaganian

G7: 30.3.1969: Alekhine

**1 e4 ♘f6 2 e5 ♘d5 3 d4 d6 4
♘f3 g6 5 ♗e2** (Later Karpov
abandoned this for 5 ♗c4 as in his
fine win against Grigorian in the
1971 USSR Ch.) **5 . . . ♗g7 6 c4
♘b6 7 ed cd 8 h3 00 9 00 ♘c6 10
♘c3 ♗f5 11 ♗f4 h6! 12 ♖c1 ?** (It
was through the bad experience of
this game that Karpov switched to
12 ♗e3 in later games.) **12 . . . e5!
13 ♗e3** (13 de de 14 ♗e3 ♘d4! is
beautiful for Black.) **13 . . . e4! 14
♘d2 ♖e8** (Black's clever idea is
that if now 15 g4 ♕h4! 16 gf gf
leaves White in a jam, e.g. 17 ♘b3
f4 18 ♗d2 f3 19 ♗×f3 ef 20 ♕×f3
♘×c4∓ ∓. After 15 g4 ♕h4!, 16
♔h2 would be met by 16 . . .
♘×d4!, e.g. 17 ♗×d4 ♗×d4 18 gf
♗e5+ 19 ♔g2 ♕g5+ 20 ♗g4
gf∓ ∓.) **15 ♘b3 d5! 16 cd ♘b4! 17
♕d2 ♘4×d5 18 ♘c5** (Karpov
does not care to try the free sample
with 18 ♘×d5 ♘×d5 19 ♗×h6
when 19 . . . e3! 20 ♗×e3 ♘×e3 21
fe ♗h6 22 ♖c3 ♖c8! 23 ♖f3 ♗e4
24 ♖g3 ♗d6 25 ♔f2 f5!, with . . . f4

to follow, is very dangerous.) **18 . . .
♘×e3! 19 fe ♕g5 20 ♔h1** (not 20
♔h2 ♖ad8 21 ♖c2 ♗e5+ 22 ♔h1
♕g3 23 ♖f4 g5!∓ ∓) **20 . . . ♖ad8**
(threatening 21 . . . ♖×d4) **21 ♖c2
♕g3** (22 . . . ♗e5 is the idea!) **22
♕c1 ♘d5! 23 ♘×d5** (23 ♘d1
♘b4 24 ♖c4 ♗×h3!) **23 . . .
♖×d5** (Now the rook is in position
to assist in wrapping up the game
with 24 . . . ♗×h3 25 gh ♕×h3+
26 ♔g1 ♖g5+ 27 ♔f2 ♕g3 mate.)
24 ♗b5 (Clearing the way for the
rook on c2 to stop the mate. 24 ♗d1
♗×h3! 25 gh ♕×h3+ 26 ♖h2
♕×f1 mate and 24 ♗c4 ♖×c5!
do not exactly serve the same
purpose.) **24 . . . ♖c8 25 ♗a4** (if
25 ♗c4 still 25 . . . ♖d×c5, e.g. 26
♗×f7+ ♔×f7 27 ♖×c5 ♖×c5 28
♕×c5 ♕×e3∓ ∓) **25 . . . b6!** (*82*)

82
25B
W

**26 ♘×e4 ♗×e4! 27 ♖×c8+ ♔h7
28 ♖c2** (The best available, e.g. 28
♖g1 ♕×h3 mate, or 28 ♕d2
♕×h3+ 29 ♔g1 ♕×c8 with a
bishop bonus.) **28 . . . ♖h5 29 ♔g1
♖×h3 30 ♖×f7 ♕h2+ 31 ♔f1
♕h1+ 32 ♔e2 ♕×g2+ 33 ♖f2
♕g4+ 34 ♔d2 ♖h1 35 ♕×h1** (or

35 ♖f1 ♕g2+) **35 . . . ♗×h1 36
♗b3 ♗f3 37 ♗e6 ♕×e6 38 ♖×f3
g5 39 ♖c7 ♔g6 40 ♖×a7 g4 41
♖f1 h5 42 ♖a6 g3 43 a4 ♗h6 44
♖f3 h4 0-1**

0908   Shteinberg–AK

G8: 1.4.1969: English

1 c4 e6 2 g3 ♘f6 3 ♗g2 c5 4 ♘f3
♘c6 5 00 d5 6 cd ♘×d5 7 d4 ♗e7 8
dc ♗×c5 9 ♘g5 ♗e7 10 ♘e4 00 11
♘bc3 ♘×c3 12 ♘×c3 ♕b6 13
♖b1 ♖d8 14 ♕a4 ♗d7 15 ♗e3
♕b4 16 ♕×b4 ♗×b4 17 ♘e4 ♗e8
18 a3 ♗e7 19 ♖fd1 b6 20 ♗f4
♖×d1+ 21 ♖×d1 ♖d8 22 ♖×d8
♘×d8 23 ♗c7 ♗c6 24 b4 b5 25
♗b8 f5 26 ♗d6 ♗×e4 27 ♗×e7
♘c6 28 ♗×e4 fe 29 ♗c5 a6 30
♔g2 ♘e5 31 ♗e3 ♔f7 32 ♗c1
♘c4 33 ♔f1 ♔f6 34 ♗e1 ♔f5 35 h3
h5 36 ♔d1 g5 37 f3 e3 38 g4+ hg 39
hg+ ♔e5 40 ♔c2 ♔d5 41 ♔b3 **0-1**

0909   Vaganian–AK

G9: 2.4.1969: Nimzo-Indian

1 d4 ♘f6 2 c4 e6 3 ♘c3 ♗b4 4 g3 c5
5 d5 ♘e4 6 ♕c2 ♕f6 7 ♘h3 ♘×c3
8 ♗d2 ♘×d5 9 cd ♗×d2+ 10
♕×d2 e5 11 d6 ♘c6 12 ♗g2 ♘d4
13 ♖d1 00 14 ♘g5 ♕g6 15 ♘e4 b6
16 e3 ♘c6 17 ♘×c5 bc 18 ♗×c6
♖b8 19 ♗f3 ♕f5 20 ♗e2 ♕h3 21
♗f1 ♕e6 22 b3 ♗b7 23 ♗c4 ♕h3
24 ♗d5 ♗a6 25 ♗c1 ♖fc8 26 ♕a5
♗d3 27 ♕d2 ♗b5 28 f3 ♖b6 29
♗c4 ♗×c4 30 ♖×c4 ♖cc6 31 ♕c2
g6 32 ♔f2 ♖×d6 33 ♖×c5 ♖bc6

34 b4 h5 35 e4 h4 36 g4 ♖f6 37 ♕e2
♖×c5 38 bc ♕×g4 39 ♖b1 ♕h3 40
♔e3 g5 41 ♖g1 ♖g6 42 ♖g4 ♔f8
43 a4 ♖c6 44 ♕d2 ♕f1 45 ♖×g5
♕a1 46 ♔f2 ♕e7 47 ♖f5 ♖g6 48
♖×f7+ ♔×f7 49 ♕×d7+ ♔f8 50
♕d8+ ♔f7 51 ♕d7+ ♔g8 52
♕d8+ ♔g7 53 ♕e7+ ♔g8 ½-½

0910   AK–Shteinberg

G10: 4.4.1969: Sicilian

1 e4 c5 2 ♘c3 ♘c6 3 g3 g6 4 ♗g2
♗g7 5 d3 d6 6 f4 e6 (Varying with,
as it turns out, good effect from
game 0902.) 7 ♘f3 ♘ge7 8 00 00 9
♗e3 ♘d4 10 ♕d2 b6 11 ♖ae1 ♗b7
12 ♗f2 ♕d7 13 ♘×d4 (13 ♘d1
♕a4!) 13 . . . cd 14 ♘e2 e5 15 c3 dc
16 ♘×c3 ♖ad8 17 ♔h1 d5 (*83*)

83
17B
W

18 ed? (This is even worse than the
alternatives 18 ♕e2 de 19 de ef 20 gf
♕d2!∓ and 18 fe d4!, both of which
are good for Black.) 18 . . . ef 19
♕×f4 ♘×d5 20 ♕d2 ♘×c3 21 bc
♗a6! (winning material) 22 ♗d4
♗×d4 23 cd ♕×d4 24 ♖e7 ♗×d3
25 ♖d1 ♕f6 26 ♖×a7 ♗e4 27

♖d7 ♖×d7 28 ♕×d7 ♗f5 29 ♕d4 ♕×d4 30 ♖×d4 ♖c8 31 h4 ♖c3 32 ♔h2 ♖a3 33 ♗d5 ♖d3 34 ♖×d3 ♗×d3 35 ♔g2 ♔g7 36 ♔f3 ♗f5 37 ♔f4 ♔f6 38 g4 ♗e6 39 g5+ ♔e7 40 ♔e5 ♗×d5 41 ♔×d5 f5 42 ♔e5 ♔d7 43 ♔d5 ♔c7 44 ♔e5 ♔c6 45 h5 gh 46 ♔×f5 ♔d6 **0-1**

0911 AK-Vaganian

G11: 5.4.1969: Alekhine

1 e4 ♘f6 2 e5 ♘d5 3 d4 d6 4 ♘f3 g6 5 ♗e2 ♗g7 6 c4 ♘b6 7 ed cd 8 h3 00 9 ♘c3 ♘c6 10 00 ♗f5 11 ♗f4 h6 12 ♗e3 d5 13 b3 bc 14 bc ♖c8 15 ♖c1 ♘a5 16 c5 ♘bc4 17 ♗f4 g5 18 ♗g3 ♕d7 19 ♗×c4 ♘×c4 20 ♕e2 ♕e6 21 ♖fe1 ♕×e2 22 ♖×e2 e6 23 ♘e4 ♗×e4 24 ♖×e4 ♘a5 25 ♗e5 ♖fd8 26 ♖b1 ♖d5 27 ♖b5 b6 28 ♗×g7 ♔×g7 29 ♖e5 ♘c4 30

♖×d5 ed 31 cb ♘×b6 32 ♖a5 ♖c1+ 33 ♔h2 ♖c7 34 ♘e5 ♔f6 35 ♘g4+ ♔f5 36 ♖c5 ♖e7 37 ♘×h6+ ♔e4 38 ♖c1 ♔d3 39 ♔g3 f6 40 ♖c6 ♖e2 41 ♘f5 ♖×a2 42 ♖×f6 ♖b2 43 ♔g4 a5 44 ♖f7 ♘c8 45 ♖f8 ♘b6 46 ♖f7 ♖×f2 47 g3 ♘c8 48 ♖d7 ♔e4 49 ♖c7 ♖×f5 50 ♖×c8 ♖f1 51 ♖a8 ♖a1 52 ♔×g5 ♔×d4 53 h4 ½-½

0912 Shteinberg-AK

G12: 7.4.1969: Spanish

1 e4 e5 2 ♘f3 ♘c6 3 ♗b5 a6 4 ♗a4 ♘f6 5 00 ♗e7 6 ♖e1 b5 7 ♗b3 d6 8 c3 00 9 h3 h6 10 d4 ♖e8 11 ♘bd2 ♗f8 12 d5 ♘e7 13 a4 ♗b7 14 c4 ♕d7 15 ♗c2 ♘g6 16 b3 ♘f4 17 ♘f1 g6 18 cb ab 19 ♗×f4 ef 20 ♘d4 ba 21 ba ♗g7 22 ♖b1 c6 23 dc ♗×c6 24 ♘×c6 ♕×c6 ½-½

10 1969 Miscellany

This section contains games from three separate events: a match between junior teams of the USSR and Yugoslavia, the 'Red Armies' team tournament in Warsaw, and the USSR Armed Forces Team Championship.

USSR-Yugoslavia

Moscow, 8-15.4.1969

1	Timoshenko	0½1½	Ljubojević	1½0½
2	Kupreichik	½0½½	Vujačić	½1½½
3	Karpov	½1½1	Evrosimovski	½0½0
4	Vaganian	½101	Kržišnik	½010
5	Sveshnikov	½111	Jakovljevski	½000
6	Romanishin	11½1	Hulak	00½0
		16		8

1001 AK-Evrosimovski

R1: Sicilian

1 e4 c5 2 ♘f3 ♘c6 3 ♘c3 g6 4 d4 cd 5 ♘×d4 ♗g7 6 ♗e3 ♘f6 7 ♗c4 ♕a5 8 00 d6 9 h3 00 10 ♗b3 ♗d7 11 ♕d2 ♘×d4 12 ♕×d4 ♘g4 13 ♕d5 ♕×d5 14 ♘×d5 ♘×e3 15 ♘×e7+ ♔h8 16 fe ♖ae8 17 ♘d5 ♖×e4 18 ♘f6 ♗×f6 19 ♖×f6 ♖×e3 20 ♖af1 ♗c6 21 ♖1f2 ♖e1+ 22 ♔h2 ♖e7 23 ♖×d6 f5 24 ♗d5 ♗×d5 25 ♖×d5 ♖c8 26 a4 ♔g7 27 c3 ♖c4 28 a5 ♖ce4 29 g3 ♖4e5 30 ♖×e5 ♖×e5 31 b4 ♔f6 32 ♔g2 ♔e6 33 ♔f3 ♖e4 34 ♖d2 ♖c4 35 ♖d3 g5 36 ♔e2 h5 37 ♖e3+ ♔f6 38 ♔d3 ♖c7 39 ♖e8 ♖d7+ 40 ♔e3 ½-½

1002 Evrosimovski-AK

R2: Hungarian

1 e4 e5 2 ♘f3 ♘c6 3 ♗c4 d6 4 d3 ♗e7 5 h3 ♘f6 6 ♘c3 ♘a5 7 ♗b3 00 8 00 h6 9 ♗e3 c6 10 d4 ♕c7 11 de de 12 ♕e2 b6 13 ♖fd1 ♘b7! 14 ♘e1 ♘c5 15 f3 (In protecting e4 and making room for his queen on f2, White weakens g3.) 15 ... ♗a6

16 ♕f2 ♖fd8 17 ♘a4 ♘×a4 18 ♗×a4 h5 19 g3 (another pawn move, this time to stop an entry at f4) 19 . . . ♖d6 20 ♖×d6 ♕×d6 21 c3 (White wants to develop his rook on d1, but now d3 and half of b3 is left unprotected.) 21 . . . ♕e6! 22 ♔h2 ♗c4! 23 a3 (23 b3 cuts off White's light-squared bishop, while 23 b4 loses control of c4. The move played deserts b3.) 23 . . . ♘f6 24 ♖d1 ♘e8 25 ♗c2 ♘d6 26 ♘d3 f5 27 ♘b4 fe 28 fe ♖f8 29 ♕g2 ♘f7! 30 ♗d3 ♗g5 31 ♗g1 (if 31 ♗×g5 ♘×g5, striking at the weaknesses at h3, f3 and e4) 31 . . . h5! 32 ♕e2 ♗b3 33 ♖f1 h4 34 g4 ♗f4+ 35 ♔g2 ♖d8 36 ♗e3 (*84*)

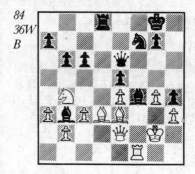

84
36W
B

36 . . . c5 37 ♗×f4 ef 38 ♘d5 (An unfortunate necessity – White loses at once after 38 ♘c2 c4 or 38 ♘a6 ♘e5.) 38 . . . ♗×d5 39 ed ♕×d5+ 40 ♗e4 ♕d2 41 ♖f2 ♕×e2 42 ♖×e2 ♘g5 43 c4 ♖d4 44 ♗b7 ♔h7 45 ♖e5 ♔h6 46 ♖d5 ♖×c4 47 ♖d6+ g6 48 ♗a6 f3+ **0–1** (White has had enough, e.g. 49 ♔g1 ♖c1+ 50 ♔h2 ♖c2+ 51 ♔h1

♘e4 52 ♖d1 ♘g3+ 53 ♔g1 ♖g2 mate.)

1003 AK–Evrosimovski

R3: English

1 c4 f5 2 ♘c3 ♘f6 3 g3 e5 4 ♗g2 ♘c6 5 ♘f3 ♗e7 6 d4 e4 7 ♘g5 0-0 8 0-0 ♕e8 9 c5 h6 10 ♘h3 d5 11 ♖b1 ♘d8 12 b4 c6 13 ♗f4 g5 14 ♗e5 ♕h5 15 f4 g4 16 ♘f2 ♕g6 17 ♕b3 h5 18 ♗×f6 ♗×f6 19 e3 h4 20 ♖fc1 ♔g7 21 b5 ♖h8 22 a4 ♕h5 23 ♘e2 ♘e6 24 ♘h1 ♖h7 25 ♔f2 ♗d7 26 ♕a2 ♕f7 27 ♖g1 h3 28 ♗f1 ♔h6 29 b6 ab 30 ♖×b6 ♖a7 31 ♕b3 ♗c8 32 ♕b4 ♗d8 33 a5 ♗×b6 34 ab ♖a2 35 ♔e1 ♗d7 36 ♘f2 ♕f8 37 ♘c1 ♖a1 38 ♔d2 ♕a8 39 ♘d1 ♖h8 40 ♘c3 ♕a3 41 ♕×a3 ♖×a3 42 ♔c2 ♖ha8 43 ♗e2 ♔g7 44 ♔b2 ♔f6 45 ♘b3 ♗e8 46 ♖c1 ♔e7 47 ♗d1 ♗d7 48 ♖a1 ♖×a1 49 ♘×a1 ♘g7 50 ♗b3 ♖a5 51 ♗c2 ♘h5 52 ♘e2 ♘f6 53 ♗b3 ♗e6 54 ♗d1 ♘d7 55 ♘b3 ♖a8 56 ♘c3 ♘b8 57 ♘c1 ♘a6 58 ♘a4 ♘b8 59 ♔a3 ♘d7 60 ♔b4 ♘f8 61 ♘b3 ♘g6 62 ♘d2 ♘h4 63 ♘f1 ♘f3 64 ♗c2 ♔f6 65 ♗b1 ♗d7 66 ♗c2 ♘e1 67 ♗b1 ♖e8 68 ♔c3 ♔g6 69 ♘d2 ♔h5 70 ♘f1 ♖a8 71 ♔b4 ½–½

1004 Evrosimovski–AK

R4: Sicilian

The complete game score is not available.

1 e4 c5 2 ♘c3 ♘c6 3 g3 g6 4 ♗g2

♗g7 5 d3 d6 6 ♗e3 e6 7 f4 ♘ge7 8 ♘f3 00 9 00 ♘d4 and Black won (**0–1**, x moves)

'Red Armies' Teams

Warsaw, 5.1969

Karpov was the reserve for the Soviet team of Geller, Lutikov, Gufeld and Savon. The event was won by·the USSR with 11½/12 (it was Gufeld who let the team down!) ahead of Poland 6, Czechoslovakia 4, and Cuba 2½. Karpov played only the one game.

1005 AK–Konikowski

Catalan

1 d4 ♘f6 2 ♘f3 d5 3 c4 e6 4 ♘c3 ♗e7 5 g3 00 6 ♗g2 ♘bd7 7 00 dc 8 e4 c6 9 a4 a5 10 ♕e2 ♘b6 11 ♖d1 ♘fd7 12 ♗f4 ♗b4 13 ♘d2 ♕e7 14 ♗e3 ♖d8 15 ♘×c4 ♘×c4 16 ♕×c4 ♘b6 17 ♕b3 ♗d7 18 ♘a2 c5 19 ♘×b4 ab (If 19 ... cb there follows 20 d5! ♘c8 21 d6! with the idea that if 21 ... ♘×d6, White gets a decisive advantage from 22 ♗c5 ♗c6 23 e5.) 20 dc ♘×a4 (*85*)

21 e5! ♖db8 (Nor are the alternatives very palatable: 21 ... ♘×c5 22 ♗×c5 ♕×c5 23 ♖×a8± ;. 21 ... ♕e8 22 c6! ♗×c6 23 ♖×d8± ± ; 21 ... ♗e8 22 ♖×d8 ♖×d8 23 ♖×a4± ± .) 22 c6! ♗×c6 23 ♗×c6 bc 24 ♖×a4 c5 25 ♖×a8 ♖×a8 26 ♕c4 **1–0**

USSR Armed Forces Team Championship

Leningrad, 6(?).1969

Karpov won the board prize for second board (Furman played on board one) ahead of three masters and four candidate masters. The event was won by Karpov's team: Leningrad.

1006 AK–Arakelov

R1(?): Spanish

1 e4 e5 2 ♘f3 ♘c6 3 ♗b5 ♘d4 4 ♘×d4 ed 5 00 c6 6 ♗a4 ♘f6 7 ♖e1 ♗e7 8 c3 00 9 d3 dc 10 bc d5 11 e5 ♘e8 12 d4 ♗f5 13 ♘d2 ♕a5 14 ♗b2 c5 15 ♘f1 b5 16 ♘e3 ♗e4 17 ♗c2 cd 18 cd ♗×c2 19 ♕×c2 ♖d8 (*86*)

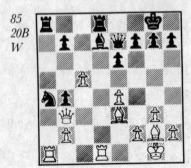

85
20B
W

86
19B
W

20 ♘f5 ♗b4 21 ♖e3 g6 22 a3 ♗d2
23 ♘e7+ ♔g7 24 ♖e2 ♖d7 25
♘c6 ♖c7 26 ♕c5 ♕b6 27 ♕×d5
♖×c6 28 ♖×d2 f6 29 ♕b3 ♖c4 30
♖e1 fe 31 de h6 32 e6+ ♔g8 33
♕d3 ♖f5 34 ♕d7 ♕c6 35 h3 ♕c8
36 ♕e7 ♖c7 37 ♖d7 **1-0**

1007   Donchenko–AK

R2(?): English

1 c4 c5 2 ♘c3 g6 3 g3 ♗g7 4 ♗g2
♘c6 5 e3 e5 6 ♘ge2 ♘ge7 7 b3 00 8
00 ♖b8 9 ♗b2 a6 10 ♘d5 b5 11 d3
d6 12 ♕d2 ♘f5 13 a4 bc 14 bc ♗e6
15 ♗c3 ♗×d5 16 ♗×d5 ♘b4 17
♗g2 a5 18 ♖a3 ♘e7 19 ♗a1 d5 20
cd ♘e×d5 21 ♘c3 ♘b6 22 ♖d1
♕e7 23 ♕e2 ♖fd8 24 ♗b2 ♖d7 25
♗h3 f5 26 e4 ♕f7 27 ef gf 28 ♘b5
♖bd8 29 ♖aa1 ♘×d3 30 ♗c3 e4
31 ♗×a5 ♗×a1 32 ♖×a1 ♘f4 33
♕e1 ♘×h3+ 34 ♔g2 ♕h5 35
♗×b6 ♘f4+ **0-1**

1008   AK–Tserdakh

R3(?): French

1 e4 e6 2 d4 d5 3 ♘d2 c5 4 ♘gf3 a6
5 ed ed 6 dc ♗×c5 7 ♘b3 ♗a7 8
♗g5 ♘f6 9 ♕e2+ ♗e6 10 ♘fd4 00
11 ♘×e6 fe 12 ♕×e6+ ♔h8 13 000
♘c6 14 ♕h3 ♕c8 15 ♕×c8
♖a×c8 16 f3 h6 17 ♗d2 d4 18 ♗d3
♘d5 19 ♖he1 ♘e3 20 ♗×e3 de 21
♗e4 ♖c7 22 c3 ♖e8 23 ♖d5 ♔g8
24 ♔d1 ♔f7 25 ♔e2 ♖e5 26 ♖ed1
♔e6 27 ♖×e5+ ♔×e5 28 ♖d5+
♔e6 29 ♘c5+ ♔f6 30 ♘d3 ♔e7
31 h4 ♖d7 32 ♖×d7+ ♔×d7 33

♗×c6+ ♔×c6 34 ♘e5+ ♔d5 35
♘g4 ♔e6 36 ♗×e3 ♔e5 **1-0**

1009   AK–E. Kogan

R4(?): Sicilian

1 e4 c5 2 ♘f3 ♘c6 3 ♗b5 g6 4 00
♗g7 5 c3 ♘f6 6 ♖e1 00 7 h3 a6 8
♗f1 b5 9 a4 b4 10 d3 d6 11 ♘bd2
♘d7 12 cb ♘×b4 13 a5 ♗b7 14
♘c4 ♘c6 15 ♗d2 ♗b5 16 d4 ♘c6
17 d5 ♘ce5 18 ♘f×e5 ♘×e5 19
♘b6 ♖a7 20 ♗c3 ♘d7 21 ♘c4
♗×c3 22 bc ♗×c4 23 ♗×c4 ♘e5
24 ♗f1 c4 25 ♕d4 (making safe the
advance f2–f4) 25 ... ♖b7 26 ♖a4
♖b5 27 ♖ea1 ♖c5 (*87*)

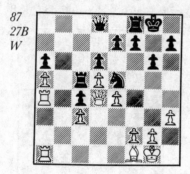

87
27B
W

28 f4 ♘d3 29 ♖×c4! ♖×c4 30
♕×c4 ♘c5 31 ♕b4 ♕c7 32 ♖b1
♖c8 33 ♔h2 ♕d7 34 ♗e2 h5 35
♕d4 ♕a4? 36 ♕×a4 ♘×a4 37
♗×a6 ♖a8 38 ♖a1 **1-0** (time)

1010   Rotov–AK

R5(?): Alekhine

1 e4 ♘f6 2 ♘c3 d5 3 e5 ♘e4 4
♘×e4 de 5 d4 ed 6 ♗×d3 ♘c6 7
♘f3 ♗g4 8 h3 ♗×f3 9 ♕×f3 ♕d4

10 00 ♕×e5 11 ♗f4 ♕f6 12 ♖ad1
g5 13 ♗×c7 ♕×f3 14 gf ♗g7 15
♗f5 00 16 ♗e4 ♖ac8 17 ♖d7 ♘e5
18 ♗×e5 ♗×e5 19 ♖×b7 ♖c7 20
♖b5 ♗f4 21 ♖d1 e6 22 c3 f5 23
♗c2♔f7 24♔f1 ♗f6 25♔e2 h5 26
♖d4 ♖f7 27 ♗d3 h4 28 a4 ♖fd7
29 ♖×d7 ♖×d7 30 a5 ♖d5 31 b4
g4 32 fg fg 33 hg h3 34 ♖×d5 ed 35
♔f3 ♔g5 36 b5 h2 37 ♔g2 ♔×g4
38 ♗e2+ ♔f5 39 ♗f3 ♔e6 40♔f1
♗c7 41 b6 ab 42 a6 ♗b8 43♔e2 b5
½–½

1011 AK–Nebolsin

R6(?): Sicilian

1 e4 c5 2 ♘f3 ♘c6 3 ♗b5 g6 4 00
♗g7 5 c3 a6 6 ♗×c6 dc 7 d3 ♘f6 8
h3 00 9 ♕e2 a5 10 ♗f4 a4 11 ♘a3
♖e8 12 ♖fd1 ♘d7 13 d4 cd 14 cd
♕a5 15 ♖ac1 ♘b6 16 ♗c7 ♕a6 17
♕e3 f5!? *(88)*

88
17B
W

18 d5? (18 ♗×b6 ♕×b6 19 ♘c4,
with quite a good position, seems
better.) 18 . . . fe 19 ♗×b6 ef 20 d6
♕e2 21 d7 ♗×d7 22 ♖×d7 ♕×e3
23 fe ♗×b2 24 ♖c4 ♗×a3 25
♖×b7 fg 26 ♔×g2 ♗d6 27 ♖×c6
♖ec8 28 ♗c7 a3 29♔f3 ♖a5 30 e4

♖g5 31 ♗×d6 ♖×c6 32 ♗×e7
♖c3+ 33♔f4 ♖g2 34 ♗f6 ♖×h3
35 ♔e5 ♖e3 36 ♖g7+ ♔f8 37
♖×h7 ♖×a2 38 ♖d7 g5 39 ♗×g5
♖b3 40 ♗e7+ ♔g8 41 ♖a7 ♖a1
42 ♗f6 a2 43 ♔d5 ♖f1 44 ♗d4
♖b4 45 ♗c3 ♖d1+ 46♔c5 ♖b3
47 ♗e5 ♖c1+ 48 ♔d6 ♖b6+ 49
♔d7 ♖c2 50 ♗a1 ♖b1 51 ♗e5
♖b5 (Karpov gives 51 . . . ♖c4 52
♔e6 ♖b6+ 53 ♔d7 ♖c2 54
♖a8+ ♔f7 55 ♗d6 ♖f2 56 ♖a7
♖b7+ 0–1) 52 ♔e6 ♖b6+ 53
♔d7 ♖f2 54 ♖a8+ ♔f7 55 ♗d6
♖c2 56 ♖a7 ♖b7+ **0–1**

1012 Karasev–AK

R7(?): Nimzo-Indian

1 d4 ♘f6 2 c4 e6 3 ♘c3 ♗b4 4 e3 00
5 ♘ge2 d5 6 a3 ♗e7 7 cd ♘×d5 8
♕c2 b6 9 ♘×d5 ed 10 ♘c3 ♗b7 11
♗d3 h6 12 00 ♘d7 13 b4 a6 14 ♕b3
♘f6 15 f3 ♖b8 16 ♗b1 c5 17 ♖d1
♕d6 18 bc bc 19 dc ♕×c5 20 ♘e2
♕c4 21 ♘d4 ♕×b3 22 ♘×b3 ♗c6
23 ♘d4 ♗a4 24 ♖d2 ♘d7 25 ♗c2
♗×c2 26 ♖×c2 ♗f6 27 ♗b2 ♖fe8
28 ♔f2 ♘e5 29 ♖d1 ♖ec8 30
♖×c8+ ♖×c8 31 ♔e2 ♘c4 32
♗c1 ♖b6 33 ♗b2 ♘a4 34 ♗a1 g6
35♔d2 ♗e7 36 ♘c2 ♘b6 37 ♗d4
♘c4+ 38 ♔d3 ♖b8 39 a4 f5 40
♔e2 ♔f7 41 ♗a1 ♔e6 42 h3 h5 43
♗d4 ♗d6 44 ♖d3 ♖b7 45 ♖d1
♗e5 46 h4 ♗×d4 47 ♘×d4+ ♔e5
48 f4+ ♔d6 49 ♖a1 ♖b2+ 50♔f3
♖d2 51 a5 ♖d3 52 ♘c2 ♔c5 53
♖a4 ♖c3 54 ♖a2 d4 55 ♔f2 d3 56
♘d4 d2 57 ♖a1 ♘×e3 **0–1**

11 World Junior Championship
Stockholm, 10-30.8.1969

We Have Waited 14 Years For This Day

A discussion with GM Semyon Furman, trainer of A. Karpov. This article appeared in *Shakhmatisti Rossii* October 1969.

I became acquainted with Anatoly Karpov at the end of last year, on the eve of the USSR Team Championship. The army chess players were taking part in a training conference in which Anatoly, representing the team on the first junior board, took part.

He was a lean, pale-faced youth, somewhat phlegmatic in appearance. It even seemed that it was with difficulty that he moved the chess pieces. Was it possible that such a one was capable of the highest sporting achievements?

When Eduard Gufeld caught sight of Anatoly for the first time he said 'this little boy will never be a grandmaster, he is too thin'.

To which Efim Geller, standing beside him, remarked, not without irony, 'Well, of course everyone judges by his own standards, you, for example, Edik became a grandmaster when your weight reached 100 kilogrammes'.

Nature did not endow Anatoly Karpov with a gigantic frame, but it conferred upon him a rare chess talent and strength of will, and also modesty and a love of hard work.

When I began to concern myself with Karpov I immediately understood that he was a very able chess player with great prospects. And I was not mistaken. In the USSR Team Championship Anatoly scored 10 11, conceding to all his young adversaries only two half points.

From this moment I, as trainer of the army chess players, took charge of Anatoly, and now I have been helping him prepare for competitions for almost a year.

In order to win the right to take part in the World Junior Championship, Anatoly had to show his superiority over two other candidates; Rafael Vaganian and Misha Shteinberg. This match-tournament of the young chess players took place last spring in Leningrad and ended in a convincing victory for Karpov.

We regard the World Junior Championship very seriously. Anatoly realized his great responsibility on behalf of millions of Soviet chess players. Fourteen years have passed since the time that Boris Spassky for the first (and last) time won for our country the title of World Junior Champion. It is time, it was already time long ago, for this title to return to the country of the chess champions.

The preparations for the World Championship consisted of various aspects. Most of all it is very important for every chess player to know himself; this is not so easy, especially at a youthful age. During work with Karpov we succeeded in bringing to light the strong and weak sides of his game and in completely assessing his capabilities. Thus, for example, it transpired that Anatoly is somewhat at odds with the theory of openings, but this circumstance even pleased me. This problem was easy to settle and we liquidated this fairly rapidly. It is true that Karpov's opening repertoire remained somewhat limited, but we did not try to broaden it. At that moment our main task consisted of achieving success in a concrete tournament and I endeavoured to deepen Karpov's knowledge of specific opening systems.

The natural feature of Karpov's chess talent delighted me; a fine positional sense. That is a special intuition which always characterized the great chess players. I also paid attention to Karpov's masterly conduct of endgames and overall accuracy of technique.

But how to take the most logical advantage of these strong sides of Karpov's chess talent in the forthcoming tournament?

On studying the games of Karpov's future opponents I formed the impression that the foreign juniors were, in general, good tacticians but weak strategists. As a rule they searched for a suitable moment to deliver a tactical blow, and rarely concerned themselves with the game as a strategic whole. Therefore we decided that Karpov would choose those openings which would not give his opponents opportunities to sharpen the game without retribution. Running in advance I remark that this line of attack proved the most expedient and completely justified itself.

It was also necessary to pay attention to Anatoly's physical preparation. Daily morning gymnastics were prescribed for him. During the training period Anatoly often played badminton and table tennis and went boating. At first we relaxed near Moscow, at Bakovka, and then we moved to Zelenogorsk, near Leningrad, with its almost Scandinavian climate. This change of venue was very expedient because the Junior

Championship would take place at Stockholm and it was essential for Anatoly to become acclimatized.

Were we confident of final success?

I must say frankly that I did not have 100% confidence in Karpov's victory. Firstly many Soviet juniors had returned from previous championships on the shield. Secondly I was not exceptionally well acquainted with the play of Anatoly's future opponents, indeed the final composition of the tournament only became known on the eve of the first round. True, I knew Karpov's strength extremely well, knew what he was capable of. But, you know, everything is relative and only seen in comparisons.

As for Anatoly himself, in general he knows his own strengths and limitations. It seems to me that before Stockholm his confidence in victory matched his strength (! – eds).

We arrived in Sweden several days before the start of the Championship in order the better to acclimatize to and acquaint ourselves with the conditions. We were shown the tournament hall, in which we had to pick our way through a forest of scaffolding and step-ladders. We were not even certain whether all the repair work would be finished before the opening of the tournament, but our fears proved to be groundless; the Swedes tried not to grieve us with troubles.

This place was received by the Stockholm Chess Federation from the municipal authorities very recently. The money for the repairs was given by chess patrons; it was even necessary to open a special fund. Now the chess players will have their own central club. It was fairly spacious for a club, but was most unsuitable for holding a major tournament. There was no big hall and in the oblong rooms where the Junior Championship took place it was very cramped, especially for the spectators (the converted building had been an ancient debtors' prison – eds.). Out TsShK (Moscow Central Chess Club; formerly the house of the Tsarist Civil Governor of Moscow –eds.) certainly would have been more suitable and spacious, but by Swedish standards even the Stockholm club was good enough.

Of course for adults to play in such conditions would have been significantly tougher, but the youngsters did not complain. True, many of them were tired out towards the end of the tournament, but I think it was the strict tournament schedule which was to blame for this. Playing off the adjourned games took place in the mornings, and only one rest day in the whole month (20 days – eds) could not have helped anyone. The only consolation was the weather. The Swedes said that they could not remember such a good summer for a long time.

During our preparation for the Championship, we had calculated that Karpov's chief rivals would be the Hungarian Adorjan, the Swede Andersson and the Scotsman McKay, but at the very last moment the Puerto Rican, Kaplan, winner of the previous World Championship, arrived in Stockholm and it became clear that he was the number one rival.

The 1969 World Junior Championship attracted a record number of participants. The Championship was contested by 38 youths from 37 countries (the Swedes were represented by two players according to the host nation's rights). True, it was unclear whether it was possible to consider England and Scotland as separate countries. However, seeing as in other forms of sport (e.g. football) they each field their own teams, no one felt able to challenge this tradition.

The participants were divided into six preliminary groups, from each of which the two winners were to make up the main final.

The system of division into such small groups involves many surprises and is fundamentally shameful. It turned out that by no means the strongest participants won through to the final. Thus the American Rogoff and the Philippino Torre failed to reach the main final, while the Colombian Castro, who reached the final, was considerably weaker than them.

Preliminary Group 2

		1	2	3	4	5	6	7	
1	**Karpov**	×	½	1	½	½	1	1	4½
2	McKay	½	×	0	1	½	1	1	4
3	Payruber	0	1	×	½	0	1	1	3½
4	Torre	½	0	½	×	½	1	1	3½
5	Hug	½	½	1	½	×	0	½	3
6	Sznapik	0	0	0	0	1	×	1	2
7	Fridjonsson	0	0	0	0	½	0	×	½

In the preliminary group Karpov was noticeably nervous. At first his rivals forged ahead and it was not clear whether Anatoly was in a position to concede any draws, or was absolutely obliged to go all out for the win. Thus, playing sharply for the win against Torre and the Swiss player Hug, Anatoly stood on the verge of defeat in these games. And in general I noticed that in the preliminaries the especially nervous ones were those participants who had every ground for aspiring to the leading places in the final.

But everything turned out favourably. Karpov did not lose a single game and even took first place in his section.

I was happy with Anatoly from the very beginning. I clearly saw his prospects in the final, and I knew that there he would play very differently, that under unworried conditions he could show his best qualities.

	1	2	3	4	5	6	7	8	9	0	1	2	
1 **Karpov**	×	½	1	½	1	1	1	1	1	1	1	1	**10**
2 Adorjan	½	×	1	½	½	½	1	1	½	½	0	1	**7**
3 Urzica	0	0	×	1	½	1	½	1	½	1	½	1	**7**
4 Kaplan	½	½	0	×	½	1	1	1	½	½	0	1	**6½**
5 Andersson	0	½	½	½	×	0	½	½	1	½	1	1	**6**
6 Neckar	0	½	0	0	1	×	1	½	1	1	½	0	**5½**
7 Juhnke	0	0	½	0	½	0	×	½	1	1	1	1	**5½**
8 Vujačić	0	0	0	0	½	½	½	×	½	1	1	½	**4½**
9 Vogt	0	½	½	½	0	0	0	½	×	½	1	1	**4½**
10 Diaz	0	½	0	½	½	0	0	0	½	×	1	1	**4**
11 McKay	0	1	½	1	0	½	0	0	0	0	×	1	**4**
12 Castro	0	0	0	0	0	1	0	½	0	0	0	×	**1½**

My forecasts were fulfilled. In the finals he played a completely different game. Karpov began to win game after game. Karpov's victories affected the play of his rivals in a fatal manner. Realizing that by 'normal play' it was impossible to catch up with Karpov, certain participants began to take too many risks and this turned out badly for them. Anatoly was able to pull ahead of his rivals. Two rounds before the end of the tournament he had assured himself first place irrespective of the outcome of the remaining games.

Of course no one could have foreseen that Karpov would succeed in winning eight consecutive games in the final. No one set him such a target and even he himself had not counted on such a series of wins. Even so, this was not fortuitous – we had succeeded in accurately defining what tactics Anatoly should follow in order to achieve maximum success. Karpov showed himself to be a remarkably able student. He succeeded in creatively developing the ideas which I showed him during the preparation for the tournament. Even those ideas which did not arise out of the given concrete opening Karpov took advantage of during the other stages of the game.

At this point the game Juhnke-Karpov is given with notes by Furman.

I have already remarked that the main strength of the foreign juniors was in tactical play, therefore the task in front of Karpov consisted of obtaining positions such that tactical contrivances by his opponents would be doomed to failure. This meant that the position must be reliable and a plan of campaign logically flow out of the requirements of the position itself.

Now part of the game Karpov–Andersson appears.

The attack in this game was carried out by Karpov on a firm positional base and was prepared for by consistently planned play. All the same, certain chess players sometimes succeeded in complicating the play and 'luring' Anatoly into the realms of tactical struggles. But then they turned out to be in unfavourable conditions because they were acting anti-positionally, for example the Colombian Castro risked using the King's Gambit against Karpov and paid heavily for it.

Castro–Karpov.

On the basis of this game it's possible to judge Karpov's tactical ability. Therefore the 'course of solidarity' is explained not by any weakness of Karpov's combinational vision, but by expediency and safety.

Karpov's magnificent play and his modest disposition aroused the regard and sympathy of the Swedish chesslovers; the local inhabitants turned to us with good wishes for success, and later with congratulations. During the period of the Championship Anatoly had a bit of a cold: the Swedes were very concerned and literally overwhelmed him with medicines, and one of them brought a thermos flask of hot tea to Anatoly at his hotel. Anatoly quickly got better, and it seemed to me that his recovery was helped not so much by the hot tea as by the warmth of the local hospitality.

The Swedish press, radio and TV publicized the Championship widely. Of course the Swedes were rooting for their own Ulf Andersson, undoubtedly a very talented player. While Ulf was still in with a chance it was impossible to get near his board. Later the spectators' interest turned to Karpov. I even recall an occasion when, under the onslaught of the public who had climbed on to the windowsill in order to get a better view of Anatoly, the radiator was torn away from the wall. Once again the repair brigade had to be brought in. . . .

On one of the days Boris Spassky and Bent Larsen, who were staying in Stockholm, visited the tournament. The famous grandmasters were themselves juniors not long ago, each of them in his time carried off the title of World Junior Champion (Larsen never won the title – he was 5th in 1951 and 8th in 1953 – eds). This symbolic meeting made an indelible impression on the youngsters.

The closing ceremony of the Championship took place in the

picturesque park of lake Skansen. The deputy mayor of Stockholm laid on a ceremonial lunch for the participants. There the prizes were distributed.

And so Anatoly Karpov won the title of World Junior Champion. In accordance with the FIDE rules he was awarded the title of international master. And what next? How will the sporting fate of the young player work out? Many grandmasters of high reputation were Junior Champions in the past, will Karpov join their ranks?

Anatoly, in my opinion, will undoubtedly become a grandmaster. When? I think a year or two, but this depends not only on his training but also on his opportunities of participating in big tournaments. The sooner that Anatoly starts to meet top-flight masters the sooner he will become a grandmaster.

Semyon Furman was talking to V. Henkin.

Also there was a lightning tournament, entitled by the tournament book 'The Unofficial World Junior Championship in Lightning Chess!':

Preliminary Group 2: Karpov 5/5, Vujačić 4, Torre 3, Øgaard 2, Bellon 1, Seret 0.

Final A: Adorjan 10½/11, Karpov 9, Andersson 7½, Kaplan 7, Ligterink 6, Torre 6, Vujačić 5½, Neckar 5½, Hug 4½, Diaz 3, Meulders 1, Weber ½.

1101 Fridjonsson–AK

PR1: 10.8.1969: Spanish

(Notes by Furman)

1 e4 e5 ♘f3 ♘c6 3 ♗b5 a6 4 ♗a4 ♘f6 5 ♕e2 b5 6 ♗b3 ♗c5 7 c3 d6 8 h3?! (Unnecessary, 8 00 is better.) 8 . . . 00 9 00 ♕e7 10 d3 h6 11 ♘bd2 ♘h5! (Already eyeing White's weaknesses; White. must do something about 12 . . . ♘g3 and also 12 . . . ♘f4.) 12 d4 ♘f4 13 ♕e3 ♗b6 (The uncertainty of his opponent's play somewhat dulls Karpov's vigilance. 13 . . . ♗a7 was more accurate, since here the bishop will subsequently be in need of support.) 14 ♖d1 ♘a5 15 ♗c2 ♕f6 (15 . . . c5 was also possible.) 16 ♔h2 c5 17 d5 ♖b8 (preparing . . . c4) 18 ♘g1 ♕g6 19 g3? (*89*) (19 ♕g3 would be better, but White is probably lost anyway.)

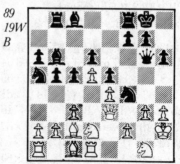

89
19W
B

19 . . . ♘×d5! (Fridjonsson must

have been reckoning on 19 ...
♘×h3 20 ♘×h3 ♕h5 21 g4.) 20
♕e2 ♘e7 21 f4 ef 22 gf ♕f6 23
♘df3 ♗g6 24 e5 de 25 fe ♗c7 **0–1**
(1·54 – 1·16)

1102   AK–Hug

PR2: 11.8.1969: Sicilian

1 e4 c5 2 ♘f3 ♘f6 3 e5 ♘d5 4 d4 cd
5 ♕×d4 e6 6 ♗e2 ♘c6 7 ♕e4 d6 8
00 de 9 ♘×e5 ♘×e5 10 ♕×e5
♕d6 11 ♗b5+ ♗d7 12 ♗×d7+
♕×d7 13 c4 ♕c7 14 ♕e2 ♘f6 15
♘c3 a6 16 ♗g5 ♗e7 17 ♗×f6
♗×f6 18 ♘d5 ♕d8 19 ♖ad1 00 20
♘×f6+ ♕×f6 21 ♖d7 b6 22 ♖fd1
♖ad8 23 g3 g6 24 b4 ♖×d7 25
♖×d7 ♖d8 26 ♖c7 ♕c3 27 c5 bc
28 bc ♕d3 29 ♕e5?? ♕d1+ ?? (29
... ♕f3∓ ∓; both players seem to
have been under considerable
tension.) 30 ♔g2 ♕d5+ 31 ♕×d5
♖×d5 32 ♔f3 ♔g7 33 ♔e3 ♔f6 34
f4 h6 35 a4 g5 36 h3 gf+ 37 gf ♖h5
38 ♔d4 ♖h4 ½–½ (1·31 – 1·15)

1103   Torre–AK

PR3: 12.8.1969: Spanish
(adjournments 13, 14.8.1969)

1 e4 e5 2 ♘f3 ♘c6 3 ♗b5 a6 4 ♗a4
♘f6 5 00 ♗e7 6 d4 ed 7 e5 ♘e4 8 b4
♘c3 9 ♘×c3 dc 10 a3 00 11 ♕d5 b5
12 ♗b3 a5 13 ♗e3 ♗b7 14 ♖ad1
ab 15 ♕×d7 ♕c8 16 e6 fe 17 ab
♔h8 18 ♗×e6 ♕×d7 19 ♖×d7
♗c8 20 ♖×c7 ♗×e6 21 ♖×c6
♗c4 22 ♖b1 ♗a2 23 ♖d1 ♗×b4
24 h3 ♖fc8 25 ♖×c8+ ♖×c8 26

♖a1 ♗c4 27 ♘e5 ♗d5 28 ♖b1
♗a3 29 ♖×b5 ♗e4 30 ♗d4 h6 31
♖b3 ♗b2 32 ♘d3 ♗a1 33 ♖a3
♗×d3 34 ♖×a1 ♗×c2 35 ♖a7
♖g8 36 h4 ♔h7 37 ♗×c3 h5 (90)

90
37B
W

38 f3 ♗f5 39 ♔f2 ♔g6 40 ♔e3 ♗e6
41 ♔e4 ♗c8 42 ♖c7 ♖e8+ 43
♗e5 ♗f5+ 44 ♔f4 ♗e6 45
♖×g7+ ♔h6 46 g4 hg 47 fg ♖f8+
48 ♔g3 ♗f7 49 ♖g5 ♖a7 50 ♗d4
♖a3+ 51 ♔f4 ♗a4 52 ♔e5 ♗b3
53 ♖h5+ ♔g6 54 ♖g5+ ♔h6 55
♔f6 ♗a6+ 56 ♔f5 ♖a5+ 57 ♗e5
♗c2+ 58 ♔f6 ♖a6+ 59 ♔e7
♖a7+ 60 ♔d6 ♖a6+ 61 ♔c5
♖a4 62 ♖g8 ♗h7 63 ♖g5 ♗c2 64
♗c3 ♗d1 65 ♗b4 ♗e2 66 ♖h5+
♔g6 67 ♖e5 ♗f3 68 h5+ ♔g7 69
♖e6 ♔f7 70 ♖g6 ♗e2 71 ♖g5
♖a8 72 ♔d5 ♖g8 73 ♖f5+ ♔g7
74 ♗c3+ ♔h6 75 ♖f6+ ♔g5 76
h6 ♖d8+ 77 ♖d6 ½–½ (4·30 – 3·25)

PR4: 13.8.1969: Karpov had a free
day, apart from his adjournment
against Torre.

1104 AK–Payrhuber

PR5: 14.8.1969: KI Attack

1 e4 c5 2 ♘f3 d6 3 g3 ♘f6 4 d3 ♘c6
5 ♗g2 g6 6 00 ♗g7 7 ♖e1 00 8 c3
♘e8 9 ♘a3 f5 10 ♘g5 ♘c7 11
♕b3+ ♔h8 12 ef ♗×f5 13 ♘f7+
♖×f7 14 ♕×f7 e6 15 ♗g5 **1-0**
(0·50 – 1·16)

1105 McKay–AK

PR6: 15.8.1969: Spanish

1 e4 e5 2 ♘f3 ♘c6 3 ♗b5 a6 4 ♗a4
♘f6 5 00 ♗e7 6 ♕e2 b5 7 ♗b3 00 8
c3 d6 9 d4 ed 10 cd ♗g4 11 ♖d1 d5
12 ed ♘a5 13 ♗c2 ♖e8 14 ♕d3
♗h5 15 ♗g5 ♗g6 16 ♕d2 ♘c4 17
♕c1 ♗×c2 ½–½ (0·31 – 1·01)

1106 AK–Sznapik

PR7: 16.8.1969: Sicilian

1 e4 c5 2 ♘f3 d6 3 c3 ♘f6 4 ♗d3
♘c6 5 00 g6 6 ♗c2 ♗g7 7 h3 00 8
♖e1 ♘e8 9 ♗b3 ♘e5 10 d3
♘×f3+ 11 ♕×f3 ♘c7 12 a4 ♗d7
13 ♘d2 ♖b8 14 ♘f1 b6 15 ♘e3 a6
16 ♘d5 ♘e6 17 ♕g3 b5 18 ab ab 19
♖a7± b4 20 ♗c4 bc 21 bc ♖b1 22
f4 ♔h8 23 ♕f2! ♗c6 24 ♘×e7
♗×c3 25 ♘×c6 ♕b6 26 ♖a6 ♕b7
27 ♗d2 ♘d4 28 ♗×c3 **1-0** (1·55 –
2·29)

1107 AK–Neckar

FR1: 18.8.1969: Alekhine

(Notes by Furman)

Neckar adopted Alekhine's
Defence, fianchettoing the king's
bishop. This system was well-
known to the Soviet player, and it
followed his game against Vaganian in the selection tournament
in Leningrad. The Czech player
repeated Vaganian's moves until
Karpov, on his 18th, diverged with
some prepared analysis and
obtained the better position. Black
defended successfully, but con-
sumed too much time. Trying to
take advantage of his opponent's
shortage of time, Karpov blundered, but Neckar did not notice it.
The game was adjourned and
White won on resumption
(19.8.1969).

1 e4 ♘f6 2 e5 ♘d5 3 d4 d6 4 ♘f3 g6
5 c4 ♘b6 6 ed cd 7 h3 ♗g7 8 ♘c3
00 9 ♗e2 ♘c6 10 00 ♗f5 11 ♗f4 h6
12 ♗e3 d5 13 b3 dc 14 bc ♘a5 15 c5
♘bc4 16 ♗f4 g5 17 ♗g3 ♕d7 18
♖e1 b6 19 cb ab 20 ♘e5 ♘×e5 21
de ♕e6 22 ♗f3 ♖ad8 23 ♗d5 ♕c8
24 ♕f3 e6 25 ♗e4 ♘c4 26 ♖ac1
♘d2 27 ♕h5 ♕a6 28 ♗×f5 ef 29
h4 f4 (*91*)

91
29B
W

30 ♗h2? (30 hg± ± with an

irresistible attack) 30 ... ♕d3 31
hg ♕f5 32 ♘e2 f3? (32 ... ♗×e5
was necessary, and on 33 ♕×h6
then 33 ... ♕g4 with a good game
for Black.) 33 ♘g3 ♕×g5 34 ♕×g5
hg 35 ♘f5 fg 36 ♔×g2 ♖d3 37
♘e7+ ♔h7 38 ♖h1 ♗h6 39 ♗g3
♘e4 40 ♖c6 f6 41 ♘f5 ♔g6 42
♘×h6 ♘×g3 43 fg ♖d2+ 44 ♔f3
♖×a2 45 ♘g4 ♖a3+ 46 ♘e3 g4+
47 ♔e4 ♖a4+ 48 ♖c4 f5+ 49 ♔f4
♖×c4+ 50 ♘×c4 b5 51 ♘d6 ♖a8
52 e6 **1–0** (2·45 – 2·40)

1108   Vujačić–AK

FR2: 19.8.1969: Spanish

White obtained nothing from the
opening. Vujačić opened the f–file,
thereby doubling his pawns, but
did not create any serious threats.
Karpov simply realized his
positional advantage – Furman.
1 e4 e5 2 ♘f3 ♘c6 3 ♗b5 a6 4 ♗a4
♘f6 5 ♕e2 b5 6 ♗b3 ♗c5 7 c3 d6 8
d3 h6 9 ♘bd2 00 10 ♘f1 ♗g4 11
♗e3 ♗×e3 12 fe ♘a5 13 ♘g3
♘×b3 14 ab g6 15 b4 ♕e7 16 00 h5
(*92*)

92
16B
W

17 h3 ♘h6 18 d4 ♗b7 19 d5 c6 20
dc ♗×c6 21 ♘d2 ♕g5 22 ♕f2
♔g7 23 ♖ad1 ♖ad8 24 ♘e2 f5 25
♘f3 ♕e7 26 ef ♘×f5 27 ♘g3 ♘h6
28 e4 h4 29 ♘e2 ♗×e4 30 ♕×h4
♕×h4 31 ♘×h4 ♖×f1+ 32 ♔×f1
♗b7 33 ♘f3 ♘f5 34 ♖a1 ♖f8 35
♔g1 ♘e3 36 ♘g5 ♔h6 37 h4
♘×g2 38 ♖f1 ♖×f1+ 39 ♔×f1
♔g7 **0–1** (2·27 – 1·55)

1109   AK–Andersson

FR3: 20.8.1969: Spanish

(Notes by Furman)

Karpov obtained a space
advantage by advancing his central
pawns, and prepared an attack on
the king's side.

1 e4 e5 2 ♘f3 ♘c6 3 ♗b5 a6 4 ♗a4
♘f6 5 00 ♗e7 6 ♖e1 b5 7 ♗b3 00 8
c3 d6 9 h3 ♘a5 10 ♗c2 c5 11 d4
♕c7 12 ♘bd2 ♗b7 13 d5 ♗c8 14
♘f1 ♗d7 15 b3 ♘b7 16 c4 ♖fb8 17
♘e3 ♗f8 18 ♘f5 ♘d8 19 ♘h2
♘e8 20 h4 f6 21 h5 ♘f7 22 ♖e3
♘g5 23 ♘h4 ♕d8 24 ♖g3 ♘c7 25
♘2f3 h6 26 ♘g6 a5 27 a4 bc 28 bc
♘a6 29 ♕e2 ♖a7 30 ♗d2 ♖ab7
31 ♗c3 ♘b4 32 ♗d1 ♘a6 33 ♘d2
♘b4 34 ♖e3 ♗e8 35 ♘f1 ♕c8 36
♘g3 ♗d7 37 ♕d2 ♘h7 38 ♗e2
♔f7 39 ♕d1 ♗e7 40 ♘f1 ♗d8 41
♘h2 ♔g8 42 ♗g4 ♘g5 43 ♗×d7
♕×d7 44 ♘f1 (*93*)
(White has a positional advantage –
he controls more space, Black's
light squares are weak and his
bishop has no prospects. White

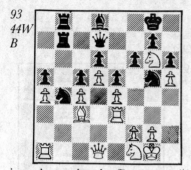

93
44W
B

intends to seize the f5 square with
the aid of the maoeuvre ♘f1–g3–f5,
followed by the pawn-storm g2–g3
and f2–f4. Not wishing to be a
passive observer of the onslaught
being prepared, Andersson tries to
free himself from White's grip on
the position.) 44 ... f5 45 ef ♕×f5
46 ♘g3 ♕f7 (If 46 ... ♕c2 then
47 f4 and 47 ... ef is not possible
because of 48 ♖e8+. The further
course of the struggle centres upon
the advance f2–f4.) 47 ♕e2!
(renewing the threat) 47 ... ♗f6 48
♖f1! ♕d7 (Black can no longer
prevent the opening up of the
position.) 49 f4 ef 50 ♖×f4 ♗×c3
51 ♖×c3 ♖e8 52 ♖e3 ♖bb8 53
♕f2 ♘h7 (Defending the f8 square
because 53 ... ♖×e3 was no good
on account of 54 ♖f8+.) 54 ♘f5
♖×e3 55 ♕×e3 ♘f6 (If 55 ...
♖e8 then 56 ♘fe7+·, but now
White wins in a different way.) 56
♘ge7+ ♔h8 (In the event of 56 ...
♔h7, White would have continued, as in the game, 57 ♘×h6,
and against 56 ... ♔f7 the simple
57 ♕g3 is decisive.) 57 ♘×h6 ♖e8
58 ♘f7+ ♔h7 59 ♖e4 ♖×e7 60

♖×c7 **1–0** (2·44 – 3·29) (The
attack in this game was carried out
by Karpov on a firm positional
basis and was prepared for by
consistently planned play.)

1110 Castro–AK

FR4: 21.8.1969: King's Gambit

(Notes by Furman)

The Colombian was in an
aggressive frame of mind at the
beginning of the game, choosing
the old Bishop's Gambit. Karpov
accepted the pawn sacrifice to
begin with, but then in his turn
sacrificed two pawns.
1 e4 e5 2 f4 (Certain of Anatoly's
rivals naively thought that it was
possible to unnerve him in this
way.) 2 ... ef 3 ♗c4 ♘f6 4 ♘c3
(Against this somewhat harmless
move, theory recommended the
reply 4 ... c6. However, Karpov
wanted to lead his opponent away
from well-trodden paths and
played a different move.) 4 ...
♗b4 (This move is also known to
theory, but it turned out not to be
known to Castro.) 5 e5 (Now a
sharp tactical skirmish, somewhat
better for Black who has a lead in
development, is brought about. 5
♘ge2 would have led to a better
game for White.) 5 ... d5 6 ♗b5+
c6 7 ef cb 8 fg ♖g8 9 ♕e2+ ♗e6 10
♕×b5+ ♘c6 11 ♕×b7 (Realizing
that the strategic battle has been
lost, Castro tries to grab as many

pawns as possible.) 11 ... ♖c8 12
♘f3 ♖×g7 13 00 ♗h3 14 ♖e1+
(otherwise g2 cannot be defended;
if 14 ♖f2 ♗c5) 14 ... ♔f8 15 ♖e2
♗g4! (*94*)

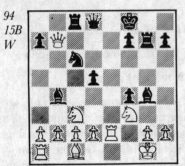

94
15B
W

16 ♖f2 (This is forced since after 16
♔h1 ♗×f3 17 gf ♖c7 18 ♕b5 ♕g5
White cannot avoid being mated.)
16 ... ♗c5 17 d4 ♘×d4 18 ♘×d4
♗×d4 19 ♗×f4 ♗×f2+ 20 ♔×f2
♖g6 21 ♔g1 d4 22 ♖f1 ♕d7 23
♕b4+ ♔g8 24 ♘e4 ♕d5 25 ♕e7
♕e6 26 ♕b7 ♗e2 27 ♖e1 ♖×c2
28 ♘g5 ♕f5 **0–1** (2·15 – 1·30)

1111 AK–McKay

FR5: 22.8.1969: Alekhine

(Notes by McKay)

1 e4 ♘f6 2 e5 ♘d5 3 d4 d6 4 ♘f3 g6
5 c4 ♘b6 6 ed cd 7 h3 ♗g7 8 ♘c3
00 9 ♗e2 ♘c6 10 00 ♗f5 11 ♗f4
d5? (11 ... h6 is better.) 12 c5 ♘c4
13 b3 ♘4a5 (Black is already in a
bad way because of this misplaced
knight.) 14 ♖c1 b6 (14 ... ♗e4,
following up with ... ♗×f3, ... e6,
... ♘e7 and ... ♘ac6, was far

better.) 15 cb ab 16 ♕d2 ♘b7 17
♘b5 ♖c8 18 ♖c3 ♕d7 19 ♖fc1 f6
(*95*)

95
19B
W

20 ♗c7! ♘cd8 (20 ... ♘b8!?, but
in the long run Black is lost
anyway.) 21 ♗×b6 ♖×c3 22
♖×c3 e5. 23 a4 ♘c6 24 b4 e4 (24
... ♘×b4?? 25 ♖c7) 25 ♘h2 ♖c8
26 a5 ♗f8 27 ♖b3 e3 28 ♕×e3 (If
28 fe ♘×b4 29 ♖×b4? ♖c2 and
Black gains material.) 28 ... ♘×b4
29 ♘g4 ♕g7 (29 ... ♗×g4 may
have been better.) 30 ♖c3 h5 31
♖×c8 ♗×c8 32 ♕e8 ♗f5 (32 ...
♗d7 33 ♕×d7) 33 ♘e3 ♗d7 34
♕b8 ♗c6 35 ♘a7 ♕d7 36 a6 ♘d6
37 ♗c5 **1–0** (1·16 – 2·22)

1112 Juhnke–AK

FR6: 23.8.1969: Spanish

(Notes by Furman)

1 e4 e5 2 ♘f3 ♘c6 3 ♗b5 a6 4 ♗a4
♘f6 5 d4 ed 6 00 ♗e7 7 e5 ♘e4 8
♘×d4 00 9 ♘f5 d5 10 ♗×c6 bc 11
♘×e7+ ♕×e7 12 ♖e1 (This is a
well-known theoretical position in
which the move 12 ... f6 is
recommended, but in one of the

semi-finals of the USSR Championship I played here, against Korelov, 12 . . . ♖e8 and obtained the advantage. During our preparatory work I showed Karpov this move and Anatoly was able to use it.) 12 . . . ♖e8 13 f3 (*96*)

96
13W
B

(This is precisely the natural reply that Black was counting on. But even after 13 b3 f6 14 f3 ♘d6! 15 ♗b2 ♘f7 16 f4 ef 17 ef ♗f5, Black's position is preferable.) 13 . . . ♘d6 14 b3 ♘f5 15 ♗a3 (or 15 ♗b2 ♗b7 with . . . c5 to follow) 15 . . . ♕g5 16 ♗b2 ♘h4 17 ♕e2 f6 18 ♕f2 ♗h3 (not immediately 18 . . . fe because of 19 f4) 19 g4 fe 20 ♘d2? (A blunder, but White's position was already hopeless.) 20 . . . ♕×d2 **0–1** (1·23 – 0·35)

1113 AK–Vogt

FR7: 24.8.1969: Pirc

Karpov did not try for a big advantage, because he was satisfied with his solid tournament position. However, his minimal positional advantage was sufficient for victory – Furman.

1 e4 g6 2 d4 ♗g7 3 ♘f3 d6 4 c3 ♘f6 5 ♗d3 0-0 6 0-0 ♘bd7 7 ♘bd2 e5 8 ♖e1 c6 9 a4 ♕c7 10 ♗f1 d5 11 de ♘×e5 12 ♘×e5 ♕×e5 13 ed ♕×d5 14 ♗c4 ♕a5 (14 . . . ♕c5 15 ♕b3 ♖b8 16 ♘e4 ♘×e4 17 ♖×e4 ♗f5 18 ♗e3 ♕d6 19 ♗f4 ♕f6 20 ♗×b8 ♗×e4 21 ♕×b7± ± Juhnke–Vogt, FR2) 15 ♘b3 ♕c7 16 ♕f3 ♗g4 17 ♕f4 ♕c8 18 h3 ♗d7 19 ♗e3 ♗e6 20 ♗×e6 ♕×e6 21 ♘c5 ♕c8 22 ♗d4 ♘d5 23 ♕d2 ♖d8 24 ♗×g7 ♔×g7 25 c4 ♘f6 26 ♕c3 ♕f5 27 ♖e5 ♕f4 28 ♖e7 ♔g8 29 ♘×b7 ♖d2 30 ♖f1 ♖b8 31 g3 ♕d4 32 ♕×d4 ♖×d4 33 b3 ♔f8 34 ♖fe1 ♖e4 35 ♖1×e4 ♘×e4 36 ♖c7 c5 37 ♔g2 a6 38 a5 ♘d2 39 ♘×c5 ♘×b3 **1–0** (1·10 – 2·30)

1114 Urzica–AK

FR8: 25.8.1969: Four Knights

(Notes by Karpov)

By now I had noticed an interesting regularity in my opponent's choice of opening. He used just the two moves: 1 e4 or 1 b4, strictly alternating the sequence. In the sixth round, against Adorjan, he had opened 1 b4, so I now expected 1 e4, though I was also ready for 1 b4.

1 e4   e5
2 ♘f3   ♘c6
3 ♘c3

In his previous games my opponent had played the Spanish with an early d4. The Four Knights came as something of a surprise.

3 ...	♘f6
4 ♗b5	♗b4
5 0-0	0-0
6 d3	d6
7 ♗g5	♗×c3
8 bc	♗d7
9 d4	h6
10 ♗h4	♖e8

10 ... ♘e7 is not on because of 11 ♗×d7 ♘×d7 12 de de 13 ♘×e5.

| 11 ♖e1 | a6 |

Now if 11 ... ♘e7, White has 12 ♖b1!

| 12 ♗d3 | ♗g4 |
| 13 d5 | |

White selects a lame plan. By closing the centre he condemns his bishops to a wretched existence.

13 ...	♘b8
14 h3	♗×f3
15 ♕×f3	♘bd7
16 ♗g3	♘c5
17 c4	

Obviously he feared 17 ... b5 after which Black would have a very strong Q-side initiative.

17 ...	♕e7
18 ♖e3	♘fd7
19 h4	♖eb8
20 ♕e2	b6

Black's last two moves do not appear very consistent. The rooks should have been placed on b8 and c8 and then Black could open up the Q-side with c7–c6.

21 a3

So that this pawn will later be defended by the rook on e3.

| 21 ... | ♘×d3 |

This bishop was no adornment to White's position, but it did stand in the way of Black's Q-side initiative.

22 ♖×d3

If 22 cd, then 22 ... b5 is good.

| 22 ... | ♘c5 |
| 23 ♖dd1 | c6! (97) |

Now White's doubled pawns become very weak.

97
23B
W

24 a4

Preventing 24 ... ♘a4 followed by ... c5 and ... b5.

24 ...	cd
25 ♖×d5	♖c8
26 f3	♖c6
27 a5	ba
28 ♖×a5	♕c7
29 ♗e1	

White is trying to block Black's passed pawn on a6.

| 29 ... | ♘e6 |
| 30 g3 | |

Apparently the only defence against the threat of 30 ... ♘f4, but now all Black's pieces penetrate into the opposing camp.

30 ...	♖×c4
31 ♕d3	♖×c2
32 ♖×a6	♖×a6
33 ♕×a6	♘d4
34 ♕d3	♕a7
35 ♔f1	♖c1

0–1

2·04   1·45

1115 AK–Adorjan

FR9: 26.8.1969: Spanish

A draw in this round guaranteed me a clear first place irrespective of further games, and I naturally did not object to this – Karpov.

1 e4 e5 2 ♘f3 ♘c6 3 ♗b5 a6 4 ♗a4 ♘f6 5 00 ♗e7 6 ♖e1 b5 7 ♗b3 d6 8 c3 00 9 h3 ♘a5 10 ♗c2 c5 11 d4 ♕c7 12 ♘bd2 ♘c6 13 de de 14 ♘f1 ♗e6 15 ♘e3 ♖ad8 16 ♕e2 c4 17 ♘f5 ♗×f5 18 ef h6 19 ♘×e5 ♘×e5 20 ♕×e5 ♗d6 21 ♕e2 ♖fe8 22 ♗e3 ♘d5 23 ♕f3 ♘×e3 24 ♖×e3 ♖×e3 25 ♕×e3 ♗c5 26 ♕e2 ♕f4 27 ♖d1 ♖×d1+ ½–½ (0·32 – 0·44)

1116 Kaplan–AK

FR10: 27.8.1969: King's Gambit

In this round came my duel with Kaplan. He was in an exceptionally aggressive frame of mind and tried, at least partially, to rehabilitate himself for his loss of the world junior title. The particular choice of opening testifies to this – Karpov.

1 e4 e5 2 f4 ef 3 ♘f3 g5 4 ♗c4 ♗g7 5

d4 d6 6 00 ♘c6 7 c3 h6 8 g3 g4 9 ♘h4 f3 10 ♕b3 ♕d7 11 ♘d2 ♘a5 12 ♕c2 ♘×c4 13 ♘×c4 ♘e7 14 ♘e3 ♕c6 15 d5 ♕c5 16 ♔h1 ♗d7 17 ♗d2 a5 18 ♕d3 h5 19 ♖ae1 ♗e5 20 ♘c4 ½–½ (1·45 – 1·20)

1117 AK–Diaz

FR11: 28.8.1969: King's Indian

1 c4 ♘f6 2 ♘c3 c5 3 ♘f3 g6 4 g3 ♘c6 5 ♗g2 ♗g7 6 00 00 7 d4 cd 8 ♘×d4 ♘×d4 9 ♕×d4 d6 10 ♕d3 ♗f5 11 e4 ♗e6 12 b3 ♘d7 13 ♗b2 ♘c5 14 ♕d2 ♕d7 15 ♖ac1 a6 16 ♖fd1 ♖fd8 17 ♘e2 ♗×b2 18 ♕×b2 f6 19 ♘f4 ♗f7 20 ♕e2 e5?! (98)

98
20B
W

21 ♗h3! f5 22 ♘d3 ♘×d3 23 ♖×d3 ♖ac8 24 ♖cd1 b5 25 ef gf 26 ♖×d6 ♕×d6 27 ♖×d6 ♖×d6 28 ♗×f5 ♖c5 29 ♕e3 ♖dc6 **1–0** (0·57 – 0·53) (30 ♗e4 ♖c7 31 ♕h6 ♗g6 32 ♗d5+ ± ±)

Prizegiving: 29.8.1969 – Anatoly Karpov declared Junior World Champion.

Our Young Champion   V. Tumanov

If at the World Junior Championship in Stockholm a special prize had
been awarded for modesty and serious application to chess then, together
with the title of Champion, it would have gone to Anatoly. In the course of
the three weeks he sat at the board calmly and in a business-like manner
and pulled off one victory after another.

'Everything depends on the finish' he replied to the importunate
questions of Swedish correspondents, although it was obvious that
everything was virtually decided already. Eight consecutive victories in
the final made his position unassailable. And it was only in the ninth round
when the Hungarian Andras Adorjan, having drawn with Karpov, shook
his hand and said 'Congratulations, you are the Champion' that Anatoly's
face lit up in a broad grin.

Many had believed in Karpov's victory. The ex-World Champion
Mikhail Botvinnik, a man of high principle and guarded in his judgements,
had spoken highly of Anatoly's play. And Boris Spassky, on the eve of
Anatoly's departure for Stockholm, had announced 'I am convinced that
Karpov will repeat my success of fourteen years ago and become the World
Junior Champion'.

On what was based the faith of the Soviet chess players in the success of
their representative? – an analysis of Anatoly's short but impressive
sporting career.

Karpov was five years old when he became acquainted with chess. He
lived at the time in Zlatoust, a small town in the Urals, far from the chess
centres. Anatoly soon stood out in the All-Russian Schools
Championships, and at the age of eleven obtained the rank of candidate
master. Quite a lot of attention was focused on the able young boy. Mikhail
Botvinnik began to concern himself with him. Even then there was already
an uncommonly striking tenacity and purposefulness in Karpov's play. It
was strange to observe how, scarcely noticeable behind the chess pieces,
the small boy sat, not stirring for five hours at a time, absorbed only by his
will to win.

At the age of fifteen Anatoly became a master, the youngest chess master
in our country. And now, at eighteen, he is World Junior Champion. Isn't
it a fact that the sporting biographies of Anatoly Karpov and Boris Spassky
are surprisingly similar, and is there not a special significance in this?

When Anatoly flew into Moscow from Stockholm not one correspondent
was able to extract an interview from him. It was not at all because Karpov
had not yet learnt to give them, it was simply that he did not have the time.

Evgeny Stepanovich Karpov, chief engineer of one of the Tula factories, drove his son, straight from the airport, back to Tula for 'repairs'. Anatoly certainly needed as much rest as possible because before him stretched a whole year of studies at the Moscow State University (MGU).

And so I was chatting to Anatoly. The World Junior Champion visited the central house of culture of the Railwaymen (Moscow – eds) where the 37th USSR Championship was taking place. He looked with interest at the games played by the young débutants in the event.

'I thought' said Anatoly, 'that Volodya Tukmakov would show up best of all, but then I was mistaken'.

The conversation turned to Anatoly's chess career.

'Up to the age of twelve' said Karpov, 'I had a very confused understanding of chess theory. I had read, all in all, two chess books, the titles of which I cannot now remember.

'When I was included in the junior *Trud* school where M. Botvinnik directed the studies, the ex-champion of the world, on becoming acquainted with my knowledge, exclaimed "he doesn't understand anything about chess". Understandably Mikhail Moiseyevich, not wanting to insult me, did not say this to my face, but I was later informed that this was the first thing he ever said about my play.

'The studies with M. Botvinnik did me a lot of good, especially the homework which he gave out. This homework taught me to work independently, forced me to sit down to work at chess books.

'Now my trainer is grandmaster Semyon Furman. He helped me to win in Stockholm and I am very grateful to him. I shall be glad if Semyon Abramovich continues to work with me. He is splendid both as a man and as a chessplayer.'

And which chessplayers have had the greatest influence on your play?

'Capablanca and Botvinnik.'

It frequently happens that parents are unhappy about the extra-curricular activities of their children, fearing that these will interfere with their studies. What was the attitude of Karpov's parents to his chess?

'They had no reason to be worried' said Anatoly, 'I always got an "excellent" for my studies, and I finished school with the gold medal, and now I am taking the first course of the Economics Faculty of the MGU.'

Well what are your interests apart from chess?

'I like pop music, Lermontov and I collect stamps.'

Anatoly looked searchingly at me, expecting some further questions, but I well realized that he had long been wanting to go to the tournament hall where it was much more interesting.

Karpov, playing on the top junior board, did not get the results to match his newly acquired title of World Junior Champion. The Hungarian team of Portisch, Lengyel, Barcza, Barczay, Forintos and Csom, *Women:* Bilek, Veröci, Karakas and Ivanka, *Juniors:* Adorjan and Ribli, proved too strong for the Russian Soviet Federative Socialist Republic team of Polugayevsky, Geller, A. Zaitsev, Antoshin, Averkin and Yuferov, *Women:* Bilunova, Tsifanskaya, Skegina and Alekhina, *Juniors:* Karpov and Sveshnikov, winning 27–21.

1201 AK–Adorjan

R1: King's Indian

(Notes by Adorjan)

1 d4 g6 2 c4 ♗g7 3 ♘c3 d6 4 ♘f3 ♘f6 5 g3 00 6 ♗g2 ♘bd7 7 00 a6!? 8 e4 c5 9 ♖e1 cd 10 ♘×d4 ♘c5 11 h3 ♗d7 12 ♗e3 ♖c8 13 ♖c1 ♕a5! (This prepares . . . b5. The immediate 13 . . . b5 would be disadvantageous because of 14 cb ab 15 b4! ♘a6 16 a3.) **14 a3 ♘a4! 15 b4!?** (A move that could be argued about; because of the weakening of White's c-pawn, it allows Black Q-side play. It is true that it only hangs by a thread that White's plan of c4–c5 is unsuccessful. After the less demanding variation 15 ♘×a4

♗×a4 16 b3 ♗e8! 17 a4 ♘d7, Black's game is easy – he has no problems.) **15 . . . ♘×c3 16 ♖×c3 ♕a4! 17 ♕b1 ♖c7 18 ♖ec1 ♖fc8 19 ♕d3 ♗e8!!** (99)

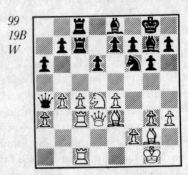

99
19B
W

(The best move of the whole game, and a very difficult decision. The text move allows ♘f6–d7–e5, against which there is no defence.)

20 ♗ f3 (The aforesaid threat could be parried by 20 f4, but the answer 20 . . . ♘h5! 21 g4 ♘×f4 22 ♗×f4 e5 23 ♗e3 ed 24 ♗×d4 ♗×d4 25 ♕×d4 b5! would be to Black's advantage.) **20 . . . ♘d7! 21 ♗ d1 ?** (21 ♕f1 was better, and would have saved him a tempo.) **21 . . . ♘e5 22 ♕f1** (22 ♗×a4 ♘×d3 23 ♖×d3 ♗×a4 24 ♖ dc3 ♗d7 25 ♕h2 f5! 26 ef gf gives Black a decisive advantage because of the threats of . . . d5 and . . . e5.) **22 . . . ♕d7 23 c5 b5! 24 ♗ b3 dc 25 ♖×c5 ♖×c5 26 bc ♘c4!** (This little combination results in a winnable position. To my great surprise, Karpov, a good defensive player, defends rather poorly and with his next hastens the end.) **27 ♗×c4 ♗×d4 28 ♖ dl e5 29 ♗×d4 ed 30 ♗ d5 ♖×c5 31 ♖×d4 ♕c8! 32 h4 ♖ c2! 33 e5 ?** (This loses a pawn without compensation. He should have tried 33 h5!?) **33 . . . ♕c3! 34 ♖ d3 ♕×e5 35 ♕g2** (or 35 ♖e3 ♕×d5 36 ♖×e8+ ♔g7 37 ♕a1+ f6 38 ♖e7+ ♔h6 39 g4 ♖d2 40 g5+ ♔h5! 41 ♖×h7+ ♔g4∓ ∓) **35 . . . ♔g7 36 ♕f3 ?** (Loses instantly. White could have prolonged the game with 36 ♕e4 ♕×e4 37 ♗×e4 ♗c6! 38 ♗×c6 ♖×c6, but without much hope.) **36 . . . ♕e1+ 37 ♔g2 ♖ c1 38 g4** (or 38 ♔h3 ♗d7+ 39 g4 f5!) **38 . . . ♕h1+ 39 ♔g3 ♖g1+ 40 ♔f4 ♕h2+ 41 ♔e4 ♕×h4 0–1**

1202 Adorjan–AK

R2: Spanish

1 e4 e5 2 ♘f3 ♘c6 3 ♗b5 a6 4 ♗×c6 dc 5 00 f6 6 d4 ♗g4 7 c3 ♗d6 8 ♗e3 ♕e7 9 ♘bd2 000 10 ♕c2 h5 11 h3 ♗×f3 12 ♘×f3 g5 13 de ♗×e5 14 ♘×e5 fe 15 ♖adl ♖×dl 16 ♖×dl g4 17 ♕d3 ♘h6 18 ♗×h6 ♖×h6 19 ♕e3 ♖d6 20 ♖×d6 cd 21 hg hg 22 ♕h6 ♕f7 23 b3 ♔c7 24 ♕g5 ♕d7 25 ♕g6 d5 26 ♕f6 ♔d6 27 ♕g7+ ♔b6 28 ed cd 29 ♕×g4 d4 30 cd ed 31 ♕e2 d3 32 ♕d2 ♕d4 33 g3 ½–½

1203 AK–Ribli

R3: Sicilian

1 e4 c5 2 ♘c3 ♘c6 3 g3 g6 4 ♗g2 ♗g7 5 d3 e6 6 f4 d6 7 ♘f3 ♘ge7 8 00 00 9 ♖b1 ♖b8 10 ♗d2 b5 11 a3 f5 12 b4 cb 13 ab a5 14 ♘a2 ab 15 ♘×b4 ♘×b4 16 ♗×b4 ♘c6 17 ♗a3 b4 18 ♗b2 e5 19 ef ♗×f5 20 ♘d2 ♕d7 21 ♘c4 ♗g4 22 ♕d2 ef 23 ♗×g7 ♔×g7 24 ♖×f4 d5 25 ♖×f8 ♖×f8 26 ♘e3 ♗f3 27 ♖f1 ♗×g2 28 ♖×f8 ♔×f8 29 ♕×g2 ♘e7 30 ♕f3+ ♔e8 31 ♕f6 ♕a7 32 ♕e5 h5 33 d4 ♕b7 34 ♔g2 ♕d7 35 ♔f3 b3 36 cb ♕×b3 37 ♕f4 ♕a2 38 ♔g5 ♕d2 39 h3 ♘f5 40 ♕×d5+ ♔c7 41 ♕f7+ ♔c8 42 ♕×g6 ♘×e3 43 ♕e6+ ♔c7 44 ♕e5+ ♔d7 45 ♔×h5 ♕e2+ 46 ♔g5 ♕f3 47 ♕f4 ♕d5+ 48 ♔g6 ♕c6+ 49 ♔g7 ♘d5 50 ♕f5+ ♔d8 51 g4 ♘e7 52 ♕f6 ♕e4 53 g5 ♔d7 54 g6 ♕d5 55 h4 ♕h5 56 ♕g5 ♕d1

57 ♕b5+ ♔d8 58 ♕e5 ♕g4 59 h5
♕d7 60 ♕a5+ ♔e8 61 ♕e5 ♔d8
62 ♔h8 ♕h3 63 ♔h7 ♕d3 64 ♔g7
♘f5+ 65 ♔f8 ♕f3 66 ♕f6+ ♔d7
67 d5 ♕×h5 ½–½

1204 Ribli–AK

R4: Spanish

(Notes by Barcza)

1 e4 e5 2 ♘f3 ♘c6 3 ♗b5 a6 4 ♗a4
♘f6 5 d4 ed 6 00 ♗e7 7 ♖e1 b5 8 e5
♘×e5 9 ♖×e5 (According to
theory, this exchange holds more
chances for Black. However, 9
♘×e5 ba 10 ♕×d4 00 11 ♕×a4
♖b8 gives Black a good game.) 9
... d6 10 ♖e1 (Now the weakened
black pawn formation gives White's
minor pieces good opportunities.)
10 ... ba 11 ♘×d4 ♗d7 12 ♕f3! 00
13 ♘c6! ♗×c6 14 ♕×c6 ♖e8
(Because of the bishop on e7 this
move is a necessary preamble to ...
♕d7, and it is only this tempo
which ensures that White, with
some positional advantage, should
regain the temporarily sacrificed
pawn.) 15 ♘c3 ♕d7 16 ♕×d7
♘×d7 17 ♘×a4 ♗f6 18 ♗d2 ♖e6
19 ♖ad1 ♖ae8 20 ♔f1 ♔f8 21 b3
♖×e1+ 22 ♗×e1! (The rook on d1
will still play a part in undermining
Black's Q-wing. It would be a pity
to exchange it.) 22 ... ♖e5 23 c4 g6
24 ♗b4 (This move thwarts, for the
moment, ... ♘c5.) 24 ... ♖f5?
(This attacking gesture is easily
countered. On the other hand,

Black is worried that the well-
placed white minor pieces do not
allow him much counterplay. 24
... h5 would have been a cold-
blooded waiting game.) 25 ♗d2!
♗d4 26 ♗h6+ ♔g7 27 ♗e3 ♘e5
28 h3! (This not only hinders ...
♘g4, but also threatens the black
rook with g4.) 28 ... ♘c6 29 c5
♔e7 30 g4! ♖e5 31 cd+ cd 32 ♘b6
(threatening both ♘c8+ and ♘c4)
32 ... ♗f8 33 ♗f4 ♖e6 34 ♖c1!
(The black army has retreated, the
Q-side pawn formation is catas-
trophically weak and material
disadvantage can no longer be
avoided, e.g. 34 ... ♘e5 35 ♗g5+
f6 36 ♘d5+ ♔f7 37 ♖c7+ is
decisive. The ensuing pawn
sacrifice is, therefore, a positional
necessity.) 34 ... d5 35 ♘×d5+
♔d7 36 ♘c7! ♖e4 37 ♗g3 f5
(Another compulsory sacrifice
because after 37 ... a5 38 ♘d5, not
only does 39 ♘f6+ win the
exchange, but 39 ♘b6+ is
threatened as well.) 38 gf gf 39
♘×a6 f4 40 ♗h4 ♖e5 41 ♖c4!
♖f5 (On 41 ... ♖a5 42 ♖×f4 ♗d6

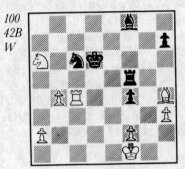

100
42B
W

43 ♖a4 followed by ♗g3 would save the knight, and the three pawns would quickly decide the issue.) 42 b4! ♔d6 (*100*)

(It looks as if the position has eased slightly for Black, as apparently . . . ♔d5 is threatened. But oh no, the following clever move thwarts this last hope.) 43 b5! ♖×b5 44 ♖×f4 ♗g7 45 ♖f7 ♗e5 46 ♖×h7 ♖a5 47 ♘b4! ♘×b4 48 ♗e7+ ♔e6 49 ♗×b4 ♖×a2 50 ♗c5 ♗f4 51 ♔g2 ♖c2 52 ♗b6 ♖b2 53 ♗d8 ♗e5 54 ♗h4 (The game was adjourned here, but next day Black resigned without resuming play.) **1–0**

13 USSR Armed Forces Team Championship zonal

Riga, ?.3–?.4.1970

Karpov played for the Leningrad team which finished second, apparently on board one (Gipslis – game 1304 – played board one for the winning team).

1301 AK–Kosenkov

R1: 24.3.1970: Sicilian

1 e4 c5 2 ♘f3 d6 3 d4 cd 4 ♕×d4 ♘c6 5 ♗b5 ♗d7 6 ♗×c6 ♗×c6 7 c4 ♘f6 8 ♘c3 e6 9 00 ♗e7 10 ♖d1 h6 11 ♕d3 00 12 ♗f4 ♕a5 13 a3 ♘×e4 14 ♘×e4 ♕f5 15 ♕e3 ♗×e4 16 ♕×e4 ♗×e4 17 ♗×d6 ♗×d6 18 ♖×d6 ♗×f3 19 gf ♖fc8 20 ♖d7 ♖×c4 21 ♖×b7 a5 22 ♖d1 ♖f4 23 ♔g2 ♖c8 24 ♔g3 g5 25 ♖e1 ♖c2 26 ♖e4 ♖f5 27 a4 ♖d5 28 h4 ♖d1 29 hg ♖g1+ 30 ♔f4 ♖×g5 31 ♔e3 ♖f5 32 ♖g4+ ♔f8 33 ♖e4 ♔g7 34 ♖b8 ♔f6 35 ♖h4 ♖e5+ 36 ♖e4 ♖f5 37 ♖h4 ½–½

1302 Alt–AK

R2: 25.3.1970: Spanish

1 e4 e5 2 ♘f3 ♘c6 3 ♗b5 a6 4 ♗a4 ♘f6 5 00 ♗e7 6 ♖e1 b5 7 ♗b3 d6 8 c3 00 9 h3 ♘a5 10 ♗c2 ♗b7 11 d4 ♘c4 12 b3 ♘b6 13 ♘bd2 ♘fd7 14 ♘f1 c5 15 de ♗×e5 16 ♘×e5 de 17

♘g3 g6 18 ♗e3 ♕c7 19 ♕e2 ♖fd8 20 ♖ed1 ♘d7 21 a4 ♗c6 22 ab ab 23 ♗d3 ♕b7 24 f3 ♘f8 25 ♕b2 ♖×a1 26 ♕×a1 ♘e6 27 ♘e2 ♕c7 28 ♕c1 ♖a8 29 ♕b2 ♗g5 30 ♗×g5 ♕×g5 31 ♘c1 ♘e6 32 ♗f1 f6 33 ♕f2 ♗e8 34 ♕d2 ♕f7 35 ♕e3 ♕e7 36 ♕d2 ♕a6 37 ♕d5 ♔f7 38 ♘e2 ♗c6 39 ♕d2 ♖a8 40 ♕e3 ♗g7 41 ♘c1 ♗e8 (*101*)

101
41B
W

42 ♕d2 ♖d8 43 ♕e1 ♖b8 44 ♕e3 ♗f7 45 ♖d2 ♘f8 46 ♖a2 ♕c7 47 ♖a3 ♘e6 48 ♖a2 h5 49 ♖a3 h4 50 ♘d3 ♖b7 51 b4 c4 52 ♘c1 ♗e8 53 ♖a8 ♕e7 54 ♘e2 ♗c6 55 ♖a6

♖c7 56 ♕f2 g5 57 ♕b6 ♔g6 58
♕e3 ♗b7 59 ♖a5 ♕d7 60 ♖a7
♕c6 61 ♕f2 ♖h7 62 ♖a5 ♗a6 63
♖a2 ♕d6 64 ♖a5 ♖d7 65 ♕e3
♕c6 66 ♖a1 ♖d3 67 ♕f2 ♗b7 68
♔h2 ♘f8 69 ♘c1 ♖d1 70 ♘b3
♖×f1 71 ♖×f1 cb 72 ♕b2 ♕c4 73
♖b1 f5 74 ef+ ♔×f5 75 ♕×b3
♕×b3 76 ♖×b3 ♘e6 77 ♖a3 ♗d5
78 ♖a5 ♗c4 79 ♖a6 ♘f4 80 ♖a8
e4 81 ♖f8+ ♔e5 82 fe ♔×e4 83
g3 hg+ 84 ♔×g3 ♔d3 85 ♖f5
♘×h3 86 ♖e5 ♘f4 87 ♖×g5 ♘e6
88 ♖g4 ♔×c3 89 ♔f2 ♔×b4 90
♔e1 ♔c3 91 ♔d1 b4 92 ♔c1 ♘d4
93 ♖g7 b3 94 ♖b7 ♘b5 **0–1**

1303 AK–Zhelyandinov

R3(?): Spanish

(Notes by Karpov)

1 e4 e5 2 ♘f3 ♘c6 3 ♗b5 a6 4 ♗a4
♘f6 5 00 ♗e7 6 ♖e1 b5 7 ♗b3 d6 8
c3 00 9 h3 h6 10 d4 ♖e8 11 ♘bd2
♗f8 12 ♘f1 ♗d7

12 . . . ♗b7 is another possible
continuation.

      13 ♘g3   ♘a5
      14 ♗c2   g6

Other continuations are 14 . . .
♘c4 and 14 . . . c5. Against 14 . . .
c5, White replies 15 b3 ♘c6 16 d5
♘e7 17 ♘h4 with advantage. I
decided to lead the game into the
position that would have arisen
from that variation.

      15 b3

This move limits the field of
operations of the knight on a5. Very
often White bases his play on
utilizing the bad position of this
knight. In the text game, the black
knight retreats to b7, but even there
it remains rather out of play. 15
♘h2 followed by f4 deserves
consideration.

      15 . . .   c5
      16 d5   ♗g7
      17 ♗e3   ♘h7

Black adopts an interesting plan.
He attempts first to restrict White's
K-side play and then to start his Q-
side counterplay. In the game
Black did not completely succeed in
effecting this idea. In the middle of
the game he starts to change plans
and suffers defeat.

      18 ♕d2   h5
      19 ♘h2   ♘b7

Now, and over the next few
moves, the continuation f4 and then
f5 would have led to very sharp
play.

      20 ♖ac1   a5
      21 a3

The idea behind the text move is
clear – White intends, at an
appropriate moment, to close the
Q-side, and also to play b4 to bury
the black knight on b7.

      21 . . .   ♕b6
      22 ♔h1

White intends to prepare and
carry out the advance f2–f4.
Therefore it is useful to remove the
king from the g1–a7 diagonal.

      22 . . .   b4
      23 ab   ab
    23 cb cb 24 a4 and the re-

deployment of a knight on c4 was possible, but at the time of the game I intended the plan with f2–f4 and I did not want to give it up. And so White succeeded in closing the Q-side, but at the same time conceded the a-file. In the outcome it transpires that the a-file does not give Black sufficient counterplay.

24 c4	♖a2
25 ♕d1	♖ea8
26 ♖f1	♕d8
27 ♘e2	

Here I intended the redeployment of knight on d3 and bishop on b2 and then the move f4. Black prevented the redeployment ♗b2, but, all the same, the white knight occupied the d3 square.

27 . . . ♗f6

Black loses the thread of the game. He makes all the subsequent moves in random order. Now if Black had decided to exchange dark-squared bishops, then a better way to do this was by 27 . . . ♕f8 and 28 . . . ♗h6.

(The game is given in *Shakhmaty v SSSR*, No. 7 1970, as continuing 27 . . . ♕e7 28 ♖b1 ♗f6 29 ♘c1 ♖2a3 30 ♘f3 ♔h8 – KJO'C.)

28 ♘f3

Preventing . . . ♗g5.

28 . . . ♔h8?

After White carries out his plan with f4 it becomes clear that the king ought to be on g8 in order to defend the f7 square.

29 ♖b1	♕e7
30 ♘c1	♖2a3
31 ♘d3	♗g7
32 ♘d2	

White is unable to transfer the bishop to b2 because of . . . f5.

32 . . .	♕f8
33 f4	ef
34 ♗×f4	♕e7
35 ♘f3	

Now White wants to carry out the advance e4–e5. If he can achieve this then the black position collapses.

35 . . . ♖a2

Against 35 . . . f6, White plays 36 ♗h2 and then ♘f4 and e5.

36 e5	♗f5
37 ♖e1	

White breaks through in the centre, after which all his pieces spring to life. At the same time, the black pieces are strewn all over the place and cannot organize effective resistance.

37 . . .	♕c7
38 ♖c1	♔g8 (*102*)

See, he's got to put the king back. But there now follows a combination and White wins quickly.

102
38B
W

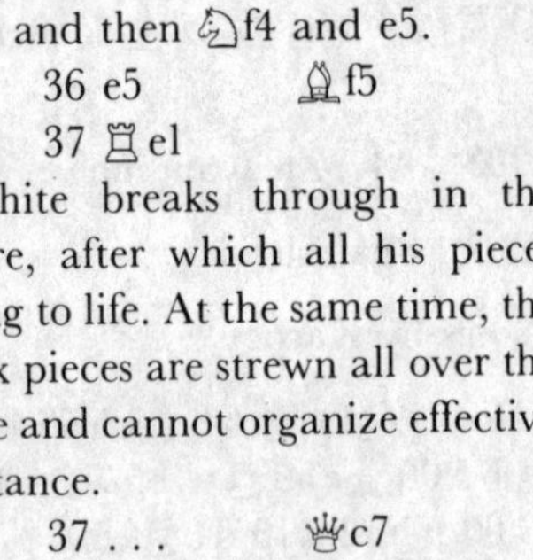

39 ed	♘×d6
40 ♘×b4	cb
41 ♗×f5	♗c3

On 41 ... gf follows 42 c5.

42 ♗b1	♖a1
43 ♖e2	**1–0**

It is typical that after the logical culmination of the plan, White succeeded in finishing the game with a combination.

1304 Gipslis–AK

R4: 28.3.1970: Spanish

1 e4 e5 2 ♘f3 ♘c6 3 ♗b5 a6 4 ♗a4 ♘f6 5 00 ♗e7 6 ♖e1 b5 7 ♗b3 d6 8 c3 00 9 h3 ♘a5 10 ♗c2 c5 11 d4 ♕c7 12 ♘bd2 ♘c6 13 d5 ♘d8 14 a4 ♖b8 15 b3 g6 16 ♕e2 ♘h5 17 ♘b1 ♗d7 18 ♗h6 ♖e8 19 ♗d3 ♗f8 20 ♗c1 ♘f4 21 ♗×f4 ef 22 ab ab 23 ♕d2 ♗h6 24 ♖a2 b4 25 ♗c4 ♘b7 26 ♖a7 bc 27 ♘×c3 ♗g7 28 ♘d1 ♕b6 29 ♖a6 ♕b4 30 ♕×f4 ♖a8 31 ♖×a8 ♖×a8 32 ♘e3 ♖e8 33 ♘f1 ♗c3 34 ♖e2 f6 35 ♖a2 ♔g7 36 ♘e3 ♖e7 37 ♖a7 ♗e5 38 ♕h4 ♗b2 39 ♘c2 ♕b6 40 ♖a6 ♕d8 41 ♖a2 ♗c1 42 ♘fe1 ♗g5 43 ♕g3 ♖×e4 44 ♘d3 f5 45 ♖a7 ♗h4 46 ♕f3 ♕b8 47 ♖a6 ♘d8 48 ♕d1 ♗f6 49 ♕d2 ♗c8 50 ♖a4 ♘f7 51 ♕a5 ♗d7 52 ♕a8 ♕×a8 53 ♖×a8 g5 54 ♖a7 ♖e7 55 ♔f1 f4 56 f3 ♗f5 57 ♖×e7 ♗×e7 58 b4 ♘e5 59 ♘×e5 de 60 d6 ♗f8 61 b5 ♗×d6 62 ♘a3 e4 63 fe ♗×e4 64 ♗e2 ♔f6 65 ♘c4 ♔e6 66 ♘d2 *(103)*

66 ... ♗f5 67 ♗g4 ♗×g4 68 hg

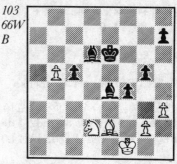

103
66W
B

♔d5 69 ♔e2 c4 70 b6 h6 71 b7 ♗c7 72 ♘f3 ♔c5 73 ♔d2 ♔d5 74 ♔e2 ♗b8 75 ♔d2 ♗a7 76 ♔e2 ♗b8 77 ♔d2 ♔e4 78 ♔e2 ♗d6 79 ♘e1 ♔d4 80 ♔d2 c3+ 81 ♔e2 ♔c4 82 ♘c2 ♗c7 83 ♘e1 ♔b3 84 ♔d1 ♔b2 85 ♘d3+ ♔b1 86 ♘b4 ♗b8 87 ♘c2 ♔b2 88 ♘b4 ♗d6 89 ♘d3+ ♔b1 90 ♘b4 ♗×b4 91 b8♕ c2+ 92 ♔e2 b1♕ 93 ♕×b4+ ♕b2+ 94 ♕×b2+ ♔×b2 ½–½

1305 AK–Chilnov

R6: 30.3.1970: Petroff/English

1 e4 e5 2 ♘f3 ♘f6 3 d3 ♘c6 4 g3 d6 5 ♗g2 ♗e7 6 00 00 7 c4 ♘e8 8 ♘c3 f5 9 ♘d5 fe 10 de ♘f6 11 ♕d3 ♘×d5 12 cd ♘b8 13 ♗d2 ♗g4 14 ♘e1 ♘d7 15 b4 c5 16 dc bc 17 ♘c2 ♗e6 18 ♘e3 ♘b6 19 f3 fcl ♕d7 20 a4 ♗g5 21 a5 ♘c8 22 ♖d1 ♕f7 23 ♖f1 ♗f6 24 ♖ac1 ♕b7 25 f4 ♖d8 26 ♕e2 ef 27 gf ♗d4 28 ♔h1 ♘e7 29 ♕d3 ♗f6 30 f5 ♗f7 31 ♘g4 ♗e5 32 ♘×e5 de 33 ♕e3 ♖e8 34 ♖c5 ♘c8 35 ♗c3 ♘d6 36 ♕g3 ♘c4 37 ♖g1 g6 38 h4 ♔f8 39 ♕g5 ♘d6 40 ♕h6+ ♔e7 41 ♖×e5+ ♔d7 42 ♖d1 ♖ad8 43 ♖×e8

♔×e8 44 ♕×h7 gf 45 ♕h8+ ♔d7
46 ♖×d6+ **1–0**

1306   Sokolov–AK

R7: 1.4.1970: Blumenfeld/Benko

1 d4 ♘f6 2 ♘f3 c5 3 d5 b5 4 c4 ♗b7
5 b3 e6 6 de fe 7 cb d5 8 ♘bd2 ♗d6
9 e4 ♘bd7 10 ed ed 11 ♗d3 0-0 12 0-0
♘e5 13 ♘×e5 ♗×e5 14 ♖b1 ♗d6
15 ♖e1 ♕c7 16 ♘f1 ♖ae8 17 ♖b2
♘e4 18 ♗×e4 de 19 ♖c2 ♖e5 20
♗e3 ♕e7 21 ♖d2 ♖e6 22 ♕h5
♖e5 23 ♕e2 ♖e6 24 ♖ed1 ♕f6 25
♕c4 ♖f7 26 ♗×c5 ♗×c5 27
♕×c5 h6 28 ♘e3 a6 29 ba ♗×a6
30 ♖c2 ♔h7 31 ♕d4 ♕f4 32 ♕d5
♖g6 ½–½

14 Kuibyshev 7.5-2.6.1970

RSFSR Championship and 38 USSR Championship semi-final

		1	2	3	4	5	6	7	8	9	0	1	2	3	4	5	6	7	8	
1	**Karpov**	×	1	½	½	½	½	1	½	1	1	1	½	½	½	1	1	½	1	**12½**
2	Krogius	0	×	½	½	1	½	½	½	1	½	1	1	½	½	1	½	½	1	**11**
3	Antoshin	½	½	×	½	½	1	½	½	0	½	0	½	1	1	1	½	1	1	**10½**
4	Dementiev	½	½	½	×	½	1	½	½	½	½	½	½	½	1	1	½	½	1	**10½**
5	Doroshkevich	½	0	½	½	×	1	0	½	½	½	1	½	1	0	½	1	1	1	**10**
6	Averkin	½	½	0	0	0	×	1	1	0	½	1	½	1	½	0	1	1	+	**9½**
7	A. Zaitsev	0	½	½	½	1	0	×	1	0	1	½	1	0	½	½	½	1	1	**9½**
8	I. Kopilov	½	½	½	½	½	0	0	×	½	½	1	1	1	½	½	½	1	½	**9½**
9	Pozdnyakov	0	0	1	½	½	1	1	½	×	1	0	½	0	½	0	1	1	½	**9**
10	Rashkovsky	0	½	½	½	½	½	0	½	0	×	½	½	½	1	1	½	1	1	**9**
11	Chernikov	0	0	1	½	0	0	½	0	1	½	×	1	½	1	1	½	½	1	**9**
12	Anikayev	½	0	½	½	½	½	0	0	½	½	0	×	1	½	0	1	½	1	**7½**
13	Zhukhovitsky	½	½	0	½	0	0	1	0	1	½	½	0	×	½	1	½	½	½	**7½**
14	Tseshkovsky	½	½	0	0	1	½	½	½	½	0	0	½	½	×	1	0	½	1	**7½**
15	Shestakov	0	0	0	0	½	1	½	½	1	0	0	1	0	0	×	½	1	½	**6½**
16	Pavlyutin	0	½	½	½	0	0	½	½	0	½	½	0	½	1	½	×	½	0	**6**
17	Tarasov	½	½	0	½	0	0	0	0	0	0	½	½	½	½	0	½	×	½	**4½**
18	Sergievsky	0	0	0	0	0	−	0	½	½	0	0	0	½	0	½	1	½	×	**3½**

1401 AK–Krogius

R1: 8.5.1970: French

(Notes by Krogius)

1 e4 e6 2 d4 d5 3 ♘d2 c5 4 ♘gf3 ♘c6 5 ed ed 6 ♗b5 ♗d6 7 00 ♘ge7 8 dc ♗×c5 9 ♘b3 ♗b6 10 ♖el 00 11 ♗e3 ♗g4 12 ♗×b6 ♕×b6 13 ♗×c6 ♘×c6 14 ♕×d5 ♘b4 15 ♕e4 ♗×f3 16 gf a5 17 a3 (17 ♘d4 is better.) 17 . . . ♘c6 18 ♕e3 ♕b5 19 a4 ♕h5 20 ♕e4 ♕g5+ 21 ♔hl ♕f6 22 ♘c5 ♖ad8? (After 22 . . . ♕×b2 23 ♘d7 ♖fd8 24 ♖abl ♕d4 the position is considerably

simplified and chances would have been level, However, I renounced that line, over-estimating Black's attacking possibilities.) 23 c3! b6 24 ♘d3 h6 25 f4 ♖d7 26 ♘e3 ♘fd8 27 ♖gl ♘e7 28 ♘e5 ♖dl 29 ♖eel ♖×el 30 ♖×el ♘f5 31 ♘g4 ♕g6 32 ♘e5 ♕h5 33 ♕f3 ♕h4 34 ♘c4 ♕f6 35 h3 ♘h4 36 ♕e4 (*104*)

104
36W
B

36 . . . ♘g6? (The decisive mistake. Black concedes the blockade square f5. 36 ... ♘f5 was necessary.) 37 f5 ♘h4 38 ♘e3 ♔h8 39 ♖e2! ♕g5 40 ♕h2 h5 41 f4 ♕h6 42 ♔g3! g5 43 fg6 ♘×g6 44 ♘f5 ♕f8 45 ♕f3 ♔g8 46 ♕×h5 ♖d3+ 47 ♔g4 ♕a8 48 ♘d4 ♖dl 49 ♘f3 ♖d5 50 ♘g5 ♕c8+ 51 ♔g3 ♖f5 52 ♕h7+ ♔f8 53 ♕h6+ ♔g8 54 ♘e6! **1–0**

1402 Chernikov–AK

R2: 9.5.1970: Nimzo-Indian

(Notes by Karpov)

1 d4 ♘f6 2 c4 e6 3 ♘c3 ♗b4 4 e3 00 5 ♘ge2 d5 6 a3 ♗e7 7 ♘g3?! c5 8

dc ♗×c5 9 b4 ♗e7 10 ♗b2 ♘c6 11 ♕c2 (intending 12 ♖dl) 11 . . . dc! 12 ♗×c4 ♕c7 13 ♘b5 (13 ♘ce4 ♘e5 14 ♗b3 ♕×c2 15 ♗×c2 ♘c4=) 13 . . . ♕b8 14 00 ♗d7 15 ♖adl ♘e5!∓ 16 ♗e2 ♖c8 17 ♕d2 ♗×b5 18 ♗×b5 a6! 19 ♗e2 ♘c4 20 ♗×c4 ♖×c4 21 ♖cl ♕c7 22 ♖×c4 ♕×c4 23 ♖cl ♕b5 24 ♗×f6 gf!∓ 25 ♘e4 f5 (25 . . . ♖d8 26 ♕b2) 26 ♘c3 ♕c6! 27 ♘bl (27 ♘e2!? ♕a4 28 ♕c3 ♖d8∓) 27 . . . ♕e8 28 ♖c4 ♗f6 29 ♕c2 ♖d8 30 ♔fl?! (30 g3) 30 . . . ♕b5 31 ♔e2 a5 32 a4 ♕d5 33 f3? (33 g3) 33 . . . ab 34 ♖c8 (34 ♖×b4 ♕d6 35 ♖×b7 ♕×h2∓∓) 34 . . . ♖×c8 35 ♕×c8+ ♔g7 36 ♕c2 b3! 37 ♕d3 ♕e5∓∓ 38 ♕×b3 ♕×h2 39 ♕×b7 ♕×g2+ 40 ♔d3 ♕fl+ 41 ♔d2 h5 42 a5 h4 43 a6 h3 44 ♕b8 ♕g2+ 45 ♔d3 h2 46 a7 hl♕ 47 ♘d2 ♕al **0–1** (48 a8♕ ♕c3 mate)

1403 AK–Sergievsky

R3: 10.5.1970: Pirc

(Notes by Karpov)

1 e4 d6 2 d4 ♘f6 3 ♘c3 ♘bd7 4 ♘ge2 b5?! 5 e5! de 6 de ♘×e5 7 ♕×d8+ ♔×d8 8 ♘×b5 a6 9 ♘bd4 ♗b7 10 ♗f4 ♘g6 11 000! ♔c8 (11 . . . ♘×f4?? 12 ♘e6+ + ♔e8 13 ♘×c7 mate!; 12 . . . ♔c8 13 ♖d8 mate!) **12 ♗d2 e6 13 ♘b3** (threatening ♘a5 and preventing . . . ♗c5) **13 . . . ♗g4 14 ♗el ♗d6 15 h3 ♘f6** (15 . . . ♘4e5 16 ♘a5±; 15 . . . ♘h2 16 ♖×d6 ♘×fl 17

♖d3 ♗×g2 18 ♖g1±) **16** ♘**a5**
♖ **d8 17 c4** ♘ **f4 18** ♘×**b7** ♔×**b7**
19 ♔**c2** ♗ **e5** (19 ... ♘×e2!? 20
♗×e2 ♗e5±) **20** ♘**c3** ♖ ×**d1 21**
♘×**d1!±** ♖ **d8 22 g3** ♘**g6 23**
♗ **g2+** ♔**b6 24** ♘**c3** ♗ **d4 25** ♘**e2!**
♗ **e5 26 f4** ♗ **d6 27** ♘**c3 c6** (*105*)

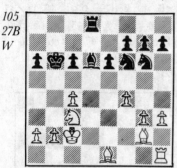

105
27B
W

28 c5+ ! ♗×**c5** (28 ... ♔×c5 29
♗f2+ ♔c4 30 b3+ ♔b4 31 a3+
♔×a3 32 ♖a1+ ♔b4 33 ♖a4
mate) **29** ♘**a4+** ♔**b5 30** ♔**b3!!**
(threatening 31 ♗ f1 mate. If 30 b3
♗b4) **30 ...** ♖ **d3+ 31** ♗ **c3**
♖×**c3+ 32** ♘×**c3+** ♔**a5 33**
♘**a4±±** ♗ **f2 34** ♖ **c1** ♘**e7 35**
♖ **c2** ♗ **e3 36** ♗ ×**c6** ♘**h5 37** ♗ **e8**
♘×**g3 38** ♔**c4** (threatening 39 b4
mate) **38 ...** ♘**d5 39 a3** ♘**b6+ 40**
♔**d3** ♘×**a4 41** ♔×**e3** ♘**f5+ 42**
♔**d3 1–0** (42 ... ♘b6 43 ♖c5
mate; 42 ... ♘d6 43 b4+ ♔b6 44
♖c6+ ♔b7 45 ♖×d6)

1404 Doroshkevich–AK

R4: 12.5.1970: Nimzo-Indian

1 d4 ♘f6 2 c4 e6 3 ♘c3 ♗b4 4 ♕c2
00 5 ♘f3 c5 6 dc ♘a6 7 ♗d2 ♘×c5
8 e3 b6 9 ♗e2 ♗b7 10 00 ♘ce4 11

♘×e4 ♗×e4 12 ♗d3 ♗×d3 13
♕×d3 ♗×d2 14 ♕×d2 d5 ½–½

1405 AK–Zhukhovitsky

R5: 13.5.1970: Spanish

1 e4 e5 2 ♘f3 ♘c6 3 ♗b5 a6 4 ♗a4
♘f6 5 00 ♗e7 6 ♖e1 b5 7 ♗b3 d6 8
c3 00 9 h3 h6 10 d4 ♖e8 11 ♘bd2
♗f8 12 ♘f1 ♗d7 13 ♘g3 ♘a5 14
♗c2 c5 15 b3 ♕c7 16 d5 ♘b7 17
♗d2 c4 18 b4 a5 19 a3 ♖a6 20 ♘h2
♖ea8 21 ♖c1 ab 22 ab ♗e7 23 f4
♘h7 24 ♘f3 ♘f8 25 ♘h5 ♗e8 26
♕e2 ♘d7 27 f5 ♘f6 28 ♘×f6+
♗×f6 29 g4 ♗e7 30 g5 hg 31 ♘×g5
♗×g5 32 ♗×g5 f6 33 ♗e3 ♕f7 34
♗d1 ♖a2 35 ♖c2 ♖×c2 36 ♕×c2
♕f8 37 ♔h2 ♕g8 38 ♖g1 ♕h7 39
♕e2 ♘d8 40 ♕g4 ♖a3 41 ♗d2
♘f7 42 ♗f3 ♕h8 43 ♕g3 ♘d8 44
♕f2 ♖a2 45 ♖g4 ♕e7 46 ♔g3
♕g8 47 ♔h2 ♘f7 48 ♖g2 ♕h8 49
♕e1 ♔f8 50 ♕g3 ♖a3 51 ♗d1 ½–½

1406 Tarasov–AK

R6: 14.5.1970: Catalan

1 d4 ♘f6 2 ♘f3 d5 3 c4 dc 4 ♕a4+
♘bd7 5 g3 a6 6 ♘c3 e6 7 ♗g2 ♖b8
8 ♕×c4 b5 9 ♕d3 ♗b7 10 00 c5 11
dc ♘×c5 12 ♕×d8+ ♖×d8 13
♖d1 ♖×d1+ 14 ♘×d1 ♗d6 15
♗f4 ♗e7 16 ♘e5 ♘d5 17 ♘e3
♘×f4 18 gf ♗×g2 19 ♔×g2 f6 20
♘c6 ♔d7 21 ♘×e7 ♔×e7 22 ♖c1
♔d6 23 f5 g6 24 b4 ♘a4 25 fe ♖e8
26 f4 ♖×e6 27 ♔f3 ♘b6 28 ♖d1+
♔e7 ½–½

1407 AK–Shestakov

R7: 17.5.1970: French

1 e4 e6 2 d4 d5 3 ♘d2 ♘f6 4 e5
♘fd7 5 c3 c5 6 ♗d3 b6 7 ♕e2 a5 8
♗b5 ♗a6 9 a4 ♕c8 10 f4 cd 11 cd
♘c6 12 ♘gf3 ♗×b5 13 ab ♘b4 14
00 ♗e7 15 ♖f2 ♖a7 16 ♘f1 00 17
♗d2 ♖c7 18 ♗×b4 ♗×b4 19 f5 f6
20 fe ♘b8 21 ♘e3 ♕×e6 22 ef
♖×f6 23 ♘g5 ♖×f2 24 ♕×f2 ♕c8
25 ♖f1 h6 26 ♘h3 ♕d8 27 ♕f5
♗d2 28 ♘×d5 ♖d7 (*106*)

106
28B
W

29 ♕e6+ ♔h8 30 ♘hf4 ♗×f4 31
♘×f4 ♖×d4 32 ♘g6+ ♔h7 33
♘f8+ ♔h8 34 ♕g6 **1–0**

1408 AK–Rashkovsky

R8: 18.5.1970: King's Indian

(Notes by Karpov)

1 c4 ♘f6 2 g3 g6 3 ♗g2 ♗g7 4 d4 00
5 ♘c3 d6 6 ♘f3 ♘c6 7 00 ♗f5 8 d5
♘a5 9 ♘d4 ♗d7 10 b3 c5 11 dc bc
12 ♗b2 c5 13 ♘c2 ♖b8 14 ♘e3
♘c6 15 ♕d2 ♘b4 16 h3 ♗c6 17
♘cd5 ♘b×d5 18 cd ♗b5 19 ♗c3
♘e8 20 ♗a5 ♕d7 21 ♖ac1 ♗a6 22

♖fe1 ♖b7 23 ♗c3 ♗×c3 24 ♕×c3
♘g7 25 ♘c2 ♖b6 26 e4 e5 27 de fe
28 ♖cd1 ♕f7 29 f4 ♘h5 30 ♖d2
♕g7 31 ♕e3 e5 32 ♖f2 ef 33 gf
♕h6 34 f5 ♕×e3 35 ♘×e3 ♘f6 36
♖d1 ♔g7 37 ♖fd2 ♘e8 38 fg hg 39
e5 de 40 ♖d7+ ♖f7 41 ♖×f7+
♔×f7 42 ♖d7+ ♔e6 43 ♖×a7
♘f6 44 ♖c7 ♗d3 45 ♖×c5 ♖a6
46 ♖c6+ ♖×c6 47 ♗×c6 ♔d6 48
♗g2 ♔c5 49 a3 ♔d4 50 ♔f2 e4
(*107*)

107
50B
W

White sealed . . .
    51 a4
One would think the position
held no difficulties for Black: the
active position of his king will
compensate for the pawn minus.

When the adjournment session
began, Rashkovsky made the
strongest move . . .
    51 . . .   ♔c3
. . . saying that after 52 ♗f1 ♘d7
53 a5 ♘c5 the game would soon be
drawn.

Since the threat of 52 ♗f1 is
easily parried, I decided to try a
different order of moves.
    52 a5   ♘d7?

The cunning is justified. Black proceeds to defend against the threat of 53 Bf1 and unexpectedly finds himself in a difficult situation. With 52 ... Kb4 he could have forced a draw.

53 h4   Kxb3

And here 53 ... Kb4 would have preserved drawing chances.

54 Nd5

Suddenly it is clear that Black's king cannot approach the pawn on a5, or attack the knight, because of Nb6+.

54 ...   Nc5
55 Ke3   Ka4

Naturally Black hastens to win back the a-pawn, thinking that with one remaining pawn, he can easily cope with the task in hand.

56 Nf4   Kxa5
57 Nxg6   Nd7

Forced. On 57 ... Kb6 there follows 58 Bh3 Bc4 59 h5 Bg8 60 h6 Kc7 61 Ne7 Bh7 62 Bf5 and if 62 ... Kd6 63 Nc8+ or 62 ... Kd8 63 Nc6+ both win.

58 Bxe4   Bc4
59 Kd4   Be2
60 Bf5   Nf6
61 Ke5   Ne8

61 ... Nh5 is no use on account of 62 Nf4. If 61 ... Ng4+ then 62 Kf4 Nh6 63 Be6 and Black's knight is snared. Or 62 ... Nf6 (instead of 62 ... Nh6) 63 Kg5 Nh7+ 64 Kh6 Nf6 65 Nf4± ±.

62 Nf4   Bd1

63 Bg6 Nc7 64 Bh5 Bxh5 65 Nxh5 Kb6 66 Nf4 Ne8 67 h5 Kc7 68 h6 Nd6 69 h7 Kd7 70 Kf6
1-0

1409   I. Kopilov–AK

R9: 19.5.1970: Sicilian

1 e4 c5 2 Nf3 e6 3 d4 cd 4 Nxd4 Nc6 5 Nc3 a6 6 Be2 Qc7 7 OO b5 8 Nxc6 Qxc6 9 Bf3 Bb7 10 Re1 Ne7 11 e5 Qc7 12 Bxb7 Qxb7 13 Ne4 Nf5 14 Nf3 Qc6 15 c3 Be7 16 Bg5 OO 17 Bxe7 Nxe7 18 Rad1 Nd5 19 Rd4 h6 ½-½

1410   AK–Anikayev

R10: 21.5.1970: Spanish

1 e4 e5 2 Nf3 Nc6 3 Bb5 a6 4 Bxc6 dc 5 OO f6 6 d4 Bg4 7 de Qxd1 8 Rxd1 Bxf3 9 gf fe 10 f4 Bd6 11 Nd2 ef 12 Nc4 OOO 13 Nxd6+ cd 14 Bxf4 Nf6 15 f3 d5 16 Bg5 de ½-½

1411   Tseshkovsky–AK

R11: 22.5.1970: Sicilian

1 e4 c5 2 Nf3 e6 3 d4 cd 4 Nxd4 Nc6 5 Nb5 d6 6 c4 Nf6 7 N1c3 a6 8 Na3 Be7 9 Be2 OO 10 Be3 Qc7 11 Rc1 Rd8 12 OO Rb8 13 Qd2 Ne5 14 f3 b6 15 Rfd1 Bd7 16 Qe1 Be8 17 Qf1 Qb7 18 Rd2 Ned7 19 Nc2 Ne5 20 Na3 Ned7 21 Rcd1 Ne5 22 Kh1 Ng6 23 Nc2 b5 24 cb ab 25 a3 Ne5 26 Nd4 b4 27 ab Qxb4 28 Ndb5 Bxb5 29 Nxb5 d5 30 Bf4 Bd6 31 Nxd6 Qxd6 32 g4 Rb4 33 Bg3 Qb8 34 Qf2

♖×b2 35 ♕d4 ♖×d2 36 ♕×d2 ♘e8 37 g5 d4 38 ♕a5 f6 39 gf gf 40 ♖g1 ♘g7 41 ♕d2 ♔c7 42 f4 ♘c6 43 f5 ♕e7 44 ♗c4 ♔h8 45 fe ♘×e6 46 ♗d5 ♘e5 47 ♕f2 d3 48 ♗×e5 fe 49 ♕g3 ♘g7 50 ♕×d3 ♘h5 51 ♗b3 ½-½

1412   AK–A. Zaitsev

R12: 25.5.1970: Caro Kann

(Notes by De Villiers)

1 e4 c6 2 d4 d5 3 ♘c3 de 4 ♘×e4 ♘d7 5 ♘f3 ♘gf6 6 ♘×f6+ ♘×f6 7 ♘e5 ♗f5 8 c3 e6 9 g4!? ♗g6 10 h4 ♗d6 11 ♕e2 (11 h5 fails to 11 . . . ♗e4 12 f3 ♗×e5.) **11 . . . c5!? 12 h5?** (12 ♗g2) **12 . . . ♗e4 13 f3 cd!** (The bishop on e4 has an ideal retreat square at d5, and the immediate 14 cd? is very bad because of 14 . . . ♗b4+ and 15 . . . ♕×d4.) **14** ♕b5+ **♘d7! 15** ♘×f7! (The best practical chance. The alternatives are all clearly in Black's favour.) **15 . . . ♗g3+ 16** ♔e2 (Nimzowitsch used to say 'My king likes going for walks'. This one is going on a very long journey.) **16 . . . d3+ ?** (He should have played 16 . . . ♕f6! when after 17 fe ♕×f7! the threatened queen entry gives White severe problems.) **17** ♔e3! ♕f6 (Now 17 . . . ♔×f7 is better.) **18** ♔×e4 ♕×f7 (*108*)

19 ♖h3 a6 20 ♕g5 h6? (Kotov and Godes both question this and give Black a win with 20 . . . e5 21 ♖×g3 ♘c5+ 22 ♔e3 00 23 ♖h3 ♖ad8 24 ♗d2 ♘e4! 25 ♔×e4

108
18B
W

♕d5+ 26 ♔e3 ♕c5+ 27 ♔e4 ♖d4+ .) **21** ♕e3! (White must be careful. 21 ♕g6? ♘c5+ 22 ♔e3 ♗f4+ 23 ♔f2 ♕×g6 24 hg d2∓ ∓) **21 . . . e5** (Black gets no win from 21 . . . ♘f6+ 22 ♔×d3 ♘×g4 23 fg, ♕×f1+ 24 ♔c2 ♕×h3 as then 25 ♕×e6+ leads to a draw by perpetual check.) **22** ♔×d3 ♗f4 **23** ♕g1 000 **24** ♔c2 ♗×c1 **25** ♖×c1! (Much better than 25 ♔×c1 ♕f4+ 26 ♔c2 e4 27 fe ♘e5 when Black once again has a good attacking position. So Karpov returns the pawn to gain the initiative and 'his sort of position'.) **25 . . .** ♕×a2 **26** ♖h2 ♖hf8 **27** ♖d2! ♕a4+ **28** ♔b1± (home at last!) **28 . . .** ♕c6 **29** ♗d3 (Karpov plays with great energy; the threat of the pin by 30 ♗f5 is sufficient to save his f-pawn.) **29 . . .** ♔c7 **30** ♗e4 ♕b6 31 ♕h2 ♖de8 32 ♖cd1 ♘f6 33 ♗g6 ♖e7 34 ♖e1 (Karpov systematically piles up the pressure on the unfortunate e-pawn.) **34 . . .** ♕b5 35 ♖de2 ♘d7 36 ♗f5!± ♖×f5 37 gf ♕d3+ 38 ♔a1 ♕×f5 39 ♕h4! ♘f6 40 ♕c4+ ♔d8 (or 40 . . . ♔b8 41

♕c5) **41 ♕c5 ♘d7 42 ♕d5 ♔c8
43 ♖e4 b5** (otherwise 44 ♖c4+ or
44 ♖b4 will be crushing.) **44
♕c6+ ♔d8 45 ♕×a6 ♕×h5 46
f4! ♕f5 47 ♕a8+ ♔c7 48 ♕a5+
♔c6 49 c4 b4 50 ♕×b4 ♖e6 51
fe± ± ♔c7 52 ♕a5+ ♔b7 53
♕b5+ ♖b6 54 ♕d5+ ♔c7 55
♔b1 ♕f2 56 ♖4e2 ♕f5+ 57 ♕e4
♕×e4+ 58 ♖×e4 ♘c5 59 ♖4e3
♘e6 60 ♔c2 g5 61 ♔c3 h5 62 b4
♖a6 63 c5 ♖a3+ 64 ♔c4 ♖×e3
65 ♖×e3 h4 66 b5 ♔d8 67 b6
♔d7 68 ♖d3+ ♔c8 69 ♖d6 h3
70 ♖×e6 g4 71 ♖h6 1–0**

1413 Averkin–AK

R13: 26.5.1970: Torre

1 d4 ♘f6 2 ♘f3 b6 3 ♗g5 e6 4 e4 h6
5 ♗×f6 ♕×f6 6 ♗d3 ♗b7 7 00 d6
8 ♘c3 ♘d7 9 ♖e1 a6 10 ♕d2 ♕d8
11 ♕f4 c5 12 dc ♘×c5 13 ♖ad1
♕f6 14 ♕e3 ♗e7 15 ♗f1 ♕g6 16
b4 ♗d7 17 ♘a4 00 18 c4 a5 19 b5
♖ab8 20 ♘d4 ♘c5 21 ♘×c5 dc 22
♘c6 ♗×c6 23 bc e5 24 c7 ♖bc8 25
♖d7 ♕c6 26 ♖ed1 ♖×c7 27 ♕h3
♖×d7 28 ♕×d7 ½–½

1414 AK–Pozdnyakov

R14: 27.5.1970: Sicilian

1 e4 c5 2 ♘f3 e6 3 d4 cd 4 ♘×d4 a6
5 ♗d3 d6 6 00 g6 7 ♗e3 ♗g7 8 f4
♘c6 9 ♘×c6 bc 10 c3 ♘e7 11 ♘d2
♖b8 12 ♖b1 00 13 ♕e2 a5 14 a4 f5
15 ♔h1 ♕c7 16 ♘f3 fe 17 ♗×e4 c5
18 ♗d3 ♗d7 19 ♗b5 ♘d5 20 ♘g5
h6 21 ♗×d7 ♕×d7 22 ♘e4 (*109*)

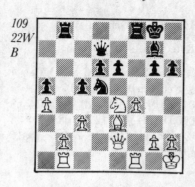

*109
22W
B*

22 ... ♖b6 23 ♖a1 ♕e7 24 ♖f2
♖fb8 25 ♗c1 ♘f6 26 ♘g3 ♕f7 27
♖f3 h5 28 c4 h4 29 ♘f1 d5 30 ♕e1
dc 31 ♕×a5 ♕e7 32 ♕e1 ♘d5 33
♕e4 c3 34 bc ♗×c3 35 ♖a2 ♕f6
36 a5 ♖b1 37 ♕c2 ♗d4 38 a6
♖1b6 39 ♗d2 ♖a8 40 ♕c4 ♘b4
41 ♗×b4 ♖×b4 42 ♕c2 ♕f5 43
♕d2 ♕e4 44 h3 ♖b1 45 ♕a5 c4 46
♕g5 ♕f5 47 ♕×h4 c3 48 ♕e7 ♗f6
49 ♕c7 ♕b5 50 ♔h2 ♕d5 51 ♖g3
g5 52 ♖a5 ♕×a5 53 ♕×a5 c2 54
♖×g5+ ♗×g5 55 ♕×g5+ ♔h7
56 ♕h5+ ♔g7 57 ♕e5+ 1–0

1415 Pavlyutin–AK

R15: 29.5.1970: Queen's Indian

1 d4 ♘f6 2 ♘f3 b6 3 c4 e6 4 e3 ♗b7
5 ♗d3 ♗e7 6 00 00 7 ♘c3 d5 8 cd
ed 9 ♘e5 c5 10 ♕e2 ♘c8 11 ♗d2
♘c6 12 ♖ac1 ♕e6 13 f4 ♖fe8 14
♘b5 ♕c8 15 dc bc 16 ♗e1 a6 17
♘c3 ♕e6 18 ♗g3 ♗d6 19 ♘a4 c4
20 ♗b1 ♘×e5 21 fe ♗×e5 22 ♘c5
♕b6 23 ♘×b7 ♕×b7 24 ♗×e5
♖×e5 25 ♖×f6 gf 26 ♖f1 ♕b6 27
♖f3 ♖ae8 28 ♖g3+ ♔f8 29 ♕g4
♖×e3 30 ♕g7+ ♔e7 0–1

1416 AK–Dementiev

R16. 30.5.1970: Spanish

1 e4 e5 2 ♘f3 ♘c6 3 ♗b5 a6 4 ♗×c6 dc 5 00 f6 6 d4 ed 7 ♘×d4 c5 8 ♘b3 ♕×d1 9 ♖×d1 ♗d7 10 ♘c3 000 11 ♗f4 ♗e6 12 ♖×d8+ ♔×d8 13 ♖d1+ ♔c8 14 ♘d5 ♗×d5 ½–½

1417 Antoshin–AK

R17: 1.6.1970: Queen's Indian

1 d4 ♘f6 2 c4 e6 3 ♘f3 b6 4 g3 ♗b7 5 ♗g2 ♗e7 6 00 00 7 ♘c3 ♘e4 8 ♘×e4 ♗×e4 9 ♘e1 ♗×g2 10 ♘×g2 d5 11 ♕a4 dc 12 ♕×c4 c5 13 dc ♗×c5 14 ♗e3 ♗×e3 15 ♘×e3 ½–½

15 Caracas 19.6-12.7.1970

Presidente de la Republica

		1	2	3	4	5	6	7	8	9	0	1	2	3	4	5	6	7	8	
1	Kavalek	×	½	0	1	½	1	½	1	½	½	½	1	1	1	1	1	1	1	**13**
2	Panno	½	×	½	½	½	½	½	1	½	½	½	1	1	½	1	1	1	1	**12**
3	Stein	1	½	×	1	½	½	½	½	1	½	0	1	½	½	1	1	1	1	**12**
4	Benko	0	½	0	×	½	½	½	1	1	½	1	½	½	1	1	1	1	1	**11½**
5	Ivkov	½	½	½	½	×	1	½	½	½	½	½	½	1	1	1	1	½	1	**11½**
6	**Karpov**	0	½	½	½	0	×	1	½	1	½	½	1	½	1	1	1	1	1	**11½**
7	Parma	½	½	½	½	½	0	×	½	½	½	1	½	½	½	½	1	1	1	**10**
8	Sigurjonsson	0	0	½	0	½	½	½	×	1	½	1	½	1	½	½	1	1	1	**10**
9	Barcza	½	½	0	0	½	0	½	0	×	½	1	½	1	1	½	1	1	1	**9½**
10	Bisguier	½	½	½	½	½	½	½	½	½	×	½	½	½	0	½	1	1	1	**9½**
11	Addison	½	½	1	0	½	½	0	0	0	½	×	½	½	½	1	1	1	½	**8½**
12	O'Kelly	0	0	0	½	½	0	½	½	½	½	½	×	½	1	½	1	½	1	**8**
13	Ciocaltea	0	0	½	½	0	½	½	0	0	½	½	½	×	1	1	½	1	½	**7½**
14	Cuellar	0	½	½	0	0	0	½	½	0	1	½	0	0	×	½	½	½	1	**6**
15	Yepez	0	0	0	0	0	0	½	½	½	½	0	½	0	½	×	½	1	1	**5½**
16	Villaroel	0	0	0	0	0	0	0	0	0	0	0	0	½	½	½	×	½	1	**3**
17	Caro	0	0	0	0	½	0	0	0	0	0	0	½	0	½	0	½	×	1	**3**
18	Slujssar	0	0	0	0	0	0	0	0	0	0	½	0	½	0	0	0	0	×	**1**

In One Bound

A. Roshal

Anatoly Karpov obtained the grandmaster norm at the first attempt. This tournament in the capital of Venezuela was in itself interesting, but the most significant aspect of it was the success of the 19-year-old Soviet player.

Anatoly, quite tired after two hard events (prior to Caracas there was Kuibyshev, where Karpov won the title of RSFSR Champion), hurried home to Tula.

The Karpov's flat is still only beginning to resemble the home of a great sportsman. There is a silver cup for winning the World Junior Championship, and behind the glassware, amidst the crockery (a special place, for the time being, not having been devised), are medals. One of them, gold, for excellent work at school.

In almost every home there is a family album; old photographs, reminiscences and old tales . . . Nina Grigorievna proudly calls her collection her son's 'archives', but shows it seemingly with the fear that 'Tolik' will accuse his mother of immodesty.

It was in his native town in the Urals, Zlatoust, that Anatoly took his first steps in chess. To begin with, when he was seven, he won the third category title, and later on all his sporting ambitions, with the exception of the second category title, at the first attempt. All this time he always worked well at school. His achievements are by no means solely in the field of chess; there were photos of the ten-year-old Anatoly with the Red Banners of the All-Russian Young Pioneer camp 'Orlenok', and a document, presented to Karpov in the seventh class of Zlatoust School No. 3, on which it stated that he was awarded the title of 'honoured pupil', and so he went down in the annals of the school. All this, together with his success in the Tula technical and mathematics olympics, precisely characterize Anatoly Karpov – a talented youth, a conscientious person, whose name is noted in the roll of honour of the Central Committee of the Young Communist League. Although externally everything is at the summit it is easy to overlook the thoughtful and tense work that has gone into it.

He is no robot, it is in his nature to be 'carried away'. He collects stamps – on the currently most popular themes of the cosmos and sport. Abroad (Anatoly has already been abroad seven times) he always acquires catalogues and more stamps, though at home he spends little time on them. This hobby is of some use for his future speciality – the political economy of foreign countries.

One of the reasons for his recent move from the Moscow State University to Leningrad University was the desire to live nearer his trainer, Semyon Furman, whom he holds in very high esteem and to whom is due no little part of the responsibility for Karpov's recent ascents.

'I have already played forty games this year, two of which I lost (in Caracas), which will suffice for the time being. Altogether in the last two years,' Karpov counts them up precisely, 'I have played 140 official games with the result $+ 75 - 9 = 56$. Now I have scored $11\frac{1}{2}$ points, but if these points had not amounted to the grandmaster title they would not have been satisfactory.'

Karpov is sober, rational, I might say has a practical outlook on life and on chess. The world's youngest grandmaster is a position player to the core.

Until the tournament in Caracas, Karpov had only played a total of five games against grandmasters: Gipslis, Krogius, A. Zaitsev and twice against Antoshin (+ 2 − 1 = 2). The young player confesses that from the very first he has exhausted his imagination in play against the bearers of the highest chess title.

1501   AK–Bisguier

R1: 20.6.1970: Spanish

(Notes by Karpov)

1 e4 e5 2 ♘f3 ♘c6 3 ♗b5 ♘f6 4 ♕e2 ♗e7 5 c3 d6 6 d4 ♘d7 7 00 00 8 ♘bd2 (I probably should have played 8 d5, but, for the time being, I was not concentrating properly.) 8 ... ♗f6 9 d5 ♘e7 10 ♗d3 c6 11 c4 a5 12 b3 g6 13 ♗a3 c5 14 ♗b2 ♗g7 15 g3 ♔h8 16 ♖ae1 (As long as Black cannot play f7–f5, there is no sense in White being in a hurry.) 16 ... ♘f6 17 ♘h4 ♘fg8 18 ♘g2 a4 19 f4 f6 20 ♘e3 ♘h6 21 ♗c3 ab 22 ab ♗h3 23 ♖f2 ♗d7 24 ♕f1 (covering h3) 24 ... ♘f7 25 f5 g5 26 ♗e2 ♘g8 (Here I began to rush things. Before opening the file I should have put my king on h1 and doubled rooks.) 27 h4 gh 28 gh ♗h6 (I had not taken this possibility into account!) 29 ♗h5 ♕e7 30 ♔h1 ♗f4 31 ♕h3 b5 32 cb ♗×b5 33 ♘dc4 ♗×e3 (Necessary. Otherwise ♘a5 and ♘ec4±) 34 ♘×e3 ♖a3 35 ♗d1 ♘gh6 36 ♗b2 ♖a2 37 ♗h5 ♖g8 38 ♘d1 ♖aa8 39 ♘c3 ♗d7 40 ♗c1 ♖ab8 41 ♗d1 ♖a8 42 ♘e2 ♖a2 43 ♖g1 ♖×g1+

44 ♔×g1 ♗b5 45 ♘c3 ♖×f2 46 ♔×f2 ♗a6 47 ♘b1 (I could not decide what to do next. It was only later, after the second adjournment, that we – Stein and I – established that in order to realize the advantage, it is necessary to exchange queens.) 47 ... ♕b7 48 ♕c3 ♘g8 49 ♗h5 ♘gh6 50 ♘d2 ♘g8 51 ♔e1 ♘gh6 52 ♔d1 ♗b5 (Now if 53 ♔c2 then 53 ... ♕a6 with the threat ... ♗e2, after which it would be impossible to punch a hole through Black's position.) 53 ♘f3 ♕a6 54 ♘g5 (*110*)

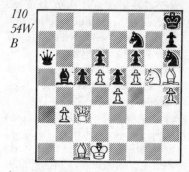

110
54W
B

(Still I could not see the right plan. It is interesting that three or four days later Bisguier told me that he could have drawn straight away with 54 ... fg 55 hg ♗e8! 56 ♗e2

♗b5 57 ♗h5, and that he felt unhappy about the thirty superfluous moves. But when I played 54 ♘g5 it was after 1 a.m. and, I can honestly say, I was totally unable to think anything out.) 54 ... ♗e8 55 ♗e2 ♗b5 56 ♗h5 ♗e8 (Finally getting the chance to adjourn, I sealed . . .) 57 ♘f3 (At 10 a.m. the same morning we resumed play.) 57 ... ♗b5 58 ♘e1 ♕a2 59 ♕b2 ♕a5 60 ♗d2 ♕a7 61 ♕c3 ♕a2 62 ♘c2 c4 63 bc ♗×c4 64 ♕a3 (After the game had finished my opponent told me that he could have exchanged queens here with an easy draw. But I do not think it is as simple as that.) 64 ... ♕b1+ 65 ♔c1 (Now he must exchange queens or give up a piece. The grandmaster preferred the second possibility.) 65 ... ♕b3 66 ♗×h6 ♕d3+ 67 ♗d2 ♕×e4 68 ♕a3 (68 ♘e3 ♗b3+ 69 ♔e2 ♗×d5 70 ♕c7 and then ♗c1–a3 would have been much better.) 68 ... ♗×d5 69 ♘e3 ♕×h4 70 ♗×f7 ♗×f7 71 ♕×d6 ♕a4+ 72 ♔e1 ♕h4+ 73 ♔d1 ♕a4+ 74 ♔c1 (The checks could have been avoided with 74 ♔e2.) 74 ... ♕a1+ 75 ♔c2 ♕a4+ 76 ♔d3 ♕b5+ 77 ♔e4 ♕b7+ 78 ♘d5 ♕b1+ 79 ♔e3 ♕g1+ 80 ♔d3 ♗×d5! 81 ♕×f6+ ♔g7 82 ♕d8+ ♕g8 83 ♕e7 ♔g3+ 84 ♗e3 h5 ½–½

This long and rather boring game demonstrates the exhausting character of the struggle at the very start of the tournament. However, I

was not too upset by the draw because, during the adjournments, I had managed to defeat the experienced Hungarian grandmaster Barcza and also grandmaster Parma.

1502 Barcza–AK

R2: 21.6.1970: English

(Notes by Ivkov and Karpov)

1 ♘f3 c5 2 c4 g6 3 g3 ♗g7 4 ♗g2 ♘c6 5 ♘c3 e5 6 d3 ♘ge7 7 0-0 0-0 8 ♘e1 (8 a3 f5!) 8 . . . ♖b8 (8 . . . d6 is also worth a try,) 9 ♘c2 a6 10 ♖b1 d6 (10 . . . b5 11 cb ab 12 b4 cb 13 ♘×b4 ♘×b4 14 ♖×b4 ♕a5 15 a3±) 11 b4 ♗e6 12 bc dc 13 ♘e3± b6 14 ♘ed5 ♗d7 (! Karpov) 15 ♗d2 ♘×d5 16 ♘×d5 ♘e7 17 ♕c1? (better 17 a4) 17 . . . ♘×d5 18 ♗×d5? ♗h3 19 ♖e1? (*111*)

111
19W
B

19 . . . b5! 20 a3 ♕d6 21 ♗f3? (21 e4 was preferable.) 21 . . . ♗e6 22 cb? ab 23 ♗e3 ♖fc8∓ 24 ♕d2 b4! 25 ab cb 26 ♗a7 ♖b5 27 ♖fc1 ♖×c1+ 28 ♕×c1 b3 29 ♕c6?? ♕×c6 30 ♗×c6 ♖a5 31 ♗e3 ♖a2

32 ♗b5 b2 33 ♔g2 e4 (! Karpov) 34 d4 ♗b3 **0–1**

1503 AK–Parma

R3: 22.6.1970: Nimzo-Indian
(Notes by Karpov)

1 c4 ♘f6 2 ♘c3 e6 3 d4 ♗b4 4 ♕c2 (When I came to the board I could not help thinking that in the next two rounds weaker opponents awaited me. I already had '+ 1' and there was no need to take risks right in the opening. To be quite frank, I would not have been terribly worried only to draw.) 4 ... 00 5 ♘f3 c5 6 dc ♘a6 7 ♗d2 ♘×c5 8 e3 b6 9 ♗e2 ♗b7 10 00 d6 11 ♖fd1 a6? 12 b3 e5 13 a3 ♗×c3 14 ♗×c3 ♕e7 15 ♘e1 ♖ac8 16 ♖ac1 ♘fe4 (Here I began to realize that to play passively for a draw was no longer possible.) 17 b4 ♘×c3 18 ♕×c3 ♘e6? (I dare say that it was because of this mistake that Black lost. The knight on e6 has nothing to do.) 19 ♕d3 ♖fd8 20 ♗f3! ♗×f3 21 ♘×f3 g6 22 ♘d2 ♘c7 23 ♘e4 ♘e8 24 ♕d5 ♔g7 25 h3 ♘f6 26 ♘×f6 ♔×f6 27 ♕e4 ♔g7 28 ♖d5 ♕c7 (It is doubtful whether White could succeed in winning by the standard method of ♕d3, e4 etc. Sensing this, I found what is, in my opinion, a very interesting solution to the position.) 29 f4 ♖e8 30 fe de 31 c5 ♖e6 32 ♕d3 bc 33 bc ♕c6 34 ♖b1 ♕c7 35 ♖f1 ♖f8 36 ♔h1 ♕c6 37 ♖b1 ♕c7 38 e4 ♖b8 39 ♖f1 ♖b7 40 ♕c3 ♖b5 41 a4 ♖b8 42 ♖c1

♖c8 43 ♖b1 ♔g8 44 ♖bd1 ♕e7 45 ♖f1 ♖c7 46 a5 ♖ec6 47 ♖c1 (*112*)

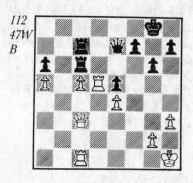

112
47W
B

47 ... f6? (Aha, the enemy can't stand the pressure!) 48 ♕d2 ♔f7 49 ♔h2 ♔e8 50 ♖d6 ♖d7 51 ♖d1 ♖c×d6 52 cd ♕e6 53 ♕d3 ♕a2 54 ♕×a6 ♕c2 55 ♕a8+ ♔f7 56 ♕d5+ ♔g7 (Deciding that my opponent was making moves out of inertia and he was about to resign, I played on at lightning speed. Meanwhile 57 a6 ♕a4 58 ♕d3 ♕c6 59 ♖a1 won immediately.) 57 ♖d2 ♕c3 58 ♖a2? h5! (Creating the threat of perpetual check after ... h4. It has become clear that my rook is wrongly placed on the second rank – its right place is on the first or third rank. It took me a long time – 40 minutes – to seal the most difficult move ...) 59 ♖d2! (Truly, for many players, to make a 'return' move is the most difficult of all. The remainder is simple.) 59 ... h4 60 ♖d1 ♕c2 61 a6 ♕a4 62 ♕d3 g5 63 ♖b1 f5 64 ♖b7 g4 65 hg fg 66 ♕e2 **1–0**

1504 Slujssar–AK

R4: 23.6.1970: QP-London

1 d4 ♘f6 2 ♘f3 c5 3 c3 b6 4 ♗f4
♗b7 5 ♘bd2 g6 6 h3 ♗g7 7 e3 00 8
♗d3 d5 9 00 ♘bd7 10 ♖e1 a6 11
♗h2 b5 12 e4 cd 13 cd de 14 ♘×e4
♘d5 15 ♕b3 ♕b6 16 ♘c3 ♘7f6 17
♖ad1 ♖ac8 18 ♗e5 ♘×c3 19 bc
♗d5 20 ♕b2 ♕c6 21 ♖e3 ♕×c3
22 ♕e2 ♕b4 23 a3 ♕a4 24 ♗f4
♗b3 **0–1**

1505 AK–Cuellar

R5: 25.6.1970: Sicilian

(Notes by Karpov)

1 e4 c5 2 ♘c3 ♘c6 3 g3 g6 4 ♗g2
♗g7 5 d3 e6 6 f4 d6 7 ♘f3 ♘ge7 8
00 00 9 ♖b1 ♖b8 10 a3 b5 11 ♗d2
a6 12 b4 cb 13 ab ♗b7 14 ♕e1?!
♘d4 15 ♘×d4 ♗×d4+ 16 ♔h1
♗g7 17 ♘d1 ♖c8 18 ♖c1 ♕d7 19
♗c3 ♗×c3 20 ♘×c3 ♖c7 21 ♘d1
f5 22 ♖f2 d5 23 ♖e2 ♘c6 24 ed ed
25 ♕c3 ♕d6 26 ♖b1 d4 27 ♕b3+
♔g7 28 ♘f2 ♖f7 29 ♖e6 ♕d7 30
♖be1 ♘d8 31 ♖6e2 ♗×g2+ 32

113
35W
B

♔×g2 ♕d6 33 ♘h3 ♖fe7 34 ♘g1
♖×e2+ 35 ♖×e2 (*113*)
35 . . . ♘f7? 36 ♘f3 ♖c3 37 ♕b1
♕d5? 38 ♕g1 ♕c6 39 ♕×d4+
♔h6 40 ♕f2 g5 41 ♔g1 ♖a3 42
♖e1 gf 43 ♘d4 ♕c7 44 gf ♕d8 45
♘×f5+ ♔g6 46 ♕c5 ♕f6 47 ♘d4
♔g7 48 ♔h1 h6 49 ♖g1+ ♔h7 50
♕f8 **1–0**

1506 Benko–AK

R6: 26.6.1970: Queen's Indian

1 d4 ♘f6 2 c4 e6 3 ♘f3 b6 4 g3 ♗b7
5 ♗g2 ♗e7 6 ♘c3 ♘e4 7 ♗d2 d5 8
♘e5 00 9 cd ♘×e3 10 ♗×e3 ed 11
♕a4 ♕d6 12 00 ♖d8 13 ♖ad1 ½–½

1507 AK–O'Kelly

R7: 27.6.1970: Spanish

(Notes by Karpov and Holmov)
1 e4 e5 2 ♘f3 ♘c6 3 ♗b5 a6 4 ♗a4
♘f6 5 00 ♗e7 6 ♖e1 b5 7 ♗b3 d6 8
c3 00 9 h3 ♘b8 10 d4 ♘bd7 11
♘bd2 (I refrained from the more
committal 11 ♘h4 and 11 c4 from
purely practical considerations . . .
opposite me sat a theoretical
expert.) 11 . . . ♗b7 12 ♗c2 ♖e8 13
♘f1 ♗f8 14 ♘g3 g6 15 a4 ♗g7 16
♗d3 d5 (16 . . . c6 is more reliable –
Holmov. Here I thought up a little
trick . . .) 17 ♗g5! (It turns out that
this move practically forces the win
of a pawn.) 17 . . . de 18 ♗×e4
♗×e4 19 ♘×e4 ed 20 ♘×d4 c5
(The threat was 21 ♘c6.) 21 ♗×f6!
♘×f6 (O'Kelly, some way back,
had not seen that 21 . . . ♗×f6
would be unplayable because of 22

♘c6 and 23 ♕×d7.) 22 ♘×c5
♖×e1+ 23 ♕×e1 b4 (*114*)

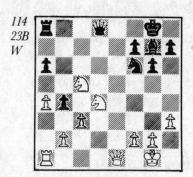

114
23B
W

24 ♖c1? (Right now I still do not
know precisely what I should have
played, but 24 ♖c1 was not much
use, that I do know – Karpov. 24
♖d1 bc 25 ♕×c3 ♖c8! 26 b4 ♘e4
27 ♕e1! – Holmov.) 24 . . . bc 25 bc
(This weakening of the Q-side
compensates Black for the missing
pawn – Holmov.) 25 . . . ♕d5 26
♘db3 ♗f8 27 ♕d1 ♕×d1+ 28
♖×d1 ♖c8 (After some unfortunate moves by White, O'Kelly
has obtained the moral right to offer
a draw, but I refused.) 29 ♘×a6
♖×c3 30 ♖b1 ♗d6 31 ♖d1 ♗f8
32 ♖b1 ♘d7? (I was already
prepared to agree a draw, but the
venerable grandmaster wants, by
taking advantage of the time
scramble, to trap my knight. This
was all that was necessary for
White. – Karpov. 32 . . . ♗d6!= –
Holmov.) 33 a5 ♖c6 34 ♖d1 ♘e5
35 ♖d5 ♘c4 36 ♘b8 ♖c8 37 ♘d7
♗e7 38 ♘b6 ♖c6 39 ♘×c4 ♖×c4
40 a6 ♖a4 41 ♖a5 **1–0**

1508   Ivkov–AK

R8: 29.6.1970: QGD

(Notes by Karpov)

1 ♘f3 ♘f6 2 c4 e6 3 ♘c3 d5 4 d4
♗e7 5 ♗g5 OO 6 e3 h6 7 ♗h4 b6 8
♗d3 ♗b7 9 OO c5 10 ♕e2 cd 11 ed
♘c6 12 ♖ad1? ♘b4 13 ♗b1 dc 14
♘e5 ♖c8 15 a3 ♘bd5 16 ♗×f6
  Here Ivkov offered a draw.
  In the street (the previous day,
Karpov and Stein had been taking
a stroll through the town and had
met Ivkov, who, upon seeing
Karpov, had called out 'already a
grandmaster!' – KJO'C), in answer
to the retort of the Yugoslav
grandmaster, I had observed that
much could still change. I was
right!
  The sporting result, the outcome
of my first games against the
grandmasters was very reassuring.
Analysis of the crosstable showed
that if I could avoid defeat against
Ivkov, Panno, Kavalek and Stein
(far off – in the penultimate
round!), there would even be real
chances of first place.
  I had wanted to get a draw,
offered to me by a participant in the
USSR–World match, up until the
grandmaster lost a pawn. Now I
somehow replied 'No', but I could
not play safely – my mind was
working hazily. Ivkov, on the other
hand, began to play with great
vigour, and within a few moves the
game which brought me not only

my first zero, but also a long depression, was decided.

16 ...   ♗×f6?

A mistake. I should have liquidated the dangerous knight with 16 ... ♘×c3!

17 ♕c2   ♖e8
18 ♕h7+   ♔f8
19 ♘e4   ♖c7
20 ♖fe1   c3

I did not sense the danger, otherwise I would have played 20 ... ♘f4.

21 ♘g3!

The terrible combinational motif ♘f5 appears, but even now all is not lost. It seems to me that 21 ... g6! gets a draw. Ivkov also, by the way, thought this. In view of the threats ... ♗g7 and ... ♘f6, it seems that White is forced to take perpetual check by 22 ♗×g6 ♗×e5 23 ♖×e5 fg.

21 ...   ♘e7
22 ♕h8+   ♘g8
23 ♗h7 (*115*)

115
23W
B

23 ...   ♗×e5?

After the game Ivkov showed me the wonderful variation: 23 ...

♔e7 24 ♘f5+ ef 25 ♘c6++ ♔d7 26 ♘×d8 g6!! 27 ♖×e8 ♗×h8 28 ♖×g8 c2 29 ♖c1 ♗×d4 30 ♘×b7 ♗×b2 31 ♖×c2 ♖×c2 and Black has an excellent position!

24 ♘f5!   ef
25 ♕×g8+   ♔e7
26 ♖×e5+   ♔f6
27 ♖×f5+   ♔e6
28 ♖e1+   ♔d7
29 ♖×e8   **1-0**

1509   AK–Panno

R9: 30.6.1970: Sicilian

(Notes by Karpov)

1 e4 c5 2 ♘f3 e6 3 d4 cd 4 ♘×d4 a6 5 ♗d3 ♗c5 6 c3 d6 7 0-0 ♘f6 8 ♕e2 ♘bd7 9 ♔h1? ♘e5 10 ♗c2 ♗d7 11 a4 ♖c8 12 ♘a3 0-0 13 f4 ♗×d4 14 cd ♘c6 15 ♕d2 d5 16 e5 ♘g4 17 ♗d1? ♕h4 18 h3 ♘h6 19 ♗c2 ♘f5 20 ♖f3 ♘g3+ 21 ♔h2 ♘e4 22 ♕e2 f5 23 ♗d2 ♗e8 24 ♖d3 ♗f7 25 ♕e1 ♕d8 26 ♘a3 ♖fc7 27 ♗f3 ♕e7 28 ♗d1 h6 29 ♖c1 ♕d8 30 ♘e3 g5 31 ♖c2 ♖g7 32 g3 ♘e7 33 ♖×c8 ♕×c8 34 ♗e1 ♘g6 35 ♘b1 ♕d8 36 ♘d2 gf 37 gf ♘h4 38 ♘×e4 fe 39 ♗×h4 ♕×h4 40 ♖d2 ♗h5 41 ♗×h5 ♕×h5 42 ♖g2 ♖×g2+ 43 ♔×g2 ♕f7 44 ♕g3 ♕e2+ 45 ♕f2 ♕h5 46 ♕g3 a5 47 ♕g4 ♕g6 48 ♔g3 ½-½

1510   Kavalek–AK

R10: 1.7.1970: Spanish

(Notes by Kavalek and Karpov)

1 e4 e5 2 ♘f3 ♘c6 3 ♗b5 a6 4 ♗a4

♘f6 5 00 ♗e7 6 ♖el b5 7 ♗b3 d6 8 c3 00 9 h3 ♘a5 10 ♗c2 c5 11 d4 ♕c7 12 ♘bd2 ♘c6 13 dc dc 14 ♘fl ♗e6 15 ♘e3 ♖ad8 16 ♕e2 c4 17 ♘f5 ♖fe8 18 ♘3h4! ♔h8 19 ♘×e7! ♕×e7 20 ♕f3 ♘d7 21 ♘f5 ♕f8 22 ♗e3 ♘c5? (I was thinking that Black should play 22 . . . f6 – Kavalek.) 23 ♖edl? (I just picked up my rook without looking at the position, and when I had the rook in my hand I saw the combination 23 ♘×g7! ♔×g7 24 ♗h6+ ! ♔×h6 25 ♕f6+ ♔h5 26 g4+ ♗×g4 27 hg+ ♔×g4 28 ♖e3 and mate – Kavalek.) 23 . . . f6 24 ♖d6 ♖×d6 25 ♗×c5 ♖dl+ 26 ♖×dl ♕×c5 27 ♖d6! (*116*)

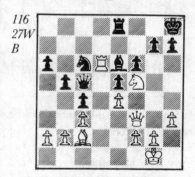

116
27W
B

27 . . . ♗f7 28 ♕dl ♘b8 29 ♖d8 ♕c7 (After the game Karpov told me that he had the better move 29 . . . ♕f8, and after 30 ♘d6 the choice between 30 . . . ♘c6 which is no good because of 31 ♘×e8 ♘×d8 32 ♘c7 winning a pawn, or 30 . . . ♗h5 after which I planned the queen sacrifice 31 ♘×e8!! ♗×dl 32 ♗×dl ♘c6 33 ♖a8 and after

White wins the black knight he has a clear advantage – Kavalek.) 30 ♘d6! (Three times on the same square. White now gets a winning endgame – Kavalek.) 30 . . . ♖×d8 31 ♘×f7+ ♕×f7 32 ♕×d8+ ♕g8 33 ♕d6 ♕e8 34 ♗dl h5 35 ♗e2 ♔h7 36 b3 cb 37 ab ♘c6 38 b4 ♔h6 39 h4 ♕c8 40 g3 ♔g6 (? Karpov) 41 ♕dl ♔f7 42 ♗×h5+ ♔e7 43 ♗g4 ♕c7 44 ♕d5 ♘d8 45 ♗f5 ♘f7 46 ♕e6+ ♔f8 47 ♕×a6 ♘d6 48 ♕a8+ ♔e7 49 ♕g8 ♘×f5 50 ef ♕×c3 51 ♕×g7+ ♔d6 52 ♕×f6+ ♔d5 53 ♕f7+ ♔e4 54 ♕b7+ ♔×f5 55 ♕×b5 ♕el+ 56 ♔g2 ♕e4+ 57 ♔h2 ♔g4 58 ♕d7+ ♔f3 59 ♕d2 **1-0**

1511   AK–Sigurjonsson

R11: 3.7.1970: Pirc

(Notes by Sigurjonsson and Karpov)

1 e4 g6 2 d4 d6 3 ♘c3 ♗g7 4 f3 c6 5 ♘ge2 b5 6 ♗e3 ♗b7 7 g4?! (7 ♕d2 ♘d7 8 ♘g3 ♘b6! is unclear.) 7 . . . h5! 8 g5 (? Karpov) 8 . . . e6 9 ♕d2 ♘e7 10 a4 b4 11 ♘dl a5 12 c3?! (12 h4!? ♗a6 13 ♘g3, again with an unclear position, is probably better.) 12 . . . bc 13 bc ♗a6! 14 ♘b2 (14 ♘g3? h4!∓) 14 . . . ♘d7 15 ♘cl (15 h4 ♕c7! is good for black, e.g. 16 ♘g3?! d5 17 e5 ♗×fl and 18 . . . 00∓ ; or 17 ♗f4?! e5!∓) 15 . . . ♗×fl 16 ♖×fl 00 17 ♗f4 e5 18 de ♘×e5 19 ♘cd3 ♘×d3+ 20 ♘×d3 ♕b6!∓ (*117*)

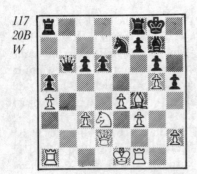

*117
20B
W*

21 ♗e3 (21 ♗×d6?! ♖fd8! 22
♗×e7? ♗×c3!∓∓ ; 22 ♗c5?! ♕a6!
23 ♖d1 ♕c4∓∓ ; 22 e5 ♘f5∓) 21
... c5 22 ♔f2 ♕b3 23 ♖fc1 ♖fd8
(23 ... ♖fb8!?) 24 ♘f4 d5 25 ♕c2
♕b8 26 ♖ab1 ♕d6 27 ♔g1 d4 (27
... de 28 fe!) 28 ♖d1 ♗e5 29 ♘h3
♕e6 30 cd ♕×h3? (30 ... cd!∓) 31
de ♕×f3 32 ♗×c5 ♕g4+ 33 ♔h1
♖×d1+ 34 ♖×d1 ♖c8 (not 34 ...
♕×g5?! 35 e6! fe 36 ♖g1 and 37
♗×e7±) 35 ♖f1! ♖×c5!= (35 ...
♕e6? 36 ♕f2!±) 36 ♕×c5 ♕×e4+
37 ♔g1 ♕g4+ 38 ♔h1 ♕e4+ ½-½

1512 AK–Villaroel

R12: 4.7.1970: English

1 c4 ♘f6 2 g3 g6 3 ♗g2 ♗g7 4 ♘c3
e6 5 e3 00 6 ♘ge2 e5 7 00 c6 8 f4
♖e8 9 h3 h5 10 e4 d5 11 cd cd 12 fe
♘×e4 13 d4 ♗e6 14 ♔h2 h4 15 gh
♘c6 16 h5 ♕h4 17 ♘×e4 de 18 hg
fg 19 ♖f4 ♕h5 20 ♖×e4 ♖ad8 21
♗f4 ♖f8 22 ♗g3 ♗d5 23 ♖h4
♕f5 24 ♗×d5+ ♖×d5 25 ♕b3
♕f7 26 ♖f4 **1-0**

1513 Yepez–AK

R13: 6.7.1970: Nimzo-Indian

(Notes by Karpov)

1 d4 ♘f6 2 c4 e6 3 ♘c3 ♗b4 4 e3 c5
5 ♗d3 00 6 ♘f3 d5 7 00 dc
♗×c4 ♘bd7 9 ♕e2 cd 10 ed b6 11
♖d1 ♗×c3? (I should have played
the normal 11 ... ♗b7.) 12 bc ♕c7
13 ♗a3 ♖e8 14 ♖ac1 ♗b7 15
♘e5! a6 16 f4? (A dubious move,
losing his opening advantage.) 16
... ♘d5 17 ♖f1 (*118*)

*118
17W
B*

(I now faced the dilemma: should I
retreat the knight, risking going
under to an attack; or allow the
creation of opposite coloured
bishops with the danger of a draw? I
decided on the latter course, and if
the worst had come to the worst
then I would have had to try for a
win against one of the stronger
players.) 17 ... f6! 18 ♘×d7 ♕×d7
19 ♗b3 b5 20 ♗c5 ♗c6 21 ♖f2 f5
22 ♕e5 ♖ac8 23 c4 bc 24 ♗×c4
♗b5 25 ♖b2 (He should not have
allowed the exchange of bishops.)
25 ... ♗×c4 26 ♖×c4 ♖c7 27

♖c1 ♖b7 28 ♖cb1 ♖×b2 29 ♖×b2 ♔f7 30 h3 h6 31 h4 ♖d8 32 g3 ♕c8 33 ♔h2 ♕a8 34 ♔g1 ♕c6 35 a3 ♖d7 36 ♔f2 ♘f6 37 ♕e1 ♘e4+ 38 ♔g1 ♘×c5 39 ♕c3 ♕e4 40 ♕×c5 (I was already starting to make my move, in this winning position, when I noticed that my opponent's flag had fallen. So why go any further? I claimed the game, but, unexpectedly, both my opponent and the controller protested – only the immediate intervention of several experienced players enabled this amusing conflict to be resolved.) **0–1** (time)

1514 AK–Caro

R14: 7.7.1970: English

(Notes by Karpov)

1 c4 e5 2 ♘c3 ♘f6 3 e4 ♗c5 4 g3 ♘c6 5 ♗g2 d6 6 h3 00 7 d3 h6 8 ♘f3 a5 9 00 ♘d4 10 ♘×d4 ♗×d4 11 ♔h2 c6 12 f4 ♔h7 13 ♕f3 a4 14 ♘e2 ♕b6 15 ♖b1 ♗c5 16 ♖d1 ♘e8 17 g4 f6 18 ♗d2 ♘c7 19 f5 ♖d8 20 h4 ♖h8 21 ♔g3? ♕g8 22 g5 hg? 23 hg ♔f7 24 ♖h1 ♗d7 25 ♕g4 ♖ag8 26 ♖×h8 ♖×h8 27 gf

♘e8 28 ♕g6+ ♔f8 29 fg+ ♘×g7 30 ♗h6 ♗f2+ 31 ♔f3 **1–0**

1515 Ciocaltea–AK

R15: 8.7.1970: Petroff

1 e4 e5 2 ♘f3 ♘f6 3 ♘×e5 d6 4 ♘f3 ♘×e4 5 ♕e2 ♕e7 6 d3 ♘f6 7 ♗g5 ♕×e2+ 8 ♗×e2 ♗e7 9 ♘bd2 ♘d5 10 ♗×e7 ♔×e7 11 000 ♘f4 12 ♗f1 h6 13 ♖e1+ ♔d8 14 h4 ♖e8 15 ♖×e8+ ♔×e8 16 g3 ♘e6 17 d4 ♘d7 18 ♗d3 ♘f6 ½–½

1516 AK–Stein

R16: 10(?).7.1970: French

1 e4 e6 2 d4 d5 3 ed ed 4 ♗f4 ♗f5 5 ♗d3 ♗×d3 6 ♕×d3 c6 7 ♘d2 ♗d6 8 ♗×d6 ♕×d6 9 ♘gf3 ♘e7 10 00 ♘d7 11 ♖e1 00 12 ♖e2 ♘g6 13 g3 ♖ae8 ½–½

1517 Addison–AK

R17: 11(?).7.1970: Petroff

1 e4 e5 2 ♘f3 ♘f6 3 ♘×e5 d6 4 ♘f3 ♘×e4 5 ♕e2 ♕e7 6 d3 ♘f6 7 ♗g5 ♕×e2+ 8 ♗×e2 ♗e7 9 ♘c3 c6 10 000 ♘a6 11 ♘e4 ♘×e4 12 de ♘c5 13 ♗×e7 ♔×e7 14 ♘d2 ½–½

16 USSR Armed Forces Team Championship Leningrad, 25.10-3.11.1970

Karpov played on board two (below Furman) for the Leningrad team which won this event (ahead of 7 other teams) with 33/49.

Not all of Karpov's games from this event are available, nor is it known how many points he scored from the seven games (Klovan won the board prize with 4½/7). However, since he could have scored a maximum of four points, this must be regarded as a disappointing result for the only grandmaster playing on second board. Karpov had received the grandmaster title (it was confirmed by the FIDE Congress at Siegen on 20 September 1970) just five days before the event began.

1601 Klovan–AK

R1: 25.10.1970: Spanish

1 e4 e5 2 ♘f3 ♘c6 3 ♗b5 a6 4 ♗a4 ♘f6 5 00 ♗e7 6 ♖e1 b5 7 ♗b3 d6 8 c3 00 9 h3 ♘a5 10 ♗c2 c5 11 d4 ♕c7 12 ♘bd2 ♘c6 13 dc dc 14 ♘f1 ♗e6 15 ♘e3 ♖ad8 16 ♕e2 c4 17 ♘f5 ♖fe8 18 ♗g5 ♘d7 19 ♘×e7+ ♘×e7 20 ♘h4 ♘c5 21 ♖ad1 f6 22 ♗e3 ♘d3 23 ♗×d3 cd 24 ♖×d3 ♗×a2 25 ♖×d8 ♖×d8 26 ♖a1 ♗c4 27 ♕g4 a5 28 ♗h6 g6 29 f4 a4 30 fe ♕×e5 31 ♘f3 ♕c5+ 32 ♔h1 ♘c6 33 ♖e1 ♘e5 34 ♘×e5 ♕×e5 35 ♗e3 ♖e8 36 ♗d4 ♕e6 37 ♕h4 f5 38 e5 ♗d5 39 ♔h2 ♗e4 40 ♖e2 ♕d5 41 ♖d2 ♕d8 42 ♕h6 ♕c7 43 ♔h1 ♕g7 44 ♕g5 h6 45 ♕h4 ♗h7 46 ♗e3 g5 47 ♕h5 ♖e6 48 ♖d6

♖×d6 49 ed ♗c6 50 ♗d4 ♕g6 ½-½

1602 AK–Tiulin

R2: 26.10.1970: Chigorin

(Notes by Karpov)

1 c4 ♘c6 2 ♘c3 ♘f6 3 d4 d5 4 cd? ♘×d5 5 e4 ♘×c3 6 bc e5 7 d5 ♘b8 8 ♘f3 ♗d6 9 ♗b5+ ♘d7 10 00 00 11 ♗×d7 ♗×d7 12 ♕b3 ♕e7? 13 a4 f5 14 ♗a3 fe 15 ♘d2 e3 ½-½

1603

R3: Karpov won his game in this round, but the game is not available and nor is it known whom it was against.

1604 Vaganian–AK

R4(?): ?.10(?).1970: Queen's Indian

(Notes by Vaganian)

1 d4 ♞f6 2 c4 e6 3 ♞f3 b6 4 a3 ♗b7 5 ♞c3 d5 6 ♗g5 ♗e7 7 e3 ♞bd7 8 cd ed (8 . . . ♞×d5 was not so good: 9 ♗×e7 ♛×e7 10 ♞×d5 ♗×d5 11 ♖c1 with the freer game for White.) **9 ♗d3 00 10 00 ♞e4 11 ♗f4 c5 12 ♖c1** (On 12 dc could follow 12 . . . ♞×c3 13 bc ♞×c5 and Black stands well, but not 13 . . . bc because of 14 ♗×h7+ ♚×h7 15 ♛b1+) **12 . . . a6** (In my opinion this is an important loss of tempo. Bearing in mind that Black is preparing to play f7–f5, it was essential to take the king off the dangerous diagonal with 12 . . . ♚h8.) **13 ♛c2 f5 14 dc bc 15 ♖fd1** (Black has a difficult game. 16 ♗×e4 fe 17 ♞×e4! de 18 ♞e5 ♗c8 19 ♛×e4 ♖a7 20 ♞c6 is already threatened.) **15 . . . ♛c8 16 b4?** (*119*)

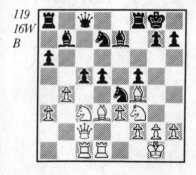

119
16W
B

(It is possible that the position does not demand such a radical solution, but I wanted to get down to concrete operations. The quiet 16 ♗f1 was not bad.) **16 . . . cb 17 ab ♗×b4 18 ♞a2** (Originally, I had planned 18 ♛b3 ♗×c3 19 ♗×e4 fe 20 ♖×c3 ♞c5 21 ♛a3 ef 22 ♖×c5, but here my opponent would have had at his disposal the unpleasant thrust 22 . . . ♛g4.) **18 . . . ♗a3** (18 . . . ♛×c2 19 ♖×c2 ♗a5 was stronger, although after 20 ♗c7 White would have, for the pawn, a position rich in possibilities.) **19 ♛b1! ♗×c1 20 ♖×c1 ♞dc5** (if 20 . . . ♞ec5 then simply 21 ♗×f5 ♖×f5 22 ♛×f5 ♛f8 23 ♛b1.) **21 ♗×e4 de 22 ♞d4 ♗d5 23 ♞b4 ♛b7** (probably the only way to escape from the pin.) **24 ♖×c5 ♖fc8?** (The losing move. It was still possible to hold on by means of 24 . . . ♖ac8 25 ♖×d5 ♛×b4 26 ♛d1 ♛a4 27 ♞e2 when, in the endgame, White does not have such an enormous advantage.) **25 ♖×d5 ♛×b4 26 ♛d1! ♛a4 27 ♖d8+ ♚f7 28 ♛h5+ 1–0**

1605

R5: 30.10.1970(?): This game is not available. Neither the opponent's name nor Karpov's result is known.

1606

R6(?): 1.11.1970(?)

This game is not available. It is not known who was White.

1607

R7: 2.11.1970(?)

This game is not available. Neither the opponent's name nor Karpov's result is known.

The following two games may have been played in this event. The other possibility is that they were played in other events in Leningrad, the first in the Leningrad Team Championship (Levy gives this game as being from the Armed Forces event), the second from the Leningrad Spartakiad. The games are given here as absolutely nothing is known concerning Karpov's participation in the two above-mentioned events.

1608   AK–Izotov

French

1 e4 e6 2 d4 d5 3 ♘c3 ♗b4 4 e5 c5 5 a3 ♗×c3+ 6 bc ♘e7 7 ♘f3 ♘bc6 8 ♗e2 ♕a5 9 00 ♗d7 10 a4 c4 11 ♕d2 000 12 ♘g5 ♖df8 13 ♗h5 g6 14 ♗g4 h6 15 ♘h3 ♘f5 16 ♗a3

♖fg8 17 ♖fb1 a6 18 ♗c5 ♕d8 19 ♖b6 ♘b8 20 ♖ab1 ♗c6 21 ♗×f5 gf 22 ♗d6 ♗b5 23 ♗×b8 ♕×b8 24 ♖d6 ♕h4 25 ♘f4 ♗×a4 26 ♖×a6 ♗d7 27 ♕c1 ♗c8 28 ♕a3 ♕d8 29 ♖a8+ ♔c7 30 ♕c5+ ♔d7 31 ♖×b7+ **1–0**

1609   AK–A. Korelov

(Leningrad Spartakiad?) Spanish

1 e4 e5 2 ♘f3 ♘c6 3 ♗b5 a6 4 ♗a4 ♘f6 5 00 ♗e7 6 ♖e1 b5 7 ♗b3 d6 8 c3 00 9 h3 ♘a5 10 ♗c2 c5 11 d4 ♕c7 12 ♘bd2 ♘c6 13 dc dc 14 ♘f1 ♗e6 15 ♘e3 ♖ad8 16 ♕e2 c4 17 ♘f5 ♘d7 18 ♘×e7+ ♘×e7 19 ♘g5 ♘c5 20 ♕h5 h6 21 ♘×e6 ♘×e6 22 ♗e3 ♘g6 23 g3 ♘c5 24 ♖ed1 ♘d3 25 ♗×d3 ♖×d3 26 a4 ♖fd8 27 ab ab 28 ♖e1 ♕c6 29 ♕f5 ♖3d6 30 h4 ♖f6 31 ♕g4 ♘f8 32 ♖ed1 ♖fd6 33 ♖×d6 ♖×d6 34 ♖a7 ♖d7 35 ♗×h6 ♕×h6 36 ♖×d7 ♘×d7 37 ♕×d7 ♕c1+ 38 ♔g2 ♕×b2 39 ♕e8+ ♔h7 40 ♕×f7 ♕×c3 41 h5 ♕d2 42 ♕f5+ ♔g8 43 ♕×e5 c3 44 ♕e8+ ♔h7 45 e5 c2 ½–½

17 38th USSR Championship
Riga, 26.11-28.12.1970

Karpov's own view of the event appeared in *64*; 'This year I participated a
great deal in competitions and already, after the first games of the Soviet
Championship final, I felt overworked and very tired. Lack of confidence
in my strength gave birth to caution – throughout the first half of the
championship I tried not to take risks and made several quick draws. I
cannot say that in the later stages I began to play better, it was simply that
the other competitors were getting even more tired. In general it is difficult
playing in the final. In international tournaments it is always possible to
find some weaker opponents, but in our championships there are no
outsiders. However, the advantage for me from playing in the tournament
is unquestionable – I gained essential experience: you know a débutant is
always a débutant!'

А. КАРПОВ.

No.	Player	Score
1	Korchnoi	16
2	Tukmakov	14½
3	Stein	14
4	Balashov	12½
5	Gipslis	12
6	**Karpov**	12
7	Savon	12
8	Averbakh	11
9	Podgayets	11
10	Bagirov	10½
11	Dementiev	10½
12	Liberzon	10½
13	Doroshkevich	10
14	Holmov	10
15	Antoshin	9½
16	I. Zaitsev	9½
17	Vaganian	9
18	Mikenas	9
19	Karasev	8½
20	Platonov	7½
21	Tseitlin	6
22	Moiseyev	5½

1701 Stein–AK

R1: 26.11.1970: Spanish

(Notes by Gufeld)

1 e4 e5 2 ♘f3 ♘c6 3 ♗b5 a6 4 ♗a4 ♘f6 5 00 ♗e7 6 ♖e1 b5 7 ♗b3 d6 8 c3 00 9 h3 ♘b8 10 d3 c5!? 11 ♘bd2 h6 12 ♘f1 ♘c6= 13 ♘g3 ♖e8 14 a4 ♗d7 15 ♗e3 ♗f8 16 ♘d2 ♘a5 17 ♗c2 d5!∓ 18 d4! cd 19 cd ed 20 ♗×d4 ♘c6 21 ♗×f6 ♕×f6 22 ab ♘b4 23 ba ♖×a6 24 ♖×a6 ♕×a6 25 ♗b1 d4 26 ♘e2 d3 27 ♘f4 ♗d6 28 ♘×d3!= ♘×d3 29 ♗×d3 ♕×d3 30 ♘f3 ♗b5 31 ♕×d3 ♗×d3 32 ♖d1 *(120)*

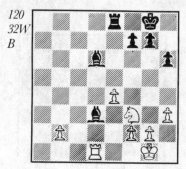

120
32W
B

32 ... ♗×e4?! (The rook ending is a safe draw, but 32 ... ♖d8 33 ♖×d3 ♗h2+, which Karpov missed, would have given him some plus.) 33 ♖×d6 ♗×f3 34 gf ♖b8 35 ♖d2 ♔h7 36 ♔g2 ♔g6 37 ♔g3 ♔f5 38 h4 g6 ½–½

1702 AK–Savon

R2: 27.11.1970: Sicilian

1 e4 c5 2 ♘f3 d6 3 d4 cd 4 ♘×d4 ♘f6 5 ♘c3 a6 6 ♗e2 g6 7 00 ♗g7 8 ♔h1 00 9 f4 ♘c6 10 ♗e3 ♗d7 11 ♘b3 b5 12 ♗f3 ♖b8 13 a3 ♕c7 14 ♖e1 e5 15 ♕d2 ef 16 ♗×f4 ♘e5 17 ♖ad1 ♖b6 18 ♗e2 ♗e6 19 ♘d4 ♖e8 ½–½

1703 Karasev–AK

R3: 28.11.1970: Queen's Indian

1 ♘f3 ♘f6 2 g3 b6 3 ♗g2 ♗b7 4 00 e6 5 c4 ♗e7 6 ♘c3 00 7 d4 ♘e4 8 ♗d2 ♘×c3 9 ♗×c3 d5 10 ♘e5 ♘d7 11 ♘d3 ♘f6 12 ♕c2 ♘e4 13 cd ed 14 ♖ac1 a5 15 ♖fd1 ♗d6 16 ♗e1 ♕e7 17 f3 ♘g5 18 ♗f2 f5 19 ♘e5 ♔h8 20 h4 ♘f7 21 f4 ♘h6 22 ♗f3 ♕e6 23 a4 ♘g4 24 ♕b3 ♘f6 25 ♔g2 ♖ac8 26 ♗e1 ♗a8 27 ♖c2 ♘e4 28 ♖dc1 ♖b8 29 ♗×e4 fe *(121)*

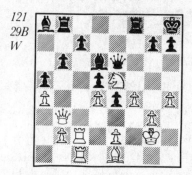

121
29B
W

30 ♖×c7!? ♗×c7 31 ♖×c7 ♖fc8 32 ♖f7 b5 33 ab ♕b6 34 ♕e3 (with the idea of f5 and ♕g5. Tal suggested 34 f5!? immediately.) 34 ... ♖b7 35 f5 ♖×f7 36 ♘×f7+ ♔g8 37 ♘e5 ♕×b5 38 ♗c3 ♖f8 39 g4 ♗b7 40 h5 ♖f6 41 ♗e1 (s) (adjournment 29.11.1970) 41 ...

♗a6 42 ♗h4 ♖b6 43 b4 (White does not really have enough for his sacrifice, but he hangs on well.) 43 ...♕×e2+ 44 ♕×e2 ♗×e2 45 ba ♖b2 46 ♔g3 h6 47 ♔f4 ♖c2 48 ♗e1 ♗b5 49 ♗b4 ♖b2 50 ♗c3 ♖b3 51 ♗d2 ♔h7 52 ♗e3 ♖b2 53 ♘g6 ♖a2 54 ♘e7 ♗c4 55 ♘c6 ♖a3 56 ♘e5 ♗a6 57 ♗d2 ♗b5 58 ♗b4 ♖b3 59 ♗d2 ♗a6 60 ♗c1 ♖c3 61 ♗d2 ♖c2 62 ♗b4 ♖f2+ 63 ♔e3 ♖b2 64 ♗d2 ♔g8 65 ♗c1 ♖e2+ 66 ♔f4 ♖c2 67 ♗e3 ♖a2 68 g5 hg+ 69 ♔×g5 ♔h7 70 ♘g4 ♗e2 71 f6 ♔g8 72 h6 gf+ 73 ♘×f6+ ♔f7 74 ♘e8 ♗d3 75 ♘d6+ ♔g8 76 ♔g6 ♖g2+ 77 ♔f6 ♔h7 78 ♔e5 ♖e2 79 ♘f5 ♗c4 80 ♗f4 ♖a2 81 ♘e3 ♗b3 82 ♘g4 ♖×a5 83 ♘f5 ♔g8 84 ♘g6 ♖a6+ 85 ♘f6+ ♔h8 86 ♔g5 ♖e6 87 ♔f5 ♖e7 88 ♗d6 ½-½

1704   AK–Antoshin

R4: 30.11.1970: Spanish

1 e4 e5 2 ♘f3 ♘c6 3 ♗b5 a6 4 ♗a4 ♘f6 5 00 ♘×e4 6 d4 b5 7 ♗b3 d5 8 de ♗e6 9 c3 ♗c5 10 ♘bd2 00 11 ♗c2 ♘×d2 12 ♕×d2 f6 13 ef (13 ♕d3!? Korchnoi) 13 ... ♖×f6 14 ♘g5 ♗f5 15 b4 ♗b6 16 ♗b3 ♘e7 17 a4 c6 18 ♖e1 ♗g6 19 ♘f3 ♘f5 20 ♘e5 ♗e8 21 ♕a2 ba 22 ♗×a4 h6 23 ♗f4 a5 24 ♘d3 ab 25 cb ♘d6= 26 ♗e5 ♖f7 27 ♘c5 ♗×c5 28 bc ♘e4 29 ♗d4 ♖fa7 30 ♕c2 ♗d7 31 f3 ♘g5 32 ♖a2 ♘e6 33 ♗f2 ♕f6 34 ♗b3 ♘d4 35 ♖×a7

♖×a7 36 ♕d3 ♘×b3 37 ♕×b3 ♖a1 38 ♕b4 ♗f5 39 h3 ♖×e1+ 40 ♕×e1 d4 ½-½

1705   Tseitlin–AK

R5: 1.12.1970: English

1 g3 c5 2 ♗g2 g6 3 ♘f3 ♗g7 4 00 ♘c6 5 c4 e6 6 ♘c3 ♘ge7 7 ♖b1 00 8 a3 d5 9 b3 b6 10 ♗b2 ♖b8 11 ♘a4 d4 12 d3 e5 13 ♗c1 ♗g4 14 ♗d2 ♕c8 15 b4 cb 16 ab ♗h3 17 b5 ♗×g2 18 ♔×g2 ♘d8 19 ♗b4 ♕d7 20 ♕c1 ♖e8 21 ♕a3 ♘b7 22 ♖fc1 ♘c8 23 c5 bc 24 ♗×c5 ♘×c5 25 ♘×c5 ♕e7 26 ♕a5 ♘d6 27 ♘a6 ♖b7 28 ♘c5 ♖b6 29 ♘d2 ♖eb8 (122)

122
29B
W

30 ♘ce4 ♘×b5 31 ♘c4 ♖6b7 32 ♕a2 ♘c3 33 ♘×c3 dc 34 ♖×b7 ♕×b7+ 35 e4 h5 36 ♖×c3 ♕d7 37 ♘e3 h4 38 ♘d5 ♖b7 39 ♕c4 ♔h7 40 ♕c8 ♕×c8 41 ♖×c8 hg 42 hg a5 43 ♖a8 ♖b3 44 ♖a7 ♔g8 (s) (adjournment 3.12.1970) 45 ♘e7+ ♔h8 46 ♘c6 a4 47 ♖a8+ ♔h7 48 ♘d8 f6 49 ♘e6 ♗h6 50 ♘c5 ♖c3 51 ♘d7 ♗g7 52 ♖a7 ♔g8 53 ♖a8+ ♔h7 54 ♖×a4 ♖×d3 55

🖤a7 ♔g8 56 ♘c5 🖤d2 57 ♔f3
♗h6 58 ♘d7 ♗g7 59 ♔e3 🖤d4 60
f4 f5 61 ef ef+ 62 gf gf 63 🖤a8+
♔f7 ½-½

1706 AK–Moiseyev

R6: 2.12.1970: QGD

1 ♘f3 d5 2 d4 ♘f6 3 c4 e6 4 ♘c3 c5
5 cd ♘×d5 6 e3 ♘c6 7 ♗d3 ♗e7 8
00 00 9 a3 ♘×c3 10 bc b6 11 c4 ♗f6
12 ♗b2 cd 13 ed ♗b7 14 🖤c1 ♕d6
15 ♗e4 ♘a5 16 ♗×b7 ♘×b7 17
♘d2 ♕f4 18 g3 ♕f5 19 ♕c2 ♕×c2
20 🖤×c2 🖤fd8 21 ♘b3 🖤ac8 22
🖤fc1 🖤d6 23 ♔f1 🖤dc6 ½-½

1707 Liberzon–AK

R7: 5.12.1970: English

1 c4 c5 2 ♘f3 ♘c6 3 ♘c3 g6 4 e3
♘f6 5 d4 ♗g7 6 d5 ♘a5 7 ♗e2 d6
½-½ The competitors were given
three rest days and the previous day
had been one of these. But there was
a football match and Liberzon is
the greatest enthusiast among the
spectators – Tal.

1708 AK–Balashov

R8: 6.12.1970: Sicilian

1 e4 c5 2 ♘f3 d6 3 d4 cd 4 ♘×d4
♘f6 5 ♘c3 a6 6 ♗e2 e5 7 ♘b3
♗e7 8 ♗g5 ♘bd7 9 a4 b6 10 ♗c4
♗b7 11 ♕e2 00 12 00 ♕c7 13 🖤fd1
🖤fc8 14 ♘d2 h6 15 ♗×f6 ♘×f6 16
♗b3 ♗f8 17 ♔f1 ♗c6 18 f3 b5 19
♘e3 ♕b6 20 ♔h1 ba 21 ♘×a4
♕b7 22 ♕d2 🖤d8 23 ♕a5 🖤db8

24 ♘c3 🖤a7 25 ♘c4 ♘e8 26 ♗a4
♗e7 27 ♗×c6 ♕×c6 28 b3 ♘c7 29
♘d5 *(123)*

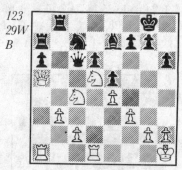

123
29W
B

29 ... ♗d8 30 ♘×c7 ♗×c7 31
♕d5 ♕×d5 32 🖤×d5 🖤d8 33
🖤a2 ♔f8 34 b4 ♕e7 35 g4 🖤aa8
36 🖤d1 a5 37 🖤da1 d5 38 ♘e3 de
39 fe 🖤d2 40 c3 🖤×a2 41 🖤×a2
♔d6 (s) (adjournment 8.12.1970)
42 ♔g2 ♘c6 43 ♔f3 ♔b5 44 ♘d5
♗d8 45 ♔e2 ♔c4 46 🖤a3 🖤a7 47
h3 g6 48 ♘e3+ ♔b5 49 ♔d3
🖤d7+ 50 ♘d5 ab 51 cb f5 52 gf gf
53 🖤a8 ½-½ Karpov outplayed
Balashov in strict positional style,
but failed to clinch it.

1709 Korchnoi–AK

R9: 7.12.1970: English

Karpov had to defend after an
opening inaccuracy and finally
slipped in the ending when he let in
Korchnoi's king.
1 c4 c5 2 ♘f3 ♘f6 3 ♘c3 d5 4 cd
♘×d5 5 d4 cd 6 ♕×d4 ♘×c3 7
♕×c3 ♘c6 8 e4 a6 9 ♗c4 ♕a5 10
♗d2 ♕×c3 11 ♗×c3 e6 12 00 🖤g8
13 🖤fd1 b5 14 ♗d3 f6 15 a4 b4 16

♗d4 ♘×d4 17 ♘×d4 ♗c5 18 ♗c4
♗×d4 19 ♖×d4 ♔e7 20 ♖ad1
♖a7 21 b3 a5 22 ♖d6 ♗d7 23 f4
♖c8 24 e5 fe 25 fe ♖c5 26 ♖e1 h6
27 h4 ♖a8 28 ♖e3 ♖c6 29 ♖d4
♖c5 30 ♖d6 ♖c6 31 ♖×c6 ♗×c6
(*124*)

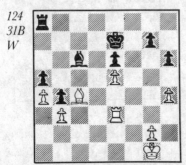

124
31B
W

32 ♖g3 ♖g8 33 ♔f2 g5 34 ♔e3 g4
35 ♔d4 h5 36 ♔c5 ♗e4 37 ♔b6
♖a8 38 ♗d3 ♗f5 39 ♖e3 ♖c8 40
♗c4 ♗c2 41 ♔b5 (41 ♔×a5?
♖×c4 42 bc b3∓ ∓) 41 ... ♖a8 (s)
(adjournment 8.12.1970) 42 ♖e2
♗g6 43 g3 ♗f5 44 ♖d2 ♗e4 45
♖d6 ♗d5 46 ♗×d5 ed 47 ♖×d5
♔e6 48 ♖c5 ♗a7 49 ♔b6 ♖d7 50
♔×a5 ♖d3 51 ♔×b4 ♖×g3 52 a5
♖g1 53 ♖c2 g4 54 ♖a2 ♖h1 55 a6
♖×h4+ 56 ♔c3 ♖h3 57 ♖g2 **1-0**

1710   AK–Podgayets

R10: 9.12.1970: Spanish

Karpov continued on his calm
drawing course (= 9 − 1 + 0 so far),
the game lasting little over an hour.
1 e4 e5 2 ♘f3 ♘c6 3 ♗b5 a6 4 ♗a4
♘f6 5 00 ♗e7 6 ♖e1 b5 7 ♗b3 d6 8
c3 00 9 h3 ♘b8 10 d4 ♘bd7 11
♘bd2 ♗b7 12 ♗c2 ♖e8 13 ♘f1
♗f8 14 ♘g3 g6 15 a4 c5 16 de de 17
b3 ♕c7 18 ♗g5 ♗g7 19 ♕e2 ♗c6
20 ab ab ½-½

1711   Averbakh–AK

R11: 10.12.1970: QGD

Averbakh failed to prove that a
more active king wins in a king and
pawn ending.
1 c4 c5 2 ♘f3 ♘f6 3 ♘c3 d5 4 cd
♘×d5 5 e3 e6 6 d4 ♘c6 7 ♗d3
♗e7 8 00 00 9 a3 ♘f6 10 dc ♗×c5
11 b4 ♗d6 12 ♘e4 ♘×e4 13 ♗×e4
♕e7 14 ♗b2 f5 15 ♗×c6 bc 16 ♗e5
♗×e5 17 ♘×e5± c5 18 ♖c1! cb 19
♘c6 ♕f6 20 ab ♗a6 21 ♖e1 ♗b5!
22 ♕d6 (threatening 23 ♘d4) 22
... ♗×c6 23 ♖×c6 ♖ae8 24 g3
♕e7 25 ♖d1 (25 ♕×e7 ♖×e7 26
♖a6 ♖b8=) 25 ... ♖f7 (25 ...
♕×d6 26 ♖d×d6 e5 27 b5 ♖b8 28
♖d5±) 26 ♕c5 (planning 27
♖dd6) 26 ... ♕×c5 27 bc ♖b7 28
♖a6 (28 ♖dd6 ♔f7) 28 ... ♖c8 29
c6 bc7 30 ♖d7! (30 ♖d6 ♔f7! 31
♖d7+ ♖×d7 32 cd ♖d8 33 ♖×a7
♔e7=) 30 ... ♖×d7! 31 cd ♖d8
32 ♖×a7 ♔f7 33 ♔g2 ♔e7 34 ♔f3
♖×d7 35 ♖×d7+ ♔×d7 36 ♔f4
♔d6 (36 ... g6? 37 ♔g5) 37 e4 fe
38 ♔×e4 ♔d7 39 ♔e5 ♔e7 40 h3
♔d7 41 h4 ♔e7 (s) (adjournment
11.12.1970) 42 f3 ♔d7 43 ♔f4 ♔e7
44 ♔g5 ♔f7 (not 44 ... ♔d6 45 h5
♔e5 46 h6 g6 47 f4+ ♔e4 48
♔f6± ±) 45 g4 ♔e7 46 h5 ♔f7 47
h6 g6 48 ♔f4 ♔f6 49 g5+ ♔f7 50
♔e5 ♔e7 51 f4 ♔f7 52 ♔d6 ♔f8!

½-½ (53 ♔×e6 ♔g8! 54 ♔e7 ♔h8
55 ♔f6 ♔g8 56 f5 gf 57 ♔×f5
♔h8=)

1712   AK-Bagirov

R12: 12.12.1970: Alekhine

(Notes by Karpov)

1 e4 ♘f6 2 e5 ♘d5 3 d4 d6 4 ♘f3
♗g4 5 ♗e2 e6 6 00 ♗e7 7 c4 ♘b6 8
ed cd 9 ♘c3 (9 h3!? ♗h5 10 ♘c3) 9
... 00 10 ♗e3 d5 11 c5 ♗×f3 12
♗×f3 ♘c4 13 ♗c1± ♘c6 14 b3
♘4a5 15 ♗e3 b6 16 ♘a4 ♖b8?! 17
♖c1 bc 18 ♘×c5 ♗f6 19 a3 ♘e7 20
♗e2 (threatening b4) 20 ... ♘f5 21
b4 ♘b7 (21 ... ♘×e3!? 22 fe ♘b7)
22 ♗f4 ♘bd6 23 ♗e5± ♗×e5 24
de ♘b7 25 ♘b3! ♕b6 26 ♗d3
♘e7 27 ♕g4 f5 28 ♕d4 (*125*)

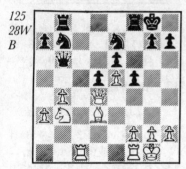

125
28W
B

28 ... ♘d8 29 b5 g5!? 30 a4 ♘g6 31
♕a1! (31 ♖fe1 ♘f7 32 ♕a1 ♖bc8
33 a5±) 31 ... ♕b7 32 ♖fe1 ♕g7
33 ♘c5 ♖f7 34 a5 ♖e7 35 ♘a6
♖a8 36 ♗f1 ♘f7 37 ♘c7 ♖d8 (37
... ♖b8 38 b6 ab 39 a6±±) 38
♖c6 ♘f8 39 b6 ab 40 a6 ♘h6 41
♖ec1 ♘g4 42 a7 ♘×e5 43 ♖6c2!
♘c4 44 a8♕ ♖×a8 45 ♘×a8 b5 46

♖a2 ♖b7 (s) **1-0** (Bagirov resigned
on 13.12.1970 as part of a chain
reaction after the 13th round –
Zaitsev resigned his adjourned
game against Bagirov, who, in turn,
resigned against Karpov – KJO'C.)

1713   Platonov-AK

R13: 13.12.1970: English

It was a poor game – Karpov.
1 c4 c5 2 ♘c3 g6 3 g3 ♗g7 4 ♗g2
♘c6 5 a3 e6 6 b4 d6 7 ♖b1 ♘ge7 8
♘h3 00 9 ♘f4 ♖b8 10 bc dc 11
♗b2 b6 12 00 ♗b7 13 ♘b5 ♘e5 14
♗×e5 ♗×e5 15 ♘d3 ♗×g2 16
♔×g2 ♗g7 17 ♘×a7 ♕d4 18 ♖c1
♖fd8 19 ♘b5 ♕d7 20 ♕b3 ♘c6 21
♖c2 ♖a8 22 ♘e1 ♖a6 23 ♘f3
♖da8 24 d3 h6 25 ♔g1 ♘a5 26
♕b1 ♘c6 27 ♕b3 ♘a5 28 ♕b1
♘c6 29 ♘d2 ½-½

1714   AK-I. Zaitsev

R14: 16 12.1970: Spanish

Karpov forced a win by steady
exploitation of a Q-side pawn
majority.
1 e4 e5 2 ♘f3 ♘c6 3 ♗b5 a6 4 ♗a4
♘f6 5 00 ♗e7 6 ♖e1 b5 7 ♗b3 d6 8
c3 00 9 h3 ♕d7 10 d4 ♗b7 11 ♘bd2
♖ae8 12 ♘f1 ♗d8 13 ♘g3 h6 14
♗c2 ♔h8 15 b3 ♘g8 16 d5 ♘ce7
17 c4 c6 18 dc ♕×c6 19 cb ab 20 b4
♗b6 21 ♗d3 d5 22 ♗b2 ♘g6 23 ed
♕×d5 24 ♗e4 ♕×d1 25 ♖a×d1
♗×e4 26 ♘×e4 ♖a8 27 a3 f5 28
♘d6 e4 29 ♘d4 ♗×d4 30 ♖×d4
♘f4 31 ♖×b5 ♘d3 32 ♖b1 ♖fb8

33 ⟋d6 ⟋×b2 34 ☖×b2 ☖×a3 35
⟋×f5 ⟋f6 36 b5 ☖a1+ 37 ⟐h2
☖a5 38 ⟋d6 ☖b6 39 ☖c2 ☖a8 40
☖c6 ☖ab8 41 ☖dc4 (*126*)

126
41W
B

41 ... ☖×b5 42 ⟋×b5 (s)
(adjournment 18.12.1970) 42 ...
☖×b5 43 ☖c2 ⟐h7 44 ☖c7 ☖d5
45 ☖e7 ☖g5 46 ☖a2 ⟋d5 47 ☖e8
⟋f6 48 ☖b8 h5 49 g3 ☖f5 50 ⟐g2
g5 51 ☖b6 g4 52 h4 ⟐g6 53 ☖a7
☖f3 54 ☖e7 ⟐f5 55 ☖b5+ ⟐g6
56 ☖g5+ **1-0**

1715   Dementiev–AK

R15: 17.12.1970: Alekhine

Dementiev's pearl was the finest
game of the round. Karpov's big
mistake was not playing 12 ...
⟋d7 and he was finally finished off
most elegantly.

1 e4 ⟋f6 2 e5 ⟋d5 3 d4 d6 4 c4
⟋b6 5 ed cd 6 ⟋c3 g6 7 ⟋f3 ♝g7 8
h3 0-0 9 ♝e2 ⟋c6 10 0-0 ♝f5 11 b3
d5 12 c5 ⟋c8? (12 ... ⟋d7,
threatening 13 ... ⟋×c5, is
correct, e.g. 13 ♝b2 ♝e4! 14 ⟋a4
e5 with a fine game.) 13 ♝f4 b6 14
♝b5 ♛d7 15 ☖c1!± a6 16 ♝×c6

♛×c6 1.7 cb ⟋×b6 18 ⟋a4 ♛b7 19
⟋c5! (stronger than 19 ☖c7 ♛b8
20 ⟋×b6 ♛×b6 21 ☖×e7 ♝e4
when Black has chances of survival)
19 ... ♛a7 20 ☖e1 ♝c8 21 ♛d2
☖e8 22 ⟋e5 ♝b7 23 a4 ☖ad8 24
♛b4 ♝×e5 25 ♝×e5 ♝c8 26 ⟋d3
(The immediate 26 ⟋×a6! is
possible.) 26 ... ⟋a8 27 ⟋c5 ⟋b6
(*127*)

127
27B
W

28 ⟋×a6! ♝×a6 29 ☖c7 ♛a8 30
♛×b6 ☖b8 31 ♛c5 ☖×b3 32
☖×e7 ♝d3 33 ♛×d5 **1-0**

1716   AK–Vaganian

R16: 19.12.1970: Grünfeld

1 c4 ⟋f6 2 ⟋c3 d5 3 cd ⟋×d5 4
⟋f3 g6 5 ♛b3 ⟋b6 6 d4 ♝g7 7
♝g5 ♝e6 8 ♛c2 ⟋c6 9 ☖d1 0-0 10
e3 ⟋b4 11 ♛b1 a5 12 ♝e2 a4 13 0-0
h6 14 ♝h4 c6 15 h3 ⟋4d5 16 ☖c1
a3 17 ⟋×d5 ♝×d5 18 b3 f5 19 ♝g3
⟋d7 20 ♝c4 ⟋f6 21 ♝e5 ⟐f7 22
♝×d5+ ♛×d5 23 ☖fd1 ☖fd8 24
⟋e1 ⟋d7 25 ♝×g7 ⟐×g7 26 ☖c3
♛d6 27 b4 ⟋b6 28 ⟋c2 ⟋d5 (*128*)
29 ☖b3 ☖a4 30 ⟋×a3 ☖da8 31
⟋c4 ♛e6 32 ☖d2 ☖8a6 33 ⟋e5

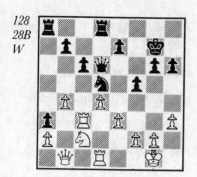

128
28B
W

♛d6 34 ♘d3 b6 35 ♖c2 e6 36 b5 cb
37 ♖×b5 ♖a7 38 ♖bb2 ♖a3 39
♘e5 ♖c3 40 ♖×c3 ♘×c3 41
♖×b6 ♛d5 (s) (adjournment
22.12.1970) 42 ♛b3 **1-0**

1717   Gipslis-AK

R17: 20.12.1970: Spanish

(Notes by Karpov)

1 e4 e5 2 ♘f3 ♘c6 3 ♗b5 a6 4
♗×c6 dc 5 00 f6 6 d4 ed
    7 ♘×d4   c5
7 . . . ♘e7 is better.
    8 ♘b3   ♛×d1
    9 ♖×d1   ♗d7
Not 9 . . . ♗d6? 10 ♘a5!±
    10 a4   b6
If 10 . . . . 000 then 11 a5 with 12
♗e3± to follow.
    11 ♘c3   000
    12 ♗f4

If 12 a5 ♔b7 (12 . . . b5? 13
♗e3±) 13 ♗f4 ♘e7 14 ♗g3 (or 14
♘a4 ♘c8!, but not 14 . . . ♘g6? 15
♗×c7 ♔×c7 16 ab+ ♔c8 17
♘×c5±, nor 14 . . . c4 15 ab cb6
16 ♘bc5+ bc 17 ♘×c5+ ♔c6 18
♖×a6+ ♔×c5 19 ♗e3+ ♔b5 20

♖b6+ ♔a5 21 ♖a1+ ♗a4 22
b4+ ± ±) 14 . . . h5 15 h4 c4 16 ♘d4
♗g4 17 f3 ♗c8.

After 12 a5, 12 . . . c4?! is met by
13 ♘d4 b5 (13 . . . ♔b7 14
♘e6± ±) 14 b3±.

    12 . . .   c4?!
    13 ♘d2

13 ♘d4!? is interesting, e.g. 13
. . . ♘e7 14 a5 b5 15 ♘d×b5± ± ; or
13 . . . ♗c5 14 b4! (14 ♘d5 c6) 14
. . . ♗×d4 (14 . . . ♗×b4 15
♘d5±±) 15 ♖×d4 ♗e6 16
♖×d8+ ♔×d8 17 b5± ±. After 13
♘d4 Black must play 13 . . . c6!?.

    13 . . .   ♗e6
    14 ♘f3   ♖×d1+
    15 ♖×d1   ♗c5
    16 ♘d4   ♗×d4
    17 ♖×d4   ½-½

1718   AK-Mikenas

R18: 21.12.1970: Alekhine

(Notes by Karpov)

Karpov justified his waiting
tactics of the early rounds by
outplaying the veteran in positional
style despite determined resistance.
Tournament bulletin.

1 e4 ♘f6 2 e5 ♘d5 3 d4 d6 4 ♘f3
♗g4 5 ♗e2 ♘c6 6 ed ed 7 c4 ♘f6 8
00 ♗e7 9 h3 ♗h5 10 d5 ♗×f3 11
♗×f3 ♘e5 12 ♗e2± 00 13 ♘c3
♘ed7 14 ♗e3 a5 15 ♛c2 ♘c5 16 a3
♘fd7?! (16 . . . ♖e8 is better,
planning . . . ♗f8, . . . g6 and . . .
♗g7.) 17 b4 ab 18 ab ♖×a1 19
♖×a1 ♘a6 20 ♛d2! (preventing

20 . . . ♗g5) 20 . . . ♘×b4 (or 20
. . . ♖e8 21 ♘a4 followed by ♖c1
and c5±) 21 ♖b1 ♘a6 22 ♖×b7
♘ac5 23 ♖a7! ♕b8 24 ♘b5 ♗d8
(24 . . . ♖c8 25 ♗g4±±) 25 ♕a2
♕b6 26 ♖a8 (planning 27 ♖c8
followed by ♕a8) 26 . . . c6 (*129*)

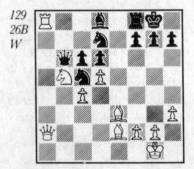

129
26B
W

27 ♘×d6 (27 dc ♕×c6 28 ♗f3
♕b6 29 ♖c8 ♗e7± or 29 . . . ♘e5
30 ♗d5 ♗e7 31 ♕a8±± is also
good.) 27 . . . cd 28 ♘c8 ♕b7 29
♗f3 ♘e4 30 cd ♘c3 31 ♕a6!
♕×a6 32 ♖×a6±± ♗f6 33 ♖a8!
♘e5 34 ♗c5 ♖d8 35 ♗b6 ♘×f3+
(35 . . . ♖f8 is comparatively best.)
36 gf ♖f8 37 ♗c5 ♖d8 (37 . . .
♖e8? 38 ♘e7+ ♔f8 39
♘g6+ + ± ±) 38 ♗e7! ♖e8 39 d6
♗×e7 40 d7 ♔f8 41 de♕+ (The
sealed move. Not 41 ♘×e7?? ♖×a8
42 ♘c8 ♖a1+! 43 ♔g2 ♖d1∓∓)
(adjournment 22.12.1970) 41 . . .
♔×e8 42 ♘d6+ + ♔d7 43 ♘×f7
♔e6 44 ♘d8+ ♔d7 45 ♘b7
♘e2+ 46 ♔h2 ♔e6 47 ♖a4 ♗f6
48 ♘c5+ ♔f5 49 ♘d3 ♕g5 50
♖a5+ ♔h6 51 f4 ♕g6 52 ♔g2 h6
53 ♔f3 ♘d4+ 54 ♔g4 ♔f7 55
♖a7+ ♔e6 56 f5+ ♔d6 57 ♖a6+

♔e7 58 ♘f4 ♔f7 59 ♖a7+ ♔g8 60
♘h5 **1-0**

1719   Doroshkevich–AK

R19: 23.12.1970: Nimzo-Indian

Karpov won yet again – 3½ out of
the last four!
1 d4 ♘f6 2 c4 e6 3 ♘c3 ♗b4 4 ♕c2
00 5 a3 ♗×c3+ 6 ♕×c3 d6 7
♗g5 ♘bd7 8 e3 (8 ♘f3
Doroshkevich–Smyslov, Riga
1968) 8 . . . b6 9 ♗d3 ♗b7 10 f3 c5!
11 ♘e2 ♖c8 12 ♖c1 h6 13 ♗h4 cd
14 ed b5! 15 b3 (15 ♕b3 bc 16
♗×c4 ♕a5+ 17 ♘c3 ♘b6 18 ♗d3
♘fd5∓) 15 . . . bc 16 bc ♗a6! 17
♗×f6!? (17 00 ♗×c4! 18 ♗×c4 d5
19 ♕b4 dc 20 ♖×c4 ♖×c4 21
♕×c4 ♕a5∓ – isolated pawns a3
and d4, weak squares for knight
outposts) 17 . . . ♕×f6 18 ♕a5
♘b8! (preparing 19 . . . d5) 19 ♖c3
(19 ♕d2 ♘c6!) 19 . . . d5! (*130*)

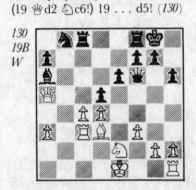

130
19B
W

20 c5 (20 cd ♗×d3 21 ♖×d3 ♕g5
22 00 ♖c2!) 20 . . . ♗×d3 21 ♖×d3
♘c6 22 ♕d2 ♖b8 23 00 ♖b7 24 f4
♖fb8 25 h3 ♖b2 26 ♕e3 ♘a5 27
♘g3 ♘c4 28 ♕e1 ♖8b3 29 ♖×b3

(29 ♖ff3 ♖b1∓∓) 29 ... ♛×d4+
30 ♔h2 ♖×b3∓∓ 31 f5 ♘e3 32
♖f3 ♛×c5 33 fe fe 34 ♘h5 ♛d6+
35 ♔g1 d4 36 ♖g3 ♖b7 37 ♛d2
♖b1+ 38 ♔f2 ♖f1+ 39 ♔e2
♛a6+ 40 ♛d3 ♖e1+ **0–1**

1720   AK–Tukmakov

R20: 24.12.1970: Spanish

1 e4 e5 2 ♘f3 ♘c6 3 ♗b5 a6 4 ♗a4
♘f6 5 00 ♗e7 6 ♖e1 b5 7 ♗b3 d6 8
c3 00 9 h3 ♘b8 10 d4 ♘bd7 11
♘bd2 ♗b7 12 ♗c2 ♖e8 13 ♘f1
♗f8 14 ♘g3 g6 15 a4 c5 16 b4 cd 17
cd d5 18 de de 19 ♘×e4 ♘×e4 20
♗×e4 ♗×e4 21 ♖×e4 ♘×e5 22
♛×d8 ♘×f3+ 23 gf ♖a×d8 24
♗e3 ♖×e4 25 fe ♖e8 26 ab ab 27
f3 f5 28 ♖a5 ½–½

1721   Holmov–AK

R21: 27.12.1970: Sicilian

Holmov outplayed Karpov, won

a pawn and seemed to have an easy
win, but allowed Black's rook too
much freedom, and, losing his
presence of mind, offered a draw in
what was still a very advantageous
situation.

1 e4 c5 2 ♘f3 ♘c6 3 d4 cd 4 ♘×d4
e5 5 ♘c3 a6 6 g3 ♘×d4 7 ♛×d4
♘e7 8 ♗f4 ♘g6 9 ♗d6 ♗×d6 10
♛×d6 ♛e7 11 ♛b6!± ♛d8 12
♘a4 ♛×b6 13 ♘×b6 ♖b8 14 000
♔e7 15 f4 d6 16 ♗g2 ♖d8 17 ♖d2
f6 18 ♖hd1 e5 19 f5 ♘h8 20 ♗f1
♘f7 21 ♗c4 ♘g5 22 ♖e2 ♗d7 23
h4 ♘f7 24 ♘×d7 ♖×d7 25 ♗e6
♖dd8 26 ♖e3 b6 27 ♖c3 ♖b7 28
♗d5 ♖a7 29 ♖c6 b5 30 ♗×f7
♔×f7 31 ♖c×d6 ♖×d6 32 ♖×d6
g6 33 g4 gf 34 gf h5 35 ♔d2 ♔e7 36
♖b6 ♖d7+ 37 ♔e3 ♖d1 38
♖e6+ ♔f7 39 ♖×a6 ♖h1 40 a4
♖h3+ 41 ♔d2 ba 42 ♖×a4 ♖×h4
43 ♖c4 ♔g7 44 b4 ♖h1 45 ♖c7+
♔h6 46 ♖c8 h4 47 ♖h8+ ♔g5 48
c4 ♖h2+ 49 ♔d3 ♖h3+ ½–½

18 Korchnoi Training Match   Leningrad, 1971

Karpov	½ 1 1 0 0 ½	**3**
Korchnoi	½ 0 0 1 1 ½	**3**

This match was played (late February/early March?) as part of Korchnoi's preparation for the Candidates'. We are grateful to Victor Korchnoi for confirming the order in which the games were played.

1801 AK–Korchnoi

G1: ?.?.1971: Spanish

1 e4 e5 2 ♘f3 ♘c6 3 ♗b5 a6 4 ♗a4 ♘f6 5 00 ♗e7 6 ♖e1 b5 7 ♗b3 d6 8 c3 00 9 h3 ♘b8 10 d4 ♘bd7 11 ♘bd2 ♗b7 12 ♗c2 ♖e8 13 ♘f1 ♗f8 14 ♘g3 g6 15 ♗g5 h6 16 ♗d2 ♗g7 17 a4 ♘b6 18 ab ab 19 b3 ♘fd7 20 ♗d3 b4 21 ♖×a8 ♗×a8 22 de ♘×e5 23 ♘×e5 de 24 ♕c2 bc 25 ♗×c3 ♕d6 26 ♘f1 ♖d8 27 ♗e2 ♕c5 28 ♘d2 ♕c6 29 ♗f1 ♗b7 30 ♕b2 ♗c8 31 ♘f3 f6 32 ♘d2 ♗e6 33 ♖c1 ♕c5 34 ♘f3 ♕d6 35 ♗a5 ♗f8 36 ♕c3 c5 37 ♗c4 b8 38 ♗×b6 ♕×b6 39 ♘h4 ♔h7 40 ♖d1 ♗×c4 41 bc ♖d8 42 ♖a1 ♕b7 43 ♕f3 ♗g7 44 ♖a5 ♖d4 45 ♖×c5 ♕b1+ 46 ♔h2 ♕×e4 47 ♕×e4 ♖×e4 48 g4 h5 49 ♔g3 hg 50 hg ♖d4 51 ♖c7 ♖d3+ 52 f3 e4 53 ♖e7 ef 54 ♘×f3 ♖c3 55 ♖c7 ♔g8 ½-½

1802 AK–Korchnoi

G2: ?.?.1971: Spanish

1 e4 e5 2 ♘f3 ♘c6 3 ♗b5 a6 4 ♗a4 ♘f6 5 00 ♘×e4 6 d4 b5 7 ♗b3 d5 8 de ♗e6 9 c3 ♗e7 10 ♘bd2 ♕d7!? 11 ♖e1 ♘c5 12 ♗c2 d4 13 ♘e4 dc 14 bc 000 15 ♕e2 ♗c4 16 ♘×c5 ♗×c5 17 ♕e4 ♔b7 18 ♗e3 ♗d5 19 ♕f4 ♗a3 20 ♖ad1 h6 (*131*)

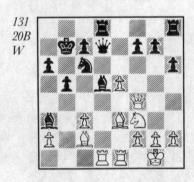

131
20B
W

21 ♖×d5 ♕×d5 22 ♗e4 ♕c4 23 ♘d4 ♕×c3 24 ♗×c6+ ♔b8 25

♖f1 ♖×d4 26 ♗×d4 ♕×c6 27
♕×f7 ♖d8 28 ♗e3 ♕d5 29 e6 ♖f8
30 ♕×g7 ♖e8 31 ♗f4 ♕c4 32 ♕g3
♗b2 33 ♖e1 ♗c3 34 ♕g6 ♗e7 35
♖e4 ♕×a2 36 h4 ♗d4 37 ♗g3 b4
38 ♔h2 ♕d5 39 ♕g4 ♗c5 40
♖×b4+ ♔a7 **1–0**

1803   AK–Korchnoi

G3: ?.?.1971: French

(Notes by Korchnoi)

**1 e4 e6 2 d4 d5 3 ♘d2 c5 4 ♘gf3
♘c6 5 ed ed 6 ♗b5 ♗d6 7 dc
♕e7+?!** (7 ... ♗×c5 8 OO
♘ge7±) **8 ♕e2!** (8 ♗e2 ♗×c5 9
♘b3±) **8 ... ♗×c5** (8 ...
♕×e2+ Tal–Korchnoi, USSR Ch
1973) **9 ♘b3 ♗b6 10 ♘e5!±
♔f8!?** (10 ... ♗d7 11 ♘×d7
♔×d7 12 ♗f4±) **11 ♗f4** (11 ♘×c6
bc 12 ♗×c6 ♗×f2+ 13 ♔d1!±±;
12 ... ♕×e2+ 13 ♔×e2 ♗a6+
with compensation for the pawn)
**11... ♕f6 12 ♗g3 h5 13 h4 ♘ge7
14 000 ♘×e5?!** (14 ... ♗e6, to be
followed by 15 ... ♖e8 and 16 ...
♘f5, is better.) **15 ♗×e5 ♕×f2**
(*132*)

132
15B
W

**16 ♗×g7+ ♔×g7 17 ♕×e7 ♗f5
18 ♕e5+!** (18 ♗d3 ♕e3+ 19
♕×e3 ♗×e3+ 20 ♔b1 ♗g4=) **18
...f6 19 ♕e7+ ♔g6 20 ♖d2!!** (20
♗d3 ♗×d3 21 ♖×d3 ♖ac8 22 c3
♖he8 is about equal; 20 ...
♖ac8!?) **20 ... ♗e3 21 ♖f1
♗×d2+ 22 ♘×d2 ♕d4!** (22 ...
♕×h4 23 ♖×f5 ♔×f5 24 ♗d3+
♔f4 25 ♕b4+ ± ±; or 22 ... ♕×g2
23 ♖×f5 ♔×f5 24 ♗d3+ ♔f4 25
♕×f6+ ± ±) **23 ♖×f5!± ♔×f5 24
♗d3+ ♔f4** (24 ... ♔g4 25 ♕e2+
♔f4 26 ♕f1+ ♔g4 27 ♕f3+
♔×h4 28 g3+ ♔g5 29 ♕f5+ ± ±)
25 ♕d6+ (25 ♕e2 ♕e3!∓) **25 ...
♕e5 26 ♕b4+ d4?!** (26 ... ♔g3
27 ♘f1+ ♔×g2 28 ♕d2+ ♔h3 29
♗f5+ ♔×h4; or 29 ♕f2 ♖g8 30
♗f5+ ♖g4) **27 ♘e4! ♔f5?± ±**
(27 ... ♔g4±) **28 ♕×b7 ♔g4** (28
...♔g6 29 ♘d6+ ± ±) **29 ♗e2+
♔×h4 30 g3+ ♔h3 31 ♘f2+
♔h2** (31 ...♔×g3 32 ♕f3+ ♔h4
33 ♘e4 and 34 ♕h1+± ±) **32
♕h1+ ♔×g3 33 ♘e4+ ♔f4 34
♕f3 mate** (One of the best games
he has played in his whole life.)

1804   AK–Korchnoi

G4: ?.?.1971: Sicilian

1 e4 c5 2 ♘f3 e6 3 d4 cd 4 ♘×d4
♘f6 5 ♘c3 d6 6 ♗e2 ♗e7 7 ♗e3
a6 8 f4 ♕c7 9 g4 d5 10 e5 ♘e4 11
♘×e4 de 12 h4 OO 13 g5 ♖d8 (*133*)
14 c3 ♘c6 15 ♕d2 ♗c5 16 h5 ♗d7
17 ♗g4 ♗e8 18 g6 ♕a5 19 gf+
♗×f7 20 ♘×c6 bc 21 ♕f2 ♗×e3
22 ♕×e3 ♖ab8 23 b4 ♕a3 24 ♕c1

133
13B
W

♕a4 25 ♗e2 c5 26 bc ♕c6 27 ♕e3 ♖b2 28 ♖g1 ♗×h5 29 ♗c4 ♕a4 30 ♗×e6+ ♔h8 31 ♗g4 ♗×g4 32 ♖×g4 ♖×a2 **0–1**

1805 AK–Korchnoi

G5: ?.?.1971: Sicilian

(Karpov)

1 e4 c5 2 ♘f3 d6 3 d4 cd 4 ♘×d4 ♘f6 5 ♘c3 g6 6 ♗e3 ♗g7 7 f3 ♘c6 8 ♗c4 00 9 ♕d2 ♗d7 10 ♗b3 ♖c8 11 000 ♘e5 12 ♗h6 ♘c4 13 ♗×c4 ♗×h6 14 ♕×h6 ♖×c4 15 h4 ♕a5 16 ♘b3 ♕e5 17 ♘d5 ♖fc8 18 c3 ♗c6 19 ♘×f6+ ♕×f6 20 ♔b1 d5 21 ed ♕f5+ 22 ♔a1 ♗×d5 23 h5 e6 24 ♘d4? ♕f6 25 hg hg 26 g4 ♕g7 27 ♕e3 ♖4c5 28 ♖h2 b5 29 ♘b3 ♖c4 30 ♖d4 ♖×d4 31 ♘×d4 b4 32 f4 a5 33 ♘b5 ♕f6 34 g5 ♕g7 35 ♔b1 f6 36 ♘d6 ♖d8 37 ♘e4 fg 38 fg ♗×e4+ 39 ♕×e4 ♕f7 40 ♖e2?? ♕f1+ 41 ♖e1? ♖d1+ 42 ♔c2 ♖×e1 43 ♕×g6+ ♔f8 **0–1**

1806 Korchnoi–AK

G6: ?.?.1971: Queen's Indian

(Notes by Korchnoi)

1 d4 ♘f6 2 c4 e6 3 ♘f3 b6 4 g3 ♗b7 5 ♗g2 ♗e7 6 00 00 7 d5 ed 8 ♘d4 ♘c6 9 cd ♘×d4 10 ♕×d4 c5 11 ♕d2!? (11 ♕d3 Uhlmann–Taimanov, USSR–World 1970) 11 ... d6 12 ♘c3 a6 13 b3?! (13 a4, planning 14 ♖b1 and b4±, is better.) 13 ... ♘d7 14 a4 ♖b8 15 ♖b1 ♗c8 16 ♖d1 ♖e8 17 ♗a3 ♕c7 18 b4 ♘e5 19 ♕f4 (19 ♕a2± is better.) 19 ... ♗d7 20 h3 ♖ec8 21 b5 (21 ♖dc1 ♕d8 threatening 22 ... ♗g5) 21 ... ♖a8 22 ♗c1 ab 23 ab ♖a5∓ 24 ♕e4 ♗f6 25 ♕c2 ♖ca8 26 ♔h2 ♘g6?! (26 ... ♕d8! with ... ♘c4∓ to follow) 27 ♗b2 ♕d8 28 f4 ♕e8 29 e4 ♗×b5 30 ♘×b5 ♖×b5 31 ♗×f6 gf 32 ♖×b5 ♕×b5 33 ♖b1 ♕a6 34 h4 (White has compensation for the pawn.) 34 ... ♔g7 35 h5 ♘f8 36 ♕d1 (36 e5!?) 36 ... h6 37 ♕g4+ ♔h8 38 ♕f5 ♘h7?! (38 ... ♔g7) 39 e5 de 40 d6!? (40 ♗e4 ♕e2+ 41 ♔h3 ♘f8

134
46B
W

42 ♕×f6+ ♔g8 43 ♕×e5±) 40...
♕e2 41 d7 ♔g7 42 ♖×b6 ♖a2 43
♕h3 ♖d2 44 ♖b2! ♖×b2!? (44...
♕d1 45 ♕g4+! ♕×g4 46 ♖×d2 ef
47 d8♕±) 45 d8♕ ♘f8 46 fe fe
(134)
47 ♕dh4? (47 ♕d5 ♘e6 48

♕f5±±; 47... ♖d2 48 ♕c6 e4 49
♕×c5 ♘e6 50 ♕e5+ ♔g8 51
♕f6±±) 47 ... ♖b4! 48 g4
(preparing ♕f3) 48 ... ♖f4! 49
♕4g3 ♘e6 50 ♕e3 ½-½ (50...
♖f2 51 ♕×e2 ♖×e2 52 ♕c3
♘f4∓)

19 Daugavpils 30.5–26.6.1971

39th USSR Championship semi-final

		1	2	3	4	5	6	7	8	9	0	1	2	3	4	5	6	7	8	
1	**Karpov**	×	½	½	1	1	½	½	1	½	½	1	1	1	1	½	½	1	1	**13**
2	Vaganian	½	×	½	0	½	½	1	1	1	0	½	1	1	½	1	1	1	1	**12**
3	Dzhindzhikhashvili	½	½	×	0	½	½	½	1	1	½	1	½	½	1	½	1	1	1	**11½**
4	Karasev	0	1	1	×	½	½	½	½	1	½	1	½	0	1	1	½	1	1	**11½**
5	Alburt	0	½	½	½	×	½	1	0	1	½	0	1	1	½	1	1	½	0	**9½**
6	Gipslis	½	½	½	½	½	×	½	1	0	½	½	½	½	1	½	½	½	½	**9**
7	Furman	½	0	½	½	0	½	×	1	½	1	1	0	1	0	0	0	1	1	**8½**
8	Shabanov	0	0	0	½	1	0	0	×	½	1	½	1	½	1	½	½	1	½	**8½**
9	V. Zhuravlev	½	0	0	0	0	1	½	½	×	½	0	1	1	½	1	1	0	½	**8**
10	Ignatiev	½	1	½	½	½	½	0	0	½	×	½	½	0	½	½	1	½	½	**8**
11	Klovan	0	½	0	0	1	½	0	½	1	½	×	0	½	1	1	1	½	0	**8**
12	Mnatsakanian	0	0	½	½	0	½	1	0	0	½	1	×	½	½	½	½	1	1	**8**
13	Lerner	0	0	½	1	0	½	0	½	0	1	½	½	×	½	½	0	½	1	**7**
14	Ruderfer	0	½	0	0	½	0	1	0	½	½	0	½	½	×	½	1	½	1	**7**
15	Ubilava	½	0	½	0	0	½	1	½	0	½	0	½	½	½	×	0	1	1	**7**
16	Petukhov	½	0	0	½	0	½	1	½	0	0	0	½	1	0	1	×	½	0	**6**
17	Kirillov	0	0	0	0	½	½	0	0	1	½	½	0	½	½	0	½	×	1	**5½**
18	Katalimov	0	0	0	0	1	½	0	½	½	½	1	0	0	0	0	1	0	×	**5**

1901 AK–Alburt

R1: 31.5.1971: Sicilian

1 e4 c5 2 ♘f3 e6 3 d4 cd 4 ♘×d4 ♘f6 5 ♘c3 ♘c6 6 ♘db5 ♗b4 7 a3 ♗×c3+ 8 ♘×c3 d5 9 ed ed 10 ♗d3 00 11 00 d4 12 ♘c2 ♕d5 13 ♘f1 ♕d6 14 ♘h5 ♘g4 15 ♗f4 ♕d8 16 ♘g3 ♕h4 17 ♘f5 ♗×f5 18 ♗×f5 ♘h6 19 ♗g3 ♕g5 20 ♗e4 f5 21 f4 ♕g6 22 ♗f3 ♘g4 23 ♕d3 ♖ad8 24 ♖fe1 ♔h8 25 ♖e2 ♖fe8 26 ♖ae1 ♖e3 27 ♕b5 ♖×e2 28 ♗×e2 ♘e3 29 ♕d3 h6 30 ♗f3 ♖e8 31 b4 a6 32 c3 ♘g4 33 ♖×c8+ ♕×c8 34 cd ♕d7 35 d5 ♘e7 36 h3 ♘f6 37 ♗h4

♕d6 38 ♕d4 b6 39 a4 a5 40 ba ba
41 ♗e1 ♘c6 42 ♕c4 ♘e7 43 ♗×a5
♘e×d5 44 ♕d4 ♕e6 45 ♗d2 ♘e4
46 a5 ♘×d2 47 ♕×d2 ♘f6 48 ♔h2
♔h7 49 ♕e2 ♘e4 50 a6 ♕c6 51 a7
♕a4 52 ♕e3 h5 53 ♗×h5 ♕a5 54
♗e2 g6 55 ♗f3 ♘d2 56 ♕e7+ **1–0**

1902 AK–Karasev

R2: 1.6.1971: English

1 c4 e5 2 ♘c3 ♘f6 3 g3 c6 4 ♘f3 e4
5 ♘d4 d5 6 cd cd 7 d3 (? Karpov) 7
. . . ♗c5 8 ♘b3 ♗b6 (? Karpov) 9
♗g2 ♗f5 10 00 e3 11 ♗×e3 ♗×e3
12 fe ♗g6 (*135*)

135
12B
W

13 ♖×f6 gf 14 ♘×d5 ♘d7 15 ♕f1
00 16 ♕f4 f5 17 ♘d4 ♘f6 18
♘×f6+ ♕×f6 19 g4 ♖ae8 20 ♖f1
♔h8 21 h4 ♕e7 (21 . . . ♕×h4 22 gf
♕×f4 23 ♖×f4 ♗h5 24 ♖h4± ±)
22 h5 fg 23 hg fg 24 ♔g3 ♖×f1+ 25
♔×f1 h5 26 ♗e4 ♕g5 27 ♕d6
♔h7 28 ♔g2 h4 29 ♕f4 ♕×f4 30 ef
♔h6 31 b4 ♖d8 32 ♘c2 ♖c8 33
♘e3 ♔h5 34 f5 gf 35 ♗×f5 ♖e8 36
♗×g4+ ♔g5 37 ♔f3 ♖f8+ 38
♘f5 ♖c8 39 ♘d4 ♖f8+ 40 ♗f5
♖h8 41 ♗h3 ♖f8+ 42 ♔g2 ♖g8

43 ♘f3+ ♔f6+ 44 ♔f2 ♖g3 45
♗f1 b6 46 e4 **1–0**

1903 Vaganian–AK

R3: 2.6.1971: Nimzo-Indian

1 d4 ♘f6 2 c4 e6 3 ♘c3 ♗b4 4 e3 c5
5 ♗d3 00 6 ♘ge2 d5 7 a3 cd 8 ed dc
9 ♗×c4 ♗e7 10 00 b6 11 ♗g5 ♗b7
12 ♕d3 ♘c6 ½–½

1904 AK–Klovan

R4: 4.6.1971: Spanish

(Karpov)

1 e4 e5 2 ♘f3 ♘c6 3 ♗b5 a6 4
♗×c6 dc 5 00 f6 6 d4 ed 7 ♘×d4
♘e7 8 ♗e3 ♘g6 9 ♘d2 ♗d6 10
c3? 00 11 ♕b3+ ♔h8 12 ♘f5?
♗×f5 13 ef ♘h4 14 ♕×b7 ♕d7 15
♕b3 ♘×f5 16 ♘c4 ♖fe8 17 ♖ad1
♖ab8 18 ♕c2 b5 19 ♖fe1 ♘×e3
20 ♘×e3 ♖be5 21 g3 ♕e6 22 b3
♔g8 23 ♘g2 ♖e2 24 ♖×e2 ♕×e2
25 ♖d2 ♕f3 26 ♔f1 ♖e5 27 ♕d3
♕×d3+ 28 ♖×d3 ♔f7 29 ♘e3
♔e6 30 ♘c4 ♖h5 31 h4 ♗c5 32
♘b2 ♖f5 33 ♖d2 h5 34 ♘d3 ♗d6
35 ♖e2+ ♔d7 36 ♖e3 (*136*)

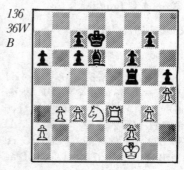

136
36W
B

36 . . . g5?? 37 c4! c5 38 ♔g2 c6 39 f3 gh 40 gh ♗f4 41 ♖ e4 ♗d6 42 f4 **1-0**

1905 Ruderfer–AK

R5: 5.6.1971: Catalan

1 d4 ♘f6 2 c4 e6 3 ♘f3 d5 4 g3 dc 5 ♗g2 b5 6 a4 c6 7 00 ♗b7 8 ♘c3 a6 9 e4 ♘bd7 10 ♕e2 ♗e7 11 e5 ♘d5 12 ♘e4 h6 13 h4 ♕c7 14 ♗d2 c5 15 ab ab 16 dc ♖×a1 17 ♖×a1 ♘×c5 18 ♘×c5 ♗×c5 19 b3 00 20 bc bc 21 ♕e4 (*137*)

137
21W
B

21 . . . ♘e3! 22 ♕f4 ♘×g2 23 ♔×g2 ♕c6 24 ♖d1 ♖d8 **0-1** (the threats of 25 . . . ♖d4 and 25 . . . c3 cannot be met.)

1906 AK–Ignatiev

R6: 6.6.1971: Sicilian

(Karpov)

1 c4 c5 2 ♘c3 ♘c6 3 ♘f3 ♘f6 4 d4 cd 5 ♘×d4 g6 6 e4 ♘×d4 7 ♕×d4 d6 8 ♗e3 ♗g7 9 f3 00 10 ♕d2 ♗e6 11 ♖c1 a6 12 ♗e2 ♕a5 13 ♘d5 ♕×d2+ 14 ♔×d2 ♗×d5 15 cd ♖fc8 16 b4? ♘d7 17 f4 ♔f8 18 a4

♔e8 19 a5 ♔d8 20 ♔d3? ♖×c1 21 ♖×c1 ♖c8 22 ♖×c8+ ♔×c8 23 g4 ♔c7 24 h4 ♗a1 25 g5 ♗b2 26 ♗g4 ♔d8 27 ♗d1 ♔c7 28 ♗a4 ♔d8 29 ♗b3 ♔e8 30 ♗c2 ♔d8 31 ♗a4 ♔c7 32 ♗c2 ♔d8 33 ♗b3 ♔e8 34 ♗d1 ♔d8 35 ♗e2 ♔c7 36 ♗f3 ♔c8 37 ♗g4 ♔d8 38 ♔c2 ♗a1 39 ♗f3 ♔c7 40 ♗e2 ♗g7 41 h5 ♗a1 42 ♔d3 ♔d8 43 ♗g4 ♔e8 44 ♗d1 ♔d8 45 ♗f3 ♔c7 46 ♗c1 ♔d8 47 ♗d1 ♔c8 48 ♗f3 ♔c7 49 ♗e2 ♔d8 50 ♔c2 ♔c8 51 ♗d1 ♔d8 52 ♗g4 ♗h8 53 ♗e2 ♗a1 54 ♗d2 ♗d4 55 ♔d3 ♗b2 56 ♔e3 ♔c8 57 ♗d1 ♔d8 58 ♗g4 ♗a1 59 ♗e2 ♗b2 60 h6 ♗a1 61 b5 ab 62 ♗×b5 ♗b2 63 ♗b4 ♗c1+ 64 ♔f3 ♗b2 65 a6 ba 66 ♗×a6 ♗d4 67 ♗b5 ♗b6 68 ♗c3 ♗c7 69 ♗d4 ♗b8 70 ♔e2 ♗c7 71 ♗e3 ♗a5 72 ♔d3 ♗c7 73 ♔c4 ♗a5 74 ♗c1 ♗e1 75 ♔d4 ♗f2+ 76 ♗e3 ♗e1 77 ♗c1 ♗a5 78 ♔c4 ♗e1 79 ♗e3 ♔c7 80 ♔d3 ♔d8 81 ♗d4 ♔e8 82 ♔e3 ♗b4 83 ♔d3 ♗a3 84 ♔e2 ♗b4 ½-½

1907 Lerner–AK

R7: 9.6.1971: Sicilian

(Karpov)

1 e4 c5 2 ♘f3 e6 3 d4 cd 4 ♘×d4 ♘c6 5 ♘c3 a6 6 g3 ♘ge7 7 ♘b3 ♘a5 8 ♗g2 ♘ec6 9 00 d6 10 ♘d2 ♗d7 11 b3 ♗e7 12 ♗b2 00 13 ♘f3 ♕c7? 14 ♘e2 ♖fd8 15 ♘f4 b5 16 h4 ♖ac8 17 ♖c1 h6 18 ♕e2 ♘b7 19 e5 ♗f8 20 ♘h5 ♗e8 21 ♖fd1 ♘b4! 22 ♕e4 d5 23 ♕g4 ♘×a2 24

萱a1 ᗡc3 25 萱d3 ᗡe4 26 ᗡd4 ᗡbc5 27 萱e3 ♛×e5 28 f4 ᗡf6 29 ᗡ×f6+ ♛×f6 30 萱b1 ♛e7 31 萱be1 f5 32 ♛h3 ᗡe4 33 g4 ♗d7 34 g5 h5 35 g6 ♗f6 36 ♗×e4 de 37 萱g3 ♗c5 38 c3 b4 39 ♔h1 bc 40 ♗×c3 ♗×d4 41 ♗×d4 ♛×d4 42 ♛g2 e3 43 ♛e2 **0-1**

1908 AK-Shabanov

R8: 10.6.1971: Bogoljubow

1 d4 ᗡf6 2 c4 e6 3 g3 ♗b4+ 4 ᗡd2 00 5 ♗g2 d5 6 ♛c2 ᗡbd7 7 ᗡgf3 c6 8 00 ♗e8 9 萱d1 b5?! 10 c5 ♗a5 11 e4 de 12 ᗡ×e4 ᗡ×e4 13 ♛×e4 ♗b7 14 ♗f4 ᗡf6 15 ♛c2 (? Karpov) 15 ... ᗡd5 16 ♗d6 (White has won the opening contest, but Black's knight at d5 could be a fine piece.) 16 ... f6 17 a3 ♛d7 18 ᗡd2 ♗d8 19 萱e1 a5 20 ♗h3! ♛f7 21 ♛e4 ♗c8 22 f4 ♗d7 (Karpov stops here, giving the end of the game as 22 ... a4 1-0. The source for the game continuation is *Shakhmatny Bulletin* No. 10 1971.) 23 萱e2 a4 24 ♛f3 ♗a5 25 ᗡe4 h6 26 ᗡf2 萱a7 27 ᗡd3 萱aa8 28 ♔h1 ♔h8 29 ♗g4! g6 (*138*)

138
29B
W

30 ♗h3 萱g8 31 ♗g2 萱ae8 32 萱f1 ♔h7 33 g4! ♗d8 34 ♛g3 ♗e7 35 g5! ♗d8 (35 ... ♗×d6 36 cd ♛f8 37 ♛h4 h5 38 gf and ᗡe5) 36 gf ♗×f6 37 ᗡe5 ♛g7 38 萱ef2! 萱c8 39 ♛h3 ♗×e5 40 fe ♛h8 41 萱f7+ 萱g7 42 ♗f8! **1-0**

1909 V. Zhuravlev-AK

R9: 11.6.1971: Sicilian

(Notes by Karpov)

1 e4 c5 2 ᗡf3 ᗡc6 3 c3 d5 4 ed ♛×d5 5 d4 e6 6 ♗d3 ᗡf6 7 00 cd 8 cd ♗e7 9 ᗡc3 ♛d6 (perhaps 9 ... ♛d8) 10 ♛e2 00 11 萱d1 ᗡd5 12 ♛e4 f5 13 ♛e1! ♗f6 14 ♗c4 ♔h8 15 ♗×d5 ed 16 ᗡb5 ♛d7 17 ♗f4 a6 18 ᗡd6 ♗e7 19 ᗡe5 ♛×d6 20 ᗡ×c6 ♛×c6 21 ♛×e7 萱e8 22 ♛a3? ♛d7 23 萱ac1? ♛e6 24 ♗e5 萱ac8 25 f4 萱×c1+ 26 萱×c1 ♗c6 27 萱c3 萱e7 28 萱g3 ♔g8 29 ♛a5 ♛d7 30 ♛b6 h6 31 b3 ♔h7 32 a4 ♛e8 33 h3 萱d7 34 ♔h2 ½-½

1910 AK-Katalimov

R10: 13.6.1971: Sicilian

(Notes by Karpov)

1 e4 c5 2 ᗡf3 ᗡc6 3 d4 cd 4 ᗡ×d4 ᗡf6 5 ᗡc3 d6 6 ♗g5 ♗d7 7 ♛d2 ᗡ×d4 8 ♛×d4 ♛a5 9 ♗d2 e5 10 ♛d3 萱c8 11 ♗g5 ♛b4 (11 ... d5 12 ♗×f6 gf 13 ♛×d5 ♗b4 14 000!±± was played in Stein-Tukmakov, Sochi 1970.) 12 000 萱×c3 13 bc ♛×e4 14 f4! ♛a4 15 萱e1 ᗡg4 16 ♛c4 h6 17 ♛×a4

♗×a4 18 ♗h4 g5 19 h3! gh 20 hg
♗g7 21 ♖×h4 ♗d7 22 g3 ♔e7 23
g5 ♗e6 24 c4 hg 25 ♖×h8 ♗×h8
26 fg f6 27 ♖e3 fg 28 ♖b3 b6 29
♖a3 a5 30 ♖b3 e4! 31 ♖×b6 ♗e5
32 ♖b3 ♗d4 33 ♖b5 ♗g4 34 ♔d2
♗c5 35 ♗e2 ♗e6 36 ♔c3 a4 37
♖a5 a3? (37 ... ♗d7!) 38 ♔b3
♔f6 39 ♖×a3! ♗×a3 40 ♔×a3
♔e5 41 c3 ♗d7 42 ♔b4 ♗c6 43 a4
♔e6 44 a5 ♔d7 45 ♔b3 *(139)*

139
45W
B

45 ...   e3
The sealed move.

45 ... ♗a8! was also possible: 46
♔c2 ♔c6! 47 ♔d2 (47 ♗g4 leads
nowhere: 47 ... ♔b7 48 ♗e6 ♔a6
49 ♗d5 ♗×d5 50 cd ♔×a5 51
♔d2 ♔b5 52 ♔e3 ♔c4! 53 ♔×e4
g4! 54 ♔f5 ♔×d5 55 ♔×g4 ♔c4
56 ♔f5 ♔×c3 57 ♔e6 ♔c4!!) 47
... ♔c5 48 ♔e3 ♗c6 (48 ... ♗b7
loses to 49 ♗f1 ♗c6 50 a6 ♔b6 51
♔d4 ♗a8 52 ♗g2 e3 53 ♗f1
♔×a6 54 c5+ ♔b7 55 cd ♔c6 56
♔e5 ♔d7 57 ♗e2± ±) 49 a6 ♔b6!
(49 ... ♗a8 50 ♗g4 ♔×c4 51 ♗c8
♔×c3 52 ♗b7) 50 ♔d4 ♗a8 51
♗f1 ♗c6 52 ♗g2 e3 53 ♗f1 ♔×a6
54 ♔×e3±.

46 c5!   dc
47 ♔c4   ♔d6
48 ♔d3   ♔c7
49 ♔×e3 ♔b8 50 ♗f3 ♗a4 51
♗d5 ♗a7 52 ♔e4 ♔a6 53 ♔f5
♔×a5 54 ♔×g5 ♗c2 55 g4 ♔a4 56
♔f6 ♔a3 57 c4 **1-0**

1911   Ubilava–AK

R11: 14.6.1971: Sicilian

(Notes by Karpov)

1 e4 c5 2 ♘f3 e6 3 ♘c3 a6 4 g3 ♘c6
5 ♗g2 d6 6 OO ♘f6 7 d4 cd 8 ♘×d4
♗d7 9 ♗e3 ♗e7 10 ♘b3 b5
(against a4) 11 f4 OO 12 e5 de 13 fe
♘×e5 14 ♗×a8 ♕×a8 15 ♗d4
♘eg4 16 ♗×f6 ♘×f6 17 ♖×f6
♗×f6 18 ♕×d7 ♖d8 19 ♕c7 b4
(140)

140
19B
W

20 ♘e2
If 20 ♘a4 ♖c8 21 ♘b6 ♖×c7 22
♘×a8, and then there are two
continuations:
a) 22 ... ♖c6 23 a3 ba 24 ♖×a3
♗×b2 25 ♖a2 ♖×c2 26 ♖×a6±;
b) 22 ... ♖c8 23 ♘b6 ♖c2 24
♘a4 ♗×b2 25 ♘×b2! ♖×b2 26

♘c5 a5 27 ♘b3 a4 28 ♘c5 a3 29 ♘d3 ♖c2 30 ♘×b4± ± .

20 . . .	♖c8
21 ♕d7	♗×b2
22 ♖f1	♗f6
23 ♕d3	½–½

If 23 . . . a5 24 ♘d2 ♕a7+ 25 ♖f2! (25 ♔g2 ♖d8 26 ♕b5 ♕a8+ 27 ♘f3 e5∓).

1912 AK–Dzhindzhikhashvili

R12: 15.6.1971: Sicilian

(Notes by Karpov)

1 e4 c5 2 ♘f3 e6 3 d4 cd 4 ♘×d4 ♘f6 5 ♘c3 d6 6 ♗e2 ♘c6 7 ♗e3 ♗e7 8 00 00 9 f4 ♗d7 10 ♔h1 (10 ♘b3!?) 10 . . . a6 11 ♕e1 ♘×d4 12 ♗×d4 ♗c6 13 ♗d3 ♘d7 14 ♖d1 e5 15 ♗e3 (15 fe!?) 15 . . . b5 16 ♘d5 ♗×d5 17 ed ½–½

1913 Mnatsakanian–AK

R13: 18.6.1971: Scotch

1 e4 e5 2 ♘f3 ♘c6 3 ♘c3 ♘f6 4 d4 ed 5 ♘×d4 ♗b4 6 ♘×c6 bc 7 ♗d3 00 8 00 d5 9 ed cd 10 ♗g5 c6 11 ♘e2 ♗d6 12 ♘d4 ♗d7 13 ♕f3 ♖e8 14 ♗×f6 ♕×f6 15 ♕×f6 gf 16 ♗f5 (? Karpov) 16 . . . ♗×f5 17 ♘×f5 ♗c5 18 ♖fe1 ♖e5 (! Karpov) 19 g4 ♖b8 20 b3 ♖b4 21 c4 dc 22 ♖ed1 h5 23 bc hg 24 ♘d4 ♖×c4 25 ♘b3 ♗b6 26 ♖ac1 ♗f4 27 ♖d2 ♖ef5 28 ♖cc2 c5 **0–1**

1914 AK–Kirillov

R14: 19.6.1971: Pirc

(Notes by Karpov)

1 e4 g6 2 d4 ♗g7 3 ♘f3 d6 4 c3 ♘f6 5 ♗d3 00 6 00 ♘bd7 7 ♘bd2 e5 8 ♖e1 c6 9 a4 a5 10 ♕c2 ♕c7 11 b3 ♖e8 12 ♗a3 b6 13 ♗f1 ♗b7 14 de de 15 ♘c4 ♗f8 16 ♗×f8 ♔×f8 *(141)*

141
16B
W

17 b4 (Inaccurate. 17 ♖ad1 ♗a6 18 ♘d6! ♖e6 19 ♕d2 ♗×f1 20 ♔×f1± is stronger.) 17 . . . ♗a6 18 ♖ad1 ♗×c4 19 ♗×c4 h6 20 ♖d2 ♔g7 21 ♖ed1 ♖e7 22 ♖d6 ♘e8 23 ♖6d2 ♘ef6 24 h3 ♘f8 25 ♘h2 ♘e6? 26 ♗×e6 ♖×e6 27 ♘g4 ♘×g4 28 hg ♖ee8 29 ♖d7 ♕b8 30 ♕b3 ♖f8 31 ♕e6 ab 32 ♖1d6 ♔g8 33 ♕×e5 ♔h7 34 ♕f6 ♔g8 35 cb ♖×a4 36 e5 **1–0**

1915 Petukhov–AK

R15: 21.6.1971: QP/English

1 d4 ♘f6 2 ♘f3 c5 3 e3 g6 4 ♗e2 ♗g7 5 00 b6 6 b3 ♗b7 7 ♗b2 00 8 c4 d6 9 ♘c3 ♘bd7 10 ♕c2 e6 11

♖fd1 ♕e7 12 ♖d2 ♖fd8 13 ♖ad1
a6 14 d5 e5 15 e4 ♗h6 16 ♖d3 b5 17
♘e1 b4 18 ♘b1 ♖f8 19 ♖h3 ♔g7
20 g4 ♗g5 21 ♘g2 ♔g8 22 ♘d2 h6
23 ♘f3 a5 24 ♖g3 ♗f4 25 ♘×f4 ef
26 ♖h3 ♘×g4 27 ♕d2 g5 28 ♘h4
gh 29 ♗×g4 ♘e5 30 ♕×f4 ♕g5 31
♕×g5 hg 32 f3 f6 33 ♔g2 ½-½

1916 AK–Furman

R16: ?.6.1971

This game is not available.

1917 Gipslis–AK

R17: ?.6.1971

This game is not available.

20 Student Olympiad   1–17.7.1971
        Mayaguez, Puerto Rico

		1	2	3	4	5	6	7	8	9	
1	USSR	×	3½	4	2½	4	4	4	4	3½	**29½**
2	USA	½	×	1½	2½	2½	3½	4	3	4	**21½**
3	Canada	0	2½	×	2	3	3½	2	4	4	**21**
4	Israel	1½	1½	2	×	2½	3½	2½	3	4	**20½**
5	Iceland	0	1½	1	1½	×	2	2½	2½	3½	**14½**
6	Brazil	0	½	½	½	2	×	2	3	2½	**11**
7	Austria	0	0	2	1½	1½	2	×	2	2	**11**
8	Puerto Rico	0	1	0	1	1½	1	2	×	2½	**9**
9	Columbia	½	0	0	0	½	1½	2	1½	×	**6**

The Soviet Union won with their accustomed ease – this was their thirteenth victory in seventeen attempts (they have been second on three occasions. There was also their 1963 'disaster' when they finished fourth). Karpov participated as the third board (four boards and two reserves), the full team being Tukmakov, Balashov, Karpov, Podgayets, Kuzmin and Razuvayev.

It was only in the last round that Karpov missed sharing the absolute best result of the event (Razuvayev had already scored 7/7), but his score of 7½/8 (93·8% was the best score by a board three and was equalled only by Kuzmin (with an identical score).

'Karpov played . . . very effortlessly and with elegance. Normally he was the first to finish his game, not using up more than an hour on the clock. It seemed that his opponents did not understand the thinking of the young grandmaster. In my opinion Karpov possesses a very original and subtle chess style, and it would be difficult to name his chess predecessor. That is always the sign of a great talent.' Grandmaster Aivar Gipslis in his report on Mayaguez in *64*.

2001   AK–Silva (Peru)

PR1: ?.7.1971: (board 3)

This game is not available.

2002   AK–Torres (PR)

PR2: ?.7.1971: (board 2)

This game is not available.

2003   AK–Markula (A)

PR4: ?.7.1971: (board 3)

This game is not available.

2004   AK–Camacho (PR)

FR3: ?.7.1971: (board 2)

2005   Amos–AK

FR4: ?.7.1971: Sicilian

(board 2) (Notes by Karpov)

1 e4 c5 2 ♘f3 e6 3 d4 cd 4 ♘×d4
♘c6 5 ♘c3 a6 6 g3 ♘ge7 (6 . . .
♘×d4 7 ♕×d4 ♘e7 8 ♗f4 ♘g6 9
♗d6 ♗×d6 10 ♕×d6 ♕e7 11
♕b6± Holmov–Karpov, USSR
Ch 1970) 7 ♘b3 ♘a5!? TN 8 ♗g2
♘ec6 9 00 d6 10 ♘d2 ♗d7 11 b3
♗e7 12 ♗b2 ♖c8 (12 . . . 00? 13 a3
b5 14 b4 ♘c4 15 ♘×c4±) 13 ♘e2
00 14 c4? (14 a3!?) 14 . . . b5 15 cb ab
16 ♘f3 b4 17 a3 ♖b8 18 a4 (18 ab
♖×b4 19 ♗a3 ♖×e4 20 ♘d2
♖b4∓) 18 . . . e5! 19 ♘d2 ♗f6 20
♖c1 ♗e6 21 f4 ef 22 ♗×f6 ♕×f6 23
♘×f4 (23 gf ♗g4∓) 23 . . . ♖fe8 24
♘d5 (24 ♘×e6!?) 24 . . . ♕d4+ 25
♔h1 ♔h8 26 ♕e2 ♘e5 27 h3 h6

(27 . . . ♕b2 28 ♖b1 ♕a2 29 ♖a1
♕c2∓) 28 ♖fd1 ♘d3 **0–1**

2006   AK–Rogoff

FR6: ?.7.1971: English

(board 3)   (Notes by Karpov)

1 c4 e5 2 ♘c3 ♘f6 3 g3 ♗b4 4 ♗g2
00 5 d3 c6 6 ♕b3 ♗a5 7 ♘f3 d5 (7
. . . e4 8 de ♘×e4 9 ♗d2) 8 00 d4 9
♘a4 ♘bd7? 10 e3 de 11 ♗×e3 ♗c7
12 a3 ♖e8 13 ♖ad1 ♗d6 14 d4 ed
15 ♘×d4 ♗f8 16 ♕c3 ♕e7 17
♖fe1 ♕e5 18 b4 ♕h5 19 h3 ♘b6 20
♘×b6 ab 21 g4 ♕g6 (*142*)

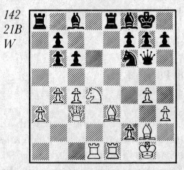

142
21B
W

22 ♗f4 ♗d7 23 ♘f3! ♖×e1+ 24
♖×e1 ♘e8 25 ♕d2!! ♖d8 26 ♘h4
1–0

2007   AK–Wittmann

FR8: ?.7.1971: King's Indian

(board 1)   (Notes by Karpov)

1 c4 ♘f6 2 ♘c3 g6 3 g3 ♗g7 4 ♗g2
00 5 ♘f3 d6 6 00 c6 7 d4 ♘a5 8 h3
e5 9 e4 ♘fd7? 10 d5 c5 11 a3± ♘a6
12 ♗e3 ♕d8 13 ♘e1 f5 14 ef gf 15 f4
e4 16 g4!± ± fg 17 hg ♘f6 18 f5 h5

19 gh ♘h7 20 h6! ♗e5 21 ♕h5
♔h8 22 ♘×e4 ♗×b2 23 ♖a2 ♘f6
24 ♕g6! ♖g8 (*143*)

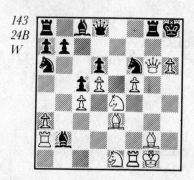

143
24B
W

25 ♖×b2! **1–0** (25 ... ♖×g6 26
fg± ±)

2008 Ruiz–AK

FR9: ?.7.1971: Sicilian

(board 3)   (Notes by de Greiff)

1 e4 c5 2 ♘c3 ♘c6 3 g3 g6 4 ♗g2
♗g7 5 d3 d6 6 f4 e6 7 ♘f3 ♘ge7 8
00 00 9 ♗e3 ♘d4 10 ♖b1 ♘ec6 11
a3 ♖b8 12 ♘e2 a5 13 c3 ♘×e2+
14 ♕×e2 a4 15 e5 ♘a5 16 ♖bd1
♕c7 17 ed ♕×d6 18 f5!± (A strong
blow, threatening ♗f4. In this
position, Karpov thought for more
than half an hour and finally
offered a draw which the
Colombian, although he has some
advantage, accepted.) ½–½

board 6	1	2	3	4	5	6	
1 Karpov	×	1	1	1	½	1*	**4½**
2 Peresipkin	0	×	1	½	1	1	**3½**
3 Veselovsky	0	0	×	1	1	1	**3**
4 Shteinberg	0	½	0	×	½	1	**2**
5 A. Petrosian	½	0	0	½	×	½	**1½**
6 Lisenko	0*	0	0	0	½	×	**½**

preliminaries	1	2	3	4	
1 Karpov	×	1	1	1	**3**
2 Lisenko	0	×	1	1	**2**
3 Gofshtein	0	0	×	½	**½**
4 Markovsky	0	0	½	×	**½**

* This game, played in the preliminaries, also counted towards the finals.

Karpov's 6½/7, on junior board for the Armed Forces team, earned him both the board prize and the absolute best result.

Results of the tournament: 1 Burevestnik 26½/45; 2 Armed Forces 26½ (losing their individual match against Burevestnik); 3 Avangard 24; 4 Spartak 20½; 5 Lokomotiv 20; 6 Trud 17½.

'On the junior board, Karpov played in a noticeably different class from the other juniors. Our youngest grandmaster has finally played his last opponent on the junior board and in future will improve in meetings with stronger opponents . . .' – Roshal.

2101   AK–Gofshtein

PR1: ?.8.1971: English

1 c4 g6 2 g3 ♗g7 3 ♘f3 f5 4 ♗g2 e5 5 d3 d6 6 00 ♘c6 7 ♘c3 ♘h6 8 ♗g5 ♕d7 9 ♘d5 ♘g8 10 b4 ♘d8 11 ♗d2 c6 12 ♘c3 ♘e7 13 ♕c1 h6 14 a4 ♘f7 15 ♘e1 00 16 b5 ♖e8 17 a5 d5 18 ♘c2 dc 19 dc e4 20 ♖d1 ♕e6 21 ♖a4 ♗d7 22 a6 ba 23 ba g5 24 ♗e1 ♘g6 25 c5 ♖ad8 26 ♘d4 ♕e7 27 ♖a5 ♘ge5 28 ♘a2 ♗c8 29 ♘b4 ♕f6 30 ♗c3 ♕g6 31 ♖a2 ♖e7 32 f4 ef 33 ef f4 34 gf gf 35 ♕×f4 ♘g5 36 ♔h1 ♖f7 37 ♕c1 ♘g×f3 **1–0** (time)

2102

This game, which Karpov won

against V. Markovsky, is not available.

2103   Lisenko–AK

PR3: ?.8.1971: English

1 c4 c5 2 g3 g6 3 ♗g2 ♗g7 4 ♘c3 ♘c6 5 e3 e5 6 ♘ge2 ♘ge7 7 ♖b1 00 8 a3 a5 9 ♘d5 d6 10 00 ♗g4 11 h3 ♗d7 12 ♘ec3 ♖b8 13 b4 cb 14 ab ♘×d5 15 ♘×d5 b5 16 d3 ab 17 ♘×b4 ♗×b4 18 ♖×b4 bc 19 ♖×b8 ♕×b8 20 dc ♖c8 21 ♗a3 ♗f8 22 ♕d3 ♗f5 23 e4 ♗e6 24 ♖c1 ♖c6 25 ♗f1 ♕c8 26 ♔h2 ♕a8 27 ♗b2 ♕b7 28 ♖c2 ♖b6 29 ♗c3 ♖b3 30 f4 ef 31 ♕d4 fg+ 32 ♔×g3 ♖×c3+ 33 ♕×c3 ♕×e4 34 ♗g2 ♕f5 35 ♖f2 ♕c5 36 ♗f1 d5 37 ♖c2 ♕g1+ 38 ♗g2 dc 39 ♕d2 ♕c5 40 ♔h2 ♗d6+ 41 ♔h1 ♗e5 42 ♖a2 c3 43 ♖a8+ ♔g7 44 ♕c1 c2 45 ♖d8 ♗f5 46 ♖d2 ♕c3 47 ♖f2 ♕g3 48 ♔g1 ♕h2+ 49 ♔f1 ♗d3+ 50 ♔e1 ♗c3+ **0–1**

FR1: Game 2103 counted as the first round of the finals.

2104   AK–A. Petrosian

FR2: ?.8.1971: Alekhine

1 e4 ♘f6 2 e5 ♘d5 3 d4 d6 4 ♘f3 g6 5 ♗e2 ♗g7 6 c4 ♘b6 7 ed cd 8 h3 00 9 00 (following Karpov's score. The Russian bulletins *Mezhdunarod-nie Vstrechi* gave the order 9 ♘c3 ♘c6 10 00.) 9 . . . ♘c6 10 ♘c3 ♗f5 11 ♗f4 h6 12 ♗e3 d5 13 b3 dc 14 bc ♖c8 15 ♖c1 ♘a5 16 c5 ♘bc4 17 ♗f4 g5 18 ♗g3 (According to Krogius, *Shakhmatny Bulletin* No. 10 1971, 18 ♗e3? was played.) 18 . . . ♕d7 19 ♖e1 b6 20 ♗×c4? (20 cb Karpov) 20 . . . ♘×c4 21 ♕e2 bc 22 d5 ♗×c3 23 ♖×c3 ½–½

2105   Veselovsky–AK

FR3: ?.8.1971: Sicilian

(Notes by Polugayevsky and Karpov)

1 e4 c5 2 ♘f3 e6 3 d4 cd 4 ♘×d4 ♘c6 5 ♘c3 a6 6 g3 ♘ge7 7 ♘de2 b5 8 a3 ♗b7 9 ♗g2 ♘c8 10 00 ♗e7 11 f4 00 12 ♔h1 ♘d6 13 g4 b4 14 ab ♘×b4 15 g5 ♖c8? (15 . . . f5! Karpov) 16 ♘g3 ♘c4 (*144*)

144
16B
W

(In order to get to c4, Black's knight has travelled via g8-e7-c8-d6-c4. White tries to drive it away so that he can develop his Q-side – Polugayevsky.) 17 b3 ♘a3 (! Polugayevsky; ? Karpov!!) 18 ♗×a3 ♖×c3 19 ♘h5 (? better 19 ♕d4 – Karpov) 19 . . . e5 (? 19 . . . ♕b6! – Karpov) (White is already in time-trouble. Nonetheless he

plays resourcefully – Polugayevsky.) 20 ♖c1 (? 20 ♘f6+ ! –
Karpov) 20 . . . ♘a2 21 ♗b2 ♖c5
22 ♖a1 ♘c3 (Karpov gives 0–1 at
this point – KJO'C.) 23 ♕e1 ♕c7
24 fe ♗×g5 25 ♘×g7 (White must
adopt violent methods otherwise he
will not survive – Polugayevsky!) 25
. . . ♔×g7 26 ♖f5 ♗e7 27 ♕e3
♔h8 28 ♕h6 (White appears to
have good chances with his attack.
He threatens 29 ♖h5. If 28 . . .
♖c6, then 29 e6 ♖×e6 30 ♕h3. On
28 . . . ♕c6 White can answer with
29 ♖f6, not 29 e6 when Black can
play 29 . . . ♕×e4. Black has to
play 28 . . . ♖×e5, but even then
his position remains quite difficult.
However, this is all academic
because what actually happened
was that White's flag fell –
Polugayevsky.) **0–1** (time)

2106   Peresipkin–AK

FR4: ?.8.1971: Sicilian

(Notes by Karpov and Polugayevsky)

1 e4 c5 2 ♘f3 e6 3 d4 cd 4 ♘×d4
♘c6 5 ♘b5 d6 6 ♗f4 e5 7 ♗e3 a6 8
♘5c3 ♘f6 9 ♗g5 ♗e7 10 ♗×f6
♗×f6 11 ♗c4 ♘a5? 12 ♗b3 0–0 13
0–0 ♗e6 14 ♘d5 ♗g5 15 ♘bc3 ♖c8
16 ♕e2 ♗h6 17 ♖fd1 ♔h8 18 ♖d3
♘c6 19 ♕d1 ♘d4 20 ♘e3 b5
(better 20 . . . ♕h4) 21 ♘cd5 ♕h4
22 f3 f5 23 ef ♘×f5 24 ♘g4 ♖c5 25
♘b6! ♕e7 (*145*) (not 25 . . . ♗c4 26
♗×c4 bc 27 ♖×d6!± ±)

145
25B
W

26 ♘×h6 (26 ♗×e6 ♕×e6 27 c3 is
more circumspect – Polugayevsky.)
26 . . . gh (Black now obtains the
g–file which, in combination with
the weak black squares, gives him a
very dangerous attack – Polugayevsky.) 27 ♗×e6 ♕×e6 28 ♘d5
♖g8 29 ♔h1 h5 30 ♕d2 h4 31 ♘e3
h3 32 gh ♘d4 (It's all over! –
Polugayevsky.) 33 ♖f1 ♕×h3 34
♖×d4 ed 35 ♕×d4+ ♖e5! 36
♕×d6? (Overlooking a mate in
two, but it no longer matters what
White plays – Polugayevsky.) 36
. . . ♕×h2+ ! **0–1**

2107   AK–Shteinberg

FR5: ?.8.1971: Sicilian

1 e4 c5 2 ♘f3 d6 3 d4 cd 4 ♘×d4
♘f6 5 ♘c3 e6 6 g4 h6 7 g5 hg 8
♗×g5 a6 9 ♕d2 ♗d7 10 0–0–0 ♘c6
11 h4 ♕c7 (Karpov gives the order
11 . . . ♗e7 12 ♗e2 ♕c7 13 f4 0–0.
The source for the text is
Mezhdunarodnie Vstrechi, Russian
bulletins which included the team
championship.) 12 ♗e2 0–0–0 13 f4
♗e7 14 h5 ♔b8 15 ♔b1 d5 16 e5
♘e4 17 ♘×e4 de 18 ♗×e7 ♘×e7

19 ♕e3 ♘f5 20 ♘×f5 ef 21 ♖hg1
♖hg8 22 b3?! (22 ♖d6! Karpov,
e.g. 22 . . . ♗e6 23 ♕d4 ♖c8 24 c3)
22 . . . ♗e6 23 ♖×d8+ ♕×d8 24
♖d1 ♕c7 25 ♖d6 g6 26 hg ♖×g6
27 ♕d4 ♖g8 28 ♔b2 ♖c8 29 c3
♖h8 30 a4 ♖h2 31 ♕e3 ♕e7 32
♖d2 ♗c8 33 ♕b6 ♕c7 34 ♕d4
♗e6 (Karpov's score stops here.) 35
♕e3 ♖g2 36 ♕d4 ♖h2 37 c4 ♖h3
38 ♗d1 ♕a5? (38 . . . a5) 39 c5
♖h4 40 b4 ♕c7 41 ♕e3 ♖h8 42
♕c3 ♖c8 43 ♖d6 ♕e7? (43 . . .

a5!) 44 ♕e3± ♖g8 45 ♗c2 ♕c7 46
♕c3 ♖c8 47 ♗b3 ♗×b3 48 ♔×b3
a5 49 ♕d4 ab 50 ♔×b4 ♕e7 51
♕e3 ♖c6 52 ♕d2 ♔a7 53 ♕d4
♕h4? 54 ♖×c6 ♕e1+ 55 ♔c4
♕e2+ 56 ♔b3± ± bc 57 ♕d7+
♔b8 58 ♕e8+ ♔b7 59 ♕×f7+
♔b8 60 ♕e8+ ♔b7 61 ♕d7+
♔b8 62 ♕d8+ ♔b7 63 ♕b6+
♔c8 64 ♕×c6+ ♔d8 65 ♕d6+
♔c8 66 e6 ♕e3+ 67 ♔c4 ♕e2+
68 ♔d5 **1-0**

22 USSR Armed Forces Team Championship
Leningrad, 16–26.8.1971

Board 1		1	2	3	4	5	6	7	8	
1 Tseshkovsky	M	×	½	½	½	½	1	½	1	4½
2 Tukmakov	(G)	½	×	1	0	0	1	1	1	4½
3 Vasyukov	G	½	0	×	1	½	1	½	1	4½
4 Gufeld	G	½	1	0	×	½	?	?	1	4
5 Karpov	G	½	1	½	½	×	0	1	½	4
6 Klovan	M	0	0	0	?	1	×	?	1	3
7 Dementiev	M	½	0	½	?	0	?	×	½	2½
8 Zhelyandinov	M	0	0	0	0	½	0	½	×	1

Karpov played board one for the Leningrad team, taking over from his trainer, Semyon Furman, who played on second board.

Result of the event: 1 Zakavkaz VO (military district) 32½/49; 2 Leningrad VO 31; 3-4 Odessa VO, Moscow VO 26½; 5 Baltic VO 25½; 6 Baltic Fleet 24½; 7 Soviet Armed Forces in Germany 15; 8 Siberia VO 14½.

2201 Zhelyandinov–AK

R1: 17.8.1971: Sicilian

(Notes by Karpov)

1 e4 c5 2 ♘f3 e6 3 ♘c3 a6 4 d4 cd 5 ♘×d4 ♘c6 6 ♗c4!? ♕c7 7 ♘×c6 ♕×c6 (7 ... bc 8 ♕e2±) 8 ♕e2 ♗b4 (8...♗e7) 9 ♗d2 ♘e7 10 0-0 0-0 11 ♗b3 b6 12 ♘d5 ♗c5 13 ♘b4 ♕c7 14 ♘d3 a5 15 ♘×c5 bc 16 ♖fe1 d6 17 ♖ad1 ♗a6 18 ♕h5 ♘g6?! 19 ♗c1 c4 20 ♗a4 e5 21 ♕g5 ♖fd8 22 h4 ♘f8 23 ♕g3 ♖ab8 24 h5 ♘e6 25 h6 f6 26 hg ♕×g7 27 ♕h3 ♕e7 28 ♗c6 ♔h8 29 ♗d5 ♘c7 30 ♖e3 ♘×d5 31 ♖×d5 a4 32 ♖a5 ♗b5 33 ♕h4 ♖g8 34 ♖f3 ♖g6 35 ♗e3 ♗d7 36 ♖a7 ♖×b2 37 ♖a8+ ♗e8 38 ♖g3 ♔g8 39 ♖a7 ♗d7 40 ♖a8+ ♗e8 41 ♖a7 ♗d7 42 ♖a8+ ♗e8 43 ♕h3 ♖b7 44 ♕c8 ♔f7 45 ♖h3 h6 46 ♖×h6 ♖×h6 47 ♗×h6 ♔g6 48 ♗e3 ♖b1+ 49 ♔h2 ♕h7+ 50 ♔g3 ♕d7 51 ♕×e8+ ♕×e8 52 ♖×e8 ♖b2 53 a3 ♖×c2 54 ♖a8 f5 55 ef+ ♔×f5 56 ♖×a4 d5 57 ♖a5

♔e4 58 ♗h6 c3 59 ♖c5 ♔d4 60 ♖c8 ♔d3 61 ♗g7 ♖e2 62 a4 ♖e1 63 a5 c2 64 ♗h6 e4 65 ♗e3 a1 66 ♖d8 ♖×a5 67 ♔f4 ♖c5 68 g4 ♔e2 69 g5 ♖c3 70 ♗c1 ♔×f2 71 ♖×d5 e3 72 ♗×e3+ ♖×e3 73 ♖c5 ♖e2 74 g6 ♔e1 75 ♔f3 ♖e6 ½-½

2202 AK–Klovan

R2: 18.8.1971: Spanish

(Notes by Karpov)

1 e4 e5 2 ♘f3 ♘c6 3 ♗b5 a6 4 ♗×c6 dc 5 OO f6 6 d4 ed 7 ♘×d4 ♘e7 8 ♗e3 ♘g6 9 ♕h5 ♗d6 10 ♘f5 OO 11 f4 ♕e8?! 12 ♘d2 ♘e7? (*146*)

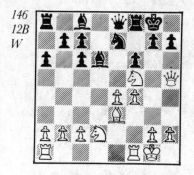

146
12B
W

13 ♘×e7+? (13 ♕×e8! ♖×e8 14 ♘×d6 cd 15 ♘c4 d5 16 ♘b6 ♖b8 17 ♗c5!±) 13 ... ♗×e7 14 ♕f3 ♗e6 15 ♖ae1 ♖d8 16 a3 c5 17 f5 ♗f7 18 ♗f4 ♗d6 19 ♕e3 (19 ♕c3 ♕d7∓; 19 ♕g3 ♕b5) 19 ... ♕c6 20 ♘f3 ♕b6 21 ♗×d6 (21 e5!? fe 22 ♗×e5 ♗×e5 23 ♘×e5 ♕×b2 24 ♕g5 h6 25 ♕g3) 21 ... cd 22 b4 ♖fe8 23 g4 ♗d5 24 bc dc 25 ♕f4 ♗c6 26 g5 ♖d7 27 gf? gf 28 ♔h1 ♕d8 29 ♖g1+ ♔h8 30 h4 ♖g8 31 h5 ♖×g1+ 32 ♖×g1 ♖d1 33 ♕h4 ♖×g1+ 34 ♔×g1 ♕d1+ 35 ♔f2 ♕×c2+ 36 ♔g3 ♔g7 37 h6+ ♔f7 38 ♕g4 ♕×e4 39 ♕g7+ ♔e8 40 ♕h8+ ♔d7 41 ♕×h7+ ♔d6 42 ♘h4 ♕e1+ (s) (adjournment 20?.8.1971) 43 ♔h3 ♕c3+ 44 ♔g4 ♕c4+ 45 ♔h3 ♕b3+ 46 ♔g4 ♕a4+ 47 ♔g3 ♕×a3+ 48 ♔g4 ♕a4+ (Karpov gives the conclusion of the game as 48 ... ♕b4+ 49 ♔g3 ♕e1+ 50 ♔h3 ♕h1+ 51 ♔g3 ♕g1+ 52 ♔h3 ♗b5 53 ♘f3 ♗f1+ 54 ♔h4 ♕g2 0–1. The source for the text continuation is *Sahs* No. 22 1971.) 49 ♔g3 ♕b3+ 50 ♔h2 ♕b2+ 51 ♔g3 ♕c3+ 52 ♔h2 ♕c2+ 53 ♔g3 ♕d3+ 54 ♔h2 ♕d2+ 55 ♔g3 ♕e3+ 56 ♔h2 ♕f4+ 57 ♔h3 ♕f1+ 58 ♔g3 ♕g1+ 59 ♔h3 ♗b5 60 ♘f3 ♗f1+ 61 ♔h4 ♕g2 **0–1**

2203 Tseshkovsky–AK

R3: 19.8.1971: Spanish

1 e4 e5 2 ♘f3 ♘c6 3 ♗b5 a6 4 ♗a4 ♘f6 5 OO ♗e7 6 ♖e1 b5 7 ♗b3 d6 8 c3 OO 9 d3 ♘a5 10 ♗c2 c5 11 ♘bd2 ♖e8 12 ♘f1 ♗b7 13 ♘e3 ♗f8 14 b4 cb 15 cb ♘c6 16 a3 a5 (16 ... d5? Tseshkovsky–Tal, Sochi 1970 – Karpov) 17 ba ♘×a5 18 ♖b1 ♕d7 19 ♗b2 ♗c6 20 ♕d2 g6 21 d4 ed 22 ♕×d4 ♗g7 23 e5 de 24 ♘×e5 ♕×d4 25 ♗×d4 ♘d7 26 ♘×c6 ♘×c6 27 ♗×g7 ♔×g7 ½-½

2204   Gufeld–AK

R4: 21.8.1971: Spanish

(Notes by Karpov and Gufeld)

1 e4 e5 2 ♘f3 ♘c6 3 ♗b5 a6 4 ♗a4
♘f6 5 00 ♗e7 6 ♖e1 b5 7 ♗b3 d6 8
c3 00 9 h3 ♘a5 10 ♗c2 c5 11 d4
♕c7 12 ♘bd2 ♘c6

    13 a3

13 ♘b3!? ♗b7 14 ♗g5; or 13 d5
♘d8 14 a4 – Gufeld.

    13 . . .   ♗d7
    14 b4   cd
    15 cd   ♖fc8
    16 ♗b3±   a5
    17 ♗b2

17 d5 ♘b8 18 ♗b2 ♘a6 19 ♖c1
♕a7 20 ♗c3 ♗d8∓ – Karpov.

    17 . . .   ab
    18 ab   ed

Gufeld gives the move order 18
. . . ♖×a1 19 ♗×a1 ed 20 ♘×d4.

    19 ♘×d4   ♖×a1
    20 ♗×a1

Gufeld–Smyslov, USSR Ch
1969, went 20 ♕×a1 ♘×d4 21
♗×d4 ♗e6 22 ♗×e6 fe ½–½ –
Karpov.

    20 . . .   ♘×d4

147
22B
W

    21 ♗×d4   ♗e6
    22 ♗×e6   fe (*147*)
    23 ♕b3

23 e5 de 24 ♗×e5 ♕c2 25 ♕e2
♖c6! – Gufeld.

    23 . . .   ♔f7
    24 e5

24 ♘f3 ♕c4 25 ♘g5+ ♔e8 26
♕×c4 ♖×c4 27 ♘×e6 ♔d7 28
♗×f6 ♗×f6 29 ♘f8+ ♔e7 30
♘×h7 ♗c3∓ – Karpov.

    24 . . .   de
    25 ♖×e5   ♕d6!

25 . . . ♕d7! 26 ♘f3 ♖c1+ 27
♔h2 ♗d6 28 g3± ; or 25 . . . ♕c6
26 ♗c5 – Gufeld.

    26 ♖e1

26 ♘f3? ♖c1+ 27 ♔h2 ♘d7; or
26 ♗b2 ♖c1+ ! – Gufeld.

    26 . . .   ♕d5
    27 ♕b2   ♔g8

27 . . . ♗d6!? – Karpov.

    28 ♖e5   ♕c6!
    29 ♕b3

29 ♗c5? ♘d7 30 ♗×e7
♕c1+ !∓ ∓ – Gufeld and Karpov.

    29 . . .   ♘d5
    30 ♗c5   ♗×c5
    31 bc   ♕×c5
    32 ♖×e6   ♕c1+
    33 ♘f1   ♕c4
    34 ♕b2!   ♘c3?
    35 ♖e7   ♕a2
    36 ♕×a2

36 ♕c1! – Karpov. 36 ♕b4?
♘d5 – Gufeld.

    36 . . .   ♘×a2
    37 ♖b7   ♖c5
    38 ♘e3   ♘c3
          ½–½

2205 AK–Tukmakov

R5: 22.8.1971: Sicilian

(Notes by Karpov)

1 e4 c5 2 ♘f3 d6 3 d4 cd 4 ♘×d4 ♘f6 5 ♘c3 a6 6 ♗e2 e6 7 00 ♗e7 8 f4 00 9 ♗e3 ♘c6 10 a4 ♕c7 11 ♔h1 ♘a5 12 ♕e1 (Tukmakov–Panno, Buenos Aires 1970, went 12 ♕d3 ♗d7 13 g4!?) 12 ... ♘c4 13 ♗c1 ♗d7 14 b3 ♘a5 15 ♗d3 ♘c6 16 ♘×c6 ♗×c6 17 ♗b2 e5 18 ♕e2 ♖ad8 19 b4! a5 (19 ... ef? 20 b5 ab 21 ab ♗d7 22 ♕d5± ±) 20 b5 ♗d7 (*148*)

148
20B
W

21 f5! ♗c8 22 ♘d1 (22 ♘d5!?) 22 ... d5 23 ed ♘×d5 24 ♕×e5 ♕×e5 25 ♗×e5 ♖ fe8 26 ♗b2 ♗c5 27 ♘c4 b6 28 ♗g3 ♗b7 29 ♔ ae1 ♗b4 30 ♖×e8+ ♖×e8 31 h4 (31 ♔g1!?) 31 ... g6 32 ♔h2 ♗c5 33 ♗f2 ♗×f2 34 ♖×f2 ♖ e1 35 ♔g3 ♘b4 36 ♔f4 ♘d5+ 37 ♔g3 ♘b4 38 ♖d2 ♘d5 39 ♘d6 ♗a8 40 ♗e4 ♘c7 41 ♗×a8 ♘×a8 42 f6 h6 43 ♘c4 ♖e8 44 ♖d6 **1–0**

2206 Vasyukov–AK

R6: 23.8.1971: Spanish

(Notes by Karpov)

1 e4 e5 2 ♘f3 ♘c6 3 ♗b5 a6 4 ♗a4 ♘f6 5 00 ♗e7 6 ♖ e1 b5 7 ♗b3 d6 8 c3 00 9 h3 ♘b8 10 d3 ♘bd7 11 ♘bd2 ♗b7 12 ♘f1 ♘c5 13 ♗c2 ♖ e8 14 ♘g3 ♗f8 15 ♘h2 d5 16 ♕f3 h6 17 ♘f5 a5 18 ♘g4 ♘×g4 19 hg (19 ♕×g4!? ♔h8 followed by ... ♖a6) 19 ... a4 20 ♗e3 ♘e6 21 ♕g3 de 22 de ♕f6 23 ♖adl ♖ad8?! (23 ... ♖ ed8) 24 ♕f3 ♘g5 25 ♕e2 ♗c6 26 ♗d3 ♖ b8 27 f3 g6 28 ♘g3 ♘e6 29 ♕f2 ♖ed8 30 a3 ♖d6 31 ♖d2 ♖ bd8 32 ♖edl ♗e8 33 ♗fl ½–½

2207 AK–Dementiev

R7: 25.8.1971: Slav

(Notes by Karpov)

1 d4 d5 2 ♘f3 ♘f6 3 c4 c6 4 e3 ♗f5 5 ♘c3 e6 6 ♗e2 (6 ♘h4 ♗g4 7 ♕b3 ♕b6 8 ♕×b6 ab 9 h3 ♗h5 10 g4 ♗g6) 6 ... ♘e4 7 00 ♗e7 8

149
30B
W

♕b3 ♕b6 9 c5 ♕c7 10 ♘×e4 ♗×e4 11 ♕c3 b6 12 cb ab 13 b4 OO 14 ♗b2 ♗d6 15 h3 f6 16 ♖fc1 ♕e7 17 a3 ♖a7 (17 ... g5!?) 18 ♕b3 ♗c7? 19 a4 g5 20 ♗a3 ♗d6 21 ♘d2 ♗g6 22 b5 cb (22 ... c5 23 e4!) 23 ♗×b5 ♔g7 24 ♘f1 h5 25 ♗×d6 ♕×d6 26 ♕d1 ♕e7 27 ♖c3 ♘a6 28 ♕b3 ♖b8 29 ♖e1 ♘c7 30 ♗c6 ♘e8 (149)
31 e4! de 32 ♗×e4 ♗f7 33 ♗d5 (33 ♗b1!?) 33 ... ♘c7 34 ♗c6 ♕d6 35 ♘e3 ♕d8 36 ♖d1 ♔h8 37 ♕b4 ♔g7 38 h4 ♘d5 39 ♗×d5 ed 40 hg fg 41 ♖c6 ♗g6 42 ♖dc1 ♗e4 43 f3 ♗h7 **1-0**

Nothing is known about this event. It is not known how many games Karpov played, nor is it known in which order the following four games were played.

2301 AK–Aronshtats (?)

Sicilian

1 e4 c5 2 ♘f3 ♘c6 3 d4 cd 4 ♘×d4 e5 5 ♘b5 a6 6 ♘d6+ ♗×d6 7 ♕×d6 ♕f6 8 ♕c7 ♘ge7 9 ♘c3 ♘b4 10 ♗d3 ♘×d3+ 11 cd 00 12 00 ♕e6 13 f4 ef 14 ♗×f4 ♕c6 15 a4 ♖fe8 16 ♕e5 f6 17 ♕d4 b6 18 ♗d6 ♗b7 19 ♖ac1 ♘c8 20 ♘b5 ab 21 ♖×c6 dc 22 ab ♘×d6 23 ♕×d6 cb 24 ♕×b6 ♖ab8 25 ♕×b5 ♔h8 26 ♕a4 ♖a8 27 ♕c2 ♖ec8 28 ♕d2 ♖d8 29 ♕e3 ♖a4 30 ♕b6 ♖d7 31 ♕e6 **1–0**

2302 Sinakov(?*)–AK

Sicilian

* Karpov, himself, was unsure of the name of his opponent.

1 e4 c5 2 ♘f3 e6 3 d4 cd 4 ♘×d4 ♘c6 5 ♘c3 ♕c7 6 ♗e3 a6 7 ♗d3 b5 8 00 ♗b7 9 ♕e2 ♘f6 10 f4 ♘×d4 11 ♗×d4 ♗c5 12 ♗×c5

♕×c5+ 13 ♔h1 b4 14 ♘d1 00 15 c4 d6 16 ♘f2 ♘d7 17 ♘g4 ♖fe8 18 ♖ae1 f5 19 ef ef 20 ♘e3 ♘f6 21 ♕d2 ♘e4 22 ♗×e4 ♖×e4 23 b3 ♖d4 24 ♕f2 ♖d3 25 ♘c2 ♗e4 (*150*)

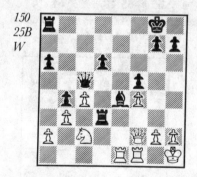

```
150
25B
W
```

26 ♖e3 a5 27 ♖×d3 ♗×d3 28 ♕×c5 dc 29 ♖c1 a4 30 ♘e3 ♗e4 31 ♔g1 ab 32 ab ♖a3 33 ♖d1 ♖×b3 34 ♖d8+ ♔f7 35 ♖c8 ♖b1+ 36 ♔f2 b3 **0–1**

2303 AK–Kozlov

Pirc/Caro Kann

(Notes by Karpov)

**1 e4 g6 2 d4 ♗g7 3 ♘c3 c6 4 ♘f3
d5 5 h3 de** (5 . . . ♘h6 6 ♗e2 00±)
**6 ♘×e4 ♗d7 7 c4 ♘gf6 8 ♘c3 00
9 ♗e2 ♕c7 10 00 e5!? 11 ♗e3
♖e8** (Planning 12 . . . ed 13 ♗×d4
♘f8 with . . . ♗f5 to follow.) **12 d5
cd 13 cd ♘b6 14 ♕b3** (14 ♖cl
♕d8! (14 . . . ♕b8?! 15 ♕b3 and 16
a4±).) **14 . . . ♗f5 15 ♖fd1** (15
♖acl!? ♕b8 16 a4±; or 15 . . .
♖ad8 16 ♘b5 ♕b8 (16 . . . ♕d7 17
♘×a7 ♘b×d5 18 ♗b5± ±) 17
♗×b6! (17 ♘c7 ♖e7 18 ♗×b6 ab
19 ♕×b6 ♘×d5) 17 . . . ab 18
♖fdl± .) **15 . . . ♖ad8 16 ♖acl**
(16 ♘b5!? ♕b8 17 ♗×b6 ab 18
♖acl±) **16 . . . ♘c8 17 ♘h4 ♗d7
18 ♘b5 ♕a5 19 a4! ♘e4** (19 . . .
a6 20 ♗d2 ♕b6 21 a5± ±) **20 d6 a6
21 ♘c7 ♖f8** (*151*)

151
21B
W

**22 ♖d5 ♕×a4 23 ♕×a4 ♗×a4 24
♖c4 ♗c6 25 ♖×e4 ♗×d5 26
♘×d5 ♖×d6 27 ♘c3± ♖c6**
(Against 28 ♖c4.) **28 ♖a4** (28
♖b4 b5=) **28 . . . ♘d6 29 ♗f3
♖6c8?** (29 . . . ♖c4 30 ♖×c4
♘×c4 31 ♗×b7 ♘×e3! (31 . . .
♘×b2 32 ♗×a6±) 32 fe ♖b8 33
♗×a6 ♖×b2=) **30 ♗d5 ♖fd8 31
g4! ♖d7 32 ♗b3! ♘e8 33 ♘d5
♖cd8 34 ♘b6 ♖d3 35 ♗c2
♖3d6 36 ♘f3 ♘c7 37 ♗e4 ♖b8**
(37 . . . ♘e6!? 38 ♖b4 (38 ♗×b7
♖b8 39 ♘c4? ♖dl+ ∓ ∓).) **38
♔g2 ♘e6 39 ♘c4 b5 40 ♖b4 a5
41 ♘×a5 ♘d4 42 ♘×d4 1–0**

2304 Orlov–AK

Sicilian

(Notes by Karpov)

**1 e4 c5 2 ♘f3 e6 3 ♘c3 ♘c6 4 d4
cd 5 ♘×d4 a6 6 g3 ♘×d4 7
♕×d4 ♘e7 8 ♗f4 ♘c6 9 ♕d2 b5**
(9 . . . d6 10 000 e5 11 ♗e3±) **10
♗g2 ♗b7 11 00** (11 ♖dl!?) **11 . . .
♘a5** (11 . . . d6!? 12 a4 (12 ♖adl
♘e5) 12 . . . b4 13 ♘d5 a5 (13 . . .
ed 14 ed ♘e5 15 ♕×b4±) 14 ♖fel
♘e5) **12 a4 b4 13 ♘dl ♖c8 14 b3
♗e7 15 ♘b2 ♗f6** (15 . . . 00?! 16
♖adl ♗f6 (16 . . . ♗c6 17 ♘d3
♕b6 18 ♗e3±) 17 e5 ♗×g2 18

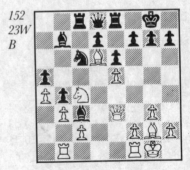

152
23W
B

♔×g2 ♗e7 19 ♗e3±) **16 ♖ab1 ♗c3 17 ♕e2 00 18 ♗d6 ♖e8 19 ♕e3 ♘c6 20 ♘c4** (If 20 ♘d3 ♘d4 21 ♘c5 ♕b6 22 ♘×b7 ♕×b7 23 e5 ♖c6 (23 . . . ♕b6 24 ♖fd1± ±); or 20 . . . ♗d4 21 ♕e2 ♕b6.) **20 . . . ♗d4 21 ♕d2 a5 22 e5 ♗c3 23 ♕e3** (*152*)

23 . . . ♗a6 24 ♖fd1 ♗×c4 25 bc ♘e7∓ **26 ♕d3 ♘f5 27 c5 ♘×d6 28 ♕×d6 ♕c7 29 f4 f6 30 c6** (30 ef ♗×f6 31 ♕×d7 ♕×c5+ ∓) **30 . . . dc 31 ef ♗×f6 32 ♕×c7 ♖×c7 33 ♖d6 c5 34 ♖×e6! ♖×e6 35 ♗d5 ♔f8 36 ♗×e6 c4∓ 37 ♖e1 g6 38 ♔f2 ♗b2 39 ♖e2 ♔g7 40 g4?** ♗c1 **0–1** (41 ♔f3 b3 42 cb c3 43 ♖c2 ♗d2∓ ∓)

24 39th USSR Championship*
Leningrad, 15.9–16.10.1971

* For the final placings of this championship see p. 173

2401 AK–Taimanov

R1: 15.9.1971: Sicilian

(Notes by Furman)

1 e4 c5 2 ♘f3 e6 3 d4 cd 4 ♘×d4 ♘c6 5 ♘b5 d6 6 ♗f4 e5 7 ♗e3 ♘f6 (Taimanov repeats the variation which he used in his match with Fischer.) **8 ♗g5 ♗e6 9 ♘1c3 a6 10 ♗×f6 gf 11 ♘a3 ♘e7** (This is, apparently, the result of his homework. The aim of this move is to save his pawn on d6 from being backward. In Fischer–Taimanov, Vancouver 1971, he played 11 . . . ♘d4 12 ♘c4 f5 13 ef ♘×f5 14 ♗d3 ♖c8 15 ♗×f5 ♖×c4 16 ♗×e6 fe 17 ♕e2 and White had some advantage.) **12 ♘c4 d5 13 ed ♘×d5 14 ♘×d5 ♗×d5 15 ♘e3 ♗c6 16 ♗c4** (This continuation guarantees White better prospects in the ending. After 16 ♕h5 ♕a5+ 17 c3 000, the position would have become sharp and Black would have good counter-chances.) **16 . . . ♕×d1+ 17 ♖×d1 ♖c8 18 ♗d5 ♗×d5 19 ♖×d5** (Black has

failed to obtain fully equal chances. With his next few moves Taimanov tries to liquidate some of the weaknesses in his pawn configuration.) **19 . . . ♔e7 20 ♔e2** (White does not have time to prevent the advance of the f–pawn with 20 g4 because of 20 . . . h5.) **20 . . . ♔e6 21 ♖hd1 f5** (*153*)

153
21B
W

22 g3! (After the natural 22 c3 f4, Black would have consolidated his position. Karpov sacrifices the pawn on c2 and thereby activates his pieces still further.) **22 . . . f4** (After the more passive 22 . . . f6 23 c3 White has held on to his positional advantage.) **23 gf ef 24**

No	Player	Total
1	Savon	15
2	Smyslov	13½
3	Tal	13½
4	**Karpov**	13
5	Balashov	12
6	Stein	12
7	Bronstein	11½
8	Polugayevsky	11½
9	Taimanov	11
10	Kapengut	10½
11	Krogius	10½
12	Lein	10
13	Platanov	10
14	Geller	9½
15	Karasev	9
16	Shamkovich	9
17	Vaganian	8½
18	Nikolayevsky	8½
19	Tukmakov	8½
20	Grigorian	8
21	Dzhindzhikhashvili	8
22	Tseitlin	8

♘g2 ♖×c2+ **25 ♔f3 ♗c5** (After 25 ... ♖×b2 26 ♘×f4+ ♔f6 27 ♖e1 Black's king is in great danger because of the threat 28 ♘h5+ .) **26 ♘×f4+ ♔f6 27 ♘d3 ♖c8 28 ♖d7 b5?** (A natural, but mistaken, move. 28 ... b6 was more far-sighted; with the bishop on c5 defended, Black would have greater chances of defending himself.) **29 ♖e1 ♔g7 30 ♖e4 ♖c4** (If Black's pawn had been on b6, he would have had the possibility of 30 ...♖c6 31 ♖f4 ♖f6, whereas now this will not do in view of 32 ♖×f6 ♔×f6 33 ♖c7 winning a piece.) **31 ♘e5** (After 31 ♖×c4 bc 32 ♘e5 ♔f6 Black would obtain counter-chances.) **31 ... ♖×e4 32 ♔×e4 ♔g8 33 f4** (Again the most accurate continuation. After 33 ♖×f7 ♗d6 Black would have chances of drawing the rook ending.) **33 ... ♗f8** (Passive defence by 33 ... ♖f8 is insufficient, although this would not be in Taimanov's style anyway.) **34 ♘×f7 ♖c2 35 ♘g5** (threatening 36 ♖d8 with 37 ♘e6 to follow) **35 ... ♗h6 36 ♘e6!** (Karpov skilfully creates an attack with his small army, taking advantage of the poor position of Black's pieces.) **36 ... ♖×h2** (36 ... ♖×b2 was somewhat better. After 37 ♔f5 ♗×f4 38 ♔×f4 ♖×h2 39 ♖g7+ ♔h8 40 ♖a7 the play would be approximately as it is in the game.) **37 ♔f5 ♗×f4** (This sacrifice is forced, because of the threatened 38 ♔f6. If 37 ... ♖g2, then 38 ♖d8+ ♔f7 39 ♖h8 and White wins.) **38 ♔×f4** (There was a quicker win with 38 ♘×f4 ♖×b2 39 ♔f6 h6 40 ♖g7+ ♔f8 41 ♘e6+ ♔e8 42 ♖e7 mate.) **38 ... ♖×b2 39 ♖g7+ ♔h8 40 ♖a7 h5 41 ♖×a6 b4** (In spite of his extra piece it is no simple matter for White to win this position because of the limited number of pawns remaining.) **42 ♘d4 ♖g2** (Here the game was adjourned.) **43 ♔f3** (43 ♘f5 was stronger.) **43 ... ♖d2 44 ♔e3 ♖b2** (Now White successfully corrects the mistake committed with his sealed move. 44 ... ♖h2, creating counter-chances by the fast advance of the h-pawn, would have been more stubborn.) **45 ♔f4 ♖d2 46 ♘f5 ♖b2** (The defensive plan of exchanging the pawn is unreal. White has time to create mating threats.) **47 ♔g5 b3 48 ♖h6+ ! ♔g8 49 ♔f6! 1–0**

2402 Vaganian–AK

R2: 16.9.1971: Réti

(Notes by Radashkovich)

1 ♘f3 ♘f6 2 c4 b6 3 g3 ♗b7 4 ♗g2 e6 5 OO ♗e7 6 b3 OO 7 ♗b2 c5 8 e3 d5 9 ♕e2 ♘c6 10 ♖d1 ♕c7 (10 ... ♖c8) **11 ♘c3 ♖ad8 12 cd ♘×d5** (12 ... ed 13 b4±) **13 ♘×d5 ♖×d5 14 d4 cd 15 ♘×d4 ♘×d4 16 ♗×d4 ♖d6?** (*154*) (16 ... ♖d7 17 ♖ac1 ♕b8 18 ♕g4 g6 19 ♗c6 ♖d6) **17 ♖dc1! ♕d7 18 ♗e5 ♖d5** (18 ...

154
16B
W

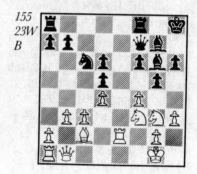

🛇d2 19 ♕g4 g6 20 🛇c7 ♕b5 21
♗c3) 19 🛇c7 ♕d8 20 🛇×b7
🛇×e5 21 🛇d1! ♕e8 22 🛇×a7 🛇a5
23 🛇b7 ♗c5 24 a4 🛇a8 25 🛇bd7
🛇b8 26 ♕b5 (intending 27 b4) 26
. . . ♗a3 27 ♗b7! **1–0**

2403   AK–Lein

R3: 17.9.1971: QGD

1 🛇f3 d5 2 c4 e6 3 d4 ♗e7 4 🛇c3
🛇f6 5 ♗g5 h6 6 ♗h4 🛇e4 7 ♗×e7
♕×e7 8 ♕c2 00 9 e3 🛇×c3 10
♕×c3 c6 11 ♗e2 dc 12 ♗×c4 b6 13
♗e2 ♗b7 14 🛇e5 🛇c8 15 ♗h5 g6
16 ♗f3 c5 17 ♗×b7 ♕×b7 18 00
🛇d7 ½–½

2404   Platonov–AK

R4: 19.9.1971: QP

1 d4 🛇f6 2 🛇f3 e6 3 e3 b6 4 ♗d3
♗b7 5 🛇bd2 c5 6 00 cd 7 ed ♗e7 8
b3 00 9 ♗b2 🛇c6 10 a3 ♕c7 11
🛇e1 🛇ac8 12 c4 d5 13 🛇c1 🛇fd8
14 ♕e2 dc 15 bc ♕f4 16 g3 ♕h6 17
🛇c2 ♕h5 18 ♕f1 🛇c7 19 ♗e2 ♕f5
20 ♗d3 ♕h5 21 ♗e2 ½–½

2405   AK–K. Grigorian

R5: 20.9.1971: Alekhine

(Notes by Tal)

1 e4 🛇f6 2 e5 🛇d5 3 d4 d6 4 🛇f3 g6
5 ♗c4 🛇b6 6 ♗b3 ♗g7 7 🛇g5 (a
little-investigated continuation) 7
. . . d5 (I think that Black's reply,
instead of 7 . . . 00, was unsuccessful
because it relieved White's centre
from any sort of trouble.) 8 00 00 9
f4 f6 10 🛇f3 ♗g4 11 🛇bd2 🛇c6 12
h3 ♗f5 13 🛇f2 ♔h8 14 c3 g5? (14
. . . 🛇a5 – Furman) 15 ef ef 16 🛇f1
h6 17 🛇g3 ♗g6 18 ♗c2 ♕e8 19 b3
🛇c8 20 ♗a3 🛇d6 21 ♗×d6 cd 22
🛇e2 ♕f7 23 ♕b1 (*155*)

155
23W
B

(The grandmaster's advantage very
quickly attained real dimensions.
After the e–file was opened Black's
pieces found themselves poorly
situated, especially helpless being
the black-squared bishop which
so often calls the tune. The Erevan
player offered a draw, but it turned
out that his information about
Karpov's peaceful nature was, as
they say, exaggerated. After a short

preparation White started the final attack.) 23 ... ♗×c2 24 ♕×c2 ♖fe8 25 ♖ael ♘e7 26 f5 ♗f8 27 ♖e6 ♘g8 28 ♘h2 ♖ec8 29 ♖1e3 ♖c6 30 ♕e2 ♖ac8 31 ♕f3 ♕c7 32 ♘e2 ♕a5 33 a4 ♖6c7 34 ♖e8 ♗g7 35 ♕h5 ♕b6 36 ♘g4 ♖×e8 37 ♖×e8 ♗e7 38 ♘×h6! ♖×e8 39 ♘f7 **mate**

2406   Geller–AK

R6: 23.9.1971: Spanish

(Notes by Furman)

1 e4 e5 2 ♘f3 ♘c6 3 ♗b5 a6 4 ♗a4 ♘f6 5 00 ♗e7 6 ♖e1 b5 7 ♗b3 d6 8 c3 00 9 h3 ♘b8 10 d4 ♘bd7 11 c4 c6 12 cb ab 13 ♘c3 ♗a6 **TN** (preparing . . . c5) 14 ♗g5 h6 15 de ♘×e5!? (15 . . . de?! 16 ♗×f6 ♗×f6 17 ♕d6) 16 ♘×e5 de= 17 ♗×f6 ♗×f6 18 ♕h5 ♕e7 19 ♖ad1 ♖ad8 20 ♘e2 ♗g5 21 ♘g3 ♕f6 22 ♖×d8 ♖×d8 23 ♖d1 ♖×d1+ 24 ♕×d1 ♗c8 25 a4 ba 26 ♗×a4 g6 27 ♘f1 ♕e6 28 ♕c2 ♗d7 29 ♘h2 ♕d6 30 ♘f3 ♗d8 31 ♕c3 ♗c7 32 h4 ♔g7 33 g3 ♔f6 34 ♔g2 ½–½

2407   AK–Dzhindzhikhashvili

R7: 24.9.1971: Scandinavian

(Notes by Gufeld)

'Karpov played simply and logically, took possession of the centre, and after a mistake by Dzhindzhikhashvili added two active bishops. But at some time the young grandmaster's attention wandered and he committed a tactical oversight on his 21st move, after which the chances were equal.' – Furman.

1 e4 d5 2 ed ♘f6 3 ♗b5+ ♗d7 4 ♗e2 ♘×d5 5 d4 ♗f5 6 ♘f3 e6 7 00± ♗c6 8 ♖e1 ♗e7 9 ♗f1 00 10 c3 ♗g4 11 ♘bd2 a6 12 ♕b3 ♗h5?! (12 . . . ♖b8±) 13 ♘e5!± ♗g6 (13 . . . ♘×e5 14 ♖×e5± ±) 14 ♘×g6 hg 15 ♘f3 ♘b6 16 ♕c2 ♕d5 17 b3 ♖fe8 18 ♗d3 ♖ad8 19 ♗f4 ♕d7 20 a4 (20 ♖ad1±) 20 . . . ♘d5 21 ♗d2 ♘db4! 22 ♕b1 (22 cb ♘×d4 23 ♘×d4 ♕×d4∓) 22 . . . ♘×d3 23 ♕×d3 ♗f6 24 b4 e5 ½–½

2408   AK–Stein

R8: 25.9.1971: Sicilian

(Notes by Furman)

1 e4 c5 2 ♘f3 ♘c6 3 d4 cd 4 ♘×d4 ♘f6 5 ♘c3 d6 6 ♗c4 ♕b6 7 ♘×c6 bc 8 00 e6 9 b3 ♗e7 10 ♗b2 00 11 ♕e2 e5 (11 . . . d5? 12 ed cd 13 ♗×d5!) 12 ♔h1 ♕c7 13 ♖ae1 ♘d7 14 ♘a4 ♗b7 (14 . . . ♗f6!?=) 15 ♗d3 ♖fe8 16 c4± ♗g5 17 ♕c2 h6 18 b4 a6 19 ♕b3 ♖ab8 20 a3 ♗c8 21 ♕c3 ♗f6 22 ♕c2 a5 (22

156
27B
W

... ♘b6!?) 23 ♗c3 ab 24 ab ♘f8 25 b5 cb?! (25 ... ♗d7!±) 26 cb± ♗d7 27 ♖b1 ♖ec8 *(156)* 28 b6! ♕b7 29 ♗b5 ♖a8 30 ♕b3 ♗e6 (30 ... ♗×b5? 31 ♕×b5 ♖×a4 32 ♕×a4 ♖×c3 33 ♕a7±±) 31 ♕b4 ♗e7 32 ♖fc1 d5 33 ♕b2 d4 34 ♗b4 ♗g5 (34 ... ♗×b4 35 ♕×b4 ♖×c1+ 36 ♖×c1 ♕×e4 37 ♘c6 ♕f4 38 ♖b1±±; 34 ... ♗×b4 35 ♕×b4 ♕×e4 36 ♘c5 and b7±±) 35 ♖×c8 ♖×c8 36 ♕e2 ♖a8 37 ♗d6±± ♘g6 38 ♕c2 ♖c8 39 ♗c7 ♗d8 40 ♘c5 ♖×c7 41 ♘×b7 ♖×c2 42 ♘×d8 (s) 42 ... ♗c8 (42 ... ♗a2 43 b7! ♗×b1 44 h4±±) 43 g3 ♖×f2 44 ♖c1 ♖f6 45 ♖×c8 ♖×b6 46 ♗c4 ♔h7 47 ♘×f7 **1-0**

2409 Smyslov-AK

R9: 27.9.1971: QGD

(Notes by Smyslov and Korchnoi)

1 c4 c5 2 ♘f3 ♘f6 3 ♘c3 d5 4 cd ♘×d5 5 e3 e6 6 d4 cd 7 ed ♗e7 8 ♗d3 00 9 00 ♘c6 10 ♖e1 ♘f6 11 a3 b6 12 ♗c2 ♗b7 13 ♕d3 ♖c8? *(157)* (13 ... g6)

157
13B
W

14 ♗g5 (14 d5! ♘a5 15 ♗g5 ♖×c3 (15 ... g6 16 d6!) 16 bc ♕×d5±; 14 ... ed 15 ♗g5 g6 16 ♖×e7 ♕×e7 17 ♘×d5 ♘×d5 18 ♗×e7±±) 14 ... g6 15 ♖ad1 ♘d5 16 ♗h6 ♖e8 17 ♗a4! a6? (17 ... ♘×c3 18 bc ♗×a3 19 c4 ♗f8 20 ♕e3/♗g5±) 18 ♘×d5! ♕×d5 (18 ... ed±) 19 ♕e3! ♗f6 (19 ... ♕h5; 19 ... ♖ed8) 20 ♗b3! ♕h5 21 d5! ♘d8 22 d6 ♖c5 23 d7 ♖e7? (23 ... ♖f8 24 ♗×f8±) 24 ♕f4! ♗g7 25 ♕b8 ♕×h6 26 ♕×d8+ ♗f8 27 ♖e3 ♗c6 28 ♕×f8+ ♕×f8 29 d8♕ **1-0**

2410 AK-Savon

R10: 28.9.1971: Sicilian

1 e4 c5 2 ♘f3 d6 3 d4 cd 4 ♘×d4 ♘f6 5 ♘c3 a6 6 ♗e2 e6 7 f4 ♗e7 8 00 ♕c7 9 ♗f3 ♘c6 10 ♗e3 ♗d7 11 a4 ♘a5 12 ♔h1 ♖c8 13 ♕d3 ♘c4 14 ♗c1 00 15 b3 ♘a5 16 ♗b2 ♘c6 17 ♖ac1 ♘×d4 18 ♕×d4 ♗c6 19 ♕d3 ♖fd8 20 ♘e2 d5 21 e5 ♘e4 22 ♘d4 ♗c5 23 ♖cd1 ♗×d4 24 ♗×d4 b5 25 ♕e3 ♕b7 26 a5 b4 27 ♗b6 ♖d7 28 ♖c1 ♗b5 29 ♖fd1 ♕c6 30 ♖d4 ♘c3 31 ♖a1 ♘e4 32 ♖ad1 ♘c3 33 ♖a1 ♘e4 34 ♖c1 ♕c3 35 ♕×c3 bc 36 ♔g1 f5 37 ef gf 38 ♗×e4 de 39 ♖×d7 ♗×d7 40 ♔f2 ♔f7 41 ♔e3 (41 ♖d1) 41 ... e5 42 fe fe 43 ♖f1+ ♔e6 44 ♖f2 h5 45 g3 ♗b5 46 ♔×e4 ½-½

2411   Kapengut–AK

R11: 1.10.1971: Sicilian

(Notes by Krogius)

1 e4 c5 2 ♘f3 e6 3 d4 cd 4 ♘×d4 ♘f6 5 ♘c3 d6 6 ♗e2 ♗e7 7 00 a6 8 f4 ♕c7 9 ♗f3 00 10 a4 ♘c6 11 ♘b3 b6 12 ♗e3 (apparently to no purpose. The immediate 12 ♕e1 was better.) 12 ... ♖b8 13 ♕e1 ♘a5 (Sensing danger, the Minsk master now made several precise defensive moves which de-fused the situation.) 14 ♘×a5 ba 15 b3 ♗b7 16 ♖d1 ♗fc8 17 ♖d3 ♗a8 18 ♗d2 ♖b4 19 f5 ♗f8 20 fe ½–½

2412   AK–Karasev

R12: 2.10.1971: English

'A draw was reached only after a tense struggle. The grandmaster obtained a more active position and it might have made things harder for Black if 16 b4 had been played instead of 16 ♖fe1. Having a white-squared bishop, Karpov tried to organize play on the white squares. There remained nothing for Karasev but to play on the black squares,' – A. Geller.

1 c4 e5 2 ♘c3 ♘f6 3 g3 ♗b4 4 ♗g2 00 5 e4 ♖e8 6 ♘ge2 ♘c6 7 a3 ♗f8 8 00 ♘d4 9 d3 ♘×e2+ 10 ♕×e2 c6 11 ♗e3 d6 12 h3 d5 13 ed cd 14 ♗g5 d4 15 ♘d5 ♗e6 16 ♖fe1 ♗×d5 17 ♗×d5 ♖b8 18 b4 h6 19 ♗×f6 ♕×f6 20 h4 g6 21 h5 ♔g7 22 c5 b6 23 cb ab 24 b5 ♗c5 25 ♖ec1 ♖e7 26 a4 ♕d6 27 ♗g2 ♖a7 28 ♖c4

♖e8 29 hg fg 30 ♕e1 ♖a5 31 ♖a2 ♖e7 32 ♗c6 h5 33 ♔g2 ♖ea7 34 ♖e2 ♖×a4 35 ♖×a4 ♖×a4 36 ♖×e5 ♖a7 37 ♖d5 ♗e7 38 ♕d2 ♕f6 39 ♖d8 ♖e2 40 ♖d7+ ♗e7 41 ♖d5 ♖e5 ½–½

2413   Bronstein–AK

R13: 3.10.1971: KI Attack

1 e4 c5 2 ♘f3 e6 3 d3 ♘c6 4 g3 ♘ge7 5 ♗g2 g6 6 ♗e3 ♗g7 7 c3 b6 8 00 d5 9 ♕c1 00 10 ♗h6 ♕c7 11 ♗×g7 ♔×g7 12 ♘bd2 ♗a6 13 ed ♘×d5 14 ♘c4 ♖ad8 15 ♖e1 h6 16 ♕c2 ♘f6 17 a4 ♖d7 18 b3 ½–½

2414   AK–Nikolayevsky

R14: 5.10.1971: Pirc

'Karpov obtained the advantage of the two bishops and began to build up against the pawn on e5. Black gave up this pawn, banking on tactical complications, which, after 28 ♗c4!, proved to be illusory. The Leningrad grandmaster conducted the technical part of the game perfectly.' – Tseitlin and Havsky.

1 e4 g6 2 d4 ♗g7 3 ♘c3 d6 4 f4 ♘f6 5 ♘f3 00 6 ♗d3 ♘c6 7 e5 de 8 fe ♘h5 9 ♗e3 ♗g4 10 ♗c4 TN ♔h8 11 ♕d2 f6 12 ef ♗×f6 13 00± ♗×f3?! (13 ... ♕d7) 14 ♖×f3 e5 15 d5 ♘d4 16 ♖f1 ♘f5 17 ♗f2 ♘d6 18 ♗b3 ♗g5 19 ♕e1 ♕e7 20 ♘e4 ♗×e4 21 ♕×e4 ♖f4 22 ♕e2 ♖af8 23 ♖ae1± a5 24 c3 (24 ♕×e5? ♕×e5 25 ♖×e5 ♗f6 and

... a4 – Korchnoi) 24 ... ♘f6
(*158*)

158
24B
W

25 ♕×e5! ♕×e5 26 ♖×e5 ♘g4 (26
... ♘e4 27 ♖×g5 ♗×g5? 28
♗d4+ ♔g8 29 d6+ ± ± –
Korchnoi) 27 ♖×g5 ♗×f2 28 ♗c4!
a4 29 ♖g3 a3 30 b3 ♘e4 31 ♖×f4
♖×f4 32 ♖e3 ♘d6 33 ♗d3 ♖f7 34
c4± ± b6 35 g3 ♔g7 36 b4 ♔f6 37
♔f2 ♖d7 38 ♗e2 ♘f5 39 ♖×a3
♔e5 40 g4 ♘h4 41 ♖e3+ (s) **1-0**

2415 Krogius–AK

R15: 6.10.1971: Queen's Indian

1 d4 ♘f6 2 c4 e6 3 ♘f3 b6 4 g3 ♗b7
5 ♗g2 ♗e7 6 00 00 7 ♘c3 ♘e4 8
♘×e4 ♗×e4 9 ♘e1 ♗×g2 10
♘×g2 d6 11 b3 ♗f6 12 ♗b2 c5 ½–½

2416 AK–Tseitlin

R16: 9.10.1971: Spanish

(Notes by Karpov)

1 e4 e5 2 ♘f3 ♘c6 3 ♗b5 f5 4 ♘c3
♘d4?! 5 ♗a4 (5 ♘×e5!) 5 ... ♘f6
6 ♘×e5 fe (6 ... ♗c5 7 ♘d3 ♗b6
8 e5± ;6 ... ♕e7!? 7 ♘f3 ♘×f3+ 8
♕×f3 fe 9 ♕g3 c6 10 00 b5 11 ♗b3
d5 12 ♖e1 and d3±) 7 00 ♗c5 (7

... ♗d6 8 ♘c4 ♗e7 9 d3 ed 10
♕×d3 ♘e6 11 ♘e5±) 8 ♘×e4
♘×e4 9 ♕h5+ g6 10 ♘×g6 (*159*)

159
10W
B

10 ... ♘f6? (10 ... ♕g5!? 11 ♕×g5
♘×g5 12 ♘×h8 b5 13 ♗b3 ♘×b3
14 ab ♗d4 15 c3 ♗×h8 16 d4± ; 12
... ♘e2+ 13 ♔h1 ♘e4 14 d3
♗×f2+ 15 ♖×f2 ♗×f2 16
♗h6±) 11 ♕e5+ ± ± ♗e7 12
♘×h8 (12 ♖e1 ♘f3+ 13 gf ♖g8 14
♕×e7+ ♔×e7 15 ♖×e7+) 12 ...
b5 13 ♕×d4 ba 14 ♖e1 ♔f8 15 d3
♖b8 16 ♕e5! ♘g8 17 ♕h5 ♔g7 18
♘f7 ♕e8 19 ♗h6+ ♘×h6 20
♕×h6+ ♔×f7 21 ♕×h7+ ♔f8 22
♖e3 ♖b6 23 ♖g3 **1-0**

2417 Shamkovich–AK

R17: 10.10.1971: English

(Notes by Gufeld)

'Karpov equalized, and with 19
... ♕a4 obtained a Q-side attack.
Shamkovich tried to hold the
position by tactical means. Thus on
24 ... ♘d3 he had prepared 25
♗×f7+ ♔h8 26 ♕f6!. On 27 ...
♘×c1, 28 ♘f5!, forcing a draw,

would have followed. But Karpov, evading his opponent's counter-chances, methodically steered the game into a better rook ending. Using the remoteness of the white king, Black won the pawn on d5 and finished an easy winner.' – Vladimirov.

1 c4 c5 2 ♘f3 ♘f6 3 ♘c3 d5 4 cd ♘×d5 5 e3 ♘×c3 6 bc g6= 7 ♗a3 ♕c7 8 ♗c4 ♗g7 9 0-0 0-0 10 ♖c1 ♘d7 11 d4 ♖b8 12 ♗b5 b6 13 ♘d2 ♖d8 14 ♕f3 a6 15 ♗e2 ♗b7 16 ♕g3 ♕c6 17 ♗b2 e5!∓ 18 e4 ed 19 cd ♕a4 20 ♗c4!? cd 21 ♗b3 ♕b5 22 ♕f4 ♖f8 23 ♘f3 ♘c5 24 ♗×d4 ♗×d4 (24 ... ♘d3?? 25 ♗×f7+ ♔h8 26 ♕f6± ±) 25 ♘×d4 ♕e8 26 ♗d5 ♘d3 27 ♕f6 (*160*)

160
27W
B

27 ... ♕d8!∓ (27 ... ♘×c1? 28 ♘f5! gf 29 ♕g5+=) 28 ♕×d8 ♖f×d8 29 ♖cd1 ♘f4 30 ♘c6 (30 ♗×b7 ♖×b7 31 ♘b3 ♘e2+ 32 ♔h1 ♖×d1 33 ♖×d1 ♘c3∓) 30 ... ♗×c6 31 ♗×c6 ♘e2+ 32 ♔h1 ♘c3 33 ♖×d8+ ♖×d8 34 ♗d5 ♔f8 35 g3 ♘×d5 36 ♖d1 ♔e7 37 ed ♖c8∓ ∓ 38 ♖d2 ♔d6 39 a4 ♖c5 40 ♖b2 b5 41 ab ab 42 ♔g2

♔×d5 (s) 43 ♖b4 ♔c6 44 ♔f3 ♖c4 45 ♖b1 b4 46 ♔e3 ♔b5 47 f4 f5 48 ♔d2 ♖c6 49 ♔d3 ♔a4 50 ♖a1+ ♔b3 **0-1**

2418   AK–Tukmakov

R18: 11.10.1971: Sicilian

(Notes by Karpov)

1 e4 c5 2 ♘f3 e6 3 d4 cd 4 ♘×d4 ♘c6 5 ♘b5 d6 6 c4 ♘f6 7 ♘1c3 a6 8 ♘a3 ♗e7 9 ♗e2 0-0 10 0-0 b6 11 ♗e3 ♗b7 12 ♖c1 ♘e5 13 ♕d4 ♘ed7 (13 ... ♘fd7 14 f3±) 14 f3?! (14 ♖fd1 ♖e8 15 ♘c2; 14 ... ♖c8 15 f3 and ♕d2) 14 ... d5! 15 ed ♗c5?! (15 ... ed 16 cd ♗c5 17 ♕d2 ♗×e3+ 18 ♕×e3 ♘×d5 19 ♘×d5 ♗×d5=) 16 ♕d2 ♗×e3+? 17 ♕×e3 ed 18 ♖fd1 ♖e8 19 ♕f2 ♖c8 20 ♖c2 ♕e7 21 ♗f1? (21 ♖cd2! b5 22 ♘×d5 ♘×d5 23 cd ♕d6 24 ♘c2±) 21 ... ♕d6 22 ♖cd2 b5 23 ♘×d5 (23 cb? ♖×c3) 23 ... ♘×d5 24 cd ♘f6 25 ♗d3 ♗×d5 26 ♗e4 ♖e5 27 ♗×d5 ♖×d5 28 ♖×d5 ♘×d5 (28 ... ♕×d5!= 29 ♖×d5 ♖c1+ 30 ♕f1 ♖×f1+ 31 ♔×f1 ♘×d5) 29 ♕d4 ♕b6 30 ♕×b6 ♘×b6 (*161*)

31 ♖d6 ♖b8 32 ♖c6!± ♔f8 33 ♘c2 ♖c8 (33 ... ♔e7 34 ♘d4) 34 ♖×c8+ ♘×c8 35 ♘b4! a5 36 ♘c6 a4 37 ♔f2 ♔e8 38 ♔e3 ♔d7 39 ♘e5+? (39 ♘d4! ♘d6 40 ♔d3 ♔c7 41 ♔c3 ♔b6 42 ♔b4±) 39 ... ♔e6 40 ♔d4 f6? (40 ... ♘e7) 41 ♘d3 ♔d6 42 ♘f4 g6 43 ♘d5 f5 44 g4 ♘a7 (s) 45 ♘b4 fg 46 fg ♘c8 47 ♘d3 (47 ♘d5 ♘a7 48 g5 ♘c6+

161
30B
W

49 ♔e4 ♘a5=) 47 . . . ♘e7 48 ♘e5
♔e6 49 a3 ♘d5 50 ♘d7! ♔d6 51
g5 (51 ♘c5 ♘b6=) 51 . . . ♘e7 52
♘f8 ♘c6+ 53 ♔c3 ♘e5? (53 . . .
♔e5 54 ♘×h7 ♔f5 55 ♔d3±) 54
♘×h7 ♘f3 55 ♔b4 **1–0** (55 . . .
♔c6 56 ♘f8 ♘×h2 57 ♘×g6 ♘f3
58 ♘e7+)

2419   Tal–AK

R19: ?.10.1971: Queen's Indian

(Notes by Karpov)

'October 13th was the day of the
USSR–N. Ireland football match.
Tal, learning in the morning of the
postponement of his game with
Karpov (who was feeling unwell),
was not very interested at first, but
then set out to find out which of the
Leningrad players lived near to the
tournament hall and had a
television set he could watch.' –
Fedorov.

1 ♘f3 ♘f6 2 g3 b6 3 ♗g2 ♗b7 4 c4
e6 5 00 ♗e7 6 d4 00 7 ♘c3 ♘e4 8
♕c2 ♘×c3 9 ♕×c3 c5 10 ♗e3
♕c7 (10 . . . ♗f6 11 ♖fd1 ♗×f3 12

♗×f3 ♘c6 13 ♗×c6 dc 14 ♕d2
Tal–Korchnoi, 1968) 11 ♖fd1 d6 12
♖ac1 ♘d7 13 a3 a5! 14 b4 (14 b3!?)
14 . . . ab 15 ab ♖a2 16 ♖d2 (16
♖a1) 16 . . . ♖×d2 (16 . . . ♖fa8 17
♖×a2 ♖×a2 18 ♕b3) 17 ♕×d2
♖a8 18 ♘e1 ♗×g2 19 ♔×g2 (19
♘×g2 ♖a4∓) 19 . . . ♖a4 20 bc bc
21 dc ♘×c5 22 ♕c2 ½–½ (22 . . .
♕c6+ 23 ♔g1 ♖a8 24 ♘d3=)

2420   AK–Balashov

R20: 14.10.1971: Sicilian

1 e4 c5 2 ♘f3 d6 3 d4 cd 4 ♘×d4
♘f6 5 ♘c3 ♘c6 6 ♗g5 ♗d7 7
♕d2 ♖c8 8 000 ♘×d4 9 ♕×d4
♕a5 10 f4 e6 11 e5 de 12 fe ♗c6 13
♗b5 ♘d5 14 ♗×c6+ (14 ♘×d5!
♗×b5 15 ♕×a7!± ± Shamkovich
and Fedorov, but 15 . . . ♗b4!
led to a drawish ending in
Hort–Panno, Palma interzonal
1970.) 14 . . . bc 15 a3 h6 16 ♗d2
♕b6 17 ♕×b6 ab 18 ♘e4 b5 19
♔b1 f5 20 ef gf 21 g4 h5 22 h3 ♗e7
23 ♖hg1 hg 24 hg ♖g8 ½–½

2421   Polugayevsky–AK

R21: 16.10.1971: English

1 c4 c5 2 ♘f3 ♘f6 3 ♘c3 d5 4 cd
♘×d5 5 g3 g6 6 ♗g2 ♗g7 7 00 00 8
♘×d5 ♕×d5 9 d3 ♘a6 10 a3 ♕h5
11 ♖b1 ♗h3 12 ♕b3 b6 13 ♕c4
♘c7 14 ♗×h3 ♕×h3 15 b4 ♘e6 16
♗e3 ♖ac8 17 ♕a6 ♘d4 18 ♗×d4
cd 19 ♕×a7 ♕e6 20 ♖fe1 ♖a8 21
♕b7 ♖×a3 22 ♘g5 ♕e5 23 ♘f3
½–½

25 Alekhine Memorial Moscow, 23.11–19.12.1971

	1	2	3	4	5	6	7	8	9	0	1	2	3	4	5	6	7	8	
1 **Karpov**	×	½	½	½	½	½	½	1	½	1	1	½	½	1	½	½	½	1	**11**
2 Stein	½	×	½	½	½	½	½	1	½	½	½	1	½	½	½	1	1	1	**11**
3 Smyslov	½	½	×	1	½	½	½	½	½	½	½	½	1	½	½	1	1	½	**10½**
4 Petrosian	½	½	0	×	½	1	½	½	½	½	1	½	½	½	1	½	1	½	**10**
5 Tukmakov	½	½	½	½	×	½	½	½	½	½	1	½	½	½	1	½	1	½	**10**
6 Spassky	½	½	½	0	½	×	½	½	½	½	0	1	1	1	½	½	½	1	**9½**
7 Tal	½	½	½	½	½	½	×	½	1	½	0	½	0	½	½	1	1	1	**9½**
8 Bronstein	0	0	½	½	½	½	½	×	½	½	0	½	½	½	1	1	1	1	**9**
9 R. Byrne	½	½	½	½	½	½	0	½	×	1	0	½	½	1	1	½	½	½	**9**
10 Hort	0	½	½	½	½	½	½	½	0	×	1	½	1	½	½	½	½	1	**9**
11 Korchnoi	0	½	½	0	0	1	1	1	1	0	×	1	½	0	1	0	½	½	**8½**
12 Gheorghiu	½	0	½	½	½	0	½	½	½	½	0	×	1	½	½	½	½	½	**7½**
13 Olafsson	½	½	0	½	½	0	1	½	½	0	½	0	×	1	0	½	½	1	**7½**
14 Savon	0	½	½	½	½	0	½	½	0	½	1	½	0	×	½	½	½	1	**7½**
15 Balashov	½	½	½	0	0	½	½	0	0	½	0	½	1	½	×	1	0	½	**6½**
16 Uhlmann	½	0	0	½	½	½	0	0	½	½	1	½	½	½	0	×	½	½	**6½**
17 Parma	½	0	0	0	0	½	0	0	½	½	½	½	½	½	1	½	×	½	**6**
18 Lengyel	0	0	½	½	½	0	0	0	½	0	½	½	0	0	½	½	½	×	**4½**

Karpov's success in this event signalled the arrival of 'Anatoly Grozny' – since this event Karpov has had only two 'failures' (2nd at Budapest and 2nd in the 1973 Soviet Championship), in every other event in which he has competed he has taken first prize (in tournaments) or has won the board prize (in team events) or has defeated his opponent (in matches). This phenomenal run of success can only be compared (in modern times) with Fischer's very similar record in the period 1963–1972.

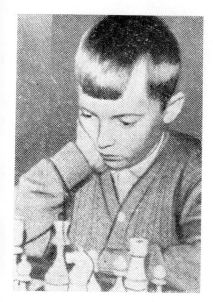

Borovichi 1961

Trud Training School, Moscow 1963. In the foreground
Botvinnik and Karpov

Leningrad 1966

Groningen 1967–8

Leningrad 1969

Before a game at Bath 1973

Leningrad Interzonal 1973

Karpov – Gligoric.

1. e4 e5 2. Kf3 Kc6 3. Cb5 a6 4. Ca4 Kf6 5. 0-0 Ce7
6. Лe1 b5 7. Cb3 d6 8. c3 0-0 9. h3 Kb8 10. d4 Kbd7 11. Kbd2
Cb7 12. Cc2 c5 13. d5 [13. Kf1!?] 13... Ke8 14. Kf1 g6 15. Ch6
Kg7 16. Ke3 Kf6 17. a4 Kph8 18. b3 [18. Фe2 c4 =] 18... Лb8
19. Фe2 Cc8 [19... Фb6] 20. ab ab 21. Лa7 Kg8 22. Cхg7+ Kpхg7
23. Лea1 Kf6 24. Cd3 Cd7 25. Фa2 Ke8?! [25... Фb6!?] 26. Фa6!
[26. Фa5 Фc8 27. Фa6 cd8 =] 26... Лb6 [26... Kc7 27. Фa5 Лa8
(27... Лc8 28. Фb6, 29. Лb7 ±) 28. Лхa8 Фхa8 29. Фхc7! Фxa1+
30. Kph2 Лd8 31. cхb5 Cхb5 32. Фхe7 Лd7 33. Фh4 Δ 34. C4, 34. Kg4+]
27. Фa5 Kf6 28. Kg4! Лb8 29. Kхf6 [29. Фc7?! Cхg4 30. hg Фхc7
31. Лхc7 cd8 32. Лc6 c4 33. bc bc 34. Лхc4 Kхg4 =] 29... cхf6
30. Фc7 Фхc7 31. Лхc7 Лfd8 32. Лaa7 Ce8 33. Лab7 [Δ 34. cхb5
C хb5 35. Л х f7+ Kpg8 36. Л хb8] 33... Kpg8 34. g4 h6 35. h4 Лхb7
36. Лхb7 c4 37. bc bc 38. Ce2 [38. Cхc4 Cd7 39. g5 Cg4!
(39... hg 40. Kхg5 ±) 40. gf Cхf3 41. Cd3 g5] 38... Лa8 39. cхc4
39... Ca4 [39... Лc8 40. Ce2 Ca4 41. g5 hg 42. Kхg5 Cхg5 43. hg
Лхc3 44 Лb6 ±] 40. Cb3! Cхb3 41. Лхb3 Лc8 [41... Лa4 42. Лb4+ –]
42. Kpg2 h5 43. gh gh 44. Лb6 Лхc3 45. Лхd6 Kpg7 46. Лc6 Лd3
[46... Лa3] 47. Лc7 Kpg6 48. Лc8 [Δ 48. Лa3 49. Лe8 Лa4 50. k+e5+]
48... Cg7 49. Лc6+ Kph7 50. Kg5+ Kpg8 51. Лc8+ Cf8 52. Лc7 f6
53. Ke6 Ch6 54. Лd7 + – Лd2 55. Kpf1 Лd1+ 56. Kpe2 Лd2+ 57. Kpe1
Лc2 58. d6 Лc1+ 59. Kpe2 Лc2+ 60. Kpf1 Лc6 61. Kpg2 Лb6
[61... Cd2 62. Лg7+ Kph8 63. d7 Лd6 64. Лe7 Ca5 65. d8Ф+ Cхd8
66. Лe8+ +–] 62. Kc7 Лb7 [62... Cf8 63. Ke8] 63. Kd5

1:0

The game Karpov-Gligoric, Leningrad 1973, in Karpov's own hand

Oscar Winner 1973 and 1974

Working hard against Kuzmin, Leningrad 1973

Nice Olympiad 1974

'Sweet dreams the Karpov way.' *British Chess Magazine*

Interview with Karpov and Furman

The discussion with Anatoly Karpov (conducted by A. Roshal and published in *64* No. 52 1971) took place in the presence of Semyon Abramovich Furman and, understandably, the trainer took part in the conversation.

AR: It is difficult to suppose that your sporting goal in this tournament was to share first place.

AK: Even some people very favourably disposed towards me hoped for a place in the top ten for me. I myself was prepared to get one of the first five places.

SF: For me personally today's success is not so unexpected, partly because during recent years his results have been stable and with every tournament they have improved. Certainly I could not have foreseen that he would share first place, but I did estimate that he would get about the same number of points as he did get. I calculated that he would get plus 4 or plus 5. One's placing in a tournament is not always decided by the total of points, everything depends on how the struggle takes shape. But the even standard of the participants suggested in advance that such a showing would achieve a very high placing.

AR: Well, how did things take shape?

AK: I was not satisfied with the way the draw worked out for me. It dictated a stormy start, and I did not feel any special wish to play. Nothing much happened. All the time I wanted a great deal, but nothing worthwhile came up, the games took shape in a difficult way. The turning point was the meeting with Vlastimil Hort, it stood out not only in a sporting but also in an artistic connection. My spirits immediately rose. In the outcome I even got the prize for the best finish. Here I emerged victor over David Bronstein and Viktor Korchnoi. True, in the game with Viktor Lvovich we both unfortunately made several mistakes. Well, and against Vladimir Savon in the last round it somehow happened that he walked into an ambush. We expected that he would adopt the Open defence in the Ruy Lopez, although to guess exactly which system was difficult. When already at the board, I recalled one of his games in which he developed in a similar fashion. I found a strong manoeuvre with the queen (18 ♕c1! – eds), which turned out to be fatal for my opponent.

SF: We had been looking at a similar idea beforehand. It should be added that Karpov embarked on this encounter with the express wish of winning. In addition he was White.

AR: Does which colour you have and fighting spirit mean much?

AK: It is undoubtedly more difficult to play Black. But it is also not bad, especially when the opponent starts to play sharply for a win. I am always disposed to fight, but nevertheless for some reason colourless games sometimes arise.

AR: To amateurs the style of the 20-year-old Karpov seems somewhat dry, rather academic. Frequent draws . . . At your age doesn't the wish arise to sacrifice a bit, to burn your bridges, and – charge!?

AK: So far I have a somewhat narrow opening repertoire – in consequence of having little spare time to work on broadening it. Of course I would like to play sharper and more modern systems, but in my opinion this is not in keeping with my style. At least I am satisfied with my style and I have not yet thought of changing it. Certainly it is possible to sacrifice pieces. Why not sacrifice? – if it is correct. But bridges I don't burn, it's not my speciality.

Draws are a separate matter. With a tournament schedule like the Memorial's they are unavoidable. It is true that they say that there is now a difficult tournament schedule everywhere, but you know you don't get such a first-class field everywhere. As regards me personally, I normally go out simply to play chess, I do not agree to draws beforehand. I settle for draws if the game which develops is not the type which I like, or if the half-points enable me to achieve the desired sporting result in the tournament. But in general it is necessary to learn not to lose, and wins will come afterwards.

SF: Prudence, or discretion – that is his characteristic feature. This particularly pleased me, even on first acquaintance; such a valuable quality is rarely met with in such young players. But for further achievements of the highest order a healthy risk is necessary; great aggressiveness. There arises a danger of changing a good quality into the opposite. Fortunately Tolya has proved, to some extent against expectation, a most dutiful student in the chess sense.

AK: Of the players in the tournament, Petrosian and Smyslov made the greatest impression on me.

SF: Clearly this is because both ex-champions are close to Karpov in their style of play, although there is not a complete resemblance. Therefore they are the most interesting for him.

AK: I don't know why. I just feel that here are chess players who understand everything, for whom there are no secrets.

AR: Do you ever experience time-trouble agonies these days?

AK: In all, two or three times in my life. This is not at all because everything is clear to me, while others think. It is simply that I don't want to make stupid mistakes, and then lose, because of time shortage. Therefore I feel compelled to content myself with normal moves (they seem good to me) instead of searching for the best ones.

AR: The burden of first place – now many people will expect a repeat of your success. Someone even laid a bet . . .

AK: . . . But I, as a rule, never bet on anything. And so far no burden of compulsion to demonstrate anything has been laid on me. One must learn to play. You know in the last count absolutely all chess players are only occupied in learning to play better.

SF: In order to achieve further goals it's probably necessary to experiment somewhere. One just cannot do this in invitation tournaments. There, as grandmaster Uhlmann puts it, 'keine fokus!'

AR: What tournaments lie ahead?

AK: Next .the international tournament at Hastings. Apparently in February, a match with the World Junior Champion, Hug, for the right of taking part in the Interzonal tournament (the match didn't take place, both players were given places in the Interzonal – eds), at the beginning of March the final of the all-Union Olympiad.

AR: Isn't that rather a lot? .

AK: In the first half of 1971 I hardly played at all, but beginning with June I scarcely left the board – June, semi-final of the Soviet Championship; July, Student Olympiad; August, two team championships (national and Armed Forces); September–October, final of the national championship. If the Alekhine tournament hadn't been so outstanding and tempting, I would have had to decline.

AR: Isn't it possible to give the All-Union Federation the individual plan of grandmaster Karpov, to have it ratified there, and afterwards to play and to occupy yourself in accordance with the plan?

SF: Unfortunately alterations, for reasons unknown to us, are quite often made. We expected that Karpov would take part in another foreign international tournament next spring. Now we again have to change all our plans.

AR: Is Anatoly really, at the same time, counted as a student of Leningrad University?

AK: I'm not just counted as one – I study the third year course in the Economics faculty. So far in my examination successes there has not yet been a 'four' and in the forthcoming session I'm desperate for an 'excellent'.

AR: Good Luck!

2501 Parma–AK

R1: 24.11.1971: Sicilian

(Notes by Gheorghiu)

Both the players and the annotator have all been World Junior Champion! 'Karpov manoeuvred calmly and White's attack did not break through. In time-trouble Parma committed an oversight which cost him a pawn, and in the adjourned position Karpov and his trainer, Furman, will most probably find a way to win.' (*64*)

1 e4 c5 2 ♘f3 e6 3 d4 cd 4 ♘×d4 ♘c6 5 ♘c3 a6 6 f4 ♕c7 7 ♗e3 b5 8 ♘b3!± ♘f6 9 ♗d3 (9 e5 b4!) 9 ... d6 10 00 ♗e7 11 ♕f3 00 12 a4! b4 13 ♘b1 a5!? (13 ... e5) 14 ♘1d2 ♗a6 15 ♗f2! ♖fc8 16 ♖ae1 d5 17 e5 ♘d7 18 ♕h3 g6 19 ♔h1 ♘d8 20 ♘f3 ♕b7 21 ♗h4!± ♗×h4 22 ♕×h4 ♘f8 23 ♘bd4! ♗×d3 24 cd ♕d7 (*162*)

162
24B
W

25 ♕g5?? (25 g4! preparing f5±) 25 ... h5! 26 ♕h6? (26 ♘h4±) 26 ... ♘c6! 27 ♘b5 ♘e7 28 ♘fd4 ♘f5!∓

29 ♘×f5 ef 30 ♕g5 ♖c2 31 b3 ♖ac8 32 ♕g3 d4! 33 ♕f3 ♖b2 34 ♖b1 ♖×b1 35 ♖×b1 ♘e6 36 ♘d6 ♖c3 37 h3 ♕c6 38 ♕g3 ♖c1+ ?! 39 ♖×c1 ♕×c1+ 40 ♔h2 ♕×f4 41 ♘c4!∓ ♕c1! (41 ... h4 42 ♕×f4 ♘×f4 43 ♘×a5 ♘×d3 44 ♘c6!=) 42 ♕f3 ♕e1 43 ♕g3 ♕c3 44 ♘×a5 ♔g7 45 ♕f3 h4 46 ♘c4! ♕×b3 47 a5 ♕a2 48 ♕b7! ♘g5 49 e6!= ♕f2! 50 ef (50 e7 ♘×h3!∓) 50 ... ♕g3+ 51 ♔h1 ♕e1+ 52 ♔h2 ♕g3+ ½–½

2502 AK–Olafsson

R2: 25.11.1971: Sicilian

1 e4 c5 2 ♘f3 ♘c6 3 d4 cd 4 ♘×d4 e6 5 ♘b5 d6 6 c4 ♘f6 7 ♘1c3 a6 8 ♘a3 ♗e7 9 ♗e2 00 10 00 b6 11 ♗e3 ♗b7 12 ♖c1 ♖b8 13 ♕d2 ♘e5 14 f3 d5 15 cd ed 16 ♘×d5 ♗×d5 17 ed ♘×d5 18 ♖fd1 ♘×e3 19 ♕×e3 ♕e8 20 ♕×e5 ½–½

2503 Lengyel–AK

R3: 26.11.1971: Catalan

(Notes by Gheorghiu)

Black defended the gambit pawn, and White's pressure along the d-file eventually became noticeable. Karpov returned the pawn in time, obtained a lot of play on the Q-side and won the exchange.' (*64*)

1 d4 ♘f6 2 c4 e6 3 g3 d5 4 ♗g2 dc! 5 ♘f3 b5 6 ♘e5 ♘d5 7 00 ♗b7 8 e4 ♘f6 9 ♖e1 ♘bd7 10 ♕e2 a6∓ 11

♘c3 ♘×e5 12 de ♘d7 13 ♖d1
♕c8 14 f4 ♗c5+ 15 ♗e3 00 16
♖d2 ♗×e3+ 17 ♕×e3 c5 18
♖ad1= ♗c6 19 ♖d6 ♖e8 20
♖1d2 ♕c7 21 ♘d1 (*163*)

163
21W
B

21 ... b4 22 ♗f1 ♗b5 23 ♗×c4
♘b6! 24 ♗×b5 ab 25 b3 ♘c8!∓ 26
♖d7 ♕b6 27 ♖c2 c4 28 ♖d4
♖a3∓ 29 ♘f2 ♘e7 30 ♕d2 c3 31
♕d3 ♘c6 32 ♖d6 ♖aa8 33 ♔g2
♖ed8 34 a3?! ♖×d6 35 ed ♘d4!∓
36 ab ♘×c2 37 ♕×c2 ♕d4 38 ♔f3
e5 39 ♘d3 ef 40 gf f6 41 e5 (s) **0–1**

2504   AK–Gheorghiu

R4: 28.11.1971: Sicilian

(Notes by Gheorghiu)

1 e4 c5 2 ♘f3 d6 3 d4 cd 4 ♘×d4
♘f6 5 ♘c3 a6 6 ♗e2 e5 7 ♘b3
♗e6 8 00 ♘bd7 9 f4 ♕c7 10 f5 ♗c4
11 a4 ♗e7 12 ♗g5 00 13 a5 ♖fc8!±
14 ♗×c4 ♕×c4 15 ♖f2 h6! 16
♗×f6 (? Karpov; 16 ♗h4!?) 16 ...
♘×f6 17 ♖a4 ♕c7 18 ♖d2 b5!∓
½–½ (19 ab ♕×b6+ 20 ♔h1 ♖×c3!
21 bc ♕c6 22 ♖a1 ♘×e4 23 ♘a5
♕×c3∓)

2505   R. Byrne–AK

R5: 29.11.1971: Sicilian

1 e4 c5 2 ♘f3 ♘c6 3 d4 cd 4 ♘×d4
e6 5 ♗e3 ♕c7 6 ♘c3 a6 7 ♗d3 b5 8
00 ♗b7 9 ♕e2 ♘f6 10 f4 ♘×d4 11
♗×d4 ♗c5 12 ♗×c5 ♕×c5+ 13
♔h1 b4 14 ♘d1 d6 15 ♘f2 e5 16
♘g4 ♘×g4 17 ♕×g4 00 18 a3 ♗c6
19 ♕f5 ba 20 ♖×a3 ♗b5 21 ♖c3
♕b4 22 ♖b3 ♕c5 23 ♖c3 ½–½

2506   AK–Balashov

R6: 30.11.1971: Spanish

(Notes by Balashov)

1 e4 e5 2 ♘f3 ♘c6 3 ♗b5 a6 4 ♗a4
♘f6 5 00 ♗e7 6 ♖e1 b5 7 ♗b3 d6 8
c3 00 9 h3 h6 10 d4 ♖e8 11 ♘bd2
♗f8 12 ♘f1 ♗b7 13 ♘g3 ♘a5 14
♗c2 ♘c4 15 b3 ♘b6 16 ♘h2
(preparing 17 f4) 16 ... d5!= 17 de
(17 ed ed∓) 17 ... ♘×e4 (17 ...
♖×e5? 18 ♘f3 ♖e8 19 e5 ♘e4 20
♘×e4 de 21 ♕×d8 ♖a×d8 22
♗×e4 ♗×e4 23 ♖×e4 ♖d1+ 24
♔h2±) 18 ♕d3 (18 ♘×e4 de 19
♕×d8 ♖a×d8 20 ♗×e4 ♗×e4 21
♖×e4 ♖d1+ 22 ♘f1 ♘d7 23 ♗b2
♖×a1 24 ♗×a1 ♖×e5= ; 18 ♘f5?
♖×e5 19 ♕g4 ♕f6∓) 18 ... ♘d7
19 f4 ♕h4 20 ♘hf1 ♘dc5 (20 ...
♗c5+ ? 21 ♔h2±) 21 ♕f3 ♘×g3
22 ♕×g3 (22 ♘×g3 d4∓) 22 ...
♗e7 23 ♗e3 ♕×g3 (23 ... ♘e4 24
♗×e4 ♕×g3 25 ♘×g3 de 26
♗f2±) 24 ♘×g3 ♗h4 25 ♔h2
♗×g3+ 26 ♔×g3 ♘e4+ 27 ♗×e4
de ½–½

2507 Uhlmann–AK

R7: 3.12.1971: English

(Notes by Uhlmann)

'In a complicated queenless middle game, the weaknesses on Black's Q-side (b4 and d5) gradually became apparent.' (*64*)

1 c4 c5 2 ♘f3 ♘f6 3 ♘c3 d5 4 cd ♘×d5 5 g3 g6 6 d3 ♗g7 7 ♗d2 b6? (7 ... 0–0 8 ♗g2±) 8 ♕a4+ ♗d7 9 ♕h4! e6 10 ♕×d8+ (10 ♗g5!±)10 ... ♔×d8 11 ♗g2 h6 12 0–0 ♘c6 13 ♘e1 ♘c7 14 a3 a5 15 ♘c2 ♖b8 16 e3 ♘e5 17 d4 ♘c4 18 ♗c1 a4 19 ♖d1 ♔e7 20 ♖b1 ♘a5 21 e4 cd 22 ♘×d4 (*164*)

164
22W
B

22 ... e5? (22 ... ♖hd8 23 ♗f1±) 23 ♘c2! ♗g4 24 ♖d3! ♗e6 25 ♗e3 ♗b3 26 ♘b4 ♖hd8 27 ♖×d8 ♔×d8 28 ♗f3 ♔e8 29 ♗e2 b5 30 ♖c1! ♔d7 (30 ... ♗c4? 31 ♗×c4 ♘×c4 32 ♘×a4 ♘×e3 33 ♖×c7 ba 34 fe ♗f8 35 ♘d5±) 31 ♗g4+ ♗e6 32 ♖d1+ ♔e8 33 ♗×e6 fe 34 ♖d6 (Uhlmann does not comment on this. Kotov queries it and gives 34 ♗a7! ♖b7 35 ♗c5!±

– KJO'C.) 34 ... ♗f8 35 ♖b6! ♖b7 36 ♖×b7? (36 ♘a6! ♖×a6 37 ♖×e6+ ♔f7 38 ♖×a6 ♘c4 39 ♗c1±) 36 ... ♘×b7 37 ♘c6 ♗g7! 38 ♘a7 ♘d6 39 ♗b6 ♘a8 40 ♗c5 ♘c4 41 ♗×b5 ♘×b2 42 ♔f1 (s) ½–½

2508 AK–Spassky

R8: 4.12.1971: Spanish

'Black played a rarely met variation with the early development of the bishop to g4. After a complicated manoeuvring fight a draw was agreed after threefold repetition of the position.' (*64*)

1 e4 e5 2 ♘f3 ♘c6 3 ♗b5 a6 4 ♗a4 ♘f6 5 0–0 d6 6 ♖e1 b5 7 ♗b3 ♗g4 8 c3 ♗e7 9 d3 0–0 10 h3 ♗h5 11 ♘bd2 ♘a5 12 ♗c2 c5 13 ♘f1 ♗×f3 14 ♕×f3 ♘d7 15 ♕g4 ♗f6 16 ♘g3 g6 17 ♗h6 ♗g7 18 ♗×g7 ♔×g7 19 f4 ♘f6 20 ♕f3 h5 21 ♖ad1 ♖c8 22 ♗b1 h4 23 ♘e2 ♘h5 24 a3 c4 25 d4 ♕e7 26 ♕g4 ♖cd8 27 ♗c2 ♘c6 28 ♔h2 ♖h8 29 ♕d2 ♘f6 30 ♕f3 ♘h5 31 ♕g4 ♘f6 32 ♕f3 ♘h5 (*165*) ½–½

165
32B
W

'I had the better position at the moment I agreed to a draw. But I couldn't help doing that, for I could not see any clear-cut plan of action.' – Karpov

166
40B
W

2509 Tal–AK

R9: 5.12.1971: Queen's Indian

'This game attracted attention with a knight manoeuvre in the opening. White's following, powerful attack on the isolated pawn gave him a clear advantage. Black managed to parry the immediate threats, but, all the same, in the adjourned position the ex-World Champion maintains the better chances.' (*64*)

1 d4 ♘f6 2 ♘f3 e6 3 c4 b6 4 g3 ♗e7 5 ♗g2 ♗b7 6 00 00 7 ♘c3 ♘e4 8 ♗d2 d5 9 cd ed 10 ♘e5 ♘d7 11 ♘d3 a5 12 ♖c1 ♘df6 13 ♗f4 c6 14 ♘e5 c5 15 dc ♘×c3 16 bc ♗×c5 17 ♗g5 ♖e8 18 ♗g4 ♗e7 19 ♗×f6 ♗×f6 20 c4 ♗e7 21 ♘e3 ♗g5 22 ♕d3 d4 23 ♗×b7 de 24 ♗×a8 ef+ 25 ♔×f2 ♗e3+ 26 ♕×e3 ♖×e3 27 ♔×e3 ♕×a8 28 ♖fd1 ♕c8 29 ♖d5 h6 30 h4 ♕g4 31 ♔f2 ♕e6 32 ♖c3 ♕h3 33 ♔g1 ♕g4 34 ♔f2 ♕h3 35 a3 ♕h2+ 36 ♔e1 ♕h1+ 37 ♔d2 ♕e4 38 ♔e1 g6 39 ♔f2 ♔g7 40 ♔e1 ♕b1+ (*166*)

41 ♔f2 (s) (adjournment 6.12.1971) 41 ... ♕e4 42 ♔e1 ♕b1+ 43 ♖d1 ♕e4 44 ♖dd3 ♕c6 45 ♔d2 g5 46 hg hg 47 ♖b3 ♔g6 48 ♖b5 f6 49 ♖d4 ♔h5 50 ♖h4+ ♔g6 51 ♖d4 ♔h5 52 ♖b3 ♕c5 53 ♖bd3 b5 54 cb ♕×b5 55 ♖d5 ♕b6 56 ♖d6 ♕b1 57 ♖6d5 ♕b6 58 ♖5d4 ♕b1 59 ♖d6 ♔g4 60 ♖f3 ♕b2+ 61 ♔e1 ♕c1+ 62 ♖d1 ♕c5 63 ♔f1 ♕e5 64 ♖d8 ♕a1+ 65 ♔f2 ♕e5 66 ♖fd3 ♕f5+ 67 ♔g1 ♕e5 68 ♖8d4+ ♔h3 69 ♔f1 ♕f5+ 70 ♔g1 ♕e5 71 ♔f2 ♕f5+ 72 ♖f3 ♕e5 73 ♖c4 ♕d5 74 ♖fc3 ♕f5+ 75 ♖f3 ♕d5 76 g4+ ♔h4 77 ♖fc3 ♕e5 78 ♖d3 ♕h2+ 79 ♔f1 ♕h1+ 80 ♔f2 ♕h2+ 81 ♔e1 ♕e5 82 ♖f3 ♕d5 83 ♖fc3 ♕e5 84 ♖d3 ♕e6 85 ♖a4 ♕e5 86 ♖ad4 ♕e7 87 ♔f2 ♕e5 88 ♔f1 ♕h2 89 ♖e3 ♕h1+ 90 ♔f2 ♕a1 91 ♖de4 ♕b1 92 ♖d3 ♕b2 93 ♔e1 ♕c1+ 94 ♔f2 ♕h1 95 ♖de3 ♕h2+ 96 ♔e1 ♕h1+ 97 ♔d2 ♕b1 98 ♔c3 ♕b6 99 ♔c2 ♕c6+ 100 ♔d1 ♕b7 101 ♔e1 ♕b1+ 102 ♔f2 ♕h1 103 ♖c4 ½-½

2510 Petrosian–AK

R10: 7.12.1971: Queen's Indian

1 d4 ♘f6 2 ♘f3 e6 3 g3 b6 4 ♗g2 ♗b7 5 c4 ♗e7 6 ♘c3 ♘e4 7 ♗d2 d5 8 cd ed 9 00 00 10 ♖c1 ♘d7 11 ♗f4 c5 12 ♘d2 ♘×c3 13 bc ♘f6 14

dc ♗×c5 15 ♘b3 ♗a3 16 ♖c2 ♖c8 ½–½

2511 AK–Hort

R11: 8.12.1971: Sicilian

(Notes by Furman)

1 e4 c5 2 ♘f3 d6 3 d4 cd 4 ♘×d4 ♘f6 5 ♘c3 e6 6 g4 ♘c6 (In my view 6 . . . h6 is preferable) **7 g5 ♘d7 8 ♗e3 a6 9 f4** (natural, but a premature advance. 9 ♖g1 was preferable.) **9 . . . ♗e7** (Hort does not utilize his opponent's inexactitude. By 9 . . . h6 Black would have obtained a definite advantage, obtaining control over e5, after 10 . . . hg, because on 10 g6 or 10 gh he can play 10 . . . ♕h4+.) **10 ♖g1 ♘×d4** (The Czech grandmaster tries rather quickly to create counterplay, but White maintains a positional advantage after this.) **11 ♕×d4 e5 12 ♕d2 ef 13 ♗×f4 ♘e5 14 ♗e2 ♗e6 15 ♘d5 ♗×d5 16 ed ♘g6** (The beginning of a dubious tactical operation. He had to reconcile himself to the more passive, but necessary plan of play – 16 . . . ♕c7, 17 . . . 000, and if 17

167
21B
W

♖g3 00 18 000 ♖ad8 with 19 . . . ♖fe8 to follow .) **17 ♗e3 h6?! 18 gh ♗h4+ 19 ♔d1 gh 20 ♗×h6 ♗f6 21 c3 ♗e5** (*167*) (At first sight it seems that Black has achieved his aims. He threatens 22 . . . ♕h4, and after 22 ♗g5 ♕b6 23 ♗e3 ♕c7 White gets nowhere. But the young grandmaster finds a strong reply.) **22 ♗g4! ♕f6** (22 . . . ♗×h2, maintaining material equality, was relatively better.) **23 h4! ♕f5 24 ♖b4 ♗f6 25 h5 ♘e7** (The knight had to retreat to a less advantageous position because on 25 . . . ♘e5 would follow 26 ♖f4 winning a piece.) **26 ♖f4 ♕e5 27 ♖f3!** (White only has one rook in play but it is working at full strength.) **27 . . . ♘×d5 28 ♖d3 ♖×h6** (Nothing better is available. On 28 . . . ♘e7, 29 ♗f4 is nasty.) **29 ♖×d5** (29 ♕×h6 would be a mistake in view of 29 . . . ♗g5 with 30 . . . ♘e3+ to follow.) **29 . . . ♕e4** (29 . . . ♕e6!? 30 ♖×d6 ♕×d6 31 ♕×d6 ♖d8 32 ♕×d8+ ± – Karpov) **30 ♖d3 ♕h1+ 31 ♔c2 ♕×a1 32 ♕×h6 ♗e5 33 ♕g5 1–0** (time) After the single inexactitude in the opening, the youngest participant in the tournament conducted the game perfectly.

2512 Tukmakov–AK

R12: 9.12.1971: Spanish

1 e4 e5 2 ♘f3 ♘c6 3 ♗b5 a6 4 ♗a4 ♘f6 5 00 ♗e7 6 ♖e1 b5 7 ♗b3 d6 8 c3 00 9 h3 ♘b8 10 d4 ♘bd7 11 c4 c6

12 cb ab 13 ᐃc3 ♗a6! 14 a3 c5= 15
dc dc 16 ♗g5 c4 17 ♗c2 ♕c7 18
ᐃh2 ♕b6 19 ᐃg4 ♖fe8 20 ♕f3
♗b7 21 ♗×f6 ½-½

2513   AK–Bronstein

R13: 12.12.1971: Sicilian

(Notes by Karpov)

'Karpov did not play 21 ♖×a6
because of the possibility of a draw
after 21 . . . ♖×a6 22 ♖×a6 ♕b7
23 ᐃa5 ♕c7 24 ᐃb3 ♕b7.
Bronstein gave up the exchange
and, although in time-trouble,
defended himself ingeniously, but
the endgame nevertheless turned
out to be lost for Black.' (*64*)

1 e4 c5 2 ᐃf3 d6 3 d4 cd 4 ᐃ×d4
ᐃf6 5 ᐃc3 a6 6 ♗e2 e5 7 ᐃb3
♗e6 8 f4 ♕c7 9 00 ᐃbd7 10 f5 ♗c4
11 a4 ♗e7 12 ♗e3 00 13 a5 b5 14 ab
ᐃ×b6 15 ♔h1 ♖fc8 16 ♗×b6
♕×b6 17 ♗×c4 ♖×c4 18 ♕e2
♖b4 19 ♖a2 h6 20 ♖fa1 ♗f8 21
♖a4!± ♖c8 22 ♖×b4 ♕×b4 23
♕×a6 (*168*)

23 . . . ♖×c3 (23 . . . ♖c4 24 ♖a4

168
23W
B

♖×e4 25 ♕f1 ♖f4 26 ♕×f4 ♕×f4
27 ♖×f4±) 24 bc ♕×e4 25 ♕d3
♕f4 26 ♖f1 ♕h4 27 ᐃd2 e4 28
♕g3 ♕×g3 29 hg d5 30 ♖b1! ♗d6
31 ♔g1 ♗×g3 (31 . . . ᐃg4 32
♖b5±) 32 ♔f1±± ᐃh5 33 ♔e2
♗f4 34 ᐃf1 ♗e5 35 ᐃe3 ♗×c3 36
♖b8+? (36 ᐃ×d5±±) 36 . . . ♔h7
37 ᐃ×d5 ♗g3+ 38 ♔f2? (38 ♔e3)
38 . . . ♗d4+! 39 ♔e1 ᐃ×f5 40
♖b4 ᐃe3 41 ♔e2 ♗c5 42 ♖b5
ᐃ×d5 43 ♖×c5 ᐃf4+ 44 ♔f2 (s)
(adjournment 14.12.1971) 44 . . .
♔g6 45 g3 ᐃe6 46 ♖d5!±± f5 47
c4 f4 48 c5 e3+ 49 ♔f3 fg 50 ♔×g3
h5 51 c6 e2 52 ♔f2 ♔f6 53 ♖d7 **1-0**

2514   Korchnoi–AK

R14: 13.12.1971: English

(Notes by Kotov)

1 c4 c5 2 ᐃf3 ᐃf6 3 g3 d5 4 cd
ᐃ×d5 5 ♗g2 g6?! 6 d4 ♗g7 7 e4
ᐃc7 8 d5 ᐃb5 9 00 00 10 ♕c2 ᐃa6
11 ♗f4 ♗g4 12 ᐃbd2± ᐃd4! 13
ᐃ×d4 cd 14 ᐃf3! ♕b6 15 ᐃe5? (15
♕d2 preparing ᐃe5 – Karpov) 15
. . . ♗×e5! 16 ♗×e5 f6 17 ♗f4
♖ac8∓ (*169*)

169
17B
W

(All of a sudden Korchnoi faces problems which are not so easy to solve: first, to find a suitable place for the queen. She can't go to d2 – that loses a bishop after g6–g5, on b1 the queen is extremely passive and, at the same time, 18 . . . ♗e2 with . . . d3 to follow would be very strong. Second, to defend himself against the threat of . . . ♘b4 followed by . . . ♖c2. Third, to defend the b–pawn. There are so many problems that even a player as ingenious as Korchnoi is unable to solve them.)

18 ♕a4 g5 19 ♗c1 ♗e2 (19 . . . ♘b4!? 20 f3 ♗h5∓ – Karpov) 20 ♖e1 d3 21 ♗f1 (offering the exchange after 21 . . . ♕b4 22 ♕×b4 ♘×b4 23 ♗×e2 ♘c2 24 ♗×d3, but Karpov is not interested in such insignificant gains.) 21 . . . ♗×f1 22 ♖×f1 ♖c2 23 ♗e3 ♘c5 24 ♕d4 (24 ♕a3!? ♖c8∓ – Karpov) 24 . . . e5 25 de ♕×e6 26 ♖ac1? (26 b4 ♘×e4 27 ♕×d3 ♖c3∓ – Karpov) 26 . . . ♖c8 27 b4 ♘×e4! 28 ♖×c2 (28 ♕×d3 ♘×f2!) 28 . . . dc 29 ♖c1 b6 30 f3 ♘d6 31 ♕d3 ♖c6! 32 a4 ♕×c4 33 ♕d2 ♘f7 34 f4 g4 35 b5 ♖c8 36 ♕d7 h5 37 ♔f2 ♕c3 38 ♕f5 ♖e8 **0–1**

2515   AK–Stein

R15: 15.12.1971: Spanish

1 e4 e5 2 ♘f3 ♘c6 3 ♗b5 a6 4 ♗a4 ♘f6 5 00 ♗e7 6 ♖e1 b5 7 ♗b3 d6 8 c3 00 9 h3 ♘b8 10 d4 ♘bd7 11 ♗g5 ♗b7 12 ♘bd2 h6 13 ♗h4 ♖e8 14

♕b1 c5 15 a4 ♕b6 16 de ♘×e5 17 ab ab 18 ♖×a8 ½–½

2516   Smyslov–AK

R16: 16.12.1971: Catalan

'A solid tournament position led to neither side taking any risk. A peaceful variation led, after exchanges, to an approximately equal ending, and the game was then agreed drawn.' (*64*)

1 d4 ♘f6 2 c4 e6 3 g3 d5 4 ♗g2 dc 5 ♕a4+ ♘bd7 6 ♕×c4 a6 7 ♘d2 c5 8 dc ♗×c5 9 ♘b3 ♗e7 10 ♘f3 b5 11 ♕d4 ♗b7 12 00 00 13 ♖d1 a5! 14 ♗g5 (14 a4 ♗d5∓ – Karpov) 14 . . . a4 15 ♘c1 h6 16 ♗×f6 ♘×f6 17 ♘d3 ♕b8 ('Black has a satisfactory game' – Furman. 17 . . . ♖c8!? – Karpov) 18 ♕e5! ♘d5 19 ♕×b8 ♖a×b8 20 a3 ♘b6 21 ♘fe5 ♗×g2 22 ♔×g2 ♖fc8 23 ♖ac1 ♘c4 24 e3 ½–½

2517   AK–Savon

R17: 18.12.1971: Spanish

'The sporting attitudes of the players were shown, in this exceptionally important game, by the choice of the Open Variation. On the 12th move Black had a choice of 12 . . . ♗g4, but he preferred a less well-known continuation. The young Leningrad grandmaster played very logically, and the Soviet champion did not equalize. The whole situation became quite tense, but on the 17th move Savon began a mistaken combination and he got tied up. Black's position immediately became critical and he soon gave up.' *(64)*

170
15W
B

1 e4 e5 2 ♘f3 ♘c6 3 ♗b5 a6 4 ♗a4 ♘f6 5 00 ♘×e4 6 d4 b5 7 ♗b3 d5 8 de ♗e6 9 c3 ♗c5 10 ♘bd2 00 11 ♗c2 ♗f5 12 ♘b3 ♗g6 13 ♘fd4 (13 a4?! ♗b6 14 ab ab 15 ♖×a8 ♕×a8 16 ♕×d5? ♘×c3∓ Tukmakov–Savon, 37th USSR Ch 1969) **13 ... ♗×d4 14 cd!** (14 ♘×d4 ♘×d4 15 cd c5 16 f3 cd) **14 ... a5 15 ♗e3** *(170)*

15 ... ♘b4 (15 ... a4 16 ♘c1 a3 – Tal and Kirillov) **16 ♗b1 a4 17 ♘d2 a3 18 ♕c1! ♖a6?!** (18 ... c5!? 19 dc d4 20 ♘×e4 de 21 ba ef† 22 ♘×f2± ; 18 ... ♘×d2 19 ♕×d2 ♘c6 20 ♖c1 – Karpov) **19 ba ♖c6** (19 ... ♘×d2 20 ♗×d2 ♘c6 21 ♗×g6 fg 22 ♕c5±± – Karpov) **20 ♕b2 ♘c2** (20 ... ♘×d2 21 ♗×d2!) **21 ♖c1!±± ♘×e3 22 ♖×c6 ♘×f2 23 ♘f1 ♕d7?** (A grave mistake in great time-trouble, but the position was already lost – Keres.) **24 ♘×e3 1–0**

26 Hastings 29.12.1971–15.1.1972

		1	2	3	4	5	6	7	8	9	0	1	2	3	4	5	6	
1	**Karpov**	×	0	1	1	½	½	½	½	½	1	½	1	1	1	1	1	**11**
2	Korchnoi	1	×	½	½	½	½	0	1	1	1	½	1	1	½	1	1	**11**
3	R. Byrne	0	½	×	½	½	1	1	½	½	½	1	0	½	1	1	1	**9½**
4	Mecking	0	½	½	×	½	1	½	½	1	½	½	1	½	1	1	½	**9½**
5	Gligorić	½	½	½	½	×	½	½	½	½	½	½	½	½	½	1	1	**8½**
6	Najdorf	½	½	0	0	½	×	1	½	½	1	½	½	1	½	½	1	**8½**
7	Andersson	½	1	0	½	½	0	×	½	½	1	½	½	½	½	½	1	**8**
8	Unzicker	½	0	½	½	½	½	½	×	½	½	1	1	½	½	½	½	**8**
9	Pfleger	½	0	½	0	½	½	½	½	×	½	½	½	½	½	1	1	**7½**
10	Kurajica	0	0	½	½	½	0	0	½	½	×	½	½	1	½	1	1	**7**
11	Ciocaltea	½	½	0	½	½	½	½	0	½	½	×	½	½	½	½	½	**6½**
12	Botterill	0	0	1	0	½	½	½	0	½	½	½	×	½	½	0	1	**6**
13	Hartston	0	0	½	½	½	0	½	½	½	0	½	½	×	½	1	½	**6**
14	Keene	0	½	0	0	½	½	½	½	½	½	½	½	½	×	½	0	**5½**
15	Markland	0	0	0	0	0	½	½	½	0	0	½	1	0	½	×	1	**4½**
16	Franklin	0	0	0	½	0	0	0	½	0	0	½	0	½	1	0	×	**3**

On February 24 1972, Anatoly Karpov discussed the Hastings tournament at the Moscow Central Chess Club.

The international tournament at Hastings, over a period of many years, took place as a rule with ten participants. In recent years this formula has begun to be outmoded. Over such a short distance the players avoided risks because even one defeat could have a fatal significance on the result. The tournament table was decorated with frequent draws. The element of fight was kept to a minimum. Such a situation did not suit either the participants or the organizers. Therefore the Englishmen came to the conclusion that it was essential to break with tradition and increase the number of participants.

This year eight grandmasters and eight masters were invited to the main tournament. At the last moment Szabo could not come and he was replaced by the 1965 World Junior Champion, Kurajica, who had been down to participate in the first subsidiary tournament (Challengers – eds). Although as a result of this change the main tournament did not forfeit its rating status the grandmaster norm turned out to be very high.

Korchnoi and I came to Hastings immediately after the Alekhine Memorial, and we felt tired. The 'echo' of the Moscow tournament was unexpectedly heard at the time of the draw.

'Of course I will draw "my" number one, that unlucky one, just as in the Alekhine Memorial', said Viktor Korchnoi as he approached the judges' dais.

Amid general laughter Viktor Korchnoi duly drew this number. But the strangest occurrence was still to come – I also got 'my' number fourteen, under which I played in Moscow! However I managed it I don't know, only unlike Viktor Korchnoi, I was not put out. It is true that I had Black against practically all my rivals, but every cloud has a silver lining: against the weakest participants I had White, and that made beating them that much easier.

Conditions in the tournament hall, although it was large enough, turned out to be very difficult. Our tournament took place parallel to the master tournament, the distance between the players and spectators was insufficient – the public were 2–3 metres away from the participants – we heard every conversation and remark. Viktor Korchnoi suffered especially – it was agonizingly painful for him to play.

The tournament began successfully for me. After drawing with Pfleger in the first round I won three successive games, and after another draw I again scored three victories. Here I felt that my strength was giving out. In the previous eight months I had played about a hundred games, and, speaking frankly, I had simply become played out. In my game against Korchnoi, who had proved to be my only rival, I could no longer fight as before – Viktor Korchnoi easily beat me.

Before the last round Viktor Korchnoi led me by half a point, and on the final day of the tournament took no risks; agreeing a quick draw with Najdorf. The question of first place was decided by my game with the Englishman Markland. At the cost of an incredible amount of effort I succeeded in overcoming this opponent and catching up with Viktor Korchnoi.

The fight for third place was between Byrne and Mecking. Success accompanied the Brazilian player, or, more accurately, not success but good luck. Thus Pfleger, in an advantageous position, forgot to make the last move before the time control.

Although Mecking succeeded in fulfilling the grandmaster norm, I don't have too high an opinion of his play. I was ever so much more pleased with the play of the Swede, Andersson – a very talented and promising player.

As for Kurajica, who in his time raised high hopes, in my opiniom he has not advanced. At any rate. there is no sign that the Yugoslav works at his chess. It is possible that he was unprepared for playing in such a strong tournament. At first Kurajica was rejoicing in his unexpected 'promotion', but later he lamented that he had accepted the invitation and moved from the master to the grandmaster tournament. . . .

I will show you two of my games, to some extent similar to each other. In both of them the Sicilian was played, an early exchange of queens took place, and an ending with opposite coloured bishops arose. In both games White succeeded in realizing a positional advantage and in getting up an attack on the black king despite the meagre quantity of material left on the board. (The games referred to are those against Byrne and Mecking – eds.).

The above article was translated from the *Central Chess Club Bulletin*.

2601 Pfleger–AK

R1: 29.12.1971: Queen's Indian

1 d4 ♘f6 2 c4 e6 3 ♘f3 b6 4 g3 ♗b7 5 ♗g2 ♗e7 6 ♘c3 ♘e4 7 ♕c2 ♘×c3 8 ♕×c3 0-0 9 0-0 d6 10 b3 c5 11 ♗b2 ♗f6 12 ♕c2!? ♘c6 13 ♖ad1 ♕e7 14 e4 g6 (14 . . . cd 15 ♘×d4±) 15 d5 ♘b4 16 ♕d2 ♗×b2 17 ♕×b2 ed 18 ed ♖ae8 19 a3 ♘a6 20 ♖fe1 ♕d8 21 ♘d2 f5 22 f4 ♘c7 23 b4 ♗a6 24 ♕c3 ♖×e1+ 25 ♖×e1 ♖e8 26 ♖×e8+ ♕×e8 27 ♔f2 ♕e7 28 ♗f1 ♘e8 29 ♗e2 ♘f6 30 ♗f3 ♔f7 31 h3 ♗c8 32 ♘f1 cb 33 ab ♕c7 34 ♘e3 h5 35 b5 a6 36 ba ♗×a6 37 g4 hg ½–½

2602 AK–R. Byrne

R2: 30.12.1971: Sicilian

(Notes by Karpov)

1 e4	c5
2 ♘f3	♘c6
3 d4	cd
4 ♘×d4	♘f6
5 ♘c3	d6

6 ♗g5   ♗d7
7 ♕d2   ♖c8
8 000   ♘×d4
9 ♕×d4   ♕a5

A well-known theoretical position has arisen.

10 f4

10 ♕d2 is another possibility.

10 ...   h6

10 ... e6 11 e5 de 12 fe ♗c6 used to be played here.

11 ♗h4   g5
12 e5 (*171*)

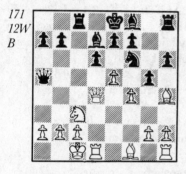

171
12W
B

This position also is not new. In one Yugoslav tournament a game went 12 ... ♗g7, which led to great complications. The variation 13 ♗e1 ♘h5 14 ♘d5 ♕×a2 15 ♘×e7 is obviously good for White. But I think that Black's idea is worth considering and is interesting to analyse.

12 ...   gh
13 ef   e6
14 ♗e2

A good move. The white bishop, depending on circumstances, can be transferred to f3 or h5, where it will control important squares.

14 ...   ♗c6
15 ♖he1   ♖g8
16 ♗f3

It is far from simple for Black to find a move, and it is no coincidence that Byrne thought for 20 minutes.

16 ...   ♔d7

Black decides on evacuating the king to the Q-side. I succeeded in finding a line which led to a clear positional advantage.

17 ♖e5!   ♕b6
18 ♕×b6   ab
19 ♗h5

Now the f-pawn cannot be defended. A series of forced moves begins – each side strives to gobble up as many pawns as possible.

19 ...   ♖×g2
20 ♗×f7   ♖×h2
21 ♗×e6+   ♔c7
22 ♖e3

White's position is better because his pawns on the f-file are more dangerous than the black pawns on the h-file. In addition to which Black's KB is, for the time-being, out of play.

Now Black faces the problem – where to put the rook which is on c8? It is possible that he should have moved it to a8, but this was a difficult decision to make; it would take the b8 square away from the king.

22 ...   ♖d8
23 ♘d5+   ♗×d5
24 ♖×d5

In spite of the opposite coloured

bishops, White's position is very much better because Black has very weak pawns.

24 ...   ♖f2

Provoking an advance of the pawn on f4, Black prepares to bring out his bishop on h6.

25 f5   h5
26 ♖c3+   ♔b8 (*172*)

172
26B
W

27 a4

I am not convinced of the correctness of the plan of attack on the king – it is possible that the correct procedure was to concern myself with the opponent's passed pawns, but this course seemed to me to be too slow.

27 ...   ♖f4
28 a5   ba
29 ♖×a5   ♖g4
30 ♖ca3   ♔c7
31 ♖b5

The pawn on b7 is in danger and there is no way to defend it. Black's only counterplay consisted of the line 31 ... ♖g1+ 32 ♔d2 ♗h6+. Byrne, however, began immediately with the second move

and allowed the white king to hide itself away on a2:

31 ...   ♗h6+
32 ♔b1   ♖g3
33 ♖a7   ♖b8
34 ♗d5   ♖g1+
35 ♔a2   ♖f1
36 ♖a×b7+   ♖×b7
37 ♖×b7+   ♔d8
38 ♗e6   h3

The last chance.

39 ♖d7+

In time-trouble, Byrne noticed that if 39 ... ♔c8 40 ♖h7+ ♔d8 41 ♖×h6 h2, White succeeds in holding the pawn by 42 ♗d5, and played ...

39 ...   ♔e8

... but after ...

40 ♖c7   **1-0**

... resigned because of the unavoidable mate.

2603   Botterill–AK

R3: 31.12.1971: QGD

(Notes by Karpov)

1 d4 ♘f6 2 c4 e6 3 ♘f3 d5 4 ♘c3 ♗e7 5 ♗g5 00 6 e3 h6 7 ♗h4 b6 8 ♗×f6 ♗×f6 9 cd ed 10 ♗e2! ♗b7 (10 ... ♗e6!?) 11 00 ♖e8?! (11 ... ♘c6!?; 11 ... ♕e7 12 ♕b3! ♖d8 13 ♖ad1 c5 14 dc ♗×c3 15 ♕×c3± Korchnoi–Geller, 5th match game 1971) 12 b4 a6 13 ♕b3 ♕d6 14 ♘d2? (14 ♘e1! with ♗f3± to follow) 14 ... ♘c6= 15 a3?! (15 ♘×d5? ♘×d4∓; 15 ♕×d5 ♘×d4 16 ♕×d6 cd∓; 15 ♗f3!) 15 ... ♘e7

16 ♗f3 ♖ad8 17 g3 ♘f5 18 ♕c2 g6
19 ♘b3 ♖e7∓ 20 ♖ad1 ♕e6 21
♘c1 ♘d6 22 ♘d3 ♕f5 23 ♗g2 g5
24 ♕b3 ♘e4 25 a4 h5 26 h3 ♗g7 27
a5 ♕e6 28 ♘a4 ♕d6 29 ♖fe1
♖de8? (29 . . . ♔h8 planning . . .
h4 and . . . f5) 30 ♘c3! ♔h8 31 b5!
(*173*)

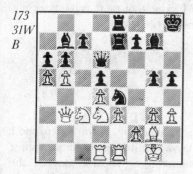

173
31W
B

31 . . . ab (31 . . . ba 32 ♘c5! ♘×c5
33 dc ♕×c5 34 ♘×d5±) 32 ♘×b5
♕h6 33 ♘c3 ♘×c3 34 ♕×c3 ba 35
♕×a5 (35 ♘c5 ♗c8) 35 . . . c6 36
♖b1 h4 37 g4 f5! 38 gf ♗c8 39 ♖b8
(39 ♖b6!? ♗×f5 40 ♘b4 ♖e6 41
♖c1 g4 is unclear.) 39 . . . ♗×f5 40
♕a8 ♕g6∓ 41 ♘b4 ♗d7 42
♖×e8+ ♖×e8 43 ♕b7 ♖e7 44
♖c1? (44 f3∓) 44 . . . g4∓∓ 45
♖×c6 ♕b1+ 46 ♗f1 (46 ♔h2 g3+
47 fg hg+ 48 ♔×g3 ♖×e3+ ∓∓)
46 . . . gh (intending . . . h2+) 47
♕b5 ♖e6 (47 . . . ♗×c6!? 48
♕×c6 ♕×b4?? 49 ♕c8+ ♔h7 50
♗d3+ ♔h6 51 ♕c6+ ±±; 48 . . .
h2+ 49 ♔×h2 ♕×f1 50 ♕c8+
♔h7 51 ♕f5+ ♔g8∓∓) 48 ♕b8+
♖e8 49 ♕d6 ♖g8! **0-1**

2604 AK–Hartston

R4: 1.1.1972: Sicilian

(Notes by Hartston)

1 e4 c5 2 ♘f3 e6 3 d4 cd 4 ♘×d4
♘c6 5 ♘b5 d6 6 c4 ♘f6 7 ♘1c3 a6
8 ♘a3 ♗e7 9 ♗e2 00 10 00 b6 11
♗e3 ♗d7!? (11 . . . ♗b7) 12 ♖c1
♕b8 13 g4!? TN (13 f3 ♖a7 12 ♘c2
♖d8 15 ♕e1 ♗e8 16 ♕f2 ♖b7 17
a4 a5= Fischer–Taimanov, Palma
interzonal 1970) 13 . . . ♖c8 14 g5
♘e8 15 f4 ♖a7 16 ♕e1 ♗b7 17
♕h4 g6! 18 ♖f3 ♘g7 19 ♖cf1 ♖e8
20 ♗d3 (20 ♘c2!? b5 21 ♘d5 ed 22
cd is unclear; 20 ♖3f2, intending
♘d5, 20 . . . ♗f8!) 20 . . . h5 21 ♕f2
♘b4! 22 ♗b1 ♗c6 23 ♖h3 (with
the idea of f5) 23 . . . ♗d7 24 ♕h4
♕c8 25 ♖c1 (preparing ♘d5) 25
. . . ♕b8 26 ♖f1 ♕c8 27 ♖hf3
d5!= 28 cd ed 29 f5 ♗c5 30 ♗×c5
♕×c5+ 31 ♕f2 ♕×f2+ 32 ♖3×f2
d4 33 ♘e2 d3 34 fg fg (34 . . . de? 35
gf+ ♔h7 36 e5+ ±±) 35 ♘f4
♖×e4 36 ♘×3 (*174*)

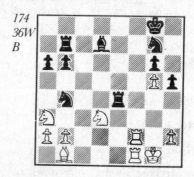

174
36W
B

36 . . . ♖g4+?! (36 . . . ♗h3!?) 37
♖g2 ♖×g2+ 38 ♔×g2 ♘×d3?!

(38 . . . ♘d5!±) 39 ♗×d3 ♘f5 40
♗×a6 ♗c6+? (40 . . . ♘e3+ 41
♔g1 ♖a7 42 ♗c4+ ♘×c4 43
♘×c4 ♗b5±) 41 ♔f2 ♖d7 42
♖c1! ♗e4 43 ♗e2 ♘d6? (43 . . .
♘d4!?) 44 ♘c4±± ♘×c4 45
♖×c4 ♗d5 46 ♖b4 ♗×a2 47
♖×b6 ♔g7 48 ♖b4 ♗b1 49 h4
♔f7 50 ♔e3 ♖e7+ 51 ♔d2 ♔e6
52 ♖b5 ♗e4 53 b4 ♖c7 54 ♔e3
♗b1 55 ♖c5 ♖e7 56 ♗f3 ♔d6+
57 ♔d4 ♖f7 58 ♖c6+ ♔d7 59
♖f6 ♖e7 60 b5 **1-0**

2605 Ciocaltea-AK

R5: 2.1.1972: Spanish

1 e4 e5 2 ♘f3 ♘c6 3 ♗b5 a6 4 ♗a4
♘f6 5 0-0 ♗e7 6 ♖e1 b5 7 ♗b3 d6 8
c3 0-0 9 h3 ♘a5 10 ♗c2 c5 11 d4
♕c7 12 ♘bd2 ♘c6 13 dc dc 14 ♘f1
♗e6 15 ♘e3 ♖ad8 16 ♕e2 c4 17
♘f5 ♗×f5 18 ef h6 19 ♘d2! (19
♘×e5? ♘×e5 20 ♕×e5 ♗d6 21
♕e2 ♖fe8=) 19 . . . ♖fe8 20 ♘e4
♘b8 21 a4! ♘bd7! (not 21 . . .
♘×e4 22 ♗×e4 ♘d7 because of 23
ab ab 24 ♖a6±) 22 ab ab 23 ♗e3
♘×e4 24 ♗×e4 ♘c5! 25 ♗×c5
♗×c5 26 ♖ed1 ♗b6 27 g3 ♕c5
½-½

2606 AK-Mecking

R6: 4.1.1972: Sicilian

(Notes by Karpov)

Mecking wanted very much to
take first place. When I had 3½/4
and my next game was with the

Romanian master Ciocaltea,
Mecking asked him,

'You are going to "get rid" of
Karpov?', 'I am going to play,'
answered Ciocaltea.

'Make sure you don't lose,
otherwise I can't be first.'

Not surprisingly, my game with
Mecking took on the character of a
needle-match.

1 e4	c5
2 ♘f3	d6
3 d4	cd
4 ♘×d4	♘f6
5 ♘c3	a6
6 ♗e2	

I frequently use this system and I
know it quite well. In games against
many foreign chess players, the
winner is often not he who plays
best, but he who has analysed the
opening variation the furthest.

6 . . .	e5
7 ♘b3	♗e6
8 f4	♕c7
9 a4 (*175*)	

175
9W
B

Here the usual replies are 9 . . .
♗e7 or 9 . . . ♘bd7, but Mecking
didn't fancy either of them. He
thought for a long time and chose a

new, but far from the strongest, continuation.

9 ...	♘c6
10 f5	♗×b3
11 cb	♛b6

If White succeeds in castling K-side and in putting his bishop on c4, his advantage will be overwhelming. Mecking hinders the achievement of this plan.

12 ♗g5	♗e7
13 ♗×f6	♗×f6
14 ♘d5	♛a5+
15 ♛d2	♛×d2+
16 ♔×d2	♗g5+
17 ♔d3	0-0
18 h4	♗d8

On h6 ths bishop might be dangerously placed (after g2–g4).

19 ♖ac1

It is not yet possible to smoke out the knight from d5 because on 19 ... ♘e7 there comes 20 ♘×e7+ ♗×e7 21 ♖c7. And if 19 ... ♘d4 then 20 b4.

19 ...	a5
20 ♔d2	♖b8
21 g4	

White's plan is clear – a pawn storm on the K-side; after ♗c4 it will be very dangerous. Appreciating this, Mecking seeks succour in the opposite coloured bishops.

21 ...	♘b4
22 ♗c4	♘×d5
23 ♗×d5	

The position has stabilized. White has a big advantage in the complete absence of counterplay for the opponent. Mecking had

placed great hopes on his next move, thinking that he would be able to blockade the K-side pawns and halt their advance.

23 ...	g5
24 fg	hg
25 ♔d3	♔g7
26 h5	♗b6

26 ... ♗g5 27 ♖c7 is no better.

27 ♖h3

In order to seize the h-file after the exchange on g6.

27 ...	♗c5
28 ♖f1	f6

Forced. 29 h6+ was threatened.

29 hg	♔×g6
30 ♖fh1	♖be8
31 ♖h7	♔g5

Mecking was in time-trouble and was afraid of mating threats after ♖h1–h5.

32 ♔e2 ♔f4

Here a devastating idea came into my head and I played ...

33 ♖1h3 (*176*)

176
33W
B

Mecking did not appreciate the threat and replied ...

33 ... ♗d4

... and after ...

34 ♖g7   **1–0**(time)

... he exceeded the time limit, although he could have resigned in view of the unavoidable mate.

But even after the best defence – 33 ... ♔×g4 34 ♖h1 ♖g8 35 ♗×g8 ♖×g8 36 ♖f1 – White wins easily.

2607   Keene–AK

R7: 5.1.1972: Sicilian

(Notes by Karpov)

1 ♘f3 c5 2 e4 e6 3 d4 cd 4 ♘×d4 ♘c6 5 ♘c3 a6 6 g3 ♘ge7 7 ♘b3 ♘a5 8 ♗g2 ♘ec6 9 00 d6 10 ♘×a5?! (10 ♘d2 ♗d7 11 b3 ♗e7 Amos–Karpov, Mayaguez 1971) **10 ...♕×a5= 11 ♘e2 ♗e7 12 b3 00** (12 ... ♗f6 13 ♗d2±) **13 ♗b2 ♗d7** (13 ... ♖d8!? planning ... b5=) **14 c4 ♖fd8** (14 ... b5 15 c5±) **15 a4± ♖ac8 16 ♗c3! ♕c7 17 ♕d2** (17 ♖a2!? planning ♕a1 and ♖d1) **17 ...b6 18 ♕b2 ♗f8 19 f4?** (19 ♖ac1 ♕b8 20 ♘d4 ♘e5 21 ♖fd1 b5 22 ab ab 23 cb ♗×b5 24 ♘×b5 ♕×b5 25 ♗×e5=) **19 ...b5!∓** (*177*)

177
19B
W

20 ab (20 cb ab 21 ♘d4 ba 22 ba ♘a5) **20 ...ab 21 cb ♕b6+ 22 ♔h1** (22 ♘d4 ♘×d4 23 ♗a5 ♕c5 24 b4 ♕c4∓; 23 ♗×d4 ♕×b5∓) **22 ...♕×b5 23 b4 d5 24 ♖ab1 ♖b8 25 ed ed 26 f5 ♘×b4 27 ♕d2 e8 28 ♘d4 ♕c4 29 ♖bd1** (29 ♖fc1!? ♘d3? 30 ♖×b8 ♖×b8 31 ♗f1 ♗×f5 32 ♘×f5 ♕e4+ 33 ♗g2±±; 29 ... ♘a2 30 ♖×b8 ♖×b8 31 ♗f1 ♕a4 32 ♖a1) **29 ...♖bc8 30 ♗a1 ♖a8 31 ♖c1 ♖a2 32 ♕g5** (32 ♖×c4 ♖×d2 33 ♖c7 ♗a4∓) **32 ...♕a6 33 ♘e6 h6 34 ♕g4 ♗×e6** (34 ... fe?? 35 fe followed by ♖×f8+±±) **35 ♗×g7 ♕e2! 36 ♕×e2 ♖×e2∓∓ 37 ♗×f8 ♖×f8 38 fe fe 39 ♖fe1 ♖f2 40 ♖×e2 ♖×e2 0–1**

2608   AK–Franklin

R8: 6.1.1972: Sicilian

1 e4 c5 2 ♘f3 a6!? 3 c3 d5 4 ed ♕×d5 5 d4 e6 6 ♗e3 cd 7 cd ♘f6 8 ♘c3 ♕a5 9 ♗d3 ♘c6 10 a3 ♗e7 11 00 00 12 ♕c2 ♗d7 13 b4 ♕h5 14 ♘e2 (threatening to trap the queen with 15 ♘f4 ♕g4 16 h3, or else win material after 15 ... ♕h6) 14 ...♘d5 15 ♗d2 ♗d6 16 ♘g3 ♗×g3 17 fg! (Karpov intends to molest the queen with a K-side pawn advance.) 17 ...♖ac8 18 ♕b2 f6 19 h3 g5 20 g4 ♕h6 21 a4! (White plans 22 b5 followed by a rook entry.) 21 ...b5 22 ab ab 23 ♖fc1 ♖b8 24 ♖c5 ♘d8 25 h4! ♕g7 (If 25 ... ♘f7, 26 ♖a5 wins the b-pawn.) 26 hg fg 27 ♘×g5 ♘b7

28 ♖cc1 ♘f4 29 ♗×f4 ♖×f4 30
♘f3 ♕×g4 (30 ... ♖×g4 31 ♖c7)
31 ♗e2 ♘d8 32 ♖c5 ♘f7 33 ♖a3!
(intending 34 ♘e5) 33 ... ♕g7 34
♖a7 ♗e8 35 ♖g5 ♕×g5 36 ♘×g5
♘×g5 37 d5! **1–0**

2609 Gligorić–AK

R9: 7.1.1972: Nimzo-Indian

1 d4 ♘f6 2 c4 e6 3 ♘c3 ♗b4 4 e3 00
5 ♗d3 c5 6 ♘f3 d5 7 00 dc 8 ♗×c4
♘c6 9 a3 ♗a5 10 ♗d3 cd 11 ed
♗b6 12 ♗e3 ♘d5 13 ♘×d5 ed 14
h3 ♘e7 TN 15 ♗g5!? (15 ♗d2) 15
... f6! 16 ♗d2 ♗f5 17 ♗b4 ♗×d3
18 ♕×d3 ♖e8 19 ♖fe1 ♕d7 20
♗c5 ♗c7 21 ♗×e7 ♖×e7 22
♖×e7 ♕×e7 23 ♕b5 ♕f7 24 ♔f1
♗d6= ½–½

2610 AK–Kurajica

R10: 8.1.1972: Sicilian

(Notes by Karpov)

1 e4 c5 2 ♘f3 ♘c6 3 d4 cd 4 ♘×d4
♕c7 5 ♘b5!? ♕b8 6 c4 ♘f6 7
♘5c3 e6 8 ♗e3 (8 f4 d6 9 ♗d3
♗e7 10 ♘d2 00 11 ♘f3±
Bronstein–Taimanov, 39th USSR
Ch 1971) 8 ... ♗e7 (8 ... b6!?
intending ... ♗c5) 9 ♗e2 d6 10 a3
b6 11 ♘d2 ♗b7 12 f4 00 13 00±
♖d8 14 ♗f3 ♗f8 15 ♗f2?! (15 b4!)
15 ... ♘d7 16 b4 g6 17 ♖c1 ♗g7
(planning ... ♘d4) 18 ♘b3 a5 (18
... ♗h6 19 g3 g5 20 ♗e3 gf 21
♗×f4± ; 19 ♕d2 ♘ce5 20 ♗e2
♘f6) 19 b5 ♘a7 20 ♘a4! ♘c8 21

♖c2 (21 f5 ♖e8 22 fe fe 23 ♘d4
♘e5 24 ♗g4 ♘×g4 25 ♕×g4
♕c7) 21 ... ♖e8 (21 ... ♕c7 22
♕e2 ♘c5 23 ♘b×c5 bc 24 e5!±)22
♕e2 ♕c7 23 ♖d1 e5 24 f5 (*178*)

178
24W
B

24 ... gf 25 ef e4 26 ♗g4 (26 ♗d4
♘c5!) 26 ... ♘e5 (26 ... ♘c5!? 27
♘b×c5 bc) 27 ♗h3 ♖b8 28 ♗d4
♗a8 29 ♖f1± ± ♕e7 (29 ... ♗f6
30 ♘c3) 30 ♘c3 d5 31 ♘×d5
♗×d5 32 cd a4 33 ♘d2 ♘f3+ 34
♘×f3 ef 35 ♕d3 **1–0**

2611 Unzicker–AK

R11: 9.1.1972: Spanish

(Notes by Karpov)

1 e4 e5 2 ♘f3 ♘c6 3 ♗b5 a6 4 ♗a4
♘f6 5 00 ♗e7 6 ♖e1 b5 7 ♗b3 d6 8
c3 00 9 h3 ♘b8 10 d4 ♘bd7 11
♘bd2 (11 c4; 11 ♗g5) 11 ... ♗b7
12 ♗c2 ♖e8 13 ♘f1 ♗f8 14 ♘g3 g6
15 ♗d2 (15 ♗g5 h6 16 ♗d2 ♗g7
17 ♕c1 ♔h7 18 h4 h5∓) 15 ...
♗g7 16 ♕c1 c5 (16 ... d5 17 ♗g5
♕c8 18 ed ed= ; 18 de ♘×e4 19
♘×e4 de 20 ♗×e4 ♘×e5=) 17
♗h6 (intending ♘f5) 17 ... ♕e7
18 ♗×g7 ♔×g7 19 ♕d2 (19 ♕g5

♔h8=) 19 . . . ♘b6 20 ♖ad1 ♖ac8
(20 . . . ♖ad8? 21 de de 22
♕g5± ±) 21 ♗b1 (21 b3 b4!) 21 . . .
♘c4 22 ♕c1 (22 ♕e2 ♕c7=) 22
. . . ♘d7! 23 b3 ½–½

2612   Andersson–AK

R12: 11.1.1972: Grünfeld

1 ♘f3 ♘f6 2 g3 c5 3 ♗g2 g6 4 00
♗g7 5 c4 d5 6 d4 cd 7 ♘×d4 00 8
cd ♘×d5 9 ♘b5 a6 10 ♘1c3 ab 11
♘×d5 ♘c6 12 ♗g5 ♗×b2 13 ♖b1
♗g7 14 ♘×e7+ ♘×e7 ½–½

2613   AK–Najdorf

R13: 12.1.1972: Sicilian

1 e4 c5 2 ♘f3 d6 3 d4 cd 4 ♘×d4
♘f6 5 ♘c3 a6 6 ♗e2 e5 7 ♘b3
♗e7 8 00 00 9 ♗g5 ♗e6 10 f4 ef 11
♗×f4 ♘c6 12 ♔h1 d5 13 e5 ♘e4 14
♘×e4 de 15 ♘d2 ♗g5 16 ♘×e4
½–½

2614   Korchnoi–AK

R14: 13.1.1972: Torre

(Notes by Korchnoi)

1 d4 ♘f6 2 ♘f3 e6 3 ♗g5 b6 (3
. . . c5 is normal.) **4 e4 h6 5 ♗×f6
♕×f6 6 ♗d3 ♗b7 7 ♘bd2 d6**
(Some sources give the order 7 . . .
a6 8 ♕e2 d6 – KJO'C.) **8 ♕e2 a6**
(I was rather expecting 8 . . . ♕d8
followed by . . . ♗e7 and . . . 00. It
is natural for such an undeveloping
move as . . . ♕d8 to go against the
grain, but I felt that the queen was

misplaced on f6 and expected
Karpov to retreat it at more than
one stage. The course of the game
repeatedly reinforced my opinion.)
9 000 ♘d7 10 ♔b1 e5 (10 . . . ♕d8
11 ♘c4) **11 c3 ♗e7** (I had still been
expecting 11 . . . ♕d8!) **12 ♘c4 00
13 ♗c2 ♖fe8** (*179*) (Perhaps 13 . . .
ed should have been played first,
even though it appears to
dangerously strengthen White's
centre; the point being that after 14
cd, 14 . . . ♖fe8 would have some
counter-attacking effect. 15 e5,
however, would still leave White on
top.)

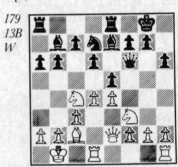

179
13B
W

14 d5! c5 (After long thought, but a
bad move. 14 . . . c6 seems
indicated.) **15 ♘e3** (Now White is
all set to start a direct attack by 16
g4.) **15 . . . ♗f8 16 g4 ♕d8 17 g5
h5** (if 17 . . . hg then 18 ♖dg1) **18
g6! fg 19 ♖hg1 ♕f6 20 ♘g5 ♗e7
21 ♘e6 ♘f8** (After the game I
asked Karpov had he overlooked
the loss of the exchange. 'No,' he
replied, 'I invited it, feeling that, in
view of the strength of your
advanced knight, it was my best

chance.' But 21 . . . ♖ ac8 seemed to me a natural measure, e.g. 22 ♖ g2 ♘ f8 23 ♖ dg1 ♔h7 24 ♘ × f8+ ♖ × f8 25 ♖ × g6 ♕ × g6 26 ♖ × g6 ♔ × g6 27 ♘ f5; White has ♗ d1, f4 etc. to follow with, probably, a winning attack, but the game is not over by any means. Whereas from now on, Black really has little or no prospect of salvation.) **22 ♘ c7 ♕ f7 23 ♖ df1 ?** (With victory in sight, I begin to relax. I have the K-side under control and should now have killed Black's prospects on the Q-side as well. I am convinced that the one correct move here was 23 a4 followed by b3, ♗ d3, ♔ c2 etc.) **23 . . .b5 ?** (Inaccurate play on both sides. 23 . . . ♖ ac8 24 ♘ × e8 ♕ × e8 would have cost me a clear tempo.) **24 ♘ × a8 ?! ♗ × a8 ?** (It would have been easier to bring the rook back into the game, after 24 . . . ♖ × a8, than to activate anew this very poor bishop.) **25 c4 ♖ b8 26 ♗ d3 ♕ e8 ?** (Black should have reconciled himself to·26 . . . b4.) **27 ♖ c1 ♗ f6 28 ♖ g2 ♕ b6 ?** (So as to play 29 . . . ♗ b7 and 30 . . . ♗ c8 but I am able to ensure that he never gets the time. Still 28 . . . b4.) **29 ♖ cg1 ♖ b8** (Forced, because White threatened 30 ♖ × g6 ♘ × g6 31 ♕ × h5.) **30 ♕ f1 b4** (After 30 . . . ♗ b7 31 cb ♗ c8 32 ba ♗ h3 33 ♕ e2 ♗ × g2 34 ♖ × g2, White should win.) **31 ♗ e2!** (Again threatening 32 ♖ × g6, and this time there is no defence.) **31 . . . h4 32 ♖ × g6 ♕ × g6** (or 32 . . . ♘ × g6 33

♕ h5± ±) **33 ♖ × g6 ♘ × g6 34 ♗ g4 ♘ f4 35 ♕ d1 b3** (agony!) **36 ab ♗ b7 37 ♘ g2 ♗ c8** (if 37 . . . ♘ × g2 then, of course, 38 ♗ e6+ ♔ f8 39 ♕ h5) **38 ♗ × c8 ♖ × c8 39 ♕ g4 ♖ e8 40 ♘ × f4 ef 41 ♕ × f4 ♗ e5 42 ♕ × h4 ♖ f8 43 b4 ♗ d4 44 bc 1-0**

2615 AK-Markland

R15: 15.1.1972: French

(Notes by Karpov)

1 e4 e6 2 d4 d5 3 ♘ c3 ♗ b4 4 e5 c5 5 a3 ♗ × c3+ 6 bc ♕ c7 7 ♘ f3 ♘ e7 8 a4 b6 9 ♗ b5+ ♗ d7 10 ♗ d3 (10 00 ♗ × b5 11 ab a5 12 ♘ g5 h6 13 ♘ h3∓) **10 . . . ♘ bc6 11 00 h6 12 ♖ e1 ♘ a5 13 ♕ d2?!** (13 ♗ e3, preparing ♘ d2, R. Byrne-Markland, same event) **13 . . . ♖ c8!** (13 . . . 00?! 14 ♕ f4 f5 15 ef ♕ × f4 16 ♗ × f4± Mecking-Markland, same event) **14 h4** (14 ♕ f4 f5 15 ♕ g3 ♔ f7 intending . . . ♖ cg8= ; 15 ef ♕ × f4 16 ♗ × f4 gf∓) **14 . . . 00 15 ♕ f4 f5 16 ef ♖ × f6 17 ♕ × c7 ♖ × c7 18 dc!±** (18 ♘ e5 cd! 19 cd ♘ ec6∓) **18 . . . bc** (18 . . . ♖ × c5? 19 ♗ a3± ±) **19 ♘ e5 ♗ c8 20 c4?!** (20 g3!? with ♗ f4 to follow) **20 . . . ♘ ac6 21 ♗ b2 ♘ b4 22 a5 ♖ f8 23 ♗ a3 dc 24 ♘ × c4 ♖ f4 25 ♘ d6!** (25 g3? ♖ × c4 26 ♗ × c4 ♘ × c2; 25 ♖ e4 ♘ × d3 26 cd ♖ × e4 27 de ♘ c6) **25 . . . ♘ × d3 26 cd ♖ × h4 27 ♘ e4** (27 ♖ ac1 a4 28 ♗ × c5 ♖ × a5? 29 ♗ b4± ± ; 28 . . . ♗ d7!) **27 . . . ♖ h5 28 ♖ ec1 ♗ b7** (28 . . . c4 29 ♗ d6

R d7 30 a6!±) **29 ♘×c5 ♗d5 30 f3 R f5** (*180*)

180
30B
W

31 a6 (31 ♘e4!?) **31 ... R f7 32 ♘e4 ♘f5** (intending ... ♘d4) **33 ♗c5 R c8 34 ♗f2 R fc7 35 R ×c7 R ×c7 36 R b1 ♘e7 37 R b8+**

♔h7 38 ♔h2 ♘g6 (38 ... R c8 39 ♘c5 with R b7 to follow) **39 ♘c5** (threatening R b7) **39 ... R c6** (39 ... ♘e5 40 R b7 ♗×b7 41 ab ♘d7 42 d4± ± ; 41 ... ♘c6 42 ♗g3±) **40 R d8** (40 R b7? R ×a6!=) **40 ... R c7 41 R d7± ± R ×d7 42 ♘×d7 ♗c6 43 ♘b8 ♗b5 44 ♗×a7 ♘e7 45 ♗b6** (45 ♗c5? ♘d5 and ... ♘c7) **45 ... ♘c8 46 ♗c5 ♔g6?** (46 ... ♗×d3 47 a7 ♘×a7 48 ♗×a7 ♗b5 49 f4± ±) **47 a7 ♘×a7 48 ♗×a7 e5 49 d4 ed 50 ♗×d4 ♔f7 51 f4 g5 52 fg hg 53 ♔g3 ♔g6 54 ♔f3 ♔f5 55 g3** (55 g4+ ?? ♔g6=) **1–0**

During the spring of 1972 Karpov and Spassky played one training game as part of the latter's preparation for the World Championship match in Reyjavik. Unfortunately, it was agreed between the players that this game should never be published.

The opening of the game was a Spanish, Closed Variation. Spassky won the game from a totally lost position.

Final A	1	2	3	4	5	6	
1 Moscow	×	5	8	5½	10	9	**37½**
2 RSFSR	7	×	6	7	6½	8	**34½**
3 Ukraine	4	6	×	5½	9	8½	**33**
4 Leningrad	6½	5	6½	×	4½	7½	**30**
5 Georgia	2	5½	3	7½	×	6	**24**
6 Latvia	3	4	3½	4½	6	×	**21**

Board 2	1	2	3	4	5	6	
1 **Karpov**	×	0	1	1	½	1	**3½**
2 Gipslis	1	×	½	½	½	½	**3**
3 Stein	0	½	×	1	1	½	**3**
4 Smyslov	0	½	0	×	1	½	**2**
5 Dzhindzhikhashvili	½	½	0	0	×	1	**2**
6 Taimanov	0	½	½	½	0	×	**1½**

Karpov played on board two (below Polugayevsky) for the RSFSR team.

2801 AK–Kudriashov

PR1: 2.3.1972: Sicilian

1 e4 c5 2 ♘f3 e6 3 d4 cd 4 ♘×d4 ♘f6 5 ♘c3 d6 6 g4 a6 7 g5 ♘fd7 8 ♗e3 b5 9 a3 ♘b6 10 ♕d2 ♕c7 11 000 ♘8d7 12 f4 ♘a4 13 ♘×a4 ba 14 ♘e2 ♗b7 15 ♗g2 ♘c5 16 ♘c3 ♗c6 17 ♗×c5 dc 18 e5 ♗e7 19 ♗×c6+ ♕×c6 20 ♕e2 c4 21 ♕e4 ♖c8 22 ♕×c6+ ♖×c6 23 ♘×a4 h6 24 h4 c3 25 ♘×c3 ♗×a3 26 ♘e4 ♗e7 27 b3 a5 28 c3 a4 29 ba ♖a6 30 ♖d4 hg 31 ♘×g5 f6 32 ♘f3 ♔f7 33 ♔c2 ♖ha8 34 ♖a1 ♔g6 35 ♖d7 ♗c5 36 h5+ ♔f5 37 ♖×g7 ♗×f4 38 ♖f1 ♖×a4 39 ef ♔e3 40 ♘e5 ♔e2 41 ♖b1 ♖d8 42 ♖d7 ♖a2+ 43 ♖b2 ♖×b2+ 44 ♔×b2 ♖b8+ 45 ♔c2 ♔e3 46 h6 ♔e4 47 ♘f7 ♗a3 48 h7 ♖b2+ 49 ♔d1 ♔e3 50 c4 **1–0**

2802 AK–Taimanov

PR2: 3.3.1972: Sicilian

(Notes by Petrosian)

1 e4 c5 2 ♘f3 e6 3 d4 cd 4 ♘×d4 a6
5 ♗d3 ♗c5 6 ♘b3 ♗b6 7 00 ♘e7 8
♕e2 ♘bc6 9 ♗e3 ♘e5 10 c4 ♗×e3
11 ♕×e3 ♕c7 12 c5! ♘×d3 13
♕×d3 b6 14 cb ♕×b6 15 ♘1d2 d5
16 e5! ♗d7 17 ♖fc1 00 18 ♕d4!
♕b8 (18 . . . ♕×d4 19 ♘×d4 ♖fc8
20 ♘2b3 ♘c6 21 ♘×c6 ♗×c6 22
♘d4±) 19 ♘f3 ♘c6 20 ♕e3 ♖c8
(20 . . . f6? 21 ♗c5± ±) 21 ♖c5 a5
22 ♖ac1 a4 23 ♘bd4 ♘a5 (23 . . .
♘×d4 24 ♕×d4±) 24 ♖×c8+
♗×c8 25 b3 ♗d7 (*181*)

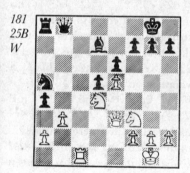

181
25B
W

26 h4 h6 27 g4! ♕b7 (27 . . . ♕d8)
28 h5 ♘c6 (28 . . . ♖c8 29 ♖×c8+
♕×c8 30 g5±) 29 g5 ♘×d4 30
♘×d4 hg 31 ♕×g5 ♔h7 32
♖c3!± ± ♕b4 33 ♖g3 ♖g8 34
♘f3 ab 35 ab ♕×b3 36 ♕c1! ♕a2
37 ♘g5+ ♔h8 38 ♘×f7+ ♔h7 39
♕g5 ♕b1+ 40 ♔h2 **1–0.** This
game also counted as the first round
of the final.

2803 Kärner–AK

PR3: 4.3.1972: Torre

(Notes by Gufeld)

1 d4 ♘f6 2 ♘f3 e6 3 ♗g5 c5 4 e3
♕b6 5 ♘bd2 ♕×b2 6 ♗d3 d5?! 7
c4! ♕c3 8 ♘e5± ♘fd7 9 ♖c1 ♕a3
10 ♘×d7 ♗×d7 11 ♗b1 h6 12 ♗f4
cd 13 00! ♗d6 14 ♗×d6 ♕×d6 15
cd ed 16 e4 ♘c6 17 ♕b3? ♘a5= 18
♕d3 ♘c6 19 ♖e1 ♗e6 20 f4? 000
21 e5 ♕b4 22 f5 ♗d7 23 e6 fe 24 fe
♗e8 25 ♘b3 ♕b6∓ ∓ 26 a4 ♔b8
27 ♖c5 ♕b4 28 ♕g3+ ♔a8 29
♖b5 ♕e7 30 ♘c5 a6 31 ♕a3 ♖b8
32 ♗d3 b6 33 a5 bc 34 ♖b6 ♖×b6
35 ab c4 36 ♕×a6+ ♔b8 37 ♖a1
♕b7 38 ♕a3 cd 39 ♕d6+ ♔c8 40
♖a8+ ♘b8 41 ♕c5+ ♗c6 42
♕d6 (*182*)

182
42W
B

42 . . . d2?? (42 . . . ♗b5∓ ∓) 43
♖×b8+ **1–0** (It's mate in two after
43 . . . ♕×b8 44 ♕×c6+ .)

2804 AK–Kuzmin

PR4: 5.3.1972: Sicilian

1 e4 c5 2 ♘f3 e6 3 d4 cd 4 ♘×d4
♘c6 5 ♘b5 d6 6 c4 ♘f6 7 ♘1c3 a6

8 ♘a3 ♗e7 9 ♗e2 00 1000 ♗d7 11 ♗e3 ♕a5 12 ♕e1 ♖fe8 13 ♖d1 ♖ad8 14 f3 ♗c8 15 ♘c2 ♕c7 16 ♕f2 ♘d7 17 ♖c1 ♗f6 18 ♘a3 ♕a5 19 ♖fd1 ♘c5 20 ♘ab1 ♖d7 21 ♗f1 ♕d8 22 ♘d2 ♔h8 23 ♘b3 b6 24 ♖d2 ♕e7 25 ♘d4 ♗×d4 26 ♗×d4 ♘×d4 27 ♖×d4 a5 28 ♖cd1 ♗b7 29 ♕g3 ♖ed8 30 ♘b5 e5 ½-½

2805   AK–Lapenis

PR5: 7.3.1972

The score of this game ($\frac{1}{2}$-$\frac{1}{2}$, x moves) is not available.

2806   AK–Gipslis

FR2: 9.3.1972: Pirc

(Notes by Boleslavsky)

1 e4 d6 2 d4 ♘f6 3 ♘c3 g6 4 ♗g5 c6 5 ♕d2 ♘bd7 6 f3 b5 7 ♘h3 ♗g7 8 ♗h6 00 9 ♘f2 e5 10 ♗×g7 ♔×g7 11 000 ♕a5 12 ♔b1 ♖e8 13 h4 h5 14 g4 ♘b6 15 g5 ♘fd7 16 a3 ♖b8 (*183*)

183
16B
W

17 f4? (White under-estimates his opponent's threats and immediately finds himself in a difficult position. It follows that he should have offered the exchange of queens with 17 ♘a2. Black can scarcely avoid the exchange without weakening his position. After 17 . . . ♕×d2 18 ♖×d2 White's game is preferable, since he will have time to double rooks on the open d–file. It is true that after 18 . . . a5 19 ♗e2 ♔f8 20 ♖hd1 ♔e7 White has no clear way to strengthen his position, but he would have the initiative.) 17 . . . ♘c4! 18 ♕e1 (An unfortunate necessity! After 18 ♗×c4 bc the threat is 19 . . . ♕×a3.) 18 . . . ef 19 ♘d3 ♘e3 20 ♖d2 c5! 21 ♖f2 b4? (This unjustified attempt to sharpen the struggle puts the game's outcome in doubt. 21 . . . cd 22 ♘e2 ♕×e1+ 23 ♘×e1 ♖×e4 gave Black a winning advantage. 22 ♖×f4 is better, but even then 22 . . . ♘c4! 23 ♘d5 ♕×e1+ 24 ♘×e1 ♖×e4 and Black's win is merely a question of time.) 22 ♘a2 ♖×e4 23 ♖×f4? (Now White perishes without a fight. After 23 dc! dc 24 ♖×f4 he could get strong counterplay and Black would have bitterly regretted his 21st move.) 23 . . . ♖×f4 24 ♘×f4 cd! 25 ab ♕f5 26 ♘d3 ♘e5' 27 ♗e2 ♗e6 28 ♘ac1 ♖c8 29 ♗d1 ♘5g4 30 ♕d2 ♔g8 31 ♗×g4 hg 32 ♘e1 ♕e4 33 ♖g1 ♗f5 34 ♕d3 ♕e5 35 ♕a6 ♕h2 **0–1**

2807 Dzhindzhikhashvili–AK

FR3: 10.3.1972: Queen's Indian

(Notes by Gufeld)

1 d4 ♘f6 2 c4 e6 3 ♘f3 b6 4 g3 ♗b7
5 ♗g2 ♗e7 6 ♘c3 ♘e4 7 ♗d2 d5 8
cd ed 9 00 00 10 ♗f4 ♘d7 11 ♕c2
(11 ♖c1 c5 12 ♘×e4 de 13 ♘d2
Dzhindzhikhashvili – Furman,
1971) 11 ... c5 12 ♘×e4 de 13 ♘e5
♘f6 (13 ... cd 14 ♗×e4 ♖c8 15
♕b1 is unclear.) 14 dc± ♗×c5 15
♗g5 ♕c7 (15 ... ♖e8 16 ♘g4?
♕c8! 17 ♘×f6+ gf 18 ♗e3 ♗×e3
19 ♕×c8 ♖a×c8 20 fe ♖c2∓; 16
♗×f6 ♕×f6 17 ♘d7±) 16 ♘c4
♗e7 17 ♖ac1 ♖fe8 18 ♘e3 ♕e5
(18... ♕×c2 19 ♖×c2 h6 20 ♗×f6
♗×f6 21 ♖fc1± ♖ac8 22 ♖×c8
♖×c8 23 ♖×c8+ ♗×c8 24 ♘d5)
19 ♗f4 ♕h5 20 h3 ♖ec8 21 ♕a4
♕×e2 22 ♖×c8+ ♖×c8 (22 ...
♗×c8?? 23 ♕c6±±) 23 ♕×a7
♕a6 24 ♕×a6 ♗×a6 25 ♘f5 ♗c5
26 ♖d1 g6 27 ♗g5 (27 ♘e3!) 27...
gf 28 ♗×f6 ♗c4 29 b3 ♗e6 30 ♗f1
♔f8 31 ♗a6 ♖a8 32 ♗b7!? (32
♖d8+ ♖×d8 33 ♗×d8 f4!) 32...
♖b8 33 ♖d8+ ♖×d8 34 ♗×d8
♔e8 35 ♗g5 ♔d7 36 ♗f4 ♗d6 37
♗e3 ♔c7 38 ♗a6 f4 39 ♗×f4
♗×h3 40 ♗c4 ♗×f4 41 gf ½–½

2808 AK–Smyslov

FR4: 11.3.1972: Petroff

(Notes by Karpov)

1 e4   e5

2 ♘f3   ♘f6
3 ♘×e5   d6
4 ♘f3   ♘×e4
5 d4   ♗e7
6 ♗d3   ♘f6

This variation came into fashion
after the game Fischer–Petrosian
(final Candidates' match, Buenos
Aires 1971) in which Black
obtained a completely equal game.

7 h3

Taking the g4 square away from
the bishop and knight.

7 ...   00
8 00   c5

But this is a new plan. Petrosian,
against Fischer, and even Smyslov,
in earlier games against Tal and
Bronstein in 1971, played 8 ...
♘bd7, ... c6 and ... ♖e8.

9 ♘c3   ♘c6
10 ♖e1

White is not bothered about the
capture on d4 because after 11 ♘b5
he regains the pawn.

10 ...   a6
11 d5

Going over to an Indian set-up.
Black's knight does not have a good
square to retreat to. On 11 ...
♘b4, both 12 ♗e4 and 12 ♗f1 ♗f5
13 ♖e2 are possible.

11 ...   ♘a7
12 a4   ♗d7
13 a5   ♖e8

13...♘b5 14 ♘a4, with 15 c4 to
follow, is bad for Black.

14 ♗f1   h6

Preparing 15 ... ♗f8; clearly
White has the better position: he

has no weakness, whilst Black has difficulty defending the pawn on d6 and, besides that, has a badly situated knight on a7. White's bishop must get on to the diagonal h2-b8, and the knight cross over from f3 to d2 and then to either c4 or e4.

15 ♗f4 ♗f8
16 ♖×e8 ♕×e8
17 ♗h2

The bishop anticipates future attacks on itself. Now 17 ... ♘e4 cannot be played in view of 18 ♘×e4 ♕×e4 19 c4 and then ♕b3 and ♖e1.

17 ... ♕d8
18 ♘d2 ♕c7

It is difficult to say what Black should play, but perhaps 18 ... ♗f5, not allowing the following move, was better.

19 ♘de4 ♘×e4
20 ♘×e4 ♗f5
21 ♘d2 ♖e8
22 c3 ♕d8
·23 ♕b3

Making the queen return to the seventh rank.

23 ... ♕d7
24 c4

The game has clarified: White is trying to make use of the position of the knight on a7, and with the move b2-b4 he will develop serious pressure on the Q-side.

24 ... ♘c8
25 g4

White does not have time to play 25 ♕a3 g5 26 b4 ♗g7 when the rook must occupy a passive position on the first rank.

25 ... ♗h7
26 ♗d3 ♗×d3
27 ♕×d3 g6
28 ♖b1! (*184*)

184
28W
B

White forces through b2-b4.

28 ... ♗g7
29 b4 cb
30 ♖×b4 ♕c7
31 ♘b3 ♗e5
32 ♗×e5 ♖×e5
33 ♕d4 g5

In the vain hope that the knight can go to f4 via e7 and g6.

34 ♔g2

Threatening 35 c5.

34 ... ♕e7

34 ... ♘e7 is not possible because of 35 ♕b6.

35 ♘d2 ♖e1
36 ♖b3 ♖e2
37 ♔f3!

On 37 ♖e3 would follow 37 ... ♕×e3!

37 ... ♖e5
38 ♖e3 f6
39 ♘e4 ♔g7
40 ♔g2 ♕c7

41 ♖f3   b5
42 ab   **1-0**

2809 Stein-AK

FR5: 13.3.1972: Grünfeld

(Notes by I. Zaitsev)

1 c4 c5 2 ♘f3 ♘f6 3 ♘c3 d5 4 cd ♘×d5 5 d4 ♘×c3 6 bc g6 7 e4 ♗g7 8 ♗b5+ ♘d7 9 00 00 10 a4 a6 11 ♗c4 ♕c7 12 ♕e2 b6 13 e5 e6 14 ♘g5 ♗b7 15 f4 h6 (*185*)

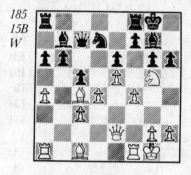

185
15B
W

16 ♘×e6!? (Another tempting possibility was 16 f5!? hg 17 f6 ♗h8 18 ♗×g5 and White, after the rook manoeuvre ♖f1-f4-h4, would have developed a strong attack.) 16 . . . fe 17 ♗×e6+ ♔h8 (17 . . . ♔h7 is more accurate.) 18 ♕g4 ♖fd8 19 f5 ♘f8 20 f6 ♘×e6 21 ♕×e6 (A line in which White risks nothing is 21 fg+ ♘×g7 22 ♕×g6 ♖c6 23 ♖f6 ♕e4 24 ♕×e4 ♗×e4 25 ♖×h6+, but he wanted more.) 21 . . . ♗f8 22 ♕h3 cd 23 cd (White overestimates his position, otherwise he would have played 23 e6 ♕×c3 24 ♕×c3 dc 25 e7, reaching a drawn ending.) 23 . . . ♖×d4 24 e6 ♗c5 25 ♔h1 (25 ♕×h6+ ♕h7 26 ♕×h7+ ♔×h7 27 ♗e3 ♖g4 does not make White's defence task any easier. 25 ♗e3 is slightly better, though after 25 . . . ♖d2 26 ♕×h6+ ♕h7 27 ♕×h7+ ♔×h7 28 ♗f2 ♖f8 29 f7 ♖e2 Black will still win.) 25 . . . h5 26 ♖a2 ♗d5 27 ♖d2 ♖×d2 28 ♗×d2 ♕e5 29 ♕d3 ♕×e6 30 ♕×g6 ♖g4 31 ♕h6+ ♔g8 32 f7+ ♗×f7 33 ♗c3 ♗d4 34 h3 ♕g7∓ 35 ♕c6 ♖d8 36 ♗×d4 ♕×d4 37 ♕b7 ♖d7 38 ♕c6 ♔g7 39 ♕c1 ♕e5 40 ♖e1 ♕f6 41 ♖f1 ♕d4 **0-1**

29 Student Olympiad   15–31.7.1972
      Graz, Austria

Final A	1	2	3	4	5	6	7	8	9	10	
1 USSR	×	2	3½	2	3½	3½	3½	3½	3½	3½	**28½**
2 Hungary	2	×	1½	2	2½	2	2½	2½	2	2½	**19½**
3 W. Germany	½	2½	×	1½	2	2½	1½	3	3½	2½	**19½**
4 USA	2	2	2½	×	2	1½	2	1½	2½	2	**18**
5 Bulgaria	½	1½	2	2	×	2½	2	2	3	2	**17½**
6 Israel	½	2	1½	2½	1½	×	1½	3	3	2	**17½**
7 Romania	½	1½	2½	2	2	2½	×	1½	2	2½	**17**
8 Cuba	½	1½	1	2½	2	1	2½	×	1	2½	**14½**
9 Denmark	½	2	½	1½	1	1	2	3	×	2½	**14**
10 England	½	1½	1½	2	2	2	1½	1½	1½	×	**14**

Board 1: Karpov 7/9 (77·8%), Hübner 9½/13 (73·1%), Rogoff 7/10 (70·0%).

The USSR team of Karpov, Balashov, Tukmakov, Vaganian, Podgayets and Anikayev was quite probably the strongest team ever seen at a student Olympiad.

Alan Perkins (of the English team) mentioned some interesting points in the *British Chess Magazine*, No. 9 1972: 'Balashov has obviously benefited from Russian training methods in one respect at least; he is noticeably physically more substantial than formerly. One feels that Karpov has scope for similar improvement (he plays well enough already). Someone asked him when he thought he would be playing Fischer – "not just yet" he said. I doubt if even Fischer had ever been photographed as much as Karpov here, but the Russian did not seem to mind.'

The tournament took place in the Congress Hall at Graz.

2901 AK–Hug

PR1: 16.7.1972: Sicilian

1 e4 c5 2 ♘f3 ♘c6 3 d4 cd 4 ♘×d4 ♘f6 5 ♘c3 e5 6 ♘db5 h6 7 ♗c4 a6 8 ♘d6+ ♗×d6 9 ♕×d6 ♕e7 10 ♕×e7+ ♔×e7 11 ♗e3 (11 b3? b5) 11 ... d6 12 000 ♗e6 13 ♘d5+ ♗×d5 14 ed (if 14 ♗×d5 ♘×d5 15 ed ♘b8 16 f4 ♘d7) 14 ... b5 15 ♗b3 ♘a5 16 f3 ♖hc8 17 g4 ♘d7 18 h4 ♘×b3+ 19 ab a5 20 ♔bl ♗a6 21 ♖hel ♘b6 22 f4 ♘d7 (22 ... f6?! 23 g5) 23 g5 h5 24 fe de 25 ♖fl a4 26 ♗d2 ab 27 ♗b4+ ♔e8 28 cb f6 29 g6 ♘f8 30 ♖gl (not 30 ♗×f8 ♔×f8 31 ♖f5? because of 31 ... ♖d6 32 ♖×h5 ♔g8 and Black has excellent winning chances.) 30 ... ♖ca8 31 ♔c2 ♖d8 32 ♔bl ♖da8 33 ♔c2 ♖d8 ½-½ ♖dl ♘d7 44 ♖hl ♘f8 45 ♖bl ♘g6 46 ♖gl ♘f4 47 ♔d2 ♘h3 48 ♖bl ♖b8 49 ♔e3 ♘f4 50 ♖dl c5 51 ♗×f4 gf+ 52 ♔f2 b4 53 cb cb 54 ab ab 55 ♖bl ♖b3 56 cb cb 57 ♔e2 b2 58 ♔d3 ♖b3+ 59 ♔c4 ♗×f3 60 ♖×b2 ♔f6 61 ♖b6+ ♔g5 62 ♔d5 ♖a3 63 ♔×e5 f3 64 ♖b8 ♔g4 65 ♖f8 ♔h3 66 ♔d6 d3+ 67 ♔c6 ½-½

2902 Balshan–AK

PR2: 17.7.1972: Spanish

1 e4 e5 2 ♘f3 ♘c6 3 ♗b5 a6 4 ♗×c6 dc 5 00 f6 6 d4 ♗g4 7 de ♕×dl 8 ♖×dl fe 9 ♖d3 ♗×f3 10 gf ♖d8 11 f4 ♘f6 12 ♘c3 ♗d6 13 f5 ♗c5 14 ♖×d8+ ♔×d8 15 ♗g5 ♔c8 16 ♖dl ♖f8 17 ♔fl g6 18 fg hg 19 ♔g2 ♗d4 20 f3 ♘h5 21 ♗cl ♗×c3 22 bc b5 23 ♗e3 ♖f6 24 ♔f2 ♖d6 25 ♖gl ♔d7 26 ♔e2 ♖e6 27 ♖dl+ ♔e8 28 ♗g5 ♖d6 29 ♖gl c5 30 ♗e3 c4 31 ♖g5 ♖e6 32 ♖gl ♔f7 33 ♖bl ♖d6 34 ♖gl ♘f6 35 ♗c5 ♖d8 36 ♗f2 ♖h8 37 ♗g3 ♔e6 38 ♖dl ♘h5 39 ♔f2 c6 40 ♖d2 a5 41 a3 ♘f6 42 ♔e3 g5 43

2903 Albano–AK

PR4: 19.7.1972: Sicilian

1 e4 c5 2 ♘f3 e6 3 d4 cd 4 ♘×d4 ♘c6 5 g3 a6 6 ♗g2 ♘×d4 7 ♕×d4 ♘e7 8 00 ♘c6 9 ♕c3 d6 10 ♗e3 ♗d7 11 ♘d2 ♖c8 12 a4 b5 13 ab ab 14 ♖fcl ♗e7 15 ♗fl ♘e5 16 ♕a5 00 17 ♗×b5 ♕×a5 18 ♖×a5 ♗×b5 19 ♖×b5 ♘d3 20 ♖al ♖×c2 21 ♖a7 ♗f6 22 ♖d7 ♘×b2 23 ♖×d6 ♘dl 24 ♖b3 g5 25 ♘fl ♘c3 26 ♖d2 ♖×d2 27 ♘×d2 g4 28 ♘bl ♘e2+ 29 ♔fl ♘d4 30 ♗×d4 ♗×d4 31 ♖d3 e5 32 ♘c3 ♖a8 33 ♘d5 ♖al+ 34 ♔g2 h5 35 ♖d2 ♖a7 36 h3 ♔g7 37 hg hg 38 f3 ♔g6 39 fg ♔g5 40 ♔h3 ♖al 41 ♖e2 ♖hl+ 42 ♔g2 ♖h8 43 ♖el ♔×g4 44 ♖fl ♖a8 45 ♖×f7 ♖a2+ 46 ♔fl ♔×g3 47 ♖f5 ♗al 48 ♘f6 ♖d2 49 ♘h5+ ♔h4 50 ♘f6 ½-½

2904 AK–Gouveia

PR5: 20.7.1972: Sicilian

1 e4 c5 2 ♘f3 e6 3 d4 cd 4 ♘×d4 a6 5 ♘c3 ♕c7 6 g3 b5 7 ♗g2 ♗b7 8

00 ♘f6 9 a3 d6 10 h3 ♘bd7 11 g4 h6
12 ♘de2 ♗e7 13 f4 ♘b6 14 ♕d3
♖d8 15 ♘g3 d5 16 e5 ♘e4 17 ♘ce2
♘a4 18 ♘d4 ♘ac5 19 ♕e3 ♘×g3
20 ♕×g3 ♘e4 21 ♕f3 ♗c5 22 c3
00 23 ♗e3 ♖de8 24 ♘b3 f6 25
♘×c5 ♘×c5 26 ♗d4 f5 27 ♕e3
♘b3 28 ♖ad1 g6 29 ♗f3 ♔h7 30
♔h2 ♕d7 31 ♖f2 ♖c8 32 ♖g1
♘×d4 33 cd ♖g8 34 ♖fg2 ♕e7 35
♕f2 ♖cf8 36 ♗e2 ♖c8 37 ♗d3
♗c6 38 h4 ♗d7 39 ♔h3 ♕f7 40
♕f3 ♖cf8 41 ♕d1 ♔h8 42 ♖g3 g5
43 gf g4+ 44 ♖×g4 ef 45 ♖×g8+
♖×g8 46 ♖×g8+ ♔×g8 47 ♗e2
♕g7 48 ♕c1 a5 49 ♔h2 ♕e7 50
♔h3 ♕g7 51 ♕c7 b4 52 ♕×a5 **1-0**

2905   AK-Stoica

FR1: 21.7.1972: Sicilian

(Notes by Ghizdavu)

1 e4 c5 2 ♘f3 d6 3 d4 cd 4 ♘×d4
♘f6 5 ♘c3 a6 6 ♗e2 e5 7 ♘b3
♗e6 8 f4 ♕c7 9 00 ♘bd7 10 f5 ♗c4
11 a4 ♗e7 12 a5 00 13 ♗e3 (13 ♗g5
♖fc8! Karpov-Gheorghiu, Moscow 1971) 13 ... b5 14 ab ♘×b6 15
♔h1 (15 ♗×b6? ♕×b6+ 16 ♔h1
♗b5!∓ Tal-Fischer, Curacao
1962) 15 ... ♖fc8 16 ♗×b6 ♕×b6
17 ♗×c4 ♖×c4 18 ♕e2 ♖ac8 (18
... ♖b4 19 ♖a2 ♕b7 20 ♘a5 ♕c7
21 ♘d5 ♘×d5 22 ed ♖b5 23 ♕d2
♕c5   24   c4± Geller-Fischer,
Curaçao 1962) 19 ♖a2 ♗d8! 20
♖fa1 ♕b7 21 ♖a4 ♖×a4 22
♖×a4 ♖c6 23 ♕d3 g6!? 24 h3
♘h5 25 ♖a1 ♘f4 26 ♕f3 ♖c4 27

♖d1 ♕c6 28 fg hg 29 ♕f1!
(threatening 30 ♖×d6 or 30 g3) 29
... ♖b4 30 g3 ♘h5 31 ♕d3 (*186*)

186
31W
B

31 ... ♖c4? (31 ... a5! 32 ♕×d6
♘×g3+ 33 ♔g2 ♕×d6 34 ♖×d6
♗h4∓ ; or 32 ♘d5 ♖×e4! 33 ♕f3!
♔f8!! 34 g4 ♘f6 35 ♘×f6 ♖e1+ ∓)
32 ♔h2 ♗c7 33 ♖f1 a5 34 ♖f2! a4?
(34 ... ♗b6! 35 ♘d5 ♔g7 36
♘×b6 ♕×b6 37 ♖×f7+ ♔×f7 38
♕×c4+ ♔g7 39 ♔g2 ♕e3 40
♕d3±) 35 ♘d2! ♖d4 36 ♕f3 ♕d7
37 ♘d5 a3 38 ♕×a3 ♗d8 39 ♕f3
1-0

2906   AK-Adorjan

FR3: 23.7.1972: Grünfeld

(Notes by Adorjan)

**1 d4 ♘f6 2 c4 g6 3 ♘c3 d5 4 cd
♘×d5 5 e4 ♘×c3 6 bc c5 7 ♗c4
♗g7 8 ♘e2 c6 9 ♗e3 00 10 00
cd 11 cd ♘a5 12 ♖c1 ♘×c4 13
♖×c4 b6 14 ♕a4 ♕d7** (14 ... a5!?
15 ♖c2 ♗a6 16 ♖d2 b5=) **15
♕a3!** (15 ♕×d7? ♗×d7 16 ♖c7
♗b5 17 ♖e1 ♖fc8 18 ♖×c7? ♗f6;
18 ♖×c8+   ♖×c8 19 ♖c1 ♖×c1+

20 ♘×c1 e6∓) **15 ... ♕b5! 16
♖fc1 e6** (16 ... ♗a6 17 ♖4c2
♖fc8? 18 ♘c3 ♕d3 19 ♖d2 ♕c4
20 ♖dd1!±±; 17 ... e6 18 ♘c3
♕a5 19 ♕×a5 ba 20 d5±) **17 ♘f4
♗b7??** (17 ... ♖d8 18 d5!? ed 19
♘×d5 ♗e6 20 ♖b4 ♕d7 21
♖d1=) **18 ♖c7?!±** (18 ♘×e6!! fe
19 ♖c7±±) **18 ... ♗×e4 19
♘×e6 ♖fe8** (19 ... ♕f5? 20 ♘×f8
♕g4 21 f3 ♗×f3 22 ♕b2 ♗×f8 23
h3 ♕g3/e4 24 ♕f2±±) **20 ♘×g7
♔×g7 21 ♗f4 ♕f5 22 ♗e5+ ♔g8
23 h4** (23 ♕e3 g5 24 h4 h6 25 hg hg
26 f3 ♗d5 27 ♔f2 f6 28 g4 ♕g6 29
♖h1 ♖ac8! 30 ♖×c8 ♖×c8 31
♗d6 ♗×a2!∓) **23 ... ♗d5 24 f3
f6 25 ♗g3 ♕e2 26 ♕e7 ♖×e7 27
♕×e7 ♕e6 28 ♕c7! ♕f7** (28 ...
♗×a2 29 ♖c6 ♕f7 30 ♕f4 ♗e6 31
d5!±) **29 ♕f4 ♖e8 30 ♖c7 ♕e7
31 ♖c8+ ♖e8??** (31 ... ♔g7 32
♕b8 ♖b7 33 ♕d6 ♖d7=) **32
♖×e8+ ♕×e8 33 ♕×f6 ♕f8 34
♕e5 ♗×a2 35 ♕c7 ♗f7 36
♕×a7 b5 37 ♕b6 ♗c4** (*187*)

*187
37B
W*

38 ♕c6?! (38 ♗e5±±) **38 ...
♕d8! 39 ♕c5?** (39 ♗e5! ♔f7!±)
39 ... ♔f7 40 h5? (40 ♔h2±) **40**

... ♕e7!= 41 ♕c6 ♕e3+ ½-½ (42
♗f2 ♕c1+ 43 ♔h2 ♕f4+ 44 g3
♕g5)

2907 Estevez–AK

FR4: 24.7.1972: Sicilian

1 e4 c5 2 ♘f3 ♘c6 3 d4 cd 4 ♘×d4
e6 5 ♘b5 d6 6 c4 ♘f6 7 ♘1c3 a6 8
♘a3 ♗e7 9 ♗e2 0-0 10 0-0 ♕a5 11
♘c2?! (11 ♗e3 is correct.) 11 ...
♖d8 12 ♗d2 ♕c7 13 ♖c1 ♗d7 14
♗e3 ♗e8 15 f3 b6 16 ♕d2 ♖a7! 17
♖fd1 ♕b8 18 ♗f1 ♖b7 19 ♕f2
♖c8 20 ♘d4 ♘e5 21 b3 h6 22 a4
♘fd7 23 ♕g3 ♔h8 24 f4 ♘c6 (*188*)

*188
24B
W*

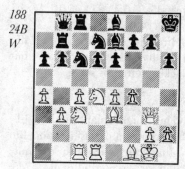

25 f5? (Both 25 ♘×c6 ♖×c6 26
♗e2 and 25 ♗e2!, with ♘×c6 and
♗f3 to follow, were better
alternatives.) 25 ... ♘×d4 26
♗×d4 ♘e5 27 fe fe 28 ♕h3 ♗g5 29
♖c2 b5 30 ab ab 31 ♖f2? (31
♕×e6? ♗e7 32 ♕f5 ♖f7 33 ♕e6
♖f6 34 ♕h3 ♗d7 35 ♕h5
♗g4∓∓, but White may be able to
hang on with 31 cb!?) 31 ... b4 32
♘b5 ♗×b5 33 cb ♖e7∓ 34 ♗e2
♕b7 35 ♗d3 ♘×d3 36 ♕×d3 e5
37 ♗b2 ♕b6 38 ♔f1 ♗e3 39 ♖f3

♗c5 40 ♗c1 ♖b8 41 ♔e2 ♖a7 42
♖df1 ♕×b5‡ ∓ 43 ♖f8+ ♔h7 44
♖×b8 ♕×b8 45 ♕h3 ♕e8 46 ♗d2
♖a2 47 ♕f5+ ♔g8 48 ♖f3 ♗d4
49 ♖d3 ♖a7 50 ♗e3 ♗×e3 51
♔×e3 ♖f7 52 ♕g4 ♖f4 53 ♕h3
♕g6 54 ♕c8+ ♔h7 55 ♕c6 ♕×g2
0-1

2908 AK-Hübner

FR6: 26.7.1972: Sicilian

(Notes by **Karpov**)

1 e4 c5 2 ♘f3 e6 3 d4 cd 4 ♘×d4 a6
5 ♗d3 ♗c5 6 ♘b3 ♗a7 7 00 ♘c6 8
♕e2 d6 9 ♗e3 ♗×e3 10 ♕×e3
♘f6 11 c4 00 12 ♖d1

Hindering the freeing . . . d5.
White has a space advantage, but
Black's position is solid.

    12 . . .   ♕c7

    13 ♘c3

The knight manoeuvre ♘b1-
d2-f3 comes into consideration. But
in that case one must carefully
watch for the possibility of . . . d5.
With the text move White
consolidates his space advantage.

    13 . . .   ♘e5

    14 ♖ac1

Indirectly defending the c-
pawn.

    14 . . .   b6

    15 ♗e2

It is useful to preserve the bishop.
If immediately 15 f4 there follows
15 . . . ♘eg4 16 ♕f3 b5!

    15 . . .   ♗b7

    16 f4   ♘g6

16 . . . ♘×c4 loses after 17 ♗×c4
♕×c4 18 ♕×b6 ♕c6 (18 . . .
♗×e4 19 ♘a5) 19 ♖×d6.

    17 g3   ♖fd8 (*189*)

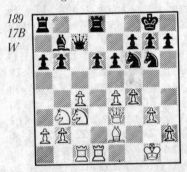

189
17B
W

This position had already
occurred in Ivkov-Hübner, Palma
interzonal 1970. Ivkov continued
18 ♖d2 ♖ac8 19 ♖cd1 ♘e7 20
♘d4 e5 21 fe de 22 ♘db5!± . I think
that, instead of 20 . . . e5, Hübner
would have got an adequate game
by means of 20 . . . ♕c5 with the
threat of . . . e5.

    18 a3

Securing the knight transfer to
d4, since . . . ♕c5 can be met by b4.

    18 . . .   ♖ac8

    19 ♘d4   ♗a8

    20 b3

Necessary in order to transfer the
bishop to the long diagonal.

    20 . . .   ♘e7

    21 ♗f3   ♖b8

    22 a4

Warding off the possibility of a
later . . . b5. Having consolidated
his centre, White is ready to
proceed, after appropriate piece
regrouping, with the storming of

Black's K-side and centre. Not wanting passively to await events, Hübner endeavours to start play in the centre, but nothing comes of this.

 22 ... ♛c5
 23 ♖d3! e5?!

(Hübner gives 23 ... ♞c6= – KJO'C.)

 24 ♞de2

Of course not 24 ♞c2 ef 25 gf ♞g6!∓ .

Having thought for 40 minutes, Hübner could find nothing better than to exchange queens and offer a draw.

 24 ... ef

After the game Hübner was in favour of 24 ... ♞c6, but 25 ♞d5 gives White an appreciable advantage.

 25 gf ♛×e3+
 26 ♖×e3

It is clear that the draw is declined since the game had decisive significance for the award of the first board-prize, and, besides that, I had sufficient reason, in purely chess terms, to continue the fight.

 26 ... ♞g6?

(Hübner gives 26 ... ♖e8 27 ♖d1 ♞c8 28 ♞g3 g6, followed by 29 ... ♝c6 and 30 ... ♖b7, as better – KJO'C.)

 27 ♖d1 ♚f8?!

During the game I thought that Black's best continuation was 27 ... ♖e8 28 ♖×d6 ♞h4 29 ♚f2 ♞×f3 30 ♚×f3 ♞×e4 31 ♞×e4 f5

32 ♞c3 fe+ 33 ♚g4. But in that case also, White has the advantage.

(Hübner gives 27 ... ♞f8!?, intending 28 ... ♞e6, as better – KJO'C.)

 28 ♖ed3 ♞e8

The only move – on 28 ... ♚e7 there follows 29 e5 de 30 ♖×d8 ♖×d8 31 ♖×d8.

 29 ♚f2 ♖dc8

Essential – the threat was e5.

 30 ♚g3 ♞e7
 31 ♞d4 ♖c5
 32 ♖1d2

Preparing 33 ♞c2. If 32 ♞c2 then 32 ... b5 is unpleasant.

 32 ... ♝b7
 33 ♞c2 g5

A questionable decision. Of course White could have prevented this by means of 33 h4, but ... you see Black is adding many weaknesses on the K-side. It is true, however, that the black pieces do obtain the e5 square.

 34 fg ♖×g5+
 35 ♚f2 ♞g6
 36 ♝h1

Defending against the threat of 36 ... ♞e5 and, at the same time, clearing the third rank for manoeuvres.

 36 ... ♖c8
 37 ♖g3 ♖cc5
 38 ♞e3 ♞e7

Black was unable to appropriate the e5 square, since that would have involved diverting the knight from the defence of d5.

 39 ♝f3 ♖×g3

40 hg   ♖ e5
41 g4

The sealed move. It seems illogical, because the pawn advances on to a square of the same colour as the bishop, but, in return, White anchors the f5 square and further hampers his opponent.

41 ...   a5

Relinquishing the struggle for ... b5 and putting the initiative completely in White's hands.

Black's position is already very difficult, and in the event of his waiting passively, White will advance his b-pawn to b5, then occupy d5 with the knight at present on c3, so that, after the exchange, the knight on e3 can attack Black's pawns from c4 or f5.

42 ♖ d1

42 ♘f5 is no good on account of 42 ... ♘×f5 43 ef ♗×f3 44 ♔×f3 h5 45 ♘d5 ♘g7! White waits for a more opportune moment and, for the time-being, withdraws his rook to the empty first rank.

42 ...   ♗ c6
43 ♘cd5   *(190)*

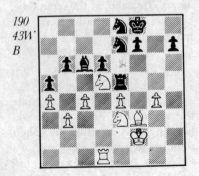

190
43W
B

A move earlier this move achieved nothing because of 42 ... ♘×d5 43 cd ♗a6. Now Black cannot capture the knight because of the unfortunate placing of the bishop.

43 ...   ♘c8
44 ♘f5   ♗×d5

The knight can no longer be endured.

45 cd   ♘e7
46 ♘e3

Directed towards c4.

46 ...   ♘g8

If 46 ... ♘f6 47 ♘c4 ♘×e4+ 48 ♔g2 ♘c3 49 ♘×e5 ♘×d1 50 ♘d7+ ♔e8 51 ♘f6+ and 52 ♗×d1 ± ±

47 ♘c4   ♖e7
48 ♘×b6

48 e5 also gave a great advantage.

48 ...   ♖b7
49 ♘c4   ♖×b3
50 ♖ a1!

In the ending the rook should be behind the passed pawn. There is no defence against 51 ♘×a5.

50 ...   ♘gf6
51 ♘×a5 ♖b2+ 52 ♔e3 ♘d7 53 ♘c6 ♖b3+ 54 ♔f4 ♘e5 55 ♘×e5 de+ 56 ♔g3 (The rest is, as they say, a matter of technique.) 56 ... ♘d6 57 ♔f2 ♖b2+ 58 ♔g1 ♖b7 59 a5 ♖a7 60 a6 ♔e7 (if 60 ... ♘b7, White wins with 61 ♗e2 ♘c5 62 ♖b1 ♘×e4 63 ♖b7 ♖a8 64 a7 ♔g7 65 ♖c7) 61 ♔f2 ♔d7 62 ♔e3 ♘c4+ 63 ♔d3 ♘b6 64 ♗e2 ♔d6 65 ♔e3 ♘d7 66 ♖h1 ♘f8 67

♖h6+ ♔e7 68 d6+ ♔d8 69 ♗b5
♖a8 70 ♖h5 f6 71 ♖h6 ♖b8 72
♗c6 ♖b3+ 73♔d2 ♖a3 74 ♖×f6
♖a2+ **1-0**

2909 AK-Markland

FR8: 28.7.1972: Sicilian

1 ♘f3 c5 2 e4 ♘c6 3 d4 cd 4 ♘×d4
♘f6 5 ♘c3 d6 6 ♗g5 ♗d7 7 ♕d2
♖c8 8 000 ♘×d4 9 ♕×d4 ♕a5 10
♗d2 a6 11 f3 ♕c5?! (11 . . . e5 is
better.) 12 ♕d3 g6 13 g4 ♗g7 14 h4
h6 15 ♔b1 ♗e6 16 ♗e3 ♕a5 17
♗d4 00 18 ♕d2! (threatening 19
♘d5) 18 . . . ♘d7 (18 . . . ♖×c3 19
♕×c3 ♕×a2+ 20 ♔c1 ♖c8 21
♕a3 leads to nothing for Black; 18
. . . ♖fe8 19 g5.) 19 ♘d5 ♕d8 20
♗×g7♔×g7 21 ♘e3 ♘e5 22 ♗e2!
(To play simply 23 f4. Karpov's
attack is simple, strong and deadly.)
22 . . . f6 23 f4 ♘c4 24 ♗×c4 ♗×c4
25 g5! (forcing the opening of lines
to Black's king) 25 . . . hg 26 hg fg
(This loses, but if 26 . . . ♖h8 or 26
. . .♗f7 then 27 gf+ , or 26 . . .♗g8
27 ♖dg1 and there is no real hope.)
27 ♕c3+ e5 28 ♘×c4 b5 29 fe
♖×c4 30 ♕h3! **1-0** (30 . . . ♖h8 31
♕×h8+ ♕×h8 32 ♖×h8 ♔×h8
33 ed ± ±)

30 Skopje Olympiad   19.9–12.10.1972

Final A	1	2	3	4	5	6	7	8	9	0	1	2	3	4	5	6	
1 USSR	×	1½	2½	2	2½	2½	3	2½	3	3½	3½	3	3½	2	3	4	**42**
2 Hungary	2½	×	2½	2½	2	2½	2½	2½	2½	3½	3½	3	2	4	1½	3½	**40½**
3 Yugoslavia	1½	1½	×	1½	2	2	2	3	3	2½	3	3	3½	3	2½	4	**38**
4 Czechoslovakia	2	1½	2½	×	1½	2½	2½	2½	2	1½	1½	2½	3½	2½	4	3	**35½**
5 West Germany	1½	2	2	2½	×	2½	2½	2½	2½	2½	2½	2	2	3	2	3	**35**
6 Bulgaria	1½	1½	2	1½	1½	×	2½	3	2½	2½	2	2½	2½	2	2½	2	**32**
7 Romania	1	1½	2	1½	1½	1½	×	2	2	3	2½	2½	2½	3½	2	2½	**31½**
8 Holland	1½	1½	1	1½	1½	1	2	×	2½	3	3	2	2½	1½	2	2½	**29**
9 USA	1	1½	1	2	1½	1½	2	1½	×	2½	3	3	1½	2½	2½	2	**29**
10 East Germany	½	½	1½	2½	1½	1½	1	1	1½	×	2½	2	2	3	4	2½	**27½**
11 Spain	½	½	1	2½	1½	2	1½	1	1	1½	×	2	3½	3	1½	3	**26**
12 Poland	1	1	1	1½	2	1½	1½	2	1	2	2	×	2	2	2	2	**24½**
13 Denmark	½	2	½	½	2	1½	1½	1½	2½	2	½	2	×	2	2½	1½	**23**
14 Argentina	2	0	1	1	1½	2	½	2½	1½	1	1	2	2	×	2½	2	**22½**
15 Sweden	1	2½	1½	0	2	1½	2	2	1½	0	2½	2	1½	1½	×	1	**22½**
16 Switzerland	0	½	0	1	1	2	1½	1	2½	1½	1	2	2½	2	3	×	**21½**

The USSR team was Petrosian, Korchnoi, Smyslov, Tal, Karpov and Savon.

Karpov's score of 86·7% was just bettered by Tal with 87·5% (the absolute best result). Karpov's score was easily the best on his board (first reserve!): 13/15 ahead of Balshan 13/16 (81·3%), Rantanen 12/15 80·0%), Csom 11½/15 (76·7%), Matulović 13½/18 (75%) etc.

Ray Keene and David Levy devoted a section of *Chess Olympiad Skopje 1972* to Hübner, Karpov and Ljubojević, entitled *Future World Champions?*

Keene and Levy posed the question 'which of this trio – if any – do you think will wrest the crown from King Bobby? Hübner – the realistic individual? Karpov – the protégé of the Soviet machine or the charismatic Ljubojević?'

Their concluding predictions were: 'David Levy believes that Karpov's all-round virtuosity backed up by the vast chess resources of the Soviet Union will one day carry him to the top, while . . . Raymond Keene adheres to the view that Hübner is likely to be Fischer's challenger in the not-too-distant future.'

From the above one can see that at this time opinion was still divided as to Karpov's likely prospects.

This is what Tal wrote about the youngest member of the Soviet Olympic team: 'To be quite frank, only now at Skopje have I realized that Karpov is really capable of the highest achievements. He had excellent results before, it is true, but from the creative point of view his play did not impress me. Now, simply as a chess player, I am enchanted with several of Karpov's games. When we are asked to show something of interest from Skopje we (the other members of the USSR team) have difficulty finding examples, but in Karpov's case there is another difficulty: he cannot decide which of his fine games could be called the best one.'

Gligorić was, if anything, even more impressed. In his introduction to the game Karpov-Ungureanu in *Chess Life and Review* he wrote: 'At the present moment, Anatoly Karpov seems to come closest to satisfying the difficult requirements (to attempt to take the title away from Fischer). He has had steadily high results, which no other young player can boast, and the experience which only a Soviet-based player can achieve. At the same time, his knowledge of the openings is more profound and up-to-date (a particular Fischer weapon) than any other representative of the coming generation. If he has any deficiencies, they could be that he is a little too cautious and physically too frail for his age'.

3001   Sloth–AK

PR2: 20.9.1972: English

(Notes by Karpov)

1 ♘f3 c5 2 g3 g6 3 ♗g2 ♗g7 4 c4 ♘c6 5 ♘c3 d6 6 a3 ♘h6 7 d3 0-0 8 ♗d2 ♘f5 (8. . . a6 9 ♖b1 ♖b8 10 b4 cb 11 ab b5=) **9 ♖b1 a5 10 0-0 ♗d7 11 e3 e6 12 ♘e1± ♕e7 13 b3 ♖ab8 14 ♘c2 ♖fd8 15 ♘b5** (15 b4 ab 16 ab ♘×b4 17 ♘×b4 cb 18 ♘b5 ♗×b5 19 cb d5=) **15 . . . b6**

(15 . . . d5 16 e4!? de 17 de ♘d6 18 ♗f4 ♘×b5 19 cb ♘e5 20 ♕e2±) **16 b4 ab 17 ab ♘e5 18 e4!± ♘h6** (18 . . . ♘d4 19 ♘c×d4 cd 20 f4±) **19 ♘c3 f5 20 b5 ♗c8 21 ♕e2 ♗b7 22 f4 ♘d7 23 ♖fe1 ♖e8 ?!** (23 . . . ♘f8) **24 ♖a1 ♕d8 25 ♖a7** (threatening 26 ♖×b7 ♖×b7 27 ef) **25 . . . ♘f8 ?** (25 . . . ♕c8) **26 h3 ?** (26 ef ♗×g2 27 fe! ♖b7 28 ♖×b7 ♗×b7 29 e7± ±) **26 . . . ♖e7 27 ♔h2 ?! ♖f7 28 ♖a4** (28 ♖a3!?) **28 . . . e5!= 29 ♘d5 ef 30**

gf? (30 ♘×f4!? g5 31 ♘h5 ♗e5 32 ef=) **30 . . . fe 31 de** ♘**e6∓ 32** ♕**d3** ♕**f8 33** ☐ **f1** ♔**h8 34** ♘×**b6** ♘×**f4** (*191*)

191
34B
W

35 ♗×**f4** (35 ☐×f4 ♗e5 36 ♗c3 ♕g7! 37 ♔h1 ☐×f4 38 ♘d7! ♗×c3 39 ♘×b8 ♗e5 40 ♘×c6 ♗×c6∓) **35 . . .** ☐×**f4! 36** ♘**d7** ☐×**f1 37** ♕×**f1** (37 ♘×f8?? ♗e5+ 38 ♕g3 ♗×g3+ 39 ♔×g3 ☐f×f8∓∓) **37 . . .** ♕×**f1 38** ♗×**f1** ☐ **d8 39** ♘**b6** ♗×**e4 40** ♘**e3?** (40 ♘e1 ♗e5+ 41 ♔g1 ♗d4+ 42 ♔h2 ☐ f8 42 ♗g2 ☐ f2∓∓) **40 . . .** ♗ **e5+ 41** ♔**g1** ♗ **d4 0–1**

3002   AK–Cobo

PR3: 21.9.1972: Sicilian

(Notes by Karpov)

1 e4 c5 2 ♘f3 d6 3 d4 cd 4 ♘×d4 ♘f6 5 ♘c3 a6 6 f4 e6 7 ♗e2 ♕c7 8 00 ♘c6 9 ♔h1 ♗d7

Black's position perhaps suffers from the slight disadvantage that the queen has gone to c7 too soon.

   10 a4   ♗e7
   11 ♘b3   0–0
   12 ♗e3

There was no point in trying to tie up the Q-side with 12 a5 as Black could break out with 12 . . . b5. But now 13 a5 is an unpleasant threat.

   12 . . .   ♘b4

Black ignores his opponent's plan. He had to play 12 . . . b6 and only then 13 . . . ♘a5 or 13 . . . ♘b4. The alternative 12 . . . ♘a5 would give White a slight advantage after 13 e5 ♘e8 14 ♘×a5 ♕×a5 15 ♕d2 and 16 ♗d4.

Now White gets a clear positional advantage.

   13 a5   ♗c6

If 13 . . . d5 14 ♗b6 ♕c8 15 e5 ♘e4 16 ♘×e4 de 17 c4.

   14 ♗b6   ♕b8

The logical continuation. Black prepares to drive the bishop away by . . . ♘d7 and follow up with . . . b5. But this plan is too slow and Black should have played 14 . . . ♕d7 after which I intended to play 15 ♗f3, preventing the freeing move . . . d5.

   15 ♕d2

An important move. White indirectly defends the e-pawn and threatens to win Black's advanced QN by 16 ♘d1 and 17 c3.

   15 . . .   d5
   16 e5   ♘d7

16 . . . ♘e4 17 ♘×e4 de 18 c4 (threatening 19 ♘c5) is horrible for Black.

   17 ♗d4   b5
   18 ♗g4

Preparing f5 and preventing Black from advancing his f-pawn.

White would have achieved nothing concrete with 18 ab ♘×b6 19 f5 because of 19 . . . ef 20 ♖×f5 ♘c4.

> 18 . . . .   g6
> 19 ♖ae1

Black's pieces are clustered on the Q-side and he takes no steps to transfer them to the defence of his king. He even removes his KR from the vital square f8 to make room for the knight.

> 19 . . .   ♖c8 *(192)*

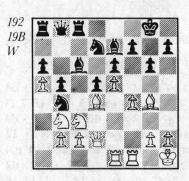

192
19B
W

> 20 f5

Decisive.

> 20 . . .   gf

If 20 . . . ef 21 e6.

> 21 ♗×f5   ♘f8

Again if 21 . . . ef, 22 e6 wins.

> 22 ♕h6   ♘g6

After 22 . . . ef White breaks open Black's position by 23 e6 f6 24 ♖×f5 ♘×c2 (24 . . . ♗e8 25 ♖×f6 and 26 ♖f7) 25 ♖g5+ ♘g6 26 ♖×g6+ hg 27 ♕×g6+ ♔h8 28 ♗×f6+ ♗×f6 29 ♕×f6+ ♔h7 30 ♖e5.

30 ♘d4 (instead of 30 ♖e5) is

tempting, e.g. 30 . . . ♘×e1 (30 . . . ♘×d4 31 ♖e3) 31 ♘f5 ♖a7 32 e7 ♖×e7 33 ♕×e7+ ♔g6 34 ♕e6+ ♔g5 (34 . . . ♔h5 35 ♕h6+ ♔g4 36 ♘e3 mate) 35 h4+ ♔g4 (35 . . . ♔h5 36 ♕h6+ ♔g4 37 ♕g5 mate) 36 ♘e3+ ♔g3 (36 . . . ♔h5 37 ♕g4+ ♔h6 38 ♘f5+ ♔h7 39 ♕g7 mate; 36 . . . ♔×h4 37 ♕g4 mate) 37 ♕g4+ ♔f2 38 ♘cd1 mate.

However, Black can avoid mate by 30 . . . ♖f8 when White has to fight to win.

> 23 ♗×g6   hg

Cobo overlooks that after 24. . . ♗f8 he loses control of h4 and White's major pieces are able to attack his king along the open h-file.

If 23 . . . fg the immediate 24 ♖f7 does not work because the black king can escape to the Q-side via e8 and d7. So I had intended to play 24 ♕h3 ♗d7 25 ♖f7 ♔×f7 26 ♕×h7+ ♔e8 27 ♕g8+ ♗f8 28 ♖f1 ♔d8 29 ♕×f8+ ♗e8 (29 . . . ♔c7 30 ♕d6+ ♔b7 31 ♕b6 mate) 30 ♗b6+ ♔d7 (30 . . . ♖c7 31 ♘c5) 31 ♖f7+ ♗×f7 32 ♕×f7+ ♔c6 33 ♘d4 mate.

> 24 ♖e3   ♗f8
> 25 ♕h4   ♗g7
> 26 ♖h3   ♗e8
> 27 ♕h7+   ♔f8
> 28 ♕×g6   f6

If 28 . . . ♗×e5 then 29 ♕×e6 with an easy win, and if 28 . . . ♘×c2 then 29 ♖h7 forces mate.

> 29 ♖×f6+   **1-0**

3003 Alvarez–AK

PR6: 24.9.1972: Sicilian

1 e4 c5 2 Nf3 e6 3 d4 cd 4 N×d4 a6 5 Nc3 Qc7 6 Be3 Bb4 7 Bd2 Nf6 8 Bd3 d6 9 00 Bc5 10 Nb3 Ba7 11 Kh1 00 12 Bg5 Nbd7 13 f4 b5 14 a3 Bb7 15 Qe2 Rfe8 16 Rad1 e5 17 Qf3 h6 18 Nh4 ef 19 Q×f4 Ne5 20 Qf3 Rae8 21 Bg3 R5e6 22 Nd5 B×d5 23 ed Re3 24 Qf4 Ne5 25 Qf5 (193)

193
25W
B

(Now Karpov wins with a neat combination.) 25 ... R×g3! 26 hg Neg4 27 Rde1 R×e1 28 R×e1 Nf2+ 29 Kh2 N6g4+ 30 Kg1 Ne4+ **0-1**

3004 Saren–AK

PR7: 25.9.1972: Sicilian

(Notes by Karpov)

1 e4 c5 2 Nf3 e6 3 d4 cd 4 N×d4 Nc6 5 Nb5 d6 6 c4 Nf6 7 N1c3 a6 8 Na3 Be7 9 Be2 00 10 00 b6 11 Be3 Bb7 12 f3 (12 Rc1) 12 ... Rb8 (12 ... Re8!?) 13 Qe1 Nd7 (13 ... Ne5 14 Qf2 Bc6±) 14 Qf2

Nc5 15 Rfd1 f5?! (15 ... Bh4 16 g3 Bf6; 16 Qf1 Qe7) 16 ef R×f5 17 Nc2 Bh4 18 g3 Be7 19 b4 Nd7 20 f4 Qf8 21 b5? (21 Bg4 Rf6 22 Ne4 Rg6 23 Bh5 Rh6 24 Bf3±) 21 ... ab 22 cb Na5 23 B×b6? (23 Rac1) 23 ... N×b6 24 Q×b6 Bd8! 25 Qa7 (25 Qe3 e5) 25 ... Rc8 26 Qe3 e5 27 Bg4 Nc4 28 Qd3?! (28 Qe2 Bb6+ 29 Kf1 R×f4+ 30 gf Q×f4+ 31 Ke1 Rf8 and 32 ... Bf2+ ∓ ∓) 28 ... Bb6+ 29 Kf1 R×f4+ 30 gf Q×f4+ **0-1**

3005 AK–Dueball

FR2: 28.9.1972: Sicilian

1 e4 c5 2 Nf3 d6 3 d4 cd 4 N×d4 Nf6 5 Nc3 g6 6 Be3 Bc6 7 f3 Bg7 8 Qd2 00 9 g4 N×d4 10 B×d4 Be6 11 000 Qa5 12 Kb1 Rfc8 13 a3 Rab8 14 g5 Nh5 15 Nd5 Q×d2 16 R×d2 B×d5 17 ed± a6 18 Rg1! b5 19 c3 a5 20 Ba7 Rb7 21 Be3 Be5! 22 Ka2 (22 a4? ba! 23 Ba6 R×c3∓ – Dueball) 22 ... Rcc7 23 Kb3 Rb8 24 Bd3 (24 Rg4?!) 24 ... Nf4 25 Be4 f5 (25 ... Rc4! 26 Bg4 a4+ 27 Ka2 Nh5 28 Bd3 R×g4 29 fg Nf4 30 Be4 Rc8 with ... Rc4= to follow – Dueball) 26 gf ef 27 Rg4 g5 (194) 28 Rg1?! (28 Bf5) 28 ... Nh3! 29 Re1 Bf4 30 Bf5 B×e3 31 R×e3 Nf4 32 Ka2 Kf8?! (32 ... a4!, fixing the Q-side pawns) 33 b4 h6 34 Kb2 Re7? (34 ... Ra7; 34 ... Ra8: Black should double rooks on

194
27B
W

the a-file) **35** ☖×**e7** ♔×**e7 36** ♔**b3±** ☖ **a8 37 c4 ab 38 ab bc+ 39** ♔×**c4** ☖**d8 40** ♔**b5!** ☖**c7** (40 ... ☖b8+ 41 ♔c6 ☖×b4 42 ♔×d6 ☖b6+ 43 ♔c5 ☖b8 44 ☖a2) **41** ☖**c2+** ♔**b7 42** ♗**d7!** ☖ **a3 43** ☖ **c6** ☖**d3** (43 ... ☖×f3 44 ☖a6±±; 43 ... ♘×d5 44 ☖×d6 ♘×b4!? 45 ☖×f6±) **44** ☖**b6+** ♔**c7 45** ♗**c6** ♘×**d5 46** ☖**b7+** ♔**c8** (46 ... ♔d8 47 ☖d7+ ♔c8 48 ☖h7±±) **47** ☖ **f7** (threatening 48 ♗×d5 ☖×d5+ 49 ♔c6; 47 ☖h7!±±) **47 ...** ♔**d8 48** ☖ **d7+** ♔**c8 49** ☖ **f7** (again 49 ☖h7!±±) **49 ...** ♔**d8 50** ♔**c4** ♘**f4 51** ☖×**f6 d5+** (51...♔c7 52 ♔b5!±±) **52** ♔**c5** ☖**e7 53** ☖×**h6** ☖ **c3+** (53 ... ☖×f3 54 ♗×d5 ♘×d5 55 ♔×d5±±) **54** ♔**b6** ☖×**f3 55 b5 g4?** (55 ... ☖b3 was the best chance, though White retains clear winning chances.) **56** ☖ **h4!±±** ☖ **h3 57** ☖×**g4** ♘ **e2 58** ♔**c7** ☖ **h7 59 b6** ♔**e6+ 60** ♔**d8!** ♘**d4!** (highly ingenious, but not quite adequate) **61** ☖×**d4** ♔**d6 62** ♗×**d5!** ♔**c5** (62 ... ☖h8+ 63 ♗g8+ ♔c6 64 ☖g4 ♔×b6 65

h4± ±; 62 ... ☖×h2 63 b7 ☖h8+ 64 ♗g8+ ♔c6 65 b8♘+! ♔b7 66 ☖b4+ ♔a7 67 ♔c7±±) **63** ☖ **d2** ♔×**b6 64** ☖ **c2 1–0**

3006 Padevsky–AK

FR4: 30.9.1972: French

(Notes by Padevsky)

1 e4 c5 2 ♘f3 e6 3 c3 d5 4 ed ed 5 d4 ♗d6 6 dc ♗×c5 7 ♗e2 ♘c6 8 00 ♘ge7 9 ♘bd2 00 10 ♘b3 ♗b6 11 ♘fd4 ♘g6 12 ♗e3 ☖e8 13 ♕c2 ♘ce5 14 ☖ad1 ♗d7 15 ♘d2 ♘g4 16 ♗×g4 ♗×g4 17 ☖de1 ☖c8 18 ♘2f3 e4 19 ♘b3 ♕d7 20 ♘d2 ☖ee8 21 f3 ♗e6 22 ♕d1 ♗c7 23 ☖f2 ♗d6 24 ♘f1 ☖a6! 25 f4 ♗d7 26 ♕b1 ♗b5!∓ 27 ♘×b5 ♕×b5 28 g3 ☖e4 29 ♗d4 ☖×e1? (29 ... ☖ce8 30 ☖×e4 de 31 ♘e3 ♘f8! 32 f5 ♘d7 and ...♘c5∓) **30** ♕×**e1** ☖ e8 31 ♕d1= a5 32 ♘e3 ☖e4 33 ♕b3 ♕×b3? (33 ... ♕d3 34 ♕×b7 ☖×e3 35 ♗×e3 ♕×e3 36 ♕c8+ ♘f8 37 ♕×c7 ♕e1+=) 34 ab± ♘e7 35 ☖d2 h5 36 ♔f2 (36 ♗a7!?) 36 ... ☖e6 37 ♔f3 g6 38 ♗c5 (*195*)

195
38W
B

38 ... ♗b6? (38 ... ♗d6!=) 39 b4
ab 40 cb ♗×c5 41 bc b6 42 b4 bc 43
bc ♔f8 44 ♘×d5 ♖c6 (44 ...
♘f5!±) 45 ♘×e7 ♔×e7 46
♖c2± ♔d7 47 ♔e4 ♖f6 48 ♖a2
♖f5 49 ♖a7+ ♔e8 50 ♖a5 ♔d8
51 ♔d4 h4 52 ♖a8+♔c7 53
♖a7+ ♔c6 54 ♔e4 ♖×c5 55
♖×f7 ♖c2 56 ♖f6+ ♔d7 57
♖×g6 ♖×h2 58 g4 h3 59 ♖h6
♖h1 60 ♔f5 h2 61 g5 ♔e7 62 g6
♖a1 63 ♖h7+ ♔f8 64 ♖×h2
♖a5+ 65 ♔f6 **1-0**

3007 Sznapik–AK

FR6: 2.10.1972: KI Attack

(Notes by Karpov)

1 e4 c5 2 ♘f3 e6 3 d3 ♘c6 4 g3 d5 5
♘bd2 ♗d6 6 ♗g2 ♘ge7 7 00 00 8
♖e1 ♗c7 9 c3 b6 10 e5 a5 11 ♘f1
♗a6 12 h4 d4 13 c4 ♕d7! 14 ♘1h2
f5 15 ef? (15 a4!±) 15 ... gf∓ 16
♘g4 e5! 17 ♗h3 ♕e8 18 ♗h6 ♖f7
19 ♗d2 ♔h8∓ 20 ♔h2 ♗c8 21
♕e2 ♗d7 22 ♘g1 f5 23 ♘h6 ♖g7
24 ♗g5 ♕g6 25 ♗g2 ♘g8 26
♘×g8 ♖a×g8 27 ♕d2 f4∓∓ 28
♗e4 ♕d6 29 ♕e2 ♗e8 30 ♗d5
♖f8 31 gf h6 32 fe ♕×e5+! 33
♕×e5 ♘×e5 34 f4 ♘g4+ 35 ♔g3
♘e3 **0-1**

3008 AK–Uddenfeldt

FR7: 3.10.1972: Sicilian

(Notes by Karpov)

**1 e4 c5 2 ♘f3 d6 3 d4 cd 4 ♘×d4
♘f6 5 ♘c3 a6 6 f4 ♕c7 7 ♗d3 e6**

**8 00 ♗e7 9 ♘f3 ♘bd7 10 ♕e1
♘c5 11 e5 ♘fd7 12 ♕g3 g6** (12
... 00 13 f5 ♘×d3 14 f6± ±; or 13
;.. de 14 ♗h6 ♗f6 15 ♗e3 b5 16
♖ad1±) **13 ♗e3** (13 f5 ♘×d3! 14
fe ♘3×e5 15 ed+ ♗×d7) **13 ... b5
14 ♗d4** (14 ♖ad1 de; 14 ed!?
♗×d6 15 ♖ad1) **14 ... ♘×d3 15
cd** (15 ed ♗×d6 16 ♗×h8 ♘×f4 17
♕h4 ♗b7) **15 ... d5?** (15 ... de 16
fe ♗b7 17 ♖ac1± ; 15 ... de 16
♘×e5: (1) 16 ... ♘f6 17 ♘g4 ♕d8
18 ♗e5; (2) 16 ... ♗f6 17 ♘e4± ;
(3) 16 ... ♗c5 17 ♗×c5 ♕×c5+
18 ♔h1 ♘×e5 19 ♗e4±) **16 ♖ac1
♕b7** (*196*)

196
16B
W

17 f5!± ± gf (17 ... ef 18 e6 ♘f6 19
ef+ ♔×f7 20 ♘g5+ ♔g7 21
♖fe1± ±) **18 ♕g7 ♖f8 19 ♘g5
♗×g5 20 ♕×g5 ♕b8 21 ♘e2
♗b7** (21 ... ♘×e5 22 ♖×c8+
♕×c8 23 ♗×e5) **22 ♘f4 ♕d8 23
♕h5!** (threatening 24 ♘×e6) **23
... ♔e7 24 ♕×h7 ♔e8** (24 ...
♖g8 25 ♘×e6! ♔×e6 26 ♕×f5+
♔e7 27 ♕×f7 mate) **25 ♘h5 ♕g5
26 ♖ c7 ♖b8 27 ♘g7+ 1-0** (27 ...
♔e7 28 ♗c5+ ♔d8 29 ♘×e6+ fe
30 ♕×d7 mate)

3009   AK–Wirthensohn

FR8: 4.10.1972: Sicilian

(Notes by Karpov)

1 e4 c5 2 ♘f3 d6 3 d4 cd 4 ♘×d4 ♘f6 5 ♘c3 a6 6 f4 e5 7 ♘f3 ♘bd7 8 ♗c4 ♗e7 9 a4 00 10 f5?! (10 00!?) 10 . . . b6 11 ♗e3 ♗b7 12 ♕d2 d5 (12 . . . ♕c7!?) 13 ♘×d5 ♘×d5 14 ♗×d5 ♗×d5 15 ed ♗c5 (15 . . . ♘c5 16 c4! ♘d3+ 17 ♔e2 ♘f4+ 18 ♔f3 ♘h5 19 g4 ♘f6 20 g5 and 21 ♘e4) 16 ♕e2 ♕h4+ 17 g3 ♕b4∓ *(197)*

197
17B
W

18 00 (18 ♖a2 ♗×e3 19 ♕×e3 ♘f6 20 c4 ♖fc8 21 00 ♘g4 22 ♕e2 ♕c5+ 23 ♔h1 ♘e3∓) 18 . . . ♕×b2 19 c4 f6 (19 . . . b5!?) 20 ♔h1 ♖fc8 (20 . . . ♕c3!? would have been better.) 21 ♕d3 ♗×e3 22 ♕×e3 a5 23 ♖fc1 ♕b4 (23 . . . ♕d4!?) 24 ♖cb1 ♕c5 25 ♕×c5 ♖×c5 26 ♔g2= ♔f8?! (26 . . . c4 27 ♔f2 ♘e5; 26 . . . h5!?) 27 ♔f3 ♔e7 28 g4 ♖h8 29 h4± ♖f8 30 ♔e3 h6 31 ♖g1 ♖cc8 32 ♖ab1 ♖b8 33 ♘e4 ♖bc8 (33 . . . ♖fc8 34 ♖gc1±) 34 ♖gc1 ♖fe8 35 ♖b5

♖ed8 36 ♔d3 ♔f8? 37 g5 hg 38 hg ♔e7 39 ♖g1 ♖h8 (39 . . . ♖g8 40 d6+ ♔f8 41 gf gf 42 ♖×g8+ ♔×g8 43 c5±±) 40 gf+ gf 41 ♖g7+ ♔d8 42 ♘d6 ♖h3+ 43 ♔e2 (some sources give 1–0 here) 43 . . . ♖h2+ 44 ♔e3 **1–0** (44 . . . ♖c7 45 ♖g8+ ♔e7 46 ♖e8+ ♔×d6 47 ♖e6 mate; or 44 . . . ♖b8 45 ♖b1 and ♖bg1±±)

3010   AK–Jansa

FR9: 5.10.1972: Sicilian

1 e4 c5 2 ♘f3 e6 3 d4 cd 4 ♘×d4 ♘c6 5 ♘b5 d6 6 c4 ♘f6 7 ♘1c3 a6 8 ♘a3 ♗e7 9 ♗e2 00 10 00 b6 11 ♗e3 ♗b7 12 ♖c1 ♘e5 13 ♕d4 ♘ed7 14 ♖fd1!? (14 f3?! d5!) 14 . . . ♕c7 15 f3 ♖fe8 16 b4!± ♖ab8 17 ♘ab1 ♗a8 18 a3 ♗f8 19 ♘d2 h6 20 f4 ♖bc8 21 ♕d3 (21 e5 de 22 fe ♘×e5 23 ♕×b6 is rather unclear but probably slightly better for White.) 21 . . . ♕b8 22 ♖c2 ♖ed8 23 ♗f3 ♗b7 24 ♖dc1 ♔h8! 25 ♕e2 ♗e7 26 h4! ♖e8 27 ♕f2 ♗a8 28 ♕e2 ♘g8 29 g3 ♗f6 30 ♕d3 ♖ed8 31 ♔g2 ♗e7 32 ♘d1 ♖c7 33 ♗d4 ♗f6 (33 . . . e5? 34 ♗f2±) 34 ♗×f6 ♘g×f6 35 ♘f2 ♖cc8 36 ♘f1 ♗c6 37 ♘e3 b5 38 g4 ♘b6= 39 g5 bc 40 ♘×c4 ♘g8 ½–½

3011   AK–Enevoldsen

FR10: 7.10.1972: French

(Notes by Karpov)

1 e4   e6

2 d4   d5
3 ♘d2   f5

This move is rare in tournament play. The theoretical recommendation is 4 ef ef 5 ♕h5+ g6 6 ♕e2+ ♕e7 7 ♘df3 with an advantage in the coming endgame. 4 e5 also gives White an advantage. However, I did not want to block the position, nor go in for the ending – I wanted a sharp, tactical game.

4 ef   ef
5 ♘df3   ♘f6
6 ♗g5

The characteristic move of the variation. Of course, 6 ♗d3, ♘e2 and 00 also gives White a lasting positional advantage.

6 . . .   ♗e7

The only move, but quite satisfactory. White was threatening ♕e2+ followed by capturing on f6.

Now came my turn to think: the early development of the bishop on g5 has not justified itself, and now White is lagging behind in the development of his K-side. I spent a long time thinking about the forthcoming sacrifice of the b-pawn.

7 ♗d3   ♘e4
8 ♗×e7   ♕×e7
9 ♘e2   ♕b4+

Black must accept the challenge because if White can get in 10 00 he will have very powerful play against the weak squares in Black's position.

10 c3   ♕×b2

11 00   00

If Black takes the second pawn he gets horribly crushed: 11 . . . ♘×c3 12 ♘×c3 ♕×c3 13 ♖c1 and 14 ♖e1+ . The black knight at e4 is the bulwark of his position and cannot be exchanged for such a small material gain.

12 c4   dc

With 12 . . . c6 13 ♘f4, Black ties himself down to the defence of his d-pawn. He could still defend it by 13 . . . ♘f6 (there is a beautiful win after 13 . . . g5 14 ♗×e4 fe 15 ♘×g5 ♖×f4 16 ♕h5 ♕×d4 17 ♕×h7+ ♔f8 18 ♕c7!, and if 16 . . . ♗f5 then 17 ♕f7+ ♔h8 18 ♕f8 mate), but then 14 ♖c1 is very strong, giving White play on the c-file after the exchange of pawns on d5.

13 ♗×c4+   ♔h8
14 ♖b1

14 ♘e5 also wins. 14 ♖b1 is the first move of a variation which should have resulted in a forced win.

14 . . .   ♕a3
15 ♘e5   g6

The only defence against 16 ♘g6+ , 17 ♖b3 and mate on the h-file.

16 ♖b3   ♕e7
17 ♘f4   ♔g7
18 ♖h3! *(198)*

White has two threats: 19 ♖×h7+ and 19 ♘f×g6; Black has the defence 18 . . . ♘g5, but then after 19 ♖e3 ♕d8 20 ♖fe1 an

198
18W
B

invasion by White's rooks along the e-file is inevitable.

18 ...   ♘c6
19 ♘f×g6

An inaccuracy. White had a beautiful way to win with 19 ♖×h7+ ♔×h7 20 ♘f×g6 (20 ♘e×g6 ♕d6 21 ♘×f8+ ♔×f8 22 ♕h5+ ♔g7 and there is no sign of any mate) 20 ... ♕d6 21 ♘×f8+ ♔g7 (21 ... ♕×f8 loses to 22 ♕h5+ ♕h6 23 ♗g8+ ♔g7 24 ♕f7+ ♔h8 25 ♘g6+) 22 ♕h5 ♘×e5 23 ♕h7+ ♔×f8 24 de! (This is the move which I didn't find in my analysis and then sprang to mind, too late, a few moves later.) 24 ... ♕d7 (24 ... ♕e7 25 ♕g8 mate) 25 ♕g8+ ♔e7 26 ♕f7+ ♔d8 27 ♕f8+ ♔e8 28 ♖d1+ ♗d7 29 ♕×f5 with e6 to follow.

19 ...   hg
20 ♘×g6   ♕f6!

The only move to keep control of h8. White has an easy win after 20 ... ♕g5 21 ♘×f8 ♔×f8 22 ♖h8+ ♔e7 23 ♖e1.

21 ♘×f8

21 ♘f4 ♕g5 22 ♕h5+ ♔g6 23

♗d3 or ♗d5 seems tempting, but after 23 ... ♕d2 there is no forced win.

21 ...   ♔×f8
22 ♖h7   ♘e7?

My opponent, tired from calculating complex variations, failed to notice that after 22 ... ♘g5, the reply 23 ♖×c7 is not possible because of 23 ... ♕d6 and White's rook suddenly finds itself trapped.

After 22 ... ♘g5 I intended to play 23 ♖h5 ♗e6 24 ♗×e6 (Black can defend himself after both 24 ♖×g5 ♗×c4 25 ♕h5 ♘e7 and 24 d5 ♗f7 25 dc ♗×c4 26 cb ♖b8 27 ♕c1 ♗×f1 28 ♕×c7 ♖×b7 29 ♕×b7 ♗e2) 24 ... ♘×e6 25 d5 ♖d8 26 ♕b3 ♘ed4 27 ♕×b7 ♖×d5 28 ♕×c7 with some advantage.

23 ♖e1

There was no point in winning the queen by 23 ♖f7+.

23 ...   ♕g6
24 ♖f7+   ♕×f7

24 ... ♔e8 loses to 25 f3 ♗e6 26 ♗×e6 ♕×e6 27 ♖h7.

25 ♗×f7   ♔×f7
26 ♕h5+   ♔f8
27 ♕h6+   ♔f7
28 ♕h7+   **1-0**

3012   Bisguier–AK

FR12: 9.10.1972: English

(Notes by Karpov)

1 c4 c5 2 ♘c3 g6 3 ♘f3 ♗g7 4 e3

♘f6 5 d4 00 6 ♗e2 cd 7 ed d5 8 00
♘c6 9 h3 ♗f5 10 ♗e3 dc 11 ♗×c4
♖c8 12 ♗e2 ♗e6 13 ♕d2 ♕a5 14
♗h6 ♖fd8 15 ♗×g7 ♔×g7 16
♖fd1 ♖d6! 17 ♕e3 ♖cd8 18 a3

A conventional opening has led
to a position which I think the
readers will find interesting. A
sharp tactical struggle is just
beginning.

     18 ...   ♗b3
     19 ♖d2

19 ♘b5 fails to 19 ... ♗×d1 20
♘×d6 ♗×e2 21 ♘×b7 ♕b6 22
♘×d8 ♗×f3.

     19 ...   ♖e6
     20 ♕f4   ♘d5
     21 ♘×d5   ♖×d5
     22 g4

White defends against the threat
of 22 ... ♖f5 followed by 23
... ♖×f3 and 24 ... ♕×d2.

If 22 ♗d3, Black gets the
advantage by 22 ... ♖f6 23 ♕e3
♖×f3 24 gf ♘×d4. This threatens
25 ... ♕×d2 with 26 ... ♘×f3+
to follow, and if 25 ♗e4 there comes
the crushing blow 25 ... ♕×d2 26
♗×d5 ♗×d5! 27 ♕e5+ (27
♕×d2 ♘×f3+) 27 ... ♔h6.

     22 ...   g5
     23 ♕g3   ♖f6
     24 ♗d1

White loses a pawn after 24 ♖d3
♗c4 25 ♖e3 ♗×e2 26 ♖×e2
♖×f3! 27 ♕×f3 ♘×d4 and 28 ...
♘×e2+ .

     24 ...   ♗c4
After 24 .. ♖×f3 25 ♕×f3 ♕×d2

26 ♗×b3 the weakness of h7 is
fatally exposed.

     25 b3   ♗a6
Of course I would have liked to
have taken the knight but after 25
... ♖×f3 26 ♗×f3 ♕×d2, White
does not play 27 ♖d1 allowing
Black to finish him off by 27 ...
♕c3 28 bc♖×d4 29 ♖×d4 ♘×d4
30♕e5+ ♔h6! but instead hurries
to exchange his bishop and draws
by 27 bc♖×d4 28 ♗×c6 bc 29
♕e5+ .

     26 b4   ♕d8
     27 ♗b3 *(199)*

It looks as though the American
grandmaster is winning but Black
has a powerful tactical riposte.

199
27W
B

     27 ...   ♘×d4
     28 ♖×d4

Bisguier does not wish to lose in a
long and gruelling endgame a
pawn down after 28 ♗×d5 ♘×f3+
29 ♗×f3 ♕×d2 30 ♖d1 ♕c3 and
rushes precipitously to his doom.

     28 ...   ♖×d4
     29 ♘×g5   ♖d3
     30 ♕h4   h6
     31 ♘×f7   ♕d4

32 ♖e1   ♖×h3!
0–1

3013   AK–Visier

FR13: 10.10.1972: Sicilian

1 e4 c5 2 ♘f3 e6 3 d4 cd 4 ♘×d4 a6 5 ♗d3 ♕c7 6 00 ♘c6 7 ♘×c6 bc 8 f4 d5 9 ♘d2 ♘f6 10 ♕e2 ♗e7 11 b3 00 12 ♗b2 a5 13 ♖f3 ♗a6 14 c3 ♖fe8 15 ♖af1 g6 16 ♔h1 a4 17 ♖h3 ab 18 ab ♗b7 19 ♗b1 de 20 ♘×e4 ♘×e4 21 ♗×e4 ♖a2 22 ♗b1 ♖×b2 23 ♕×b2 c5 24 ♕e2 ♖d8 25 ♖d3 ♖×d3 26 ♗×d3 ♕c6 27 ♖e1 ♗h4 28 ♗e4 ♕b6 29 ♖b1 ♗f6 30 ♗×b7 ♕×b7 31 ♕d3 ♕b6 32 c4 ♗e7 33 ♕c3 ♕c7 34 ♖f1 ♗d6 35 ♕e3 h5 36 g3 ♗e7 37 h3 ♗f6 38 g4 hg 39 hg ♔g7 40 ♕f3 ♕c8 41 ♔g2 ♕a6 42 ♔h3 ♕c8 43 ♖d1 ♕h8+ 44 ♔g2 ♕c8 45 ♖d6 ♕b8 46 ♖d7 ♗d4 47 f5 ef 48 gf **1–0**

3014   Hase–AK

FR14: 11.10.1972: Centre Game

1 e4 e5 2 d4 ed 3 ♕×d4 ♘c6 4 ♕e3 d6?! (4 . . . ♘f6 is probably best, and 4 . . . ♗b4+ , 4 . . . ♗e7 and 4 . . . g6 are all preferable to the text.) 5 ♘c3 ♘f6 6 ♗d2 ♗e7 7 000 00 8 ♕g3 a6 9 f4 b5 10 e5 ♘d7 11 ♘f3 ♖b8 12 ♘d5 ♘c5 13 ♗e3 ♘e4 14 ♕e1 f5 15 h3 ♗e6 16 ♖g1 ♔h8 17 g4 de 18 ♘×e7 ♕×e7 19 ♘×e5 ♘×e5 20 fe ♖bd8 21 ♗d3 ♗d5 ½–½ (White could well continue with 22 gf ♕×e5 23 ♕h4± , but a

package deal of four draws was agreed between the team captains – surprising since Korchnoi was also in trouble, while none of the Argentinians was losing.)

3015   AK–Ungureanu

FR15: 12.10.1972: Sicilian

(Notes by Karpov)

1 e4 c5 2 ♘f3 ♘c6 3 d4 cd 4 ♘×d4 ♘f6 5 ♘c3 d6 6 ♗g5 e6 7 ♕d2 e7 8 000 00 9 f4 ♘×d4 10 ♕×d4 a5 11 ♗c4 ♗d7 12 e5 de 13 fe ♗c6 14 ♗d2! ♘d7 (14 . . . ♖fd8? 15 ♘d5 ♖×d5 16 ♗×a5± ±) **15 ♘d5 ♕d8 16 ♘×e7+ ♕×e7 17 ♖he1** (17 h4!?) **17 . . . ♖fc8 18 ♕f4 a5 19 ♔b1 ♘b6** (19 . . . b5 20 ♗d3 ♘c5; 20 ♗f1±) **20 ♗d3 ♘d5 21 ♕g4 ♕c5 ?!** (21 . . . b5; 21 . . . ♘b4!?) **22 ♖e4! b5** (22 . . . ♘b4 23 ♖c4±) **23 ♕h3** (threatening 24 ♕×h7+ and 24 ♖h4) **23 . . . ♘b4** (*200*)

200
23B
W

24 ♗e3!± ± (24 ♖×b4 ab 25 ♕×h7+ ♔f8 26 ♕h8+ ♔e7 27 ♕h4+ g5± ; 24 ♗×b4 ab 25

♕×h7+ ♚×h7 26 ♖c4± +) **24 . . .**
♗×**e4** (24 . . . ♕e7 25 ♖×b4
♕×b4 26 a3!! ♕a4 27 ♕×h7+
♚f8 28 ♗c5+ ♚e8 29 ♕g8+ ♚d7
30 ♕×f7+ ♚d8 31 ♕e7 mate) **25**

♗×**e4** ♕×**e5 26** ♕×**h7+** ♚**f8 27**
♗×**a8** ♚**e7** (27 . . . ♖×a8 28
♕h8+ ♚e7 29 ♕×a8 ♕×e3 30
♕d8 mate; 27 . . . g6 28 ♖f1± ±)
28 ♕**e4** ♕**c7 29** ♕**b7 1–0**

18.11–14.12.1972

Church's Fried Chicken

	1	2	3	4	5	6	7	8	9	0	1	2	3	4	5	6	
1 **Karpov**	×	½	0	1	½	½	1	½	½	1	1	½	½	1	1	1	**10½**
2 Petrosian	½	×	½	1	½	½	½	1	1	½	½	½	½	1	1	1	**10½**
3 Portisch	1	½	×	0	1	1	½	1	½	½	½	½	1	½	1	1	**10½**
4 Gligorić	0	0	1	×	½	½	1	½	½	1	1	½	½	1	1	1	**10**
5 Keres	½	½	0	½	×	1	½	1	1	1	½	0	½	1	1	½	**9½**
6 Hort	½	½	0	½	0	×	½	0	1	½	1	½	1	1	1	1	**9**
7 Suttles	0	½	½	0	½	½	×	½	½	½	½	1	1	1	1	1	**9**
8 Larsen	½	0	0	½	0	1	½	×	0	1	0	1	1	1	1	1	**8½**
9 Mecking	½	0	½	½	0	0	½	1	×	½	1	½	1	1	½	1	**8½**
10 D. Byrne	0	½	½	0	0	½	½	0	½	×	0	1	½	1	1	1	**7**
11 Browne	0	½	½	0	½	0	½	1	0	1	×	½	1	0	0	1	**6½**
12 Evans	½	½	½	½	1	½	0	0	½	0	½	×	0	½	½	1	**6½**
13 Kaplan	½	½	0	½	½	0	0	0	0	½	0	1	×	1	½	0	**5**
14 Campos-Lopez	0	0	½	0	0	0	0	0	0	0	1	½	0	×	1	½	**3½**
15 Saidy	0	0	0	0	0	0	0	0	½	0	1	½	½	0	×	1	**3½**
16 Smith	0	0	0	0	½	0	0	0	0	0	0	0	1	½	0	×	**2**

The growing interest in Karpov, and his future potential, was noted by the late Kühnle-Woods in *Chess Express*: 'The chess world was eager to see how Karpov would fare, who is already now and somewhat prematurely labelled as opponent for Fischer in 1975. He did not disappoint and captured first place.'

3101   Saidy–AK

R1: 19.11.1972: KI Reversed

(Notes by Larsen)

1 ♘f3 ♘f6 2 g3 b5!? 3 ♗g2 ♗b7 4 00 e6 5 d3 ♗e7 (This is much better than 5. . . d5 6 e4! Black must keep things quiet in the centre until he has castled.) **6 e4 d6 7 a4 a6 8 ab** (Not a bad idea. Another one was 8 c3 followed by ♘a3. In such an unknown position there is plenty of scope for imagination and originality.) **8 . . . ab 9 ♖×a8 ♗×a8 10 ♘a3 b4 11 ♘c4 00 12 ♗d2 ♘c6 13 ♕a1?** (A blind alley. 13 ♖e1 was good. White has a nice position without pawn weaknesses, while the far advanced black b-pawn might be considered weak.) **13 . . . d5 14 ed ♘×d5 15 ♕a6? ♗f6 16 ♖a1? h6! 17 ♖e1** (A sad retreat, but Karpov's last move prevented tricks like 17 ♕b5 ♕d7 18 ♖a6 ♖b8 19 ♕×b8+ ♘×b8 20 ♖×a8 ♕c8 21 ♘a5 because of 21 . . . ♔h7! 22 ♘c6 ♕b7.) **17 . . . ♕e7 18 ♘a5** (Why not to e5?) **18 . . . ♕d6** (After 18 . . . ♘×a5 19 ♕×a5 ♗×b2 20 ♖b1 ♗c3 21 ♗×c3 bc 22 ♘d4 Black cannot hold the plus pawn.) **19 ♘c4 ♕c5 20 ♗e3** (Probably best. White has lost the initiative, but he still has a playable game.) **20 . . . ♘×e3 21 fe ♘e7!** (Otherwise White would get the advantage with ♘fd2.) **22 ♘fd2 ♗d5 23 ♘e4 ♗×e4 24 ♗×e4 h5!? 25 ♕a1?!** (Seeing the beginning of a black attack, White retires.   25 ♖a1! was more energetic.) **25 . . . g6 26 ♕d1 h4 27 ♕e2 ♕g5 28 ♗f3 ♔g7 29 ♕f4 ♕c5 30 ♖a1 ♘d5 31 ♕f2 c6** (31 . . . ♗g5 is not very good because of 32 ♖a5 ♕×e3 33 ♘×e3 ♗×e3 34 ♗×d5. Saidy was short of time, so Karpov was hoping for a chance.) **32 ♖a5 ♕e7 33 g4?** (Helping Black. 33 ♗f3, threatening e4, probably was best.) **33 . . . ♕c7 34 ♖a1 ♗g5 35 ♔h1 ♕h6 36 ♖g1?** (Again, better ♗f3. But, having played 33 g4?, White could not play e4 as the black knight would go to f4.) **36 . . . ♘f6 37 ♗f3 ♖d8** (201)

201
37B
W

38 ♖a1? b3! (After this Black's advantage is probably decisive.) **39 ♖a6 bc 40 ♕×c2 ♘d5** (Adjourned. White has too many weaknesses.) **41 ♕d2 c5 42 ♕e2 ♘b4 43 ♖a3 ♗g7 44 ♗g2 ♗f6 45 ♗f1 ♘c6! 46 ♕f2 ♘e5 47 ♘×e5 ♕×e5 48 b3 ♖d7** (Black wants to play . . . ♗g5, forcing e4, after which White will be terribly weak on the black squares. But first he

prevents ♖ a7.) **49 e4** ♕ **g5 50** ♕ **e2**
♖ **b7 51** ♕ **f3** ♗ **e5** (A nice position!
Karpov has slowly and patiently
collected important positional
advantages. The game might still
take a long time without the
following blunder, but there is no
reason to doubt that he would have
won.) **52** ♖ **a5 ??** ♕ **d2 0–1**

3102 AK–Browne

R2: 20.11.1972: English

(Notes by Karpov)

1 c4	c5
2 b3	♘f6
3 ♗b2	g6
4 ♗×f6!?	

An original idea: in exchange for
giving up his good bishop, White
takes control of d5. If Black does not
like the position which arises after
White's fourth move, he could have
played 3 . . . e6 instead of 3 . . . g6.
This entire idea needs verifying,
and it is for this reason that this
game is interesting from the
theoretical point of view.

4 . . .	ef
5 ♘c3	♗g7
6 g3	♘c6
7 ♗g2	f5

This advance, as it turns out, is
hasty. On f5, the pawn hems in the
white-squared bishop. Possibly
better was 7 . . . d6, so as on 8 e3 to
reply 8 . . . ♘b4, retaining the
possibility of finding an active spot
for the white-squared bishop.

| 8 e3 | 00 |

Now it would have been
thoughtless to continue 8 . . . ♘b4
inasmuch as the check on d3 is not
dangerous for White; he could play
either 9 ♕b1, defending against 9
. . . ♘d3+ , or 9 ♘ge2, allowing 9
. . . ♘d3+ .

9 ♘ge2	a6
10 ♖c1	

In order, on 10 . . . b5, to have
the possibility 11 d3 and on 11 . . .
bc, of recapturing with the d-pawn.
10 00 is also good.

10 . . .	b5
11 d3	

Of course, 11 cb was dangerous:
11 . . . ab 12 ♘×b5 ♖×a2 13 ♖×c5
♕a5 and on 14 ♘bc3 there follows
14 . . . ♖×d2!

11 . . .	♗b7
12 0–0	d6
13 ♕d2	♕a5

Black is in serious difficulties.
The b-pawn needed defending. It
could only be defended by the
queen, but that piece is not well
placed on a5. On the other hand,
both the exchange on c4 and the
advance 13 . . . b4 were unpleasant
for Black. Browne selected the lesser
evil.

14 ♖fd1	♖ab8
15 ♘d5	♕×·d2
16 ♖×d2	b4

Black must move the b-pawn,
since to exchange it on c4 serves no
purpose and it is impossible to
maintain the tension on the Q-side,
for White threatened 17 cb ab 18 d4

cd 19 ♖×c6 ♗×c6 20 ♘e7+ and
21 ♘×c6.

17 d4 (202)

202
17W
B

The game is strategically won: d5
is firmly held, Black's pawns on the
K-side have been stopped and
White's extra pawn in the centre
promises him all the winning
chances.

17 ...   ♖fd8

Forced, inasmuch as after 17 . . .
cd there would follow a massive
exchange of pieces which would not
be in Black's favour: 18 ♘×d4
♘×d4 19 ♘e7+ ♔h8 20 ed.

18 ♖cd1

An inaccuracy. White has an
overwhelming advantage after 18
dc dc 19 ♖cd1, threatening 20
♘e7+ .

18 ...   cd
19 ed   ♔f8
20 c5?

A serious error, letting slip the
lion's share of White's advantage.
The quiet 20 ♘e3 was much
simpler and stronger, and found
when my head was clear; but,
during the game . . .

20 ...   ♘a7!

The point! The knight will have
a wonderful post on b5, from where
it can go to c3 and attack the d-
pawn. Any other move in this
position would be much weaker.

21 ♘e3

White gets nothing with 21 cd
♗×d5 (21 . . . ♖×d6 is worse: 22
♘e3 ♗×g2 23 ♔×g2 and 24 d5
with good prospects) 22 ♗×d5
♖×d6 and 23 . ∴. ♘b5; also the
simple 21 ♘×b4 does not work due
to 21 . . . ♗×g2 22 ♘×a6 ♗f3 23
♘×b8 ♖×b8. The text was
probably the only possibility of
preserving the knight and fighting
for a further advantage.

21 ...   ♗×g2
22 ♔×g2   dc
23 dc   ♖×d2
24 ♖×d2   ♖c8 (203)

203
24B
W

White has a clear theoretical
advantage thanks to the presence of
an extra passed pawn on the Q-side,
but, for the moment, he must tend
to its defence. I decided to
exchange the c-pawn for the b-

pawn, loosening Black's hold on the strongpoint at c3.

25 ♘d5

After 25 ♖c2 ♘b5, Black is on his way to seizing the initiative.

25 ...	♖×c5
26 ♘×b4	a5
27 ♘d5	♖c6

This move and those following were made by Browne in time-pressure, and therefore I succeeded in increasing my advantage and winning. Of course, the normal result from this position would be a draw.

This move is the first mistake. 27 ... ♘c6, without fearing 28 ♘b6, was more precise.

28 ♘e3	♖c5
29 ♘f4	♗h6
30 ♖d5	

White goes in for an exchange of pieces so that he can take advantage of his extra pawn on the Q-side.

30 ...	♖×d5
31 ♘f×d5	♗×e3?

From this moment on White again has real winning chances. It was necessary to keep the bishop and continue 31 ... ♘c6; then White's winning chances would be extremely problematical.

Now both opponents, as is usually the case in endgames, bring their kings to the centre.

32 ♘×e3	♔e7
33 ♘c4	♘c6
34 ♔f3	♔e6
35 ♔e3	♔d5

36 a3

Preparing the king's entry to d3. Now 36 ... a4 is impossible due to 37 ♘b6+ .

36 ...	♔e6
37 ♔d3	♔d5
38 f3	h6
39 ♔c3	h5
40 ♔d3	f6
41 f4!	

Zugzwang. Black cannot move his king to c5 due to 42 ♘×a5 and 43 b4+ ; the knight cannot leave the defence of the a-pawn.

41 ...	g5
42 ♘e3+	♔e6
43 h4	

Blockading the pawns and guaranteeing the win.

43 ... gh 44 gh ♘e7 45 ♔c4 ♘g6 46 ♘g2 ♔d6 47 ♔b5 ♔d5 48 ♔×a5 ♔e4 49 b4 ♔f3 50 b5 ♔×g2 51 b6 ♘f8 52 ♔b5 ♘d7 53 a4 ♘×b6 54 ♔×b6 ♔f3 55 a5 ♔×f4 56 a6 ♔e3 57 a7 f4 58 a8♕ f3 59 ♕e8+ **1-0**

3103 Larsen-AK

R3: 21.11.1972: Queen's Indian (Notes by Larsen)

1 d4 ♘f6 2 ♘f3 e6 3 c4 b6 4 g3 ♗b7 5 ♗g2 ♗e7 6 00 00 7 b3 (Of course, the most common move is 7 ♘c3. I played the text move in order to get into less explored territory. By the way, Karpov knows the continuation 7 ♘c3 ♘e4 8 ♕c2 ♘×c3 9 ♕×c3 c5!? very well. It was rehabilitated by

Korchnoi a few years ago, at a time when he was working with Furman – and later Furman became Karpov's trainer!) **7 ... c5** (If Karpov had answered 7 ... d5, I would have played 8 cd, hoping to transpose into my game against Evans in the previous round. I would like to have the white pieces once in that position!) **8 ♗b2 cd 9 ♕×d4 ♘c6 10 ♕f4 d5** (After 10 ... ♕b8, White would play either 11 ♘c3 or 11 ♕×b8 ♖a×b8 12 ♘c3 followed by pressure against Black's d-pawn.) **11 ♖d1 ♕c8?** (11 ... ♕b8 must be the right continuation, which I would proably have answered by 12 ♘e5. 12 ♕×b8 ♖a×b8 13 ♘e5 ♖bc8 leads to a very drawish position. One of the ideas behind the text move is 12 ♘c3 dc 13 ♕×c4 ♘b4, so I preferred ...) **12 ♘bd2 ♖d8 13 ♖ac1 ♕b8 14 ♘e5 ♗d6 15 ♘×c6** (The best answer to 15 ♘df3 seems to be 15 ... ♘e7.) **15 ... ♗×c6 16 ♕h4 ♗e5** (16 ... ♗e7 17 cd ♗×d5 18 ♘e4 does not look very attractive for Black.) **17 ♗×e5 ♕×e5** (*204*)

204
17B
W

18 ♘f3 (I find it hard to explain why I abandoned my original plan: 18 cd ♗×d5 19 e4 ♗b7 20 ♘c4 ♖×d1+ 21 ♖×d1 ♕c7 (21 ... ♕c3? 22 ♕f4!) 22 e5 ♘d5 (22 ... ♗×g2?? 23 ef ♗f3 24 ♕g5!) 23 ♘d6. Really, the black position would be very difficult to defend, for instance 23 ... ♗c6 24 ♖c1. I remember seeing 23 ... ♕c2 24 ♕h5 g6 25 ♕f3 ♘c3! 26 ♕×b7 ♕×d1+ 27 ♗f1 ♖f8 – but this is all nonsense! White should just play 24 ♖f1, with the double threat 25 ♘×b7 and 25 ♗e4. I did not look deep enough and rejected a promising continuation for no good reason. Maybe drawing a game in round three does not decide the outcome of the tournament, but I had the feeling that this was where I lost first prize!) **18 ... ♕b8?** (18 ... ♕e4! was correct. The ending after 19 ♕×e4 is tenable for Black. It looks as though the majority on the Q-side should offer White winning chances, but the white bishop is misplaced.) **19 ♘d4 ♗b7 20 cd ♘×d5 21 ♘c6?** (For the second time, a very tame continuation. 21 ♘b5! offered winning chances. One of the ideas is 21 ... ♖c8 22 ♗×d5! ♗×d5 (22 ... ed gives White a clear positional advantage.) 23 e4 ♗c6 24 ♘×a7! ♕×a7 25 ♖×c6, the back rank mating threat nets White an important pawn.) **21 ... ♗×c6 22 ♖×c6 ♕e5 23 ♕e4** (The only good continuation. A good reply to

23 ♕c4? is 23 . . . ♘e3!, for instance 24 ♖×d8+ ♖×d8 25 ♖c8! ♕a1+ 26 ♕c1 ♕×c1+ 27 ♖×c1 and White(!) can just hold the ending.) **23 . . . ♕×e4 24 ♗×e4 ♘f6 25 ♖×d8+ ♖×d8 26 ♗d3** (I believed that I still had some chances with ♗ v ♘ in a rather open position with a more active rook. But Black has a very good defence, pointed out by Karpov after the game: 26 . . . ♘e8 followed by the centralization of the king. White cannot find any weak spots in the black fortress.) **26 . . . ♘d5 ? 27 a3 ♔f8 28 ♗b5** (Preventing 28 . . . ♔e7 because of 29 e4. Black now has some problems, but finds a good defence.) **28 . . . g5! 28 ♔f1** (Honestly, I did not see Black's following manoeuvre, but also after 29 ♔g2 g4! there would not be many winning chances. The advance of the black g-pawn prevents White from a slow, broad advance on the K-side.) **29 . . . ♘e7!** (Exactly on time, before the white king reaches e1.) **30 ♖c7 ♖d1+ 31 ♔g2 ♖b1 32 ♗c4 a6! 33 a4 ½-½** (Because of 33 . . . b5, eliminating all pawns on the Q-side.)

3104 AK–Campos-Lopez

R4: 23.11.1972: Alekhine

(Notes by Larsen)

1 e4 ♘f6 2 e5 ♘d5 3 d4 d6 4 ♘f3 g6 5 ♗c4 c6 (Most players prefer 5 . . . ♘b6 as did Fischer in the 13th match game in Reykjavik. Spassky continued very badly so that game was of no great importance for opening theory. 6 ♗b3 ♗g7 7 ♘g5!? 00 8 f4 is probably critical, but there are not too many good master games available yet with this ambitious attempt to build a strong centre and lock up the black fianchetto bishop.) **6 00 ♗g7 7 ed** (There are other continuations, for example 7 ♖e1 or 7 h3, but the text move is not bad. The position now looks more like a Caro-Kann than an Alekhine.) **7 . . . ♕×d6 8 h3 00 9 ♘b3 ♗f5** (Another possibility is 9 . . . b5!? followed by . . . ♘d7 and . . . ♗b7.) **10 ♖e1 ♖e8 11 ♘bd2 b5!? 12 a4 ♘d7 13 c4 ♘b4??** (Running completely wild. After 13. . . bc it would have been a normal game. Did Black see some danger for his QB? It is not there, as 14 ♘×c4 ♕c7 15 g4? ♗e6 16 ♘g5 ♘f8 only weakens White's own position.) **14 c5 ♕f6 15 ♘e4 ♗×e4 16 ♖×e4 e5** (To prevent ♖f4. The black position is already hopeless.) **17 ab** (Cat and mouse! 17 de was not bad either.) **17 . . . ♖ad8 18 ♗g5 ♕f5 19 ♗×d8 ♖×d8** (or 19 . . . ♕×e4 20 ♗×f7+ !) **20 ♕e2 cb 21 ♖×a7 ♘c6 22 ♖c7 ♘a5 23 ♗d5 1-0**

3105 Suttles–AK

R5: 24.11.1972: Sicilian

(Notes by Karpov)

1	g3	c5
2	♗g2	♘c6
3	e4	g6
4	♘e2	♗g7
5	0-0	d6
6	c3	

In comparison to the Closed Variation of the Sicilian, White has a somewhat better position as a result of his intricate move order. First of all, he has rapidly developed his K-side pieces; secondly, ♘c3 has been omitted, which allows White to occupy the centre with his pawns. Naturally Black will try to prevent this by any means at his disposal.

6	...	e5
7	♘a3	

The knight is headed for c2, from where it will be able to support the thrust d4, while, at the same time, it could go to d5 via e3.

Another possibility for White was to play 7 d3 followed by ♗e3 and d4.

7	...	♘ge7
8	♘c2	♕b6!?

First and foremost, consistency!

| 9 | ♘e3 | |

The plan 9 ♖b1 and 10 b4 is too slow.

9	...	0-0
10	d3	♗e6
11	♔h1	♕d8

The queen has done her job on b6. The way is now cleared for the Q-side pawns, while the queen goes to support an eventual ... d5. After

White plays f4, the queen may go to d7 to help prevent f4-f5.

12	f4	f5

The aforementioned 12 ... ♕d7 was also possible.

13	♘d5	♔h8

Black retreats his king to avoid checks, in certain variations, from e7 and f6, while the square g8 can be used later by the bishop on e6.

14	fe?!	

This demands timing; 14 ♗e3 should be played first.

14	...	de
15	♗g5	h6
16	♘×e7	♘×e7
17	♗e3	♕c7

With this move, Black not only protects his pawns, but frees the d-file, preparing to put pressure on White's weakened central pawns.

18	♕d2	

18 d4 leads to complications which are unfavourable for White.

18	...	♔h7
19	b3	♖ad8
20	c4	

Hoping to control d5, but this meets with an elegant refutation.

20	...	g5!
21	ef	

Practically forced; f5-f4 was threatened.

21	...	♗×f5
22	♖×f5	

At first glance, the exchange sacrifice looks attractive, but no more than equal compensation for it is obtained. True, this is the only way out of the position for White.

22 ...	♘×f5
23 ♗e4	♔h8
24 ♘c3	

This looks very good for White, occupying the central squares, but Black shatters the illusions with one move.

24 ...	♘d6

Now the white-squared bishop must be exchanged, for to remove it from e4 would allow Black to free his black-squared bishop via e5–e4.

25 ♘d5	

25 ♗d5 is no better, for Black follows up 25 ... e4 with the advantage.

25 ...	♘×e4
26 de	♕c8!

The blockade g3–g4 cannot be allowed. To prevent that, I had to agree to the loss of an important central pawn on c5.

27 ♕e2	g4
28 ♔g2	

Black succeeds more readily in realizing his exchange advantage after this passive move. White had to accept Black's dangerous gift with 28 ♘e7 ♕e6 29 ♗×c5 b6 30 ♗a3.

28 ...	♖f3
29 ♖d1	♖d7

Black has managed to defend his weaknesses and strengthen f3.

30 h4	h5
31 ♗g5	♕f8 *(205)*
32 ♘f4	

Despair.

32 ...	♕e8

32 ... ef also wins: 33 ♖×d7

205
31B
W

♖×g3+ 34 ♔f1 (34 ♔h1 ♖h3+ 35 ♔g1 ♗d4+ and wins) 34 ... ♗d4! (threatening mate on g1!) 35 ♔e1 (35 ♕h2 ♖f3+) 35 ... ♖g1+ 36 ♔d2 f3 37 ♕d3 f2 38 e5!?? (mate almost seems inevitable, but 38 ... f1♘+ or 38 ... ♖d1+ leads to an easy win).

33 ♖×d7	♕×d7
34 ♘d5	

After 34 ♘×h5 ♕d3, White would be forced to exchange queens and knight for bishop. In the ensuing endgame, Black's rook would create havoc among the white pawns on the Q-side.

34 ...	♕c6
35 ♗e3	♔h7
36 ♗f2	b6
37 ♗e1	♕b7
38 ♗c3	♖f8!

The rook frees f3 for the queen. The exchange is unavoidable; the rest of the game is easy.

39 ♗e1	♕f7
40 ♗d2	♕f3+
41 ♕×f3	♖×f3
42 ♗c3	♖d3
43 ♔f2	♖f3+

44 ♔g2   ♚g6
45 b4

White comes to the realization that his position is hopeless. I intended to transfer the king to e6, the bishop to d8 and break with . . . a6 and . . . b5.

45 . . .   cb
46 ♗×b4 ♖d3 47 ♘e7+ ♚f7 48 ♘c8 ♚e6 49 ♘×a7 ♖d4 50 a3 ♖×c4 51 ♘b5 ♗h6 52 ♚f2 ♖c2+ 53 ♚e1 ♗e3 54 ♚d1 ♖g2 55 ♘c7+ ♚f7 56 ♘d5 ♖×g3 57 a4 ♗d4 58 a5 ba 59 ♗×a5 ♖h3 60 ♗d8 g3 **0–1**

3106   AK–D. Byrne

R6: 26.11.1972: Sicilian

1 e4 c5 2 ♘f3 d6 3 d4 cd 4 ♘×d4 ♘f6 5 ♘c3 g6 6 ♗e3 ♗g7 7 f3 00 8 ♕d2 ♘c6 9 ♗c4 a5 10 a4! (The only way for White to extract any advantage from Donald Byrne's pet variation.) 10 . . . ♘×d4 11 ♗×d4 ♗e6 12 ♗b5 ♖c8 13 000 ♘d7 14 ♗×g7 ♚×g7 15 f4 ♘f6 16 ♖he1 ♕c7 17 ♕d4 ♖fd8 18 ♖d2 d5 19 ed ♗×d5 20 ♕e5 e6 21 ♖ed1 *(206)*

206
21W
B

(Now Byrne wanted to play 21 . . . ♕×e5, but he noticed that after 22 fe ♘g4 23 ♘×d5 ♖×d5 24 ♖×d5 ed 25 ♖×d5 ♖×c2+ 26 ♚×c2 ♘e3+ 27 ♚c3 ♘×d5+ 28 ♚d4 and 29 ♚c5, he loses the ending. So to make the line playable he found . . .) 21 . . . b6?? (. . . which prevents the entry of the white king, but which loses even sooner. Probably best was 21 . . . ♖h8 followed by . . . h5, when White's advantage is so slight that Karpov was unable to win a single variation in the post-mortem analysis.) 22 ♗a6 h5 23 ♗×c8 ♖×c8 24 h3 ♕×e5 25 fe ♘e4 26 ♘×e4 ♗×e4 27 ♖e2 ♗d5 28 ♖d4 ♖c5 29 h4 f5 30 ef+ ♚×f6 31 ♖f4+ ♚g7 32 ♖e5 ♗c7 33 g3 ♖c6 34 ♚d2 ♗c7 35 b3 ♖d7 36 ♚e3 ♖e7 37 g4 hg 38 ♖×g4 ♚f6 39 ♖eg5 ♖h7 40 ♖×g6+ (1–0 at this point in the tournament book) 40 . . . ♚e5 **1–0**

3107   Petrosian–AK

R7: 27.11.1972: Queen's Indian

(Notes by Keene)

1 d4 ♘f6 2 c4 e6 3 ♘f3 b6 4 e3 ♗b7 5 ♘c3 d5 6 ♗d3 ♗e7 7 00 00 8 b3 c5 9 ♗b2 cd 10 ♘×d4?! (10 ed) 10 . . . dc 11 ♗×c4 a6!? (11 . . . ♘c6 12 ♘×c6 ♗×c6 13 ♗e2=) 12 ♗e2 b5 13 ♗f3 ♖a7! 14 ♗×b7 ♖×b7 15 ♕f3 ♖d7 16 a4 ba (16 . . . b4 17 ♘ce2±) 17 ♘×a4 ♕c7 18 ♖fc1 ♕b7 19 ♘c5 ♕×f3 20 gf ♗×c5 21 ♖×c5 h6 22 ♚g2 ♖b7 (planning

... ♘bd7 and ... e5) 23 f4 ♔h7 24
♖ac1 ♖d8 25 ♖1c2 ♘e4 26 ♖c7
♖d7 27 ♖×b7 ♖×b7 28 ♗a3 g5=
29 ♔f3 ♘f6 ½-½

3108 AK–Gligorić

R8: 29.11.1972: Spanish

(Notes by Karpov)

1 e4 e5 2 ♘f3 ♘c6 3 ♗b5 a6 4 ♗a4
♘f6 5 00 ♗e7 6 ♖e1 b5 7 ♗b3 d6 8
c3 00 9 h3 ♘b8

10 d3

The 9 ... ♘b8 variation has
recently become a frequent feature
of international competition. 10 d4
is considered the normal continuation. In that way White exerts
pressure against the enemy centre,
maintaining the initiative. With 10
d3 White defers the start of active
play for a while.

10...   ♘bd7
11 ♘bd2   ♗b7
12 ♘f1   ♘c5
13 ♗c2   ♖e8
14 ♘g3   ♗f8

This system is considered one of
the best replies to the variation
selected by White. Black has
succeeded in regrouping his forces
and is prepared for a battle in the
centre.

15 b4

This is the only way to drive
away Black's knight. 15 d4 is
impossible because of the
insufficient defence of e4.

15...   ♘cd7

16 d4   h6
17 ♗d2

Defending against the possibility
of ... d5.

17 ...   ♘b6

For some reason Gligorić
declines to play the known 17 ... a5
which gives Black a completely
equal game. Nevertheless, his move
merits consideration.

18 ♗d3

This move blocks the incursion of
Black's knight at c4 and halts the
advance of Black's a-pawn at the
same time.

18 ...   ♖c8
19 ♕c2!? (207)

207
19W
B

At first glance a strange
continuation – White places his
queen on the same file as Black's
rook. But the c-file will not, in fact,
be opened, either by the immediate
19 ... c5 20 bc dc 21 d5, or after the
preliminary exchange 19 ... ed 20
cd c5 21 bc dc 22 d5 with a very
sharp position.

19 ...   ♕d7

A lethargic move that will cost
Black dearly. Not only does it lose
an important tempo, but the queen

has taken the d7 square away from Black's knights, limiting their manoeuvrability.

20 ♖ad1   ♕c6
21 ♗e3   ♘a4

This is the only way to gain time to defend against the threatened ♘f3–d2–b3–a5. 21 ... ♘c4 was impossible in view of 22 d5 ♕d7 23 ♗×c4 bc 24 ♘d2 and 25 ♘×c4.

22 ♖c1   ♘b6
23 ♕b1

The immediate 23 ♘d2 is better; then 23 ... d5 is not dangerous since e4 is safely defended, e.g. 24 de ♖×e5 25 ♗d4! (25 f4? de with a winning position for Black) 25 ... de 26 ♘d×e4. There is no defence against ♘d2–b3–a5.

23 ...   ♕d7
24 ♘d2   c5

A forced action. Now White gets a strong, defended passed pawn on d5.

25 bc   dc
26 d5   ♘a4
27 c4   b4
28 ♖f1

Black's trouble is that he cannot find a satisfactory defence against the break-through f2–f4, initiating a fearsome assault on the King's position. Q-side counterplay is hopelessly late.

28 ...   ♕c7
29 f4   ♘d7
30 ♕c2   ♘c3

This advance of Black's knight loses a pawn by force after the transfer of White's bishop to d2, but

a retreat to b6 would be even gloomier.

31 f5   ♘f6
32 ♘e2?!

Of course it would have been better to win the pawn by 32 ♘f3, 33 ♗d2 and 34 ♗×c3, but it seemed to me that Black was defenceless against a K-side pawn storm. However, it turns out that Black's king is able, a little at a time, to escape from its insecure refuge.

32 ...   ♘×e2+
33 ♗×e2   ♗d6
34 g4   ♔f8
35 h4   ♔e7
36 g5   hg
37 hg   ♘d7
38 ♗g4

White's pieces have turned out to be unprepared for such a swift unfolding of events. The decisive thrust requires regrouping and the supplying of new pieces to the K-side.

38 ...   ♖g8

White was threatening 39 f6+ gf 40 gf+ ♘×f6 41 ♗g5. But Black will hardly be able to manage without the advance ... f6. Thus 38 ... f6 was better here.

39 ♔f2   ♖h8
40 ♖h1   ♖cg8 *(208)*

It is vital for the black king to be able to escape to the Q-side without interference. Now White has an excellent chance to resolve the struggle in his favour by 41 a3 a5 42 ♕a4! ♘b6 43 ♕b5! and Black cannot trap the queen since on 43 ... 罝×h1 44 罝×h1 罝a8 there follows the deadly 45 f6+, and Black has no time for . . . f6 because of the manoeuvre ♘b3 with attacks on a5 and c5. But I bypassed this opportunity and made a not completely successful move.

208
40B
W

41 ♕d1 ♔d8

The sealed move. Gligorić, as previously, refrains from advancing . . . f6. 41 . . . ♘b6 loses because of 42 f6+ gf 43 ♕f3 ♘d7 44 ♘b3 with threats of ♗×d7 and ♘×c5. 41 . . . a5 42 ♕a4 ♘b6 43 ♕b5 is also bad.

42 ♕g1 ♘b6
43 罝h2 ♕e7?

This is a serious mistake. It is necessary to push the Q-side pawns. White's knight immediately occupies a5 and the game ends quickly.

44 ♘b3 ♔c7
45 ♔f3

Yet another little stratagem; White's king move frees the second rank for his rooks and open the g1-a7 diagonal for his queen.

45 . . . ♘d7

46 a3 ba
47 罝a2 罝h4
48 罝×a3 罝gh8
49 罝b1

Black lacks the strength to defend all his weak points, and the game ends very quickly.

49 . . . 罝b8?

An error which does not change matters. All the same, 49 . . . f6 was more tenacious.

50 ♕e1 罝×g4

On 50 . . . 罝hh8 there would follow 51 ♕a5+ ♔c8 52 f6 gf 53 ♘×c5.

51 ♔×g4 ♗c8
52 ♕a5+ **1-0**

On 52 . . . 罝b6, 53 ♘×c5 ♗×c5 54 罝×b6 ♗×b6 55 ♗×b6+ ♘×b6 56 c5 is decisive.

3109 Portisch–AK

R9: 30.11.1972: Nimzo-Indian

(Notes by Portisch)

1 d4 ♘f6 2 c4 e6 3 ♘c3 ♗b4 4 e3 c5 5 ♗d3 00 6 ♘f3 d5 7 00 dc 8 ♗×c4 ♘bd7 9 ♕e2 cd (Slightly unusual. 9 . . . b6 at once is the normal move.) **10 ed b6?!** (Rather dubious. In any event White has good compensation for the isolated d-pawn, but after Black's move the problem of the isolated pawn is immediately solved.) **11 d5 ♗×c3 12 de ♗b4 13 ed ♕×d7 14 a3!** (After 14 ♘e5 ♕f5, Black has equalized completely – 15 ♗d3 ♕e6. My move forces the bishop to a less favourable square. If it retreats to e7, the black queen has no good square.) **14 ... ♗d6 15 ♖d1?** (A hallucination. I had wanted to play 15 ♗g5 ♕e7 16 ♕×e7 ♗×e7 17 ♖fe1, but after 17 ... ♗d6 I analysed a position in which my QB was still on c1 and I could find nothing better than 18 ♖d1. But of course with the rooks united, I would leave my KR on e1 and play 18 ♖ad1 with a very good game.) **15 ... ♕c7 16 h3** (16 ♗g5 ♗g4 17 ♗×f6 gf 18 ♖d4 ♗h5 gives White nothing.) **16 ... ♗b7 17 ♗e3 ♖ae8** (At this point Karpov thought that he had the better game, so he gave me some chances by trying for a win. But in fact the chances are equal. Instead of the text, 17 ... ♖ac8 18 ♗a6 leaves White with the smallest of advantages.) **18 ♖ac1 ♕b8 19 ♗b5 ♖e7 20 ♗c6** (A risky move because now the coming sacrifice is forced.) **20 ... ♗×c6** (Better than 20 ... ♗c5!? 21 ♘d4 ♗×d4 (21 ... ♕e5 22 ♕f3) 22 ♖×d4 ♖c8 23 ♖dc4 ♗a6 24 ♗b5 with a slight advantage to White.) **21 ♖×c6 ♗c5 22 ♖×f6** (Necessary. If 22 ♘d4 ♕e5! and White has some problems.) **22 ... gf** (If 22 ... ♗×e3 then 23 ♖fd6 ♗g5 24 ♕d3 ♗f6 25 b4 with a slight plus for White, but Black's game would be tenable.) **23 ♘d4 ♗×d4** (The only move. If White's knight is allowed to reach f5, Black's game collapses.) **24 ♖×d4** (Stronger than 24

♕g4+ ♔h8 25 ♗×d4 ♖e6! White needs his rook in the middle of the board from where it can quickly come into the attack.) **24 ... ♕e5 25 ♕f3** *(209)*

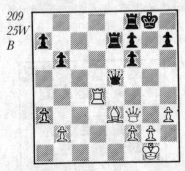

209
25W
B

25 ... ♔h8?? (25 ... f5 was essential: 26 ♖d5 ♕×b2 27 ♗d4 ♕c1+ 28 ♔h2 ♖e6 29 ♖×f5 and White has compensation for the exchange in his control of Black's weak dark squares and his attacking prospects against Black's king, e.g. 29 ... f6? 30 ♕b3! or 29 ... ♖g6 30 h4.) (Robert Byrne, in *The New York Times*, suggested, after 25 ... f5 26 ♖d5 ♕×b2 27 ♗d4, 27 ... ♕b1+ 28 ♔h2 f6 29 ♖×f5 ♕e4 as better for Black, casting doubt on the exchange sacrifice – KJO'C.) **26 ♖d5 1-0** (There is no defence to the mate threat. If 26 ... ♕×b2 27 ♗d4 ♕c1+ 28 ♔h2 followed by ♗×f6+ etc.)

3110   AK–Smith

R10: 1.12.1972: Sicilian

Karpov experiences surprising

difficulty in defeating the tail-ender.

1 e4 c5 2 ♘f3 d6 3 d4 cd 4 ♘×d4 ♘f6 5 ♘c3 e6 6 g4 h6 7 g5 hg 8 ♗×g5 a6 9 ♕d2 ♗d7 10 000 ♘c6 11 h4 ♕c7 12 ♗e2 000 13 f4 ♗e7 14 h5 ♔b8 15 ♔b1 ♗e8 16 ♗f3 ♘a5 17 ♕e2 ♘c4 18 ♖he1 ♖c8 19 ♖d3 ♘g8 20 ♕g2 ♗f8 21 ♖h1 ♘e7 22 b3 ♘a3+ 23 ♔b2 ♘b5 24 ♘c×b5 ab 25 ♕d2 ♕b6 26 ♗h4 b4 27 ♗f2 ♕a5 28 ♗e1 e5 29 ♘e2 ♘c6 30 f5 f6 31 ♖d5 ♕a3+ 32 ♔b1 ♗f7 33 ♖d3 b6 34 ♗f2 ♔b7 35 c3 bc 36 ♖×c3 ♗e7 37 ♖g1 ♖hg8 38 ♕b2 ♕×b2+ 39 ♔×b2 ♘a7 40 ♖×c8 ♘×c8 41 ♘c3 ♗d8 42 ♗e2 ♘e7 43 ♗c4 ♗×c4 44 bc ♖h8 45 ♖h1 ♔c6 46 ♔b3 ♖h7 47 ♗e3 ♖h8 48 ♔b4 ♖h7 49 ♘d5 ♘×d5 50 cd+ ♔b7 51 ♔b5 ♗c7 52 a4 ♖h8 53 ♗d2 ♖h7 54 ♗b4 ♖h8 55 ♖g1 ♖h7 56 ♖g6 ♗b8 57 h6 gh 58 ♖×f6 h5 59 ♗×d6 ♗×d6 60 ♖×d6 h4 61 ♖×b6+ ♔a7 62 ♖g6 h3 63 ♖g1 ♖h4 64 ♖g7+ ♔a8 65 f6 ♖f4 66 f7 h2 67 ♖h7 ♖×f7 68 ♖×h2 ♖f4 69 d6 ♖×e4 70 ♖h8+ **1-0**

3111   Evans–AK

R11: 3.12.1972: English

(Notes by Evans)

1 c4 c5 2 ♘c3 ♘c6 3 g3 g6 4 ♗g2 ♗g7 5 a3 d6 6 ♖b1 a5 7 ♘f3 e5 8 00 ♘ge7 9 d3 00 10 ♗d2 ♖b8 11 ♘e1 ♗e6 12 ♘c2 d5 13 cd ♘×d5 14 ♘×d5 ♗×d5 15 b4 (15 ♗×d5! ♕×d5 16 b4 ab 17 ab e4 18 ♗f4!; 17

... cb 18 ♘×b4 ♘×b4 19 ♗×b4 ♖fc8 20 ♕b3±) 15 ... ♗×g2 16 ♔×g2 b5 17 ba ♘×a5 18 ♘e3 e8 19 ♕c1 ♗f8 20 ♗×a5 ♕×a5 21 ♘d5 ♖e6 (*210*)

22 e4 ♕a4 23 f4 (23 ♕c3) 23 ... ♕d4 24 fe (24 f5 ♖d6) 24 ... ♕×e5 (24 ... ♕×d3 25 ♕f4 ♖b7 26 ♖bd1!) 25 ♖f3 ♖a6 26 ♖b3 f5 27 ♕b1 ba8 28 ♖×b5 ♖×a3 29 ♖b7 (29 ♖f2) 29 ... ♖a2+ 30 ♖f2 (30 ♔h3 ♖h8! with ... fe and ... ♕h5+ to follow) 30 ... ♖×f2+ 31 ♔×f2 fe 32 de c4 33 ♔g2 ♖c8 (33 ... ♖a1 34 ♕c2 ♕d4 35 ♕×c4! ♕×c4 36 ♘f6+ ♔h8 37 ♖×h7 mate; 33 ... ♗c5 34 ♖c7 ♕d4 35 ♘f6+!) 34 ♘b6 ♖e8 ½-½ (35 ♘×c4 ♕×e4+ 36 ♕×e4 ♖×e4=)

3112   Hort–AK

R12: 4.12.1972: Sicilian

1 e4 c5 2 ♘c3 e6 3 ♘f3 ♘c6 4 d4 cd 5 ♘×d4 a6 6 g3 ♘ge7 7 ♗g2 ♘×d4 8 ♕×d4 ♘c6 9 ♕e3 d6 10 b3 ♗e7 11 ♗b2 00 12 00 ♖b8 13 ♘e2 b5 14 ♖ac1 ♕a5 15 a3 ♕b6

16 ♕d2 a5 17 ♖fd1 ♖d8 18 ♘f4 ½-½

3113   AK–Kaplan

R13: 5.12.1972: Sicilian

(Notes by Kaplan)

1 e4 c5 2 ♘f3 ♘c6 3 d4 cd 4 ♘×d4 g6 5 c4 ♘f6 6 ♘c3 d6 7 ♘c2 ♗g7 8 ♗e2 00 9 00? (9 ♗e3! ♘d7 10 ♕d2) 9 ... ♘d7∓ 10 ♕d2?! (10 ♗d2; 10 ♗e3 ♗×c3!∓) 10...♘c5 11 f3 f5 12 ef ♗×f5 13 ♘e3 ♘d4 (13 ... a5) 14 ♘×f5 ♘×f5 15 ♖b1 e6 (preparing ... d5) 16 ♕e1 a6? (planning ... ♗d4?!; 16 ... a5! 17 ♗d2 d5∓) 17 ♔h1 ♗d4 18 ♗d2 ♕e7 19 f4 ♖ae8? (19 ... a5) 20 b4!± ♘d7 21 ♗d3 e5!? 22 fe ♘×e5 23 ♕e4! ♗a7 24 ♕d5+ ♔g7 25 ♖be1? (25 ♗×f5 ♖×f5 26 ♖×f5 gf 27 ♖f1±) 25...♕f7!∓ (25...♕h4 26 ♗×f5 ♘g4 27 ♕×b7+ ♔h8 28 h3!; 28 ♗×g4?? ♕×e1!∓∓) 26 ♗×f5 ♕×d5 27 ♘×d5 (27 cd!?) 27 ... ♖×f5 28 ♗c3 ♔f7 29 ♖×f5+ gf 30 c5 ♘d3! (211) 31 ♖f1 (31 ♖×e8 ♔×e8 32 cd ♘f2+ 33 ♔g1 ♘e4+ 34 ♔f1 ♘×c3 35 ♘×c3 ♔d7∓; 32 ♘f6+ !=) 31 ... ♖e2∓ 32 ♖×f5+ ?! ♔e6 33 ♖h5 dc 34 bc ♗×c5 34 a4∓ (Here Karpov offered a draw. I had about three minutes left and decided to see if I could quickly find a forced win. Engrossed in the analysis, I forgot about the clock and almost let my flag fall! Having only a few seconds left I was happy to accept the offer.) ½-½

211
30B
W

3114   Keres–AK

R14: 8.12.1972: Nimzo-Indian

1 d4 ♘f6 2 c4 e6 3 ♘c3 ♗b4 4 e3 c5 5 ♗d3 00 6 ♘f3 d5 7 00 dc 8 ♗×c4 cd 9 ed b6 10 ♗g5 ♗b7 11 ♕e2 ♘bd7 12 ♖ac1 ♖c8 13 ♘e5 h6 14 ♗f4 ♘×e5 15 ♗×e5 ♕e7 16 ♗a6 ♗×a6 17 ♕×a6 ♗×c3 18 bc ♘d5 19 c4 ♘b4 20 ♕a3 f6 21 ♗g3 ½-½

3115   AK–Mecking

R15: 10.12.1972: Sicilian

1 e4 c5 2 ♘f3 d6 3 ♗b5+ ♗d7 4 ♗×d7+ ♕×d7 5 00 ♘c6 6 c4 ♘f6 7 ♘c3 g6 8 d4 cd 9 ♘×d4 ½-½

32 Budapest 13.2–2.3.1973

	1	2	3	4	5	6	7	8	9	0	1	2	3	4	5	6	
1 Geller	×	½	½	1	1	½	½	½	1	½	½	1	1	½	½	1	**10½**
2 **Karpov**	½	×	1	½	1	1	½	½	½	½	½	1	½	½	½	½	**9½**
3 Vaganian	½	0	×	½	½	½	½	1	½	½	1	½	½	½	½	1	**8½**
4 Szabo	0	½	½	×	½	1	½	½	½	½	½	½	1	1	½	½	**8½**
5 Adorjan	0	0	½	½	×	½	½	½	½	½	1	1	½	1	1	½	**8½**
6 Hort	½	0	½	0	½	×	½	1	½	1	1	0	1	1	½	½	**8½**
7 Bilek	½	½	½	½	½	½	×	½	½	½	½	½	½	1	½	½	**8**
8 Antoshin	½	½	0	½	½	0	½	×	1	½	½	0	½	1	1	1	**8**
9 Csom	0	½	½	½	½	½	½	0	×	½	½	1	½	½	½	1	**7½**
10 Ribli	½	½	½	½	0	½	½	½	½	×	½	½	1	0	½	½	**7**
11 Ciocaltea	½	½	0	½	0	0	½	½	½	½	×	1	½	½	½	½	**6½**
12 Sax	0	0	½	½	0	1	½	1	0	½	0	×	½	0	1	½	**6**
13 Hecht	0	½	½	0	½	0	½	½	½	0	½	½	×	1	1	0	**6**
14 Velimirović	½	½	½	0	0	0	0	0	½	1	½	1	0	×	½	1	**6**
15 Forintos	½	½	½	½	0	½	½	0	½	½	½	0	0	½	×	½	**5½**
16 Lengyel	0	½	0	½	½	½	½	0	0	½	½	½	1	0	½	×	**5½**

Geller, in *64* No 11 1973, tells the story of Karpov at Budapest: 'After six rounds he was one point behind me. In the remaining eight rounds a real race developed with the interesting consequence that we, one with the other, as if by agreement, began to play in synchronization: if one day one of us won, then the other was also victorious.

'A. Karpov's play is distinguished by the confidence in his strength for rapid and correct calculation of variations, the highest technique in playing typical endings (for example in his game against Hort). And here, in Budapest, Anatoly played confidently, easily, was boldly combinative, but sometimes he showed, I dare say, insufficient sporting staying-power. He sometimes let slip an advantage in the struggle against stubborn opponents. (Geller here points out the win Karpov missed against Ribli-eds).

'Usually Karpov goes straight towards the goal by simple means. However, when that does not work, he can abruptly switch to a sharp combinative struggle.'

3201 AK-Hecht

R1: 13.2.1973: English

1 c4 e5 2 ♘c3 ♘f6 3 ♘f3 ♘c6 4 g3 ♗b4 5 ♘d5 e4 6 ♘h4 ♗c5 7 ♗g2 d6 8 00 ♗e6 9 d3 ♘×d5 10 cd ♗×d5 11 de ♗e6 12 ♗d2 ♕d7 13 ♗c3 00 14 ♘f3 ♗h3 15 ♕d5 ♗×g2 16 ♔×g2 ♖ae8 17 e5 ♕e6 18 ♖ad1 ♕×d5 19 ♖×d5 ♘e7 20 ♖d3 ♘c6 21 ed ♗×d6 22 e3 f6 23 ♖fd1 ♖d8 24 ♘h4 g6 25 f4 f5 26 ♘f3 ♗c5 27 ♖d7 ♖×d7 28 ♖×d7 ♖f7 29 ♖×f7 ♔×f7 30 e4 ♗e7 31 ef gf 32 ♘g5+ ♔g6 33 ♘e6 ♗d6 34 ♔f3 h5 35 h3 ♘e7 36 ♗e5 ♘c6 37 ♗c3 ♔f7 38 ♘g7 ♔g6 39 a3 a6 40 ♘e8 ♗f7 41 ♘f6 ♔g6 42 ♘d5 ♘e7 43 ♘f6 ♘c6 44 ♔e2 b5 45 ♔d3 h4 46 gh ♗×f4 47 h5+ ♔g5 48 h4+ ♔×h4 49 ♘d5 ♗h6 50 ♘×c7 ♔×h5 51 ♘×a6 ♗f8 52 ♘c7 b4 53 ab ♘×b4+ ½-½

3202 AK-Hort

R2: 14.2.1973: French
(Notes by Karpov)

1 e4 e6 2 d4 d5 3 ♘d2 ♘f6 4 e5 ♘fd7 5 c3 c5 6 ♗d3 ♘c6 7 ♘e2 ♕b6 8 ♘f3

8 00!? cd 9 cd ♘×d4 10 ♘×d4 ♕×d4 11 ♘f3 is also possible.

8 ...   cd
9 cd   f6

10 ef   ♘×f6
11 0-0   ♗d6
12 ♘c3!?   0-0
13 ♗e3   ♕d8

Not 13 ... ♕×b2? 14 ♘b5 ♗e7 15 ♖b1 ♕×a2 16 ♖a1 ♕b2 17 ♖a4! followed by 18 ♗c1 trapping the queen.

14 ♗g5   ♗d7
15 ♖fe1   ♕b8

If 15 ... ♖c8 16 ♗c1 followed by ♗b1 and ♕d3 with advantage.

16 ♗h4!   a6
17 ♖c1   b5
18 ♗b1   ♗f4
19 ♗g3

19 ♖c2 ♕d6 20 ♖ce2 gives no more than equal chances.

19 ...   ♗×g3
20 hg   ♕b6
21 ♘e2

21 ♕d3! and if 21 ... ♖ae8 22 ♘e5!

21 ...   ♖ae8
Intending 22 ... e5, keeping White's advantage to a minimum.

22 ♘f4   ♘×d4
23 ♕×d4

23 ♘×d4! was correct, e.g. 23 ... e5 24 ♘×d5 ♕×d4 25 ♘×f6+ ♖×f6 26 ♕×d4 ed 27 ♖×e8+ ♗×e8 28 ♖c8 ♔f7 29 ♖d8±

23 ...   ♕×d4
24 ♘×d4   e5

25 ♘fe6! ♗×e6
26 ♖×e5 ♗d7
27 ♖×e8 ♖×e8
28 f3 ♖c8
29 ♖×c8+ ♗×c8
30 ♔f2 ♔f7
31 ♔e3 ♔e7
32 b4 g6
33 g4 ♘d7
34 f4 (212)

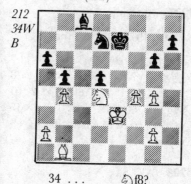

212
34W
B

34 ... ♘f8?

34 ... ♘b6 35 ♘c6+ ♔d6 36 ♘e5 ♘c4+ 37 ♔d4 is also good for White. Black's only chance was 34 ... ♔d6!? 35 g5! ♘b6 36 ♗d3±.

35 g5 ♔d6
36 ♔f3 ♘e6?
37 ♘×e6 ♗×e6
38 ♔e3±± ♗g4
39 ♗d3 ♗e6
40 ♔d4 ♗g4
41 ♗c2 ♗e6
42 ♗b3 ♗f7
43 ♗d1 ♗e6
44 ♗f3 ♗f7
45 ♗g4 **1-0**

3203 Geller–AK

R3: 15.2.1973: Spanish

1 e4 e5 2 ♘f3 ♘c6 3 ♗b5 a6 4 ♗a4 ♘f6 5 OO ♗e7 6 ♖e1 b5 7 ♗b3 d6 8 c3 OO 9 h3 ♘b8 10 d4 ♘bd7 11 ♘bd2 ♗b7 12 ♗c2 ♖e8 13 ♘f1 ♗f8 14 ♘g3 g6 15 a4 c5 16 d5 c4 17 ♗g5 h6 18 ♗e3 ♘c5 19 ♕d2 ♔h7 20 ♖a3± ♕c7 21 ♖ea1 ♗g7 22 ♕d1! ♖ab8 23 ab ab 24 ♖a7 ♕b6 25 ♖1a5 ♖a8 26 ♕a1 ♖×a7 27 ♖×a7 ♘fd7 28 h4 (28 ♘d2!? intending b4) 28 ... ♖b8! 29 h5 ♕d8 30 ♘d2 ♖a8 31 b4 (Velimirović suggests 31 ♖×a8!? ♕×a8 32 ♕×a8 ♗×a8 33 ♘b1 ♗b7 34 ♘a3 ♗a6 35 hg+ fg 36 ♘e2 with ♘c1–a2–b4 to follow.) 31 ... cb 32 ♘×b3 ♘×b3 33 ♗×b3 ♖×a7 34 ♕×a7 ♕a8 35 ♕×a8 ♗×a8 36 c4 bc 37 ♗a4 ♘b8 38 ♗a7 ♘a6 39 ♗b5 (White can make no progress in the ending.) 39 ... ♗b7 40 ♗×c4 ♗f6 41 ♘f1 ♗g5! 42 ♗b5 ♔g7 43 hg fg 44 f3 ♔f7 45 ♔f2 ♔e7 46 ♘e3 ♗×e3+ 47 ♔×e3 g5 48 ♔d3 ♘c7 49 ♔c4 ♗c8 50 ♗e3 ♗d7 51 ♗c6 ♗c8 52 ♗b5 ♗d7 53 ♗c6 ♗c8 ½-½

3204 AK–Szabo

R4: 16.2.1973: Sicilian

1 e4 c5 2 ♘f3 d6 3 d4 cd 4 ♕×d4 ♘c6 5 ♗b5 a6 6 ♗×c6+ bc 7 OO e5 8 ♕d3 ♗e7 9 c4 ♘f6 10 ♘c3 ♘d7 11 b4! OO 12 ♗e3 a5 13 b5 ♗b7 14 a4 c5 15 ♘d2 ♗b6 16 ♖fd1?! (16 f4!) 16 ... ♕c8 17 f3 ♕e6 18 ♘d5 ♗×d5 19 cd ♕g6 20 ♘c4 ♘×c4 21 ♕×c4 ♗g5 22 ♗f2 ♖ab8 (22 ... f5!?) 23 g4 h5 24 h3 ♕h6 25 ♔g2

♗e3 26 ♗×e3 ♕×e3 27 ♕d3
♕×d3 28 ♖×d3 h4 29 ♖b3 ♖b6
30 g5 f5 31 gf ♖×f6 32 ♔f2 ♖g6 33
♖bb1 ♔f7 34 ♖g1 ♖×g1 35
♖×g1 ♔f6 36 ♔e3 g5 37 ♔d3
♖b8 38 ♖b1 ♖b6 ½-½

3205　Ciocaltea–AK

R5: 18.2.1973: KI Attack

1 e4 c5 2 ♘f3 e6 3 d3 ♘c6 4 g3 g6 5
♗g2 ♗g7 6 00 ♘ge7 7 c3 00 8 ♘h4
d5 9 f4 f5 10 ef ef 11 ♘a3 ♖b8 12
♘f3 ½-½

3206　AK–Lengyel

R6: 19.2.1973: Spanish

1 e4 e5 2 ♘f3 ♘c6 3 ♗b5 a6 4 ♗a4
♘f6 5 00 ♗e7 6 ♖e1 b5 7 ♗b3 d6 8
c3 00 9 h3 ♘b8 10 d3 ♘bd7 11
♘bd2 ♘c5 12 ♘f1 ♖e8 13 ♘g3
♗b7 14 ♗c2 ♗f8 15 b4 ♘cd7 16 d4
g6 17 a4 ♗g7 18 ♗d3 c6 19 ♗g5 h6
20 ♗e3 ♕c7 21 ♖c1 ♖ad8 22 ♕d2
♔h7 23 ♕a2 ♖e7 24 c4 ed 25
♗×d4 ♘e5 26 ♗e2 ♘×c4 27
♗×c4 bc 28 ♕×c4 ♖de8 29 e5
♘d5 30 ed ♖×e1+ 31 ♘×e1

♕×d6 32 ♗×g7 ♔×g7 33 ♘d3
♘b6 34 ♕c3+ ♔f6 35 ♕c2 ♘d7
36 a5 c5 37 bc ♖c8 38 ♕b3 ♗c6 39
♘b4 ♖b8 40 ♕a3 ♘e5 (213)
41 ♖d1? (41 ♘×c6) 41 . . . ♗×g2!
42 ♔×g2 ♖×b4 43 ♕×b4 ♕f3+
44 ♔g1 ♕×d1+ 45 ♘f1 ♘f3+ 46
♔g2 ♘e1+ 47 ♔g1 ♘f3+ 48 ♔g2
♘e1+ 49 ♔g1 ½-½

3207　Antoshin–AK

R7: 20.2.1973: Queen's Indian

1 d4 ♘f6 2 c4 e6 3 ♘f3 b6 4 g3 ♗b7
5 ♗g2 ♗e7 6 00 00 7 ♘c3 ♘e4 8
♘×e4 ♗×e4 9 ♘e1 ♗×g2 10
♘×g2 d5 11 ♕a4 ♕d7 12 ♕×d7
♘×d7 13 cd ed 14 ♘f4 ♘f6 15 ♗e3
c5 16 dc bc ½-½

3208　AK–Sax

R8: 21.2.1973: King's Indian

(Notes by Meleghegyi)

1 d4 ♘f6 2 c4 g6 3 ♘c3 d6 4 g3 ♗g7
5 ♗g2 00 6 ♘f3 c5 7 d5 e5 8 00 (8
de?! ♗×e6 9 ♘g5 ♗×c4! 10 ♗×b7
♘bd7) 8 . . . ♘a6 (8 . . . ♘bd7) 9
e4 ♘c7 10 a4 b6 11 ♘e1 ♘h5 12

213
40B
W

214
20B
W

♘d3 (12 f4 ef 13 gf? ♗d4+ 14♔h1
♕h4∓ ∓) 12 . . . f5 13 ef ♗×f5 14
♘e4 ♕d7 15 f3 ♘f6 16 ♘df2
♗×e4 17 fe! a6 18 ♗e3 ♖fb8 (18
. . . b5 19 ♗h3 ♕e7) 19 ♗h3 ♕e7
20 ♕d2 b5 *(214)*

21 b4!? cb 22 ab ab 23 c5 ♖a4 24
♖ac1 ♘ce8 (24 . . . ♘fe8 25 ♘g4
♘f6 26 ♗g5!± ±) 25 c6 ♘c7 26
♖a1 ♘a6 (26 . . . ♖ba8) 27 ♕d3
♘c7 28 ♖ab1 ♘a6 29 ♖a1 ♘c7 30
♕b3 ♖ba8 31 ♖×a4 ♖×a4 32
♗d2 ♘a6 33 ♕d3 ♖a5 (33 . . .
♘c7) 34 ♕e2 ♕a7 35 ♗e3 ♘c5?
36 ♖c1 ♘e8 37 ♕g4! b3 38♔g2 b2
39 ♖b1 ♖a3 40 ♗×c5 dc 41 ♖×b2
♕b8 42 ♕e6+ **1–0**

3209   Forintos–AK

R9: 23.2.1973: QGD

1 d4 ♘f6 2 c4 e6 3 ♘f3 d5 4 ♘c3
♗e7 5 ♗f4 00 6 e3 b6 7 ♗d3 ♗b7 8
00 c5 9 ♕e2 ♘c6 10 dc bc 11 cd ed
12 ♖fd1 ♕a5 13 a3 ♖fd8 14 ♕c2 c4
15 ♗e2 ♗c8 16 ♘e5 ♘×e5 17
♗×e5 ♗e6 18 ♗f3 ♖d7 19 h3
♖ad8 20 ♘e2 ♘e8 21 ♘f4 ♗f6 22
♗×f6 ♘×f6 23 b3 cb 24 ♕×b3 h6
25 ♖d4 ♖c8 26 ♖a4 ♕c5 27 ♕d3
♕c3 28 ♕×c3 ♖×c3 29 ♖a5 ♔f8
30 ♖b1 ♖c8 31 ♖d1 g5 32 ♘h5
♘×h5 33 ♗×h5 ♔e7 34 ♗f3 ♖c3
35 ♖d4 ♔f6 36 ♔h2 ♖c2 37 ♔g3
♖b7 38 ♖b4 ♖×b4 39 ab ♖c4 40
♗×d5 ♗×d5 41 ♖×d5 ♖×b4 42
♖d6+ ♔g7 43 ♖a6 ♖b7 44 h4
♖b4 45 hg hg 46 ♖×a7 ♔g6 47
♖a6+ f6 48 f3 ♖b2 49 e4 ♖e2 50
♔h3 ♔g7 51 g3 ♔g6 52 ♖a3 ♖e1

53 ♔g4 ♖e2 54 ♖b3 ♖e1 55 ♖b4
♖e3 56 ♖b6 ♖e2 57♔h3 ♖e3 58
♔g4 ♖e2 59 ♖b3 ♖e1 60 ♖b4
♖e3 61 f4 ♖×e4 62 ♖×e4 f5+ 63
♔f3 fe+ 64 ♔×e4 ½–½

3210   AK–Adorjan

R10: 24.2.1973: Grünfeld

(Notes by Adorjan)

**1 c4 g6 2 d4 ♘f6 3 ♘c3 d5 4 ♘f3
♗g7 5 ♗g5 ♘e4 6 cd ♘×g5 7
♘×g5 e6 8 ♕d2 h6 9 ♘h3 ed 10
♘f4 00! 11 g3** (11 ♘f×d5 c6∓; 11
e3 c5!) **11 . . . ♘c6!?** (11 . . . c6 12
♗g2 ♗f5 13 00 ♘d7=) **12 e3 ♘e7
13 ♗g2 c5! 14 dc** (14 00 cd 15 ed
♘c6 16 ♘ce2 g5! 17 ♘h5 ♗h8 18
f4 ♗g4 19 ♗f3 ♗×f3 20 ♖×f3
g4∓) **14 . . . d4 15 ♘d1** (15 ♖d1
♗g4!; 15 000 dc!?) **15 . . . de 16
♘×e3 ♕×d2+ 17 ♔×d2 ♗×b2
18 ♖ab1 ♗a3!** (18 . . . ♗d4 19
♖fc1±; 18 . . . ♖d8+ 19♔e2 ♗a3
20 ♗×b7 ♗×b7 21 ♖×b7 ♗×c5
22 ♖c1 ♗d6 23 ♘d3±) **19 ♘d3
♖d8 20 ♔c3!** (20 ♔c2 ♘f5!; 20
♔e2 ♘f5!) **20 . . . a5!** (20 . . . ♗e6
21 ♖×b7 ♘d5+ 22 ♗×d5 ♗×d5
23 ♘×d5 ♖×d5 24♔c4 ♖ad8 25
♘b4±) **21 ♖hd1 ♗e6 22 ♗×b7**
(22 ♖×b7 ♘d5+ 23 ♘×d5 ♗×d5
24 ♗×d5 ♖×d5=) **22 . . . ♖ab8
23 c6 ♗d6 24 ♗c4 ♘d5+ 25♔b2
♘e7 26 ♔c3** (26 ♗×a5 ♘×c6!)
26 . . . ♘d5+ 27♔c2? (27♔b2=)
**27 . . . ♗f5 28 a3 ♗c7 29 ♖b5
♘e7 30 f3 h5?** (time-trouble; 30
. . . ♖d4! 31 ♘e3?! ♖bd8∓ ∓; 31

♔c3 ♖bd8 32 ♘cb2∓) **31 ♔c3 ♘d5+ 32 ♔b2 ♘e7 33 ♘f2 ♖×d1 34 ♖×d1 h4! 35 gh♗ d3 36 ♔c3 ♗e2 37 ♘de3 ♗×f3 38 ♘×a5** *(215)*

215
38W
B

38 ... ♗×a5 ?? *(38 ... f5∓)* **39 ♖×a5 ♘×c6** *(39 ... ♗×c6)* **40 ♖a8!± ± ♖×a8 41 ♗×a8 ♘e5 42 ♗×f3 ♘×f3 43 a4 ♘e5 1-0**

3211 Ribli-AK

R11: 25.2.1973: Sicilian

1 e4 c5 2 ♘f3 e6 3 d4 cd 4 ♘×d4 ♘c6 5 ♘c3 ♕c7 6 ♗e2 ♘f6 7 00 a6 8 ♗e3 ♗b4 9 ♘a4 00 10 ♘×c6 dc 11 ♗b6 ♕f4 12 ♗d3 ♘d7 13 g3 ♕f6 14 a3 ♗e7 15 ♗c7 e5 16 b4 b5 17 ♘b6 ♘×b6 18 ♗×b6 ♗h3 19 ♖e1 ♖fb8 20 ♗e3 a5 21 c3 ab 22 cb ♖d8 23 ♗b6 ♖d7 24 ♕c2 ♖b8 25 ♗a5 c5 26 ♗e2 c4 27 a4 ba 28 ♖×a4 ♖d4 29 b5 ♖×b5 30 ♗c3 ♖d8 31 ♖d1 ♖c8 32 ♖×c4 *(216)* 32 ... ♖bc5? (32 ... ♖×c4 33 ♗×c4 ♕f3 34 ♗f1 ♗×f1 35 ♖×f1 ♖c5 36 ♖c1 h5!∓ ∓ – Geller) 33 ♖×c5 ♗×c5 34 ♗f1 ♗×f1 35 ♔×f1 ♗×f2 36 ♕×f2 ♖×c3 37

♔g2 h5 38 ♖d5 ♔h7 39 ♕f5+ ♕×f5 40 gf f6 41 h4 c6 42 ♔f3 g6 43 fg+ ♔×g6 44 ♖d8 ♖c3+ 45 ♔f2 ♖f5 46 ♖h8 ♖c2+ 47 ♔e3 ♔g4 48 ♖g8+ ♔f5 49 ♖h8 ♖c3+

216
32W
B

50 ♔f2 e4 51 ♖g8 ♖a3 52 ♖e8 ♖a4 53 ♖g8 ♖a2+ 54 ♔e3 ♖g2 55 ♖g7 ♔e5 56 ♖e7+ ♔d5 57 ♖d7+ ♔e6 58 ♖a7 ♖×g3+ 59 ♔×e4 ♖g4+ 60 ♔f3 ♔f5 61 ♖a5+ ♔g6 62 ♖b5 ♖×h4 63 ♖a5 ♖h1 64 ♔g2 ♖h4 65 ♔f3 ♖b4 66 ♖c5 ♖b8 67 ♖c4 ♔g5 68 ♖c5+ f5 69 ♖c4 h4 70 ♔g2 ♖b2+ 71 ♔h3 ♖b3+ 72 ♔g2 ♖g3+ 73 ♔f2 g4 74 ♖c8 h3 75 ♖a8 ♖b4 76 ♔g3 ♖b3+ 77 ♔h2 f4 78 ♖g8+ ♔h4 79 ♖h8+ ♔g4 80 ♖g8+ ♔f5 81 ♖f8+ ♔e4 82 ♖e8+ ♔f3 83 ♖f8 ♖b7 84 ♖a8 ♖e7 85 ♖a6 ♖e1 86 ♖a8 ♔f2 87 ♔×h3 f3 88 ♖a2+ ♔e2 89 ♖a1 ½-½

3212 AK-Vaganian

R12: 26.2.1973: French

(Notes by Karpov)

1 e4 e6 2 d4 d5 3 ♘d2 c5 4 ♘gf3

♘c6 5 ed ed 6 ♗b5 ♗d6 7 dc ♗×c5 8 00 ♘ge7 9 ♘b3 ♗b6 10 ♖e1 00 11 ♗g5!? h6 12 ♗h4 g5 (12 ... f6!? 13 ♗g3 ♘f5 with an unclear position) 13 ♗g3 ♘f5 (if 13 ... ♗g4 14 ♕d3 followed by ♘fd4) 14 ♕d2 ♘×g3 15 hg ♕f6 16 c3 ♗f5 17 ♕×d5 ♖ad8 18 ♕c4 ♗d3 19 ♕a4 ♗×b5 20 ♕×b5 g4 21 ♘fd4 ♘×d4 22 cd (22 ♘×d4? a6 23 ♕h5 ♗×d4 24 cd ♖×d4) 22 ... a6 23 ♕h5 ♗×d4 24 ♕×g4+ ♕g7 25 ♕f3 ♗×b2 26 ♖ad1 b6 27 ♕b7 ♖×d1! 28 ♖×d1 ♕g4 29 ♖b1 ♖d8 30 ♕×a6 ♖d1+ 31 ♖×d1 ♕×d1+ 32 ♕f1 ♕c2 33 ♕b5 ♗a3 34 ♕d5 *(217)*

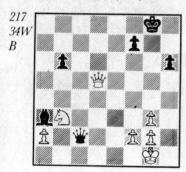

217
34W
B

34 ... ♗f8 (34 ... ♗c5!) 35 ♕d2 ♕e4 36 ♔h2 ♗c5 37 ♘c1 ♔g7 38 ♘d3 ♕d4 39 ♕e2 ♗d6?! (39 ... ♕c4!?) 40 ♔h3 ♕d5 41 ♘f4 ♗×f4 42 gf ♔f8 43 ♔g3 b5 44 ♕b2 ♕d3+ 45 ♔h4 ♕d8+ 46 ♔g3 ♕d3+ 47 ♔h2 ♔g8 48 a3 ♕d6 49 ♕b4 ♕f6 50 f3! ♕h4+ 51 ♔g1 ♕h5? (51 ... ♕f6) 52 ♕e7 ♔h7 (if 52 ... ♕g6 53 ♕e8+ and 54 ♕×b5± ; or 52 ... ♕f5 53 ♕e8+ ♔g7 54 ♕e5+ ♕×e5 55 fe ♘g6 56

f4 ♔f5 57 g3 h5 58 ♔f2 ♔g4 59 ♔e3!♔×g3 60 f5 h4 61 e6 f2 62 fe h3 63 e7 h2 64 e8♕ h1♕ 65 ♕g8+ ♔h3 66 ♕h8+ ± ±) 53 g4 ♕h3 54 ♕×f7+ ♔h8 55 ♕e8+ ♔h7 56 ♕e4+ ♔g8 57 f5 ♕g3+ 58 ♔f1 ♕h3+ 59 ♔e2 ♕g2+ **1-0**

3213 Bilek–AK

R13: 27.2.1973: English

1 c4 c5 2 g3 g6 3 ♗g2 ♗g7 4 ♘c3 ♘c6 5 e3 e6 6 ♘ge2 ♘ge7 7 00 00 8 d4 cd 9 ♘×d4 d5 10 cd ♘×d4 11 ed ♘×d5 12 ♘×d5 ed 13 ♗e3 ♗e6 14 ♕d2 ♕d7 ½-½

3214 AK–Csom

R14: 1.3.1973: Sicilian

(Notes by Geller)

1 e4 c5 2 ♘f3 d6 3 d4 cd 4 ♕×d4 ♘c6 5 ♗b5 ♕d7!? 6 ♗e3 a6 7 ♗a4 b5 8 ♗b3 ♘a5 9 00 e6 10 ♖d1 ♗b7 11 ♘c3 ♗e7 12 e5 ♘×b3 13 ab ♖d8 (A questionable decision. He should have played 13 ... ♕c6, creating pressure on the a8-h1 diagonal and controlling the e4 square. In that case 14 ed ♗×d6 15 ♕d4 is not difficult on account of 15 ... 000 and the line 16 ♕×g7 ♘e7 17 ♕×f7 ♖hg8 leads to a suspect position for White.) 14 ♘e4! ♕c6 15 ♘×d6✝ ♗×d6 16 ed ♖×d6 17 ♗d2 ♘e7 18 ♗b4 ♖d5 (18 ... ♖d7 is more reliable.) 19 c4! bc 20 bc ♕×c4 21 ♗×e7 ♔×e7 22 ♘e5 ♕e4? (He should have defended by 22 ... ♕b5.) 23 ♕g5+ ♔f8 *(218)*

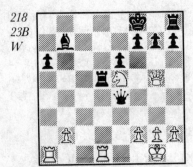

218
23B
W

24 f3 (White wins the exchange, but now he obtains a technically difficult ending, ultimately finishing up as a draw. A win is reached with 24 ♘d7+ ♔e8 25 ♕×g7 ♔×d7 26 ♕×h8 ♕×g2+ 27 ♔×g2 ♖×d1+ 28 f3 ♖×a1 29 ♕×h7 and the h-pawn decides the game's outcome.) 24 ... ♕×e5 25 ♕×e5 ♖×e5 26 ♖d8+ ♔e7 27 ♖×h8 ♖g5! 28 ♖a3 ♖b5? (28 ... h5!) 29 ♖×h7 ♔f6 30 b3 ♖b6 31 ♖h4 ♗d5 32 b4 g5 33 ♖g4 ♔f5 34 ♖a5 f6 35 ♔f2 ♔e5 36 ♔e3 ♖c6 37 ♖c5 ♖b6 38 ♖d4 f5 39 h4? f4+ 40 ♔d3 gh 41 ♔c3 ♖b7 42 ♖d2 ♖h7 ½-½

3215   Velimirović–AK

R15: 2.3.1973: Spanish

1 e4 e5 2 ♘f3 ♘c6 3 ♗b5 a6 4 ♗a4 ♘f6 5 OO ♗e7 6 ♖e1 b5 7 ♗b3 d6 8 c3 OO 9 h3 ♘a5 10 ♗c2 c5 11 d4 ♕c7 12 ♘bd2 ♘c6 13 ♘b3 ♗b7 14 d5 ♘b8 15 c4 ♘bd7 16 ♗d2 b4 17 ♘c1 ♘e8 18 ♘d3 g6 19 ♗h6 ♘g7 20 g4 ½-½

33 USSR National Teams Match-Tournament
Moscow, 24–30.4.1973

Karpov	1 ½		Karpov	1 ½
Spassky	0 ½		Taimanov	0 ½

Karpov played on board one for the USSR Youth team (the other two teams were USSR-1 and USSR-2), and captured the board prize with 3/4 (this was jointly the absolute best result). Karpov also won the best game prize for his win against Spassky. Team results: USSR-1 23½, USSR Youth 18½, USSR-2 18.

3301 Taimanov–AK

R1: 24.4.1973: Nimzo-Indian

(Notes by I. Zaitsev)

1 d4 ♘f6 2 c4 e6 3 ♘c3 ♗b4 4 e3 c5 5 ♗d3 00 6 ♘f3 d5 7 00 dc 8 ♗×c4 cd 9 ed·b6 10 ♕e2 ♗b7 11 ♖d1 ♘bd7 12 ♗d2 ♖c8 13 ♗a6 ♗×a6 14 ♕×a6 ♗×c3 15 bc ♖c7 16 ♖ac1 ♕c8 17 ♕a4 *(219)*

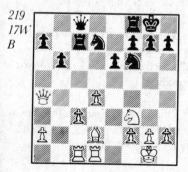

219
17W
B

17 ... ♖c4! 18 ♕×a7 (Now White has a material advantage, Black a positional advantage.) 18 ... ♕c6 19 ♕a3 ♖c8 20 h3 h6 21 ♖b1 ♖a4 22 ♕b3 ♘d5 23 ♖dc1 ♖c4 24 ♖b2 (On 24 ♕b5 Karpov intended 24 ... ♕×b5 25 ♖×b5 ♖a8 26 ♖c2 f6 27 ♔f1 ♔f7 28 ♔e2 e5 29 ♘d3 ♖aa4 30 ♖b3 ♔e6 and White is suddenly threatened with 31 g4 e4+ ! 32 ♔×e4 ♘c5 mate!) 24 ... f6 25 ♖e1 ♔f7 26 ♕d1 ('I cannot be worse here', Taimanov stated definitely.) 26 ... ♘f8 27 ♖b3 ♘g6 28 ♕b1 ♖a8 29 ♖e4 (Perhaps this was the right time to 'mix it' with 29 ♕d3 ♖×a2 30 ♖×e6!? ♔×e6 31 ♕×g6.) 29 ... ♖ca4 30 ♖b2 ♘f8 31 ♕d3 ♖c4 32 ♖e1 ♖a3 (32 ... ♘g6 33 ♖×e6!?; 32 ... ♘×c3 33 ♗×c3

♖×c3 34 ♖×b6 ♖×d3 35 ♖×c6).
33 ♕b1 ♘g6 34 ♖c1 (White goes
over entirely to defence. 34 ♕d3
deserved consideration – setting a
trap: 34 . . ♘×c3? 35 ♖b3!, and
intending to strike a blow against
e6: 36 ♖×e6.) **34 ... ♘×c3 35
♕d3 ♘e2+ ! 36 ♕×e2 ♖×c1+ 37
♗×c1 ♕×c1+ 38♔h2 ?** (38 ♘e1
was essential.) **38 ... ♖×f3! 39 gf
♘h4! 0–1** (time) (40 ♖×b6?
♕c7+ ; 40 ♔g3 ♕g5+ ; 40 ♖b3
♕g5! 41 ♕f1 ♕f4+ 42♔g1 and 42
... ♘×f3+ or 42 ... ♕×d4)

3302 AK–Spassky

R3: 26.4.1973: Spanish

(Notes by Karpov)

The prize of the weekly *64* for the
best game of the match tournament
was awarded to Karpov for this
game. The prize was a cut crystal
(or glass) bowl – KJO'C.
1 e4 e5 2 ♘f3 ♘c6 3 ♗b5 a6 4 ♗a4
♘f6 5 00 ♗e7 6 ♖e1 b5 7 ♗b3 d6 8
c3 00 9 h3 ♘b8 10 d3 ♗b7 11 ♘bd2
♘bd7 12 ♘f1 ♘c5 13 ♗c2 ♖e8 14
♘g3 ♗f8 15 b4 ♘cd7 16 d4

All this has been seen more than
once. Now White is forced to push
the d-pawn, otherwise Black will
intercept the initiative with the
liberating pawn advance d6–d5.

16 ...   h6
17 ♗d2   ♘b6
18 ♗d3   g6

Spassky deviates from my game
against Gligorić (3108) in which 18

... ♖c8 was played.

19 ♕c2

A regrouping of forces. The
queen frees d1 for the rooks and, at
the same time, protects the e4
square.

19 ...   ♘fd7

If White has surplus defence of
c4, it is essential to organize rapid
pressure against the neighbouring
d4 square with the help of the
bishop on g7.

20 ♖ad1   ♗g7
21 de

Here I thought for more than 30
minutes. Black has disposed his
pieces very adroitly and, therefore,
it is not easy to get any advantage.
The standard plan of a K-side
attack, or undermining the centre
by f2–f4, will not do, since in each
case Black has time to strike a
counter-blow in the centre with d6–
d5. I came to the conclusion that
White is almost forced to carry out
this central exchange.

21 ...   de

This move undoubtedly cannot
be called a mistake, but maybe one
should exchange knights.

22 c4

This follows straight away; there
is no time to prepare it, for example
22 ♗e3 ♕e7 23 ♘d2 c5 with
equality.

22 ...   bc

On 22 ... c5 a piece sacrifice was
possible: 23 cb c4 24 ♗×c4 ♖c8 25
♗×f7+ ♔×f7 26 ♕b3+ .

23 ♗×c4   ♕e7 *(220)*

But this is an inaccuracy. Allowing the dangerous 'Spanish bishop' to escape with his life, Black subjects himself to great difficulties. After 23 ... ♘×c4 24 ♕×c4 chances would have been level.

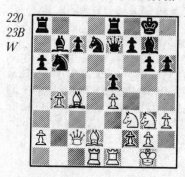

220
23B
W

24 ♗b3! c5
25 a4

Of course, in making this move, I foresaw the exchange sacrifice and considered its consequences. As a matter of fact, I had decided on this line a move earlier, and there is no going back now, nor is there any need to do so.

25 ... c4

25 ... cb and 25 ... ♖c8 were both bad on account of 26 a5, Black replying, according to his 25th move, either 26 ... ♖c8 or 26 ... cb, and then 27 ♕a2 ♘a8 28 ♗×b4!

26 ♗a2 ♗c6
27 a5 ♗a4
28 ♕c1 ♘c8

28 ... ♗×d1 was hardly better for Black: 29 ♖×d1 ♘a4 30 ♗×h6 ♗×h6 31 ♕×h6 and not 31... ♘c3 because of 32 ♗×c4 with the

threat of 33 ♕×g6+, while on 31 ... ♘f8 White has excellent attacking prospects with 32 ♖c1.

29 ♗×h6 ♗×d1
30 ♖×d1 ♘d6?

After this move there follows an utterly unexpected dénouement.

30...♗×h6 also loses: 31 ♕×h6 ♘d6 32 ♘g5 ♘f8 33 ♘h5 gh 34 ♖×d6 ♖ac8 35 ♖f6.

30 ... ♖a7 appears to be the best, but even then, after 31 ♗×g7 ♔×g7 32 ♕×c4, White gets more than enough compensation for the exchange.

31 ♗×g7 ♔×g7 *(221)*

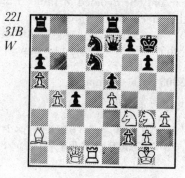

221
31B
W

32 ♕g5!

Here is the surprise! White quite unexpectedly offers the exchange of queens, which Black cannot accept in view of the piece that would be lost.

Black would suddenly be winning after 32 ♕d2 ♖ad8 33 ♕×d6? ♘f8.

32 ... f6

32 ... ♖ac8 only drags out the struggle; after 33 ♖×d6 ♕×g5 34

♘×g5 ♘f6 35 ♘e2 c3 36 ♗×f7, White ought to realize his material advantage.

33 ♕g4   ♔h7

The only defence against 34 ♖×d6 and ♘f5+ , but the position is quite hopeless.

34 ♘h4   **1-0**

Some might think this a somewhat premature surrender, but, with a survey of the following variations, they will be convinced that Black's position is hopelessly indefensible:

a) 34 ... ♖g8 35 ♗×c4 ♖g7 36 ♖×d6 ♕×d6 37 ♘hf5 and mate can only be avoided at the cost of the queen (37 ... ♕d1+) or;

b) 34 ... ♘f8 35 ♘×g6 with 36 ♕h5+ and 37 ♖×d6 to follow.

3303   AK-Taimanov

R4: 27.4.1973: Sicilian

1 e4 c5 2 ♘f3 ♘c6 3 d4 cd 4 ♘×d4 e6 5 ♘b5 d6 6 c4 ♘f6 7 ♘1c3 a6 8 ♘a3 ♗e7 9 ♗e2 00 10 00 b6 11 ♗e3 ♗b7 12 ♖c1 ♖c8 13 ♕d2 ♘e5 14 ♕d4 ♘ed7 15 ♖fd1 ♖e8 16 ♘c2 ♕c7 17 ♔h1 h6 18 f3 d5 19 cd ed 20 ed ♗c5 21 ♕d2 ♗×e3 22 ♘×e3 ♕f4 23 ♘g4 ♘×d5 24 ♗×a6 ♗×a6 25 ♕×d5 ♘c5 26 ♖b1 ♗b7 27 ♕d2 ♘e6 28 ♘b5 h5 29 ♘f2 ♕a4 30 ♘c3 ♕h4 31 ♘fe4 ♗×e4 32 ♘×e4 ♖ed8 33 ♕e3 b5 34 ♖dc1 ♖a8 35 a3 ♖d4 36 ♖d1 ♖ad8 37 ♘c3 b4 38 ab ♖×b4 39 ♘d5 ♖b5 40 ♕e4 ♕×e4 41 fe ♖b3 42 ♘e7+ ♔f8 43 ♖×d8+ ♘×d8 44 ♘d5 ♔e8 ½-½

3304   Spassky-AK

R6: 29.4.1973: English

1 c4 ♘f6 2 ♘c3 c5 3 ♘f3 d5 4 cd ♘×d5 5 e3 ♘×c3 6 bc g6 7 d4 ♗g7 8 ♗d3 ♕c7 9 00 00 10 ♗a3 ♘bd7 11 e4 e5 12 ♗b5 a6 13 ♗×d7 ♗×d7 14 ♗×c5 ♖fe8 15 ♘×e5 ♗b5 16 c4 ♗×e5 17 de ♕×c5 18 cb ab ½-½

34 Leningrad Interzonal 2–27.6.1973

		1	2	3	4	5	6	7	8	9	0	1	2	3	4	5	6	7	8	
1	**Karpov**	×	½	½	1	½	½	1	1	½	½	1	½	1	1	1	1	1	1	**13½**
2	Korchnoi	½	×	1	½	1	1	½	½	1	1	1	1	1	½	0	1	1	1	**13½**
3	R. Byrne	½	0	×	½	1	½	½	½	1	½	1	1	1	½	1	1	1	1	**12½**
4	Smejkal	0	½	½	×	0	0	½	1	1	½	0	1	1	1	1	1	1	1	**11**
5	Larsen	½	0	0	1	×	1	1	0	½	0	0	1	½	1	1	½	1	1	**10**
6	Hübner	½	0	½	1	0	×	½	1	½	1	½	1	1	½	½	½	0	1	**10**
7	Kuzmin	0	½	½	½	0	½	×	0	½	1	½	½	½	1	1	1	1	½	**9½**
8	Gligorić	0	½	½	0	1	0	1	×	½	0	½	½	1	½	½	0	1	1	**8½**
9	Taimanov	½	0	0	0	½	½	½	½	×	½	½	1	½	½	1	½	1	½	**8½**
10	Tal	½	0	½	½	1	0	0	1	½	×	1	1	0	½	0	1	0	1	**8½**
11	Quinteros	0	0	0	1	1	½	½	½	½	0	×	0	½	0	½	1	½	1	**7½**
12	Radulov	½	0	0	0	0	0	½	½	0	0	1	×	1	1	½	½	1	1	**7½**
13	Torre	0	0	0	0	½	0	½	0	½	1	½	0	×	½	½	1	1	1	**7**
14	Uhlmann	0	½	½	0	0	½	0	½	½	½	1	0	½	×	½	½	½	1	**7**
15	Rukavina	0	1	0	0	0	½	0	½	0	1	½	½	½	½	×	0	1	½	**6½**
16	Tukmakov	0	0	0	0	½	½	0	1	½	0	0	½	0	½	1	×	½	1	**6**
17	Estevez	0	0	0	0	0	1	0	0	0	1	½	0	0	½	0	½	×	1	**4½**
18	Cuellar	0	0	0	0	0	0	½	0	½	0	0	0	0	0	½	0	0	×	**1½**

The tournament, played in the Dzerzhinsky House of Culture, was a very great success for Karpov.

When he was interviewed after the Interzonal, Korchnoi was full of praise for the maturity of Karpov's play: 'He is becoming a great tournament fighter who does not avoid risks when they are necessary and who is capable of fighting for a win in each individual game. In this he is very practical and he does not make big mistakes. His play reminds me of Spassky in his better years – his level of concentration in each game, his evenness of play in all stages of the game and the way in which he plays without making blunders.

'It might appear that Karpov's performance in this Interzonal was uneven. In the second half he scored more points than in the first. In fact he just happened to have more difficult opponents in the first half of the tournament.'

3401 Estevez–AK

R1: 3.6.1973: QGD

'Equal for a long time, but, on move 33, the Cuban mistakenly exchanged queens to go into a marginally worse ending. He could still have held the game by blockading Karpov's b-pawn; he allowed the black bishop pair too much activity.' *World Championship Interzonals.*

1 d4 ♘f6 2 c4 e6 3 ♘f3 d5 4 ♘c3 ♗e7 5 ♗g5 OO 6 e3 h6 7 ♗h4 b6 8 ♗e2 ♗b7 9 ♗×f6 ♗×f6 10 cd ed 11 b4 (11 OO!?) 11 . . . c6 12 OO a5 13 a3 ♕d6 14 ♕b3 ab 15 ab ♘d7 16 ♖fd1 ♖×a1 17 ♖×a1 ♗e7 (Karpov wants to play for a win and is not afraid of dancing on the edge of a precipice. 17 . . . ♖a8 18 ♖×a8+ ♗×a8 19 ♕a4 ♗b7 20 ♕a7 ♕b8, with the likely result a draw, was also possible.) 18 ♖a7 ♖b8 19 ♘a2 ♗c8 20 ♕c2 ♗f6 21 ♘c1 ♘f8 22 ♘d3 ♗f5 23 ♕a4 ♘d7 24 ♖a8 (24 ♕a6!? threatening 25 b5!?) 24 . . . ♖×a8 25 ♕×a8+ ♔h7 26 ♕a6 g6 27 ♕b7 ♔g7 28 h3 h5 29 ♕a7 ♗d8 30 ♕b7 (30 ♘de5 is met by 30 . . . ♗e7 followed by . . . f6, . . . ♗f5–e6–f7 and . . . g5.) 30 . . . ♕c7 31 ♕a8 ♗e7 *(222)*

32 ♘de5 (White would probably do better to play 32 b5 cb 33 ♕×d5

222
31B
W

b4 34 ♘de5 ♘×e5 35 ♘×e5 ♗f6 with a sharp game.) 32 . . . ♗×b4 33 ♕×c6?! (33 ♘×c6! ♗d6 34 ♗b5=) 33 . . . ♕×c6 34 ♘×c6 ♗d6 35 ♗b5?! (35 ♘a7 with good drawing chances) 35 . . . ♘f6 36 ♘d2 ♘e8! 37 f3 ♘c7 38 ♗e2 ♗c2! 39 ♔f2 ♗a4 40 ♘e5 b5 41 ♘d3 (s) (adjournment 6.6.1973) 41 . . . h4! 42 ♘b2 (42 e4!? and ♔e3 or 42 ♘c1!? followed by ♗d3 and ♘db3 would have been better.) 42 . . . ♗b4 43 ♘b1 ♗b3 44 ♗d3 ♗c4! 45 e4 g5 46 ed ♗×d5 47 ♘d1 ♗c6 48 ♘bc3 ♗d7 49 ♘e4 ♗e7 50 ♘c5? (50 ♔e2∓) 50 . . . ♗×c5!∓ ∓ 51 dc ♘e6 52 ♘c3 b4 53 ♘e4 b3 54 ♘d2 ♘×c5 55 ♗b1 ♔f6 **0–1** (time) (3·30 – 2·56)

3402 AK–Hübner

R2: 4.6.1973: Sicilian

(Notes by Hübner)

1 e4 c5 2 ♘f3 e6 3 d4 cd 4 ♘×d4

**a6 5 ♗d3 ♘f6 6 00 ♕c7 7 ♕e2 d6
8 c4 g6 9 ♘c3** (9 b3!?) **9 ... ♗g7
10 ♗e3 00 11 ♖ac1** (11 f4! and if 11
... ♘c6 then 12 ♘×c6 bc 13 f5!) **11
... ♘c6 12 ♘×c6 bc 13 f4** (13 c5?
d5 14 ed ♘×d5 15 ♘×d5 ed∓) **13
... c5 14 ♖fd1 ♗b7** (14 ...
♖b8!?) **15 a3 ♗c6 16 b4** (16 e5 de
17 ♗×c5 ♗f3 18 ♕×f3 ♕×c5+ 19
♔h1 ef 20 ♕×f4 a5∓) **16 ... cb 17
ab ♕b7 18 e5** (18 b5 ab 19 cb
♗×e4 20 ♘×e4 ♘×e4 21 ♗×e4
♕×e4 22 ♖×d6 ♗a2 23 ♖d2
♗d4!∓∓; or 18 ♗d2 ♕×b4 and
(1) 19 ♘b5 ♕c5+ 20 ♗e3 ♕h5∓;
(2) 19 ♘d5 ♕b8 20 ♘e7+ ♔h8 21
♘×c6 ♕b6+ 22 ♘d4! ♘d7 23 e5
de 24 c5 ♘×c5 25 ♖b1 ♕d8!) **18
... de 19 fe ♘d7 20 b5 ab 21 cb
♗d5 22 ♗d4 ♕b8 23 ♖e1 ♗b7
24 b6 ♖d8** (24 ... ♖c8 25 ♗b5
♘c5 26 ♖b1±) **25 ♗b5 ♖a5! 26
♕e3 ♗a8?** (26 ... ♗a8! and 27
... ♕b7) **27 ♕f2 ♗a6 28 ♖b1
♗×b5 29 ♖×b5?** (29 ♘×b5! ♕d5
30 ♘d6 ♘×e5·31 ♗×e5 ♗×e5 32
♕×f7+ ♔h8 33 ♘e8±±) **29 ...
♖×b5 30 ♘×b5 ♕a5 31 ♘d6**
(223)

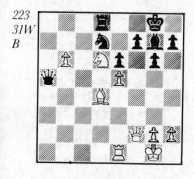

223
31W
B

31 ... ♘×e5! 32 ♗×e5 (32 ♘b7?
♘f3+! 33 gf ♕g5+ ∓∓; not 32 ...
♘g4? 33 ♘×a5 ♗×d4 34 ♕×d4
♖×d4 35 ♖b1±±) **32 ... ♖d6
33 ♗×g7** (33 ♗×d6? ♗d4!; 33 b7
♖b6! and (1) 34 ♖a1 ♗×e5 35
♖×a5 ♖b1+; (2) 34 b8♕+ ♖×b8
35 ♗×b8 ♗d4) **33 ... ♔×g7 34
♖b1 ♖d8 35 ♕b2+ ♔g8** (35 ...
e5!?) **36 b7 ♖b8** (36 ... ♕c5+! 37
♔h1 ♖b8 38 ♖c1? ♖×b7; 38 ♖a1
♕c6) **37 ♕c2 ♔g7 38 ♕c8 ♕a2
39 ♕c3+ ♔g8 40 ♖a1 ♕d5 41
♕c8+** (s) ½-½ (2.37 - 2.27) (41 ...
♔g7 42 ♕×b8 ♕d4+ 43 ♔f1
♕×a1+ 44 ♔f2 ♕d4+=).

3403   Tukmakov–AK

R3: 5.6.1973: Spanish

(Notes by Karpov)

1 e4 e5 2 ♘f3 ♘c6 3 ♗b5 a6 4 ♗a4
♘f6 5 00 ♗e7 6 ♖e1 b5 7 ♗b3 d6 8
c3 00 9 h3 ♘b8 10 d4 ♘bd7 11 c4 c6
12 ♗g5

In our game in the 1971 Alekhine
Memorial, Tukmakov played 12 cb
ab 13 ♘c3 ♗a6 14 de de 15 ♗g5
but did not achieve anything with
it. So he decided to change the
order of moves. However, I doubt
whether this innovation will find
many followers.

12 ...   h6

Opening manuals state that
Black also has a good game after 12
... bc 13 ♗×c4 ♘×e4 14 ♗×e7
♕×e7 15 ♖×e4 d5 16 ♖e2 dc. I
think that 12 ... h6 is stronger and

even allows Black to count on some advantage.

    13 ♗h4   ♘h5!

The dark-squared bishops are exchanged and the knight gets to f4, where it can harass the white king.

    14 ♗×e7   ♕×e7
    15 cb   ab
    16 ♘c3

This is a serious inaccuracy, allowing Black to intercept definitively the initiative. The modest 16 ♘bd2 should have been chosen.

    16 ...   b4
    17 ♘b1

The knight would be clumsily placed on e2.

    17 ...   ♘f4
    18 ♘bd2   ed
    19 ♘×d4   ♘e5! *(224)*

224
19B
W

Black's pieces have taken up ideal positions. The centrally placed knights keep almost the whole of the board under control. White's king is in difficulties. There is also an unpleasant threat of 20 ... ♕g5; with his following move White defends against that particular assault.

    20 ♘2f3   ♕f6
    21 ♘×e5

He must submit to the opening of the d-file, otherwise White would find it extremely difficult to unravel the tangle of central pieces.

    21 ...   de
    22 ♘f5

Practically forced. 22 ♘f3 is bad because of 22 ... ♖d8 23 ♕c2 ♘×h3+, while after 22 ♘e2 Black has the sacrificial line: 22 ... ♖d8 23 ♕c2 ♘×h3+ 24 gh ♕f3.

    22 ...   ♗×f5
    23 ef   ♖ad8

Acquiring a pawn (23 ... ♕×f5) would lose the initiative and, after 24 ♕f3, trying to convert the extra pawn would be a protracted business. I wanted more than that.

    24 ♕f3   ♖d2
    25 ♖e3

25 ♖ac1 loses to 25 ... ♕×f5 26 ♖×c6? ♘×h3+! 27 ♕×h3 ♕×f2+ and 28 ... ♕×e1, but after 25 ♖ad1 Black can simply take the pawn – 25 ... ♖×b2. Tukmakov seeks counterplay by attacking the e-pawn.

    25 ...   ♖×b2
    26 ♖ae1   ♖e8
    27 ♖e4   ♘d5
    28 ♕g3   ♘c3
    29 ♖×b4

White also loses the exchange after 29 ♖×e5 ♘e2+ (but not 29 ... ♖×e5 30 ♕×e5) 30 ♖1×e2 ♖×e2.

    29 ...   ♘e2+
    30 ♖×e2   ♖×e2

31 Rb7?

White misses his last chance to fight for a draw – 31 Qg6!

31 ...	Re7
32 Rb8+	Kh7
33 Kf1	

Of course, if 33 Qg6+, Black should play 33 ... Q×g6, avoiding perpetual check.

33 ...   Rd2

0–1

2·22   1·55

Black has avoided the last snare: 33 ... Rb2 34 Qg6+ !! fg (or 34 ... Q×g6 35 fg+ K×g6 36 B×f7+ K×f7 37 R×b2=) 35 Bg8+ Kh8 36 Bb3+ with perpetual check. White can also draw after 33 ... Re4 with 34 Qg6+ !! Q×g6 35 fg+ K×g6 36 Bc2.

3404 AK–Korchnoi

R4: 7.6.1973: Pirc

1 e4 d6 2 d4 Nf6 3 Nc3 g6 4 Nf3 Bg7 5 Be2 00 6 00 Nc6 7 d5 Nb8 8 h3 c6 9 a4 a5 10 Bg5 Bd7 11 Re1 Na6 12 dc B×c6 13 Bb5 Nb4 14 Qe2 h6 15 Bf4 e5 16 Bh2 Rc8?! (16 ... Nd7! 17 Radl Nc5 18 Rd2 Qe7 is probably good for Black.) 17 Radl Qe7 18 Bd2 h5!? ½-½ (1·45 - 1·40) (19 Rfdl Rfd8 20 Qe3 Qf8!; 19 Qe3!? Ng4! 20 hg hg 21 Qg5 Q×g5 22 N×g5 Bh6 23 R×d6! – Nitkin, 'Karpov and Korchnoi spent the next three to four hours in the special players' room, out of reach of the swarming journalists, fiercely debating some of the later positions of their game.'–Wade.)

3405 Taimanov–AK

R5: 8.6.1973: Nimzo-Indian

(Notes by Shamkovich)

1 d4 Nf6 2 c4 e6 3 Nc3 Bb4 4 e3 00 5 Ne2 d5 6 a3 Be7 7 cd N×d5 8 Bd2 TN N×c3 9 N×c3 c5 10 dc B×c5 11 Ne4 Be7 12 Bc3 Nc6 13 Bb5 (13 Bc4!, threatening 14 Qg4, e.g. 13 ... Q×d1+ 14 R×d1 Rd8 15 Ke2 b6 16 R×d8+ B×d8 17 Rd1 Be7 18 Nd6) 13 ... a6 14 B×c6 bc 15 Qf3 Qc7 16 Rc1 Rb8 17 00 f6 (17 ... e5, with ... f6 and ... Be6 to follow, would have been better.) 18 Qe2 Rd8 19 Rc2 Qb6 (19 ... e5 20 Qc4+ Rd5? 21 Bb4!) 20 Rfcl Qb5 21 Qe1! (threatening 22 Ba5) 21 ... f5!? (21 ... e5 fails to 22 Ba5 Rd5 23 Bc7 Bf5 24 Nc3 and 21 ... Rd5 to 22 Bd4!) 22 Nd2 Bb7 23 f3 (if 23 Nf3 then 23 ... c5 24 Ne5 Be4! with a good game for Black) 23 ... Bf8 24 Qg3 Rbc8 25 Be5 Rd5 26 Nc4 Rcd8 27 h4 c5= 28 Kh2 Rd1 29 Qf4 R×c1 30 R×c1 Bd5 31 Rc3 Rd7 32 b3 B×c4 33 Q×c4 (33 bc? Qb1, threatening 34 ... Rd1) 33 ... Q×c4 34 R×c4 Rd3 35 Rc3 c4! (A very sly move, played in his opponent's time-trouble.) 36 R×c4 (if 36 b4?? Bd6!∓ and if 36 bc Bd6! 37 f4 R×c3 38 B×c3 B×a3 with the better ending for Black) 36 ... R×e3 37 f4 R×b3 38

a4! (The threat is 39 ♖ c6.) 38 . . .
♗ e7 (not 38 . . . ♖ a3? 39 ♖ c8 ♔ f7
40 ♖ × f8+ ± ±) 39 ♖ c7 (39 ♖ c8+
leads nowhere: 39 . . . ♔ f7 40 ♖ c7
♔ e8, threatening 41 . . . ♗ × h4.)
39 . . . ♗ f6 40 ♗ × f6 ½–½
(2·26–2·27)

3406 Cuellar–AK

R6: 9.6.1973: English

'Cuellar began an adventurous
attack with the bizarre g4, but
Karpov did not counter in the
centre as theory demands. This
resulted in Cuellar having
dangerous K-side chances for a long
time, but his e6 sacrifice was not
adequate and Karpov consolidated
to reach a won ending.' *World
Championship Interzonals.*

1 d4 ♞ f6 2 ♞ f3 c5 3 c4 cd 4 ♞ × d4
♞ c6 5 ♞ c3 ♛ b6 6 e3 e6 7 ♗ e2
♗ e7 8 00 00 9 b3 a6 10 ♗ b2 d6 11
♛ d2 ♗ d7 12 ♖ ad1 ♖ fd8 13 g4
♛ a7 14 g5 ♞ e8 15 ♞ f3 ♖ ab8 16 e4
♗ f8 17 ♛ f4 ♞ e7 18 ♞ h4 (18 a4
♛ b6! 19 ♞ d2 ♛ a5 – Nitkin) 18 . . .
b5 19 ♖ d2 ♗ c6 20 ♖ fd1 ♛ a8 21
♗ d3 ♖ d7 22 ♛ g4 ♞ c7 23 ♞ d5 bc

225
26B
W

24 ♞ × e7+ ♗ × e7 25 bc g6 26 ♗ c3
a5 (*225*) (26 . . . ♞ e8!?)
27 ♗ c2 (27 ♞ f5 seems to 'on' here:
27 . . . gf? 28 ef± ± ; 27 . . . ef 28 ef
♛ a7 29 fg fg and (1) 30 ♗ e4 ♗ × e4
31 ♛ × d7 ♗ f8 32 ♗ d4 ♛ a8 33
♛ × c7 ♖ b7 trapping the queen –
Zaitsev; (2) 30 ♗ × g6! hg 31 ♛ h4
♖ f8 32 ♛ h6 ♔ f7 33 ♖ e1 ♛ c5 34
♛ g7+ ♔ e8 35 ♗ f6 ♖ f7 36 ♛ × g6
d5 37 ♖ de2 – Nikitin.) 27 . . . ♞ e8!
28 ♞ f3 (28 ♞ f5 is definitely no
good now: 28 . . . ef 29 ef ♗ f8 and
. . . ♗ g7.) 28 . . . ♖ dd8 29 ♞ d4
♗ d7 30 e5 ♗ f8 31 ♞ e2 d5 32 ♖ d3
(32 ♞ f4!?) 32 . . . ♖ bc8! (Karpov
retains his composure even in time-
trouble.) 33 cd (33 ♛ h4 ♖ × c4 34
♞ d4 ♖ dc8 35 ♖ h3 h5! 36 gh
♖ × c3 – Cuellar) 33 . . . ed 34 ♛ h4
♗ f5 35 e6 fe 36 ♞ d4 ♛ g7!∓ ∓ 37
♞ × f5 ♞ × f5 (threatening 38 . . .
d4) 38 ♛ a4 ♗ g7 (38 . . . d4 39
♗ × d4 ♞ h4 was another way to
win.) 39 ♗ × g7 ♔ × g7 40 ♗ b3 ♖ c5
41 ♖ e1 ♛ c6 42 ♛ f4 ♛ d6 43 ♛ d2
♔ g8 44 f4 ♞ g7 45 ♖ d4 (s)
(adjournment 10.6.1973) 45 . . .
♛ b6 46 ♔ h1 ♖ b5 47 ♖ c1 ♖ f8 48
♖ d3 ♖ b4 49 ♖ f3 ♛ d6 50 f5 ♞ × f5
51 a3 ♖ h4 52 ♗ d1 ♛ e5 53 ♛ f2
♖ e4 54 ♔ g2 ♞ h4+ 55 ♔ h3 ♞ × f3
56 ♗ × f3 **0–1** (3·00 – 3·05)

3407 AK–Kuzmin

R7: 12.6.1973: French

(Notes by Karpov).

1 e4   e6

| 2 d4 | d5 |
| 3 ♘d2 | |

At the present time this continuation is squeezing out 3 ♘c3, which used to be more popular. It leads to a small, but long-term (and I mean long-term) advantage for White.

3 ...	c5
4 ed	ed
5 ♘gf3	♘c6
6 ♗b5	♗d6

If 6 ... cd Black must reckon with 7 ♕e2+, and the ending arising from 7 ... ♕e7 is in White's favour. Therefore he spends a tempo on 6 ... ♗d6, so as to use his KN as a screen on e7.

7 dc

After 7 00 cd 8 ♘×d4 ♗×h2+ Black has a good game.

7 ...	♗×c5
8 0-0	♘ge7
9 ♘b3	♗d6

9 ... ♗b6 also leads to a complicated position with a small advantage for White.

10 ♗g5

The bishop is going to g3.

| 10 ... | 0-0 |
| 11 ♗h4 | ♕c7 |

A waste of time. He should have played 11 ... ♗g4 to begin fighting for the central squares. I intended to answer 12 ♗g3 ♗×g3 13 hg ♕b6 14 ♗d3 (threatening 15 ♗×h7+ ♔×h7 16 ♘g5+) and after 14 ... ♘f5 15 ♗×f5 ♗×f5 16 c3 White maintains some advantage.

| 12 ♗g3 | ♗×g3 |

As before, 12 ... ♗g4 was better.

13 hg	♗g4
14 ♖e1	♖ad8
15 c3	♕b6
16 ♗d3	*(226)*

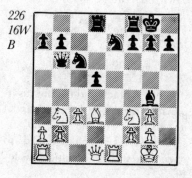

226
16W
B

The side with the isolated pawn tries either for an initiative on the K-side or to advance the pawn. Here Black has no attack, so there is just the one plan left: to push through d5–d4. If he fails in this, then White will have a clear advantage.

16 ... ♘g6

On 16 ... d4 then 17 c4 would, of course, follow.

| 17 ♕c2 | ♗×f3 |
| 18 gf | ♖d6 |

After 18 ... d4 19 f4 (19 c4? ♘b4) 19 ... dc 20 bc an interesting positions arises, in which the white pawns restrain Black's knights on both wings.

19 f4 ♖fd8

20 a3!

Now the d-pawn cannot advance. White's plan is clear:

transfer the knight to f3, double rooks on the e-file, and then, according to circumstances, activate the f-pawn and the Q-side pawns. Black tries to create counterplay by advancing his h-pawn, but is not successful.

20 ...	h5
21 ♔g2	h4
22 ♖e2	♘f8
23 ♘d2	♖h6
24 ♘f3	

What is Black to do about his h-pawn? It cannot be defended, and if it advances to h3 it will be surrounded. Its exchange leads to open lines which are dangerous for Black.

24 ...	hg
25 fg	♘d7
26 ♖ael	♔f8

No other means of defending the back rank is apparent. Now the white pawns rush ahead and completely disorganize the opponent's pieces.

27 g4	♕c7
28 g5	♖h8
29 ♔g3	♘c5
30 ♗f5	g6
31 b4!	

Before retreating the bishop the knight must be dislodged.

31 ...	♘e4+

31 ... gf was plain bad: 32 bc ♕d7 33 ♖h2 ♔g7 34 ♘h4, as was 31 ... ♘d7 32 ♗×g6 fg 33 ♕×g6 with an irresistible attack.

32 ♗×e4	de
33 ♕×e4	♔g7

34 b5	♘a5
35 ♕e7!	

Forcing a winning ending, because 35 ... ♕×c3 is bad: 36 ♖e3 ♕b2 37 ♖e5.

35 ...	♕×e7
36 ♖×e7	♖d3
37 ♖c7	♘b3
38 ♔g4	♖f8
39 ♖ee7	**1–0**
1·41	2·29

There is no defence to the threats of 40 ♖×f7+ ♖×f7 41 ♖×f7+ ♔×f7 42 ♘e5+ and 40 ♘e5.

3408 Tal–AK

R8: 15*.6.1973: Spanish

(* The 8th round took place on 13.6. This game was postponed because Tal was ill.)

(Notes by Shamkovich)

1 e4 e5 2 ♘f3 ♘c6 3 ♗b5 a6 4 ♗a4 ♘f6 5 00 ♗e7 6 ♖e1 b5 7 ♗b3 d6 8 c3 00 9 h3 ♘b8 10 d4 ♘bd7 11 ♘bd2 ♗b7 12 ♗c2 ♖e8 13 b4 ♗f8 14 ♗b2 a5 15 ♗d3 c6 16 a3 ♘b6 17 ♖c1 ed! 18 ♘×d4 (if 18 cd ab 19 ab d5! 20 e5 ♘e4 21 ♘×e4 de 22 ♗×e4 ♗×b4 23 ♖e2 ♘d5 with strong counterplay for Black) **18...♘fd7 19 ♘2b3! ♘e5!?** (19 ... ab would have been still better: 20 cb ♘e5 21 ♘a5 ♖×a5! 22 ba ♘×d3 23 ♕×d3 ♘c4 24 ♗c3 ♘×a5 with sufficient compensation for the exchange. 25 ♘f5 g6 26 ♕d4 is no threat – 26 ...

🖢 e5! 27 f4 ♘b3.) **20 ♘× a5 🖢× a5
21 ba ♘bc4 22 🖢 c2 ♕× a5** (22 . . .
♘× d3 23 ♕× d3 ♖× a5 and if 24
♗cl d5! threatening 25 . . . c5) **23
♗ f1!** (23 ♗cl ♘× d3 as above) **23
. . . ♘× b2 24 🖢× b2 ♕× c3** (after
24 . . . ♕× a3 25 ♕d2 Black has to
reckon with the threat of c4, e.g. 25
. . . ♕c5 26 c4! ♘× c4 27 ♗× c4
♕× c4 28 🖢cl and the queen is
lost.) **25 🖢 b3 ♕ a5 26 ♕ b1** (Now
27 ♘× b5 cb 28 🖢× b5 is
threatened.) **26 . . . ♕ a7** (26 . . .
♗ a8!?) **27 🖢 d1 ♘ d7?** (27 . . . g6
was better: 28 ♗× b5 cb 29 ♘× b5
♕a5 30 ♘× d6 (30 🖢× d6 ♘c4!) 30
. . . ♗× d6 31 🖢× b7 ♕× a3 with no
problems.) **28 ♘ f5 🖢 e6 29 ♘ d4
🖢 e8 30 ♗× b5! cb 31 ♘× b5 ♕ c5
32 ♘× d6 ♗× d6 33 🖢× b7 ♘ f6 34
♕ b3** (Black has lost several tempi
compared with the variation in the
last note.) **34 . . . ♗ c7** (34 . . . 🖢 e6!?
35 🖢 b6 ♔f8! – Zaitsev) **35 ♕ b5
♕ c2 36 ♕ b1! ♕× b1!** (Black
cannot avoid the exchange of
queens in view of 37 🖢cl.) **37
🖢 d× b1 ♗ d6 38 a4 🖢× e4 39
🖢 d1** (39 a5! 🖢 a4 40 🖢 a7 ♔f8 41
g3 ♘e8 42 🖢 a8 ♔e7 43 🖢 b3!) **39
. . . ♘ e8 40 a5 ♔ f8 41 a6!** (s) *(227)*
('We looked a little at the position
and then Anatoly went to bed. In
his dreams he saw a ferocious move
for White, after 41 . . . 🖢 a4, in 42
🖢 a7. He began to seek a defence
and, in his dream, he found it in 42
. . . g5. His brain continued to
work. Again he saw a terrible
continuation for White in 43 🖢 a8

227
41W
B

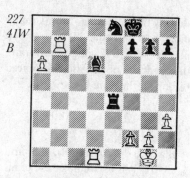

♗ e5 44 f4 when, if Black takes on f4
with bishop or pawn, 45 🖢 dd8 is
decisive. After he woke up, we
found the best defence was 44 . . .
🖢× f4, but Tal did not play this
dangerous line.' – Furman)

(adjournment 19?.6.1973) **41 . . .
🖢 a4 42 🖢 a7 g5! 43 🖢 a8 ♗ e5 44
g3 ♔ e7 45 🖢 e1 f6 46 a7 ♘ c7 47
🖢 h8 🖢× a7** ½-½ (2·57 – 2·25)

3409 AK–Quinteros

R9:14.6.1973: Sicilian

(Notes by Karpov)

1 e4 c5 2 ♘f3 d6 3 d4 cd 4 ♘×d4
♘f6 5 ♘c3 a6 6 ♗g5 e6 7 f4 ♕b6 8
♘b3

A small concession to Black, but I
have obtained good tournament
positions without going in for wild
variations involving the sacrifice of
a pawn after 8 ♕d2. To be fair, one
should note that 8 ♕d2 is the only
way to obtain an opening
advantage.

8 . . .   ♗e7
After 8 . . . ♕e3+ 9 ♕e2
♕×e2+ 10 ♗×e2 White has a

slightly better ending. I think that a more precise order of moves is to play 8 ... ♘bd7, not determining the position of the black-squared bishop for the time-being.

```
9  ♕f3      h6
10 ♗h4      ♘bd7
11 0-0-0    ♕c7
```

Black is preparing b7–b5 and ♗c8–b7. White, to make use of his lead in development, must start play in the centre as quickly as possible. My next move serves this aim.

```
12 ♗g3      b5
13 e5       ♗b7
14 ♕e2      de
```

14 ... ♘d5 offered better prospects. 15 ed ♘×c3 16 dc ♘×e2+ 17 ♗×e2 ♖c8 18 f5 e5 and 15 ♘×d5 ♗×d5 16 ed ♕×d6 17 f5 ♕b6 promise White nothing. But there is a tempting exchange sacrifice: 15 ♘×d5 ♗×d5 16 ♖×d5 ed 17 e6 ♘f6 (17 ... fe is bad because of 18 ♕×e6.) 18 ef+ ♔×f7 19 ♕f3 to be followed by ♗f1–d3, ♗g3–f2 and a pawn storm on the K-side. The consequences of this sacrifice are very difficult to calculate.

```
15 fe       ♘h7
```

Sadly the knight must retreat to the edge of the board. 15 ... ♘d5 will not do in view of 16 ♘×d5 ♗×d5 17 ♖×d5 ed 18 e6.

```
16 ♘e4
```

The knight speeds towards d6, at the same time preventing castling:

16 ... 00? 17 ♘f6+ ♗×f6 18 ef with a strong attack.

```
16 ...      ♗g5+
```

Obviously, 16 ... ♘×e5 is dangerous because of 17 ♘ec5, and on 16 ... ♘g5 I had intended to play 17 ♘f6+ gf 18 ef ♕c4 19 ♕×c4 bc 20 ♘a5± .

```
17 ♔b1      0-0
18 h4       ♗e7
19 ♘d6      ♗d5? (228)
```

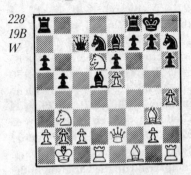

228
19B
W

Black's position is unattractive. His pieces are scattered and the knight on h7 is cut off from the centre of affairs. Nonetheless, Black can defend himself by playing 19 ...♗c6 or 19 ... ♖ad8.

After the move played White obtains a decisive attack on the king by sacrificing the exchange.

```
20 ♖×d5     ed
21 ♘f5
```

Threatening 22 ♘×e7+ and 22 e6. Black's reply is forced.

```
21 ...      ♕d8
22 ♕g4      g6
23 ♘×h6+    ♔g7
24 ♘f5+
```

A quicker route to victory is: 24

♘d4 ♚×h6 25 h5 (25 ♘f5+ gf 26 ♗f4+ ♘g5 27 hg++ ♚g7 28 ♕×f5 ♖h8 29 ♖h6, with a mating attack, is probably an even more effective winning procedure.); on 25 . . . g5 there is the beautiful mate 26 ♘f5, and on 25 . . . ♚g7 then 26 hg fg 27 ♘e6+ or 26 . . . ♘g5 27 ♘f5+ ♚g8 28 g7.

 24 . . .   ♚h8
 25 ♗d3   ♖g8

After 25 . . . gf 26 ♕×f5, Black cannot avoid being mated (26 . . . ♘hf6 27 ef ♘×f6 28 ♗e5).

 26 ♘h6   ♖g7
 27 h5   ♕e8

The only way to defend g6. On 27 . . . ♘df8, 28 hg fg 29 e6 could follow.

 28 e6   ♘df6
 29 ef   ♕d8

On 29 . . . ♕f8 White can win simply by 30 ♕d4, or beautifully (as pointed out by Tseitlin) with 30 hg ♘×g4 31 ♘×g4 ♗d6 (defending against 32 ♗e5) 32 ♘f6 ♗×g3 33 ♘×h7 ♕d6 34 ♘f6+ ♗h2 35 ♘e8! ♖×g6 36 ♗×g6.

 30 ♕d4   ♘×h5
 31 ♗e5   ♗f6
 32 ♖e1   ♗×e5
 33 ♖×e5 ♘5f6
 34 g4   ♕f8
 35 g5   ♘e4
 36 ♗×e4 de
 37 ♕×e4 **1–0**
  2·04   1·58

3410 Larsen–AK

R10: 16.6.1973: English

'Larsen made no attempt to prove the advantage of the white pieces.' – Wade.

1 c4 c5 2 g3 g6 3 ♗g2 ♗g7 4 ♘c3 ♘c6 5 a3 e6 6 ♖b1 a5 7 ♘h3 ♘ge7 8 ♘f4 0-0 9 d3 ♖b8 10 ♗d2 b6 11 0-0 ♗b7 12 ♖e1 d6 13 ♘b5 ♘d4 14 ♘×d4 ♗×d4 15 ♗×b7 ♖×b7 16 ♕a4 ♕d7 17 ♕×d7 ♖×d7 18 ♗c3 ♗g7 19 ♗×g7 ♚×g7 20 b4 ab 21 ab ♖a8 ½–½ (0·55 – 0·57)

3411 AK–R. Byrne

R11: 17.6.1973: Sicilian

1 e4 c5 2 ♘f3 d6 3 d4 cd 4 ♘×d4 ♘f6 5 ♘c3 a6 6 ♗e2 e5 7 ♘b3 ♗e6 8 f4 ♕c7 9 f5 ♗c4 10 a4 ♘bd7 11 ♗e3 ♗e7 12 a5 0-0 13 0-0 b5 14 ab ♘×b6 15 ♚h1 ♖fc8 16 ♗×b6 ♕×b6 17 ♗×c4 ♖×c4 18 ♕e2 ♖ac8 19 ♖a2 ♗d8 20 ♖fa1 ♕b7 21 ♖a4 ♖×a4 ½–½ (0·37 – 0·31)

3412 Uhlmann–AK

R12: 18.6.1973: QGD

'Karpov took the opportunity to share the lead by beating Uhlmann in a dour positional game. Karpov had the two bishops, but Uhlmann had a good centre until his poor 29th move allowed Black to dominate the whole board.' – *World Championship Interzonals*.

1 c4 c5 2 ♘f3 ♘f6 3 ♘c3 d5 4 cd ♘×d5 5 e3 e6 6 d4 ♘c6 7 ♗d3 cd 8

ed ♗e7 9 00 00 10 ♖e1 ♘f6 11 a3
b6 12 ♗e3 ♗b7 13 ♖c1 ♖c8 14
♗b1 ♖c7 15 ♕d3 ♖d7 16 ♕c2 g6
17 ♗a2 ♘g4 (17 ... ♘d5 18
♘×d5 ed 19 ♘e5 ♘×e5 20 de±)
18 ♖cd1 ♘×e3 19 fe ♗f6 20 ♕f2
♗g7 (20 ... e5!?) 21 ♖d2 ♘e7 (21
... e5!?) 22 e4 h6 (22 ... e5!?) 23
♖ed1 ♕b8 24 ♕e3 ♖fd8 25 h3
♔h7 26.♔h1 a6 27 ♖f2 ♘g8 28
♖df1 b5 *(229)*

229
28B
W

29 h4? (29 d5!?; 29 e5!?) 29 ... ♘f6
30 ♘e5? (30 ♘h2!?) 30 ... ♖×d4
31 ♖×f6 ♕×e5! 32 ♖×f7 ♖8d7
33 ♖×d7 (33 ♕h3!? e.g. 33 ...
♖×f7 34 ♖×f7 ♗×e4 35 ♕×e6 –
Kondratiev) 33 ... ♖×d7 34 ♕h3
♖d6 35 ♗b1 ♖d2 36 h5 gh 37 ♘d1
♗c6! ('This is typical of Karpov's
mastery of the art of chess' –
Kotov.) 38 ♕f3 ♗e8 39 b4 ♗g6 40
♘f2 ♕d4 41 ♘h3 (s) (adjournment
19.6.1973?) 41 ... e5 42 ♘f2 ♖b2
43 ♔h2 ♕c4 44 ♖d1 ♖b3 45 ♘d3
♕×e4 **0-1** (3·04 – 2·54)

3413 AK–Gligorić

R13: 21.6.1973: Spanish

(Notes by Karpov)

1 e4 e5 2 ♘f3 ♘c6 3 ♗b5 a6 4 ♗a4
♘f6 5 00 ♗e7 6 ♖e1 b5 7 ♗b3 d6 8
c3 00 9 h3 ♘b8 10 d4 ♘bd7 11
♘bd2 ♗b7 12 ♗c2 c5

Gligorić plays this variation
regularly, for instance, his games
with Keres, San Antonio 1972, and
with Tal in the interzonal. Both
Keres and Tal continued with the
manoeuvre ♘d2-f1–g3. I decided
to close the centre.

    13 d5   ♘e8

Black plans to play g7-g6,
♘e8-g7 and f7-f5.

    14 ♘f1   g6
    15 ♗h6

After this Black does not succeed
in advancing f7-f5.

    15 ...   ♘g7
    16 ♘e3   ♘f6

The only possibility of counterplay is to eject the annoying bishop
from h6. Otherwise, after g2-g4,
♔h2 and ♖g1, White prepares the
standard Spanish attack with
♘e3-f5.

    17 a4   ♔h8
    18 b3

I rejected the immediate 18 ♕e2
because of 18 ... c4. It would take a
long time to prepare a siege of the c-
pawn because it cannot be
undermined by b2-b3 as the pawn
on e4 is attacked.

The move played is slow, but it
hinders the advance to c4 and
thereby Black's counterplay on the
Q-side.

    18 ...   ♖b8

Otherwise it will be difficult to defend the b-pawn.

19 ♕e2   ♗c8

I would have preferred 19 ... ♕b6. True, this move is not 'Spanish', but there is no white bishop on e3 and therefore it is perfectly playable. It is important for Black to prevent his opponent's rook getting to the seventh rank.

20 ab   ab
21 ♖a7   ♘g8
22 ♗×g7+   ♔×g7
23 ♖ea1

While Black has been getting rid of the bishop on h6, White has firmly entrenched himself on the a-file.

23 ...   ♗d7

(In his notes for *The Chess Player*, Karpov mistakenly gave the order 23 ... ♘f6 24 ♗d3 ♗d7. – KJO'C)

24 ♗d3   ♘f6
25 ♕a2

White intends to play ♕a5, offering an exchange of queens. After that his rooks would run riot on the seventh rank.

25 ...   ♘e8
25 ... ♕b6!?
26 ♕a6

On 26 ♕a5 Black would avoid the exchange by 26 ... ♕c8, and then drive the queen back with ♗e7 d8.

26 ...   ♖b6

Now White's positional advantage becomes menacing. Why did the Yugoslav grandmaster refrain

from 26 ... ♘c7.? After 27 ♕a5 ♖a8 (27 ... ♖c8 is bad because of 28 ♕b6 and ♖a7–b7 to follow.) both players looked at the following forced variation: 28 ♖×a8 ♕×a8 29 ♕×c7 ♕×a1+ 30 ♔h2 ♖d8 31 ♗×b5 ♗×b5 32 ♕×e7 ♖d7. White has a pawn for the exchange. I supposed that I had sufficient compensation; after 33 ♕g5 or 33 ♕h4 White has good chances of an attack. Gligorić rejected this variation because of 33 ♘f5+. However, this sacrifice does not give White any more than perpetual check.

27 ♕a5   ♘f6 *(230)*

The only move because of the threat 28 ♖×d7. The rook could not return to b8 because of the exchange of queens and 29 ♖b7 winning the b-pawn.

230
27B
W

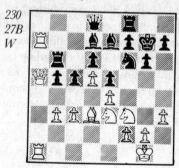

28 ♘g4

Threatening 29 ♘×f6 and 30 ♖×d7. The rook has to move from b6 and thereby give White's pieces access to c7.

28 ...   ♖b8
29 ♘×f6

29 ♛c7 would seem stronger, and after 29 ... ♜c8 then 30 ♛×d8 and 31 ♜b7. However, Black would have continued 29 ... ♝×g4 30 hg ♛×c7 31 ♜×c7 ♝d8. After 32 ♜c6 c4 33 bc bc 34 ♜×c4 ♞×g4 the weakness of f2 would have given him counterplay.

29 ...　　　♝×f6

Taking with the king is impossible because of 30 ♛c7.

30 ♛c7　　　♛×c7
31 ♜×c7　　　♜fd8
32 ♜aa7　　　♝e8
33 ♜ab7

Threatening 34 ♝×b5 ♝×b5 35 ♜×f7+ , then exchange on b8 and taking a bishop.

33 ...　　　♚g8

Apparently the only move.

34 g4

White's plan is to play g4–g5 and, driving the enemy bishop off the h4–d8 diagonal, to secure access to e7. The other possibility was to restrict the activity of the bishop on f6 by means of h3–h4 and g2–g3, but I rejected it because in some variations after h7–h5 the enemy bishop can get out on h6.

34 ...　　　h6
35 h4　　　♜×b7

Otherwise 36 g5 follows. After 36 ... hg 37 hg ♝g7, the manoeuvre ♞f3–h2–g4 gives White the win. If he does not exchange on g5 and retreats the bishop by 36 ... ♝g7, then White himself exchanges on h6 and plays ♞g5. After the forced exchange of the knight, Black cannot avoid the loss of the pawn on b5. The move played does not save him either.

36 ♜×b7　　　c4
37 bc　　　bc
38 ♝e2

38 ♝×c4 will not do because of 38 ... ♝d7 39 g5 ♝g4! After 40 gf ♝×f3 41 ♝d3 g5! Black has the possibility of invading with his rook.

38 ...　　　♜a8

Now 38 ... ♝d7 is meaningless because on 39 g5 Black does not have the move 39 ... ♝g4 as the knight is defended, and 39 ... hg 40 ♞×g5 does not promise Black any good.

39 ♝×c4　　　♝a4

39 ... ♜c8 has been recommended in the tournament bulletin and by other commentators. I would have continued 40 ♝e2, to which Black only has one answer – 40 ... ♝a4 (40 ... ♜×c3? 41 ♜b8 ♚f8 42 g5!). Then 41 c4 ♝c2 42 g5 hg 43 ♞×g5 ♝×g5 44 hg ♝×e4 45 ♜d7 and it is not apparent how Black defends his pawn on d6 (on 45 ... ♜a8 follows 46 f3! defending against perpetual check). So after 39 ... ♜c8 Black remains a pawn down without sufficient compensation for it.

40 ♝b3　　　♝×b3
41 ♜×b3　　　♜c8

The best chance. Black keeps control of the back rank, otherwise after a check the white rook would occupy the c-file with decisive effect. 41 ... ♖a4 is no good because of 42 ♖b4 and then ♖b4–c4.

42 ♔g2 *(231)*

The sealed move. (adjournment 24.6.1973)

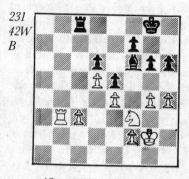

231
42W
B

42 ...   h5

I had not looked at this reply in my adjournment analysis. After the game Gligorić said that he, in his turn, had not foreseen my sealed move. The Yugoslav grandmaster had only considered variations with 42 h5 and had come to the conclusion that Black loses.

However, 42 h5 allows the enemy bishop freedom, and therefore I preferred 42 ♔g2.

I thought that Black had to defend against the manoeuvre ♖b3–b6 with the exchange of the c- for the d-pawn being to White's advantage. In so far as the d-pawn could not be defended by the rook, because of ♖c6, I analysed the continuations 42 ... ♔f8, 42 ... ♗d8 and 42 ... ♗e7. The idea of the last move is to obtain

counterplay by f7–f5, when I planned to play 43 ♔g3 f5 44 gf gf 45 ♘d2 ♔f7 46 ♔h3! (it is important that the black pawn lands on f4 without check!). In a word, Black does not obtain counterplay.

43 gh

43 g5 is also possible in that Black can never play f7–f6 because of the exchange on f6 and then ♘g5. Black would not have the strength to suffer this knight and its exchange would lead to a winning endgame for White.

43 ...   gh
44 ♖b6   ♖×c3
45 ♖×d6   ♔g7
46 ♖c6   ♖d3

Black's desire to hinder the manoeuvre ♘f3–d2–c4 and to hold up the advance of the d-pawn is easy to understand. However, 46 ... ♖d3 meets with a forced refutation.

46 ... ♖a3 or 46 ... ♖b3 would have been more stubborn. But then with straightforward play by White the game cannot be saved. On 46 ... ♖b3, for example, there might follow 47 ♘g5, and then f2–f3, ♔g2–g3 and in the end Black would be forced to face an unfavourable endgame.

47 ♖c7   ♔g6

Otherwise 48 ♘g5. However, White will now take the e-pawn with check. This is very important, because it does not allow Black to attack the pawn on e4.

48	♖c8	♗g7
49	♖c6+	♔h7
50	♘g5+	♔g8
51	♖c8+	♗f8
52	♖c7	f6
53	♘e6	

Now even the naked eye can see that Black's position is hopeless.

| 53 | ... | ♗h6 |
| 54 | ♖d7 | |

Guaranteeing the advance of the d-pawn. The bishop cannot leave h6 because of 55 ♖g7+ and ♖g7-f7, and the king does not have a move because of 55 ♖f7. The rook is obliged to watch the d-pawn.

54	...	♖d2
55	♔f1	♖d1+
56	♔e2	♖d2+
57	♔e1	♖c2

There are no more checks or moves with other pieces so the rook has to leave the d-file. Now White's passed pawn comes into action.

58	d6	♖c1+
59	♔e2	♖c2+
60	♔f1	♖c6
61	♔g2	

After this, except for ... ♖b6 and ... ♖a6, Black does not have a single move. The rook cannot move away from the sixth rank because of 62 ♖e7 and if 61 ... ♗d2, then 62 ♖g7+ ♔h8 63 d7 ♖d6 64 ♖e7 is decisive.

| 61 | ... | ♖b6 |
| 62 | ♘c7 | ♖b7 |

If 62 ... ♗f8, then 63 ♘e8; if 62 ... ♗d2, then 63 ♘d5; if 62 ... ♔f8, then 63 ♖h7 ♗g7 64 d7.

| 63 | ♘d5 | **1-0** |
| | 3·00 | 4·00 |

3414 Rukavina–AK

R14: 22.6.1973: English

'Karpov moved into the sole lead for the first time by beating Rukavina who suicidally saddled himself with doubled, isolated c-pawns, and it was merely a question of time before the front one disappeared.' *World Championship Interzonals.*

1 c4 ♘f6 2 ♘c3 e6 3 ♘f3 c5 4 d4 cd 5 ♘×d4 ♗b4 6 ♘c2? (6 ♘db5; 6 ♗d2; 6 ♕b3) 6 ... ♗×c3+ 7 bc ♕a5 8 ♘b4 (8 ♕d3!? ♘c6 9 ♗f4) 8 ... 00 9 e3 b6 10 ♗e2 ♗b7 11 00 ♖c8! 12 f3 ♘c6 13 ♕b3 ♕e5! *(232)*

232
13B
W

14 ♘×c6 ♖×c6 15 ♗d2 ♕c7 16 ♕a4 a5 17 ♖fb1 ♗a6 18 ♖b2 (not 18 ♕b3 ♖b8) 18 ... ♗×c4 19 ♗×c4 ♖×c4 20 ♕b5 ♖c6 21 e4 d6 22 ♕g5 ♘d7 23 ♕e7 ♘e5! 24 ♕×c7 ♖×c7 25 ♖b5 (not 25 ♖×b6 ♘c4) 25 ... ♘c4 26 ♗c1 ♖ac8 27 ♖ab1 ♖c5 28 ♔f1 ♔f8 29

♔e2 ♕e7 30 ♖5b3♔d7 31 a4♔c7
32 ♗f4♕b7‡ ∓ 33 ♗e3 ♖5c6 34
♗d4 f6 35 ♖d1 ♖d8 36 f4 d5 37
♗f2 ♖cd6 38 ♗c5 ♖c6 39 ♗f2
♖dd6 40 ed ♖×d5 41 ♖×d5 ed 42
♖b5 ♕e6+ 43 ♔d3 ♔c6 44 g3
♖e7 45 ♖b1 ♖b7 46 ♖b5 ♘d6 47
♖b2 b5 48 ab+ ♖×b5 49 ♖e2 (s)
0–1 (2·56 – 2·11)

3415 AK–Radulov

R15: 23.6.1973: English

1 c4 e5 2 ♘c3 c5 3 g3 g6 4 ♗g2 ♗g7
5 ♘f3 ♘e7 6 00 00 7 ♘e1 ♘bc6 8
♘c2 d6 9 ♘e3 ♗e6 10 a3 ♕d7 11
d3 ♗h3 12 ♘ed5 ♗×g2 13 ♔×g2
♘×d5 14 ♘×d5 ♘e7 15 ♘×e7+
♕×e7 16 e4 f5 17 f3 h5 18 ♗d2
♔h7 19 b4 ♗h6 20 ef ♖×f5 21
♗×h6♔×h6 22 ♕d2+ ♔g7 23 bc
dc 24 ♖ae1 ♖d8 25 ♖e3 ♖d4 26
♕e2 ♕d6 27 ♖b1 ♖f7 28 a4 b6 29
♖e1 ♖d7 30 h4 ♖×d3 31 ♖×d3
♕×d3 32 ♕×e5+ ♔h7 33 ♕e6
♕f5 34 ♕×f5 gf 35 ♔f2 ♔g7 36 a5
♖d4 37 ab ab 38 ♖e6 ♖×c4 39
♖×b6 f4 ½–½ (2·06 – 1·42)

3416 Smejkal–AK

R16: 25.6.1973: Sicilian

(Notes by Taimanov)

**1 e4 c5 2 ♘f3 e6 3 d4 cd 4 ♘×d4
♘c6 5 ♘c3 a6 6 ♗e2 ♕c7 7 00
♘f6 8 ♗e3 ♗b4 9 ♘a4 00 10
♘×c6 bc 11 ♘b6 ♖b8 12 ♘×c8
♖f×c8 13 ♗×a6 ♖d8!** (13 . . .
♖e8 14 ♗d3 ♗d6 15 ♔h1 ♗e5 16

c3! ♖×b2 17 ♕c1! ♕b7 18 f4 ♗c7
19 e5 ♘d5 20 ♗c5 ♕b8 21 c4 ♘e7
22 ♗a7! ♕b7 23 ♗d4 ♖b4 24 ♗c5
♖a4 25 ♗×h7+ ± ± Kochiev-
Ruderfer, Odessa 1972; 17 . . ♘g4
18 f4 (18 ♕×b2 ♗×c3!) 18 . . .
♘×e3 19 ♕×b2 ♗×f4 20 ♕f2!±
Taimanov and Vasyukov) **14 ♗d3
♗d6 15 ♔h1 ♗e5 16 c3 ♖×b2 17
♕c1 ♘g4 18 f4 ♘×e3 19 ♕×b2
♗×f4 20 ♕f2 ♘×f1 21 ♖×f1**
(233)

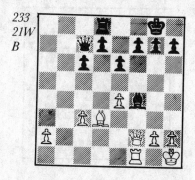

233
21W
B

21 . . . e5 ?! (21 . . . g5 22 g3 ♕d6 23
♗e2 ♗e5 24 ♕×f7+ ♔h8 is
better.) **22 g3 ♕d6 23 ♗e2 g5
24 ♕×f7+ ♔h8 25 a4** (Black has
not solved all his problems and
White's passed pawn is likely to be
troublesome.) **25 . . . ♗e7 26 a5
♖f8 27 ♕c4 ♖×f1+ 28 ♗×f1
♕f6 29 ♔g2 ♕f8 30 ♗e2 ♗c5 31
♗g4 ♕f2+ ?!** (31 . . . d6 was
correct: if 32 ♕e6, then 32 . . . g6; if
32 ♗d7, *then* 32 . . . ♕f2+.) **32
♔h3 d6 33 ♗d7 ?!** (33 ♕e6 was
correct, e.g. 33 . . . g6 34 ♕e7!, or
33 . . . ♕f1+ 34 ♔h4 ♕f6+ 35
♕×f6 gf 36 ♗d7 and the endgame

promises Black no good.) **33 . . . g6 34 ♗×c6 ♔g7** (Now that his king is out of trouble Black has no difficulty neutralizing the passed pawn.) **35 ♗b5 ♕b2! 36 a6 ♗g1 37 ♕e2 ♕×c3 38 ♗c4 ♕c1 39 ♕f1 ??** (39 ♔g2) **39 . . . ♕h6+ 40 ♔g2 ♕×h2+ 41 ♔f3 ♕h5+ 42 ♔g2 ♕h2+** (s) (adjournment 26.6.1973) **43 ♔f3 ♗d4 44 ♗d5 ♗c5 45 ♗c6 ♗d4** *(234)*

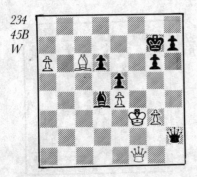

234
45B
W

46 ♗b7? (46 ♗d5) **46 . . . g5! 47 ♔g4 h5+ 48 ♔f5** (48 ♔×g5 ♕×g3+ 49 ♔×h5 ♗f2! and White will be mated.) **48 . . . ♕×g3 49 ♔e6 ♕f2! 50 ♕b5** (Black wins the ending only because White's bishop is on b7. If it were on, say, d5, then 50 ♕×f2 ♗×f2 51 ♕f5! g4 52 ♗c4 g3 53 ♗f1 would draw.) **50 . . . ♕f6+ 51 ♔d5 g4 52 ♗c8 ♕e7 53 ♗f5 ♔h6 54 ♕f1 ♕c7 55 ♕e2 ♕c5+ 56 ♔e6 ♔g5 57 ♕f1 ♕a3 58 ♕e2 ♗c5 59 ♕d2+ ♕e3 60 ♕a5 ♗b6 61 ♕a2 ♕f2 62 ♕b1 g3 63 ♗h3 ♔h4 64 ♗g2 ♕g1 65 ♕×g1** (65 ♕b2 ♗f2) **65 . . . ♗×g1**

66 ♔×d6 ♗d4 67 a7 ♗×a7 68 ♔×e5 g4 69 ♔d5 h4 70 e5 h3 (70 . . . ♗b6 71 e6 ♗d8 is even simpler.) **71 ♗×h3+ ♔×h3 72 e6 ♗c5! 0–1** (4·06 – 4·02)

3417   AK–Torre

R17: 27.6.1973: Alekhine

(Notes by Karpov)

1 e4 ♘f6 2 e5 ♘d5 3 d4 d6 4 ♘f3 g6 5 ♗c4 ♘b6 6 ♗b3 ♗g7 7 ♘g5 d5 8 f4 ♗c6 9 c3 (so that if 9 . . . ♘a5, then 10 ♗c2) **9 . . . f6 10 ♘f3 ♗f5 11 00 ♕d7** (11 . . . 00 12 ♘bd2±) **12 ♘bd2** (12 ♘h4?! ♗g4 13 ♕e1 000 and 14 . . . g5) **12 . . . fe** (12 . . . ♗h6 13 ♘h4) **13 fe 00 14 ♖f2!** ♘a5 **15 ♗c2 ♗×c2 16 ♕×c2 ♕f5?!** (16 . . . e6) **17 ♕d1 e6** (17 . . . ♕d3 18 ♘e1± and if 18 . . . ♕e3 19 ♘df3) **18 ♘f1 c5** *(235)*

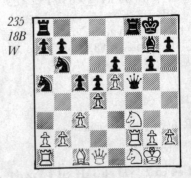

235
18B
W

19 h3! (if 19 ♘e3 then (1) 19 . . . ♕g4 20 ♘×g4± ±; (2) 19 . . . ♕e4 20 ♘g5 ♕h4 21 ♖×f8+ ♖×f8 22 ♘×e6 ♕f2+ 23 ♔h1± ±; (3) 19 . . . ♕h5 20 g4 ♕h3 21 ♘g5 ♕h4)

19 . . . cd 20 cd ♘ **c6 21 b3** ♘ **d7 22** ♗ **a3**± ± ♖ **f7** (22 . . . ♖ fd8 23 ♘ g3 ♕ f4 24 ♘ e2 ♕ e4 25 ♘ g5 ♕ e3 26 ♗ c1± ± ; 24 . . . ♕ f7 25 ♘ g5) **23 g4!** (23 ♘ g3 ♕ f4 24 ♘ e2 ♕ e3? 25 ♗ c1 ♕ e4 26 ♘ g3± ± ; 24 . . . ♕ f5 25 g4 ♕ ×f3 26 ♖ ×f3 ♖ ×f3) **23 . . .** ♕ **e4** (23 . . . ♕ f4 24 ♗ c1 ♕ e4 25 ♘ g3± ±) **24** ♘ **g5 1–0** (1·23 – 2·26)

	1	2	3	4	5	6	7	8	
1 USSR	×	5½	5	5½	5½	6½	5½	7	**40½**
2 Yugoslavia	2½	×	4½	6	6½	4½	4½	5½	**34**
3 Hungary	3	3½	×	6½	5½	5½	5½	3½	**33**
4 Poland	2½	2	1½	×	5	4	5½	4½	**25**
5 W. Germany	2½	1½	2½	3	×	4½	4½	5½	**24**
6 England	1½	3½	2½	4	3½	×	4½	4½	**24**
7 Romania	2½	3½	2½	2½	3½	3½	×	5	**23**
8 Switzerland	1	2½	4½	3½	2½	3½	3	×	**20½**

Once again Karpov received a board prize (his score was 5/6) and registered an advance within his own team of two boards compared with Skopje. The USSR team was Spassky, Petrosian, Korchnoi, Karpov, Tal, Smyslov, Geller, Kuzmin, Tukmakov and Balashov.

3501 AK–Whiteley

R1: 6.7.1973: Sicilian

(Notes by Karpov)

1 e4 c5 2 ♘f3 d6 3 ♘c3 g6 4 d4 cd 5 ♘×d4 ♘f6 6 ♗e3 ♗g7 7 ♗c4 ♘c6 8 f3 00 9 ♕d2 ♗d7 10 000 ♕a5 11 ♗b3 ♖fc8 12 h4 ♘e5 13 ♔b1 (13 h5 ♘×h5 14 ♗h6 ♘d3+ 15.♔b1 ♘×b2 16 ♔×b2 ♗×h6 17 ♕×h6 ♖×c3!) 13 ... ♘c4 14 ♗×c4 ♖×c4 15 ♘b3 ♕d8 (15 ... ♕a6? 16 e5 ♘e8 17 ♘d5± ; 16 ... de 17 ♘c5± ±) 16 ♗h6 ♕f8?! (16 ...

♗h8) 17 ♗×g7± ♕×g7 18 g4 (threatening 19 e5 de 20 g5) 18 ... ♗e6 19 ♘d4 ♘d7 20 h5 ♖ac8 21 hg hg (236)

236
21B
W

22 ♘ce2! (22 ♘f5 ♗×f5 23 gf
♖×c3 24 bc ♕×c3 25 fg fg) 22 ...
♖4c5 (22 ... ♘e5 23 c3) 23 c3 ♘f8
24 ♖dg1 (preparing ♘f5) 24 ...
♕e5 25 ♘g3± ± g5 (25 ... ♖a5 26
a3 with 27 f4 or 27 ♘gf5 to follow)
26 ♘gf5 ♗×f5 27 gf f6 28 f4
♕×e4+ 29 ♔a1 ♔f7 (29 ... ♘h7
30 ♕h2± ±) 30 fg fg 31 ♕×g5 ♘e5
(31 ... ♔e8 32 ♖e1± ±) 32 ♕h5+
1–0

3502 Ghizdavu–AK

R2: 7.7.1973: Sicilian

(Notes by Karpov)

**1 e4 c5 2 ♘f3 d6 3 d4 cd 4 ♘×d4
♘f6 5 ♘c3 a6 6 f4 ♘bd7 7 a4 g6 8
♗d3 ♗g7 9 ♘f3 00 10 00 ♘c5!?**
(10 ... e5 intending ... ♕c7 and
... b6) **11 ♕e1 ♖b8** (11 ... ♗g4?!
12 ♕h4 ♗×f3 13 ♖×f3 and 14
♖h3±) **12 ♕h4 b5 13 ab ab 14
e5?!** (14 ♔h1) **14 ... ♘×d3 15 cd**
(15 ef? ♗×f6 16 ♘g5 ♗×g5 17 fg
♘×c1∓∓; 15 ♘g5 de 16 fe h6) **15
... ♘e8** (15 ... b4 16 ef ♗×f6 17
♘g5 ♗×g5 18 fg bc∓) **16 d4** (16
♘d4? de 17 fe b4; 16 ♘d5 and (1)
16 ... f6?! 17 ♘d4 and if 17 ... de
18 ♘c6; (2) 16 ... ♖b7 17 ♖a8 de)
16 ... ♘c7 17 ♘e4 f5! (17 ...
♗b7 18 f5!; 17 ... ♗f5 18 ♘g3
♗d3 19 ♖d1) **18 ♘eg5 h6 19 ♘h3
♗e6 20 ♕g3 ♗f7 21 ♖e1 b4 22
♔h1** (22 ♘h4 de) **22 ... ♘d5?!**
(22 ... ♖b7; 22 ... ♕d7? 23 ♘h4
♔h7 24 ♖a7±) **23 ♕h4** (23 ♘h4
♔h7 24 ♘f3 e6∓) **23 ... ♖b7 24**

♘hg5 e6 25 ♘×f7 (25 ♖a6 hg 26
♘×g5 ♖e8 27 ♖×d6 ♕c8∓) **25
... ♕×h4 26 ♘×h4 ♔×f7 27
♘f3 de 28 de ♗c8∓ 29 ♘d4 ♗f8
30 ♖a6** *(237)*

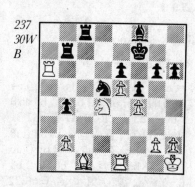

237
30W
B

30 ... ♖b6 (30 ... ♗c5! 31 ♘×e6
♗b6∓∓; 31 ♘b3 ♗b6∓) **31
♖a7+ ♖c7 32 ♖a8 b3 33 ♖a4
♗c5 34 ♘e2 ♗b4?!** (34 ... ♘e3!)
35 ♖d1 bc6 36 ♖a1 ♖b6 (36
... ♖c2 37 ♘d4 ♖f2 38 ♘g1±)
**37 ♖d3 ♗e7 38 g3 ♖c4 39 ♔g2
♖c2 40 ♔f3 ♖b4** (40 ... ♖b7!?
with 41 ... ♗c5 to follow) **41 h4?**
(41 ♖a7 ♖e4 42 ♗d2 ♖×b2 43
♖b7∓; 41 ... ♖bc4 42 ♖×b3
♖×e2 43 ♔×e2 ♖×c1 44 h4!∞) **41
... ♗c5?** (41 ... ♖e4+∓ 42 ♗d2
♖×b2 43 ♘d4 ♖a2; 42 ♘d4 ♖h2
and either 43 ... ♗c5 or 43 ...
♗e1) **42 ♗d2 ♖e4 43 ♖c1 ♗b4
44 ♖×c2 bc 45 ♗c1** (45 ♗×b4
♖×e2) **45 ... ♖c4 46 ♗d4 ♖c7
47 b3 ♗e1** (47 ... ♗c3 48 ♖c4
♖b7 49 b4; 47 ... ♗a5!? 48 ♖c4
♖×c4 49 bc ♘c3 50 ♘×c3
♗×c3∓∓) **48 ♖c4 ♖×c4 49 bc
♘c3** (49 ... ♗b4 50 ♔e3 ♘a2 51

♗d2) **50 ♘×c3?** (50 ♘d4 ♘e4 51
♘×c2 ♗×g3 52 h5∓) **50 ...
♗×c3∓ ∓ 51 g4 fg+ 52 ♔×g4
h5+ 53 ♔f3 ♗e1 54 ♔e2 ♗×h4
55 ♔d3 ♗f2 56 ♔×c2 h4 57 ♔d3
h3 0-1**

3503   Matanović–AK

R4: 9.7.1973: Spanish

1 e4 e5 2 ♘f3 ♘c6 3 ♗b5 a6 4 ♗a4
♘f6 5 00 ♗e7 6 ♖e1 b5 7 ♗b3 d6 8
c3 00 9 h3 ♘b8 10 d4 ♘bd7 11
♘bd2 ♗b7 12 ♗c2 ♖e8 13 b4 ♗f8
14 a4 a5 15 ba ♖×a5 16 ♖b1 ♗a6
17 ab ♖×b5 18 ♗a1 ♖b6 19 ♗b3
h6 20 ♕c2 ♗b7 21 ♗a4 ♖a6 22
♗b2 ♕a8 23 ♗b5 ♖×a1 24 ♖×a1
♕c8 25 ♖e1 ♕a8 26 ♖a1 ♕c8 27
♖e1 ½-½

3504   AK–Schauwecker

R5: 10.7.1973: English

1 ♘f3 ♘f6 2 c4 c5 3 ♘c3 e6 4 g3
♘c6 5 ♗g2 d6?! (5 ... d5) 6 00
♗d7 7 d4 cd 8 ♘×d4 a6 9 b3±
♗e7 10 a4 00 11 ♗a3 ♕b8 12 ♖a2!
♖d8 13 ♖d2 ♘×d4 (13 ... ♗e8!?)
14 ♖×d4 ♗c6 15 ♕d2 ♘e8 16.
♖d3 ♕c7 17 ♖d1 ♖d7 (17 ...
♗×g2!?) 18 ♘d5!± ed (18 ...
♗×d5 19 cd e5 20 ♖c1 ♕b6 21
♗h3 ♖dd8 22 e3± ±) 19 cd ♗×a4
20 ba ♗f6 (20 ... ♕b6!?) 21 ♕b4
♖e7 22 ♗f3 ♗e5 23 ♖b3 g6 24
♖db1 ♖b8 25 e4 ♘f6 26 ♗g2 ♕c2
27 ♖c1 ♕e2 28 h3! g5 29 ♖e3 ♕h5
30 ♕b6 ♘e8 31 ♗b4 ♕g6 32 ♕a7
♖d8 33 ♗a5± ± ♖d7 34 ♖c8

♕g7 35 ♕b8 f6 36 ♗d8 ♖f7 37
♗b6 ♖fe7 38 a5! h5 39 ♗f3 ♔h6
40 ♗d1 *(238)*

238
40W
B

40 ... f5 41 ef ♕f7 42 ♗a4 ♘f6 43
♖f8 ♕g7 44 ♖h8+ ♘h7 45 ♖g8
1-0

3505   Hecht–AK

R6: 11.7.1973: French

(Notes by Hecht)

**1 e4 c5 2 ♘f3 e6 3 c3 d5 4 e5 ♗d7
5 d4 ♕b6** (5 ... ♕a5!? Dueball) **6
♗e2 ♗b5 7 00 ♗×e2 8 ♕×e2
♕a6 9 ♕d1 c4** (9 ... ♘c6 Hecht-
Tröger, Bad Pyrmont 1963) **10
♖e1 ♘c6 11 ♘bd2 000** (11 ...
♘ge7) **12 ♘f1 ♖d7!** (with ideas of
... ♘d8 and ... f6; ... b5 and ...
♖b7; ... ♕b6 and ... ♕d8) **13
♗f4!?** (13 h4 ♘d8 14 ♗f4) **13 ...
♘ge7! 14 h4 h5** (14 ... ♘g6 15
♗g5? h6 16 h5 ♘g×e5!∓; 15 ♗g3!
and ♘e3) **15 ♗g3 ♘g6 16 ♗g5
♗e7 17 ♕d2 ♕b6! 18 ♗×e7
♖×e7 19 ♖e2** (intending ♕g5) **19
... ♕d8!** (preparing ... ♖c7 and
... ♘×h4, and if 20 b3?! ♘a5! 21

b4 ♘c6 22 b5 ♘b8∓ rather than 20
... cb!? 21 ab ♖c7 22 b4 ♘×h4 23
♘×h4 ♕×h4 24 b5 ♘b8 25 ♖×a7
which is unclear.) **20 ♘f1 f6 21
♘1h2! fe 22 ♘×e5! ♘×h4?** (22
... ♘c×e5 23 de ♖f8 24 g3 and f4;
22 ... ♘g×e5 23 de ♖d7 and ...
d4=) **23 ♘×c6 bc 24 b3!** (The
position is rather unclear.) **24 ...
cb 25 ab ♔b7?!** (25 ... ♖h6!? 26
♕d3 ♔b8 27 g3 ♘g6) **26 ♕d3
♔a8 27 g3 ♘f5 28 ♘f3± h4 29 g4**
(29 ♘e5 ♖c7) **29 ... ♘d6 30 ♘e5
♖c7 31 ♖ea2 ♘c8 32 ♖a6 ♕e8
33 ♕d2** (with ideas of ♕a2–a4 or
♕f4. 33 c4!?) **33 ... h3 34 ♔h2 c5**
(34 ... ♖f8 35 ♖1a2 and ♕e3–g3)
35 dc ♖×c5 36 ♕d4 ♖c7 *(239)*

239
36B
W

37 f4?? (37 c4! dc? 38 ♕e4+ ♖b7
39 ♘×c4 and ♘a5±±; 37 ...
♖f8!? 38 cd ed 39 ♕×d5+ ♖b7 40
♖1a2±) **37 ... ♕b5!⁼** (Black
threatens ... ♕e2+) **38 ♖6a2**
(preparing for c4) **38 ... ♕×b3 39
♘c6! ♕b7** (39 ... ♖×c6? 40
♖×a7+ ♔b8 41 ♖a8+ ♔c7 42
♕×g7+ ♔d6 43 ♕e5+ ♔d7 44

♖1a7+ ±±) **40 ♘×a7 ♘×a7 41
♖×a7+ ♕×a7 42 ♖×a7+ ♖×a7
43 ♕b6!** ½–½ (43 ... ♖h6 44
♕d8+ ♔b7 45 ♕d7+ ♔b6 46
♕d6+ ♔b5 47 ♕b8+=) (The
players spent a considerable
amount of time looking at this game
in the analysis room, and they both
had great fun doing so – they were
so busy laughing that Hecht seemed
not in the least worried about the
probable win he missed – KJO'C.)

3506   AK–Ribli

R7:12.7.1973: Sicilian

1 e4 c5 2 ♘f3 d6 3 ♗b5+ ♗d7 4
♗×d7+ ♕×d7 5 c4 e5 6 ♘c3 ♘c6
7 00 ♘ge7 8 ♘d5 ♘×d5 9 cd ♘d4
10 ♘×d4 cd 11 d3 ♗e7 12 ♕b3 00
13 f4 ♖ac8 14 ♗d2± f6 15 h3 ♖c7
16 ♖f2 ♖fc8 17 ♖af1 ♖c2 18 g4 a6
19 a4 ♖8cb 20 ♗b4 ♖×f2 21 ♔×f2
♖c7 22 ♗d2 ♖c8 23 ♖e2 ♖c5 24
f5 ♗d8 25 ♕a3 ♔f7 26 ♖b1 ♔e7
27 ♔d1 ♕d7 28 b4 ♖c8 29 ♕a2
♗b6 30 ♗e1 ♔f7 31 ♖a1 ♗d8 32
♗d2 ♗b6 33 a5 ♗d8 34 ♕a4
♕×a4+ 35 ♖×a4 ♔e8 36 h4 h6 37
♖a2 ♔d7 38 ♗e1 ♗e7 39 ♖g2
♗d8 40 ♗d2 ♗e7 41 ♖g3 ♖h8 42
♔c2 ♖c8+ 43 ♔b2 ♖h8 44 ♖g2
♖c8 45 ♖g1 ♖h8 46 ♔c2 ♖c8+
47 ♔d1 ♖h8 48 ♗e1 ♖c8 49 ♖g2
♖h8 50 ♖b2 ♖c8 51 ♗d2 ♗d8 52
b5 ab 53 ♖×b5 ♔c7 54 ♔e2
♔b8 55 ♗b4 ♗c7 56 a6 ♔a7 57 ab
♖b8 58 ♗d2 ♖×b7 59 ♖×b7+
♔×b7 *(240)*

240
59B
W

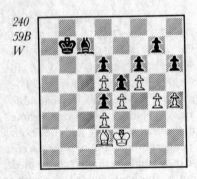

60 g5 (threatening ♔e2–f3–g4–h5–

g6) 60 ... hg (60 ... h5 61 g6 and
62 ♗×h6± ±) 61 hg ♗d8 (61 ... fg
62 ♗×g5 ♔c8 63 ♗e7 and 64
♗f8± ±) 62 ♔f3 ♔c8 63 ♔g4 ♔d7
64 ♔h5 ♔e8 65 ♗b4! fg (65 ...
♗e7 66 gf gf 67 ♔g6 and
♗b4–e1–h4, or if 67 ... ♔f8 68
♗×d6! ♗×d6 69 ♔×f6± ±) 66
♗×d6 ♗f6 67 ♗b4 ♔f7 68 ♗d2
♗e7 (68 ... g4 69 ♔×g4 g6 70
♗g5± ±) 69 ♗×g5 ♗a3 70 ♗d8
♗d6 71 ♔g5 **1–0**

36 41st USSR Championship

Moscow, 2–26.10.1973

	1	2	3	4	5	6	7	8	9	0	1	2	3	4	5	6	7	8	
1 Spassky	×	½	½	½	½	½	½	½	½	1	0	½	1	1	1	1	1	1	**11½**
2 **Karpov**	½	×	1	1	0	½	½	½	½	½	1	½	1	½	½	½	½	1	**10½**
3 Korchnoi	½	0	×	½	½	½	½	½	½	½	1	½	1	1	½	1	1	½	**10½**
4 Kuzmin	½	0	½	×	½	½	½	½	½	1	½	½	½	1	1	1	1	½	**10½**
5 Petrosian	½	1	½	½	×	½	½	½	1	½	½	½	½	½	½	½	1	1	**10½**
6 Polugayevsky	½	½	½	½	½	×	½	1	1	½	½	½	1	½	½	½	½	1	**10½**
7 Geller	½	½	½	½	½	½	×	½	½	0	½	1	½	0	½	1	1	0	**8½**
8 K. Grigorian	½	½	½	½	½	0	½	×	1	½	+	½	½	1	½	0	0	½	**8½**
9 Tal	½	½	½	½	0	0	½	0	×	0	½	1	½	½	1	½	½	1	**8**
10 Taimanov	0	½	½	0	½	½	1	½	1	×	½	½	0	½	½	½	½	½	**8**
11 Savon	1	0	0	½	½	½	½	–	½	½	×	½	½	½	½	½	½	1	**8**
12 Keres	½	½	½	½	½	½	0	½	0	½	½	×	½	½	½	½	½	1	**8**
13 Rashkovsky	0	0	0	½	½	0	½	½	½	1	½	½	×	½	½	½	½	1	**7½**
14 Tukmakov	0	½	0	0	½	½	1	0	½	½	½	½	½	×	½	½	½	1	**7½**
15 Averkin	0	½	½	0	½	½	½	½	0	½	½	½	½	½	×	½	0	1	**7**
16 Smyslov	0	½	0	0	½	½	0	1	½	½	½	½	½	½	½	×	½	½	**7**
17 Sveshnikov	0	½	0	0	0	½	0	1	½	½	½	½	½	½	1	½	×	0	**6½**
18 Belyavsky	0	0	½	½	0	0	1	½	0	½	0	0	0	0	0	½	1	×	**4½**

Karpov's impressions of the tournament (from *64*):

'Spassky played excellently throughout the whole tournament and completely deserved his success. As usual Korchnoi played in a fighting spirit and also at a high level.

'I began the tournament, if you take the number of points obtained as the criterion, like never before. But all the same, even in those games which I won, such as those against Savon and Belyavsky, a feeling of dissatisfaction with my play never left me. I never felt that my game got going. When, in the all-important meeting with Spassky, I not only let slip a tremendous advantage, but even obtained the inferior position, it became clear to me that I could have wished for better form.

'Although I was not very satisfied with the place I obtained, nevertheless I consider my overall result satisfactory, the more so because towards the end I succeeded in overcoming the slump in my play. Although in the later stages I scored fewer points than at the start, nevertheless the quality of my play was higher.'

3601 AK–Savon

R1: 2.10.1973: English

1 ♘f3 ♘f6 2 c4 b6 3 g3 ♗b7 4 ♗g2 c5 5 00 g6 6 d3 ♗g7 7 e4 00 8 ♘c3 ♘c6 9 ♖b1 ♘e8 10 ♗e3 ♘d4 11 ♘e2 e5 (11 ... ♘×f3+ also deserves consideration.) 12 b4 d6 13 bc dc 14 ♘e×d4 cd (14 ... ed 15 ♗f4 h6 is also possible.) 15 ♗d2 ♘c7 16 ♘e1 ♘e6 (16 ... ♘a6 Korchnoi-Kuzmin, Leningrad interzonal 1973; 16 ... f5!?) 17 ♗b4 ♖e8 18 f4 ef 19 gf ♕c7 20 ♕g4 ♘c5 21 ♗×c5! bc 22 ♖b2 ♖ab8 23 ♖bf2 ♗c8 24 ♕g3 ♖b1 25 h4 h5 26 ♘f3! ♖×f1+ 27 ♗×f1 ♗h6 28 ♘d2 ♔h7 29 ♔h2 ♗g4 30 e5 f5?! (30 ... ♗g7) 31 ♕g2 ♖b8 *(241)*

241
31B
W

(Black should be trying to create counter-threats based on variations such as 31 ... ♕d8 32 ♔g3 ♗g7 33 ♘f3 ♗×f3 34 ♕×f3 ♗f6 35 ♖h2 ♖×e5 36 fe ♗×e5+ 37 ♔h3 ♗×h2 38 ♔×h2 ♕×h4+) 32 ♔g3± ♖d8 33 ♘f3 ♖d7?! (33 ... ♖b8! with ♗h6-f8-e7 and ♕c7-d8 to follow–Suetin) 34 ♖b2 ♕a5 35 ♕d2 ♕c3 36 ♗g2 ♖d8? (The decisive mistake. 36 ... ♗×f3 was correct: 37 ♗×f3 ♕×d2 38 ♖×d2±) 37 ♖b3 ♕a1 38 ♖b7+ ± ♔h8 (38 ... ♗g7 39 ♘g5+ ♔g8 40 ♖×g7+ wins a piece.) 39 ♕e1! (threatening 40 e6! followed by 41 ♕e5+ !) 39 ... ♕c3 40 e6 ♕×e1+ 41 ♘×e1 **1-0** (2·27 – 2·34) (There is no defence against the threat of 42 e7 and 43 ♗c6.)

3602 Taimanov–AK

R2: 3.10.1973: Nimzo-Indian

1 d4 ♘f6 2 c4 e6 3 ♘c3 ♗b4 4 e3 c5 5 ♘f3 00 6 ♗d3 d5 7 00 dc 8 ♗×c4 ♘c6 9 a3 ♗a5 10 ♗a2 a6 11 ♘e2 cd 12 ♘e×d4 ♘×d4 13 ♘×d4 ♗c7 14 ♗d2 ♗d6 15 ♖c1 ♗d7 16 ♗b1 ♖c8 17 ♕b3 ♖×c1 18 ♖×c1 ♕b8 19 h3 ♖c8 20 ♖×c8+ ½-½ (0·55 – 0·50)

3603 AK–Sveshnikov

R3: 4.10.1973: Sicilian

1 e4 c5 2 ♘f3 e6 3 d4 cd 4 ♘×d4
♘c6 5 ♘b5 ♘f6 6 ♘1c3 d6 7 ♗f4
e5 8 ♗g5 a6 9 ♘a3 b5 10 ♘d5 ♗e7
11 ♗×f6 ♗×f6 12 c3! 00 13 ♘c2
♗g5 (13 . . . ♖b8! Sveshnikov) 14
a4 ba (14 . . . ♖b8!?± Kupreichik-
Sveshnikov, USSR 1973) 15 ♖×a4
a5 16 ♗c4 ♖b8? (16 . . . ♗d7) 17
b3 (17 ♕a1!) 17 . . . ♗e6 18 ♕a1 g6
19 00 ♕d7 20 ♖d1 f5 21 ef gf 22 b4
(22 ♘a3!?) 22 . . . ab 23 cb ♔h8 24
b5 ♗×d5! (Much more accurate
than 24 . . . ♘e7 25 ♖a7 ♖b7 26
b6±) 25 ♖×d5 ♘e7 *(242)*

242
25B
W

26 ♕×e5+ (White wins a pawn but
loses the initiative. 26 ♖d3 would
have been better, e.g. 26 . . . ♗f6 27
♖a7 ♕d8 28 ♕d1! ♘c8 29
♖a6± – Shamkovich) 26 . . . de 27
♖×d7 ♘c8! 28 ♖c7 ♗d8 29 ♖c6
♘b6 30 ♖b4 ♘×c4 31 ♖c×c4
♗b6 32 ♔f1 (32 g3 f4!) 32 . . . ♖fd8
33 ♔e2 ♗a5 34 ♖b3 ♖d2+ 35
♔e3 f4+ 36 ♔e4 ♖×f2 37 ♔×e5
♖×g2 38 ♘d4 ♖×h2 39 ♖c6 ♗b6
40 ♘e6 f3! 41 ♖×f3 ♖h5+ 42 ♔f6

♖×b5 43 ♖d6 ♗b2 44 ♔e7 ♗a5
½-½ (1·35 – 2·34)

3604 Belyavsky–AK

R4: 6.10.1973: Nimzo-Indian

1 d4 ♘f6 2 c4 e6 3 ♘c3 ♗b4 4 e3 c5
5 ♗d3 00 6 ♘f3 d5 7 00 dc 8 ♗×c4
cd 9 ed b6 10 ♗g5 ♗b7 11 ♕e2
♘bd7 (better 11 . . . ♗e7 followed
by . . . ♘c6) 12 ♖c1 ♖c8 13 ♘e5
♕c7 14 ♗b5 ♕d6 15 ♖fd1 ♗×c3
16 bc± ♕d5 17 f4! ♕d6 (not 17 . . .
♘×e5? 18 fe ♘e4 19 c4!–Suetin) 18
c4! ♕c7 19 ♗a4 a6 20 ♗c2 g6 21
♕e1 ♔g7 22 ♗a4 h6 23 ♗h4 b5 24
cb ♕d6 25 ba ♗×a6 26 d5! ♖×c1
(not 26 . . . ed? 27 ♘×d7 ♗×d7 28
♗e7!± ± – Suetin) 27 ♖×c1 ♗c8
(243)

243
27B
W

28 ♗×d7? (Belyavsky overlooks a
clear win: 28 ♘×f7! (1) 28 . . .
♔×f7 29 de+ ♕×e6 30 ♗b3 ♘d5
31 ♕×e6+ ♔×e6 32 ♖c6+ !±±;
(2) 28 . . . ♖×f7 29 de ♖e7 30
♖×c8± ± . Zaitsev's 28 ♘×d7 may
also be sufficient to win.) 28 . . .
♘×d7 29 de ♕×e6 30 ♘c4 ♗a6 31
♕×e6 fe 32 ♗g3 (32 ♘e5 ♖×f4!=)

32 ... ♖c8 33 ♖d1 ♗×c4 34 ♖×d7+ ♔f6 35 a3 ♗d5 36 h3? (Belyavsky, in time-trouble, misses 36 ♗h4+, drawing easily.) 36 ... ♖c1+ 37 ♔f2 ♖c2+ 38 ♔e3 ♖c3+ 39 ♔f2 ♖×a3 40 ♗h4+ g5 41 fg+ hg 42 ♗g3 ♖a2+ 43 ♔e3 ♖×g2∓ 44 ♗c7 (s) (adjournment 9.10.1973) 44 ... ♖a2 45 ♖h7 ♖a8 46 ♔f2 ♔g6 47 ♖d7 ♖a3 48 ♖d8 ♖f3+ 49 ♔g1 ♖×h3∓∓ 50 ♖f8 ♖c3 51 ♗d6 ♖c2 52 ♖f2 ♖c6 53 ♗e5 g4 54 ♖f6+ ♔g5 55 ♖f8 ♗f3 56 ♗f4+ ♔g6 57 ♔f2 ♖c2+ 58 ♔g3 ♖g2+ 59 ♔h4 ♖e2 60 ♗g3 e5 61 ♖b8 e4 62 ♖b5 ♖e3 63 ♖b6+ ♔f7 64 ♔g5 ♖d3 65 ♔f5 e3 66 ♖d6 ♖b3 67 ♖d7+ ♔e8 68 ♔e6 e2 69 ♖e7+ ♔f8 70 ♔f6 ♗d5 71 ♗h4 ♖f3+ 72 ♔g6 ♗f7+ **0-1** (4·25 – 3·15)

3605   AK–Tal

R5: 7.10.1973: Slav

(Notes by Tal)

1 ♘f3 d5 2 c4 c6 3 d4 ♘f6 4 ♘c3 c6 5 e3 ♘bd7 6 ♗d3 ♗b4 7 00 (7 a3!?) 7 ... 00 8 a3 ♗d6 (8 ... ♗a5 9 ♗d2 ♕e7? 10 ♘×d5± ±) 9 ♕c2 dc 10 ♗×c4 ♕e7 (10 ... e5!?) 11 h3! e5 12 ♗a2! a5!? (12 ... ed 13 ed!± ; 12 ... ♖e8 13 ♘g5!±) 13 a4?! (13 ♗d2 b5! 14 ♖ac1 b4 is unclear; 13 de! ♘×e5 14 ♘d4±) 13 ... ♗b4! 14 ♖d1 b6?! (14 ... ♔h8!∓) 15 de ♘×e5 16 ♘d4 ♗d7 17 ♗d2 ♖ad8 18 ♗e1 ♘g6= 19 ♘f3 ♘e5 20 ♘d4 ♘g6 21 ♘f3 ♘e5= ½-½ (1·30 – 1·40)

3606   Korchnoi–AK

R6: 8.10.1973: Irregular

1 ♘f3 ♘f6 2 g3 b5 3 c3!? ♗b7 4 a4 a6 5 e3 ♘c6 6 d4 e6 (6 ... e5 was also possible.) 7 b4 ♗e7 8 ♘bd2 ♘a7 9 ♗d3 00 10 e4 d6 (preparing c7–c5, closing the centre) 11 00 c5! 12 bc (12 ♗b2 cb 13 cb d5) 12 ... dc 13 ♗b2 ♘c6 (This pawn sacrifice leads to sharp play. 13 ... c4!? may have been better.) 14 e5?! (14 ab ab 15 ♗×b5 ♕b6 16 c4 would have been a better way for Korchnoi to take the pawn.) 14 ... ♘d5 15 ab ab 16 ♕b1 cd 17 cd (After 17 ♗×h7+ ♔h8 18 cd g6 19 ♗×g6 fg 20 ♕×g6 ♕e8 21 ♕×e6 ♗f7, Black's extra piece will prove stronger than White's pawns.) 17 ... h6 18 ♗×b5 ♕b6 19 ♗e2 (19 ♗d3, to transfer the bishop to e4 is not a bad alternative.) 19 ... ♖×a1 20 ♗×a1 ♕a7 21 ♘c4 (21 ♘e4! intending 22 ♘c5!= – Botvinnik) 21 ... ♖b8 22 ♗b2 ♗a6 23 ♕c2 ♕b7 24 ♗a1 ♘cb4 25 ♕d2 ♖c8∓ 26 ♘e3 ♘×e3 27 ♕×e3 (not 27 ♗×a6 ♕×f1, nor 27 fe ♖c2) 27 ... ♗×e2 (Both players were already in time-pressure.) 28 ♕×e2 ♖c2 29 ♕d1 ♕c6 30 h3 (30 d5! ♕×d5 31 ♕×d5 ♘×d5 32 ♗d4= – Botvinnik) 30 ... ♘d5 31 ♕d3 ♕a4 32 ♘d2 ♖a2 33 ♘b3 ♘b4 34 ♕b1 ♘d5 35 ♖c1 ♕a8 36 ♖c8+ ♕×c8 37 ♕×a2 ♕c4 38 ♕b1 ♕e2 (*244*)

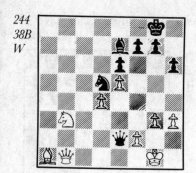

244
38B
W

39 ♕c1 ? (The decisive mistake. 39 ♘c5∓ is best.) **39 ... ♗g5∓∓ 40 ♕f1 ♕f3** (threatening 41 ... ♕×b3) **41 h4** (s) **0–1** (2·30 – 2·28) (Black has a forced win with 41 ... ♗e3! and (1) 42 ♕g2 ♗×f2+ 43 ♕×f2 ♕×b3 44 ♔h2 ♕d3 45 ♗b2 ♘e3 46 ♔h3 h5! 47 ♕f3 ♕d2 and 48 ... ♘g4; (2) 42 fe ♕×g3+ 43 ♔h1 ♕×h4+ 44 ♔g1 ♕g3+ 45 ♔h1 ♘×e3. So Korchnoi resigned without resuming.)

3607 AK–Spassky

R7: 11.10.1973: Spanish

(Notes by Karpov)

1 e4 e5 2 ♘f3 ♘c6 3 ♗b5 a6 4 ♗a4 ♘f6 5 00 ♗e7 6 ♖e1 b5 7 ♗b3 d6 8 c3 00 9 h3 ♘a5 10 ♗c2 c5 11 d4 ♕c7 12 ♘bd2 ♘c6 13 d5 ♘d8 14 a4 ♖b8

It is interesting that this same line was employed in the first game of the Spassky-Korchnoi match (Kiev 1968).

15 ab

The immediate 15 b4 is also good.

15 ...   ab
16 b4   c4
17 ♘f1   ♘e8

In my opinion this is an inaccuracy, since Black shows his hand too soon. It is not advisable to take away the e8 square from the black rook at such an early stage. Taking advantage of this I succeeded in thinking up a comparatively new plan involving the moves ♘f3–h2 and f2–f4.

Black should have played 17 ... ♗d7.

18 ♘3h2   f6

I think that 18 ... ♗f6 would have been better.

19 f4   ♘f7
20 ♘f3

Here White has many varied possibilities. Thus 20 f5 g6 21 g4 ♘g7 seems natural, and now, by playing 22 ♗e3, White firmly seizes the a-file. This line is perfectly sound, but it is not clear that dominating the only open file would have got me anywhere.

20 ...   g6
21 f5   ♘g7
22 g4   ♗d7
23 ♗e3   ♖a8
24 ♕d2

Probably this is not best, even though it forces the black queen to b7. 24 ♖c1 was more consistent, so that if 24 ... ♖a2, the rook can be repelled from the second rank with 25 ♗b1 and only then play 26 ♕d2.

24 . . .   ♕b7
25 ♖ac1

A crucial decision – to concede the a-file to the opponent. On the other hand, if one pair of rooks is exchanged then White is left with fewer winning chances. If you want to win – give your opponent counterplay!

25 . . .   ♖a2
26 ♘g3   ♖fa8
27 h4   ♗d8
28 ♔h1   ♗b6
29 ♖g1   ♗×e3
30 ♕×e3   ♕a7
31 ♕d2   ♗e8

I do not think very much of this manoeuvre – the black pieces have become very passive. In guarding g6 an extra time, Black finally unties his opponent's hands and leaves them free for a K-side attack. I think that transferring the queen to d8 by ♕a7–b6–d8 was more useful here.

32 g5   ♕e7
33 ♖cf1   fg

Black must go in for this exchange immediately, otherwise White plays 34 ♘h2 and eliminates even this possibility.

34 hg   ♕d7
35 ♘h2

I dare say that the simplest move was 35 ♖f2, keeping in reserve the threat f5–f6. That would have posed Black very difficult problems, the more so because at this moment Spassky only had four minutes left on his clock. But instead of this I

made some unimportant moves.

35 . . .   ♕d8 (245)

245
35B
W

36 f6

It seemed to me that after 36 fg hg 37 ♘g4 ♕×g5 38 ♘f6+ ♔h8 39 ♕h2+ ♕h6 40 ♖g2 (not diverting the other rook which can still prove useful on the f-file) 40 . . . ♖a1 41 ♗b1 ♕×h2+ 42 ♖×h2+ ♘h5 43 ♘g×h5 gh there is nothing clearly forcing and Black's position is holding together. If, all the same, White plays 40 ♖f2, then again 40 . . . ♖a1 41 ♕×h6+ ♘×h6 42 ♖h2 ♘h5 43 ♘g×h5 gh and g8 is protected. It is true that in each case Black's position remains shaky, and I should have sought an improvement in one of these variations.

36 . . .   ♗d7

Black, on the other hand, has no pretensions, he just makes the best moves.

37 fg

(Bondarevsky, Spassky's trainer, suggested sacrificing a piece instead of taking one: 37 ♖f2 ♘e8 38 ♘f5 with an attack – KJO'C.)

37 ...   ♕×g5

38 ♕g2

38 ♕f2 was stronger, and after the forced 38 ... ♕f4–39 ♘f5, and White again has the advantage, and a significant one at that.

38 ...   ♖b2

39 ♖b1

Again 39 ♕f2 was better here. The variations arising from that move I analysed at home because they could have a bearing on the adjourned position:

39 ... ♕e7 40 ♘f5 gf 41 ef ♖aa2 (41 ... ♕f6 42 ♘g4 ♕g5 43 ♖g2 and White has a tremendous advantage) 42 f6 ♕e8 43 ♖c1 ♘h6 44 ♖g5 (preventing ♗f5) 44 ... ♕f7 45 ♔g1 ♗f5 (45 ... ♘f5 46 ♘g4; 45 ... e4 46 ♕h4 ♕×f6 47 ♖f1) 46 ♕b6 (The tempting 46 ♖×f5 ♕g6+ 47 ♔h1 ♘×f5 48 ♗×f6 ♖×f2 49 ♗e6+ ♕f7 50 ♘g4 unfortunately does not work because of 47 ... ♖×c2 48 ♖×c2 ♖a1+ .).

It is clear that 45 ... ♗c8 is preferable (instead of 45 ... ♗f5): 46 ♘f1 ♖×c2 47 ♖×c2 ♖×c2 48 ♕×c2 ♕×f6 49 ♖g2 ♘g4 50 ♘e3 h5 (50 ... ♘×e3 51 ♕×h7+ ♔×h7 52 g8♕+) 51 ♘×g4 ♗×g4 52 ♕f2 ♔×g7 53 ♕e3 and White's position is slightly better.

Instead of 39 ... ♕e7, 39 ... ♕f4 deserves consideration. Also in this case it seems possible to play 40 ♘f5 ♕×f2 41 ♖×f2 gf 42 ef and, with f5–f6 to follow, White sets his opponent difficult problems. If

Black prevents this then the following piquant ending arises: 42 ... ♖aa2 43 ♘g4 ♔×g7 44 ♘h6+ and all the king's moves lead to mate. If he plays immediately 41 ... ♖aa2, then 42 ♘e3 in conjunction with ♘h2–f3–g5–e6 also gives White the advantage.

Finally, I was aware that all the preceding variations were similar and required further checking.

39 ...   ♖ba2

40 ♕e2   ♕h4

41 ♖bf1

The sealed move. (adjournment 14.10.1973) In the adjourned position, despite White's extra piece, Black already has some advantage.

41 ...   ♗h3

42 ♖f2   ♘g5

43 ♕e3   ♗g4

Move by move Black introduces threats, each time forcing White to make practically the only reply.

44 ♖gf1   ♔×g7

45 ♗d1

I do not see any other satisfactory reply.

45 ...   ♗×d1

46 ♖×d1   ♖a1

47 ♖df1

47 ♖ff1 is unsatisfactory on account of 47 ... ♖8a2, and 47 ♖fd2 because of the same reply.

47 ...   ♖×f1+

48 ♖×f1   ♖a2

49 ♖f2   ♖a1+

50 ♖f1   ♖a2

51 ♖f2   ♖a1+

52   ♖f1   ♖×f1+
53   ♘×f1   ♕×e4+
54   ♔g1 *(246)*

246
54W
B

54 ...   ♕×e3+

In my opinion this exchange is not forced. Black had the useful 54 ... ♕h4 (54 ... h6 is not possible in view of 55 ♕a7+ ♔f6 56 ♕d7), with the idea of the manoeuvre ♘g5-h3-f4. White is practically forced to play 55 ♕a7+ ♔h6 56 ♕e3. The endgame which arises after the text is also favourable for Spassky.

55   ♘×e3   ♘e4
56   ♘d1   ♘f6

(Bondarevsky gave 56 ... ♔f6 as practically winning – KJO'C.)

57   ♘e3   h5

I think the immediate king thrust, 57 ... ♔h6, (while the white knights are unable to create a barrier) was better.

58   ♘f3   ♘e4
59   ♘d1   ½-½

3·23   3·54

The ending still retains its tension, e.g.: 59 ... ♔f6 60 ♘e1 ♔f5 61 ♘c2 ♘f6 62 ♘a3; or 59 ...

g5 60 ♘e1 ♘f6 61 ♘e3 ♔g6 (61 ... ♘e8 62 ♘f3 ♔g6 63 ♘d2 ♘f6 64 ♘d×c4 bc 65 b5 ♔f7 66 b6 ♘d7 67 b7 and Black's d-pawn is lost just the same) 62 ♘1c2 ♘e8 63 ♘a3 (The immediate 63 ♘×c4 is possibly more accurate.) 63 ... ♘c7 64 ♔g2 g4 65 ♘e×c4 bc 66 b5 ♘×d5 67 ♘×c4 h4 68 ♘×d6 and, although Black is certainly not risking defeat, the white pawns could become strong.

3608 Petrosian–AK

R8: 12.10.1973: Queen's Indian

1 d4 ♘f6 2 ♘f3 e6 3 c4 b6 4 e3 ♗b7 5 ♘c3 ♗e7 6 ♗d3 d5 7 00 00 8 ♕e2 c5 9 dc dc (9 ... ♗×c5!?) 10 ♗×c4 ♗×c5 11 e4! (11 ♖d1 Petrosian-Kotov, USSR Ch 1958) 11 ... ♘bd7 12 e5 ♗×f3 13 gf ♘h5 14 ♖d1 ♕e7 15 f4 g6 16 f5! ef 17 e6 ♘df6 18 ef+ ♔g7 19 ♕×e7 ♗×e7 20 ♘b5 ♖ac8 21 ♗b3 a6 22 ♘d4 ♖×f7 (22 ... ♔h8 23 ♗h6 ♘g7 24 ♗×g7+ ♔×g7 25 ♘e6+) 23 ♗e3 ♘g4 24 ♗×f7 (24 ♘e6!?) 24 ... ♔×f7 25 ♖ac1 ♖c5 26 ♔g2 ♘hf6 27 ♗d2 ♖d5 28 ♗e1 a5 29 ♘f3 ♖×d1 30 ♖×d1∓ (Petrosian now produces a model example of how to realize a material advantage in the endgame.) 30 ... ♘e4 31 ♘d2 ♘d6 32 b3 ♘e5 33 ♘b1 ♔e6 34 ♘c3 ♘ef7 35 f3 ♗d8 36 ♗f2 ♘c8 37 ♘b5 ♘cd6 38 ♘d4+ ♔d7 39 ♗g3 ♗e7 40 ♔f1 ♗f6 *(247)*

41   ♘b5   (s)   (adjournment 14.10.1973) 41 ... ♗e7 42 h4 ♔e6

247
40B
W

43 ♘d4+ ♔d7 44 ♔g2 ♗f6 45
♘b5 ♗e7 46 a4 h6 (46 . . . ♔e6 47
♘d4+ ♔d7 48 h5; 46 . . . ♔c6 47
♖c1+ ♔d7 48 ♖c7+ ; 46 . . . h6 47
h5! g5 48 f4! g4 49 ♗f2 ♗d8 50
♘d4 ♔e8 51 ♘e6± ±) 47 h5!± ±
gh 48 ♗f2 ♗d8 49 ♘d4 f4 50 ♘e2
♔c6 51 ♘×f4 h4 52 ♘g6 ♗b7 53 f4
♗f6 54 ♖c1+ ♘c5 55 ♔h3 ♘d6
56 ♗×c5! (forcing yet another
weakness in Black's position and
making the win very simple) 56 . . .
bc 57 ♘×h4 h5 58 ♘f3 ♔d5 59
♖d1+ ♗d4 60 ♘d2 ♔e6 61 ♔g3
♘f5+ 62 ♔f3 h4 63 ♘c4 ♗c3 64
♔g4♗b4 65 ♖d3 **1–0** (3·47 – 3·05)

3609 AK–Kuzmin

R9: 13.10.1973: Sicilian

1 e4 c5 2 ♘f3 d6 3 d4 cd 4 ♘ × d4 ♘f6
5 ♘c3 a6 6 f4 ♕c7 7 a4 g6 8
♘f3 ♗g4 9 ♗d3 ♘c6 10 h3 ♗×f3
11 ♕×f3 ♗g7 12 00 00 13 ♗d2 e6
14 ♘e2± ♖ ac8? (Both 14 . . . ♘b4
15 ♗×b4 ♕b6+ followed by 16
. . . ♕×b4, and 14 . . . ♘d7 15
♗c3 ♗ × c3 16 bc♕d8! would have
been better; White would have
found it difficult to increase his K-

side initiative.) 15 ♔h1 e5 16 ♘c3
ef 17 ♗×f4 ♘b4 18 ♗d2 ♘d7 19
♕g3 ♕c6 20 ♗g5 ♖ce8 21 ♖ad1
(*248*)

248
21W
B

21 . . . ♘e5 (21 . . . h6!?) 22 ♕h4
♘e×d3 (22 . . . ♖e6, followed by
23 . . . f6, might have been better.)
23 cd ♕d7 24 ♗f6 a5 25 d4 ♖e6 26
e5 d5 (26 . . . de 27 de ♕c6 28 ♘e4)
27 ♗×g7 ♔×g7 28 ♖f6 h6 29
♖dfl ♖×f6 30 ♖×f6 ♖e8 31 ♘e2
♘c6 (or 31 . . . ♖e6 32 ♘f4 ♖×f6
33 ♕×f6+ and 34 e6± ±) 32
♖d6± ± ♕f5 33 ♘g3 ♕d3 34
♖×d5 ♖e6 35 ♕f4 ♖e7 36 ♔h2
♔g8 37 ♕×h6 ♕c4 38 ♘e4 **1–0**
(2·10 – 2·25)

3610 Averkin–AK

R10: 15.10.1973: Réti

1 ♘f3 ♘f6 2 c4 b6 3 b3 ♗b7 4 ♗b2
e6 5 e3 ♗e7 6 ♗e2 00 7 00 d5 8
♘c3 c5 9 cd ♘×d5 10 d4 ♘×c3 11
♗×c3 ♘c6 12 ♖c1 ♖c8 13 dc
♗×c5 14 ♕×d8 ♖f×d8 15 ♗b2
♘b4 16 ♖fd1 ♗×a2 17 ♖×d8+
♖×d8 18 ♗a1 ♘b4 19 ♖×a7 ♗d5
20 ♘d4 h6 21 ♖c7 ♖a8 22 ♗f1

♗d6 23 ♖c1 ♗e5 24 ♖a1 ♖×a1
25 ♗×a1 ♗f6 26 ♗c4 ♗×c4 27 bc
♔f8 28 ♔f1 ♗e7 29 ♗c3 ½-½
(1·10 – 1·55)

3611   AK–Geller

R11: 16.10.1973: Spanish

1 e4 e5 2 ♘f3 ♘c6 3 ♗b5 a6 4 ♗a4
♘f6 5 00 ♗e7 6 ♖e1 b5 7 ♗b3 00 8
a4 ♗b7 9 d3 d6 10 ♘c3 ♘a5 11
♗a2 b4 12 ♘e2 c5 13 c3 c4 14 ♘g3
(14 dc ♘×e4? 15 cb ♕b6 16 ba
♕×f2+ 17 ♔h1 ♕c5 18 ♖f1 ♘f2+
19 ♖×f2 ♕×f2 20 ♕e1; 14 . . .
♗×e4! 15 cb ♘c6 16 b5 ♘b4 17
♘c3) 14 . . . cd 15 ♗g5 h6 16 ♗×f6
♗×f6 17 ♖e3 bc 18 bc ♕c7 19
♖×d3 ♖ad8 20 ♘e1 g6 21 ♘c2
♗g7 22 ♘e3 ♔h8 23 ♖b1 ♗c8 24
♖b2 ♘b7 25 ♘d5 ♕d7 26 ♘b6
♕c7 27 ♘×c8 ♖×c8 28 h4 ♘c5 29
♖d5 h5 30 ♖bd2 ♕e7 ½-½
(2·20 – 2·22)

3612   Tukmakov–AK

R12: 17.10.1973: Sicilian

(Notes by Tukmakov)

**1 e4 c5 2 ♘f3 e6 3 d4 cd 4 ♘×d4
a6 5 ♗d3 ♘f6 6 00 ♕c7 7 ♘d2
♘c6 8 ♘×c6 bc 9 f4 d5 10 b3 ♗e7
11 ♗b2 a5 12 c4** (12 ♕e2 deserved
consideration as a more natural
place for the queen than the one I
chose.) **12 . . . 00** (Karpov made
this move after long thought – 36
minutes. In castling, Black was
obliged to look at the consequences

of the sacrifice 13 e5 ♘d7 14
♗×h7+ ♔×h7 15 ♕h5+ ♔g8 16
♖f3 f5 17 ♖h3. After 17 . . . ♖d8
White has a draw but no more.) **13
♕c2 h6! 14 ♔h1 ♕b6** (The threat
was 15 cd.) **15 ♖ ael ?** (I thought
for a long time about the position
after the exchange sacrifice and it
seemed to me really formidable; in
reality it was not so simple. 15 ♘f3
was quieter and better.) **15 . . .
♘g4** *(249)*

249
15B
W

16 ed (16 ♘f3 ♗c5) **16 . . . cd 17
cd ♘f2+ 18 ♖×f2 ♕×f2 19 ♖e2**
(After 19 ♖f1 ♕c5 White has no
compensation for the exchange.) **19
. . . ♕×f4** (19 . . . ♕c5 is bad: (1)
20 de ♕×c2 21 ef+ with sufficient
compensation; (2) 20 ♘c4 ed 21
♗a3 dc 22 ♕h7+ ! ♔h8 23 ♗×c5.)
(Lilienthal, however, recommends
19 . . . ♕c5, analysing: (1) 20 de
♕×c2 21 ef+ ♖×f7 22 ♗×c2 ♗a6
and if 23 ♖e4 then 23 . . . ♗b4 24
♘c4 ♗b7 with advantage to Black;
(2) 20 ♗c4 ed 21 ♘e4 ♕c6! again
with better chances for Black; (3) 20
♘c4 ed 21 ♗a3 ♕d4! 22 ♗×e7 dc
23 ♗h7+ ♔h8 24 ♗×f8 ♗g4! and

Black has good chances – White has an extra piece, but all his pieces are out of play. KJO'C.) **20 ☒ e4 ♕ d6** (20 . . . ♕g5 was possible. White can draw with 21 ☒ e5 ♕f4 22 ☒ e4, but it is not easy to find more, if indeed it is possible. However, the text move is better.) **21 ♘ c4 ♕×d5 22 ☒ g4!** (Immediately regaining the exchange does not work: 22 ♘b6 ♕b7 23 ♕c3 e5! 24 ♘×a8 ♕×a8 and Black is a pawn up.) **22 . . . e5 23 ☒ g3 ☒ a6** (23 . . . ♕e6!– Lilienthal) **24 ♘×e5** *(250)*

250
24W
B

(Here my opponent thought for a long time – 12 minutes – and it seemed to me that in playing 23 . . . ☒ a6, Karpov had overlooked, in the variation 24 ♘×e5 ☒ e6 25 ♗ c4 ☒ ×e5, the move 26 ☒ ×g7+ ! Now I had ten minutes left and Karpov twenty.) **24 . . . ♗ f6** (24 . . . ☒ f6 25 ♘c6!) **25 ♗ c4 ♕ d6** (Lilienthal also mentions 25 . . . ♕b7 26 ♗ ×a6 ♕×a6 27 ♘c4 ☒ e8 with some positional plus for Black – KJO'C.) **26 ♘ × f7!** ☒ × f7 **27 ♗ ×f6** (27 ♗ ×f7+ loses to 27 . . .

♔×f7 28 ♗ ×f6 ♗ f5 29 ☒ ×g7+ ♔f8!) **27 . . . ♗ e6!** (if 27 . . . ♕×f6 28 ♗ ×f7+ ♕×f7 29 ♕×c8+) **28 ☒ d3 ♕ c7** (After 28 . . . ♗ ×c4 29 ☒ × d6 ☒ ×d6 30 bc, White is not risking anything.) **29 ☒ d8+ ♕ × d8!** (If 29 . . . ☒ f8 there would have followed the stunning blow 30 ☒ ×f8+ ♕×f8 31 ♗ ×g7+! The bishop is immune: 31 . . . ♕×g7 32 ♕f2+ and 33 ♗ ×a6; or 31 . . . ♔×g7 32 ♕b2+ and 33 ♗ ×a6. That leaves 31 . . . ♔g8, but then 32 ♗ b2 and White has two pawns for the exchange, which, together with the position of the black king, gives White at least equal chances.) **30 ♗ ×d8 ♗ ×c4 31 h3!** (If 31 ♕×c4 ☒ c6! and it is not possible to defend against the two mates at f1 and c1 except by going into a lost endgame with 32 ♕×f7+ .) **31 . . . ♗ f1** (31 . . . ♗ d5 was best of all in this position.) **32 ♕ e4! a4 33 ba ☒ d6 34 ♗ a5 ☒ df6 35 ♗ e1 ♗ a6 36 ♔ h2 ♗ b7 37 ♕ c4 ☒ c6 38 ♕ b3 ☒ g6 39 ♗ g3 ☒ g5 40 ♕ c4 ♗ d5 41 ♕ c8+** (s) (adjournment 18.10.1973) **41 . . . ☒ f8 42 ♕ c2 h5 43 a5!** ½-½ (2·55–3·00) (The ending after 43 . . . h4 44 ♗ ×h4 ☒ ×g2+ 45 ♕×g2 ♗ ×g2 46 ♔×g2 cannot be won.)

3613 AK–Polugayevsky

R13: 20.10.1973: Slav

1 d4 d5 2 c4 c6 3 ♘f3 ♘f6 4 ♘c3 e6 5 e3 ♘bd7 6 ♗d3 dc 7 ♗×c4 b5 8 ♗d3 ♗b7 9 e4 b4 10 ♘a4 c5 11 e5

♘d5 12 dc ♘×c5 (12 . . . ♗×c5) 13
♘×c5 ♗×c5 14 00 h6 15 ♕e2 ♕b6
16 ♗d2 ♔f8 17 ♖ac1? (17 h4! g6 18
h5!) 17 . . . ♖d8 18 ♖c2 g6 19 ♖fc1
♗e7 20 ♗c4 ♖c8! 21 ♗×d5 ♖×c2
22 ♖×c2 ♗×d5= 23 ♖c8+ ♔g7
24 ♖×h8 ♔×h8 25 ♗×h6 ♕c7 26
b3 ♕c3 27 h4 a5 28 ♗g5 ♗×f3 29
♕×f3 ♗×g5 30 hg ♕e1+ 31 ♔h2
♕×e5+ 32 ♕g3 ♕b2 33 ♕b8+
♔g7 34 f4 ♕×a2 35 ♕e5+ ½–½
(2·27 – 2·17)

3614   Keres–AK

R14: 21.10.1973: Queen's Indian

1 d4 ♘f6 2 c4 e6 3 ♘f3 b6 4 g3 ♗b7
5 ♗g2 ♗e7 6 00 00 7 ♘c3 ♘e4 8
♕c2 ♘×c3 9 ♕×c3 c5 10 ♖d1 d6
11 ♕c2 ♘c6 12 dc bc 13 b3 a5 14
♗b2 ♕c7 15 ♕c3 ♗f6 16 ♕d2
♗×b2 17 ♕×b2 a4 18 e3 h6 19
♖d2 ab 20 ab ♖×a1+ 21 ♕×a1
♖a8 22 ♖a2 ♖ × a2 23 ♕ × a2 ½–½
(1·10 – 0·50)

3615   AK–K. Grigorian

R15: 23.10.1973: QGD

1 ♘f3 c5 2 c4 ♘f6 3 ♘c3 d5 4 cd
♘×d5 5 d4 e6 6 e4 ♘×c3 7 bc cd 8
cd ♘c6 9 ♗c4 ♗b4+ 10 ♗d2 ♕a5
11 d5!? (11 ♖b1?! ♗×d2+ 12
♕ × d2 ♔e7! and 13 . . . ♖d8; 11 a3
♗×d2+ 12 ♕×d2 ♕×d2+ 13
♔×d2) 11 . . . ♗×d2+ 12 ♘×d2
♘e7! 13 00 (13 d6!?) 13 . . . ed 14 ed
00 (not 14 . . . ♘×d5?? 15 ♕b3± ±)
15 ♖e1 ♘f5 16 ♗b3 ♘d6 (Kotov
recommends 16 . . . b5 followed by

. . . ♗b7 and . . . ♖ad8) 17 ♘e4
(251)

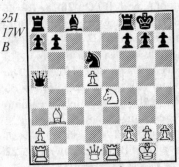

251
17W
B

17 . . . ♕b4! (17 . . . ♕d8 is strongly
met by ♕d1–f3–f4.) 18 ♕f3
(Karpov spent 62 minutes on this
move.) 18 . . . ♖e8 19 a3 ♕a5! 20
♖e3 ♘×e4 21 ♖×e4 ♖×e4 22
♕×e4 ♗d7 23 h3 ♕c3?! (23 . . .
♖e8=) 24 ♕b1! ♕c5 (if 24 . . .
♖e8?! then 25 ♕d1 followed by
♖c1 and d6±) 25 ♗c2 ♕×d5 26
♗×h7+ ♔h8 27 ♗e4 ♕d4 28
♖a2 ♖e8 29 ♗×b7 ♖b8 30 ♕e4!
♕d1+ 31 ♔h2 ♗e6! 32 ♖b2 (32
♖c2?? ♖×b7) 32 . . . ♕d6+ 33 g3
♕×a3 34 ♕e5 ♖d8 35 ♗e4 ♔g8
36 ♖b8 ♕e7 37 h4 a5 38 ♕h5? (38
♖b5! a4 39 ♖a5 should win.) 38
. . . f5!= 39 ♖×d8+ ♕×d8 40
♗×f5 ♗×f5 41 ♕×f5 a4 (s)
(adjournment 25.10.1973) 42 ♕c2
♕a5 ½–½ (2·40 – 2·40)

3616   AK–Rashkovsky

R16: 24.10.1973: Benoni

1 c4 g6 2 d4 ♘f6 3 ♘c3 c5 4 d5 d6 5
♘f3 ♗g7 6 e4 00 7 ♗e2 e6 8 00
♖e8 9 h3 ed 10 ed ♘e4? 11 ♘×e4

☖×e4 12 ♗d3 ☖e8 13 ♗g5 ♛b6
14 ☖b1 ♗d7 15 a3 a5 16 b3 ♛c7 17
♛d2 a4 18 ♗h6 ab 19 ♗×g7
♔×g7 20 ☖×b3 ♗c8 21 ♛b2+
♔g8 22 ♘d2 f5 (*252*)

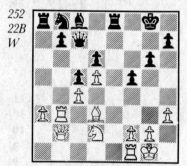

252
22B
W

23 ♘f3 (23 ♗×f5! ♗×f5 24 ☖×b7;
23 ... gf 24 ☖g3+ ♔f8 25 ♛h8+
♔e7 26 ☖e1+) 23...♘d7 24 ♘g5
♘f8 25 ♛d2 ♛e7 26 f4 ♛e3+ 27
♛×e3 ☖×e3 28 ♔f2 ☖e7 29 ☖a1
♘d7 30 ♘f3 ♔f8 31 ♘d2 ♘f6 32
a4 ☖a5 33 ♗c2 ♔e8 34 ♔f3 ♔d8
35 ☖bb1 ☖a6 36 a5 ☖a7 37 ☖g1

☖a6 38 ♘b3 ♗d7 39 ☖gb1 ☖a7
40 ♘d2 ♗c8 41 ♘f1 ☖a6? (s) (the
losing move) (adjournment
25.10.1973) 42 ☖b6!± ± h6 43
☖×a6 ba 44 ☖b1 g5 45 ♘g3 g4+
46 hg fg+ 47 ♔f2 ♘e8 48 ♗g6
☖g7 49 ♗×e8 ♔×e8 50 ♘e4 ♔e7
51 ☖b8 ♗d7 52 ♔g3 ☖g6 53 ☖b7
♔d8 54 ☖b6 **1-0** (3.03 - 3.25)

3617 Smyslov–AK

R17: 26.10.1973: Sicilian

1 e4 c5 2 ♘f3 d6 3 d4 cd 4 ♘×d4
♘f6 5 ♘c3 a6 6 ♗e2 e5 7 ♘f3 ♗e7
8 00 00 9 ☖e1 ♘bd7 10 a4 ♛c7 11
♘d2 ♘c5 12 ♗f3 ☖b8 13 a5 ♘e6
14 ♘b3 b5 15 ab ☖×b6 16 ♗e3
☖b4 17 ♗e2 ♗b7 18 f3 d5 19
♘×d5 ♘×d5 20 ed ♘d4 21 ♘×d4
ed 22 c3 dc 23 bc ♛×c3 24 ♗×a6
♗c5 25 ♗×c5 ♛×c5+ 26 ♔h1
♗×a6 27 ☖×a6 ☖d4 28 ♛a1
♛×d5 29 ☖a5 ½-½ (2.06 - 1.36)

		1	2	3	4	5	6	7	8	9	0	1	2	3	4	5	6	
1	**Karpov**	×	½	½	½	1	1	½	½	½	1	½	1	1	1	1	½	**11**
2	Tukmakov	½	×	½	½	½	½	1	0	1	1	1	½	1	1	½	1	**10½**
3	Furman	½	½	×	½	1	1	½	½	½	½	1	0	1	½	1	1	**10**
4	Hort	½	½	½	×	½	½	1	1	½	½	½	½	½	1	½	1	**9½**
5	Uhlmann	0	½	0	½	×	½	½	½	1	1	½	1	½	1	1	1	**9½**
6	Andersson	0	½	0	½	½	×	½	½	1	½	½	1	1	1	½	1	**9**
7	Portisch	½	0	½	0	½	½	×	½	½	1	1	1	½	½	1	1	**9**
8	Browne	½	1	½	0	½	½	½	×	½	½	½	1	1	½	1	0	**8½**
9	Ljubojević	½	0	½	½	0	0	½	½	×	½	1	1	½	1	1	1	**8½**
10	Planinc	0	0	½	½	0	½	0	½	½	×	1	0	1	0	1	1	**6½**
11	Panno	½	0	0	½	½	½	0	½	0	0	×	½	1	½	1	½	**6**
12	Calvo	0	½	1	½	0	0	0	0	0	1	½	×	½	½	0	½	**5**
13	Kaplan	0	0	0	½	½	0	½	0	½	0	0	½	×	1	½	1	**5**
14	Pomar	0	0	½	0	0	0	½	½	0	1	½	½	0	×	½	1	**5**
15	S. Garcia	0	½	0	½	0	½	0	0	0	0	0	1	½	½	×	½	**4**
16	Bellon	½	0	0	0	0	0	0	1	0	0	½	½	0	0	½	×	**3**

Karpov took first prize. He also picked up the Best Game Prize and the prize for scoring the best result in the last four rounds (3½/4).

This tournament re-inforced Karpov's position as number two in the world (after Fischer), though Spassky still had some claims to share this place. Golombek, the tournament arbiter, made some interesting comments in *The Times*: 'Anyone who had watched his play at Madrid would have come away with the conviction that if he does manage to make his way successfully through the series of Candidates' matches then Karpov will give the world champion a really hard fight for the title. His play at Madrid had that sort of universal quality that characterizes the really great player and, in a tournament which was toughly contested he, as far as I could distinguish, made only one mistake, in his draw with Portisch.'

1973 Chess Oscar

1973 was a magnificent year for Karpov – he lost only one game (against Petrosian in the USSR Championship) and finished with the excellent overall score of + 32 − 1 = 41 (71%) which recalls Fischer's results of 1970: + 48 − 3 = 23 (80%).

The year's achievements were crowned when he was awarded the chess oscar at the end of the Madrid tournament (In 1972 Karpov had also been in the running for this prize: 1 Fischer, 2 Spassky, 3 Portisch, 4 Karpov).

If one can draw conclusions from history then the list of previous oscar winners is most interesting: 1967 Bent Larsen; 1968, 1969 Boris Spassky; 1970, 1971, 1972 Robert Fischer.

Karpov was also voted one of the Soviet Union's top ten sportsmen of the year (No. 1 chessplayer) in an annual poll of Soviet sports writers.

3701 AK–Pomar

R1: 26.11.1973: Caro Kann

1 e4 c6 2 ♘c3 d5 3 ♘f3 ♗g4 4 h3 ♗×f3 5 ♕×f3 e6 6 a3 de 7 ♘×e4 ♘f6 8 ♘c3 d5 9 ♗e2 ♘d7 10 0-0 ♕f6 11 ♕×f6 ♘7×f6 12 ♗f3 ♗d6 13 d3 0-0 14 g3 ♖fe8 15 ♖e1 ♖e7 16 ♘b1 ♖ae8 17 ♘d2 e5 18 b3 e4! 19 ♘×e4 (19 de ♗e5 20 ♖b1 ♘c3 21 ♖b2∓) 19 ... ♗e5 20 ♗g5 (20 ♖b1 ♘×e4 and 21 ... ♘c3) 20 ... ♗×a1 21 ♖×a1 h6 22 ♘×f6+ ♘×f6 23 ♗d2 (23 ♗×f6 ♖e1+ ∓∓) 23 ... ♘d7 24 a4 ♘e5 25 ♗g2 c5 (25 ... ♘d7!?) 26 ♗e3 ♘c6 27 ♗×c6 bc 28 a5 *(253)*

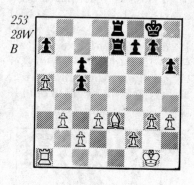

253
28W
B

28 ... ♖e5?! (28 ... ♖×e3 29 fe ♖×e3=) 29 a6 ♖d5 30 ♔f1 ♔f8 31 ♔e2 ♔e7 32 ♔d2 ♔d7 33 c4 ♖h5 34 h4 ♔c7 35 f4 ♖f5 36 ♖a5 g5 37 hg hg 38 b4! gf 39 gf ♔b8 40 ♖×c5 ♖×c5 41 ♗×c5 ♖h8 42 ♔c3 ♖h1

43 b5 ♖b1 44 bc ♔c7 45 d4 ♔×c6 46 ♗×a7 ♖a1 47 d5+ ♔d7 48 ♗b8 ♖×a6 49 c5 ♖a4 50 c6+ ♔c8 51 ♗d6 f6 52 ♗b4 ♔c7 53 ♔b3 ♖a1 54 ♔c4 ♔b6 55 ♗c5+ ♔c7 56 ♔b5 ♖b1+ 57 ♗b4 **1–0** (2·28 – 3·32)

3702 Panno–AK

R2: 27.11.1973: Réti

1 c4 ♘f6 2 g3 c6 3 ♘f3 d5 4 b3 ♗f5

5 ♗g2 e6 6 00 ♗e7 7 ♗b2 h6 8 d3 00 9 ♘bd2 ♗h7 10 a3 ♘bd7 11 b4 a5 12 ♕b3 ab 13 ab ♕b6 14 ♗c3 ♖fc8 15 ♕b2 ♗f8 16 h3 ♕d8 17 ♖a5 ♖×a5 18 ba b6 19 ab ♕×b6 20 ♖al ♕×b2 21 ♗×b2 ♗b4 22 cd cd 23 ♖cl ½-½ (2·22 - 1·27)

3703   AK-Andersson

R3: 28.11.1973: Bogoljubow

1 d4 ♘f6 2 c4 e6 3 ♘f3 b6 4 g3 ♗b4+ 5 ♘bd2 ♗b7 6 ♗g2 00 7 00 c5 8 a3 ♗×d2 9 ♗×d2 cd? (9 ... d6; 9 ... d5; 9 ... ♘e4) 10 ♗b4! ♖e8 (10...d6 11 ♕×d4 and the d-pawn falls.) 11 ♗d6! (Black never escapes the bind.) 11 ... ♘e4 (11 ... ♗×f3!? 12 ♗×f3 ♘c6) 12 ♕×d4 ♘a6 13 b4 ♖c8 14 ♖acl ♘×d6 15 ♕×d6 ♘c7 16 ♖fdl ♗e7 17 ♕d3 (threatening 18 ♘g5±±) 17...♗×f3 (17...d5 18 e4±) 18 ♗×f3 ♘e8 19 ♗b7! ♖c7 (254)

254
19B
W

20 ♗a6! ♖c6 21 ♕b3 ♕b8 (or 21 ... ♖d6 22 ♖×d6 ♘×d6 23 c5 bc 24 ♖×c5±) 22 ♕a4! (threatening 23 ♖×d7) 22...♖c7 23 ♕b5 ♘f6 24 f3 d5 (24 ... ♕e8 25 ♖d6±±)

25 c5! h5 26 a4!± ± ♖e8 27 cb ab 28 a5 ♖×cl 29 ♖×cl ♕e5 (29 ... ba 30 ♕×b8 ♖×b8 31 ba) 30 ♕×b6 d4 31 ♔hl ♕e3 32 ♖fl e5 33 ♗d3 h4 34 gh ♕f4 35 ♖gl ♕×h4 36 a6 g6 (36 ... e4 37 fe ♘×e4 38 ♕c6±±) 37 a7 ♔g7 38 ♗×g6! **1-0** (1·52 - 2·28) (38 ... fg 39 a8♕ ♖×a8 40 ♕b7+) 'This game came very much into the reckoning for the best game prize, but, in the opinion of the judges, Karpov played another game later on that was even more worthy of the prize.' - Golombek (tournament arbiter).

3704   Tukmakov-AK

R4: 30.11.1973: Queen's Indian

1 ♘f3 ♘f6 2 c4 e6 3 d4 b6 4 g3 ♗b7 5 ♗g2 ♗e7 6 00 00 7 ♘c3 ♘e4 8 ♕c2 ♘×c3 9 ♕×c3 d6 10 b3 ♘d7 11 ♗b2 ♘f6 12 ♖fdl c5 13 ♘el ♗×g2 14 ♘×g2 cd 15 ♕×d4 ♕b8 16 ♖acl ♖d8 17 ♘e3 ½-½ (0·15 - 0·17)

3705   AK-Bellon

R5: 1.12.1973: English

(Notes by Bellon)

1 c4 e5 2 ♘c3 ♘c6 3 g3 f5 4 ♗g2 ♘f6 5 d3 ♗c5 6 e3 f4!? 7 ef 00 8 ♘ge2 d6 9 00 ♕e8! 10 ♘a4 ♗d4! 11 ♘×d4? (11 fe! de 12 ♘×d4 ed±) 11 ... ed 12 a3 a5! 13 b3 ♗f5 14 ♗b2 (14 ♖el ♕g6 15 ♗fl h5∓) 14 ...♕g6 15 ♕c2 ♘d7! 16 ♖el ♘c5

17 ♗f1 ♖a6! 18 ♗d2 ♖b6 19
♗×a5 ♖×b3? (19 ... ♘×a5 20 b4
♘ab3! 21 ♖a2 ♖a8 22 bc ♘×c5∓)
20 ♗d2 (20 ♗×c7? ♖c8∓∓) 20
... ♖a8 21 a4 h5 22 h3 ♖a6 (22
... ♘b4! 23 ♗×b4 ♖×b4 24 ♖a3
♖a5∓) 23 a5 *(255)*

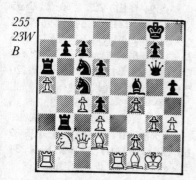

255
23W
B

23 ... ♘b4 (23 ... ♔h7 Saidy-
Fischer, New ·York 1969!!-
KJO'C) 24 ♗×b4 ♖×b4 25 ♖a3!
b6 26 ♖ea1 ♕e6? (26 ... ♔h7!) 27
ab ♖a×b6 28 ♖a8+ ♔h7 29 ♕d1!
g6 (29 ... ♕g6) 30 ♘a4! ♘×a4 31
♖8×a4 ♖×a4 32 ♖×a4? (32
♕×a4! ♗×h3 33 ♗×h3 ♕×h3 34
♕e8!±) 32 ... ♗×h3 33 ♖a7
♗×f1! 34 ♖×c7+ ♔h6 35 ♕×f1
h4! 36 ♔g2! ♖b2! 37 ♔f3?! (37 ♔h1
♖×f2+! 38 ♔×f2 ♕e3+=; 37
♕c1? ♕e2! 38 f5+ g5; 37 f5
♕e3!∓) 37 ... d5! 38 gh! (38 g4 g5
39 fg+ ♔g6!!∓) 38 ... ♖b3
(intending ... ♕e4+!) 39 cd
♕×d5+ 40 ♔g3 ♕f5 41 f3 ♖×d3
42 ♖c6 (42 ♖e7 ♖d2 and ...
♕c2) 42 ... ♖c3 43 ♖d6 ♕h5! 44
♔g2! ♖c2+ 45 ♔g3 ♖c3 46 ♔g2
♕×f4 47 ♖d5+ (47 ♕b5+

♔×h4∓∓) 47 ... ♔h6 (47 ...
♕×h4?? 48 ♕h1+∓∓) 48 ♕e2!
♕c1 49 ♖h5+! ½-½ (2·27 – 3·01)

3706 Ljubojević–AK

R6: 2.12.1973: Sicilian

1 e4 c5 2 ♘f3 e6 3 d4 cd 4 ♘×d4
♘c6 5 ♘b5 d6 6 c4 ♘f6 7 ♘5c3
♗e7 8 ♗e2 00 9 00 b6 10 ♗f4! ♗b7
11 ♘bd2 a6! (11 ... d5 12 cd ed 13
e5 ♘e4 14 ♘d×e4 de 15 ♗c4!
Ljubojević–de Castro, Manila
1973) 12 a3 ♘d4 13 ♗d3 ♘d7! (13
... b5?! 14 cb ab 15 b4!) 14 ♗e3
♗f6 15 ♖c1 ♘e5 16 ♗b1 ♘ec6 17
♖e1 ♖b8 18 b4 b5 19 ♗a2 ♗a8
20 ♘d5! ed 21 cd a5 (21 ... ♘e7 22
♘f1 ♕b6 23 ♘g3! g6 24 ♕d2 ♖fc8
25 ♖×c8+ ♖×c8 26 ♖d1±±) 22
dc ♘×c6 23 ♕b3 ab 24 ab ♘e5 25
h3 ♕e7 26 ♗b1 ½-½ (1·45 – 1·36)

3707 AK–Browne

R7: 4.12.1973: Benoni

(Notes by Browne)

1 d4 c5 2 d5 ♘f6 3 ♘c3 d6 4 e4 g6 5
♘f3 ♗g7 6 ♗e2 00 7 00 ♘a6 8 ♗f4
♘c7 9 a4 (9 h3!?) 9 ... ♗g4 10 h3
♗×f3 11 ♗×f3 ♘d7 12 ♕d2 a6 13
♗e2 ♖b8 14 ♗h6 (14 a5 ♘b5!) 14
... b5 15 ♗×g7 ♔×g7 16 ♘d1
♘f6 17 ♗f3 e6 (17 ... e5!=) 18 ab
ab 19 ♘e3 ed 20 ed ♖e8 21 ♖a7
♖e5 22 b4!± c4 23 ♕d4 ♖a8 24
♖fa1 ♖×a7 25 ♖×a7 ♔b8 26 g3
h5 27 ♗g2 (intending f4) 27 ...
♔g8! 28 g4 (28 f4 ♖e7 29 ♔f2
♘f×d5! 30 ♗×d5 ♘×d5 31 ♘×d5

♕×a7!∓) 28 ... hg 29 hg
♘f×d5!= 30 ♘×d5 ♘×d5 *(256)*

256
30B
W

31 ♖d7? (31 ♗×d5 ♖×d5 32
♕×d5=) 31 ... ♕b6? (31 ... ♖e7!
32 ♖×e7 ♘×e7 33 f4∓) 32 ♕×b6
♘×b6 33 ♖×d6 a4 34 ♗d5
♖e1+ 35 ♔h2 ♘c3 36 ♖×g6+
♔f8 37 ♖g5 ♖e2 38 ♔g2 ♖×c2 39
♖f5 ♘×d5 40 ♖×d5 ♖b2 41
♖×b5 c3 42 ♔g3 c2 43 ♖c5 ♖×b4
44 ♖×c2 ♔g7 45 ♖c5 ♖b3+ 46
♔f4 ♖b2 47 f3 ♖b3 48 ♖c6
♖b4+ 49 ♔g3 ♖b3 50 g5 ♖a3 51
♔g4 ♖a4+ 52 f4 ♖b4 53 ♖d6
♖a4 54 ♔f5 ♖a1 55 ♖d4 ♖e1 ½–½
(2·45 – 3·08)

3708 S. Garcia–AK

R8: 5.12.1973: Sicilian

1 e4 c5 2 ♘f3 e6 3 d4 cd 4 ♘×d4
a6 5 ♗d3 ♘f6 6 00 d6 7 c4 ♕c7 8
♕e2 g6 9 f4 ♗g7 10 ♔h1 00 11
♘c3 b6 12 ♗d2 ♗b7 13 ♘f3 ♘c6
14 ♖ac1 ♖ae8 15 ♕f2?! (15 a3)
15 ... ♘g4 16 ♕g1 (16 ♕h4 f5!)
16 ... f5 17 ef (17 ♘a4 ♘b4 18
♗×b4 fe) 17 ... gf 18 h3?! (18
♘d5! ♕f7 19 ♘×b6 ♕h5 is

unclear; 18 ... ♕d8 19 ♘×b6
♗b2 20 ♖b1±) 18 ... ♘f6 19
♘d5 ♕d8 (19 ... ed? 20 cd ♘×d5
21 ♗c4; 19 ... ♘×d5? 20 cd ed 21
♘d4) 20 ♕×b6? (20 ♘×b6) 20
... ♕×b6 21 ♘×b6 ♘e4! 22
♗×e4 (22 ♗e1!? ♘c5 23 ♗c2
♗×b2 24 ♖b1) 22 ... fe 23 ♘g5
♘d8! 24 ♖fe1 (24 h4 h6 25 ♘h3
♗×b2 26 ♖b1 ♗d4∓) 24 ... d5
25 ♘d7 h6 26 ♘×e4 de 27 ♘×f8
♖×f8∓ 28 b4 ♗c6 29 a4!? (29
♖b1 ♖f5 30 ♔g1 ♗d4+ 31 ♗e3!
♗×e3+ 32 ♖×e3 ♖×f4 33 b5 ab
34 cb ♗d5 is unclear – Griffiths.) 29
... ♗×a4 30 ♖×e4 ♗c6 31 ♖e2
h5 32 ♔h2 h4 33 g3 hg+ 34
♔×g3 ♗h7 35 ♗c3 h6 (35 ...
♖×f4 36 ♔×f4 ♗h6+ 37 ♔e5
♗×c1 38 ♔d6± ±) 36 ♖f1 ♖g8+
37 ♔h2 ♗f7 38 ♗e5 ♘×e5 39 fe
♗g7 40 ♖f7 (40 ♖fe1!?) 40 ...
♔h6 41 h4 (41 ♖c7 ♗f3 42 ♖e3
♗×e5+ 43 ♖×e5 ♖g2+ 44 ♔h1
♖g5+) 41 ... ♔h5 42 ♔h3 ♗e8
43 ♖a7 ♗g6 44 ♖×a6 ♗d3 45
♖f2! ♗×c4 46 ♖a3 *(257)*

257
46W
B

46 ... ♗h6? (46. ... ♗×e5 47 ♖a5
♖g3+ and 48 ... ♖e3+ or 48 ...

♗d5∓∓) **47 ♖g3 ♖a8 48 ♖f7
♖a1 49 ♖h7 ♖h1+** (avoiding the
mate!) **50 ♔g2 ♖×h4 51 ♔g1** (51
♔f2!?) **51...♗e2 52 ♔f2 ♗g4 53
b5 ♗f5 54 ♖h8 ♖b4 55 ♖g1
♖b2+ 56 ♔f3 ♖b3+ 57 ♔f2
♗e4 58 ♖g3 ♖b2+ 59 ♔g1 ♗f5
60 ♖g2 ♖×g2+ 61 ♔×g2 ♗e4+
62 ♔g3 ♔g6 63 b6 ♗d5 64 ♖b8**
(64 ♖d8 ♔f5! 65 ♖d7 ♗f4+ 66
♔f2 ♗×e5 67 b7 ♔e4!∓∓) **64...
♔f5 65 b7 ♔×e5 66 ♔g4 ♗e3 67
♔g3 ♗g5 68 ♔f2?** (68 ♔g4 ♗e3
69 ♔h3! ♗d4 70 ♔h2 ♗b6 71 ♖c8
♗×b7 72 ♖b8=; 68 ... ♗f6 69
♔g3! ♔f5 70 ♔f2 ♗d4+ 71 ♔e2
♔e5 72 ♔d3 ♗b6 73
♔c3= –Griffiths) **68 ... ♗e7 0–1**
(4·03 – 2·30)

3709 AK–Hort

R9: 7.12.1973: Caro Kann

1 e4 c6 2 d4 d5 3 ♘d2 de 4 ♘×e4
♗f5 5 ♘g3 ♗g6 6 ♘f3 ♘d7 7 h4
h6 8 h5 ♗h7 9 ♗d3 ♗×d3 10
♕×d3 ♘gf6 11 ♗d2 e6 12 ♕e2
♕c7 13 000 c5 14 ♖h4 ♗e7 15 dc
♘×c5 16 ♖d4 00 17 ♗f4 ♕a5 18
♔b1 ♖fd8 19 ♗e5 ♖×d4 20
♗×d4 ½–½ (1·02–1·00)

3710 AK–Furman

R10: 8.12.1973: Spanish

1 e4 e5 2 ♘f3 ♘c6 3 ♗b5 a6 4
♗×c6 dc 5 d4 ed 6 ♕×d4 ♕×d4 7
♘×d4 ♗d6 8 ♘c3 ♘e7 9 ♗e3
♗d7 10 000 000 11 ♘b3 ♔b8 12 f4
f6 13 f5 b6 14 ♘d2 ♗e5 15 ♘c4

♗×c3 16 bc c5 17 ♗f4 ♔c8 18 g4
♗b5 19 ♖×d8+ ♖×d8 20 ♘d2
♖e8 21 h4 ♘c6 22 g5 ♘a5 23 gf ½–½
(0·45 – 1·02)

3711 Kaplan–AK

R11: 9.12.1973: Sicilian

1 e4 c5 2 ♘f3 e6 3 d4 cd 4 ♘×d4
♘c6 5 ♘c3 a6 6 ♗e2 ♕c7 7 00 ♘f6
8 ♔h1 ♗b4 9 ♘×c6 bc 10 ♕d4 c5
11 ♕e3 d6 12 ♕g3 (12 ♗d2 00 13
a3 ♗a5 14 f4; 12 f4) 12...♗×c3 13
♕×c3 00 14 f3 ♗b7 15 ♗f4 (15 b3;
15 b4!?) 15 ... ♘h5 16 ♗g5 e5 17
♖ad1 f5! 18 ♕d3 h6 19 ♗c1 ♖ad8
20 ef d5! 21 f4 (21 g4 ♘f4 22 ♗×f4
ef and ... ♖de8, ... ♖e3, ...
♖fe8, ... d4) 21 ... ♘×f4 22
♗×f4 ef 23 ♗g4 d4 24 ♕d2 h5 25
♗×h5 ♖×f5 26 ♗g4 ♖f6 27 ♕e2
♗d5 28 ♖de1 c4 29 ♕e5 ♕×e5 30
♖×e5 d3 31 cd cd 32 b3 ♖g6 33 h3
d2 34 ♖d1 ♗f7 35 ♔g1 ♖c6 36
♔f2 ♖c2 37 ♖a5 ♖d6 38 ♗e2
♖c1 39 ♗f3 ♔h8 40 ♖e5 ♖c2 41
♖a5 ♗g6 42 ♖d5 ♖×d5 43 ♗×d5
♗d3 44 a3 g5 *(258)*

258
44B
W

45 ♗c4?? (45 g3! fg+ 46 ♔c3 ♗f5

47 ♖×d2= ; 45 . . .♔g7 46 gf gf 47 ♔f3 ♔f6 48 ♗e4! ♗×e4+ 49 ♔×e4 ♔g5 59 ♔d3=) 45 . . . ♖cl!∓ ∓ 46 ♗×d3 ♖×dl 47 ♔e2 ♖gl 48 ♔×d2 ♖×g2+ 49 ♔c3 ♖g3 50 ♔c2 ♖×h3 51 ♗×a6 g4 52 a4 g3 **0–1** (3·30 – 2·20)

3712　AK–Uhlmann

R12: 11.12.1973: French

At the start of this round Uhlmann was leading the tournament with 8½ and Karpov was on 7½. At the end of this round Karpov was joint leader. This game had the added bonus of winning the best game prize.

1 e4 e6 2 d4 d5 3 ♘d2 c5 4 ed ed 5 ♘gf3 ♘c6 6 ♗b5 ♗d6 7 dc ♗×c5 8 00 ♘ge7 9 ♘b3 ♗d6 10 ♗g5 00 11 ♗h4 ♗g4 12 ♗e2 ♗h5 (12 . . . ♕b6? 13 ♗×e7! Kuzmin–Uhlmann, Leningrad interzonal 1973; 12 . . . ♖e8 R. Byrne–Uhlmann, Leningrad interzonal 1973) 13 ♖el ♕b6 14 ♘fd4 ♗g6 15 c3 (15 c4 ♗b4) 15 . . . ♖fe8 16 ♗fl ♗e4 17 ♗g3 ♗×g3 18 hg a5?! (18 . . . a6; 18 . . . ♖ad8) 19 a4! ♘×d4

259
21B
W

20 ♘×d4! ♘c6 (20 . . . ♕×b2?? 21 ♘b5 and ♖e2 or ♘c7) 21 ♗b5 ♖ed8 (*259*)

22 g4! ♘×d4?! (better 22 . . . ♕c7 and if 23 c4, then 23 . . . ♘b4) 23 ♕×d4 ♕×d4 24 cd ♖ac8? (24 . . . ♔f8 25 ♖e2 ♖ac8 26 f3 ♗g6 27 ♖ael and ♖e7) 25 f3 ♗g6 26 ♖e7 b6 (26 . . . ♖c2!?) 27 ♖ael h6?! (27 . . . h5) 28 ♖b7 ♖d6 (28 . . . ♖c2) 29 ♖ee7 h5 30 gh ♗×h5 31 g4 ♗g6 32 f4 ♖cl+ 33 ♔f2 ♖c2+ 34 ♔e3 ♗e4 (34 . . . ♖e6+ 35 ♖×e6 fe 36 ♖×b6 ♖×b2 37 ♖×e6± ±) 35 ♖×f7 ♖g6 36 g5 ♔h7 37 ♖fe7 ♖×b2 38 ♗e8 ♖b3+ 39 ♔e2 ♖b2+ 40 ♔el ♖d6 41 ♖×g7+ ♔h8 42 ♖ge7 **1–0** (2·31–2·32)

3713　Calvo–AK

R13: 12.12.1973: KI Attack

1 e4 c5 2 ♘f3 e6 3 d3 ♘c6 4 g3 d5 5 ♘bd2 ♗d6 6 ♗g2 ♘ge7 7 00 00 8 ♖el ♕c7 9 b3?! (9 c3) 9 . . . ♗d7 10 ♗b2 d4! 11 ♘c4 e5 12 a4 b6 13 ♕d2? (13 ♘×d6 ♕×d6 14 ♘d2 and ♘c4) 13 . . . f6 14 h4 ♕b8 15 ♗a3 ♗c7 16 ♖ebl ♗e6 17 ♔h2 ♕c8 18 ♕e2 ♗g4 19 ♕fl f5 20 ♘cd2 f4 21 ♗h3 h5 22 ♕g2 ♗g6 23 ♘g5? (23 b4 cb 24 ♗×b4 ♘×b4 25 ♖×b4, followed by ♖c4, was the only chance of counterplay.) 23 . . . ♗d8 24 ♘gf3 ♗e7 25 ♖gl ♕e6 26 ♖afl ♖f7 27 ♖hl ♖af8 28 ♔gl ♕d6 29 ♔h2 a6 30 ♔gl ff 31 ♗×g4 hg 32 ♘g5 f3 33 ♕h2 ♘h8 34 ♖cl ♖h6 35 ♘c4 ♕c7 (*260!!*) **0–1** (2·00 – 1·48)

260
35B
W

3714 AK–Portisch

R14: 13.12.1973: Spanish

1 e4 e5 2 ♘f3 ♘c6 3 ♗b5 a6 4 ♗a4
♘f6 5 00 ♗e7 6 ♖e1 b5 7 ♗b3 d6 8
c3 00 9 h3 ♘b8 10 d4 ♘bd7 11
♘bd2 ♗b7 12 ♗c2 ♖e8 13 ♘f1
♗f8 14 ♘g3 g6 15 a4 c5 16 d5 ♘b6
17 a5 ♘c4 18 b4 cb 19 cb ♖c8 20
♗d3 ♗g7 21 ♖a2 ♖f8 22 ♖c2
♕d7 23 ♘h2 ♕h8 24 h4 h5 25 ♕e2
♔g8 26 ♗×c4 ♖×c4 27 ♖×c4 bc
28 ♕×c4 ♘e8 29 ♖f1 ♘c7 30 f4 ef
31 ♗×f4 ♘b5 32 ♕d3 ♖c8 33
♗d2 ♖c7 34 ♘e2 ♗c8 35 ♘f3
♕e7 36 ♗g5 f6 37 ♗f4 f5 38 ♘g5 fe
39 ♕×e4 ♕×e4 40 ♘×e4 ♖c4 41
♘×d6 ♗×d6 42 ♗×d6 ♖×h4 43
♗c5 ♖e4 44 ♘f4 ♔h7 45 ♘e6
♗×e6 46 de ♖×e6 47 ♖f7 ♔h6 48
♖b7 ♖e4 49 ♔f2 ♗d4+ 50 ♗×d4
♖×d4 ½–½ (2·44 – 2·58)

3715 Planinc–AK

R15: 15.12.1973: Sicilian

1 e4 c5 2 ♘f3 e6 3 d4 cd 4 ♘×d4 ♘c6
5 ♘c3 a6 6 f4 ♕c7 7 ♘×c6 ♕×c6 8
♗d3 b5 9 ♕e2 ♗b7 10 ♗d2?! (10
00) 10 . . . ♗c5 11 ♕g4?! (11 a3) 11
. . . g6 12 a3 (12 ♕h4 b4 13 ♘d1
♗e7 14 ♕h3 ♘f6 15 ♘f2 d5!∓
Planinc-Suetin, Ljubljana 1973) 12
. . . f5! 13 ef? (13 ♕h4) 13 . . . ef 14
♕e2+ ♔f7! 15 000 ♖e8 16 ♕f1
♘f6 17 a4 *(261)*

261
17W
B

17 . . . ♕×g2 18 ♕×g2 ♗×g2 19
♖he1 b4 20 ♘a2 a5 21 ♔b1 ♗f3 22
♖c1 ♘e4 23 ♗×e4 ♗×e4 24 ♔a1
d5 25 ♗e3 ♗×e3 26 ♖×e3 d4 27
♖e2 ♗c6 28 ♖d2 ♖e4 29 ♖cd1
♗×a4 30 b3 ♗c6 31 ♖×d4 ♖×d4
32 ♖×d4 ♖e8 33 ♖c4 ♖e1+ 34
♔b2 ♗e4 35 ♘c1 ♖h1 36 ♖c7+
♔g8 37 ♘e2 ♖×h2 38 ♘d4 h5 39
♘e6 h4 40 ♘g5 h3 41 ♖c8+ ♔g7
42 ♖c7+ ♔f8 **0–1** (2·40 – 1·25)

38   Candidates' Quarter-Final
Moscow, 16.1–4.2.1974

Karpov	½	½	½	1	½	1	½	1	**5½**
Polugayevsky	½	½	½	0	½	0	½	0	**2½**

The match became a theoretical duel centering upon the Nimzo-Indian and the Sicilian Najdorf. Polugayevsky had his chances (notably in the fourth game where he was clearly winning at one stage), but Karpov's 3–0 victory confirmed, for some observers, that he was beginning to beat an inexorable path to the door of Robert Fischer.

In view of the semi-final draw, and the results, it is interesting to note Spassky's evaluation of Karpov's victory. 'Karpov is a methodical chess player. His evaluation of a position conforms to a concrete calculation. In this harmony, it nevertheless seems to me, Karpov is more inclined to an intuitive manner of play than to a concrete one. It is no coincidence that he has lately made his leap in the field of tactics and a sharper manner of conducting the fight. I think that this is connected with an accumulation of experience, with a growth of confidence in his own strengths, with youth, energy, and ambition, so necessary for the attainment of victory.' In the above Spassky goes a long way to exploding the common belief that Karpov is, first and foremost, a strategist, a view which was also attacked by Polugayevsky who maintained that Karpov is stronger in tactics.

Karpov's comment was also interesting: 'For me it is very bad to play Polugayevsky in the first match because if I win I still have to play Spassky and if I lose it is terrible. It would be much better if I played Spassky first and if I won then I would have a free road to the World Championship Match.'

3801   Polugayevsky–AK

G1: ?.1.1974: Nimzo-Indian

1 d4 ♘f6 2 c4 e6 3 ♘c3 ♗b4 4 e3 0 0 5 ♗d3 c5 6 ♘f3 d5 7 00 dc 8 ♗×c4 ♘c6 9 a3 ♗a5 10 ♗d3 cd 11 ed ♗b6 12 ♗e3 ♘d5 13 ♗g5! (13 ♘×d5 Gligorić–Karpov, 2609) 13

... f6 14 ♗e3 ♘ce7 15 ♕c2 ♘×e3 16 fe g6 17 ♗c4 (17 ♘a4! ♗d7 18 b4! and ♘c5 – Botvinnik) 17 ... ♘f5! 18 ♖fe1 ♗g7 19 ♖ad1 ♗d7 20 ♔h1 ♖c8 21 ♗a2 ♘d6= 22 ♕d3 ♘e7 23 e4 ♘f7 24 e5 (24 d5 ♘e5 25 ♘×e5 fe=) 24 ... fe 25 ♘×e5 (25 d5 ♗c7 26 ♘e4 ed 27 ♗×d5 ♗c6=) 25 ... ♘×e5 26 ♖×e5 (262)

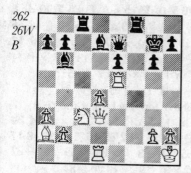

262
26W
B

26 ... ♖f5 (26 ... ♕h4 27 ♗×e6 ♕×d4 28 ♕×d4 ♗×d4 29 ♗×d7 ♗×e5 30 ♗×c8 ♖×c8 31 ♖d7+ ♔h6 32 ♖×b7 ♗×c3 33 bc ♖×c3 34 h4 ♖×a3= ; 28 ♕e2!±± – Botvinnik) 27 ♘d5 (27 ♖ee1!?) 27 ... ♕d6 (27 ... ♕g5 is also possible.) 28 ♘×b6 ♕×b6 29 ♕e2 ♕d6 30 h3 ♖cf8 31 ♔g1 ♗a4 32 ♖d2 ♗d7 ½-½

3802 AK–Polugayevsky

G2: ?.1.1974: Sicilian

1 e4 c5 2 ♘f3 d6 3 d4 cd 4 ♘×d4 ♘f6 5 ♘c3 a6 6 ♗e2 e5 7 ♘b3 ♗e7 8 00 ♗e6 9 f4 ♕c7 10 a4 ♘bd7 11 ♔h1 00 12 ♗e3 ef 13 ♖×f4 ♖fe8 14 ♘d4 ♘e5 15 ♘f5

♘g6 16 ♖f1 ♗f8 17 ♕d4 ♘e5 18 ♗g5 ♘fd7 19 ♖ad1 ♘c5 20 ♘×d6 ♗×d6 21 ♕×d6 ♕×d6 22 ♖×d6 ♗d7 23 b3 (23 ♗e3 ♘×a4 24 ♘d5± Karpov; ± Botvinnik; 24 ... ♖ac8= Spassky) 23 ... ♗c6 24 ♗f3 f5 25 ♗e3? (25 ef!± Botvinnik) 25 ... ♘×e4 26 ♗×e4 fe 27 h3 ♖ad8 28 ♖×d8 ♖×d8 29 ♔g1 ♘g6 30 ♘e2 ♗f8 31 ♖d1 ♘h4 32 ♗c5 ♖c8 33 ♗e7 ♘f5 34 ♖d8+ ♖×d8 35 ♗×d8 h5 36 c4 e3 37 ♗g5 ♗e4 38 a5 ♔f7 39 ♘c3 ♗c2 40 b4 ♘d6 ½-½

3803 Polugayevsky–AK

G3: ?.1.1974: Nimzo-Indian

1 d4 ♘f6 2 c4 e6 3 ♘c3 ♗b4 4 e3 00 5 ♗d3 c5 6 ♘f3 d5 7 00 dc 8 ♗×c4 ♘c6 9 a3 ♗a5 10 ♗a2 a6 11 ♘a4 cd 12 ed h6 13 ♗f4 ♗c7 14 ♗×c7 ♕×c7 15 ♕e2 ♖d8 16 ♖fd1 ♗d7 17 ♖ac1 ♗e8 18 ♘c3 ♖d6 19 d5 ed 20 ♘×d5 ♖×d5 21 ♖×d5 ♖ad8 ½-½

3804 AK–Polugayevsky

G4: ?.1.1974: Sicilian

1 e4 c5 2 ♘f3 d6 3 d4 cd 4 ♘×d4 ♘f6 5 ♘c3 a6 6 ♗e2 e5 7 ♘b3 ♗e7 8 00 ♗e6 9 f4 ♕c7 10 a4 ♘bd7 11 ♔h1 00 12 ♗e3 ef 13 ♖×f4 ♘e5 14 ♘d4 (14 a5!) **14 ... ♖ad8 15 ♕g1** (if 15 a5 d5 16 ♘×e6 fe 17 ♗b6± , but 15 ... ♕d7 or 15 ... ♖d7) **15 ... ♖d7 16 ♖d1 ♗e8 17 ♘f5 ♗d8! 18 ♘d4 ♘g6** (18 ... ♗c4!?) **19 ♖ff1 ♘e5**

20 ♗f4 ♕c5 (also 20 . . . ♕a5 with
the idea . . . ♕b4 and . . . ♗b6) **21
♘×e6 ♕×g1+ 22 ♖×g1 ♖×e6
23 ♗f3 ♘eg4 24 ♖gf1 ♗b6 25
♖d2 ♗e3 26 ♗×e3** (better 26
♗×g4 – Botvinnik) **26 . . . ♘×e3
27 ♖b1 ♔f8 28 ♔g1 ♖c7 29
♔f2 ?!** (29 ♖e2 ♘c4 30 ♘d1=) **29
. . . ♘c4 30 ♖d3** (263)

263
30W
B

30 . . . g5 ?! (30 . . . ♖e5 31 ♘d5
♘×d5 32 ♖×d5 ♖×d5 33 ed
♘b6∓∓; 31 b3! ♗a3 32 ♖b2!
♖ec5 33 ♘e2 ♖×c2 34 ♖×c2
♖×c2 35 ♖×d6∓ – Botvinnik) **31
h3 h5** (31 . . . ♖e5) **32 ♘d5
♘×d5 ?** (32 . . . ♖c5∓) **33 ♖×d5
♘e5 34 c3 h4** (34 . . . ♖f6 and 35
. . . g4) **35 ♖bd1 ♔e7 36 ♖1d4
f6 ?** (36 . . . ♖f6=; 36 . . . b6=) **37
a5 ♖c6** (37 . . . ♘c4 38 ♗e2; 37
. . . ♘c6 38 ♖c4 ♖e5 39 ♗g4± ±) **
38 ♗e2 ♗d8 ?** (38 . . . ♘g6!?) **39
c4 ♔c7 40 b4± ± ♘g6 41 b5 ab**
(41 . . . ♖c5 42 b6+ ♔c8 43 ♗d1
♖×d5 44 ♖×d5± ±) **42 cb ♖c2
43 b6+ ♔d7 44 ♖d2! ♖×d2 45
♖×d2 ♖e5** (or 45 . . . ♖×e4 46

♗b5+ ♔c8 47 ♖c2+ ♔b8 48 a6
ba 49 ♗×a6 ♖e8 50 b7 ♘e7 51
♖e2± ±) **46 a6 ♔c6 47 ♖b2 ♘f4
48 a7 ♖a5 49 ♗c4 1–0**

3805   Polugayevsky–AK

G5: ?.1.1974: Nimzo-Indian

**1 d4 ♘f6 2 c4 e6 3 ♘c3 ♗b4 4 e3
00 5 ♗d3 c5 6 ♘f3 d5 7 00 dc 8
♗×c4 ♘c6 9 a3 ♗a5 10 ♗a2 a6**
(10 . . . ♗b6) **11 ♖b1 ♗b6 12
♕c2! g6 ?** (12 . . . cd 13 ed ♘×d4 14
♘×d4 ♗×d4 15 ♗g5±; 14 . . .
♕×d4 15 ♗e3 ♕d6 16 ♗g5 is
better for Black than the text.) **13
dc** (13 ♖d1) **13 . . . ♗×c5 14 b4
♗e7 15 ♗b2 e5 16 ♖d1 ♕e8 17
b5 ab 18 ♘×b5 ♗f5 19 ♕e2
♗×b1** (19 . . . e4 20 ♘h4 ♗g4 21 f3
ef 22 gf ♗h5 23 ♘c7 ♕c8 24 ♘×a8
♕h3 is about equal, but 20 ♘d2
♖d8 21 h3±) **20 ♘c7 ♕b8 21
♘×a8 ♗f5** (21 . . . e4 22 ♖a×b1 ef
23 ♕×f3 ♕×a8 24 ♗×f6± ±) **22
♘b6 e4 23 ♘d4** (23 ♘e1 ♗g4 24
f3 ef 25 ♘×f3; 23 . . . ♘g4!?) **23 . . .
♘×d4 24 ♗×d4 ♗g4 25 f3!** (if 25
♕b2, then 25 . . . ♗×d1 26 ♗×f6
♗×f6 27 ♕×f6 and 27 . . . ♕d8!=
ràther than 27 . . . ♗g4 28 ♘d5
♖e8 29 ♕d4 with ♘f6+ to follow) **
25 . . . ef 26 gf ♗e6 27 ♖ac1** (27
♕b5 and ♕e5± ±) **27 . . . ♖d8 28
♕b2 ♘e8 29 ♗e5 ♗d6 30 ♗×d6**
(30 ♖×d6 ♘×d6 31 ♕b4 and
♕d1; 30 . . . ♖×d6! 31 ♕b4 ♕d8
32 ♗×d6 ♘×d6) **30 . . . ♖×d6**
(264)

264
30B
W

31 ♕b4? (31 ♕b5! ♕d8 32 ♖×d6
♕×d6 33 ♕×e8+ ; 32 . . . ♘×d6
33 ♖d1) **31 . . . ♕d8! 32 ♖×d6
♘×d6 33 ♖d1 ♕g5+ 34 ♔f2
♘f5 35 ♕f4 ♕f6 36 ♘a4** (36 ♘d7
♕b2+ 37 ♔g1 ♕×a3? 38 ♘f6+
♔g7 39 ♘h5+ ! gh 40 ♕g5+ ; 37
. . . ♗×d7 38 ♖×d7 ♕×a3 39
♖d8+ ±) **36 . . . ♗b3 37 ♖d2**
(37 ♖e1) **37 . . . g5! 38 ♕b8+** (38
♕e4 ♗×a4 39 ♕×a4 ♕e5) **38 . . .
♔g7 39 ♘b2 ♗d5 40 ♘d3 ♘d6
41 ♘f4!= gf 42 ♖×d5 ♕b2+ 43
♔f1 fe 44 ♕g5+** ½-½ (44 . . . ♔h6
45 ♕×d6+ ♔×g5 46 ♕e7+ and
♕×e3=)

3806 AK–Polugayevsky

G6: ?.1.1974: Sicilian

1 e4 c5 2 ♘f3 d6 3 d4 cd 4 ♘×d4
♘f6 5 ♘c3 a6 6 ♗e2 e5 7 ♘b3
♗e7 8 00 ♗e6 9 f4 ♕c7 10 a4
♘bd7 11 ♔h1 00 12 ♗e3 ef 13
♖×f4 ♘e5 14 a5! ♘fd7 15 ♖f1
♗f6 16 ♘d5! ♗×d5 17 ♕×d5!
♕×c2! (17 . . . ♘c6 18 c3 ♖fe8 19
♖ad1± – Botvinnik) 18 ♘d4!
♕×b2 19 ♖ab1 ♕c3 20 ♘f5 ♕c2

21 ♖be1= (21 ♖fe1!± – Botvinnik)
21 . . . ♘c5?! (21 . . . ♖ad8 22
♘×d6 ♘b8= – Botvinnik) 22
♘×d6 ♘cd3 23 ♗×d3 ♘×d3 24
♖d1 ♘b4 25 ♕×b7?! (25 ♕f5; 25
♕h5) 25 . . . ♖ab8 26 ♕a7 (265)

265
26W
B

26 . . . ♕c6? (26 . . . ♕e2! 27 ♖de1
♕h5=) 27 ♗f4! ♖a8 28 ♕f2 ♖ad8
29 ♕g3 ♕c3 30 ♖f3 ♕c2 31 ♖df1
♗d4 32 ♗h6 ♘c6 33 ♘f5 ♕b2 (33
. . . ♗e5 34 ♗×g7! ♗×g3 35
♖×g3 h5 36 ♗f6+ ♔h7 37 ♖g7+
♔h8 38 ♖×f7+ ♔g8 39 ♘h6
mate) 34 ♗c1! ♕b5 35 ♘h6+ ♔h8
36 ♘×f7+ ♖×f7 37 ♖×f7 ♗f6 38
♕f2 ♔g8 39 ♖×f6 gf 40 ♕×f6 **1-0**

3807 Polugayevsky–AK

G7: ?.1?.1974: Nimzo-Indian

1 d4 ♘f6 2 c4 e6 3 ♘c3 ♗b4 4 e3 00
5 ♗d3 c5 6 ♘f3 d5 7 00 dc 8 ♗×c4
♘c6 9 a3 ♗a5 10 ♗a2 ♗b6 11 dc
♗×c5 12 b4 ♗d6 13 ♗b2 ♕e7 14
♕c2 ♗d7 15 ♖fd1 (15
♖ad1!± – Botvinnik) 15 . . . ♘e5
16 ♘g5 ♖ac8 17 f4 ♘g6 18 ♕e2=
♗b8 19 ♕f3 h6! 20 ♘h3 ♗c6! 21
♕g3 ♘e4 22 ♘×e4 ♗×e4 23 ♘f2

♗c2 24 ♖d2 ♖fd8! 25 ♗d4 b6 26
♖c1 ♗a4 27 ♖×c8 ♖×c8 28 ♘d3
♗c2 29 ♕g4 ♗×d3 30 ♖×d3
♖c1+ 31 ♖d1 ♕h4 32 ♕f3
♖×d1+ 33 ♕×d1 e5 34 g3 ♕d8 35
fe ♘×e5 36 ♕h5 ♕f6 37 ♗×e5
♗×e5 38 ♗×f7+ ♕×f7 39 ♕×e5
♕b3 40 b5 ♕×a3 41 ♔g2 ½-½

3808   AK–Polugayevsky

G8:?.2.1974: Sicilian

**1 e4 c5 2 ♘f3 d6 3 d4 cd 4 ♘×d4
♘f6 5 ♘c3 a6 6 ♗e2 e5 7 ♘b3
♗e7 8 00 ♗e6 9 f4 ♕c7 10 a4
♘bd7 11 ♔h1 00 12 ♗e3 ef 13
♖×f4 ♘e5 14 a5! ♖fe8!** (In the
sixth game, Polugayevsky failed to
obtain counterplay with 14 . . .
♘fd7) **15 ♗b6 ♕d7 16 ♖a4!** *(266)*

266
16|1
B

16 . . . ♖ac8 (This allows White to
transfer his rook to the d-file,
increasing the pressure on the d-
pawn. 16 . . . ♗d8 is answered by
17 ♖d4 and Black has no time for
17 . . . ♗×b6 in view of 18 ♖×d6.
However, Botvinnik suggests 16 . . .
♘c6! and then 17 ♘d5 ♗×d5 18 ed

♘e5 followed by 19 . . . ♗d8± .) **17
♖d4 ♕c6** (Polugayevsky questions
this and suggests instead the tactical
solution to his problems: 17 . . .
♖×c3 18 bc ♕c6 upon which he
bestows an exclamation mark,
assessing the position as unclear, yet
this seems to founder upon 19 ♕e1!
♘fd7 20 ♖b4.) **18 ♖d2!±**
(Clearing a retreat for the bishop on
b6 and threatening ♘d4.) **18 . . .
♗×b3** (or 18 . . . ♘g6 19 ♘d4±)
19 cb ♘fd7 20 ♗g1 (20 ♗e3 was
also possible.) **20 . . . ♗g5!?** (20 . . .
♖cd8!? was also tempting, the idea
being 21 b4 ♗g5 22 ♖×d6 ♗×f4
23 ♖×c6 ♘×c6, but White has the
simple 21 ♖f1!) **21 ♖×d6 ♗×f4 22
♖×c6 ♖×c6 23 b4! ♘f6?!** (23 . . .
♖cc8!?, uniting the rooks, was
preferable to this plan of laying
siege to the e-pawn, but even then
24 b5 looks promising.) **24 b5
♖ce6 25 ba ba 26 g3** (Clearly
better than 26 b4 which robs the
knight of its support and would
allow Black's rooks to penetrate
along the c-file; 26 ♕b3 ♗d2 with
threats against the e-pawn; 26 ♕f1
♗d2 and the e-pawn is again in
trouble, though 26 ♘d5 ♘g6 27
♘×f4 ♘×f4 28 ♗c4 ♖×e4 29
♗×a6 should lead to a win with
accurate play, but Black's rooks
would have a great deal more scope
than they get in the game.) **26 . . .
♗g5 27 h4 ♗h6 28 ♗b6!** (28 g4 g5
29 ♗e3 looks tempting, but then 29
. . . ♘g6 30 hg ♗×e4 with counter-
chances. The text move lays siege to

the a-pawn.) **28 . . . ♘ed7 29 ♗c4 ♖e5** (29 . . . ♖6e7 30 ♗f2) **30 ♕b3!± ±** (30 ♗g1 ♘f8 31 ♕b3 was another way.) **30 . . . ♖b8 31 ♗×f7+ ♔h8 32 ♕c4! ♗d2** (or 32 . . . ♘×b6 33 ab ♖e7 34 e5! ♖×e5 35 b7 and 36 ♕c8+ cannot be prevented.) **33 ♗c7 ♖c5** (The

only move; if 33 . . . ♖c8 34 ♕×a6! Now White exchanges into a won ending.) **34 ♕×c5 ♘×c5 35 ♗×b8 ♗×c3 36 bc ♘f×e4 37 c4 ♘d7 38 ♗c7 g6 39 ♗e6 ♘ec5 40 ♗×d7 ♘×d7 41 ♗d6 1–0** (41 . . . ♘f6 42 ♗e5 ♔g7 43 c5 ♔f7 44 c6 wins easily.)

39 Candidates' Semi-Final
Leningrad, 12.4–10.5.1974

Karpov	0	$\frac{1}{2}$	1	$\frac{1}{2}$	$\frac{1}{2}$	1	$\frac{1}{2}$	$\frac{1}{2}$	1	$\frac{1}{2}$	1	**7**
Spassky	1	$\frac{1}{2}$	0	$\frac{1}{2}$	$\frac{1}{2}$	0	$\frac{1}{2}$	$\frac{1}{2}$	0	$\frac{1}{2}$	0	**4**

The opening ceremony of the Candidate's semi-final between Spassky and Karpov took place in Leningrad on the 9th April. Dr Euwe, President of FIDE, was in attendance at the opening. The match took place in the Palace of Culture which seats 1,000 spectators–tickets were sold out almost instantly. The opening game was postponed as Karpov was indisposed with influenza, which may account for his loss in that game.

In the openings of his games with Spassky, Karpov was very clever. He repeatedly selected systems and variations that enabled him to side-step any theoretical traps that Spassky had hoped to set. In the first game of the match Karpov was playing under the handicap of a high temperature but after that he was never in any real danger of losing the match. He surprised Spassky by opening with 1 d4 in the majority of his games with the white pieces and Spassky was so ill-prepared for this switch that he was criticized afterwards in the Soviet press. The newspaper *Komsomolskaya Pravda* wrote: 'There were shortcomings in his theoretical and psychological preparation for the match, and they were caused primarily by underestimation of his opponent.'

And of Karpov, *Pravda* wrote: 'Karpov's play evoked general admiration. He displayed an ability to solve strategic problems in a very well-considered way; to manoeuvre with precision and to be precise in endgames too. His famous defensive skills have long been known, but now we have seen Karpov as a master of attack.'

Keres, in *Chess Life and Review*, summed up the match as follows: 'I have the feeling that Spassky lost this match mainly for psychological reasons. I do not know why, but he apparently felt unsure in the handling of certain opening set-ups, and some strategical problems. Some games give me the strong impression that Spassky has lost faith in his own abilities, with a consequent reduction in his usual fighting spirit. Psychological disadvantages are sometimes sufficient to decide the issue in an encounter between equal opponents.'

Karpov took the win as a matter of course.

3901 AK–Spassky

G1:12.4.1974: Sicilian

(Notes by Tal)

1 e4 c5 2 ♘f3 d6 3 d4 cd 4 ♘×d4 ♘f6 5 ♘c3 e6 6 ♗e2 ♗e7 7 0-0 0-0 8 f4 ♘c6 9 ♗e3 e5 10 ♘b3 a5 11 a4 ♘b4 12 ♗f3 ♗e6 (threatening 13 ... ef 14 ♗×f4 ♘×c2! and 15 ... ♕b6+ winning a pawn) **13 ♔h1 ♕c7 14 ♖f2 ♖fd8 15 ♖d2 ♗c4! 16 ♘b5 ♗×b5 17 ab a4 18 ♘c1 d5! 19 fe** (clearly not 19 c3 de) **19 ... ♘×e4 20 c3** (20 ♖e2 a3!) **20 ... ♘×d2 21 ♗×d2** (After 21 ♕×d2 d4 22 ♗×d4, both 22 ... ♕×e5 23 ♘e2 and 22 ... ♘d5 23 ♘d3 give White a pawn and the initiative in compensation for the exchange, but 22 ... ♘c2! 23 ♕×c2 ♖×d4 24 ♗e4 ♖dd8 25 ♗×h7+ ♔h8 is good for Black.) **21 ... ♕×e5! 22 cb** (The black knight isn't going anywhere and 22 g3! deserved serious consideration, though Black isn't doing too badly after 22 ... d4 23 cb ♕×b5.) **22 ... ♕×b2 23 ♘d3 ♕d4 24 ♖a3 ♕b6! 25 ♕e2** (Not 25 ♗c3 on account of 25 ... d4 and after 25 ♖×a4 Black has 25 ... ♕×b5 (25 ... ♕d4 is less clear in view of 26 ♗e2) 26 ♖×a8 ♖×a8 27 ♗e2 ♗f6 with an extremely difficult

defensive task for White.) **25 ... ♖e8 26 ♗×d5 ♗×b4 27 ♗×f7+ ♔×f7** (267)

267
27B
W

28 ♕f3+ (White's position was very difficult, now it is lost. 28 ♕h5+ was necessary: 28 ... ♔g6 (28 ... ♔g8 29 ♗×b4 and the b5 pawn is defended) 29 ♕f3+ ♕f6 30 ♗×b4 (30 ♕×f6+ gf 31 ♗×b4 ♖ad8 is weaker) 30 ... ♕×f3 31 gf and White's position is defensible since 31 ... ♖e3 can easily be met by 32 ♗c5!) **28 ... ♔g8 29 ♗×b4 ♕×b5 30 h3 ♖ad8 31 ♗d2 ♕d5 32 ♕f2 b5 33 ♗a5 ♖d7 34 ♘f4 ♖f7! 35 ♖f3 ♕c4 36 ♗d2 b4 37 ♕b6 b3 38 ♔h2 ♕c2** (38 ... ♖ef8!∓ ∓) **39 ♗c3! ♕e4** (not 39 ... ♖×f4 40 ♕×c7) **40 ♕d6 h6** (40 ... a3 would be met by 41 ♕×a3 ♖×f4 42 ♕a7!, but 40 ... ♕e7 would have reduced Black's technical difficulties in the ending.) **41 ♗b2** (The adjourned position.

White has a number of tactical resources, e.g. 41 . . . ☐ ef8? 42 ☐ g3!; 41 . . . ☐ c8 42 ♗×g7.) **41 . . . ♕c2** (s) (adjournment 13.4.1974) **42 ♕d5** (42 ♕d4 ☐ e4 43 ♕d5 ♕c4) **42 . . . ♕f5** (of course not 42 . . . ♕×b2?? 43 ♘g6) **43 ♕c6 ♕d7 44 ♕g6 ☐ ee7! 45 ♕a6 ♕b7! 46 ♕×a4 ☐ e4 47 ♕×b3 ☐ b4** (47 . . . ♕×b3? 48 ☐×b3 e×f4 is almost certainly drawn.) **48 ♕e6 ☐×b2 49 ☐ g3 ☐ b6 50 ♕e8+ ♔h7 51 ♕e3 ☐ d6 52 ♕c5 ♕c7 53 ♕b4 ♕d7 54 ♘h5** (White's knight is forced out of play by the threat of 54 . . . ☐ d4.) **54 . . . ☐ g6 55 ☐×g6 ♕×g6 56 ♘g3 ♕d3 57 h4 ♔h7 58 h5 ☐ d7 59 ♕c5 ☐ d4 60 ♕e7 ☐ g4 61 ♕e5 ☐ h4+ 62 ♔g1 ♕d1+ 63 ♔f2 ♕d4+ 0–1**

3902 Spassky–AK

G2:15.4.1974: Caro-Kann

1 e4 c6 2 d4 d5 3 ♘c3 de 4 ♘×e4 ♗f5 5 ♘g3 ♗g6 6 ♘f3 ♘d7 7 ♗d3 e6 8 00 ♘gf6 9 c4 ♗d6 10 b3 00 11 ♗b2 c5 12 ♗×g6 hg 13 ☐ e1 ♕c7 14 dc ♗×c5 15 ♕c2 ☐ fd8 16 ♘e4 ♘×e4 17 ♕×e4 ½-½

3903 AK–Spassky

G3:17.4.1974: King's Indian

1 d4 ♘f6 2 c4 g6 3 ♘c3 ♗g7 4 e4 d6 5 ♘f3 00 6 ♗e2 c5 7 00 ♗g4 8 d5 ♘bd7 9 ♗g5 a6 10 a4 ♕c7 11 ♕d2 ☐ ae8 12 h3 ♗×f3 13 ♗×f3 e6 14 b3 ♔h8 (14 . . . ed 15 ed!±)

15 ♗e3 ♘g8 16 ♗e2= (16 ☐ ac1± –Botvinnik) **16 . . . e5** (better 16 . . . ♕a5 17 ☐ ac1 ed! 18 ed f5! 19 ♗d3 f4 20 ♘b1 ♕×d2 21 ♗×d2 ♘e5= –Botvinnik) **17 g4 ♕d8** (17 . . . f5 18 ef gf 19 gf±) **18 ♔g2 ♕h4!?** (18 . . . a5 19 h4! ♕×h4 20 ☐ h1 ♕e7 21 ☐×h7+ !) **19 f3** (if 19 ♗g5, then 19 . . . ♗h6 20 ♗×h4 ♗×d2) **19 . . . ♗h6?** (19 . . . f5!, though White retains an edge with 20 ☐ ad1 or 20 ☐ a2.) **20 g5± ♗g7 21 ♗f2 ♕f4 22 ♗e3 ♕h4 23 ♕e1! ♕×e1 24 ☐ f×e1 h6** (24 . . . a5 25 ♘b5± ±) **25 h4 hg?** (25 . . . f6!±) **26 hg ♘e7 27 a5! f6 28 ☐ ebl! fg 29 b4!** (*268*)

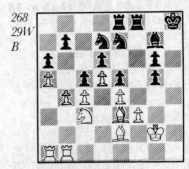

268
29W
B

29 . . . ♘f5 (or 29 . . . g4 30 bc ♘×c5 31 ♗×c5 dc 32 ☐×b7 g5 33 ☐ b6+± ±) **30 ♗×g5!** (30 ef e4 31 ♗d2 ef+ 32 ♗×f3 gf is not clear.) **30 . . . ♘d4** (30 . . . ♗h6 31 ef! ♗×g5 32 ♘e4+± ±) **31 bc ♘×c5 32 ☐ b6!± ± ♗f6** (32 . . . ☐ d8 33 ♗×d8 ☐×d8± ; 33 ♗e7!± ±) **33 ☐ h1+** (33 ☐×d6 ♔g7!) **33 . . . ♔g7** (33 . . . ♔g8 34 ☐×d6!) **34 ♗h6+ ♔g8 35 ♗×f8 ☐×f8 36 ☐×d6 ♔g7 37 ♗d1 ♗e7** (37 . . .

♗d8 38 ♘a4 ♗c7 39 ♘×c5 ♗×d6
40 ♘×b7 and c5± ±) **38 ♖ b6 ♗ d8**
39 ♖ b1 ♖ f7 (39 . . . ♗×a5 40
♘a4 ♘×a4 41 ♖×b7+ ♖ f7 42
♖×f7+ ♔×f7 43 ♗×a4± ±) **40**
♘ a4 ♘ d3 (40 . . . ♘×a4 41 ♗×a4
♗×a5 42 c5!± ±) **41 ♘b6 g5 42**
♘ c8! ♘ c5 (42 . . . g4 43 ♘d6 gf+
44 ♔f1± ±) **43 ♘ d6 ♖ d7 44**
♘ f5+ ♘×f5 **45 ef e4** (s)
(adjournment 18.4.1974) **46 fe**
♘×e4 **47 ♗ a4 ♖ e7 48 ♖ be1!**
♘c5 **49 ♖×e7+ ♗×e7 50 ♗ c2**
♗ d8 **51 ♖ a1 ♔f6** (51 . . . ♗c7 52
♔f3 ♔f6 53 ♔g4± ±) **52 d6 ♘ d7**
53 ♖ b1 ♔e5 54 ♖ d1 ♔f4 55
♖ e1! 1-0

3904   Spassky-AK

G4: 19.4.1974: Caro-Kann

1 e4 c6 2 d4 d5 3 ♘c3 de 4 ♘×e4
♗f5 5 ♘g3 ♗g6 6 h4 h6 7 ♘f3
♘d7 8 h5 ♗h7 9 ♗d3 ♗×d3 10
♕×d3 e6 11 b3?! (11 ♗d2) 11 . . .
♘gf6 12 ♗b2 ♕a5+ ! 13 ♗c3 (13
c3 c5; 13 ♔e2 ♘d5; 13 ♘d2 ♗a3)
13 . . . ♗b4 14 ♗×b4 ♕×b4+ 15
♕d2 (if 15 c3, then 15 . . . ♕d6 and
. . . c5=) 15 . . . ♕×d2+ 16 ♔×d2=
c5 17 c4 cd! 18 ♘×d4 a6 19 ♔e3
(better 19 ♘ge2 to be followed by f3
and g4, or the immediate 19 f3 with
the same idea) 19 . . . ♖ c8∓ 20
♖ ac1 ♔e7 21 f3 ♖ c5! 22 ♘de2 (22
b4 ♖ c7) 22 . . . ♖ hc8 23 f4 b5
(better 23 . . . ♖ 5c7 and then 24
. . . b5–Botvinnik) 24 cb ab 25
♖×c5 ♖×c5 26 ♖ c1 ♘d5+ 27
♔f3 ♖×c1 28 ♘×c1 f5 29 ♘d3

♕d6 (29 . . . b4 30 ♘f1 ♘7f6 31
♘e3= ; 29 . . . ♘c3 30 ♘e3! ♘×a2
31 ♔d2± ± ; Karpov thought for 39
minutes before playing the text.) 30
a4!= ba 31 ba ♘7f6 32 ♘e5 ♔c5
33 ♘f7 ♘b4 34 ♘d8 ♘c7 35 ♘e2
♘×h5 36 ♘d4 ♘d5 37 ♘8×e6
♘e7 38 ♘×f5 ♘×f5 39 g4 ♘h4+
40 ♔f2 ♘×f4 41 ♘×f4 ♔×a4 42
♘e6 ♘g6 ½-½

3905   AK–Spassky

G5: 22.4.1974: Nimzo-Indian

1 d4 ♘f6 2 c4 e6 3 ♘c3 ♗b4 4 ♘f3
c5 5 e3 d5 6 ♗d3 00 7 00 ♘c6 8 a3
♗×c3 9 bc dc 10 ♗×c4 ♕c7 11
♗d3 e5 12 ♕c2 ♖ e8 13 ♘×e5
♘×e5 14 de ♕×e5 15 f3 ♗e6 16 e4
♖ ad8 17 ♗e2 (17 ♗e3 ♘d5; 17 f4
♕d6) 17 . . . b6 18 a4 (18 c4!? ♘h5!)
18 . . . ♗d7! 19 ♖ d1 (19 a5) 19 . . .
♗c6 20 ♖×d8 ♖×d8 21 ♗e3 (21
♗d2 ♘×e4! 22 fe ♗×e4∓ ∓) 21
. . . h6! 22 ♗f2 ♘h5 23 g3 (better
23 ♗f1!= or, perhaps, 23 ♗c4) 23
. . . g5!∓ 24 ♗b5 ♗b7 25 ♖ d1? (25
♖ e1 ♘f6∓ ; Black will follow up
with g4.) 25 . . . ♖×d1+ 26 ♕×d1
♘f6!∓ 27 g4 ♕×c3 28 ♗g3 (28
♕d8+ ♔g7 29 ♕c7 ♕×f3! 30
♕×b7 ♘×g4∓ ∓) 28 . . . ♔g7 29
♗e2?! *(269)* (29 ♕d3)
29 . . . ♗c6? (29 . . . h5! 30 ♕d6 hg!
31 ♗e5 ♕e1+ 32 ♗f1 ♕e3+ 33
♔h1 ♕×f3+ 34 ♗g2 ♕f2∓ ∓; 30
h3 ♘×e4!∓ ∓; 30 ♗e1 ♕b2∓ ∓) 30
♕d6! (intending 31 ♗e5) 30 . . .
♕d4+ 31 ♕×d4 cd 32 a5= ba
33 ♗e5 ♔g6 34 ♗×d4 ♘e8 35

269
29W
B

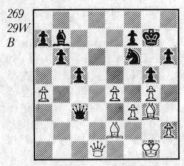

♗×a7 h5 36 gh+ ♔×h5 37 ♔f2
♔g6 38 ♗d3 ♘g7 39 ♗b6 a4 40
♗c5 ♘e6 41 ♗d6 ♔h5 (s) ½-½

3906   Spassky–AK

G6: 24.4.1974: Caro-Kann

**1 e4 c6 2 d4 d5 3 ♘c3 de 4 ♘×e4
♗f5 5 ♘g3 ♗g6 6 ♘f3 ♘d7 7
♗d3 e6 8 00 ♘gf6 9 c4 ♗d6 10 b3
00 11 ♗b2 ♕c7 12 ♗×g6 hg 13
♕e2 ♖fe8 14 ♘e4!** (14 ♘e5 c5=)
14 . . . ♘×e4 15 ♕×e4 ♗e7 (if 15
. . . e5, then 16 ♖ad1± or 16 c5 ♗f8
17 ♕h4±) **16 ♖ad1 ♖ad8 17
♖fe1 ♕a5** (17 . . . ♗f6±) **18 a3
♕f5 19 ♕e2 g5 20 h3** (20 d5!? ed
21 ♘d4 ♕g6 22 cd cd 23 ♕b5!± ;
21 . . . ♕e5!?; 21 . . . ♕e4=) **20 . . .
g4 21 hg ♕×g4 22 d5!± cd 23 cd
e5!** (23 . . . ed 24 ♖×d5±) **24 d6!**
(24 ♘×e5 ♕×e2 25 ♖×e2 ♗d6 26
♖de1 ♘×e5 27 ♗×e5
♗×a3= ; 24 ♕b5 ♗c5! 25 ♘×e5
♘×e5 25 ♗×e5 ♗×f2+ 27 ♔×f2
♖×e5∓) **24 . . . ♗f6 25 ♘d2 ?!** (25
♕b5! e4 26 ♘h2 and if 26 . . . ♕g5
then 27 ♖d5!±) **25 . . . ♕×e2** (25
. . . ♕e6=) **26 ♖×e2 ♖c8 27 ♘e4**
(27 ♘c4) **27 . . . ♗d8 28 g4 f6**

(intending . . . ♘f7 and . . . ♔e6)
29 ♔g2 ♔f7 30 ♖c1 (30 ♖d5; 30
a4) **30 . . . ♗b6 31 ♖ec2 ♖×c2 32
♖×c2 ♔e6∓ 33 a4 a5 34 ♗a3
♖b8! 35 ♖c4** (35 ♘d2) **35 . . .
♗d4 36 f4 g6 37 ♘g3 ef 38 ♖×d4
fg 39 ♔×g3** (39 g5!?) **39 . . . ♖c8
40 ♖d3 g5!∓ 41 ♗b2** (s)
(adjournment 25.4.1974) **41 . . . b6
42 ♗d4** (42 ♖c3 ♖×c3+ 43
♗×c3 is unclear; 42 . . . ♖h8!∓)
42 . . . ♖c6 43 ♗c3 ♖c5! (43 . . .
♖×d6 44 ♖×d6+ ♔×d6 45 b4=)
44 ♔g2 ♖c8 45 ♔g3 (45 ♔f2!?)
45 . . . ♘e5 46 ♗×e5 fe (*270*)

270
46B
W

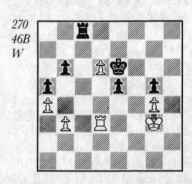

47 b4 ? (47 ♔f3! ♖d8 48 b4∓)
Black would have good chances e.g.
48 . . . ♖×d6 49 ♖b3 ♖d4! 50 ba
♖f4+ ! 51 ♔e3 ♖×g4! 52 ♖×b6+
♔f5 and . . . ♖×a4∓ ∓) **47 . . .
e4!∓ ∓** (47 . . . ab 48 d7 ♖d8 49
♖b3 ♖×d7∓) **48 ♖d4 ♔e5 49
♖d1 ab 50 ♖b1** (50 d7 ♖d8 51
♔f2 b3 52 ♔e3 b2 53 ♖b1 ♖×d7
54 ♖×b2 ♖d3+ ∓ ∓) **50 . . .
♖c3+ 51 ♔f2 ♖d3 52 d7 ♖×d7
53 ♖×b4 ♖d6 54 ♔e3 ♖d3+ 55
♔e2 ♖a3 0–1**

3907 AK–Spassky

G7: 26.4.1974: Dutch

1 d4 d5 2 c4 e6 3 ♘c3 c6 4 e3 f5 5 f4!? ♘f6 6 ♘f3 ♗e7 7 ♗e2 00 8 00 ♘e4 9 ♕c2 ♘d7 10 b3 ♘×c3? (10 ... ♖f6 11 a4 b6 12 cd ed= –Botvinnik) 11 ♕×c3 ♘f6 12 ♘e5 ♗d7 13 a4 ♘e4? (13 ... ♖e8! 14 ♗a3 ♘d7± –Botvinnik; 13 ... c5!?) 14 ♕d3 ♘f6 (14 ... ♗e8!?) 15 ♗a3 ♖e8 16 ♗h5! g6 17 ♗f3 ♗×e5 (17 ... b5!? Cherepkov) 18 de! h5 19 ♗×e4!± fe 20 ♕d2 ♔f7 21 a5 ♖h8 22 ♗d6 ♖h7 23 ♕b4 ♗c8 24 ♖a2 ♔g8 25 h3 a6 26 g3 ♗d7 27 ♕×b7 ♗e8 28 ♕b4 ♖aa7 29 ♖g2 ♖b7 30 ♕c3 ♖bf7 31 ♗c5 g5! *(271)*

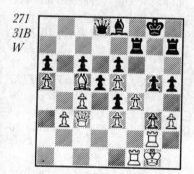

271
31B
W

32 ♗b6? (32 cd! cd 33 ♗b6± ±; 32 ... ed 33 f5± ±) 32 ... ♕d7 33 cd ed 34 g4 hg 35 hg gf! 36 ef ♖h4 37 f5 ♖fh7 38 e6 (38 ♔f2!?; 38 ♕d2!?) 38 ... ♕d6 39 ♕g3 ♖h1+ 40 ♔f2 ♕b4 41 ♕e3 (s) ½-½ (41 ... ♖1h3 42 ♖g3=; 42 ♕g5+ ♔h8 43 ♕f6+= –Botvinnik, or 42 ... ♖g7!? e.g. 43 ♕d8 c5! 44 ♕×d5 ♖d3 45

♕×c5 ♖f3+ 46 ♔g1 ♖×f1+ 47 ♔×f1 ♗b5+ 48 ♖e2 ♕d2!∓ ∓)

3908 Spassky–AK

G8: 1.5.1974: Caro-Kann

1 e4 c6 2 d4 d5 3 ♘c3 de 4 ♘×e4 ♗f5 5 ♘g3 ♗g6 6 h4 h6 7 h5 ♗h7 8 ♘f3 ♘d7 9 ♗d3 ♗×d3 10 ♕×d3 ♘gf6 11 ♗d2 ♕c7 12 c4 e6 13 ♕e2 ♗d6!= 14 ♘f5 ♗f4 15 ♗×f4 (15 ♘×g7+ ♔f8∓; 15 ♗c3 000 16 ♘e3 ♘e4) 15 ... ♕×f4 16 ♘e3 ♕c7 17 000 b5? (17 ... c5! and 18 dc ♘×c5= or 18 d5 000= Botvinnik; 17 ... 000 18 c5!±) 18 cb cb+ 19 ♔b1 00 20 g4!± (20 ♕×b5 is unclear.) 20 ... ♘e4 21 ♖hg1 (21 ♖dg1 ♕f4!) 21 ... ♘g5 22 ♘×g5 hg *(272)*

272
22B
W

23 d5?! (23 ♕×b5! ♖ab8 24 ♕e2 ♖b4 25 ♖d2 ♖fb8 26 ♖c1 ♕f4 27 d5! ♘b6 28 d6± Botvinnik) 23 ... a6! 24 h6 gh 25 ♖h1 (25 de fe 26 ♘f5 ef 27 ♕e6+ ♖f7∓ ∓) 25 ... ♘f6! (25 ... ♔g7 26 f4!) 26 ♖×h6 (26 d6 ♕c6) 26 ... ♔g7 27 ♖hh1 ♖ad8 28 de fe 29 ♘c2 ♕f4 30 f3 (30 ♖×d8 ♖×d8 31 ♕×e6 ♕e4!; 30

♕×e6 ♖×d1+ 31 ♖×d1 ♕×g4=)
30 . . .♔f7 31 a3 e5 32 ♘b4 e4 33 fe
♖×d1+ 34 ♖×d1 ♖e8! (34 . . .
♕×g4 35 ♕×g4 ♘×g4 36 ♖f1+
♔e8 37 ♖g1) 35 ♘×a6 ♕×e4+ 36
♕×e4 ♖×e4 37 ♘c7 b4 38 ab
♖×b4 39 ♖f1 ♖f4 ½-½

3909   AK–Spassky

G9: 3.5.1974: Sicilian

1 e4 c5 2 ♘f3 e6 3 d4 cd 4 ♘×d4
♘f6 5 ♘c3 d6 6 ♗e2 ♗e7 7 0 0 0 0 8
f4 ♘c6 9 ♗e3 ♗d7 10 ♘b3 a5 11
a4 ♘b4 12 ♗f3 ♗c6 (12 . . . e5) 13
♘d4 g6 14 ♖f2! e5 15 ♘×c6 bc (15
. . . ♘×c6 16 f5±) 16 fe de 17 ♕f1
♕c8? (17 . . . ♘d7! 18 ♖d1 ♕c7 19
♕c4 ♖ab8 20 ♔h1 ♔g7=; 18 ♕c4
♘b6 19 ♕b3 ♗g5 20 ♗c5 ♗e7=
Botvinnik) 18 h3 ♘d7 (18 . . . ♕e6
has been recommended, but
Botvinnik gives 19 ♖c1 ♖ad8 20
♗e2 ♖d4! 21 b3!!±±) 19 ♗g4 h5
20 ♗×d7 (20 ♗×h5!? gh 21 ♕e2 is
unclear.) 20 . . . ♕×d7 21 ♕c4
♗h4 22 ♖d2 ♕e7 23 ♖f1! (23 ♗c5
♕g5 24 ♖d7 ♘×c2 is unclear.) 23
. . . ♖fd8 *(273)*

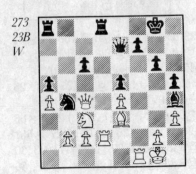

273
23B
W

24 ♘b1!±± ♕b7 25 ♔h2!
(intending g3) 25 . . . ♔g7 26 c3
♘a6 (26 . . . ♖×d2 27 ♘×d2 ♘a6
28 ♘b3±±) 27 ♖e2! ♖f8 28 ♘d2
♗d8 (28 . . . ♕×b2? 29 ♘f3) 29
♘f3 f6 30 ♖d2 ♗e7 31 ♕e6 ♖ad8
32 ♖×d8! (32 ♖fd1 ♖×d2 33
♖×d2 ♖d8) 32 . . . ♗×d8 (32 . . .
♖×d8 33 ♘×e5!) 33 ♖d1 ♘b8 34
♗c5 ♖h8 35 ♖×d8! **1–0** (35 . . .
♖×d8 36 ♗e7)

3910   Spassky–AK

G10: 8.5.1974: Spanish

1 e4 e5 2 ♘f3 ♘c6 3 ♗b5 a6 4 ♗a4
♘f6 5 0 0 ♗e7 6 ♖e1 b5 7 ♗b3 d6 8
c3 0 0 9 h3 ♘b8 10 d4 ♘bd7 11
♘bd2 ♗b7 12 ♗c2 ♖e8 13 ♘f1
♗f8 14 ♘g3 g6 15 a4 c5 16 d5 c4 17
♗g5 ♖b8! (17 . . . ♗e7 Ciocaltea-
Spassky, Dortmund 1973) 18 ♕d2
♗c8 19 ab ab 20 ♖a2 ♗g7 21
♖ea1 ♘c5 22 ♕e3 ♖e7 23 ♘d2
♖c7 24 b3± cb 25 ♘×b3 ♗d7 (25
. . . ♘a4 26 ♘e2) 26 ♘×c5 (26
♘a5 ♖a7 27 ♘c6 ♖×a2 28 ♖×a2
♗×c6 29 dc ♕c7∓ Botvinnik) 26
. . . ♖×c5 27 ♕d2 ♕c8 28 ♘e2
♘e8 (28 . . . ♖c4!?) 29 ♗d3 f5 30
♗e3 ♖c7 31 f3 f4 (31 . . . ♘f6!?) 32
♗a7 ♖bb7 33 ♕e1 ♕d8 34 ♕f2
♖c8 35 ♖a6! ♗f6 36 ♗b6 ♕e7 37
♖a7 ♖cb8! (37 . . . ♗h4 38 ♕×h4
♕×h4 39 ♖×b7 ♘f6 40 ♗f2± or
38 ♖×b7) 38 ♖×b7 ♖×b7 39 ♔f1
♗h4 40 ♕g1 ♔g7 41 ♖a7 (41
♖a8!?) 41 . . . ♖×a7 42 ♗×a7
♕d8 43 ♕b6 ♕c7!= (43 . . .
♕×b6 44 ♗×b6±) 44 ♕×c7

♘×c7 45 ♗b8 ♘e8 46 ♘c1 (s)
(adjournment 9.5.1974) 46 ...
♗d8 47 ♗a7 ♗a5 48 c4 (48 ♘a2
♘c7=) 48... bc 49 ♗×c4 ♔f7 50
♘b3 ♗c7 51 ♗f2 g5 52 ♗e1 h5 53
♘c1 ♘f6 54 ♘d3 ♔g6 55 ♗a6 g4
56 hg hg 57 ♘b2 ♘h7 58 ♘c4 ♘g5
59 ♔f2 ♔f6 60 ♗b4 ♔f7 ½-½

3911   AK–Spassky

G11: 10.5.1974: QGD

1 d4 ♘f6 2 c4 e6 3 ♘f3 d5 4 ♘c3
♗e7 5 ♗g5 h6 6 ♗h4 00 7 e3 b6 8
♗e2 ♗b7 9 ♗×f6 ♗×f6 10 cd ed
11 00 ♕d6 12 ♖c1 a6 13 a3 ♘d7 14
b4 ♗b5 15 ♘e1= (15 ♘d2!?) 15 ...
c6 16 ♘d3 ♘b6?! (16 ... a5) 17 a4!
♗d8?! (17 ... ♘c4! 18 ♘c5
♖ab8± Botvinnik; also 17 ...
♖ae8 with the follow-up ... ♖e7
and ... ♖fe8) 18 ♘c5± ♗c8 19 a5
♗c7 20 g3 ♘c4 21 e4! ♗h3 22 ♖e1

de 23 ♘3×e4 ♕g6 (better 23 ...
♕d8 Botvinnik) 24 ♗h5 ♕h7 (24
... ♕f5 25 ♖c3! and g4) 25 ♕f3! f5
(274) (better 25 ... ♕f5±
Botvinnik)

274
25B
W

26 ♘c3 g6 27 ♕×c6!±± gh 28
♘d5 f4 (28 ... ♗d6 29 ♖×c4±±)
29 ♖e7! ♕f5 (29 ... fg 30 ♘f6+!
♖×f6 31 ♕×a8+ ♖f8 32 ♕×f8+
♔×f8 33 ♖×h7±±) 30 ♖×c7
♖ae8 31 ♕×h6 ♗f7 32 ♖×f7
♔×f7 33 ♕×f4 ♖e2 34 ♕c7+ ♔f8
35 ♘f4 **1-0**

Final A	1	2	3	4	5	6	7	8	9	10	11	12	13	14	15	16	
1 USSR	×	2½	3	2	3	2	3½	3½	3	3	3½	4	2½	2½	4	4	**46**
2 Yugoslavia	1½	×	1½	2	2½	1	2½	2	3½	2	3	3½	3	3½	2	4	**37½**
3 USA	1	2½	×	1½	2½	2	1½	3	2½	3	2	3	3½	2½	3½	2½	**36½**
4 Bulgaria	2	2	2½	×	2	1½	2	2	2	3	3	3	3	2	2½	4	**36½**
5 Holland	1	1½	1½	2	×	2	2	2	2½	2½	3½	2½	2½	3	3	4	**35½**
6 Hungary	2	3	2	2½	2	×	2½	1	1½	2½	1	2½	2½	3½	3	3½	**35**
7 West Germany	½	1½	2½	2	2	1½	×	2	2	2½	2½	2½	2	2½	3	3	**32**
8 Romania	½	2	1	2	2	3	2	×	2	2	2	2	3	1	2½	2½	**29½**
9 Czechoslovakia	1	½	1½	2	1½	2½	2	2	×	3	1	1½	2	3	3½	2½	**29½**
10 England	1	2	1	1	1½	1½	1½	2	1	×	2	2	2	2	2	3½	**26**
11 Philippines	½	1	2	1	½	3	1½	2	3	2	×	1	1	2	2½	2½	**25½**
12 Spain	0	½	1	1	1½	1½	1½	2	2½	2	3	×	2	2½	1½	3	**25½**
13 Sweden	1½	1	½	1	1½	1½	2	1	2	2	3	2	×	2	1½	2½	**25**
14 Argentina	1½	½	1½	2	1	½	1½	3	1	2	2	1½	2	×	2	1½	**23½**
15 Finland	0	2	½	1½	1	1	1	1½	½	2	1½	2½	2½	2	×	2½	**22**
16 Wales	0	0	1½	0	0	½	1	1½	1½	½	1½	1	1½	2½	1½	×	**14½**

As usual the Soviet Union took first place. Karpov, despite twice being in trouble (against Pritchett and Hartston) captured the prize for the best score on top board with 12/14. The USSR team was Karpov, Korchnoi, Spassky, Petrosian, Tal and Kuzmin.

In general Karpov's play reflected the anticlimax that he must have felt, playing in an event with a number of weak opponents.

4001 AK–Pritchett

PR1: 7.6.1974: English

(Notes by Pritchett)

1 ♘f3 c5 2 c4 ♘c6 3 ♘c3 ♘f6 4 d4 cd 5 ♘×d4 e6 6 g3 ♕b6 7 ♘b3 ♗b4!? 8 ♗g2 d5 9 ♘d2!? d4 10 ♘a4 ♕c7 11 00 ♗e7! (Otherwise 12 c5 is embarassing.) 12 a3 00 13 b4 e5 14 ♕c2 ♗e6 15 ♘b3 ♖ad8 16

♘ac5 ♗c8 17 e4?! (A critical
moment. My immediate recation to
this move, notwithstanding that my
opponent was Karpov, was that this
was weak because of the following
pawn sacrifice disrupting White's
position. Maybe 17 ♘e4 is better.)
17 . . . ♗×c5(!) (17 . . . ed was also
playable.) 18 ♗×c5 d3! 19 ♘×d3
(White must accept. 19 ♕c3? ♘d4
20 ♕×d3 ♗g4 is much better for
Black.) 19 . . . ♘d4 20 ♕b2 ♗g4 21
♖e1 (If 21 f3 ♘×f3+ 22 ♗×f3
♖×d3 is better for Black.) 21 . . .
♖fe8! (*275*)

275
21B
W

22 f4?? (loses by force) 22 . . . ef??
(Well, I was short of time, but that
is hardly an excuse for missing 22
. . . ♘e2+ 23 ♖×e2 ♗×e2 24
♕×e2 ♕×c4 25 ♗f1 – what else? –
25 . . . ♕d4+ and wins. 24 ♘×e5
♗×c4 is better, but hardly good
enough.) 23 ♗×f4 ♕×c4 24 ♘e5
♕c2 25 ♖a2 ♕×b2 26 ♖×b2 ♗e6
27 a4 (Now White is better and,
really short of time, I managed to
speed the win.) 27 . . . ♘d7 28 ♘d3
♘b6?! 29 ♘c5 ♘c4 30 ♖f2 ♗c8??
(30 . . . b6 is much better.) 31 ♗c7

b6 32 ♗×d8 bc 33 ♖c1 ♘e5 34
♖×c5 ♗g4 35 ♖d5 ♘df3+ 36
♔h1 f6 37 ♗c7 ♖c8 38 ♖d8+
♖×d8 39 ♗×d8 ♔f7 40 h3 **1-0**

4002   Zalm–AK

PR2: 8.6.1974: Nimzo-Indian

1 d4 ♘f6 2 c4 e6 3 ♘f3 c5 4 e3 b6 5
♘c3 cd 6 ed ♗b7 7 ♗e2 ♗b4 8 00
00 9 ♕b3 ♗e7 10 ♗e3 d5 11 c5
♘c6 12 cb ♘a5 13 ♕d1 ab 14 ♘e5
♖c8 15 ♗d3 ♘c4 16 ♕e2 ♘×e3 17
♕×e3 ♘e8 18 ♘e2 ♘d6 19 b3 b5
20 ♖ad1 b4 21 f4 g6 22 g4 ♘e4 23
f5 ♗g5 24 ♕h3 ♕e7 25 ♘f4 ♗×f4
26 ♖×f4 f6 27 ♗×e4 fe **0–1**

4003   AK–Al Mallah

PR3: 9.6.1974: French

1 e4 e6 2 d4 d5 3 ♘d2 c5 4 ed ed 5
♘gf3 c4 6 ♗e2 ♘f6 7 00 ♗e7 8 b3
cb 9 ab ♘c6 10 ♗b2 ♗e6 11 ♘e5
♘×e5 12 de ♘d7 13 ♘f3 a6 14
♘d4 00 15 f4 ♘c5 16 f5 ♗d7 17 f6
gf 18 ef ♗×f6 19 ♘c6 ♕e8 20 ♖×f6
♕e3+ 21 ♔h1 ♖ae8 22 ♖f3
♕×e2 23 ♖g3+ ♗g4 24 ♖×g4+
1-0

4004   AK–Schmidt

PR5: 11.6.1974: English

1 c4 g6 2 ♘c3 c5 3 ♘f3 ♗g7 4 a3
♘f6 5 g3 00 6 d3 ♘c6 7 ♗g2 ♖b8 8
♗e3 d6 9 00 a6 10 ♘e1 ♗d7 11
♘c2 b5 12 cb ab 13 b4 cb 14 ♘×b4
♘g4 15 ♗d2 ♘ge5= 16 ♕b1
♘×b4?! 17 ab ♗c6 18 ♘e4 ♖a8 19
♗c3 ♖c8 20 ♗b2 ♕d7 21 ♖a5

♗×e4? (21 . . . f5!?±) 22 ♗×e4± d5
23 ♗g2 ♖fd8 24 ♕a1 d4 25 ♖c1
♖×c1+ 26 ♕×c1 ♖c8 27 ♖a8!
♖×a8 28 ♗×a8 h5 29 ♕c5 h4 30
♗g2! h3 31 ♗f1±± g5 32 f3 g4 33 fg
♕×g4 34 ♕×e7 ♕f5 35 ♕d8+
♔h7 36 ♕h4+ ♔g8 37 ♗×h3 **1–0**

4005   Wiliams–AK

PR8: 14.6.1974: Nimzo-Indian

(Notes by Keene)

**1 d4 ♘f6 2 c4 e6 3 ♘c3 ♗b4 4
♗g5 h6 5 ♗h4 c5 6 d5 d6 7 e3
♗×c3+ 8 bc e5 9 ♗d3 ?** (This
move is condemned by theory,
since Black's inevitable . . . e4 will
now gain a tempo. Preferable
alternatives are 9 f4!? or 9 ♕c2.) **9
. . . e4! 10 ♗c2** (10 ♗×e4? g5!; 10
♗×f6 ♕×f6 11 ♗×e4 ♕×c3+ is
also unhappy for White.) **10 . . . g5
11 ♗g3 ♕e7 12 h4 ♖g8 13 hg hg
14 ♘e2** (Taimanov recommends
the immediate 14 ♕b1, but I do not
see that it makes any difference.) **14
. . . ♘bd7 15 ♕b1 ♔d8** (An
excellent strategic idea.) **16 a4** (In a
way this looks quite logical, but
Karpov's reply leaves White's K-
bishop without any good squares,
while the resultant 'weakness' of the
black b-pawn is illusory.) **16 . . . a5!
17 ♖a2 ♔c7 18 ♖h6 ♖a6!** (*276*)
19 ♕b5 (This is a complete waste of
energy. Maybe the time had come
for the 'desperation' piece sacrifice:
19 ♘d4?! cd 20 cd. It must surely be
unsound, but it would have granted

276
18B
W

White temporary dynamic play.
After the text White is pushed back
in confusion.) **19 . . . ♔b8 20 ♖b2
♔a7 21 ♕b3 ♘g4 22 ♖h1 f5 23
♔d1 ♖b6 24 ♕a2 ♖×b2 25
♕×b2 b6 26 ♗b3 ♗a6 27 ♘c1
♘de5 28 ♕e2 ♘g6 29 ♔d2 ♘f6
30 ♕d1 f4 0–1** (After 31 ♗h2 ♖h8
White can hardly move.)

4006   AK–Hort

FR2: 16.6.1974: Pirc

(Notes by Karpov)

**1 e4 d6 2 d4 ♘f6 3 ♘c3 g6 4 ♘f3
♗g7 5 ♗e2 00 6 00 c6** (6 . . . ♘c6;
6 . . . ♗g4) **7 h3 b5 8 e5 ♘e8 9
♘e4** (9 ♗f4!?; 9 ♖e1) **9 . . . ♗f5!
10 ♘g3 ♗e6 11 a4 b4 12 c4 bc 13
bc ♗d5** (13 . . . ♘d7?! 14 ♘g5 de
(14 . . . ♗d5 15 c4± ±) 15 ♘×e6 fe
16 de±) **14 ♖e1 ♘d7 15 ♗f4** (15
ed!? ♘×d6 16 a5 and ♖a4 and c4
to follow with some advantage to
White) **15 . . . de 16 ♘×e5 ♘×e5
17 ♗×e5 ♗×e5 18 de ♕a5= 19
♕d4 ♘g7** (19 . . . ♖d8 20 ♕b4±)
20 c4 (20 ♕×b4 ♕×b4 21 cb ♘e6=)
20 . . . ♗e6 21 ♗f3 ♖ad8 22 ♕h4

♕c7 23 ♕e4 c5 24 ♖edl ♖×dl+ (24 . . . ♘f5 25 ♘e2; 24 . . . ♕a5 25 ♕c6 ♗×c4 26 ♖×d8 ♖×d8 27 ♖cl ♗b3 28 ♕×c5 ♕×c5 29 ♖×c5 ♗×a4 30 ♖a5=) **25 ♖×dl ♖b8** (25 . . . ♕a5 26 ♕c6) **26 ♘e2 ♖b4** (26 . . . ♕a5 27 ♘f4 ♕×a4 28 ♘d5±) **27 ♘f4 ♘f5** (27 . . . ♖×c4?? 28 ♘×e6±) **28 ♘×e6** (28 ♗g4?! ♗×c4! 29 ♖cl ♘d4; 29 ♗×f5 ♗b3! 30 ♕a8+ ♖b8∓ ∓) **28 . . . fe 29 ♗g4 ♘d4 30 h4** (30 ♖×d4 cd 31 ♗×e6+ ♔g7 32 ♕×d4 ♖×a4? 33 ♕f4 ♕d8 34 ♕f7+ ♔h8 35 c5±±; 32 . . . ♕b6! 33 ♕d7 ♖bl+ 34 ♔h2 ♕×f2 35 ♕×e7+ ♔h6∓ ∓) **30 . . . ♔g7** (30 . . . ♖×c4?? 31 ♗×e6+; 30 . . . ♖×a4?! 31 h5 ♔g7 32 ♕f4±) **31 h5** *(277)*

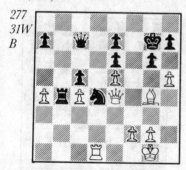

277
31W
B

31 . . . ♖b8? (31 . . . ♕b7! 32 ♕f4 ♖bl 33 ♖×bl ♕×bl+ 34 ♔h2=) **32 ♕e3 gh 33 ♗×h5 ♘f5 34 ♕f4 ♖d8 35 ♖bl ♔h8** (35 . . . h6!? 36 ♕g4+? ♔h8!; 36 ♕e4 ♖d4 37 ♖b7 ♕a5 (37 . . . ♖×e4 38 ♖×c7 ♖×c4 39 ♖×a7±) 38 ♕e2 ♕×a4 39 ♗g4 (39 g4? ♕al+ 40 ♔h2 ♖dl∓) 39 . . . ♕×c4 40 ♕×c4

♖×c4 41 ♗×f5=) **36 ♗f7 ♕d7 37 a5± ♔g7 38 ♗h5 ♕d3?** (38 . . . ♕d4? 39 ♕g5+ ♔h8 40 ♖dl ♖g8 41 ♖×d4 ♖×g5 42 ♖d8+ ♖g8 (42 . . . ♔g7 43 g4 ♘d4 44 ♖×d4! cd 45 f4±±) 43 ♖d7±) **39 ♖dl ♕×dl+ 40 ♗×dl ♖×dl+ 41 ♔h2±± ♖d4 42 ♕cl h5 43 ♕g5+ ♔f8 44 ♕g6 ♘g7 45 ♕bl ♖h4+! 46 ♔gl ♖×c4 47 ♕b8+ ♔f7 48 ♕×a7 ♖cl+ 49 ♔h2 c4 50 ♕d4! ♖c2 51 ♕al ♘e8 52 a6 ♘c7 53 a7 ♖d2 54 ♕a5 ♖d7 55 ♕a4 1-0**

4007 Hartston–AK
FR3:17.6.1974: Sicilian

1 e4 c5 2 ♘f3 e6 3 d4 cd 4 ♘×d4 ♘c6 5 ♘c3 a6 6 ♗e2 ♕c7 7 00 ♘f6 8 ♔h1!? ♗e7 9 f4 d6 10 ♗e3 00 11 ♕el ♗d7 12 ♕g3 b5 13 a3 (13 e5 Tal-Hartston, Hastings 1973–4, 1–0, 27) 13 . . . ♖ab8 14 e5 ♘e8 (14 . . . de 15 fe ♘×e5 16 ♗h6! ♘e8 17 ♗f4 f6 18 ♗g4) 15 ♗d3 b4 16 ♘e4 ('Karpov described Black's position hereabouts as "normal"; Tal said it was terrible.' Hartston) 16 . . . ba 17 ba g6? (17 . . . de!?) 18 ♘f3 ♘a5 19 ♗d4 ♗b5 20 ed ♘×d6 21 ♘f6+ ♗×f6 22 ♗×f6 ♗×d3 23 cd ♖b5 24 ♖ael ♖f5 25 ♘e5 ♘c6 26 ♗al ♖d8 27 ♖cl (27 ♘h4!?) 27 . . . ♕b7 28 ♕h4! (threatening both 29 ♖×c6 ♕×c6 30 ♕×d8+ and 29 ♘g5) 28 . . . f6 *(278)*
29 ♗×f6? (29 ♖×c6! ♕×c6 30 ♘d4 ♕d5 31 ♘×f5 ♕×f5 32 ♕×f6 ♕×f6 33 ♗×f6±) 29 . . . ♖f8 30 ♗e5 ♘b5 31 a4 (31 ♖×c6!? ♕×c6

278
28B
W

32 a4 Hartston) 31 . . . ♘×e5 32 fe
♘c7 33 ♕e7 ♖8f7 34 ♕d6♔g7 35
♕c6 ♕b3 36 ♖fd1 ♕b2 37 ♕c2
♕b4 38 ♕c4 ♕b2 39 ♕c2 ♕b4 40
♕c4 ♕b2 ½-½

4008   AK-Unzicker

FR4: 18.6.1974: Spanish

(Notes by Karpov)

1 e4 e5 2 ♘f3 ♘c6 3 ♗b5 a6 4 ♗a4
♘f6 5 00 ♗e7 6 ♖e1 b5 7 ♗b3 d6 8
c3 00 9 h3 ♘a5 10 ♗c2 c5 11 d4
♕c7 12 ♘bd2 ♘c6 13 d5!

　13 de de 14 ♘f1±

　　13 . . .　　　　♘d8
　　14 a4　　　　　♖b8
　　15 ab　　　　　ab
　　16 b4　　　　　♘b7!?

16 . . . c4 17 ♘f1 ♘e8 18 ♘3h2 f6
19 f4± Karpov-Spassky, USSR Ch
1973.

　　17 ♘f1　　　　♗d7
　　18 ♗e3

18 ♗d2?! ♖a8 with the idea 19
. . . ♖×a1 20♕×a1 cb.

　　18 . . .　　　　♖a8
　　19 ♕d2　　　　♖fc8

　　20 ♗d3±　　　g6
20 . . . c4?! 21 ♗c2±
　　21 ♘g3　　　　♗f8
　　22 ♖a2

22 ♕b2!? (intending 23 ♖a3
followed by 24 ♖eal) and 22 . . .
♗g7 23 ♖a3 ♘e8 (23 . . . cb 24 cb
♘×d5? 25 ed e4 26 ♗d4! ♗×d4 27
♘×d4± ±) 24 ♖eal ♖×a3 25
♕×a3 (25 ♖×a3 cb 26 cb f5) 25 . . .
cb 26 cb f5? 27 ♖cl±±, or 22 . . .
♕d8? 23 ♖×a8 ♖×a8 24 bc ♘×c5
25 ♗×c5 dc 26 ♘×e5± ±

　　22 . . .　　　　c4

22 . . . cb!? 23 cb ♖×a2 24 ♕×a2
♕c3 25 ♕b1 ♕a3±

　　23 ♗b1

23 ♗f1?! ♘e8 with . . . f5 to
follow.

　　23 . . .　　　　♕d8(279)

279
23B
W

　　24 ♗a7!±　　♘e8

24 . . ♕c7 (preparing 25 . . .
♘d8 and 26 . . . ♕b7) 25 ♖a6
♘d8 (25 . . . ♘a5 26 ♗b6± ±) 26
♕a2±

　　25 ♗c2　　　　♘c7

Or 25 . . . ♘g7 26 ♖eal f5 27 ef
gf 28 ♘g5± but not 28 ♕h6?! ♕e8
29 ♘h4 ♕f7∓

26 ♖ea1   ♕e7
27 ♗b1   ♗e8
28 ♘e2   ♘d8
29 ♘h2

29 ♗e3 ♖×a2 30 ♖×a2 ♗a8 31 ♖×a8 ♘×a8 32 ♕a2 ♕b7 33 ♕a5 ♗e7±

29 ...   ♗g7
30 f4   f6

If 30 ... ef then 31 ♘×f4 with the idea 32 ♘f3 followed by ♘d4±

31 f5   g5?!
32 ♗c2± ±   ♗f7
33 ♘g3   ♘b7

Or 33 ... h5 34 ♘h1 h4 35 ♘f1 planning 36 g3 hg 37 ♘×g3 followed by ♘g4, ♕h2 and h4.

34 ♗d1   h6
34 ... ♕e8 35 ♗f3 followed by ♕d1 and ♗h5.

35 ♗h5   ♕e8
36 ♕d1   ♘d8
37 ♖a3   ♔f8
38 ♖1a2   ♔g8
39 ♘g4   ♔f8

39 ... ♗×h5 40 ♘×h5 ♕×h5?? 41 ♘×f6+ ♗×f6 42 ♕×h5± ±

40 ♘e3   ♔g8
41 ♗×f7+   ♘×f7
42 ♕h5   ♘d8
43 ♕g6   ♔f8
44 ♘h5   **1-0**

'One is permitted to lose to Karpov with Black.' – Unzicker.

4009   Andersson–AK

FR7: 21.6.1974: Queen's Indian

1 c4 ♘f6 2 ♘f3 c5 3 ♘c3 e6 4 g3 b6 5 ♗g2 ♗b7 6 00 ♗e7 7 d4 cd 8 ♕×d4 ♘c6 9 ♕f4 00 10 ♖d1 ♕b8 11 ♕×b8 (11 e4!?) 11 ... ♖a×b8 12 ♗f4 ♖bc8 13 ♘e5 ½-½

4010   AK–Kavalek

FR8: 22.6.1974: Sicilian

(Notes by Karpov)

1 c4 c5 2 ♘f3 g6 3 d4 cd 4 ♘×d4 ♘c6 5 e4 ♘f6 6 ♘c3 d6 7 ♗e2 ♘×d4 8 ♕×d4 ♗g7 9 ♗g5 00 10 ♕d2 (10 ♕e3) **10 ... ♗e6** (10 ... ♗d7 11 00 a6±) **11 ♖c1** (11 00? ♖c8 12 b3 b5!∓) **11 ... ♕a5 12 f3** (intending ♘d5!) **12 ... ♖fc8 13 b3** (13 ♘d5 ♕×d2+ 14 ♔×d2 ♘×d5 15 cd ♗d7= 16 ♖×c8+ ?! ♖×c8 17 ♗×e7?? ♗h6+ 18 ♔d3 ♗b5+ ∓ ∓; 18 ♔d1 ♖c1 mate; 18 ♔e1 ♖c1+ ∓) **13 ... a6 14 ♘a4! ♕×d2+** (14 ... ♕d8 15 ♗e3±) **15 ♔×d2± ♖c6** (15 ... ♘d7 16 ♖c2 and ♖hc1±; 16 ♗×e7? ♗h6+) **16 ♘c3 ♖ac8 17 ♘d5 ♔f8** (17 ... ♗×d5 18 cd ♖×c1 19 ♖×c1 ♖×c1 20 ♔×c1±; 18 ed ♖6c7 19 g4±) **18 ♗e3 ♘d7 19 h4** (19 ♘f4 ♘c5 20 ♘×e6+ ♘×e6=) **19 ... ♗×d5** (19 ... h5?! 20 ♘f4±) **20 ed ♖6c7 21 h5 ♔g8 22 f4! ♘c5 23 ♗g4! ♘e4+ 24 ♔d3 f5 25 ♗f3 b5 26 g4** (26 ♗×e4? bc+ 27 ♖×c4 ♖×c4 28 bc fe+ 29 ♔×e4 ♖×c4+ ∓) **26 ... bc+ 27 ♖×c4** (27 bc?! ♘c3!∓) **27 ... ♖×c4 28 bc ♘c5+ 29 ♗×c5 ♖×c5** (29 ... dc 30 h6± ±) **30 h6! ♔f8** (30 ... ♗h8 31 ♖b1 ♖c8 32 g5± ± – the plan is ♖b7, ♗d1, ♗a4 and ♗d7.)

31 ♔c3! (31 g5 ♖a5 32 ♖b1 ♔f7! 33 ♖b7 ♖a3+ !± ; 32 ... ♖a3+ 33 ♖b3 ♖×b3+ 34 ab a5 35 ♔d4 ♔f7 36 c5! dc+ 37 ♔e5!± ± ; 32 ... ♖×a2 33 c5 dc 34 d6±) **31 ... fg** (31 ... ♔f7 32 g5± ± ; 31 ... ♖a5 32 ♔b3 and g5± ±) **32 ♗×g4** (*280*)

280
32W
B

32 ... ♔f7 33 ♗e6+ ♔f6 34 ♗g8 ♖c7 35 ♗×h7 (35 ♔d3? ♗×h6! 36 ♖×h6 ♔g7=) **35 ... e6** (35 ... e5? 36 fe+ ± ±) **36 ♗g8 ed 37 h7** (37 ♗×d5? ♖h7=) **37 ... ♗g7?**± ± (37 ... ♖×c4+ 38 ♔d3 ♗g7 39 ♗×d5± ; 39 h8♕ ♗×h8 40 ♖×h8 ♖c8= ; 40 ... ♔g7? 41 ♗×d5 ♖c5 42 ♖g8+ ♔h7 43 ♗e6± ±) **38 ♗×d5 ♗h8 39 ♔d3 ♔f5 40 ♔e3 ♖e7+ 41 ♔f3 a5 42 a4 ♖c7** (42 ... ♖e8 43 ♖g1± ±) **43 ♗e4+ ♔f6 44 ♖h6 ♖g7** (44 ... ♔g7 45 ♖×g6+ ♔×h7 46 ♖g1+ ♔h6 47 ♖h1+ ♔g7 48 ♖h7+ ± ±) **45 ♔g4 1-0**

4011   Gheorghiu–AK

FR9: 23.6.1974: Queen's Indian

(Notes by Gheorghiu)

1 c4 c5 2 ♘f3 ♘f6 3 ♘c3 e6 4 g3 b6 5 e4 ♗b7 6 d3 d6 7 ♗g2 ♗e7 8 00 00 9 ♖e1 (9 h3 Smyslov) 9 ... ♘c6 (9 ... a6!?) 10 d4 cd (10 ... e5 11 de de 12 ♘d5±) 11 ♘×d4 ♘×d4 12 ♕×d4 ♘c7 (12 ... ♘g4!= Smyslov) 13 b3 ♖fd8 14 ♗b2 ♖ac8 15 ♖ad1± ½-½

4012   AK–Westerinen

FR11: 25.6.1974: Spanish

(Notes by Chistiakov)

1 e4 e5 2 ♘f3 ♘c6 3 ♗b5 a6 4 ♗a4 d6 5 00 ♗d7 6 d4 ♘f6 7 c3 ♗e7 (7 ... ♘×e4 is not good because of 8 ♖e1.) 8 ♘bd2 00 9 ♖e1 ♖e8 10 ♘f1 h6 11 ♘g3 ♗f8 12 ♗d2 b5 (12 ... g6, depriving the 'Spanish' bishop of f5, is better.) 13 ♗c2 ♘a5 14 b3 c5 15 d5 (Preventing any counterplay on the c-file. Also, the knight on a5 will be bad for the whole of its life.) 15 ... ♘h7 16 h3 ♗e7 (16 ... ♘g5 17 ♘×g5 hg 18 ♕h5 ♗e7 19 ♘f5 gives White good attacking chances.) 17 ♘f5 ♘b7 (17 ... ♗×f5 18 ef ♘f6, planning e5–e4, would give greater chances of counterplay.) 18 a4 ba? (*281*) (If Black still did not want to exchange on f5, then 18 ... ♕c7 was acceptable.)

19 b4! a5 20 ♗×a4 ab 21 cb ♗f8 (21 ... cb is bad because of 22 ♗×d7 ♕×d7 23 ♘×e5! de 24 ♕g4 winning the queen; or 22 ... ♖×a1 23 ♕×a1 ♕×d7 24 ♕a7 ♘c5 25 ♕×d7 ♘×d7 26 ♗×b4 winning a

281
18B
W

pawn. Now, however, disaster
strikes on the Q-side.) 22 ♗c6! ♕c7
(After 22 ... ♗×c6 23 dc Black
loses his knight.) 23 b5 ♘f6 24 ♕c2
♖eb8 25 ♘e3 ♗c8 26 ♘c4 ♗e7 27
b6 ♕d8 28 ♖a7 ♘d7 29 ♕a4
♖×a7 30 ba ♖a8 31 ♕a6 ♕c7 32
♗×d7 ♕×d7 33 ♘b6 ♘d8 34
♕a1! **1-0**

4013 Radulov–AK

FR12: 26.6.1974: Caro-Kann

1 e4 c6 2 d4 d5 3 ♘c3 de 4 ♘×e4
♘d7 5 ♗c4 ♘gf6 6 ♘g5 e6 7 ♕e2
♘b6 8 ♗d3 c5 9 dc ♗×c5 10 ♘1f3
♕c7 11 ♗d2 h6 12 ♘e4 ♗e7 13
♗c3 ♘bd5 14 ♘×f6+ gf 15 ♗d2
♗d7 16 00 ♘f4 17 ♗×f4 ♕×f4 18
♗b5 000 ½-½

4014 AK–Pomar

FR13: 27.6.1974: Caro-Kann

1 e4 c6 2 d4 d5 3 ♘c3 de 4 ♘×e4

♗f5 5 ♘g3 ♗g6 6 ♘f3 ♘d7 7 h4
h6 8 h5 ♗h7 9 ♗d3 ♗×d3 10
♕×d3 ♕c7 11 ♗d2 e6 12 ♕e2
♘gf6 13 c4 ♗d6 14 ♘f5 000 (14 . . .
♗f4 15 ♗×f4 ♕×f4 16 ♘e3±) 15
♘×d6+ ♕×d6 16 ♗a5! ♖de8 (16
. . . b6 17 ♗c3 and a Q-side pawn
storm with a2-a4-a5) 17 ♘e5 ♕e7
18 ♗c3!? ♖d8 19 f4± ♗×e5 20 fe
♘h7 21 000 ♘g5 22 a3 f5 23 ef gf 24
♖hf1 ♖he8 25 ♖de1± ♕f7 26 g4
♖f8 27 ♕c2 ♕g8 28 ♗b4 (28
♕g6!±± Geller) 28 . . . ♖f7 29
♕g6 ♕×g6 30 hg ♖g7 31 ♖×f6
♖dg8 32 ♖ef1 ♖×g6 33 ♖×g6
♖×g6 34 ♖f8+ ♔c7 35 ♗a5+! b6
36 ♗d2 ♘e4 37 ♗f4+ ♔b7 38
♖f7+ ♔a8 (38 . . . ♔a6? 39 ♗b8)
39 ♖f8+ ♔b7 40 b4 ♖×g4 41
♖f7+ ♔a8? (41 . . . ♔c8! 42 ♗e5
c5!± Geller) 42 ♔c2 h5 43 a4 h4 44
♔d3 ♖g5 (*282*)

282
44B
W

45 ♖f8+ ♔b7 46 ♖b8+ ♔a6 47
♗d2 ♖g3+ 48 ♔c2 **1-0**

41 Candidates' Final Moscow, 16.9–22.11.1974

	1	2	3	4	5	6	7	8	9	0	1	2	3	4	5	6	7	8	9	0	1	2	3	4	
Karpov	½	1	½	½	½	1	½	½	½	½	½	½	½	½	½	½	1	½	0	½	0	½	½	½	**12½**
Korchnoi	½	0	½	½	½	0	½	½	½	½	½	½	½	½	½	½	0	½	1	½	1	½	½	½	**11½**

The final match of the men's Candidates' series began in the middle of September. This match provided the centre of attention for almost the whole chess world during the next two months. The match began at a cracking pace. In the first game Karpov employed a defence which Furman, his trainer, had used to good effect against Uhlmann at Madrid some months earlier, but there was a hole in it (17 ♘d5!) which none of the eminent grandmasters involved had spotted and which Korchnoi also missed during the game. In the second game Karpov produced a crushing victory. There followed three draws and then another crushing defeat for Korchnoi in what Spassky called a suicidal game. Indeed why had Korchnoi switched from the French Defence which proved such a trusty weapon in the fourth game, and later in the match, to a risky variation of the Petroff?

After the match Karpov stated that with the exception of his two mistakes (analysis of the continuation of the nineteenth game and the opening in the 21st game) there were no gross faults in the match. Yet this statement is difficult to reconcile with the facts, even in just the first six games. Would Fischer have allowed Karpov's defence to go unpunished in the first game? In the third game Anatoly failed to convert a clearly favourable endgame into a win and, in the fourth game, he was over-ambitious in the opening and Korchnoi could have obtained a superior ending.

However, at the beginning of October Karpov had a clear lead of two points. There followed ten straight draws with Karpov apparently happy to play quietly and carefully to maintain his lead, but the temperature of the match was nearing boiling point as these 'dull' draws followed one after another: in the eleventh game Korchnoi chose an inferior move in the middle game apparently banking on Karpov refraining from a complicated path to advantage in favour of a safe course to equality, and he was right; in both the thirteenth and fifteenth games Korchnoi missed winning continuations. There followed another 'up and down' draw. Then, at the very end of the month, came the crucial seventeenth game – Korchnoi got the better of the opening, probably could have won, but pressed too hard, blundered and lost.

Karpov began November with a 3–0 lead and, at most, seven more games to play. Almost everyone now wrote Korchnoi off (even his friends and fellow grandmasters tried to persuade him to resign the match), but the real excitement was still ahead. Karpov remained content to draw, but then in the nineteenth game Korchnoi registered his first victory. The 20th game saw Korchnoi opt for an ultra sharp defence with Karpov trying to find a simple path through to a draw. In the 21st game–sensation, Karpov loses in 19 moves! Korchnoi now had some practical chances of levelling the match, but Karpov hung on grimly to his lead. Thus the 23-year-old Soviet superstar became the only player since Tal to make his way through to a World Championship match at the first attempt.

4101 Korchnoi–AK

G1: 16.9.1974: English

1 c4 ♘f6 2 ♘c3 e6 3 ♘f3 b6 4 e4 ♗b7 5 ♕e2 ♗b4 6 e5 ♘g8 7 d4 d6 8 ♗d2 de 9 de ♘a6 10 000 ♕e7 11 g3 000 12 ♗g2 ♘c5 13 ♗g5 f6 14 ♖×d8+ ♕×d8 15 ♖d1 ♕e8 16 ef gf (*283*)

283
16B
W

17 ♗d2?! (17 ♘d5! e.g. 17 . . .

♗×d5 18 cd fg 19 ♘d4 or 17 . . . ♕a4 18 ♘×b4 ♕×b4 19 ♗h3 in each case with a strong attack) 17 . . . ♘e7 18 ♘e4! (18 ♗h3 ♔b8 19 ♘e1 ♘c6= Uhlmann-Furman, Madrid 1973) 18 . . . ♘×e4 19 ♗×b4 ♘c6 20 ♗a3 (20 ♗e1!? Petrosian) 20 . . . f5 21 ♘e1 (21 ♘h4 ♕f7 22 ♗×e4 fe 23 ♕×e4 ♕×f2 24 ♕×e6+ ♔b8= Kotov; 21 ♘d2!? Petrosian; 21 ♕e3! followed by b3 and ♗b2± Botvinnik) 21 . . . ♕g6 22 f3 ♘g5 23 f4?! (23 ♘d3 ♕f6= Petrosian; 23 ♕e3!? Kotov; 23 b3 e5 24 ♗b2 ♖e8 25 ♕f2 e4= Botvinnik) 23 . . . ♘e4 24 ♘f3 ♕f6 25 ♕e3 ♖d8 26 ♖×d8+ ♘×d8 27 ♘g5 ♕g6! 28 ♘f3 (28 ♘×e4 ♗×e4 29 ♗×e4 fe= Petrosian) 28 . . . ♕f6 29 ♗b4 c5 30 ♗e1 ♘f7 31

♗f1 ♗c6 32 ♗d3♔b7 33 h3 (33 g4
♕h6= Petrosian) 33 . . . ♕h6 34 h4
♕g7 35 ♘g5 ♘fd6 36 ♘f3 ♘f7 37
♘g5 ♘fd6 ½–½ (2·24 – 2·05)

4102 AK–Korchnoi

G2: 18.9.1974: Sicilian

**1 e4 c5 2 ♘f3 d6 3 d4 cd 4 ♘×d4
♘f6 5 ♘c3 g6 6 ♗e3 ♗g7 7 f3
♘c6 8 ♕d2 OO 9 ♗c4 ♗d7 10 h4
♖c8** (The main line since 10 . . .
♕a5 lost its popularity following
some severe reverses.) **11 ♗b3 ♘e5
12 OOO ♘c4 13 ♗×c4 ♖×c4 14 h5
♘×h5 15 g4 ♘f6** (So far the game
has followed Geller-Korchnoi,
Candidates' 1971. That game
continued 16 ♗h6 ♘×e4 17 ♕e3
♖×c3 18 bc ♘f6 19 ♗×g7 ♔×g7
20 ♖h2 ♕a5 (20 . . . ♖g8!) 21
♘b3 ♕×a2 22 ♕×e7 and White
won. Hartston and Keene, in
Karpov-Korchnoi 1974, mention that
at Nice Korchnoi could be seen
surreptitiously hiding Levy's *The
Sicilian Dragon* under a pile of other
chess literature. The first edition of
that book, however, considered
only 16 ♗h6 and 16 ♖dg1.) **16
♘de2!** (So simple. Black's
counterplay in this line is almost
invariably based on . . . ♖×c3 at
some stage to weaken White's Q-
side pawn structure. Karpov denies
Black this counterplay.) **16 . . .
♕a5 17 ♗h6 ♗×h6 18 ♕×h6
♖fc8 19 ♖d3!** TN *(284)*

19 . . . ♖4c5? (19 . . . ♕d8 20 g5
♘h5 21 ♘f4 ♕f8 22 ♕×f8+ ♔×f8

284
19W
B

(22 . . . ♖×f8!?) 23 ♘×h5 gh 24
♖×h5 ♕g7±; 19 . . . ♗e6 20 g5
♘h5 21 ♘f4 ♕e5! 22 ♘×h5 gh 23
♕×h5 ♔f8! is probably better.) **20
g5!** ♖×g5 (Or 20 . . . ♘h5 21 ♘f4
♖×g5 22 ♘cd5 and Black is
crushed.) **21 ♖d5!** (White's last
two moves impressed Petrosian
sufficiently to give them both two
exclamation marks!) **21 . . . ♖×d5
22 ♘×d5** (This is the point of
White's 20th move – to play ♘d5
without allowing . . . ♖×d5.) **22
. . . ♖e8** (Everything loses, e.g. 22
. . . ♕d8 23 ♘×f6+ ef 24 ♘f4 ♖c5
25 ♕×h7+ ♔f8 26 ♕h8+ ♔e7 27
♘d5+ . The idea of the text is that if
23 ♘×f6+ and 24 ♕×h7+ then
the king can creep out via e7.) **23
♘ef4!** (Threatening simply 24
♘×f6+ and 25 ♘d5 sealing off e7.)
23 . . . ♗c6 (*285*) (Or 23 . . . ♗e6
24 ♘×e6 fe 25 ♘×f6+ ef 26
♕×h7+ ♔f8 27 ♕×b7±±)
24 e5! (24 ♘×f6+ ef 25 ♘h5 fails to
25 . . . ♕g5+ . The text blocks the
black queen's route to g5.) **24 . . .
♗×d5** (24 . . . de 25 ♘×f6+ ef 26
♘h5! leads to mate.) **25 ef ef 26
♕×h7+ ♔f8 27 ♕h8+ 1–0** (0·48

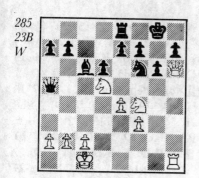

285
23B
W

– 1·09) (After 27 ... ♔e7 28 ♘×d5+ ♕×d5 29 ♖e1+ it is all over.)

4103 Korchnoi–AK

G3: 20.9.1974: English

1 c4 ♘f6 2 ♘c3 e6 3 ♘f3 b6 4 e4 ♗b7 5 ♕e2 ♗b4 6 e5 ♘g8 7 d4 ♘e7! 8 ♗d2 00 9 000 d5! 10 h4 (10 cd ♗a6 11 ♕e3 ♗×f1 12 ♖h×f1 ♗×c3 and ... ♕×d5= Kotov; 11 ♕e4! ♗×c3 12 bc ♗×f1 13 ♖h×f1 ♕×d5 14 ♕c2± Botvinnik) 10 ... ♗×c3! 11 ♗×c3 dc 12 ♕×c4 (12 ♘g5 ♗d5 13 ♕h5 h6 14 ♖h3 is unclear.) 12 ... ♗a6! 13 ♕a4 ♗×f1 14 ♖h×f1 ♕d5!∓ 15 ♔b1 (15 ♘e1!? Gufeld) 15 .·. a5 16 ♕c2 h6 17 ♖fe1 ♘a6 18 ♕e4! ♖fd8 (18 ... ♘b4!? 19 ♗×b4 ab 20 ♕×d5 ♘×d5∓; 19 ♕×d5!? Gufeld) 19 ♕×d5 ♖×d5 (19 ... ♘×d5! 20 ♗d2 ♖d7 21 ♖c1 c5!∓ Botvinnik) 20 ♖d2 ♖ad8 21 ♖ed1 h5 22 ♔c2 ♘f5 23 g3 f6?! (23 ... ♘b8!?) 24 ef gf 25 ♘g1! ♘e7 26 ♘e2 ♘g6 27 ♖d3 ♘b4+ 28 ♗×b4 ab 29 a3! ba 30 ♖×a3 ♖8d7 31 ♖e1?! (31 ♖ad3=) 31 ... ♔f7? (31 ...

e5!∓ /∓) 32 ♖d3 ♖f5 (32 ... e5? 33 de ♖×d3 34 e6+ ! Balashov) 33 f3 c5 34·f4! ♘e7 35 dc ♖×c5+ 36 ♘c3 dc7 37 ♔d2 ♘f5 38 ♖a1 ♖c4 39 ♖a6 b5?! (39 ... ♖b4!) 40 b3! ♖b4 41 ♘e2 ♔e7 42 ♖a8! ♖d7 43 ♖×d7+ ♔×d7 44 ♖h8 ♖×b3= (s) (adjournment 21.9.1974) 45 ♖×h5 ♘×g3 46 ♘×g3 ♖×g3 47 ♖×b5 f5 48 ♔e2 ♖g4 49 ♔f3 ♖×h4 50 ♖b6 ♖h1 51 ♖a6 c1 52 ♔g3 ♖c4 53 ♔f3 ♖c3+ 54 ♔f2 ♖c6 55 ♖a1 ♖c4 56 ♔f3 ♔d6 57 ♖e1 ♖c3+ ½-½ (2·51 – 3·08)

4104 AK–Korchnoi

G4: 22.9.1974: French

1 e4 e6 2 d4 d5 3 ♘d2 c5 4 ed ed 5 ♘gf3 ♘c6 6 ♗b5 ♗d6 7 dc ♗×c5 8 00 ♘e7 9 ♘b3 ♗d6 10 c3 ♗g4 11 ♘bd4 00 12 ♕e2 ♖e8 13 ♖e1 a6 14 ♗g5 h6 (14 ... ♕c7?! 15 h3 ♗h5 16 ♗×e7 ♘×e7 17 ♘h4± Balashov) 15 ♗h4 ♕b6 16 ♕b3 ♗c5 17 ♕×b6 ♗×b6 18 ♗d3 ♔f8 (18 ... ♘×d4 19 ♘×d4 ♗×d4 20 ♗×e7± Balashov; 20 cd ♘f5= Botvinnik) 19 a3 ♘×d4 20 ♘×d4 ♗×d4 21 cd (21 ♗×e7+ ! ♖×e7 22 cd± Botvinnik) 21 ... ♘f5 22 f3 ♘×h4 23 fg ♘g6 24 g3?! (24 ♗×g6=) 24 ... ♘e7!∓ 25 ♗f1 (25 ♖ac1 ♘c6 26 ♖×e8+ ♖×e8 27 ♗×a6 ♘×d4 28 ♗f1 ♘e2+ 29 ♗×e2 ♖×e2 30 ♖c8+ ♔e7 31 ♖c7+ ♔e6 32 ♖×b7 d4= Balashov) 25 ... ♘c6 26 ♗g2 ♖×e1+ 27 ♖×e1 ♖d8 28 ♔f2 ♖d6 29

🨶d1 🨔e7 30 b4 🨶d8 31 🨔e3 🨔d6
32 🨶f1 f6 33 🨶c1 🨶c8 34 🨶c5
🨞e7 35 🨗f1?! (35 🨶×c8 🨞×c8
36 a4! Botvinnik) 35 ... 🨶e8!
36 🨔d2 (36 🨔d3! f5 37 🨗e2 fg 38
🨗×g4 🨶f8 39 🨶c2= Balashov) 36
... f5! 37 🨗e2 (37 b5!? fg 38 ba ba
39 🨶a5! Balashov; 37 gf?! 🨞×f5 38
🨗g2 🨞e3∓ Petrosian) 37 ... fg (37
... g5!? Petrosian) 38 🨗×g4 🨶f8
39 🨶c2 (39 🨔e3!? 🨶f1 40 🨗c8
Balashov) 39 ... g6?! (39 ... 🨶f1!∓
Botvinnik) 40 🨔e3 h5 (40 ... 🨶f1
41 🨶f2!= Botvinnik) 41 🨗h3 🨞c6
42 🨶d2 b5? (s) (42 ... g5! 43 🨗g2
a5 44 b5! 🨞e7 45 🨔d3!! 🨞c8 46 b6!
🨞×b6 47 🨶b2 🨞c8 48 🨔e3! b6 49
🨶b5 🨶f5 50 🨗e4! Botvinnik)
(adjournment 23.9.1974) 43 🨗g2
a5 44 h4! ab 45 ab 🨶e8+ ½–½ (2·41
– 3·12)

4105 Korchnoi–AK

G5: 25.9.1974: Queen's Indian

**1 c4 🨞f6 2 🨞c3 e6 3 🨞f3 b6 4 g3
🨗b7 5 🨗g2 🨗e7 6 d4 00** (6 ...
🨞e4!= Petrosian) **7 ♕c2 c5 8 d5
ed 9 🨞g5 g6 10 ♕d1 ?!** ('What a
funny move. Why don't you play cd
and mate him?' asked Keene. 'I
didn't think of that ... it can't be
good,' replied Korchnoi. However,
after some analysis, Korchnoi was
convinced that it was a good idea
and said that he would try it the
next chance he got.) **10 ... d6 11
cd 🨞a6 12 00 🨞d7 13 🨞f3 🨞c7
14 a3 🨗f6 15 e4 b5 16 🨗f4 🨞b6
17 🨶e1 a5 18 ♕c2** (18 🨗×d6

♕×d6 19 e5 🨗×e5 20 🨞×e5
🨞b×d5 21 🨞e4 ♕×e5 22 🨞×c5
♕d6 23 🨞×b7 ♕c6= ; 18 e5 de 19
🨞×e5 🨞b×d5 20 🨞×f7 🨶×f7 21
🨗×c7= Petrosian) **18 ... 🨗g7** (18
... b4?! 19 ab ab 20 🨶×a8 🨗×a8
21 🨞d1± Flohr; 21 🨞b1±
Petrosian) **19 🨶ad1 b4 20 🨞b1
🨗a6 21 h4 🨶e8 22 🨗g5 ♕d7** (22
... f6!? Petrosian) **23 🨔h2 ba 24
🨞×a3 ♕a4 25 e5! 🨗f8** (25 ...
♕×c2! Flohr) **26 ♕×a4 🨞×a4 27
ed 🨗×d6 28 🨗c1! 🨶a8 ?!** (better
28 ... 🨶×e1 29 🨶×e1 🨶e8±
Botvinnik) **29 🨞d2!± 🨗e2** (29 ...
🨞×b2 30 🨗×b2 🨶×b2 31 🨞dc4
🨶×e1 32 🨶×e1 🨶b3 33 🨞×d6
🨶×a3 34 🨶e7 🨞b5 35 🨞×b5
🨗×b5 36 d6± Petrosian) **30 🨞dc4
🨗×d1 31 🨶×d1 🨗ed8 32 🨞×d6
🨶×d6 33 🨞c4 🨶f6 34 🨗f4** (34
🨔g1! Flohr) **34 ... 🨶×f4 35 gf
🨞×b2** (?! Botvinnik) **36 🨶b1 a4 37
d6 🨞e6 38 🨗d5!± ± a3** (286)

286
38B
W

39 🨞×a3 ?= (39 🨗×e6! fe 40
🨞×a3± ± ; 39 ... a2 40 🨶a1 fe 41
🨞e5± ± Flohr/Dvoretsky) **39 ...
🨞×f4 40 🨗f3 🨶b4 ?!** (40 ... 🨔f8!
41 🨞c4 🨞fd3! Botvinnik) **41 d7** (s)

(adjournment 26.9.1974) **41 ...
♘e6 42 ♘c2 ♖b8 43 ♘e3 ♔f8 44
♘c4 ♖b4! 45 ♗d5 ♖×c4 46
♗×e6 ♔e7! 47 ♖×c4 ♘×c4 48
♖d1 ♔d8 49 ♔g3 ♘e5 50 ♔f4
♘×d7 51 ♔g5 ♔e7 52 ♔h6 ♘e5
53 ♔×h7 ♘f3! 54 ♖h1 ♔e6 55
♔g7 c4 56 ♖h3 ♘e5 57 ♖a3 ♔f5
58 ♖c3 ♔e4 59 ♖c1 ♔d4 60 f4
♘d3 61 ♖f1 ♔e4 62 f5 ♘e5 63
♔f6 ♔g4+ 64 ♔g5 ♘e3 65 fg fg
66 ♖c1 ♔d3 67 ♔×g6 ♘g2 ½–½**
(4·26 – 4·11)

4106   AK–Korchnoi

G6: 27.9.1974: Petroff

**1 e4 e5 2 ♘f3 ♘f6 3 ♘×e5 d6 4
♘f3 ♘×e4 5 d4 d5 6 ♗d3 ♗e7 7
00 ♘c6 8 ♖e1 ♗g4 9 c3 f5 10
♕b3 00 11 ♘bd2 ♔h8** (11 ...
♘×d2? 12 ♘×d2 ♖b8 13 ♘f1 f4 14
♗e4 ♗e6 15 ♗×h7+ ± R. Byrne;
11 ... ♘a5 12 ♕b5 c6 13 ♕a4
b5 14 ♕c2 ♘c4= Botvinnik
12 h3 TN (12 ♘f1? ♗×f3
Capablanca–Kostić, match 1919)
12...♗h5 (12 ...♗×f3! 13 ♘×f3
♖b8± Suetin) **13 ♕×b7 ♖f6 14
♕b3** (*287*)

287
14W
B

14 ... ♖g6? (14 ... ♕d6 15 ♗b5!
♖b8 16 ♕a4± ; 14 ... g5!?
Botvinnik) **15 ♗e2!± ♖h4** (15 ...
♕d6? 16 ♘e5!; 15 ... ♘×f2 16
♔×f2 ♗h4+ 17 ♔f1 ♗×e1 18
♘×e1 ♗×e2+ 19 ♔×e2 ♕e7+ 20
♔f1 ♖e8 21 ♕d1± ± Botvinnik; 15
... ♗×f3 16 ♘×f3 ♖b8 17 ♕c2
♗d6 Kotov) **16 ♖f1 ♗×f3** (16 ...
♕e7 17 ♕d1!± R. Byrne) **17 ♘×f3
♗×f2+? 18 ♖×f2 ♘×f2** (18 ...
♕d6 19 ♘h4! R. Byrne) **19 ♔×f2
♕d6 20 ♘g5! ♖f8 21 ♕a3 ♕d8
22 ♗f4 h6 23 ♘f3± ± ♖e8 24
♗d3 ♖e4 25 g3! ♖f6 26 ♕c5**
(better 26 h4 Botvinnik) **26 ... g5
27 ♘×g5 hg** (27 ... ♖×f4+ 28 gf
hg 29 fg ♖d6 30 h4± ± Suetin) **28
♗×g5 ♖ee6 29 ♖e1 ♕g8 30 h4!
♖g6 31 ♖×e6 1–0** (time) (1·15 –
2·30) (31 ... ♖×e6 32 ♗b5 ♘d8
33 ♕×c7± ± R. Byrne; 31 ...
♕×e6 32 ♕f8+ ! Suetin)

4107   Korchnoi–AK

G7: 30.9.1974: English

**1 c4 ♘f6 2 ♘c3 e6 3 ♘f3 b6 4 e4
♗b7 5 ♕e2 ♗b4 6 e5 ♘g8 7 d4
♘e7 8 ♕d3 d5 9 ed cd 10 a3
♗×c3+ 11 ♕×c3 00 12 b4?!** (12
b3!? Kan, 12 ... ♘d7 13 ♗b2?!
♖c8 14 ♗e2 b5!∓ ; 13 ♗e2!=
Polugayevsky; 12 ♗e2!± Botvinnik) **12 ... ♘d7 13 ♗e2 ♖c8 14
00** (14 ♕b3!? Kan; 14 a4! ♗a6 15
b5 ♗b7 16 ♗e3± Botvinnik) **14
...♗a6!= 15 ♕b3 d5 16 b5 ♗b7**
(16 ... dc! Botvinnik) **17 cd ♗×d5
18 ♕b4 ♘g6 19 ♗g5 ♕c7 20**

♖ fc1 ♕ b8 21 ♘ d2 (better 21
♖×c8 Gufeld; 21 ♘e1 Botvinnik)
21 ... ♘ f6 (21 ... h6! 22 ♗ e3
♘h4!∓; 22 ♗ e7 ♖×c1+ 23 ♖×c1
♖ c8 24 ♖×c8+ ♕×c8 25 ♗ d6
♘h4!∓ Polugayevsky) 22 ♗×f6 gf
23 g3 ♖ fd8 24 ♘ f1 f5 25 ♘ d2 (25
♘e3!? Polugayevsky) 25 ... ♕ b7
26 a4!= ♖ d7 27 a5 dc7 28
♖×c7 ♖×c7 (28 ... ♕×c7 29 ab
ab 30 ♗f3! ♗×f3 31 ♘×f3 ♕c3! 32
♕×c3 ♖×c3 33 ♔g2 ♖ b3 34 d5!
♖×b5 35 de fe 36 ♘d4 ♖ e5 37
♖ b1= Polugayevsky) 29 ab ab 30
♘ c4 ♗×c4 31 ♗×c4 ♕ e4 32 ♗ f1
♖ c2 33 ♕ b1! ♘e7 34 ♕ d1 ♕ b2
35 ♗ g2 ♕ c2 36 ♕×c2 ♖×c2 37
h3 ♖ b2 38 ♗ c6! f4?! (38 ...
♘×c6! 39 bc ♖ c2 40 ♖ a8+ ♔g7
41 ♖ c8 b5= Polugayevsky) 39 gf
♘ f5 40 ♖ d1 ♘ e7 41 ♗ d7 ♔f8!
42 ♖ a1 (42 f5! ♘×f5 43 d5 Flohr;
43...♔e7! Botvinnik) 42...♖ b4
43 ♖ a8+ ♔g7 44 ♖ a7 ♔f6 45 d5
(s) (adjournment 1.10.1974) 45 ...
♘×d5 46 ♗ e8 ♖×f4 (46...♘e7
47 ♖ b7 Kan) 47 ♖×f7+ ♔e5 48
♖×h7 ½-½ (3·15 – 2·11) (48 ...
♘f6 49 ♖ h8 ♘×e8 50 ♖×e8 ♖ b4
51 ♖ h8 ♔d6 52 ♖ h5 e5= Kan)

4108 AK–Korchnoi

G8: 2.10.1974: French

1 e4 e6 2 d4 d5 3 ♘ d2 c5 4 ed ed 5
♘ gf3 ♘ c6 6 ♗ b5 ♗ d6 7 dc
♗×c5 8 0-0 ♘ e7 9 ♘ b3 ♗ d6 10 c3
♗ g4 11 ♘ bd4 0-0 12 ♕ a4 ♗ h5 13
♖ e1 ♕ c7 14 h3 ♗ g6 (14...a6 15
♗ d3! Botvinnik) 15 ♗ g5 a6 16

♗ f1 h6 17 ♗×e7 ♘×e7! (17 ...
♗×e7 18 ♘×c6 bc 19 ♘e5 fc8 20
♘×c6± Botvinnik) 18 ♖ ad1 ♘ c6
19 ♗ d3 ♗ h5 20 g4 ♗ g6 21 ♕ c2!
(21 ♗×g6 fg 22 ♘e6 ♕f7 23 ♕×f8
♕×f3∓ Polugayevsky; 21 ♘f5
♗×f5! 22 ♗×f5 ad8∓ Zaitsev)
21 ...♗×d3 22 ♕×d3 ♖ ad8 23
♖ e2 (23 ♘×c6 bc!) 23 ... ♖ fe8
(288) (23 ... ♗c5! Botvinnik)

288
23B
W

24 ♘ f5 (24 ♖×e8+ ♖×e8 25
♘×c6 bc 26 ♕×a6± Polugay-
evsky; ± Botvinnik; 26 ... f5!?) 24
... ♖×e2 25 ♕×e2 ♗ f4 26 ♖ e1
g6 (26 ... ♔f8 27 ♘3d4±
Averbakh) 27 ♘ e7+ ♗×e7 28
♕×c7 ♖ b6 29 ♔g2 ♔g7 30 ♖ d1
♗ d6 31 ♕ e2 ♖ c7 32 ♖ d3 ♕ e6
33 ♕ d1 ♗ b6 (33 ... b5!?
Polugayevsky) 34 ♖ d2± (34 b3
♕f6! 35 ♖×d5 ♖×d5 36 ♕×d5
♕×c3= Averbakh) 34...♕ e4 35
b3 ♖ d6 (better 35...h5! 36 gh gh
37 c4 ♖ d6 38 ♖×d5 ♖ g6+ or 35
...♗c5! 36 c4 d4= Botvinnik) 36
c4 h5! 37 ♖×d5?! (37 g5 d4 38 b4
♗ d8= Averbakh; 39 c5 ♖ d5 40
♖×d4 ♖×d4 41 ♕×d4 ♕×d4 42
♘×d4 ♗×g5 43 c6 bc 44 ♘×c6

♗f4 45 a4 ♗c7 46 a5 ♔f6 47 b5 ab 48 a6 ♗b6 49 a7 ♗×a7 50 ♘×a7 b4± Botvinnik) **37 ... ♖×d5 38 ♕×d5 ♖×d5** (38 ... ♕c2? 39 ♕d2! Averbakh) **39 cd hg 40 hg ♔f6 41 ♔f1 ♔e7** (s) (adjournment 3.10.1974) **42 ♘d2 ♗c7 43 ♘e4 f5 44 gf gf 45 ♘c5 ♗d6 46 ♘×b7+ ♔×d5 47 b4 ♔c4 48 ♘c5 ♗b6 49 ♘×a6 ♗b5 50 ♘c5 ♔×b4 51 ♘b3 ♔a3** ½-½ (2·34 – 3·00)

4109 Korchnoi–AK

G9: 4.10.1974: English

1 c4 ♘f6 2 ♘c3 e5 3 ♘f3 ♘c6 4 g3 ♗b4 5 ♗g2 00 6 00 e4 7 ♘e1 ♗×c3 8 dc h6 9 ♘c2 b6 10 ♘e3 ♗b7 11 ♘d5 (better 11 b3, intending 12 a4, 13 ♖a2 and 14 f4! Botvinnik) 11 ... ♘e5 12 b3 ♖e8 13 a4 (13 ♘e3!? Kotov) 13 ... d6 14 ♖a2 ♘ed7 15 h3?! (15 a5!? Suetin; 15 f4± Botvinnik) 15 ... a5 (15 ... a6! Botvinnik) 16 ♗e3 ♘×d5 17 cd ♕f6 18 c4 ♕g6 19 ♕b1 ♗c8 20 ♗d4= (better 20 b4! ab 21 ♕×b4 ♖a5 22 ♕b3 ♘c5 23 ♕c2 ♗d7 24 ♖fa1 with 25 ♗d2 and 26 a5 to follow – Botvinnik) 20 ... ♘c5 21 ♔h2 ♗d7 22 ♖g1 h5 23 ♖b2 ♖e7 24 ♕c1 ♕f5 25 ♕e3 f6 26 ♖c2 ♘f7 27 ♖c3 ♖ae8 28 ♖f1 ♔g8 29 ♕c1 ♕g5 30 ♕×g5 fg 31 ♖e3 ♔h7 32 ♖h1 ♔g6 33 ♔g1 ♘a6 34 ♔h2 ♘b4 35 ♖c1 g4 36 h4 ♗f5 37 ♔g1 ♔h7 38 ♔f1 ♗g6 39 ♔e1 ♖f7 40 ♗h1 ♔g8 41 ♗g2 (s) (adjournment 5.10.1974) 41 ... ♔h7 42 ♗h1 ½-½ (2·57 – 2·17)

4110 AK–Korchnoi

G10: 9.10.1974: French

1 e4 e6 2 d4 d5 3 ♘d2 c5 4 ed ed 5 ♘gf3 ♘c6 6 ♗b5 ♗d6 7 00 ♘e7 8 dc ♗×c5 9 ♘b3 ♗d6 10 ♘bd4 00 11 c3 ♗g4 12 ♕a4 h5 13 ♗d3 h6 14 ♗e3 a6 15 ♖fe1 ♕c7 16 h3 ♘a5! 17 ♘h4 (17 ♖ad1 ♘c4 18 ♗c1 ♘e5 19 ♗e2= Antoshin; 18 ... b5 19 ♕c2 ♗c5! 20 g4 ♗g6 21 ♗×g6 fg 22 ♔g2 ♖f7; 20 b3 ♘d6= Botvinnik) 17 ... ♘c4 18 ♕c2 ♘×e3 19 ♖×e3 ♗h2+ (19...♗c5 20 ♖ae1 ♘c6 21 g4! Botvinnik) 20 ♔h1 ♗f4 21 ♖ee1 ♗g5 22 ♘hf5 ♘×f5 23 ♘×f5 (23 ♗×f5!? ♗f6 24 g4! ♗×d4 25 cd ♕×c2 26 ♗×c2 ♗g6 27 b3! ♗e4+ 28 ♔h2 f5 29 ♖e3± Antoshin) 23 ... ♗g6 24 ♘d4 (better 24 ♖e2 Botvinnik) 24 ... ♗×d3 25 ♕×d3 ♖fe8 26 ♕f3 ♖b6 27 ♖e2 ♗f6 (27 ... ♖e4! Botvinnik) 28 ♖d1 ♖e4 29 ♘f5 ♖ae8 30 ♘e3 ♕e6 31 ♖×d5 ♗g5 32 ♖d4?! (32 ♕f5 ♕×f5 33 ♖×f5 ♗×e3= Antoshin; 32 ♖ed2! ♗×e3 33 fe ♖×e3 34 ♕f4= Botvinnik) 32 ... ♖×d4 33 cd ♕×a2 34 ♘c4 ♖d8 35 ♕d3 b5 (35 ... ♗f6!? Antoshin) 36 ♘e3 ♕e6 37 d5 ♕d7 38 b4 ♗d6 39 ♕d4 ♔f8 40 ♕e4! ♗×e3?! (40 ... g6!∓ Botvinnik) 41 ♖×e3 ♕×d5 42 ♕h7 (s) (adjournment 10.10.1974) 42 ... f6= 43 ♔g1! ♕a2 44 ♔h2 ♕×f2 45 ♖g3 ♕f4 46 ♕×g7+ ♔e8 47 ♕b7 h5 (47 ... ♖d7= Antoshin) 48 ♕c6+ ♖d7 49 ♕c8+ ♔e7 50 ♕c5+ ♔d8 51

♕×h5 ♖d3 52 ♕h8+ ♔c7 53
♕h7+ ♖d7 54 ♕c2+ ♔b7 55
♕b3 ♖d4 (55 ... ♖g7 56 ♕f3+ ±
Antoshin) 56 ♕f7+ ♔b6 57 ♕e6+
♔b7 58 ♕e7+ ♔b6 ½-½ (3·04 –
3·40)

4111 Korchnoi–AK

G11: 11.10.1974: Queen's Indian

**1 d4 ♘f6 2 ♘f3 e6 3 g3 b6 4 ♗g2
♗b7 5 c4 ♗e7 6 ♘c3 0-0 7 ♕d3 d5
8 cd ♘×d5 9 ♘×d5 ed 10 0-0 ♘d7
11 ♗f4 c5 12 dc bc 13 ♖fd1
♘f6= 14 ♕c2** (14 ♗e5!? Gufeld)
14 ... ♕b6 15 ♘d2 (15 ♘h4 g6= ;
15 ♖ac1!? Polugayevsky) **15 ...
♖fe8!** (15 ... ♘h5 16 ♗e5 f6 17
♗c3 d4 18 ♘c4± Polugayevsky)
16 ♕b3! ♗a6! 17 e3 (17 ♘f1!?
♗c6 18 ♕c2 ♖ac8 19 ♘e3 d4 20
♗×c6 ♕×c6 21 ♘c4 ♘d5= ; 19
♗h3 ♖cd8 20 ♗c7 ♖a8∓
Polugayevsky) **17 ... ♗c6 18 ♕c2
♗a4?!** (18 ... d4!? Polugayevsky;
18 ... ♗b7!? Gufeld) **19 b3 ♗c6
20 ♖ac1** (20 ♗e5!? Gufeld) **20 ...
♗f8 21 ♘f3 ♗b7** (21 ... ♘d7! 22
♘d4 ♗b7 23 ♘f5 ♕e6 24 ♗h3
♕c6= Polugayevsky) **22 ♗e5 ♘e4**
(22 ... ♘g4 23 ♗b2 d4 24 ed ♖e2
25 ♖d2±) **23 ♗a1 ♖ad8?!** (23 ...
♖ac8! Botvinnik) **24 ♘e5 ♕b6** (24
... ♕e6 25 ♘d3± Gufeld) **25
♗×e4** (25 b4 cb 26 ♕c7 ♕×c7! 27
♖×c7 ♗a8± Botvinnik; 28 ♘×f7
♖c8∓ Polugayevsky) **25 ... de 26
♕c4?!** (26 ♘d7 ♕b5 27 ♘×f8
♖×f8= ; 26 ♖d7! ♖×d7 27 ♘×d7
♕e6 28 ♘×f8 ♖×f8 29 ♕×c5±

Gufeld) **26 ... ♕c7 27 b4
♖×d1+ ?!** (27 ... ♗d6!! 28 ♘g4
cb 29 ♕×c7 ♗×c7 30 ♖×d8+
♗×d8∓ Polugayevsky; 29 ♕d4
♗e5!!= Gufeld) **28 ♖×d1 ♗c8!**
(28 ... ♖×e5 29 ♗×e5 ♕×e5 30
♖d7± ± Flohr) **29 bc!** (29 ♖d7
♗×d7 30 ♕×f7+ ♔h8 31 ♘×d7
♖a8∓ ∓ Polugayevsky) **29 ...
♗e6!** (29 ... ♖×e5? 30 ♗×e5
♕×e5 31 ♖d8 ♗h3 32 ♕d4 ♕c7
33 ♕d6± ± Gufeld) **30 ♕a4** (30
♕×e4 ♕×c5∓ Gufeld) **30 ...
♖c8 31 ♗d4** (31 c6?! f6 32 ♖d7
♕b6 33 ♖b7 ♕c5∓ Gufeld) **31 ...
f6 32 ♕a6** (32 ♘c4!?) **32 ... ♗d5**
(32 ... ♖e8!? 33 ♘c4 ♗×c5 34
♗×c5 ♕×c5= Polugayevsky) **33
♘c4** (33 ♗b2 ♕×c5 34 ♗a3!!
♕c2 35 ♖×d5 fe 36 ♕e6+ ± 33 ...
♕b7= Polugayevsky) **33 ... ♕c6!**
(33 ... ♗×c5? 34 ♗×c5 ♕×c5 35
♖×d5 ♕×c4 36 ♖d8+ Polugayevsky) **34 ♕×c6 ♖×c6 35 ♗c1** (35
♘a5!? ♖c7 36 ♘b3 ♗×b3 37 ab
♗×c5 38 ♖c1 ♗b6 39 ♖×c7
♗×c7 40 ♗×a7; 35 ... ♖a6 36
♗c3 ♗×a2 37 c6 Gufeld) **35 ...
♔f7** (35 ... ♗×c5? 36 ♘a5± ±
Gufeld) **36 a3 ♖a6 37 ♗c3 ♔e6
38 ♗d2 ♔d7 39 f3! ef** (39 ... f5!?
Polugayevsky) **40 ♔f2 ♖a5** (40
... ♖a4! Polugayevsky) **41 e4
♗c6** (s) (adjournment 12.10.1974)
42 ♔×f3 ♔e6 (42 ... ♖a4 43 ♔e3
g6 44 ♗×f6 ♖×a3 45 ♖×a3
♗×c5+ 46 ♗d4 ♗×a3 47 ♗×a7
♗c1= Gufeld) **43 ♔e3 ♖a4 44
♗b3** (44 ♘c4=) **44 ... g6 45 ♔d3
a6! 46 ♗e3 ♗b5+ 47 ♔c2 f5** (47

. . . ♗g7!? 48 ♘f3 ♖×e4 49 ♘d4+
♔d5 50 ♘×b5 ab 51 ♔d3 ♖a4=
Polugayevsky) **48 ef+ gf** (48 . . .
♔×f5=) **49 ♗f2 ♗g7** (49 . . .
♖g4!? Polugayevsky) **50 ♖e3+**
♔**d7 51 ♖f3 ♗e6 52 ♖e3+ ♔d7**
53 ♖f3 ♗e6 54 ♔b3 g5 ? (54 . . .
♖g4= Gufeld) **55 ♖e3+ ♔d7 56**
♘**f3!± ♗f6** (*289*)

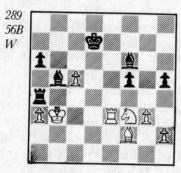

289
56B
W

57 ♖e1 ? (57 ♘e5+ ! ♔c7 58 ♘g6;
57 . . . ♔c8 58 ♘f7 f4 59 ♘d6+
♔d7 60 gf ♖×f4 61 ♗g3±
Polugayevsky) **57 . . . f4 58 ♘e5+**
(58 ♗d4!? ♗×d4 59 ♖d1 ♗e2 60
♖d2!!± ± ; 59 . . . fg 60 ♘×d4♔c7
61 hg ♖c4= Gufeld) **58 . . . ♔c8**
(58 . . . ♔c7 59 gf ♖×f4 60 ♗g3
Gufeld) **59 ♘f7 fg 60 ♘d6+** (60
♗×g3 h4!=) **60 . . . ♔d7 61 hg**
♖**g4!** (61 . . . h4 62 ♘e4 ♗e7 63 gh
♗c6 64 ♘g5 ♗×g5 65 hg Gufeld)
62 ♘×b5 ab 63 ♖h1 ♔c6!! (63
. . . ♖g5± Gufeld) **64 ♖×h5 ♗d4!**
65 ♗×d4 ♖×d4 66 ♖g5 ♖e4 67
g4 ♖a4 68 ♔b2 ♖f4 69 ♔c2 (69
♖g8 ♔×c5 70 g5 ♖g4 71 g6 ♔b6
72 g7 ♔b7= Gufeld) **69 . . .** ♖**f3**
70 ♔b2 ♖f2+ 71 ♔c3 ♖f3+ 72
♔**d4 ♖f4+ 73 ♔e5 ♖a4 74 ♖g8**

♖×**a3 75 g5 ♔×c5 76 g6 ♖g3 77**
♖**c8+ ♔b4 78 ♔f6 ♖f3+ 79**
♔**e6 ♖g3 80 ♔f7 ♔a3 81 g7 ♖g7** ½-½
(4·35 - 4·33)

4112   AK–Korchnoi

G12: 14.10.1974: French

1 e4 e6 2 d4 d5 3 ♘d2 c5 4 ed ed·5
♘gf3 ♘c6 6 ♗b5 ♗d6 7 00 cd 8
♘b3 ♗e7 9 ♘b×d4 00 10 c3 ♗g4
11 ♕a4 ♗h5 12 ♗e3 ♕c7 13 h3
♘a5 14 ♗d3 (better 14 ♖ad1
Botvinnik) 14 . . . ♘c4! 15 ♘b5
♕d7! 16 ♗×c4 dc 17 ♖fd1 ♘f5!
(17 . . . a6? 18 ♖×d6 ♕×b5 19
♕×b5 ab 20 ♘d4± Gufeld) 18
♕×c4 ♗×f3 19 gf ♘×e3! 20 fe
♕×h3 21 ♘×d6= (21 ♖×d6? a6!∓
Suetin) 21 . . . ♕g3+ 22 ♔f1
♕×f3+ (22 . . . ♕h3+= Suetin)
23 ♔e1 ♕g3+ ½-½ (0·37 - 1·31)

4113   Korchnoi–AK

G13: 16.10.1974: Queen's Indian

1 ♘f3 ♘f6 2 d4 e6 3 g3 b6 4 ♗g2
♗b7 5 c4 ♗e7 6 ♘c3 00 7 ♕d3 d5
8 cd ♘×d5 9 ♘×d5 ed 10 00 ♘d7
11 ♖d1 (11 ♗f4= 4111) 11 . . . ♖e8
12 ♗e3 ♗d6 13 ♖ac1 a5 14 ♕c2 c6
15 ♘e1 ♘f6 16 ♗f3 ♖c8 17 ♘g2
h6 18 ♗f4 (18 ♗h4!? ♕d7 Zaitsev)
18 . . . c5 19 ♗×d6 ♕×d6 (19 . . .
cd?! 20 ♗c7 ♕d7 21 ♕b3! ♖×c7
22 ♕×b6± ± Zaitsev) 20 dc ♖×c5
21 ♕d2 ♘e4 22 ♕f4 ♕c6 23 ♖×c5
bc 24 ♘e3?! (24 ♕c1!? Euwe) 24
. . . d4 25 ♘c4 ♕a4! 26 ♖c1 (26 b3
♕×a2 27 ♗×e4 ♗×e4 28 ♘d6

Re7 29 N×e4 Q×e2; 27 Ne5 Ng5!∓ Zaitsev) 26 ... Ng5! 27 Qf5 N×f3+ ?! (27 ... B×f3 28 ef Ne6∓ Euwe; 28 ... Q×a2 29 Q×c5 N×f3+ 30 Kg2 Qb3! 31 N×a5 Qd3 Botvinnik) 28 ef Ba6 (28 ... Qc6!?) 29 Nd6 Re7 30 Q×c5 d3 31 Qd5! Qb4 (31 ... Qc2! 32 R×c2 Re1+ 33 Kg2 dc= Zaitsev) 32 Kg2 Q×b2?! (32 ... d2! 33 Rd1 Re1 34 Q×f7+= ; 33 Rc6 d1 Q! 34 Q×d1 Re1 35 Q×e1 Q×e1 36 R×a6= Botvinnik) 33 Rc6 Qe5 34 Q×e5? (34 Nc8! B×c8 35 R×c8+ Kh7 36 Q×d3+ g6 37 Qd8 Zaitsev) 34 ... R×e5 35 Ne4 Bb5?! (35 ... Bb7= Euwe) 36 Rd6 f5 37 Nc3 Bc4 38 f4 Rc5 39 Kf3 Kf7 (39 ... B×a2 40 N×a2 Rc2= Zaitsev) 40 Ke3 Ke7 41 Rb6 Rc8 42 Rb7+ Kf8 43 Ra7 Rc5 (290)

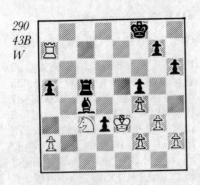

290
43B
W

44 h4 (s) (adjournment 17.10.1974) 44 ... h5 45 a3 Ba6! 46 Kd2 (46 R×a6 R×c3 47 R×a5 g6=) 46 ... Rc6 47 Rd7 Bc4 48 Nd1 Bb5 49 Ne3 g6 50 Rd5! Rb6 51 Nd1 (51 Rc5!? Zaitsev) 51 ... Kf7 52 Nb2

Ba6 53 Na4 Rc6 54 Rc5 Re6 55 Re5 Rc6 56 Nc5 Bc4 57 Na4 Ba6 58 Rc5 Re6 59 Rc7+ Ke8 60 Nc3 Rb6 61 Nd1 Re6 62 Ne3 Rb6 63 Rc5 Rb2+ 64 Kc3 R×f2 65 R×a5 Bb7 66 K×d3 Rf3 67 Kd4 Kd7 68 Nc4 R×g3 69 a4 Kc7 70 Rc5+ Kb8 71 Ne5 Be4 72 Rc3 (72 a5!? Polugayevsky) 72 ... Rg1 73 Kc5 Kc7! 74 a5 Ra1 75 Kb5 Kd6 76 a6 Rb1+ 77 Ka5 Ra1+ 78 Kb6 Rb1+ 79 Ka7 Kd5 80 Rc6 Rf1 (80 ... Kd4? 81 Rb6 Rf1 82 N×g6 Zaitsev) 81 Kb6 Kd4 82 Rc4+ Ke3 83 Ra4 Ba8 84 N×g6 Kf3 85 Kc7 Rd1 86 a7 Kg4 87 Ra6 Kg3 88 Ra3+ (88 Rf6 Ra1 89 R×f5 R×a7+ 90 Kb8 Ba6 91 Rg5+ Kf3 92 f5 Be4 93 R×h5 Rf6= Zaitsev) 88 ... Kg4 89 Ra5 Rb1= 90 Ra6 Rd1 91 Rd6 Ra1 92 Kb8 Be4 93 Rd7 Kf3 94 Rg7 Ra6 95 Kc8 Kg3 96 Kd8 Ba8 ½-½ (6·15 - 5·44)

4114   AK–Korchnoi

G14: 18.10.1974: French

1 e4 e6 2 d4 d5 3 Nd2 c5 4 ed ed 5 Ngf3 Nc6 6 Bb5 Bd6 7 00 cd 8 Nb3 Nge7 9 Nb×d4 00 10 c3 Bg4 11 Qa4 Bh5 12 Bd3 Bc5 13 Re1 h6 14 Be3 Bb6 15 h3 Qd6 16 Be2 Rfe8 17 Rad1 Qf6 18 Nh2 B×e2 19 R×e2 N×d4 20 B×d4 Qc6 21 Q×c6 bc 22 Rde1 B×d4 23 cd Kf8 24 Nf3 Ng6 25 g3 R×e2 26 R×e2 f6 27 Kf1 Rb8 28 Rc2 Rb6 29 Ke2 Ra6 30 b3 Ke7 ½-½ (1·32 – 1·47)

4115   Korchnoi–AK

G15: 23.10.1974: English

1 ♘f3 ♘f6 2 g3 d5 3 ♗g2 ♗f5 4 c4 c6 5 cd cd 6 ♕b3 ♕c8 7 ♘c3 e6 8 d3 ♘c6 9 ♗f4 ♗e7 10 00 00 11 ♖ac1 ♗g6! 12 ♘e5 ♗d7 13 ♘×g6 hg 14 h4 (14 e4 ♘c5 15 ♕d1 d4 16 ♘d5! Murei; 15 ... de! 16 ♘×e4 ♘×e4 17 ♗×e4 ♕d7 Botvinnik) 14 ... ♘c5 15 ♕d1 ♕d8 16 d4! ♘d7 17 e4 ♘b6 18 e5?! (18 ed ed 19 ♕g4 ♘×d4 20 ♖fd1± Zaitsev; 18 ... ♘×d5 19 ♘×d5 ed 20 h5! gh 21 ♕×h5± Botvinnik) 18 ... ♖c8 19 ♗h3 (better 19 ♖e1 with ♗f1 to follow – Botvinnik) 19 ... a6 20 ♔g2 ♘c4! (20 ... g5 21 hg ♗×g5 22 ♕h5; 22 ♖h1± Gufeld) 21 b3 ♘a3 22 ♗a4 ♘b4 23 ♕d2 *(291)* (23 ♘c5 is better, e.g. 23 ... ♗×c5 24 ♖×c5 ♖×c5 25 dc d4∓ Gufeld)

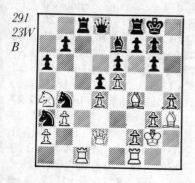

291
23W
B

23 ... b5? (23 ... ♘bc2!! and then ... ♖c6, ... ♕c7 and ... ♖c8∓ Botvinnik) 24 ♘c5 ♗×c5 25 dc? (25 ♖×c5± e.g. 25 ... ♖×c5 26 ♕×b4) 25 ... ♘c6 26 ♖fe1 d4 27

♗g4?! (27 ♔g1!? Zaitsev) 27 ... ♕a5 28 ♕×a5 ♘×a5 29 ♗d2 ♘c6 30 ♗f3 d3! 31 ♖e3 (31 ♗×c6 ♖×c6 32 ♖ed1 ♘c2 33 ♗a5 ♖×c5 34 ♗b4 ♖×e5 35 ♗×f8 ♔×f8 36 ♔f1 d5 37 ♖d2 e5∓ Zaitsev) 31 ... ♘c2 32 ♖×d3 ♘×e5 33 ♖d6 ♖×c5 34 ♗e4 ♖fc8 35 ♗d1 (35 ♗f4 ♘g4= Botvinnik, 36 ♗f3! ♘f6 37 ♖×a6± Gufeld) 35 ... ♘c6 36 ♗g5 a5 37 ♖d7 ♘6b4 38 ♖b7 ♘d5 39 ♗×d5 ed 40 ♗e7 ♖5c7 41 ♖×c7 ♖×c7 42 ♗d8 ♖d7 43 ♗×a5 d4 44 a4 (44 ♔f1!? Botvinnik) 44 ... ba 45 ba ♖a7 46 ♗b6 ♖×a4 (s, but 'open') (adjournment 24. 10.1974) 47 ♔f1 ½–½ (3·05 – 2·07)

4116   AK–Korchnoi

G16: 25.10.1974: French

1 e4 e6 2 d4 d5 3 ♘d2 c5 4 ed ed 5 ♘gf3 ♘c6 6 ♗b5 ♗d6 7 00 cd 8 ♘b3 ♘e7 9 ♘b×d4 00 10 c3 ♗g4 11 ♕a4 ♕d7 12 ♗e3 a6 13 ♗e2 ♘×d4 14 ♕×d4 ♘c6 15 ♕d2 ♖fe8 16 ♖ad1 ♖ad8 17 ♗b6 ♗c7 (17 ... ♖c8 18 ♖fe1 ♗b8 19 ♕×d5 ♕×d5 20 ♖×d5 ♗e6 21 ♖dd1 ♗×a2 22 ♖d7± Lilienthal) 18 ♗×c7 ♕×c7 19 ♖fe1 h6 20 h3= ♗f5 21 ♗f1 ♖×e1! 22 ♕×e1 ♕b6 23 ♖d2 ♗e4 24 ♕e2 ♘a5 (24 ... ♗×f3 25 ♕×f3 d4= Flohr) 25 ♕d1 ♕f6 26 ♘h2 ♕b6 27 ♘f3 (27 ♘g4 ♘c6 28 ♘e3 d4 Lilienthal) 27 ... ♘c6 (27 ... ♕f6= Lilienthal) 28 ♘d4 ♘e5 29 f3 ♗g6 30 ♕e1!± ♘d7 (30 ... ♘c4!? O'Kelly) 31

♕f2 ♕a5 32 a3 ♕c7 33 ♘b3 ♗f5
34 ♘d4 ♗g6 35 ♘c2 (*292*)

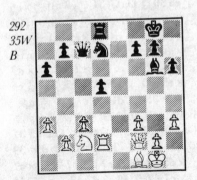

292
35W
B

35 ... ♘f6?! (35 ... ♗×c2=) 36
♘e3± ♕e5? (36 ... ♕e7!? Flohr;
36 ... ♖d7± Botvinnik) 37 c4! b5
(37 ... d4 38 ♘d5 ♘×d5 39
♕×d4; 37 ... ♖d7 38 cd ♘×d5 39
f4 Flohr) 38 cd h5 (38 ... ♘×d5 39
f4! ♕e4 40 f5 ♗h7 41 ♕f3!
Lilienthal; 41 ♘×d5 ♖×d5 42
♕c5 ♖×c5 43 ♖d8+ Gufeld) 39
a4 ♖e8 (± Gufeld) 40 ab ab (40 ...
♕×e3 41 ♕×e3 ♖×e3 42 ba±±
Lilienthal) 41 ♗×b5 (s) (= ; 41
♘d1± Botvinnik) (adjournment
26.10.1974) 41 ... ♕×e3 42 ♗×e8
♕×e8 43 d6 ♗f5 44 ♖d1 ♕b5 45
♕d4 ♘d7 46 ♖e1 ♗e6 47 ♔h2
♕g5 48 h4 ♕d8 49 b4 ♘f6 50 ♕e5
(better 50 ♖e5 Botvinnik) 50 ...
♘e8! 51 ♖e4 ♕×d6 52 ♕×d6
♘×d6 53 ♖d4 ♘b7 54 g4 ♔h7 55
♔g3 ♔g6 56 ♔f4 hg 57 fg f6 58
♖d1 ♔h6 59 ♖d4 ♔g6 60 h5+
♔h6 61 b5 g6 62 hg ♔×g6 63 b6
♔f7 64 ♖d2 ♘e7 65 ♖c2 ♗d5 66
♖c7+ ♔e6 67 ♖h7 ♘d6 ½-½ (3·46
-4·23)

4117 Korchnoi–AK

G17: 30.10.1974: Catalan

**1 d4 ♘f6 2 c4 e6 3 g3 d5 4 ♗g2 dc
5 ♘f3 c5 6 00 ♘c6 7 ♕a4 ♗d7 8
♕×c4 cd 9 ♘×d4 ♖c8 10 ♘c3
♕a5!?** (10 ... ♘×d4 11 ♕×d4
♗c5 seems simpler. Lutikov
suggested 10 ... ♕b6!?) **11 ♖d1!**
(11 ♗×c6 ♗×c6 12 ♘×e6 is
refuted by 12 ... ♗d7.) **11 ...
♗e7** (11 ... ♕b4 12 ♕×b4 ♗×b4
13 ♘db5!± Lutikov; 11 ... ♗b4!?
R.Byrne) **12 ♘b3 ♕c7 13 ♘b5** (13
♗f4! e5 14 ♗g5 ♗e6 15 ♕a4 00 16
♗×f6 ♗×f6 17 ♘c5 Botvinnik) **13
... ♕b8 14 ♘c5 a6! 15 ♘×d7
♘×d7 16 ♘c3** (16 ♘d4!
Botvinnik) **16 ... ♘de5 17 ♕a4**
(17 ♕b3! 00 18 ♗f4 to be followed
by 19 ♗×e5 or 19 ♗×c6
Botvinnik) **17 ... 00 18 ♗f4 ♕a7
19 ♗×e5** (19 ♗×c6 ♘×c6 20
♖d7± Suetin, endorsed by
Botvinnik) **19 ... ♘×e5 20 ♕e4
♘c6 21 ♖d7 ♗f6 22 ♖ad1 ♕b6
23 ♕c2** (23 ♘a4 ♕b5 24 e3 Geller)
**23 ... ♘a5! 24 ♖1d3 h6 25 a3
♖c7** (25 ... ♕b3!? Lutikov; 25 ...
♖fd8 Botvinnik) **26 b4 ♘×d7 27
♖×d7 ♖c8 28 ♖d3?!** (28 ♘d5
♖×c2 29 ♘×b6 ♖c1+ 30 ♗f1
♘b3= Lutikov; 28 ♘a4 ♖×c2 29
♘×b6 ♖c1+ 30 ♗f1 ♘b3 31 e3=
Botvinnik) **28 ... ♘c4 29 ♘e4
♕c7!** (*293*)
30 ♘c5? (30 ♘×f6+ ± Zaitsev, 30
... gf 31 ♗f1= Botvinnik) **30 ...
♘e5∓ ∓** (30 ... ♘b2!∓ ∓
Botvinnik) **31 ♖d2** (31 ♖c3 b6∓ ∓

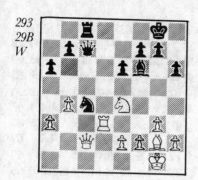

293
29B
W

Gufeld) **31 ... b6 32 f4 bc 33 fe ♕×e5 34 ♗b7 ♖c7 35 ♕e4 ♕a1+** (35 ... cb? 36 ♖d8+ !± ± Gufeld) **36 ♔g2 ♕×a3 37 bc ♖×c5 38 ♖d3 ♕a5 39 ♕f3 ♕b6 40 ♖d7 ♖f5 41 ♕g4 ♕f2+ 42 ♔h3 g6 0–1** (2·30 – 2·28)

4118 AK–Korchnoi

G18: 1.11.1974: French

1 e4 e6 2 d4 d5 3 ♘d2 c5 4 ed ed 5 ♘gf3 ♘c6 6 ♗b5 ♗d6 7 00 ♘e7 8 dc ♗×c5 9 ♘b3 ♗d6 10 ♗g5 00 11 ♖e1 ♕c7 12 c3 ♗g4 13 h3 ♗h5 14 ♗e2 h6 15 ♗×e7 ♘×e7 16 ♘fd4± ♗×e2 17 ♕×e2 a6 18 ♕f3 ♖ad8 19 ♖ad1 ♖d7 20 ♘f5 ♘×f5 21 ♕×f5 ♖fd8 22 ♖e3 g6 23 ♕f3 ♗f8 24 ♖ed3 ♕c6 25 ♘d4 ♕a4 26 a3 h5 27 ♖1d2 ♗h6 28 ♕d1 ♕c4 29 ♖e2 ♕c7 30 ♘c2 b5! 31 ♘e3 (31 ♘b4 ♕b7 32 ♖e5 d4! 33 cd ♗g7! O'Kelly) 31 ... ♕c5 32 ♖ed2 ♗×e3 33 ♖×e3 ♖e7 34 ♖×e7 ♕×e7 35 g3 (35 ♖×d5 ♖×d5 and ... ♕e1+ O'Kelly) 35 ... ♕e6 36 h4 ♔g7 37 ♔g2 (37 ♖d4!? ♕f5 38 a4 ba 39 ♖×a4 ♖d6 40 ♖d4 ♖b6 41 ♕d2 a5 42 ♖×d5 ♖×b2 43 ♕×b2 ♕×d5 44 c4+ Kotov) 37 ... ♕e4+ 38 ♔h2 ♕f5 39 ♔g2 ♕e4+ 40 ♕f3= (40 ♔g1! Botvinnik) 40 ... ♕×f3+ 41 ♔×f3 ♔f6 42 ♔f4 ♖e8 ½–½ (2·13 – 2·26) (43 ♖×d5 ♖e2 44 f3 ♖×b2 45 ♖d6+ ♔g7 46 ♖×a6 ♖b3= Gufeld)

4119 Korchnoi–AK

G19: 4.11.1974: QP

1 d4 ♘f6 2 ♗g5 e6 3 e4 h6 4 ♗×f6 ♕×f6 5 ♘f3 d6 6 ♘c3 g6 7 ♕d2 ♕e7 8 000 a6 9 h4 ♗g7 10 g3 b5 11 ♗h3 b4 12 ♘d5± ed 13 ♗×c8 00 14 ♗b7 ♖a7 15 ♗×d5 c6 16 ♗b3 ♕×e4 17 ♕d3= (17 ♕f4! ♕×f4 18 gf and 19 h5 or 19 f5± Dvoretsky) **17 ... ♕×d3 18 ♖×d3 ♘d7 19 ♖e1 ♘b6 20 a4! ba 21 ba a5 22 ♖de3** (22 ♗a2!? Murei; better 22 a4 Botvinnik) **22 ... ♗f6** (22 ... a4 Botvinnik) **23 a4 c5** (23 ... ♖c7! 24 g4 c5 25 dc dc 26 g5 hg 27 hg ♗d8 Geller, Fridshtein; 24 e4! d5 25 ♖4e3 c5 26 dc ♖×c5= Botvinnik) **24 dc dc 25 ♘d2! ♔g7 26 ♖f3± ♖c7 27 ♘c4 ♘×c4 28 ♗×c4 ♖d8 29 c3 ♖cd7 30 ♔c2 ♖d2+ 31 ♔b3 ♖d1 32 ♖×d1 ♖×d1 33 ♗b5! ♖d5** (33 ... ♖d2 34 ♔c4 ♖c2= Zaitsev; 33 ... ♖c1 34 ♔c4 ♖c2 35 ♗c6 ♖c1 36 ♗d5 ♖c2 37 ♔b5 ♖×c3 38 ♔×a5 ♖×f3 39 ♗×f3 ♗d4 40 ♗d5 c4!= Botvinnik) **34 ♖e3** (34 ♔c4! Botvinnik) **34 ... ♖e5 35 ♖d3 ♖e2 36 ♖f3 ♖e5** (36 ... ♖d2 37 ♔c4 ♖c2 Gufeld; 36 ... ♖e1 37 ♔c4 ♖c1=)

Botvinnik) **37 ♔c4! ♖f5 38 ♖d3 ♖×f2 39 ♔×c5 ♗e5 40 ♔b6 ♖g2 41 c4!** (s) (adjournment 5.11.1974) **41 ... ♖×g3** (41 ... ♗×g3? 42 ♖×g3 ♖×g3 43 c5 g5 44 hg hg 45 c6 ♖c3 46 c7 ♖×c7 47 ♔×c7 f5 48 ♔b6± ± Zaitsev) **42 ♖d7!** (42 c5 ♖×d3 43 ♗×d3 ♗d4 44 ♔b5 ♔f6 45 c6 ♔e7 46 ♔×a5 ♔d6= Zaitsev) **42 ... g5 43 hg hg 44 c5 ♖c3 45 c6 g4 46 c7 g3 47 ♗c6 ♗×c7+ 48 ♖×c7** (294)

294
48W
B

48 ... ♔h6? (48 ... ♖×c6+ ! Konopleva: 49 ♖×c6 f5 50 ♖c1 ♔f6! 51 ♔×a5 f4 52 ♖g1 ♔f5 53 ♔b4 ♔g4 54 a5 f3 55 a6 f2 56 ♖a1 g2 57 a7 g1♕ 58 a8♕ ♕e1+ = ; 51 ♖g1 f4 52 ♔c5 ♔e5 53 ♖e1+ ♔f5 54 ♔d4 ♔g4! 55 ♔d3 g2! 56 ♖e8 ♔g3= Zaitsev) **49 ♖c8 f5 50 ♖f8 ♖×c6 + ?!** (50 ... ♖c2!? Gufeld; 50 ... ♔g5! 51 ♗a8 f4 52 ♔×a5 ♖b3!! Botvinnik) **51 ♔×c6± ± ♔g5 52 ♖g8+ ♔f4 53 ♔b5 f3 54 ♔×a5 f4** (54 ... g2 55 ♔b4! ♔f2 56 ♔c3! g1♕ 57 ♖×g1 ♔×g1 58 ♔d3! ♔h2 59 a5 f4 60 a6 f3 61 ♔e3! ♔g3 62 a7 f2 63 ♔e2 ♔g2 64 a8♕+ ± ± Zaitsev) **55 ♔b4 ♔g2**

(55 ... g2 56 ♔c3 ♔f2 57 ♔d4 f3 58 ♔e4± ± Gufeld) **56 a5 f3 57 a6 f2 58 a7 f1♕ 59 a8♕+ ♕f3 60 ♕a2+ ♕f2 61 ♕d5+ ♕f3 62 ♕d2+ ♕f2 63 ♔c3 ♔g1** (63 ... ♕×d2+ 64 ♔×d2 f2 65 ♖f8+ !± ±) **64 ♕d1+ ♔g2 65 ♕d3 ♔c5+ 66 ♔b3 ♕b6+ 67 ♔c2 ♔c6+ 68 ♔d2 ♕h6+ 69 ♕e3 ♕h4 70 ♖b8 ♕f6 71 ♖b6 ♕f5 72 ♖b2 ♔h2 73 ♕h6+ ♔g1 74 ♕b6+ ♔h2 75 ♕b8 ♔h3 76 ♕h8+ ♔g4 77 ♖b4+ ♔f3 78 ♕h1+ ♔f2 79 ♖b2 1-0** (4·59 - 3·26)

4120 AK-Korchnoi

G20: 8.11.1974: Spanish

1 e4 e5 2 ♘f3 ♘c6 3 ♗b5 a6 4 ♗a4 f5!? 5 d4 ed 6 e5 ♗c5 7 00 ♘ge7 8 ♗b3 d5 9 ed ♕×d6 10 ♖e1 h6 11 ♘bd2 b5 12 a4 ♗b7 13 ab ab 14 ♖×a8+ ♗×a8 15 ♖e6 (15 ♘f1! and then ♘g3 Botvinnik) 15 ... ♕d7 16 ♕e2 (16 ♕e1!± Taimanov) 16 ... d3! 17 cd ♗d8! 18 ♘f1 ♖e8 19 ♘g3 (19 ♗e3!? Taimanov) 19 ... ♘d4 20 ♘×d4 ♗×d4 21 ♗e3 ♗×e3 22 ♕×e3 ♗d5! 23 ♗×d5 ♘×d5 24 ♖×e8+ ♕×e8 25 ♕d4 (25 ♕×e8+!? ♔×e8 26 ♘×f5± Taimanov, 26 ... ♔f7 and ... ♘b4 with compensation - Matanović) 25 ... ♕d7 26 h4 ♔c8 27 ♔h2 f4 28 ♘e2 ♕f7 29 ♕e4 c6 30 ♘d4 ♕f6 31 ♘×b5 ♕×h4+ (31 ... ♕×b2! Taimanov; 31 ... cb 32 ♕×d5 ♕×b2= Matanović) 32 ♔g1 ♕e7 33 ♘d4 ♕f6 34 ♕f5+

♕×f5 35 ♘×f5 ♘b4= 36 d4 ♘d3
37 ♘×g7 ♘×b2 38 ♘f5 ♕d7 39
♘×h6 ♔e6 40 ♔f1 ♔d5 41 ♘f5
♔e4 42 ♘e7 ♔×d4 43 ♘×c6+
♔e4 44 ♔e2 ♘c4 45 f3+ ♔d5 (s)
(adjournment 9.11.1974) 46 ♘b4+
♔e5 47 ♘c2 ♔f5 48 ♔d3 ♘e5+
49 ♔d4 ♘g6 50 ♔d5 ♘h4 51 ♘e1
♘g6 ½–½ (2·40 – 3·01)

4121 Korchnoi–AK

G21: 11.11.1974: Queen's Indian

**1 d4 ♘f6 2 ♘f3 e6 3 g3 b6 4 ♗g2
♗b7 5 c4 ♗e7 6 ♘c3 0-0 7 ♕c2!
c5 8 d5 ed 9 ♘g5 ♘c6?!** (9 . . . g6
4105) **10 ♘×d5 g6 11 ♕d2!
♘×d5?** (One mistake follows
another. Here 11 . . . ♖e8,
preparing ♗e7–f8–g7, would have
been better.) **12 ♗×d5 ♖b8??**
(*295*) (The final error. Karpov's last
chance of salvation lay in 12 . . .
♗×g5 13 ♕×g5 ♕×g5 14 ♗×g5,
though White would have had a
vastly superior ending.)

295
12B
W

13 ♘×h7! ♖e8 (Black could
resign. 13 . . . ♔×h7 loses to 14
♕h6+ ♔g8 15 ♕×g6+ ♔h8 16

♕h6+ ♔g8 17 ♗e4 f5 18 ♗d5+
♖f7 19 ♕g6+. The probable
reason for Karpov's delayed
resignation is that he must have
been in a state of shock – he had, in
home analysis, reached and looked
at the position after Black's twelfth
move, but he had failed to notice
anything the matter with it . . . that
is until he had just made the move
on the board against Korchnoi,
when he suddenly realized. . . .) **14
♕h6 ♘e5 15 ♘g5 ♗×g5 16
♗×g5 ♕×g5** (or 16 . . . ♕c7 17
♗f6 and mates) **17 ♕×g5 ♗×d5**
(18 . . . ♘f3+ is the forlorn hope.)
18 0-0 ♗×c4 19 f4 1–0 (0·24 – 0·38)

4122 AK–Korchnoi

G22: 15.11.1974: Catalan

**1 ♘f3 ♘f6 2 c4 e6 3 g3 d5 4 d4 dc 5
♕a4+ ♘bd7 6 ♕×c4 b6 7 ♗g2
♗b7 8 0-0 c5 9 ♖d1 a6 10 dc ♗×c5
11 b4 ♗e7 12 ♗b2 b5 13 ♕d4 ♖c8**
(13 . . . ♕b6! 14 ♕f4 ♘d5 15 ♕g4
♘7f6 16 ♕×g7 ♖g8 17 ♕h6
♘g4‡ Balashov; 14 a4! Taimanov)
**14 ♘bd2 0-0 15 a3 ♖c2 16 ♘e1 ♖c7
17 ♗×b7 ♖×b7 18 ♘b3 ♕a8 19
♖ac1 ♖c8 20 e4 ♖bc7 21 ♖×c7
♖×c7 22 f3 ♕c8 23 ♖c1 ♖×c1 24
♘×c1 ♗d8 25 ♕c3 ♕a8** (25 . . .
♕×c3 26 ♗×c3 ♘b6 27 ♘c2 ♘c4
28 ♘d3 ♘d7= Taimanov; 27
♘cd3 ♘c4 28 ♘c2= Balashov) **26
♕d3 ♘b6 27 ♘c2 ♘c4 28 ♗d4
♕c8 29 ♕c3 ♕d7 30 ♘d3 h5 ½–½**
(1·48 – 2·20)

4123 Korchnoi–AK

G23: 18.11.1974: Queen's Indian

(Notes by Tal)

1 d4 ♘f6 2 c4 e6 3 ♘f3 b6 4 g3 ♗b7
5 ♗g2 ♗e7 6 ♘c3 ♘e4 7 ♗d2 ♗f6
8 00 00 9 ♕c2 ♘×d2 10 ♕×d2 d6
11 ♖ad1 ♘d7 12 ♘e1 (12 e4 c5 13
d5 ♗×c3! 14 ♕×c3 ed= ; 12 b4!?)
12 … ♗×g2 13 ♘×g2 ♕e7 14
♘e1 c5 15 ♘c2 (15 ♘f3!?) 15 …
♖ac8 16 b3 ♖fd8 17 e4 ♘b8 18
♖fe1 (18 d5!? ♗×c3! 19 ♕×c3 ed
20 ♖×d5! ♕×e4 21 ♖g5 g6 22
♖e1 ♕b7 23 ♘e3±) 18 … cd! (18
… ♘c6 19 ♘d5! ed 20 ed ♕d7 21
dc ♕×c6 22 ♘e3!!±) 19 ♘×d4
♕b7 20 ♖e3 a6 21 ♕e2 ♘c6 22
♘×c6 ♕×c6 23 ♖ed3 h6 24 a4
♕c5 25 ♕d2 b5 26 ab ♗×c3ˑ 27
♕×c3 ab 28 ♖d4 (28 e5? d5) 28 …
♕c7 (28 … d5 29 ed ed 30 b4 and
c5) 29 ♕b4 e5 ½-½ (2·10 – 1·48) (30
♖×d6 ♖×d6 31 ♕×d6 ♕×d6 32
♖×d6 bc 33 bc ♖×c4=)

4124 AK–Korchnoi

G24: 22.11.1974: QGA

1 ♘f3 d5 2 d4 ♘f6 3 c4 dc 4 e3 g6 5
♗×c4 ♗g7 6 00 00 7 b3 c6 8 ♗b2

♗g4 9 ♘bd2 ♘bd7 10 h3 ♗f5 11
♖e1 ♘b6 12 ♗f1 ♘e4 13 ♘×e4
♗×e4 14 ♘d2 ♗f5 15 ♖c1± ♖c8
16 ♕e2 ♖c7 17 a4 ♗c8 18 ♗a3
♗e6 19 ♕d1 ♖e8 20 ♘e4 f5 21
♘c5 ♗f7 22 ♗b2 ♘d7 23 ♘d3
♖c8 24 b4 a5 25 ba ♕×a5 26 ♗c3
♕a7 27 a5 c5 28 ♕a4 ♘b6 (28 …
b6 29 dc ♘×c5 30 ♘×c5 bc 31
♗c4± Furman) 29 ♕a1 ♘d5? (29
… ♘d7± Suetin) 30 ♘×c5!
♘×c3 (30 … ♖×c5 31 dc ♘×c3
32 ♖×c3 ♖a8 33 a6 ♗×c3 34
♕×c3 ba; 33 ♖b1 ♗×c3 34 ♕×c3
♕×a5 35 ♕e5± Zaitsev) 31
♕×c3± (296) ½-½ (1·46 – 2·13)

296
31W
B

Korchnoi; a pawn down, offered
the draw which Karpov required to
win the match and, as it turned out,
the title of World Champion.

Chess Oscar 1974

Karpov received the annual oscar for the second consecutive year.

12th World Champion

As it turned out Karpov's victory in the match against Korchnoi earned
him the title of World Champion. At the time the match was being played,

Fischer was being asked, by FIDE, to reconsider his decision to resign his title as a protest against FIDE's refusal to agree entirely with his conditions for a championship match. Fischer was given until April 1st 1975 to make up his mind. An extraordinary meeting of the FIDE General Assembly also was held from March 18–20, 1975; the main item on the agenda was the men's world championship match and the two conditions which FIDE had refused to accept – on this occasion one was accepted, the other rejected. The deadline for Fischer to respond came and went.

On April 24th 1975 Anatoly Karpov was formally crowned as the 12th chess champion of the world in a glittering ceremony at Moscow's Central House of Trade Unions.

The small gold medallion of champion was presented to Karpov by Dr Max Euwe, president of FIDE. In his speech of acceptance, Karpov pledged that he would devote the three years of his reign to active chess competition.

42 Ljubljana–Portoroz

3rd Vidmar Memorial

		1	2	3	4	5	6	7	8	9	0	1	2	3	4	5	6	
1	**Karpov**	×	½	½	½	½	½	1	½	1	1	½	1	1	1	1	½	**11**
2	Gligorić	½	×	½	½	½	½	0	1	½	1	1	½	1	1	½	1	**10**
3	Ribli	½	½	×	1	½	½	½	½	½	½	1	½	½	1	1	½	**9½**
4	Furman	½	½	0	×	1	½	½	½	½	1	½	1	½	1	1	½	**9½**
5	Hort	½	½	½	0	×	½	½	½	½	1	1	½	1	½	1	1	**9½**
6	Parma	½	½	½	½	½	×	½	½	½	½	½	1	½	½	½	1	**8½**
7	Portisch	0	1	½	½	½	½	×	1	0	1	0	1	0	1	½	1	**8½**
8	Ljubojević	½	0	½	½	½	½	0	×	½	½	½	½	1	½	1	1	**8**
9	Velimirović	0	½	½	½	½	½	1	½	×	0	0	1	1	0	1	1	**8**
10	Barle	0	0	½	0	0	½	0	½	1	×	1	1	½	1	½	1	**7½**
11	Planinc	½	0	0	½	0	½	1	½	1	0	×	0	0	1	½	1	**6½**
12	Mariotti	0	½	½	0	½	0	0	½	0	0	1	×	½	½	1	1	**6**
13	S. Garcia	0	0	½	½	0	½	1	0	0	½	1	½	×	½	½	½	**6**
14	Musil	0	0	0	0	½	½	0	½	1	0	0	½	½	×	½	½	**4½**
15	Osterman	0	½	0	0	0	½	½	0	0	½	½	0	½	½	×	½	**4**
16	Karnar	½	0	½	½	0	0	0	0	0	0	0	0	½	½	½	×	**3**

Amazingly, Karpov's victory in this tournament was the first time that a reigning World Champion has finished ·outright first in a major international tournament since Alekhine won the tournament at Zürich in 1934!!

For anyone still needing to be convinced that Anatoly Karpov is one of the world's greatest ever players, this surprising fact should be the clincher.

4201 AK–Portisch

R1: 2.6.1975: Slav

(Notes by Zaitsev)

1 ♘f3 d5 2 d4 ♘f6 3 c4 c6 4 ♘c3 dc5 a4 ♗f5 6 e3 e6 7 ♗×c4 ♗b4 8 00 00 9 ♘h4 ♗g4 10 f3 ♗h5 (10 ... ♘d5 11 fg ♕×h4 12 ♕f3!±) 11 g4 ♗g6 12 ♘×g6 (Portisch, White, chose 12 e4 against Hort, Petropolis interzonal 1973.) 12 ... hg 13 ♕b3 ♕e7 14 g5! ♘d5 15 e4 ♘b6 16 ♘a2! ♗a5 (16 ... ♕d8? fails to 17 ♗×e6!; 16 ... ♗c5!? 17 ♗e3± and 16 ... ♘×c4 17 ♘×b4 ♘d6 18 ♗f4 ♘d7 19 ♘d3± are both good for White.) 17 ♗e2 e5 18 ♕c2 ♘6d7 (After 18 ... ed, White's threat of b2–b4 would come into operation since d4 would no longer be accessible to the black queen: 19 b4 ♗×b4 20 ♘×b4 ♕×b4 21 ♗a3.) 19 de ♕×e5 20 ♔h1! ♖e8 21 ♗c4 ♘b6 (After 21 ... ♗c7 22 ♘b4 ♘b6 23 ♘d3 ♕×h2+ 24 ♕×h2 ♗×h2 25 ♗×f7+ the ending is bad for Black.) 22 ♗d3 ♘a6 (if 22 ... ♘8d7, then 23 b4 ♕×a1 24 ba ♘c8 25 ♘c3 and Black's queen is

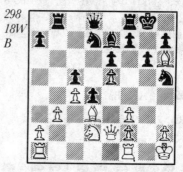

297
27W
B

trapped.) 23 ♗×a6 ba 24 ♖d1 c5 25 ♗e3 ♕ac8 26 ♘c3 ♘c4 27 ♗c1 (297)

27 ... ♖b8? (27 ... ♗×c3 was correct. 28 ♖d5 ♗×b2 29 ♖×e5 ♗×e5 30 ♖b1 ♘d6 would give Black quite good drawing chances. However, after 28 ♕×c3 the ending is good for White.) 28 ♘d5! ♘×b2 29 ♗f4 ♕e6 30 ♖db1! (30 ♗×b8 ♘×d1 31 ♗c7? ♕×d5) 30 ... ♕h3 31 ♗×b8 ♖×b8 32 ♖×b2 1–0

4202 Osterman–AK

R2: 3.6.1975: Queen's Indian

1 d4 ♘f6 2 c4 e6 3 ♘f3 b6 4 e3 ♗b7 5 ♘c3 d5 6 ♗d3 ♗e7 7 00 00 8 ♕e2 c5 9 dc bc 10 e4 d4 11 ♘b1 ♘bd7 12 e5 ♗×f3 13 gf ♘e8 14 ♗f4 ♖b8 15 b3 g6 16 ♘d2 ♘g7 17 ♔h1 ♘h5 18 ♗h6 (298)

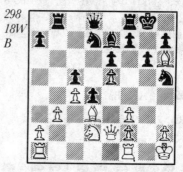

298
18W
B

18 ... ♗g5 19 ♗×f8 ♕×f8 20 ♖g1 ♗f4 21 ♘e4 ♗×e5 22 ♘g3 ♘f4 23 ♕d2 ♗c7 24 ♖f1 ♕d6 25 ♖e1 f5 26 ♗e2 ♔f7 27 ♖b1 a5 28 a3 h5 29 ♖ge1 h4 30 ♘f1 ♕e7 31 ♘e3 ♘f6 32 ♗d1 de 33 fe ♖d8 34 ♕c2 ♘d3

35 ♖ f1 e5 36 e4 ♖ d4 37 ef gf 38 b4
ab 39 ab cb 40 ♕ g2 e4 41 fe ♕ ×e4
42 ♗ f3 ♕ e5 43 ♖ a1 b3 44 ♖ a7 b2
45 ♖ b7 ♖ ×c4 46 ♗ d1 ♖ c1 **0–1**

4203 AK–Parma

R3: 4.6.1975: Spanish

1 e4 e5 2 ♘ f3 ♘ c6 3 ♗ b5 f5 4 ♘ c3
fe 5 ♘ ×e4 d5 6 ♘ ×e5 de 7 ♘ ×c6
♕ g5 8 ♕ e2 ♘ f6 9 f4 ♕ h4+ 10 g3
♕ h3 11 ♘ e5+ c6 12 ♗ c4 ♗ c5 13
d3 ♘ g4 14 d4 ♘ ×e5 15 ♕ ×e4
♗ ×d4 16 fe ♕ g4 17 ♕ ×g4 ♗ ×g4
18 c3 ♗ ×e5 19 00 000 20 ♗ g5
♖ df8 21 ♔ g2 h6 22 ♗ e3 b6 23
♖ ae1 ♖ ×f1 24 ♗ ×f1 ♗ f6 ½–½

4204 Furman–AK

R4: 5.6.1975: Slav

1 d4 d5 2 c4 c6 3 ♘ f3 ♘ f6 4 ♘ c3 e6
5 e3 ♘ bd7 6 ♗ d3 dc 7 ♗ ×c4 b5 8
♗ d3 b4 9 ♘ e4 ♘ ×e4 10 ♗ ×e4
♗ b7 11 00 ♗ e7 12 ♕ e2 00 13 ♖ d1
♕ b6 14 ♗ d2 c5 ½–½

4205 AK–Barle

R5: 7.6.1975: King's Indian

(Notes by Zaitsev)

**1 c4 ♘ f6 2 ♘ c3 g6 3 e4 d6 4 d4
♗ g7 5 f3 00 6 ♗ e3 c5 7 dc dc 8
♕ ×d8 ♖ ×d8 9 ♗ ×c5 ♘ c6 10
♘ d5! ♘ ×d5 11 cd ♗ ×b2 12 ♖ b1
♗ c3+ 13 ♔ f2 b6** (Black should
have resigned himself to the worse
ending after 13 ... ♗ d4+ 14

♗ ×d4 ♘ ×d4 15 ♔ e3 e5.) **14 ♗ a3**
(299)

299
14W
B

14 ... ♘ e5 (14 ... ♗ d4+ may
have been Black's only chance,
though White still comes out on top
after 15 ♔ g3 h5!? 16 h4 g5 17 hg
h4+ 18 ♖ ×h4 ♗ ×g1 19 dc ♖ d2 20
♖ h6.) **15 ♘ e2! ♗ d2 16 ♗ ×e7
♖ e8** (16 ... ♘ d3+ 17 ♔ g3 ♗ e3
18 ♗ ×d8?? ♗ f2 mate; 18 h4± ±)
**17 ♗ f6 ♘ d3+ 18 ♔ g3 ♗ d7 19
♖ d1 ♗ e1+ 20 ♖ ×e1 ♘ ×e1 21
♘ d4 ♖ ac8 22 ♗ b5 ♗ ×b5 23
♘ ×b5 ♖ c1 24 d6 1–0** (24 ... ♖ d1
25 ♘ d4)

4206 Ljubojević–AK

R6: 8.6.1975: Ponziani

No quiet grandmaster draw!
1 e4 e5 2 ♘ f3 ♘ c6 3 c3 d5 4 ♕ a4 de
5 ♘ ×e5 ♕ d5 6 ♘ ×c6 bc 7 ♗ c4
♕ d7 8 d3 ed 9 00 ♗ d6 10 ♘ d2
♘ e7 11 ♘ e4 00 12 ♖ d1 ♖ e8 13
♗ g5 h6 14 ♗ ×h6 ♘ d5 15 ♗ ×d5
♗ ×h2+ 16 ♔ ×h2 ♕ ×d5 17 ♘ f6+
gf 18 ♕ h4 ♗ f5 19 ♕ ×f6 ♕ d6+
½–½

4207   AK–S. Garcia

R7: 9.6.1975: Sicilian

(Notes by Zaitsev)

1 e4 c5 2 ♘f3 ♘c6 3 d4 cd 4 ♘×d4 g6 5 ♘c3 ♗g7 6 ♗e3 ♘f6 7 ♗c4 00 8 ♗b3 d6 9 f3 ♗d7 10 ♕d2 ♕a5 11 h4 ♖fc8 12 000 ♘e5 13 ♔bl b5?! 14 ♘c×b5! ♕a6 15 ♘c3 ♘c4 16 ♕d3 ♖ab8 17 ♗cl ♖b4 (*300*)

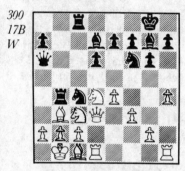

300
17B
W

18 h5! ♕b7 (18 . . . ♘×h5 19 ♘d5!) 19 hg hg 20 ♗h6 ♗×h6 (or 20 . . . ♗h8 21 ♗g5) 21 ♖×h6 ♔g7 22 ♖dh1 ♕b6 23 ♘de2 (23 ♘d5 is also possible.) 23 . . . e6 24 g4 ♔f8 (Black's king tries to escape from the danger zone, but White's pieces dominate the board.) 25 ♖h8+ ♔e7 26 ♖×c8 ♘e5 27 ♕d1 ♗×c8 28 g5 ♘fd7 29 a3! ♖×b3 30 cb ♘×f3 31 ♘f4 (threatening both 32 ♕×f3 and 32 ♘d5+) 31 . . . ♕f2 32 ♘×g6+!± ± fg 33 ♖h7+ ♔d8 34 ♕×d6 ♕d4 35 ♕e7+ **1–0**

4208   AK–Hort

R8: 10.6.1975: Caro-Kann

1 e4 c6 2 d4 d5 3 ♘d2 de 4 ♘×e4

♗f5 5 ♘g3 ♗g6 6 h4 h6 7 ♘f3 ♘d7 8 h5 ♗h7 9 ♗d3 ♗×d3 10 ♕×d3 ♘gf6 11 ♗d2 e6 12 ♕e2 ♕c7 13 c4 000 14 c5 ♖g8 15 b4 g6 16 ♖bl gh 17 ♔fl ♖g4 18 ♖b3 ♔b8 19 ♘×h5 ♘×h5 20 ♖×h5 ♘f6 21 ♖e5 ♗g7 22 b5 ♘d5 23 b6 ab 24 cb ♕d6 25 ♖e4 ♖×e4 26 ♕×e4 f5 27 ♕c2 ♗f6 28 ♕c4 ♖g8 29 ♕a4 h5 30 ♗b4 ♘×b4 31 ♖×b4 ♖g4 32 ♖c4 ♖g8 33 ♘el ♔c8 34 ♘d3 ♖g4 35 ♘c5 ♖×d4 36 ♖×d4 ♗×d4 37 ♘×b7 ♕×b7 38 ♕a7+ ♔c8 39 b7+ ♔d7 40 b8 ♕+ ♗×a7 41 ♕×a7+ ♔d8 42 ♔gl c5 43 ♕a4 ♕d5 44 ♕a5+ ♔e7 ½–½

4209   Musil–AK

R9: 13.6.1975: Sicilian

1 e4 c5 2 ♘f3 e6 3 d4 cd 4 ♘×d4 a6 5 ♗d3 ♘f6 6 00 d6 7 ♕e2 g6 8 c4 ♗g7 9 ♘c3 00 10 ♗e3 ♕c7 11 ♖acl ♘bd7 12 f3 b6 13 ♕f2 ♗b7 14 ♖fd1 ♘h5 15 ♗fl ♖ac8 16 ♖c2 ♖fe8 17 ♖cd2 ♗f8 18 ♘db5 ab 19 ♘×b5 ♕b8 20 ♘×d6 ♘c5 21 ♘×e8 ♖×e8 22 b4 ♘a4 23 a3 ♗c6 24 ♖cl ♕c7 25 ♕el ♖c8 26 ♕dl

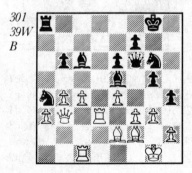

301
39W
B

♗e8 27 ♕b3 h6 28 ♖cd1 g5 29
♗f2 ♘f4 30 ♗g3 ♗g7 31 ♕e3
♖a8 32 ♖c1 ♗e5 33 ♗f2 ♘g6 34
g3 ♕e7 35 ♕b3 ♕f6 36 ♔g2 h5 37
♖d3 h4 38 ♗e2 ♗c6 39 ♔g1 (*301*)
39 ... ♘f4! 40 ♖d2 ♘c3 41 gf
♕×f4 42 ♖×c3 ♕×h2+ 43 ♔f1
♕h1+ 44 ♗g1 ♗h2 **0–1**

4210 AK–Velimirović

R10: 14.6.1975: Sicilian

(Notes by Zaitsev)

1 e4 c5 2 ♘f3 d6 3 d4 cd 4 ♘×d4
♘f6 5 ♘c3 g6 6 ♗e3 ♗g7 7 f3 00 8
♕d2 ♘c6 9 ♗c4 ♗d7 10 000 ♕b8
11 ♗b3 a5 12 ♘db5 a4!? 13 ♗×a4!
(13 ♘×a4 ♘a5) 13 ... ♖c8 (13 ...
♘a5 14 ♕e2) 14 ♔b1 ♘a5 15 ♗b3
♘c4 16 ♕e2! ♘×e3 17 ♕×e3 ♖c5
18 ♘d4 ♕a7 19 a3 ♖a5 20 ♕d2
(*302*)

302
20W
B

20 ... ♘e8?! (20 ... e5 21 ♘de2
d5!? seems more promising: 22 ed e4
23 fe. Now after 23 ... ♘×e4 24
♘×e4 ♖×a3 25 ba ♕×a3 26 c3
♕×b3+ 27 ♕b2 ♕c4 28 ♘d4 and
23 ... ♖×a3 24 ba ♕×a3 25 ♘a2

♘×e4 26 ♕c1, White should win.
However, the outcome is not so
clear after either 23 ... ♘g4 or 23
... b5.) 21 ♘d5! e6 22 ♕b4 ♗c7 23
c3 ♘a6 24 ♘dc2 ♗c5 25 ♕×d6
♗b5 26 ♗a2 ♘a4 27 ♕c7! ♗e8 28
♖d8 ♗f6 29 ♖×a8 ♕×a8 30 ♕f4
♕d8 31 ♕e3 ♕c7 32 f4 ♘b6 33
e5± ± ♗e7 34 ♘d4 ♘c4 35 ♗×c4
♕×c4 36 ♖d1 ♗a4 37 ♕d3 ♕c8
38 ♖d2 ♕f8 39 g3 ♖c5 40 ♕e4
♖c7 41 ♖d3 ♕c8 42 g4 (s)
(adjournment 16?.6.1975) 42 ...
♗d7 43 ♖bc2 ♖c5 44 ♕e1 ♕c7 45
h4 h6 46 g5 h5 47 b4 ♖c4 48 ♘e3
♖c6 49 ♘×c6 ♗×c6 50 ♖d4 **1–0**

4211 Planinc–AK

R11: 15.6.1975: Sicilian

1 e4 c5 2 ♘f3 e6 3 d4 cd 4 ♘×d4 a6
5 ♗e2 ♘f6 6 ♘c3 ♕c7 7 00 ♗b4 8
♕d3 ♘c6 9 ♔h1 ♘×d4 10 ♕×d4
♗c5 11 ♕d3 b5 12 ♗f3 ♖b8 13
♗g5 ♗e7 14 ♖ad1 b4 15 ♘e2 d6
16 ♗f4 ♖b6 17 ♗e3 ♖b8 18 ♗f4
♖b6 19 ♗e3 ½–½

4212 AK–Mariotti

R12: 17.6.1975: Spanish

(Notes by Zaitsev)

1 e4 e5 2 ♘f3 ♘c6 3 ♗b5 ♗c5 4 00
♕f6 5 c3 ♘ge7 6 b4 ♗b6 7 ♗a3! g5
8 d4! g4 9 ♘×e5 ♘×e5 10 de ♕×e5
11 ♕×g4 ♕×c3 12 ♖b1 ♖g8 13
♕h5 ♕g7 (before White can play
♖b1–b3–g3. However, Karpov has
a huge lead in development.) 14 g3

c6 15 ♗d3 d6 16 ♘c4 ♗g4 17 ♕h4 ♘c8 18 e5! de 19 ♗h6! (19 ♘×e5 ♕×e5 20 ♗b2 was also possible.) 19 ... ♗d8 20 ♗×g7 ♗×h4 21 ♗×e5 f5 (otherwise 22 ♗×h7 or 22 ♗h7) 22 ♘a5! **1–0**

4213 Ribli–AK

R13: 18.6.1975: English

1 c4 ♘f6 2 ♘f3 b6 3 g3 ♗b7 4 ♗g2 e6 5 00 ♗e7 6 b3 00 7 ♗b2 c5 8 ♘c3 d5 9 cd ♘×d5 ½–½

4214 AK–Gligorić

R14: 19.6.1975: Spanish

1 e4 e5 2 ♘f3 ♘c6 3 ♗b5 a6 4 ♗a4 ♘f6 5 00 ♗e7 6 ♖e1 b5 7 ♗b3 d6 8 c3 00 9 h3 ♘b8 10 d4 (10 d3 3108) 10 ... ♘bd7 11 ♘bd2 ♗b7 12 ♗c2 ♖e8 (12 ... c5 3413) 13 ♘f1 ♗f8 14 ♘g3 g6 15 a4 c5 16 d5 ♘b6 17 ♘d2

c4 18 a5 ♘bd7 19 b3 cb 20 ♗×b3 ♘c5 21 ♗c2 ♗c8 22 ♗a3 ♕c7 23 ♗b4 ♗d7 24 ♕f3 ♗g7 25 ♗d3 ♘×d3 26 ♕×d3 ♖ec8 27 ♖acl ♘e8 ½–½

4215 Karnar–AK

R15: 21.6.1975: Réti

1 g3 ♘f6 2 ♗g2 d5 3 c4 c6 4 b3 ♗f5 5 ♘f3 e6 6 00 h6 7 ♗b2 ♘bd7 8 d3 ♗h7 9 ♘bd2 ♗e7 10 ♗c3 a5 11 a3 b5 12 cb cb 13 b4 a4 14 ♖c1 ♖c8 15 ♗b2 00 16 ♖×c8 ♕×c8 17 ♕al ♕b7 18 ♖cl ♘b8 19 ♖c2 ♖c8 20 ♕cl ♖×c2 21 ♕×c2 ♘e8 22 ♘bl ♔f8 23 ♔fl ♗d6 24 ♗e5 ♔e7 25 ♔el f6 26 ♗×d6+ ♘×d6 27 ♕c5 ♘d7 28 ♕cl e5 29 ♘fd2 ♗g8 30 ♘c3 ♔d8 31 e3 ♗e6 32 ♘e2 g5 33 h3 ♔e7 34 ♕c2 ♕b6 35 ♘bl f5 36 ♘bc3 ♘f6 37 ♘dl g4 38 h4 ♘d7 39 ♘dc3 ♕b7 40 ♕cl e4 41 d4 ½–½

Appendix

43 6th USSR Spartakiad

4301 AK–Spassky
PR2: Queen's Indian

1 d4 ♘f6 2 c4 e6 3 ♘f3 b6 4 g3 ♗b7 5 ♗g2 ♗e7 6 ♘c3 OO 7 ♕c2 d5 8 cd ♘×d5 9 OO ♘d7 10 ♘×d5 ed 11 ♖d1 ♘f6 12 ♘e5 c5 13 dc ♗×c5 14 ♘d3 ♗d6 15 ♗f4 ♖e8 16 e3 ♘e4 17 ♗×d6 ♕×d6 18 ♘f4 ♖ac8 19 ♕a4 ♕e7 20 ♕×a7 ♘×f2 21 ♘×d5 ♗×d5 22 ♕×d1 23 ♖c1 ♖b8 24 ♕b4 ♗×g2 25 ♔×g2 ♕e3+ 26 ♔g1 ♗e6 27 ♕f4 ♖d8 28 ♕×d4 ♖de8 29 ♕d7 ♘g4 30 ♖c8 ♘f6 31 ♖×e8+ ♖×e8 32 ♕b7 ♖e6 33 ♕b8+ ♘e8 34 a4 g6 35 b4 ♔g7 36 ♕b7 h5 37 h3 ♔f6 38 ♔g2 ♖d6 39 a5 ba 40 ba ♖e6 41 a6 ♘c7 42 a7 ♖e7 43 ♕c6+ ♔e5 44 ♔f3 **1–0**

4302 L. Grigorian–AK
PR3: Queen's Indian

1 c4 c5 2 ♘f3 ♘f6 3 ♘c3 e6 4 g3 b6 5 ♗g2 ♗b7 6 OO ♗e7 7 d4 cd 8 ♕×d4 d6 9 ♗g5 a6 10 ♗×f6 ♗×f6 11 ♕d3 ♗e7 12 ♖fd1 ♖a7 13 ♘e4 OO 14 ♖ac1 ♗a8 15 ♕e3 ♘c6 16 ♘c3 ♕b8 17 ♘d4 ♘e5 18 b3 ♖c8 19 ♗×a8 ♕×a8 20 ♘f3 ♘×f3+ 21 ef ♕c6 22 a4 ♖d7 23 ♖d3 ♕c5 24 ♖cd1 ♗f8 25 ♘e4 ♕c6 26 ♘c3 ♖cd8 27 ♕d2 h6 28 h4 ♕c5 29 ♘e4 ♕a3 30 ♕c1 ♕×c1 31 ♖×c1 d5 32 ♖cd1 ♗b4 33 ♖×d5 ♗×c3 34 ♖×c3 d4 35 ♖c2 e5 36 ♖e2 ♖e8 37 ♖de1 f6 38 ♔g2 ♔f7 39 f4 d3 40 ♖e3 e4 41 f3 f5 42 h5 g6 43 hg+ ♔×g6 44 ♔f2 h5 45

4303 AK–Kupreichik
PR4: Slav

1 d4 d5 2 c4 c6 3 ♘c3 ♘f6 4 ♘f3 dc 5 a4 ♗f5 6 e3 e6 7 ♗×c4 ♗b4 8 OO OO 9 ♕h4 ♗g4 10 f3 ♗d5 11 fg ♕×h4 12 ♕f3 ♘d7 13 ♗d2 a5 14 ♖ad1 ♖ad8 15 ♗b3 ♘5f6 16 h3 c5 17 ♗e1 ♕g5 18 ♗g3 cd 19 ed e5 20 ♘b5 ed 21 ♘×d4 ♕c5 22 ♗f2 ♕e5 23 ♗g3 ♕c5 24 ♕f5 ♕b6 25 ♔h1 ♘c5 26 ♗c2 ♖de8 27 ♖f4 ♘cd7 28 ♖f3 g6 29 ♕f4 ♗c5 30 ♖b3 ♗b4 31 ♖f3 ♗c5 32 ♘b5 ♖e2 33 ♗d3 ♖×b2 34 ♕g5 ♔g7 35 ♖df1 ♕c6 36 ♕c1 ♗a2 37 ♕c4 ♗d2 38 ♗f4 ♖b2 39 ♕c3 ♗b4 40 g5 ♗d4 41 ♕×c6 bc 42 ♘×d4 **1–0**

4304 AK–Gurgenidze
FR1: Sicilian

1 c4 ♘f6 2 ♘c3 c5 3 ♘f3 g6 4 d4 cd 5 ♘×d4 ♘c6 6 e4 ♘×d4 7 ♕×d4 d6 8 ♗g5 ♗g7 9 ♕d2 ♗e6 10 ♖c1 ♖c8 11 b3 b5 12 ♗×f6 ♗×f6 13 ♘×b5 ♕b6 14 ♗e2 ♕c5 15 ♖c2 OO 16 OO a6 17 ♘c3 ♗d4 18 ♗d3 a5 19 ♘b5 ♖a8 20 a3 ♖fc8 21 b4 ab 22 ab ♕b6 23 ♖fc1 ♗d7 24 ♘×d4 ♕×d4 25 ♕c3 ♕×c3

26 ♖×c3 ♖cb8 27 ♖b1 ♖c8 28 f3
♖a2 29 b5 ♔g7 30 e5 ♖c5 31 ed ed 32
♖c2 ♖×c2 33 ♗×c2 ♖×c4 34 ♗e4
♖c8 35 b6 ♖b8 36 b7 ♗f5 37 ♗×f5 gf
38 ♔f2 ♔f6 39 ♔e3 ♔e5 40 ♖b5+
♔e6 41 ♔d4 f4 **1-0**

4305 Tal–AK

FR2: Queen's Indian

1 d4 ♘f6 2 ♘f3 e6 3 c4 b6 4 e3 ♗b7 5
♘c3 d5 6 ♗d3 ♘bd7 7 00 ♗e7 8 ♕e2
00 9 e4 de 10 ♘×e4 c5 11 ♖d1 ♕c7 12
♗g5 ♖fe8 13 dc bc 14 ♖d2 h6 15 ♗h4
♘×e4 16 ♗×e4 ♗×h4 17 ♘×h4
♗×e4 18 ♕×e4 ♖ad8 ½-½

4306 AK–Petrosian

FR3: Spanish

1 e4 e5 2 ♘f3 ♘c6 3 ♗b5 a6 4 ♗a4
♘f6 5 00 ♗e7 6 ♗×c6 dc 7 d3 ♘d7 8
♘bd2 00 9 ♘c4 f6 10 ♘h4 ♘c5 11 ♘f5
♗×f5 12 ef ♕d5 13 ♕g4 e4 14 ♘e3
♕e5 15 ♘c4 ♕d5 ½-½

44 Milan

4401 Petrosian–AK

R1: 20.8.1975: Nimzo-Indian

1 d4 ♘f6 2 c4 e6 3 ♘c3 ♗b4 4 e3 00 5
♗d3 c5 6 ♘f3 d5 7 00 cd 8 ed dc 9
♗×c4 b6 10 ♗g5 ♗b7 11 ♕e2 ♗×c3
12 bc ♘bd7 13 ♗d3 ♕c7 14 c4 ♘g4 15
♗e4 ♗×e4 16 ♕×e4 ♘gf6 17 ♕d3 h6
18 ♗×f6 ♘×f6 19 a4 ♖ac8 20 ♖fc1
♖fd8 21 h3 e5 22 ♘×e5 ♕×e5 23 de
♖×d3 24 ef ♖d4 25 a5 gf 26 ab ab 27
♖ab1 ♖x×c4 28 ♖×c4 ♖×c4 29
♖×b6 ½-½

4402 AK–Smejkal

R2: 21.8.1975: English

1 c4 e5 2 ♘c3 ♘c6 3 ♘f3 ♘f6 4 g3 ♘d4
5 ♗g2 ♘×f3+ 6 ♗×f3 ♗b4 7 00 00 8
♕c2 ♖e8 9 d3 c6 10 ♗g2 h6 11 ♖b1 d5
12 cd cd 13 ♕b3 ♗×c3 14 bc b6 15 a4

4307 Belyavsky–AK

FR4: Nimzo-Indian

1 d4 ♘f6 2 c4 e6 3 ♘c3 ♗b4 4 e3 c5 5
♗d3 00 6 ♘f3 d5 7 00 dc 8 ♗×c4 cd 9
ed b6 10 ♗g5 ♗b7 11 ♕e2 ♗×c3 12 bc
♘bd7 13 ♗d3 ♕c7 14 c4 ♘g4 15 ♖e2
♗×e4 16 ♕×e4 ♘gf6 17 ♕e2 ♖ac8 18
♖ac1 ♗b7 19 ♕b2 ♕a6 20 ♕b3 ♗c6
21 ♖c2 ♖fc8 22 ♖fc1 h6 23 ♗f4 ♕a5
24 ♗d2 ♕f5 25 d5 ♘c5 26 ♕e3 ♖d8
27 ♘d4 ♕d3 28 ♘c6 ♕d7 29 ♘e5
♕×e3 30 ♗×e3 ♗b7 31 ♖d1 ♘cd7 32
♘c6 ♘b8 33 ♘×b8 ♖b×b8 34 ♗d4
♘×d5 35 ♖cc1 ♘b4 36 a4 ♖c6 37
♗e3 ♖bc8 38 ♖d7 a6 39 h3 ♖×c4 40
♖×c4 ♖×c4 41 ♗×b6 ♘d5 42 a5
♖c6 43 ♗d4 f6 44 ♖h2 h5 45 g3 ♔h7
46 h4 ♔g6 47 ♔g2 ♖c4 48 ♗b6 ♖b4
49 ♖d6 ♔f5 50 ♖c6 g6 51 ♗a7 ♖b7
52 ♗d4 e5 53 ♗b6 ♖d7 54 ♔f3 ♘e7
55 ♖c2 ♔e6 56 ♗e3 ♖d5 57 ♗b6
♖d6 58 ♖c7 ♖d3+ 59 ♔g2 ♖d7 60
♖c1 ♖d6 61 ♖c7 ♘d5 62 ♖b7 ♘×b6
63 ab ♔d5 64 ♖g7 ♖×b6 65 ♖×g6 a5
66 g4 hg 67 h5 ♔e6 68 h6 ♖b8 69
♖×g4 ♖a8 70 ♖g7 ½-½

20.8.–14.9.1975

♗g4 16 ♖e1 ♕d7 17 ♗d2 ♖ac8 18 a5
ba 19 ♕a3 ♖b8 20 ♖×b8 ♖×b8 21 f3
♗h3 22 ♗×h3 ♕×h3 23 ♕×a5 ♕d7
24 ♗e3 ♖b7 25 ♖a1 e4 26 de de 27
♗d4 ♖b2 28 ♖a2 ♖×a2 29 ♕×a2 ef
30 ef ♕c6 31 ♔f2 a6 32 ♕b3 ♘d5 33 c4
♘c7 34 ♗e3 a5 35 ♗f4 ♕c5+ 36 ♔g2
♘e6 37 ♗e3 ♕c6 38 ♕b8+ ♔h7 39
♕b5 ♕a8 40 ♕a4 ♘g5 41 ♗×g5 hg 42
c5 ♕d5 43 ♕×a5 g4 44 ♕c3 gf+ 45
♔f2 ♕e4 46 ♕e3 ♕d5 47 g4 g5 48 h3
♔g6 49 ♔g3 ♕d1 50 ♕e4+ ♔g7 51
♕c4 ♕h1 52 ♕c2 f6 53 ♕f2 ♔f7 54 c6
♔e6 55 ♕d2 ♕g2+ ½-½

4403 Ljubojević–AK

R3: 22.8.1975: Spanish

1 e4 e5 2 ♘f3 ♘c6 3 ♗b5 a6 4 ♗a4
♘f6 5 00 ♗e7 6 d4 ed 7 e5 ♘e4 8

Nxd4 00 9 Nf5 d5 10 ed Bxf5 11 de Nxe7 12 Bb3 Qxd1 13 Rxd1 Rad8 14 Re1 Nc5 15 Nc3 Rd7 16 Be3 Nxb3 17 cb Rfd8 18 Rad1 f6 19 Rxd7 Rxd7 20 Rd1 Rxd1+ 21 Nxd1 Nd5 22 Nd2 Rb1 23 a3 Qc2 24 Ne3 Nxe3 25 Bxe3 Nxb3 26 f3 Qf7 27 Bf4 c6 28 Bd6 Qe6 29 Bf8 g6 30 Kf2 a5 31 Ne3 b6 32 h4 c5 33 g4 Bd1 34 Ke4 a4 35 h5 gh 36 gh f5+ 37 Ke3 Kd5 38 h6 Kc4 39 f4 Kb3 40 Bg7 Kc2 41 Ne5 Bh5 42 Bf6 Bf7 43 Be5 Bb3 44 Bg7 b5 45 Bf8 c4 46 Bg7 b4 47 Kd4 c3 48 bc ba 49 c4 a2 50 Kc5 Kb1 51 Kb4 a1Q 52 Bxa1 Kxa1 53 c5 Kb2 54 c6 a3 55 c7 Ne6 56 Kc5 a2 57 Kd6 Nc8 **0-1**

4404 AK-Unzicker
R4: 23.8.1975: Spanish
1 e4 e5 2 Nf3 Nc6 3 Bb5 a6 4 Ba4 Nf6 5 00 Be7 6 Re1 b5 7 Bb3 d6 8 c3 00 9 h3 Na5 10 Bc2 c5 11 d4 Qc7 12 Nbd2 Bd7 13 Nf1 Rfe8 14 d5 Nb7 15 N3h2 g6 16 Ng3 c4 17 f4 ef 18 Bxf4 Bf8 19 Bg5 Be7 20 Qd2 Bc8 21 Rf1 Nd7 22 Ng4 **1-0**

4405 Browne-AK
R5: 24.8.1975: Queen's Indian
1 d4 Nf6 2 c4 e6 3 Nf3 b6 4 g3 Bb7 5 Bg2 Be7 6 Nc3 Ne4 7 Nxe4 Bxe4 8 00 00 9 Ne1 d5 10 Bxe4 de 11 Nc2 c5 12 b3 cd 13 Qxd4 f5 14 Bb2 Bf6 15 Qxd8 Rxd8 16 Bxf6 gf 17 Rad1 ½-½

4406 AK-Gligorić
R6: 26.8.1975: Spanish
1 e4 e5 2 Nf3 Nc6 3 Bb5 a6 4 Ba4 Nf6 5 00 Be7 6 Re1 b5 7 Bb3 d6 8 c3 00 9 h3 Nb8 10 d4 Nbd7 11 Nbd2 Bb7 12 Bc2 Re8 13 Nf1 Bf8 14 Ng3 g6 15 a4 c5 16 d5 Nb6 17 Be2 Nxa4 18 Bxa4 ba 19 Rxa4 Bg7 20 c4 Bc8 21 Bd2 Bb8 22 Rb1 Re7 23 Ne1 Reb7 24 Nd3 Rb3 25 bal Ne8 26 Bc3 Qh4 27 R1a3 f5 28 Be1 Qe7 29 Rxb3 Rxb3 30 Ncl Rb8 31 Nd3

Rb3 32 f3 Qg5 33 Kh2 Nf6 34 Qc2 Rb8 35 b4 fe 36 Nxe4 Nxe4 37 fe Qe3 38 bc Qxe4 39 cd Bf5 40 Ra3 Rc8 41 Rc3 Bf8 42 Bf2 Qxd6 43 Qa2 a5 44 c5 Qd7 45 Ra3 Bb5 46 cd Bxd3 47 d7 Rd8 48 Rxd3 Qxd3 49 d6+ Kh8 50 Bxa5 **1-0**

4407 Tal-AK
R7: 27.8.1975: Petroff
1 e4 e5 2 Nf3 Nf6 3 d4 Nxe4 4 Bd3 d5 5 Nxe5 Bd6 6 00 00 7 c4 Bxe5 8 de Nc6 9 cd Qxd5 10 Qc2 Nb4 11 Bxe4 Nxc2 12 Bxd5 Bf5 13 g4 Bxg4 14 Ne4 Nxal 15 Nc3 Bh3 16 Re1 f5 17 ef Rae8 18 Bd2 Rxe4 19 Nxe4 Qc2 20 Rcl Nd4 21 Rxc7 Rf7 22 Rxf7 Nf3+ 23 Kh1 Kxf7 24 fg Kxg7 25 Be3 b6 26 Nd2 Nxd2 27 Bxd2 a5 28 f3 a4 29 Kgl Be6 30 a3 ½-½

4408 AK-Andersson
R8: 28.8.1975: Sicilian
1 e4 c5 2 Nf3 e6 3 d4 cd 4 Nxd4 Nc6 5 Nb5 d6 6 c4 Nf6 7 N1c3 a6 8 Na3 Be7 9 Be2 00 10 00 b6 11 Be3 Bb7 12 Rc1 e8 13 Nb3 Bd7 14 Rfd1 Rc8 15 Rd2 Nc7 16 Rd1 Nb8 17 f3 Ba8 18 Qf1 Nce5 19 Nab1 Nf6 20 Nh1 h6 21 Rddl Bf8 22 Nd2 Rcd8 23 Qf2 Ned7 24 a3 d5 25 cd ed 26 ed Bd6 27 Nf1 Rxe3 28 Nxe3 Bxh2 29 Nf1 Bf4 30 Rc2 b5 31 Nd3 Bb6 32 Be4 Nc4 33 a4 Re8 34 ab ab 35 Re2 Be5 36 Qc5 Nd6 37 Na2 Ndxe4 38 fe Bd6 39 Qc2 e5 40 g3 Qe8 41 Rde1 Bb7 42 Kgl Nh7 43 Ncl Ng5 44 Nd2 Bb4 45 Kf2 Bxd2 46 Rxd2 Nxe4+ 47 Rxe4 Rxe4 48 Be2 Bc8 49 Nc3 Rel 50 Ne2 al 51 Rd4 Qd8 52 Qc6 Bd7 53 Qd6 Qe8 54 Nf4 Qc8 55 b4 Bh3 56 Qe4 Qf5 57 Qe3 Qc2 58 g4 Bd7 59 Qe4 Qb3 60 Qd3 Qb2 61 Qe4 Ra8 62 Qe3 Ra2 63 d6 Ra8 64 Re4 Bc6 65 Qd4 Qb1 66 Re7 Qh1 67 Qf4 Qg2+ 68 Rel Ral+ 69 Kd2 Qd5+ 70 Qd4 Ra2+ 71 Kc3

♕f3+ 72 ♖e3 ♖a3+ 73 ♔d2 ♖a2+ 74 ♔e1 ♕h1+ 75 ♔f2 ♕h2+ 76 ♔e1 ♕h1+ 77 ♔f2 ♕a1 78 ♖c3 ♕g2+ 79 ♔e3 ♕f3+ **0-1**

4409   Larsen–AK
R9: 30.8.1975: English
1 c4 ♘f6 2 ♘c3 e5 3 ♘f3 ♘c6 4 d3 d6 5 g3 g6 6 ♗g2 ♗g7 7 00 00 8 ♘b1 a6 9 b4 ♗d7 10 a4 ♕c8 11 ♗g5 ♘h3 12 b5 ab 13 cb ♗×g2 14 ♔×g2 ♘e7 15 ♕b3 ♕d7 16 ♘d2 ♘f5 17 ♗×f6 ♗×f6 18 ♘de4 ♗d8 19 ♖fc1 ♔g7 20 e3 c6 21 bc bc 22 ♕b7 ♖a7 23 ♕×d7 ♖×d7 24 ♘e2 ♘e7 25 d4 f5 26 ♘g5 ♖f6 27 ♖d1 ♘d5 28 de de 29 e4 ♘fd6 30 ed ♗×g5 31 dc ♖×d1 32 ♖×d1 ♖×d1 33 c7 ♖d8 34 cd ♗×d8 35 ♘c1 ♗f6 36 ♘b3 ♔e6 37 a5 ♔d5 38 a6 ♗b6 39 ♘f1 e4 40 ♔e2 ♔c4 41 ♘d2+ ♔b5 ½-½

4410   Portisch–AK
R10: 31.8.1975: Queen's Indian
1 ♘f3 ♘f6 2 c4 b6 3 g3 ♗b7 4 ♗g2 e6 5 00 ♗e7 6 ♘c3 00 7 ♖e1 ♘e4 8 ♘×e4 ♗×e4 9 d3 ♗b7 10 d4 ♗e4 11 d5 ♗f6 12 ♘d2 ♗×g2 13 ♕×g2 d6 14 ♘e4 ♘d7 15 ♕c2 ♘c5 16 ♘×c5 bc 17 de ½-½

4411   AK–Mariotti
R11: 1.9.1975: Sicilian
1 c4 ♘f6 2 ♘c3 g6 3 e4 d6 4 d4 c5 5 ♘f3 ♗g7 6 ♗e2 00 7 00 cd 8 ♘×d4 ♘c6 9 ♗e3 ♗d7 10 ♕d2 ♘×d4 11 ♗×d4 ♗c6 12 f3 ♘d7 13 ♗e3 a5 14 b3 ♘c5 15 ♖ac1 ♕b6 16 ♘b5 ♖fc8 17 ♖fd1 ♕d8 18 ♖c2 b6 19 ♗f1 ♕d7 20 ♘c3 ♗b7 21 ♕f2 ♘a6 22 ♖cc1 a4 23 ♘d5 ♗×d5 24 cd ab 25 ab b5 26 f4 b4 27 ♖c4 ♖×c4 28 ♗×c4 ♘c7 29 ♕e2 ♖a5 30 ♗f2 ♘b5 31 ♖c1 ♘c3 32 ♕d3 ♕a8 33 g3 ½-½

semi-final

4412   AK–Petrosian
G1: 3.9.1975: Spanish
1 e4 e5 2 ♘f3 ♘c6 3 ♗b5 a6 4 ♗a4 ♘f6 5 00 ♗e7 6 ♖e1 b5 7 ♗b3 d6 8 c3 00 9 h3 ♘a5 10 ♗c2 c5 11 d4 ♕c7 12 ♘bd2 ♗d7 13 ♘f1 ♘c4 14 ♘e3 ♘×e3 15 ♗×e3 fc8 16 ♖c1 ♗c6 17 ♘d2 cd 18 cd ♕b7 19 d5 ♗e8 20 ♘e2 ♗d8 21 b4 ♗b6 22 ♗d3 ♗×e3 23 ♕×e3 ♖×c1 24 ♖×c1 c8 25 ♘b3 ♖×c1+ 26 ♕×c1 ♗d7 27 ♔h2 ♕b6 28 ♕d2 ♕c7 ½-½

4413   Petrosian–AK
G2: 4.9.1975: Queen's Indian
1 d4 ♘f6 2 ♘f3 e6 3 c4 b6 4 g3 ♗b7 5 ♗g2 ♗e7 6 ♘c3 ♘e4 7 ♗d2 ♗f6 8 ♕c2 ♘×d2 9 ♕×d2 00 10 00 d6 11 e4 ♘d7 12 d5 ♕e7 13 ♖fe1 ♗×c3 14 ♕×c3 e5 15 b4 a5 16 a3 ♖a7 17 ♘h4 g6 18 ♘h3 ♖fa8 19 ♗g2 ♗c8 20 ♘e3 ♘f6 21 ♗×c8 ♖×c8 22 f3 ♖ca8 23 ♖ec1 ♘d7 24 h4 ♕e8 25 ♕b2 ♖a6 26 b5 ♖a7 27 a4 ♕e7 28 ♔g2 ♘c5 29 ♕c2 ♖f8 30 ♖h1 ♖aa8 31 ♖ae1 ♖ae8 32 g4 h6 ½-½

4414   AK–Petrosian
G3: 5.9.1975: Queen's Indian
1 c4 ♘f6 2 ♘c3 e6 3 ♘f3 b6 4 g3 ♗b7 5 ♗g2 ♗e7 6 00 c5 7 d4 cd 8 ♕×d4 00 9 ♖d1 ♘c6 10 ♕f4 ♕b8 11 e4 ♕×f4 12 ♗×f4 ♖fd8 13 e5 ♘e8 14 ♘d4 ♘a5 15 b3 ♗×g2 16 ♔×g2 d6 17 ed ♗×d6 18 ♗×d6 ♘×d6 19 ♖d2 ♔f8 20 ♖ad1 ♔e7 21 f4 ♖ac8 22 ♔f3 ♘c6 23 ♘×c6+ ♖×c6 24 ♘e4 ♘b7 25 ♖×d8 ♘×d8 26 ♔e3 ♘b7 27 ♖d4 h6 28 b4 f6 ½-½

4415   Petrosian–AK
G4: 8.9.1975: English
1 c4 ♘f6 2 ♘c3 e5 3 ♘f3 ♘c6 4 g3 ♗b4 5 ♘d5 ♘×d5 6 cd ♘d4 7 ♗g2 ♘×f3+ 8 ♗×f3 00 9 00 d6 10 ♗g2 ♗c5 11 b3 ♗d4 12 ♖b1 ♗f5 13 d3 ♕d7 14 ♗b2 ♗×b2 15 ♖×b2 ♗h3 16 ♗×h3 ♕×h3 17 ♖c2 ♕d7 18 ♕c1 ♖fc8 19 ♕e3 c5 20 dc ♖×c6 21 ♖×c6 bc 22 d4 ♖e8 23 ♖e1 h6 24 ♔g2 a5 25 h3 ed 26 ♕×d4 c5 27 ♕d5 a4 28 ba ♕×a4 29 ♕×d6 ♕×a2 30 ♕×c5 ½-½

final

4416 Portisch–AK

G1: 9.9.1975: Nimzo-Indian

1 d4 ♘f6 2 c4 e6 3 ♘c3 ♗b4 4 e3 c5 5
♗d3 00 6 ♘f3 d5 7 00 dc 8 ♗×c4 cd 9
ed b6 10 ♗g5 ♗b7 11 ♖c1 ♘c6 12 a3
♗e7 13 ♕d3 ♖c8 14 ♖fd1 ♘d5 15
♗×d5 ♗×g5 16 ♘×g5 ♕×g5 17 ♗e4
h6 18 ♕e3 ♖fd8 19 ♕×g5 hg 20 d5 ed
21 ♖×d5 ♖×d5 22 ♗×d5 ♘a5 23
♗a2 ♘c4 24 ♘b5 ♘d6 25 ♖×c8+
♘×c8 26 f3 ♔f8 27 ♔f2 ♗c6 28 ♗c4
♔e7 29 ♔e3 a5 30 ♔d4 ♗×b5 31
♗×b5 ♔d6 32 ♗c4 f6 33 ♗d3 ♘e7 34
♗e4 ♘c8 ½–½

4417 AK–Portisch

G2: 10.9.1975: Spanish

1 e4 e5 2 ♘f3 ♘c6 3 ♗b5 a6 4 ♗a4 d6 5
00 ♗e7 6 ♗×c6+ bc 7 d4 ed 8 ♘×d4
c5 9 ♘c6 ♕d7 10 ♘a5 ♗f6 11 ♕d3
♘e7 12 ♘c3 ♖b8 13 ♖b1 00 14 ♗d2
♗×c3 15 ♗×c3 ♘c6 16 a3 ♘×a5 17
♗×a5 ♖e8 18 ♖fe1 ♖e6 19 c4 ♗b7 20
f3 ♖be8 21 ♕d2 ♗c6 22 b3 ♕e7 23
♕f4 ♖b8 24 ♖c3 f6 25 ♔f2 ♕f7 26 h4
♖ee8 27 g4 ♖b7 28 ♖b2 ♖eb8 29
♖eb1 ♗f8 30 ♖g1 ♗e8 31 ♕e3 ♕e6
32 ♕d3 ♗c6 33 b4 cb 34 ab ♗e8 35
♖d2 ♖b6 36 ♕d4 ♕e5 37 ♕×b6
♕h2+ 38 ♔e1 ♗×d2+ 39 ♔×d2 cb
40 ♖a1 ♗f7 41 ♖×a6 ♖b8 42 ♗d3 h5
43 b5 hg 44 fg ♖c8 45 ♖a4 ♗e6 46 g5
f5 47 ef ♗×f5+ 48 ♔d4 ♕f7 49 ♗b4
♔e6 50 ♖a6 ♖b8 51 h5 ♗g4 52 h6 gh
53 gh ♗f5 54 ♗d2 ♖g8 55 ♗f4 ♖b8
56 ♖a7 ♔f6 57 ♖g7 ♗e6 58 ♖c7 ♖h8
59 ♖c6 ♖g8 60 ♖×d6 ♔f5 61 ♖×b6
♖g4 62 ♖×e6 ♔×e6 63 ♔e4 ♖g1 64
b6 1–0

4418 Portisch–AK

G3: 11.9.1975: Queen's Indian

1 c4 ♘f6 2 ♘c3 e6 3 ♘f3 b6 4 g3 ♗b7 5
♗g2 ♗e7 6 00 00 7 ♖e1 d5 8 cd ♘×d5
9 ♘×d5 ed 10 d4 ♘d7 11 ♗f4 c5 12 dc
bc 13 ♘d2 a5 14 ♖c1 ♖a7 15 ♘b1
♘b6 16 b3 d4 17 ♗×b7 ♖×b7 18 e4 a4
19 ♕d3 ab 20 ab ♘d7 21 h4 h6 22 e5
♖b6 23 ♕a3 ♗e6 24 ♘c4 ♕b8 25 h5
♖e8 26 ♖b1 ♘b6 27 ♗d2 ♗×c4 28 bc
♕a8 29 ♖a1 ♕b7 30 ♖ab1 ♕a8 ½–½

4419 AK–Portisch

G4: 12.9.1975: Spanish

1 e4 e5 2 ♘f3 ♘c6 3 ♗b5 a6 4 ♗a4
♘f6 5 00 ♗e7 6 ♖e1 b5 7 ♗b3 d6 8 c3
00 9 h3 ♘b8 10 d4 ♘bd7 11 ♘bd2
♗b7 12 ♗c2 ♖e8 13 ♘f1 ♗f8 14 ♘g3
g6 15 a4 c5 16 d5 c4 17 ♗e3 ♘c5 18
♕e2 ♘fd7 19 ♘d2 ♕c7 20 ♖a3 ♘b6
21 ab ab 22 ♖ea1 ♖×a3 23 ♖×a3
♗c8 24 ♕d1 ♗d7 25 ♕a1 ♘ba4 26 b3
½–½

4420 Portisch–AK

G5: 13.9.1975: Nimzo-Indian

1 c4 ♘f6 2 ♘c3 e6 3 d4 ♗b4 4 e3 c5 5
♗d3 00 6 ♘f3 d5 7 00 cd 8 ed dc 9
♗×c4 b6 10 ♗e1 ♗b7 11 ♗d3 ♘c6 12
a3 ♗e7 13 ♗c2 ♖e8 14 ♕d3 ♖c8 15
d5 ed 16 ♗g5 ♘e4 17 ♗×e4 de 18
♕×e4 g6 19 ♕h4 h5 20 ♖ad1 ♕c7 21
♗×g6 fg 22 ♕c4+ ♕g7 23 ♗f4 ♗a6
24 ♕c3+ ♖f6 25 ♗×c7 ♗×c3 26
♖×e8 ♖×e8 27 bc ♗e2 28 ♖e1 ♖c8
29 ♖×e2 ♖×c7 30 ♖e6 ♘d8 31 ♖e3
♔f6 32 ♔f1 ♗e6 33 g3 g5 34 h3 ♖c5 35
♘d2 ♖d5 36 ♔e2 ♘c5 37 c4 ♖d4 38
♖e8 h4 39 ♖f8+ ♔e7 40 ♖h8 hg 41 fg
½–½

4421 AK–Portisch

G6: 14.9.1975: English

1 ♘f3 c5 2 c4 ♘f6 3 ♘c3 d5 4 cd ♘×d5
5 g3 ♘c6 6 ♗g2 ♘c7 7 d3 e5 8 ♘d2
♗d7 9 00 ♗e7 10 ♘c4 f6 11 f4 b5 12
♘e3 ef 13 ♖×f4 00 14 ♘ed5 ♘e6 15
♖f8 ♖b8 16 ♗d2 ♘e5 17 ♖c1 ♗f7 18
♘×e7+ ♕×e7 19 b4 c4 20 ♘d5 ♕d8
21 ♗c3 ♘g4 ½–½

Index of Openings

No. in italics indicates Karpov was White

	AK White			AK Black		
	+	=	−	+	=	−
1 c4 c5						
2 ♘c3 ♘f6 3 ♘f3 e6 4 d4 3406, 3414, *4001*	1	·	·	2	·	·
2 ♘c3 ♘f6 3 ♘f3 d5 1709, 2417, 2421, 2507, 3304, *4421*	·	1	·	1	3	1
2 ♘c3 ♘c6 3 g3 g6 4 ♗g2 ♗g7 *0805*, 1007, 1502, 1705, 1713, 2103, 3001, 3111, 3213, 3410, *4004*	2	·	·	4	5	·
Other 0908, 1707, 2514, 3012, *3102*, *3504*, *3601*	3	·	·	3	1	·
1 c4 e5						
2 ♘c3 f5 *1003*, *2101*	1	1	·	·	·	·
2 ♘c3 ♘f6:						
3 e4 *1514*	1	·	·	·	·	·
3 ♘f3 ♘c6 4 g3 *3201*, 4109, *4402*, 4409, 4415	·	2	·	·	3	·
3 g3 0401, *1902*, *2006*, *2412*, *3705*	2	2	·	1	·	·
2 ♘c3 other 0119, 0510, *3415*	·	1	·	2	·	·
1 c4 ♘f6						
2 ♘c3 e6 3 ♘f3 b6 4 e4 4101, 4103, 4107	·	·	·	·	3	·
Other *0511*, *1512*, *1716*, 4213	3	·	·	·	1	·
1 d4 d5						
2 ♘c3 *0809*	1	·	·	·	·	·
2 c4 dc *4124*	·	1	·	·	·	·
2 c4 c6 3 ♘f3 ♘f6:						
4 ♘c3 dc *4201*, *4303*	2	·	·	·	·	·
4 ♘c3 e6 5 e3 *3605*, *3613*, 4204	·	2	·	·	1	·
4 e3 ♗f5 *2207*	1	·	·	·	·	·
2 c4 ♘c6 *1602*	·	1	·	·	·	·
2 c4 e6						
3 ♘c3 c5 *1706*, 1711, 2409, 3412, *3615*	·	2	·	1	1	1
3 ♘c3 ♘f6:						
4 e3 b6 0130	·	·	·	1	·	·
4 ♘f3 ♗b4 0705	·	·	·	·	1	·
4 cd 0202, 0209	·	·	·	·	2	·
4 ♗f4 3209	·	·	·	·	1	·
4 ♗g5 0102, 0131, 0136, 0215, 0305, 0514, 1508, *2403*, 2603, 3401, *3911*	1	1	·	6	2	1

Opening	+	=	−	+	=	−
1 d4 c5 *3616, 3707*	1	1	·	·	·	·
1 d4 ♞f6 2 ♞f3 c5 1306, 1915	·	·	·	·	2	·
1 d4 ♞f6 2 ♞f3 e6:						
3 e3 2404	·	·	·	·	1	·
3 ♗f4 0416	·	·	·	1	·	·
3 ♗g5 0211, 0221, 0506, *0507*, 0802, 1413, 2614, 2803	1	·	·	1	4	2
1 d4 ♞f6 other *0208*, 1504, 4119	1	·	·	1	·	·

1 d4 ♞f6 2 c4 e6 3 ♞c3 ♝b4

	+	=	−	+	=	−
4 a3 0106, 0804	·	·	·	2	·	·
4 ♛b3 0307	·	·	·	1	·	·
4 ♛c2 0512, 1404, *1503*, 1719	1	·	·	2	1	·
4 ♞f3 0705	·	·	·	·	1	·
4 g3 0909	·	·	·	·	1	·
4 ♗g5 0408, 4005	·	·	·	2	·	·
4 e3						
4 . . . b6 4002	·	·	·	1	·	·
4 . . . 00						
5 ♞e2 1012, 1402, 3405	·	·	·	2	1	·
5 ♞f3 c5 6 ♗e2 0905	·	·	·	1	·	·
5 ♗d3 c5						
6 ♞e2 1903	·	·	·	·	1	·
6 ♞f3 d5 7 00						
7 . . . dc 1513, 2609, 3109, 3114, 3301, 3602, 3604, 3801, 3803, 3805, 3807, 4307, 4401, 4416, 4420	·	·	·	3	11	1
7 . . . ♞c6 *3905*	·	1	·	·	·	·
7 . . . ♞bd7 0810	·	·	·	1	·	·
1 d4 ♞f6 2 c4 e6 3 ♞f3 ♝b4+ *1908, 3703*	2	·	·	·	·	·

1 d4 ♞f6 2 c4 e6 3 ♞f3 b6

	+	=	−	+	=	−
4 a3 0402, 1604	·	·	·	·	·	2
4 e3 0901, 1415, 3107, 3608, 4202, 4305	·	·	·	3	2	1
4 g3 0107, 0410, 0508, 0904, 1417, 1506, 1703, 1806, 2415, 2419, 2509, 2510, 2601, 2807, 3103, 3207, 3614, 3704, 4009, 4011, 4105, 4111, 4113, 4121, 4123, *4301*, 4302, 4405, 4410, 4413, *4414*, 4418	1	1	·	1	28	1
1 d4 ♞f6 2 c4 e6 3 ♞f3 d5 0404, *1005*, 1406, 1905, 2503, 2516, 4117, *4122*	1	1	·	3	3	·
1 d4 f5 *0605*, 3907	·	1	1	·	·	·

1 d4 ♞f6 2 c4 g6

3 ♞c3 ♝g7 4 e4 d6:

	+	=	−	+	=	−
5 f3 *0115, 0409, 4205*	3	·	·	·	·	·

	+	=	−	+	=	−
5 ♘f3 *3903*	1	·	·	·	·	·
3 ♘c3 d5:						
4 cd 2809, *2906*	·	1	·	1	·	·
4 ♘f3 0139, *1716, 3210*	2	·	·	1	·	·
3 g3 d6 *1117, 1201, 1408, 2007, 3208*	4	·	1	·	·	·
3 g3 d5 2612	·	·	·	·	1	·

1 e4 c5

	+	=	−	+	=	−
2 ♘c3 ♘c6 3 g3:						
3 . . . e6 *0308*	1	·	·	·	·	·
3 . . . g6 4 ♗g2:						
4 . . . ♖b8 *0302*	1	·	·	·	·	·
4 . . . ♘f6 *0220*	1	·	·	·	·	·
4 . . . ♗g7:						
5 d3 *0210, 0214, 0216, 0236, 0501, 0502, 0513, 0706, 0902, 0910,* 1004, *1203, 1505,* 2008	6	5	1	1	1	·
5 ♘ge2 *0110, 0133, 0135, 0203, 0205, 0304, 0407, 0413, 0420*	7	2	·	·	·	·
2 ♘f3						
2 . . . a6 0703, *2608*	1	·	·	1	·	·
2 . . . ♘f6 *1102*	·	1	·	·	·	·
2 . . . ♘c6						
3 ♗b5 *0807, 1009, 1011*	1	1	1	·	·	·
3 c3 1909	·	·	·	·	·	1
3 d4 cd 4 ♘×d4						
4 . . . ♕c7 *2610*	1	·	·	·	·	·
4 . . . e5 *2301*	1	·	·	·	·	·
4 . . . g6:						
5 ♘c3 *1001*	·	1	·	·	·	·
5 c4 *1906, 3113, 4010, 4304, 4411*	2	3	·	·	·	·
4 . . . ♘f6 5 ♘c3						
5 . . . d6 6 ♗c4 *2408*	1	·	·	·	·	·
5 . . . d6 6 ♗e3 *0109*	·	1	·	·	·	·
5 . . . d6 6 ♗g5 *1910, 2420, 2602, 2909, 3015*	4	1	·	·	·	·
5 . . . e5 *2901*	·	1	·	·	·	·
2 . . . d6						
3 ♗b5+ *3115, 3506*	1	1	·	·	·	·
3 c3 *1106*	1	·	·	·	·	·
3 g3 *1104*	1	·	·	·	·	·
3 d4 cd						
4 ♕×d4 *1301, 3204, 3214*	·	3	·	·	·	·
4 ♘×d4 ♘f6 5 ♘c3						
5 . . . a6						
6 ♗e2 e5 *1708, 2504, 2513, 2606, 2613, 2905, 3411, 3617, 3802, 3804, 3806, 3808*	6	5	·	·	1	·
6 ♗e2 e6 *2205, 2410*	1	1	·	·	·	·

	+	=	−		+	=	−
6 ♗e2 g6 *1702*	·	1	·		·	·	·
6 f4 *3002, 3008, 3009*, 3502, *3609*	4	·	·		1	·	·
6 g3 *0419*	·	1	·		·	·	·
6 ♗g5 *3409*	1	·	·		·	·	·
5 . . . e6 — 2 . . . e6							
5 . . . g6 6 ♗e3 ♗g7 7 f3 ♘c6 8 ♕d2 00:							
9 ♗c4 *0704, 1805, 3106, 3501, 4102, 4207, 4210*	6	·	1		·	·	·
9 g4 *3005*	1	·	·		·	·	·
2 . . . e6							
3 c3 *0709*, 3006, 3505	1	·	·		·	1	1
3 ♘c3 1911	·	·	·		·	1	·
3 d3 2413, 3007, 3205, 3713	·	·	·		2	2	·
3 d4 cd 4 ♘×d4							
4 . . . a6							
5 ♘c3 *2904*, 3003	1	·	·		1	·	·
5 ♗d3 *1414, 1509, 2802, 2908, 3013, 3402*, 3612, 3708, 4209	4	2	·		2	1	·
4 . . . ♘c6							
5 ♘b5 d6 6 c4 1411, *2418, 2502, 2604, 2804,* 2907, 3004, *3010, 3303,* 3706, *4408*	2	4	1		2	2	·
5 ♘b5 d6 6 ♗f4 2106, *2401, 3603*	1	1	·		1	·	·
5 g3 2903	·	·	·		·	1	·
5 ♘c3 a6:							
6 ♗c4 2201	·	·	·		·	1	·
6 ♗e2 ♕c7 7 00:							
7 . . . b5 1409	·	·	·		·	1	·
7 . . . ♘f6 8 ♗e3 3211, 3416	·	·	·		1	1	·
7 . . . ♘f6 8 ♔h1 3711, 4007, 4211	·	·	·		1	2	·
6 ♗e3 ♕c7 7 ♗d3 b5 2302, 2505	·	·	·		1	1	·
6 f4 2501, 3715	·	·	·		1	1	·
6 g3 ♘×d4 1721, 2304	·	·	·		1	1	·
6 g3 ♘ge7 1907, 2005, 2105, 2607, 3112	·	·	·		4	1	·
4 . . . ♘f6							
5 ♘c3 ♘c6 6 ♘db5 *1901*	1	·	·		·	·	·
5 ♗d3 *0417*	·	1	·		·	·	·
5 f3 *0118*	·	1	·		·	·	·
5 ♘c3 d6:							
6 ♗e2 *1804, 1912,* 2411, *3901, 3909*	1	1	2		·	1	·
6 g4 *2107, 2511, 2801, 3110*	4	·	·		·	·	·
2 g3 *0306, 0504,* 3105	1	1	·		1	·	·
1 e4 c6							
2 ♘c3 *3701*	1	·	·		·	·	·
2 d4 d5							
3 ♘c3 g6 *0137, 2303*	1	1	·		·	·	·
3 ♘c3 (♘d2) de 4 ♘×e4:							
4 . . . ♘d7 *0138, 1412,* 4013	1	1	·		·	1	·

	+	=	−		+	=	−
4 . . . ♗f5 *3709*, 3902, 3904, 3906, 3908, *4014*, *4208*	1	2	·		1	3	·
4 . . . ♘f6 0204	·	·	·		1	·	
1 e4 d5 *0206*, 2407	·	1	1		·	·	
1 e4 d6 2 d4 ♘f6 *0224*, *0601*, *0603*, 1113, *1403*, *1914*, *2414*, *2806*, 3404, 4006	7	2	1		·	·	

1 e4 e5

2 ♘c3 0808	·	·	·		1	·	
2 ♗c4 0406	·	·	·		·	·	1
2 d4 3014	·	·	·		·	1	·
2 ♘f3 ♘c6:							
3 c3 *0132*, 4206	·	·	·		1	1	
3 ♘c3 0223, *0711*, 1114, *1913*	·	·	·		2	2	
3 ♗c4 0127 *1002*	·	·	·		2	·	
3 d4 0122	·	·	·		·	1	·
2 ♘f3 d6 *0222*	·	1	·		·	·	
2 ♘f3 ♘f6 *0212*, 0219, *0312*, 0505, *1305*, 1515, 1517, *2808*, *4106*, 4407	5	·	·		·	5	·
2 f4 0103, 1110, 1116	·	·	·		2	1	·

1 e4 e5 2 ♘f3 ♘c6 3 ♗b5

3 . . . ♗c5 *4212*	1	·	·		·	·	
3 . . . ♘d4 *1006*	1	·	·		·	·	
3 . . . d6 *0108*	1	·	·		·	·	
3 . . . f5 *0310*, 2416, *4203*	2	1	·		·	·	
3 . . . ♘f6 *1501*	·	1	·		·	·	

3 . . . a6

| 4 ♗×c6 *0117*, 0217, *0311*, 0418, 0421, 0503, 1202, *1410*, *1416*, 1717, *1904*, *2202*, 2902, *3710* | 2 | 4 | 1 | | 2 | 5 | · |

4 ♗a4

4 . . . b5 *0140*	1	·	·		·	·	
4 . . . d6 *0123*, *0201*, *0708*, *0811*, *2508*, *4012*, *4417*	5	2	·		·	·	
4 . . . f5 *4120*	·	1	·		·	·	

4 . . . ♘f6

5 ♘c3 0101	·	·	·		1	·	
5 d3 *0218*, 0313	·	1	·		1	·	
5 d4 0602, 0604, 1112, 1204	·	·	·		2	1	1
5 ♕e2 0301, *0405*, *0509*, *0906*, 1101, 1108	3	·	·		3	·	

5 00

| 5 . . . ♘×e4 *0234*, *1704*, *1802*; *2517* | 2 | 2 | · | | · | · | |

5 . . . ♗e7

6 ♗×c6 0806, *4306*	·	1	·		1	·	
6 d4 1103, 4403	·	·	·		1	1	
6 ♕e2 0124, 0213, 0303, *0707*, 1105	·	1	·		1	3	

6 ♖e1 b5 7 ♗b3

| 7 . . . 00 8 a4 *0226*, *0235*, *3611* | 2 | 1 | · | | · | · | |

	+	=	−	+	=	−
7 . . . d6						
8 ♘c3 0128	·	·	·	1	·	·
8 c3 00						
9 d4 ♗g4 0207, *0403*, 0801	1	·	·	2	·	·
9 h3						
9 . . . ♘a5 0104, *0105*, 0111, *0112*, 0120, 0121, 0141, 0225, 0233, *0309*, 0515, *1109*, *1115*, 1302, 1304, 1510, 1601, *1609*, 2203, 2204, 2605, 3215, *3607*, *4008*, *4404*, *4412*	4	6	·	5	9	2
9 . . . ♘b8 10 d3 1701, 2206, *3108*, *3206*, *3302*	2	1	·	·	2	·
9 . . . ♘b8 10 d4 *1507*, *1710*, *1720*, *1801*, 2406, 2512, *2515*, 2611, 3203, 3403, 3408, *3413*, 3503, *3714*, 3910, *4214*, *4406*, *4419*	3	7	·	1	7	·
9 . . . ♕d7 *1714*	1	·	·	·	·	·
9 . . . h6 0912, *1303*, *1405*, 2506	1	2	·	·	1	·
1 e4 e6						
2 d4 c5 *0702*	1	·	·	·	·	·
2 d4 d5						
3 ♘c3 ♗b4 *1608*, *2615*	2	·	·	·	·	·
3 ♘c3 (♘d2) de 0113, 0126	·	·	·	2	·	·
3 ♘d2 c5 *1008*, *1401*, *1803*, 3006, *3212*, *3407*, *3712*, *4003*, *4104*, *4108*, *4110*, *4112*, *4114*, *4116*, *4118*	7	7	·	·	·	1
3 ♘d2 f5 *3011*	1	·	·	·	·	·
3 ♘d2 ♘f6 *0142*, *1407*, *3202*	3	·	·	·	·	·
3 ed *0114*, *0116*, *0134*, *1516*	3	1	·	·	·	·
3 e5 *3505*	·	·	·	·	1	·
1 e4 ♘f6						
2 ♘c3 *1010*	·	·	·	·	1	·
2 e5 ♘d5 3 d4 d6:						
4 c4 ♘b6 5 ed *0129*, *1715*	1	·	·	·	·	1
4 ♘f3 ♗g4 *1712*, *1718*	2	·	·	·	·	·
4 ♘f3 g6:						
5 c4 *1107*, *1111*	2	·	·	·	·	·
5 ♗c4 *2405*, *3104*, *3417*	3	·	·	·	·	·
5 ♗e2 *0803*, *0903*, *0907*, *0911*, *2104*	·	4	1	·	·	·
1 e4 g6 *0125*, *1511*, *2303*	2	1	·	·	·	·
1 ♘f3 ♘f6 2 g3 b5 *3101*, *3606*	·	·	·	2	·	·
1 ♘f3 d5 2 c4 *0701*, *2402*, *3610*, *3702*, *4115*, *4215*	·	·	·	1	4	1
1 f4 *0606*	·	·	·	·	1	·

Index of Endings

A

Pawn 0131, 0910, 1304, 1711, 3102, 3209

♘v♘ 0116, 0118, 0209, 0212, 0217, 1408, 2418, 3102, 3210, 3904, 4120

♘+♘v♘+♘ 0118, 3904

♗v♗ 0113, 0901, 0910, 1010, 1910, 2807, 3202, 3416, 3502, 3506, 4403, 4407

♗+♗v♗+♗ 2807

♖v♖ 0107, 0109, 0123, 0131, 0134, 0222, 0419, 0706, 0804, 0911, 1001, 1102, 1701, 1709, 1711, 1721, 2201, 2417, 2902, 3006, 3110, 3204, 3209, 3211, 3707, 3714, 3906, 4103, 4111, 4302, 4304, 4307, 4401

♖+♖v♖+♖ 0107, 0119, 0138, 0222, 0311, 1001, 1301, 3204, 4302, 4401

♕v♕ 0234, 1202, 1509, 1510, 1609, 2107, 3212, 3613, 3615, 3807, 4208, 4402

B

♘v♗ 0117, 0126, 0405, 0406, 0602, 0908, 1008, 1304, 3808, 4108, 4409, 4416

♘+♘v♘+♗ 1108

♘+♘v♘+♗ 3808

♘+♗v♘+♗ 0124, 0420, 1008, 1408, 2615, 3201, 3202, 3401, 3502, 3610, 3802, 4403, 4407, 4416

♘+♗v♗+♗ 1304, 1906, 3203, 3905

♖+♘v♖+♘ 0209, 0217, 0418, 0911, 1012, 1113, 1406, 2204, 2205, 2418, 3006, 3303, 3908, 4103, 4114, 4414, 4420

♖+♘v♖+♗ 0109, 0126, 0134, 0136, 0139, 0402, 0405, 0406, 0419, 0602, 0705, 0811, 1002, 1009, 1507, 1701, 1705, 1708, 1801, 1904, 2302, 2401, 2414, 2417, 2801, 2902, 2903, 2908, 3005, 3103, 3413, 3414, 3616, 3707, 3715, 3804, 3906, 4014, 4104, 4107, 4113, 4115, 4307

♖+♗v♖+♗ 0113, 0226, 0410, 0706, 0807, 0901, 0910, 1010, 1103, 1204, 1709, 1720, 2304, 2410, 2602, 2604, 3110, 3209, 3405, 3506, 3604, 3711, 3714, 4010, 4111, 4119, 4304, 4417

♕+♘v♕+♘ 0116, 0810, 1203, 2501, 3206

♕+♘v♕+♗ 0218, 1402, 1510, 1901, 2202, 3212, 4402

♕+♗v♕+♗ 0401, 0417, 1501, 1601, 1704, 2904, 2906, 3416, 3615

♕+♖v♕+♖ 0236, 0909, 1102, 1202, 1503, 2907, 3211, 3402, 3705, 4415

C

♖v♘ 0108, 0508, 1412, 2513, 4105

♖v♗ 0220, 3701, 3711, 4417

♖v♘+♗ 0103, 0308, 1302, 1902, 4116

♖v♗+♗ 0404, 0510, 3708

♖+♘v♖ 1107, 2401

♖+♘v♘+♗ 1718, 2513, 3608

♖+♗v♖ 2201, 3305

♖ + ♗*v*♘ + ♘ 1403

♖ + ♗*v*♘ + ♗ 0220, 0605, 1703, 3105, 3903

♖ + ♗*v*♗ + ♗ 1910

♖ + ♗*v*♘ + ♗ + ♗ 0308

♕*v*♖ + ♘ 4006, 4301

♕*v*♖ + ♗ 0210, 2614

♕*v*♖ + ♖ 2509, 3505

♖ + ♖*v*♖ + ♘ 0142, 0408, 0508, 0804, 1412, 1714

♖ + ♖*v*♖ + ♗ 1011, 3106, 3214, 3701

♖ + ♖*v*♖ + ♘ + ♗ 3408

♖ + ♖*v*♖ + ♗ + ♗ 0606, 3708

Index of Opponents

Italics indicate that Karpov was White

	+	=	−
Abetisian 0416	1	·	·
Addison 1517	·	1	·
Adorjan 0503, *0513,, 1115,* *1201,* 1202, *2906,* *3210*	1	5	1
Ageichenko 0711	·	1	·
Albano 2903	·	1	·
Alburt *1901*	1	·	·
Alexeyev *0118,* 0211, *0216,* 0221	·	4	·
Alt 1302	1	·	·
Alvarez 3003	1	·	·
Amos 2005	1	·	·
Andersson *1109,* 2612, *3703,* 4009, *4408*	2	2	1
Anikayev *1410*	·	1	·
Antoshin 0402, 1417, *1704,* 3207	·	3	1
Arakelov *1006*	1	·	·
Arbakov *0226*	1	·	·
Aronshtats(?) *2301*	1	·	·
Aroshiov 0126	1	·	·
Augustin *0304*	1	·	·
Averbakh 1711	·	1	·
Averkin 1413, 3610	·	2	·
Bagirov *1712*	1	·	·
Balashov *1708, 2420, 2506*	·	3	·
Balshan 2902	·	1	·
Barcza 1502	1	·	·
Barle *4205*	1	·	·
Bellon *3705*	·	1	·
Belyavsky 3604, 4307	1	1	·
Benko 1506	·	1	·

	+	=	−
Bilek 3213	·	1	·
Bisguier *1501,* 3012	1	1	·
Bitman *0709*	1	·	·
Blatny 0303	·	1	·
Bokuchava *0412*	·	·	1
Botterill 2603	1	·	·
Botvinnik *0137*	·	1	·
Bronstein 2413, *2513*	1	1	·
Browne *3102, 3707,* 4405	1	2	·
Budakov *0105*	·	1	·
Byrne D. *3106*	1	·	·
Byrne R. 2505, *2602, 3411*	1	2	·
Calvo 3713	1	·	·
Camacho *2004*	1	·	·
Campos-Lopez *3104*	1	·	·
Caro *1514*	1	·	·
Castro 1110	1	·	·
Chechelian *0417*	·	1	·
Chernikov 1402	1	·	·
Chilnov *1305*	1	·	·
Chistiakov *0210,* 0215, *0220*	2	1	·
Ciocaltea 1515, 2605, 3205	·	3	·
Ciric 0515	·	1	·
Cobo *3002*	1	·	·
Csom *3214*	·	1	·
Cuellar *1505,* 3406	2	·	·
Dementiev *1416,* 1715, *2207*	1	1	1
Detkov *0403*	1	·	·
Diaz *1117*	1	·	·
Didishko *0206*	·	·	1
Dobkin *0420*	·	1	·
Donchenko 1007	1	·	·
Doroshkevich 1404, 1719	1	1	·

	+	=	−
Drizgalovich 0139	1	·	·
Dueball *3005*	1	·	·
Dvoretsky *0409*	1	·	·
Dzhindzhikhashvili *1912*, 2407, 2807	·	3	·
Enevoldsen *3011*	1	·	·
Estevez 2907, 3401	2	·	·
Estrin *0707*	·	1	·
Evans 3111	·	1	·
Evrosimovski *1001*, 1002, *1003*, 1004	2	2	·
Fedin *0133*	1	·	·
Forintos 3209	·	1	·
Franklin *2608*	1	·	·
Fridjonsson 1101	1	·	·
Furman *1916*, *3710*, 4204	·	3	·
Gaimaletdinov *0108*	1	·	·
Garcia S. 3708, *4207*	2	·	·
Geller 2406, 3203, *3611*	·	3	·
Gheorghiu *2504*, 4011	·	2	·
Ghizdavu 3502	1	·	·
Gik *0704*	1	·	·
Gipslis 1304, 1717, 1917, 2806	·	3	1
Gligorić 2609, *3108*, *3413*, *4214*, *4406*	3	2	·
Gofshtein *2101*	1	·	·
Gouveia *2904*	1	·	·
Grigorian K. *2405*, *3615*	1	1	·
Grigorian L. 0411, 4302	1	·	1
Gufeld 2204	·	1	·
Gurgenidze *4304*	1	·	·
Hampyuk 0141	1	·	·
Hartston *2604*, 4007	1	1	·
Hase 3014	·	1	·
Hatlebakk 0233, *0234*	1	1	·
Hecht *3201*, 3505	·	2	·
Holmov 1721	·	1	·
Hort *2511*, 3112, *3202*, *3709*, *4006*, *4208*	3	3	·
Hostalet *0507*, 0512	1	1	·
Hramtsov 0701	1	·	·
Hübner *2908*, *3402*	1	1	·
Hug *1102*, 2901	·	2	·
Ignatiev *1906*	·	1	·
Ivkov 1508	·	·	1
Izotov *1608*	1	·	·
Jacobsen *0605*, 0606	·	1	1
Jansa *3010*	·	1	·
Juhnke 1112	1	·	·
Kalashnikov 0107, *0117*, 0121, 0132	2	2	·
Kalinkin 0111	·	1	·
Kapengut 2411	·	1	·
Kaplan 1116, *3113*, 3711	1	2	·
Karasev 1012, 1703, *1902*, *2412*	2	2	·
Karin *0125*	1	·	·
Karnar 4215	·	1	·
Kärner 2803	·	·	1
Katalimov *1910*	1	·	·
Kavalek 1510, *4010*	1	·	1
Keene 2607	1	·	·
Keres 3114, 3614	·	2	·
Kirillov 0119, *1914*	2	·	·
Kirpichnikov 0806	1	·	·
Klovan 1601, *1904*, *2202*	1	1	1
Kogan E. *1009*	1	·	·
Kolishkin 0120, 0124	1	1	·
Konikowski *1005*	1	·	·
Kopilov I. 1409	·	1	·
Korchnoi 0122, 1709, *1801*, *1802*, *1803*, *1804*, *1805*, 1806, 2514, 2614, *3404*, 3606, 4101, *4102*, 4103, *4104*, 4105, *4106*, 4107, *4108*, 4109, *4110*, 4111, *4112*, 4113, *4114*, 4115, *4116*, 4117, *4118*, 4119, *4120*, 4121, *4122*, 4123, *4124*	7	23	6
Korelov A. *1609*	·	1	·
Kornasiewicz 0310	1	·	·
Korotayev 0130	1	·	·
Kosenkov *1301*	·	1	·
Kozlov *2303*	1	·	·
Krasnov 0705	·	1	·
Krogius *1401*, 2415	1	1	·
Kudishevich 0209, 0225	1	1	·
Kudriashov *2801*	1	·	·
Kupka *0311*	·	1	·
Kupreichik 0301, *4303*	2	·	·
Kurajica *2610*	1	·	·
Kushnir *0235*	1	·	·

	+	=	−
Kuzmin *2804*, *3407*, *3609*	2	1	·
Lapenis *2805*	·	1	·
Larsen 3103, 3410, 4409	·	3	·
Lazarev 0102	1	·	·
Lein *2403*	·	1	·
Lengyel 2503, *3206*	1	1	·
Lepeshkin 0713	·	1	·
Lerner 1907	1	·	·
Lewi 0510	1	·	·
Liberzon 1707	·	1	·
Ligterink *0504*, 0514	·	2	·
Lilein *0205*, *0419*	·	2	·
Lisenko *0807*, 2103	1	1	·
Ljubojević 3706, 4206, 4403	1	2	·
Lukin 0408	1	·	·
Maeder *0502*	1	·	·
Maksimov *0115*	1	·	·
Al Mallah *4003*	1	·	·
Manakov 0128	1	·	·
Mariotti *4212*, 4411	1	1	·
Markland *2615*, *2909*	2	·	·
Markovsky 2102	1	·	·
Markula *2003*	1	·	·
Maroszczyk 0305	·	1	·
Matanović 3503	·	1	·
McKay 1105, *1111*	1	1	·
Mecking *2606*, *3115*	1	1	·
Mikenas *1718*	1	·	·
Miklyaev *0811*	1	·	·
Mnatskanian 1913	1	·	·
Moiseyev *1706*	·	1	·
Moles *0509*	1	·	·
Mukhudulin *0109*	·	1	·
Musil 4209	1	·	·
Najdorf *2613*	·	1	·
Nebolsin *1011*	·	·	1
Neckar *1107*	1	·	·
Nedelin *0112*	1	·	·
Nepomnyashchy *0201*	·	1	·
Nikolayevsky *2414*	1	·	·
Nisman 0804	1	·	·
Nizovsky *0405*	1	·	·
Noakh *0212*, 0217, *0222*	2	1	·
Nowak E. *0309*	·	1	·
Nowak V. 0307	1	·	·
O'Kelly *1507*	1	·	·
Olafsson *2502*	·	1	·

	+	=	−
Orekhov *0142*	1	·	·
Orlov 2304	1	·	·
Osterman 4202	1	·	·
Padevsky 3006	·	·	1
Palatnik *0407*, 0421	1	1	·
Panno *1509*, 3702	·	2	·
Parma *1503*, 2501, *4203*	1	2	·
Pavlyutin 1415	1	·	·
Payruber *1104*	1	·	·
Peresipkin 2106	1	·	·
Peshina *0805*	1	·	·
Petrosian A. *2104*	·	1	·
Petrosian T. 2510, 3107, 3608, *4306*, 4401, *4412*, 4413, *4414*, 4415	·	8	1
Petrov *0134*	1	·	·
Petukhov 1915	·	1	·
Pfleger 2601	·	1	·
Piskunov *0129*	1	·	·
Planinc 3715, 4211	1	1	·
Platonov 1713, 2404	·	2	·
Podgayets *1710*	·	1	·
Polugayevsky 2421, *3613*, 3801, *3802*, 3803, *3804*, 3805, *3806*, 3807, *3808*	3	7	·
Polyakov *0140*	1	·	·
Pomar *3701*, *4014*	2	·	·
Ponomarev *0116*	1	·	·
Popov 0418, 0801	2	·	·
Portisch 3109, *3714*, *4201*, 4410, 4416, *4417*, 4418, *4419*, 4420, *4421*	2	7	1
Pozdnyakov *1414*	1	·	·
Pritchett *4001*	1	·	·
Pronin *0702*	1	·	·
Quinteros *3409*	1	·	·
Radulov *3415*, 4013	·	2	·
Rashkovsky *1408*, *3616*	2	·	·
Ravinsky 0213, *0218*, 0223	1	2	·
Reiman 0810	1	·	·
Ribli *1203*, 1204, 3211, *3506*, 4213	1	3	1
Rogoff *2006*	1	·	·
Romanishin *0809*	1	·	·
Rotov 1010	·	1	·
Ruderfer 1905	1	·	·
Ruiz 2008	·	1	·

	+	=	−
Rukavina 3414	1	·	·
Rutka 0313	1	·	·
Sadovsky 0401	1	·	·
Saidy 3101	1	·	·
Samadov 0204	1	·	·
Sangla 0802	1	·	·
Saren 3004	1	·	·
Savon *1702, 2410, 2517, 3601*	2	2	·
Sax *3208*	1	·	·
Sazontiev 0136, *0208*	2	·	·
Schaufelberger *0501*	1	·	:
Schauwecker *3504*	1	·	·
Schmidt *4004*	1	·	·
Schoupal *0312*	1	·	·
Sergievsky *1403*	1	·	·
Shabanov *1908*	1	·	·
Shakarov 0202	·	1	·
Shamkovich 2417	1	·	·
Shefler *0114*	1	·	·
Shestakov *1407*	1	·	·
Shneider 0103	1	·	·
Shteinberg *0902*, 0904, *0906*, 0908, *0910*, 0912, *2107*	4	2	1
Shusharin 0101	1	·	·
Sigurjonsson *1511*	·	1	·
Sikora *0308*	1	·	·
Silva *2001*	1	·	·
Simanov *0135*	1	·	·
Sinakov (?) 2302	1	·	·
Skvortsov 0712	·	1	·
Sloth 3001	1	·	·
Slujssar 1504	1	·	·
Smejkal *0302*, 3416, *4402*	2	1	·
Smith *3110*	1	·	·
Smyslov 2409, 2516, *2808*, 3617	1	2	1
Sokolov 1306	·	1	·
Spassky *0138, 2508*, 2701, *3302*, 3304, *3607, 3901*, 3902, *3903*, 3904, *3905*, 3906, *3907*, 3908, *3909*, 3910, *3911, 4301*	6	10	2
Stein *1516*, 1701, *2408, 2515*, 2809	2	3	·
Stoica *2905*	1	·	·
Sukhanov *0706*	1	·	·
Suttles 3105	1	·	·

	+	=	−
Sveshnikov *3603*	·	1	·
Szabo *3404*	·	1	·
Sznapik *1106*, 3007	2	·	·
Taimanov *2401, 2802*, 3301, *3303*, 3405, 3602	3	3	·
Tal 2419, 2509, 3408, *3605*, 4305, 4407	·	6	·
Tarasov 1406	·	1	·
Tarinin 0104, *0123*	1	·	1
Timman 0506, *0511*	1	1	·
Timoshenko 0113, 0207, 0406	2	·	1
Tiulin *1602*	·	1	·
Torre 1103, *3417*	1	1	·
Torres *2002*	1	·	·
Tsamryuk *0413*	1	·	·
Tseitlin 1705, *2416*	1	1	·
Tserdakh *1008*	1	·	·
Tseshkovsky 1411, 2203	·	2	·
Tsikhelashvili *0203*, 0808	2	·	·
Tukmakov *1720, 2205, 2418*, 2512, 3403, 3612, 3704	3	4	·
Ubilava 1911	·	1	·
Uddenfeldt *3008*	1	·	·
Uhlmann 2507, 3412, *3712*	2	1	·
Ungureanu *3015*	1	·	·
Unzicker 2611, *4008, 4404*	2	1	·
Urzica 1114	1	·	·
Vaganian 0410, *0803*, 0901, *0903*, 0905, *0907*, 0909, *0911*, 1604, *1716*, 1903, 2402, *3212*	4	6	3
Vasyukov 2206	·	1	·
Vatnikov 0711	·	1	·
Velimirović 3215, *4210*	1	1	·
Veselovsky 2105	1	·	·
Vibornov 0703	1	·	·
Villaroel *1512*	1	·	·
Visier *3013*	1	·	·
Vogt *1113*	1	·	·
Volpert *0236*	1	·	·
Vujačić 1108	1	·	·
Vujaković *0601*, 0602, *0603*, 0604	3	1	·
Walica *0306*	1	·	·
Westerinen *4012*	1	·	·
Whiteley *3501*	1	·	·

	+	=	–		+	=	–
Williams 4005	1	·	·	Zakhvatov 0404	·	1	·
Wirthensohn *3009*	1	·	·	Zalm 4002	1	·	·
Wittman *2007*	1	·	·	Zara 0505, 0508	·	2	·
Yepez 1513	1	·	·	Zhelyandinov *1303*, 2201	1	1	·
Zadneprovsky 0106	1	·	·	Zhukhovitsky 1405	·	1	·
Zaitsev A. *1412*	1	·	·	Zhuravlev V. 1909	·	1	·
Zaitsev I. *0214*, 0219, *0224*,				Zilbert *0708*	1	·	·
1714	1	3	·	Zyulyarkin *0110*, 0127, 0131	3	·	·